# VENGEANCE 1

READINGS IN MEDIEVAL CIVILIZATIONS AND CULTURES: XIII
series editor: Paul Edward Dutton

# VENGEANCE
# IN MEDIEVAL EUROPE

## A READER

edited by

DANIEL LORD SMAIL and KELLY GIBSON

University of Toronto Press

LIBRARY AND ARCHIVES CANADA CATALOGUING IN PUBLICATION

   Vengeance in medieval Europe : a reader / edited by Daniel Lord Smail and Kelly Gibson.

(Readings in medieval civilizations and cultures ; 13)
Includes index.
ISBN 978-1-4426-0126-0 (pbk.).—ISBN 978-1-4426-0134-5 (bound)

   1. Revenge—Europe—History—To 1500.  2. Revenge—Political aspects—Europe—History—To 1500.  3. Revenge—Social aspects—Europe—History—To 1500.  4. Revenge—Religious aspects—Christianity.  5. Middle Ages.  I. Smail, Daniel Lord .II. Gibson, Kelly, 1982–   III. Series: Readings in medieval civilizations and cultures ; 13

KJ147.V45 2009    306.2094'0902    C2009-902850-6

We welcome comments and suggestions regarding any aspect of our publications – please feel free to contact us at news@utphighereducation.com or visit our internet site at www.utphighereducation.com.

*North America*
5201 Dufferin Street
Toronto, Ontario, Canada, M3H 5T8

2250 Military Road
Tonawanda, New York, USA, 14150

ORDERS PHONE: 1-800-565-9523
ORDERS FAX: 1-800-221-9985
ORDERS EMAIL: utpbooks@utpress.utoronto.ca

*UK, Ireland, and continental Europe*
NBN International
Estover Road, Plymouth, PL6 7PY, UK
TEL: 44 (0) 1752 202301
FAX ORDER LINE: 44 (0) 1752 202333
enquiries@nbninternational.com

This book is printed on paper containing 100% post-consumer fibre.

The University of Toronto Press acknowledges the financial support for its publishing activities of the Government of Canada through the Book Publishing Industry Development Program (BPIDP).

Book design and composition by George Kirkpatrick.

*Printed in Canada*

# CONTENTS

# INTRODUCTION

As users of this series have long appreciated, the many kinds of sources that have survived from medieval Latin Christendom – from the Iberian peninsula to the Baltic frontier, from the Mediterranean islands to the North Atlantic, from the fall of Rome to the sixteenth century – offer an extraordinary wealth of material to students of the past. Medieval sources have long been celebrated for what they tell us about the history of Europe: its peoples, institutions, ideas, art forms, and innovations. From these sources we can learn about the histories of power, of religion, of warfare and crusades, of families and women, of cities, economies, and culture. To this array of subjects we can now add the new history of emotion, and specifically, in the case of this reader, the emotions of anger, hatred, and rage: in a word, vengeance.

As we hope to illustrate in this collection, medieval European culture had a rich and complex understanding of the idea and practice of vengeance. Terms for vengeance or the emotions and practices associated with it, including peacemaking, are scattered, thinly but meaningfully, across an astonishing array of sources, ranging from the lives of saints and papal letters to learned treatises, chronicles, and court cases. The broad reach of the language of vengeance reveals the pervasiveness of the idea. We might expect to find that medieval authors cast a jaundiced eye on both emotions of hate and the practice of vengeance, and they often did. But vengeance, in certain contexts, was sometimes given a positive spin. This is, in part, because the principle of revenge was so thoroughly embedded in the Old Testament, one of the sources used by people in the Middle Ages when they wanted to think about matters. Revenge, notably, was celebrated in the law of the talion, which called for taking an eye for an eye, a tooth for a tooth. Vengeance wasn't just the lawless retaliation that our own culture deems it. Vengeance was justice, an integral part of the language of medieval law and legal culture.

The nature of vengeance and the emotions associated with it were much discussed by clerics and other writers throughout the Middle Ages. Their own ideas were powerfully shaped not only by what they found in the Bible, but also in the commentaries of Church Fathers like Augustine and Jerome. The redactors of the Germanic law codes, in turn, were influenced by Roman legal ideas about homicide and vengeance, and later, by the twelfth and thirteenth centuries, Roman legal understandings would have an even more obvious influence on the law of homicide. The worldview of medieval authors was not framed entirely by written sources, however. Early medieval thinkers, all of whom had been raised in a society that was very familiar with feud and other forms of customary vengeance, thought about and presented concepts such as the Last Judgment and historical causation within the framework and language of vengeance. They talked about how rulers "took vengeance" on the wicked for their crimes and, in so doing, established peace. Saints and their relics "avenged" misdeeds in a similar way. Both minor conflicts between local powers and major wars between kingdoms were conceived of and described within the framework of vengeance. Many crusade chronicles are filled with talk of the vengeance exacted by Christians upon Muslims and pagans in response to the atrocities that they thought had been committed against the churches and Christians in the Holy Land (Docs. 62 and 63), as if the crusades were just one enormous bloodfeud. Wherever commentators discussed hostile relations between individuals or groups, whatever the scale, there the modern reader can find talk of hatred and vengeance.

Vengeance could be a "one time only" riposte. It could also settle into a long-term state marked by constant emotion and episodic violence: something we might now call a feud or a vendetta. Yet many languages of medieval Europe, such as Old Icelandic and legal Latin, never actually developed a word for "feud." Instead, they described a vengeful state of relations between two individuals or kin groups as a coldness, an enmity, or even a state of "unfriendship" (óvinr, inimicitia), a negative counterpart to the bonds of kinship and friendship. Vengeance, in a sense, was the action, but emotions provided the reason and context, which is why vengeance cannot be studied independently of the language of emotion.

Vengeance was not always forever, however, and all forms of vengeance, in turn, could lead to acts of peacemaking, where hatred turned to love and was sealed, often, by the kiss of peace. The possibility of turning hatred into peace was always there, for as long as people had been writing about vengeance. As medieval sources grow ever richer, from the thirteenth century onward, we find more and more evidence for the practice of peacemaking. Peacemaking was a standard component of sermons delivered by members of the mendicant orders, and a great number of peace acts have survived in local archives. The widespread insistence on peacemaking is a reminder of how the medieval culture of vengeance was twinned with an equally pervasive culture of peacemaking.

Not everyone, of course, had the automatic right to pursue vengeance. In major passages in the Old Testament, vengeance was seen as God's prerogative; it was not up to the victim or the victim's kin to avenge injuries. In the early Middle Ages, God's vengeance was channeled through the saints. By the twelfth century, kings, or more accurately the chroniclers and panegyrists who wrote about kings, routinely claimed the right to exercise vengeance in God's name. The claim to exercise legitimate vengeance was routinely made by the military aristocracy of the High and later Middle Ages, from which it may be possible to trace the history of the duel. But the right to revenge filtered even further down the social and political hierarchy. Thus, in 1361 a shepherd named Guilhem de Bessa came before a public notary of the city of Marseille to declare, formally, that he had taken vengeance on his employer, who had shamefully beaten him, and went on to announce his plan to avenge himself on the other parties to the beating (Doc. 120j). It is doubtful that the learned opinions of his day, whether from kings, jurists, preachers, or confessors, would have agreed with him, but the point for the modern reader is that the claim to exercise legitimate vengeance was in some respects a claim to be an autonomous or free individual. The same goes for the freedom to make peace and accept compensation from one's enemies (see Doc. 83). In other words, vengeance wasn't about violence. As these sources will make clear, it was about justice, political autonomy, honor, and a great many other things. The long history of vengeance may be a history of the civilizing process – how states and societies repressed the urge to do violence – but it may also be a history of how individuals like Guilhem de Bessa, who prized their honor, gradually found their freedoms eroded. The story of vengeance is not just a story about law, but also a story about politics, culture, religion, family – everything, in fact, that has made medieval Europe such a fascinating field of study.

*Vengeance in Medieval Europe* offers a wide temporal, geographic, and cultural perspective on vengeance, supplying primary sources from Late Antiquity through the late Middle Ages, from northern to Mediterranean Europe, and from ecclesiastical exegetes and royal advisers to shoemakers and shepherds. This volume offers materials for the study of vengeance by juxtaposing the ecclesiastical rhetoric of peacemaking, along with the flat condemnations of violence made by centralizing states, with the more shadowy world of minor jurisdictions and lay society in the central and later Middle Ages. We hope to provide sources that will help students appreciate the commonplace notion that state-building means, among other things, the attempt to monopolize the exercise of violence; that is to say replacing private vengeance with state vengeance. Students will have a chance to explore both "unofficial" and "official" justice in an age when the distinction between the two was rather fuzzy, where a private hostility could lead either to a feud or to a lawsuit and where both were readily trumped by God's justice. Material gathered in this volume will also suggest that the art and practice of litigation, perfected by the fourteenth century, borrowed far more heavily from the culture of vengeance than has hitherto been appreciated. Generally, the state-building process, when confronted with a culture of vengeance, is successful where it manages to channel, not suppress, the desire for vengeance. Vengeance was channeled not only by limiting it to certain days of the week (Docs. 47 and

68) but by directing it against criminals and enemies of the church or king. The culture of vengeance that existed in the Middle Ages, therefore, played a prominent role in shaping the developing European legal systems of the period.

The fact that almost everyone reading this volume has experienced their own feelings of anger and desire for vengeance makes it impossible to avoid inviting comparisons with modern society. As students examine the language and practice of vengeance, they will approach an understanding of the medieval world as its contemporaries saw it, and, in the process, perceive similarities with as well as differences from our world and mentalities. When one looks at modern society, one may realize that the Middle Ages is not such a distant, violent world. Even the most casual of Internet searches will show how the emotional language of hatred and vengeance suffuses the way we think about certain aspects of criminal and civil law, politics, policy, and "the clash of civilizations." Our own students have filled their course blogs with examples drawn from their knowledge of schools, sports, inner-city gangs, and personal relationships. People sometimes feel frustrated by a legal system that doesn't allow as much vengeance as they would like.

Given this climate, it seems important to learn about the medieval practice of vengeance, to know what people thought about it then, and how they understood its function in their own society. The principle of feuding and vengeance-taking, as many of the texts in this collection will illustrate, was a legal principle in medieval European society. Vengeance had its own rules and codes, even if these codes were usually unwritten. In its own way, the threat of vengeance arguably served to place limits on unfettered violence, for who would not be at least somewhat cautious about doing an injury if the inevitable riposte was vengeance? Above all, as many of the texts here make clear, the vengeance practiced in medieval Europe was invariably paired with peacemaking. The culture celebrated both the vengeance-takers and the peacemakers. This, the act of peace, is almost invariably forgotten in the modern rush to dismiss the Middle Ages as a violent and vengeful age. Yet we forget it, perhaps, at our peril.

We have divided this collection into three major sections, and have grouped the sources within each section into four chapters with the following themes: laws and statutes; sermons, exegesis, and other forms of moral regulation; histories, lives of saints, and other narrative sources; and documents of practice. The idea is to allow readers to track instances of vengeance and vengeful emotions in a variety of contexts. In many cases we have excerpted passages from longer texts in the hope that interested readers can follow up where they might desire. In other cases, we have preferred to include the entire source, deeming it better to enable readers to develop an extended familiarity from one source rather than to merely provide snippets from many. A number of the sources have been translated here for the first time, and these include statutes, court cases, saints' lives, sermons, and moral literature. The material within each part is organized chronologically, in order to reveal historical changes in both practice and discourse across the period. Text in italic type indicates foreign words; in addition, we use italics in document introductions and also for paraphrases that are intended to bridge a gap between two selections. Square brackets enclose editorial comments, either by the original editor or translator or by us. These comments are intended to clarify a foreign term or to contextualize a word or a phrase. Round brackets in a document enclose words that belong to the text.

We warmly thank those who contributed original translations to this volume: Louis Hamilton, Nina Melechen, Laura K. Morreale, Lori Pieper, Susanne Pohl, Kathleen M.M. Smail, and Jennifer Speed. In addition, Elizabeth Kamali was instrumental in selecting some relevant passages from the London Coroner's Rolls. Dan Smail originally began this volume in collaboration with Dr. Susanne Pohl, and he would like to thank her not only for her inspiration and for much of the original design of the collection but also for kindly allowing him to complete the volume with a new co-editor when circumstances made it difficult for Susanne to carry on. Some of the translations for this volume were enabled by a grant from the Ames Fund of the Graduate School of Arts and Sciences at Fordham University; Dan Smail gratefully acknowledges this material assistance. Benjamin Arnold, Tom Head, and Kate Jansen provided helpful suggestions and feedback on some elements of this reader, and we benefited greatly from the editorial insights of Maryanne Kowaleski. Barbara Rosenwein of Loyola University Chicago and Oren Falk of Cornell University reviewed the manuscript and provided invaluable comments and corrections, though we alone are responsible for errors and oversights that remain. Finally, we would like to thank Paul Dutton for his advice and editorial leadership and for bearing with this project over its very long gestation.

# PART I.
## PROLOGUE: ANCIENT SOURCES FOR
## MEDIEVAL CONCEPTS OF VENGEANCE

*Much of the language used in medieval European sources to describe both vengeance and peacemaking was borrowed or adapted from the books of the Christian Bible. The laws constructed to deal with the effects of vengeance, in turn, were influenced by the legal traditions of Rome. Knowledge of Roman law was passed on to medieval scholars and rulers through collections of Roman laws compiled by late Roman or Byzantine emperors, particularly those of Theodosius II (r. 408–450) and Justinian I (r. 527–565). Part I provides a sampling of some relevant biblical texts and Roman laws.*

# CHAPTER ONE: THE OLD TESTAMENT

*The Old Testament is the source for much of the language of vengeance that was used in medieval discourse. The "Old Testament God" is often depicted as vengeful and punishing; the famous law of the talion in Exodus 21:24 – an eye for an eye, a tooth for a tooth – neatly summarizes what has been seen by many as the retributive legal nature of the Hebrew God.*

*The Old Testament, however, is a document that was compiled over many hundreds of years following the emergence of the Israelite kingdom, approximately three thousand years ago (ca 1000 BCE). One result of this extended process of compilation, with its multiple authors, is the absence of a single, coherent Old Testament stance on violence and vengeance. Were members of the ancient Hebrew nation free to avenge any wrongs committed against them, as might be interpreted by the law of the talion, or did they have to rely on God's assistance? Collectively, the texts tend to urge peace within family units or larger groups while insisting on the need for God's vengeance against more distant enemies.*

*The Douay-Rheims translation of the Bible, used here, is an English translation of the version of the Latin Bible known as the Vulgate. The Vulgate, translated into Latin from Hebrew and Greek by Jerome (ca 347–420), was the standard version of the Bible used throughout most of the Middle Ages.*

Source: The Old Testament (Douay-Rheims version), trans. from the Latin Vulgate by Gregory Martin, et al. (Douay: The English College, 1609–10), rev. Richard Challoner (1749–52).

## 1. THE POLLUTION OF KIN-SLAYING

*The bloodfeud, with its potential for never-ending tit-for-tat vengeance, is often considered a characteristic of lawless, anarchic societies. But, as many anthropologists and historians have observed, the bloodfeud is actually constrained, typically, by sets of informal rules or customs that are widely shared and appreciated by the members of the society in which it operates. In a feuding society, vengeance is necessary to restore a family's honor and restore societal balance. But what happens when a killing takes place within a family? Under these conditions, a family can't take vengeance on itself. Consequently, kin-slayings were often seen as polluting to both family and society, and required different solutions. This extract is from Genesis 4:1–16.*

1 And Adam knew Eve his wife: who conceived and brought forth Cain, saying: I have gotten a man through God.

2 And again she brought forth his brother Abel. And Abel was a shepherd, and Cain a husbandman [farmer].

3 And it came to pass after many days, that Cain offered, of the fruits of the earth, gifts to the Lord.

4 Abel also offered of the firstlings of his flock, and of their fat: and the Lord had respect to Abel, and to his offerings.

5 But to Cain and his offerings he had no respect: and Cain was exceeding angry, and his countenance fell.

6 And the Lord said to him: Why art thou angry? and why is thy countenance fallen?

7 If thou do well, shalt thou not receive? but if ill, shall not sin forthwith be present at the door? but the lust thereof shall be under thee, and thou shalt have dominion over it.

8 And Cain said to Abel his brother: Let us go forth abroad. And when they were in the field, Cain rose up against his brother Abel, and slew him.

9 And the Lord said to Cain: Where is thy brother Abel? And he answered, I know not: am I my brother's keeper?

10 And he said to him: What hast thou done? the voice of thy brother's blood crieth to me from the earth.

11 Now, therefore, cursed shalt thou be upon the earth, which hath opened her mouth and received the blood of thy brother at thy hand.

12 When thou shalt till it, it shall not yield to thee its fruit: a fugitive and a vagabond shalt thou be upon the earth.

13 And Cain said to the Lord: My iniquity is greater than that I may deserve pardon.

14 Behold thou dost cast me out this day from the face of the earth, and I shall be hidden from thy face, and I shall be a vagabond and a fugitive on the earth: every one, therefore, that findeth me, shall kill me.

15 And the Lord said to him: No, it shall not be so: but whosoever shall kill Cain, shall be punished sevenfold. And the Lord set a mark upon Cain, that whosoever found him should not kill him.

16 And Cain went out from the face of the Lord, and dwelt as a fugitive on the earth, at the east side of Eden.

## 2. THE LAW OF THE TALION

*The law of the talion (Exodus 21:24) is often seen as the most significant statement to be found in the Hebrew Bible concerning the need for tit-for-tat vengeance. The sentiments expressed in the verses selected below (Exodus 21:12–29) duplicate the principles of retaliation described in the famous early written law code of Hammurabi, king of Babylon (1792–1750 BCE). The Code of Hammurabi decreed that whoever damaged an eye or limb of another would themselves lose an eye or limb. Damage to a slave or freedman's eye or limb was punished with a monetary fine. The influence of that code can be seen in the famous chapter from Exodus that follows. It is important, when reading it, to think about whether the text below permits family vengeance or calls for judicial vengeance.*

12 He that striketh a man with a will to kill him, shall be put to death.

13 But he that did not lie in wait for him, but God delivered him into his hands: I will appoint thee a place to which he must flee.

14 If a man kill his neighbor on set purpose and by lying in wait for him: thou shalt take him away from my altar, that he may die.

15 He that striketh his father or mother, shall be put to death.

16 He that shall steal a man, and sell him, being convicted of the guilt, shall be put to death.

17 He that curseth his father, or mother, shall die the death.

18 If men quarrel, and the one strike his neighbor with a stone or with his fist, and he die not, but keepeth his bed:

19 If he rise again and walk abroad upon his staff, he that struck him shall be quit, yet so that he make restitution for his work, and for his expenses upon the physicians.

20 He that striketh his bondman, or bondwoman with a rod, and they die under his hands, shall be guilty of the crime.

21 But if the party remain alive a day or two, he shall not be subject to the punishment, because it is his money.

22 If men quarrel, and one strike a woman with child, and she miscarry indeed, but live herself: he shall be answerable for so much damage as the woman's husband shall require, and as arbiters shall award.

23 But if her death ensue thereupon, he shall render life for life,

24 Eye for eye, tooth for tooth, hand for hand, foot for foot,

25 Burning for burning, wound for wound, stripe for stripe.

26 If any man strike the eye of his manservant or maidservant, and leave them but one eye, he shall let them go free for the eye which he put out.

27 Also if he strike out a tooth of his manservant or maidservant, he shall in like manner make them free.

28 If an ox gore a man or a woman, and they die, he shall be stoned: and his flesh shall not be eaten, but the owner of the ox shall be quit.

29 But if the ox was wont to push with his horn yesterday and the day before, and they warned his master, and he did not shut him up, and he shall kill a man or a woman: then the ox shall be stoned, and his owner also shall be put to death.

# 3. VENGEANCE AND EMOTION

*Passages in Leviticus 24 (Doc. 3b) reiterate the tit-for-tat stance on vengeance that was proposed in Exodus 21. However, Leviticus 19 (Doc. 3a) expresses an important sentiment about emotional states that appears to be somewhat contrary to the principles that are written down in Leviticus 24.*

## a. Seek not revenge

19:17 Thou shalt not hate thy brother in thy heart, but reprove him openly, lest thou incur sin through him.

18 Seek not revenge, nor be mindful of the injury of thy citizens. Thou shalt love thy friend as thyself. I am the Lord.

## b. Eye for eye, tooth for tooth

24:17 He that striketh and killeth a man, dying let him die.

18 He that killeth a beast, shall make it good, that is to say, shall give beast for beast.

19 He that giveth a blemish to any of his neighbors: as he hath done, so shall it be done to him:

20 Breach for breach, eye for eye, tooth for tooth, shall he restore. What blemish he gave, the like shall he be compelled to suffer.

21 He that striketh a beast, shall render another. He that striketh a man shall be punished.

22 Let there be equal judgment among you, whether he be a stranger, or a native that offends: because I am the Lord your God.

# 4. THE PRINCIPLE OF SANCTUARY

*In many societies, it is considered normal for killers or lawbreakers of all kinds to seek sanctuary in consecrated buildings or in similar protected spaces, such as the household, the court, or the marketplace. By doing so, a killer is safe from the threat of vengeance posed by their victim's kin as long as they stay in sanctuary. The extract below from Deuteronomy 19 cannot be said to have invented the principle of sanctuary; instead, the text translates a common practice into a formal legal principle that would come to have a great deal of influence on the idea of sanctuary in medieval Europe (see, e.g., Docs. 11k, 16c, 26b, 124, and 125). Deuteronomy 32 provides a very powerful statement to the effect that vengeance belongs to the Lord and therefore cannot or should not be undertaken by mere mortals.*

## a. The three cities of sanctuary

19:1 When the Lord thy God hath destroyed the nations, whose land he will deliver to thee, and thou shalt possess it, and shalt dwell in the cities and houses thereof:

2 Thou shalt separate to thee three cities in the midst of the land, which the Lord will give thee in possession,

3 Paving diligently the way: and thou shalt divide the whole province of thy land equally into three parts: that he who is forced to flee for manslaughter, may have near at hand whither to escape.

4 This shall be the law of the slayer that fleeth, whose life is to be saved: He that killeth his neighbor ignorantly, and who is proved to have had no hatred against him yesterday and the day before:

5 But to have gone with him to the wood to hew wood, and in cutting down the tree the axe slipped out of his hand, and the iron slipping from the handle struck his friend, and killed him: he shall flee to one of the cities aforesaid, and live:

6 Lest perhaps the next kinsman of him whose blood was shed, pushed on by his grief should pursue, and apprehend him, if [because] the way be too long, and take away the life of him who is not guilty of death, because he is proved to have had no hatred before against him that was slain.

7 Therefore I command thee, that thou separate three cities at equal distance one from another.

8 And when the Lord thy God shall have enlarged thy borders, as he swore to the fathers, and shall give thee all the land that he promised them,

9 (Yet so, if thou keep his commandments, and do the things which I command thee this day, that thou love the Lord thy God, and walk in his

ways at all times) thou shalt add to thee other three cities, and shalt double the number of the three cities aforesaid:

10 That innocent blood may not be shed in the midst of the land which the Lord thy God will give thee to possess, lest thou be guilty of blood.

11 But if any man hating his neighbor, lie in wait for his life, and rise and strike him, and he die, and he flee to one of the cities aforesaid,

12 The ancients of his city shall send, and take him out of the place of refuge, and shall deliver him into the hand of the kinsman of him whose blood was shed, and he shall die.

13 Thou shalt not pity him, and thou shalt take away the guilt of innocent blood out of Israel, that it may be well with thee.

### b. Revenge is mine

32:35 Revenge is mine, and I will repay them in due time, that their foot may slide: the day of destruction is at hand, and the time makes haste to come.

36 The Lord will judge his people, and will have mercy on his servants: he shall see that their hand is weakened, and that they who were shut up have also failed, and they that remained are consumed.

37 And he shall say: Where are their gods, in whom they trusted?

38 Of whose victims they ate the fat, and drank the wine of their drink offerings: let them arise and help you, and protect you in your distress.

39 See ye that I alone am, and there is no other God besides me: I will kill and I will make to live: I will strike, and I will heal, and there is none that can deliver out of my hand.

40 I will lift up my hand to heaven, and I will say: I live for ever.

41 If I shall whet my sword as the lightning, and my hand take hold on judgment: I will render vengeance to my enemies, and repay them that hate me.

42 I will make my arrows drunk with blood, and my sword shall devour flesh, of the blood of the slain and of the captivity, of the bare head of the enemies.

43 Praise his people, ye nations, for he will revenge the blood of his servants: and will render vengeance to their enemies, and he will be merciful to the land of his people.

44 So Moses came and spoke all the words of this canticle in the ears of the people, and Josue the son of Nun.

## 5. THE LEVITE'S CONCUBINE

*In matters concerning vengeance, the Old Testament book of Judges was not especially influential in medieval Europe. Nonetheless, the story told below provides a vivid statement about the practice of vengeance in Israelite society.*

19:1 There was a certain Levite, who dwelt on the side of mount Ephraim, who took a wife of Bethlehem Juda:

2 And she left him, and returned to her father's house in Bethlehem, and abode with him four months.

3 And her husband followed her, willing to be reconciled with her, and to speak kindly to her, and to bring her back with him, having with him a servant and two asses: and she received him, and brought him into her father's house. And when his father in law had heard this, and had seen him, he met him with joy,

4 And embraced the man. And the son in law tarried in the house of his father in law three days, eating with him and drinking familiarly.

5 But on the fourth day, arising early in the morning, he desired to depart. But his father in law kept him, and said to him: Taste first a little bread, and strengthen thy stomach, and so thou shalt depart.

6 And they sat down together, and ate and drank. And the father of the young woman said to his son in law: I beseech thee to stay here to day, and let us make merry together.

7 But he rising up, began to be for departing. And nevertheless his father in law earnestly pressed him, and made him stay with him.

8 But when morning was come, the Levite prepared to go on his journey. And his father in law said to him again: I beseech thee to take a little meat, and strengthening thyself, till the day be farther advanced, afterwards thou mayest depart. And they ate together.

9 And the young man arose to set forward with his wife and servant. And his father in law spoke to him again: Consider that the day is declining, and draweth toward evening: tarry with me to day also, and spend the day in mirth, and to morrow thou shalt depart, that thou mayest go into thy house.

10 His son in law would not consent to his words: but forthwith went forward, and came over against Jebus, which by another name is called Jerusalem, leading with him two asses loaden, and his concubine.

11 And now they were come near Jebus, and the day was far spent: and the servant said to his master: Come, I beseech thee, let us turn into the city of the Jebusites, and lodge there.

12 His master answered him: I will not go into the town of another nation, who are not of the children of Israel, but I will pass over to Gabaa:

13 And when I shall come thither, we will lodge there, or at least in the city of Rama.

14 So they passed by Jebus, and went on their journey, and the sun went down upon them when they were by Gabaa, which is in the tribe of Benjamin:

15 And they turned into it to lodge there. And when they were come in, they sat in the street of the city, for no man would receive them to lodge.

16 And behold they saw an old man, returning out of the field and from his work in the evening, and he also was of mount Ephraim, and dwelt as a stranger in Gabaa; but the men of that country were the children of Jemini.

17 And the old man lifting up his eyes, saw the man sitting with his bundles in the street of the city, and said to him: Whence comest thou? and whither goest thou?

18 He answered him: We came out from Bethlehem Juda, and we are going to our home, which is on the side of mount Ephraim, from whence we went to Bethlehem: and now we go to the house of God, and none will receive us under his roof:

19 We have straw and hay for provender of the asses, and bread and wine for the use of myself and of thy handmaid, and of the servant that is with me: we want nothing but lodging.

20 And the old man answered him: Peace be with thee: I will furnish all things that are necessary: only I beseech thee, stay not in the street.

21 And he brought him into his house, and gave provender to his asses: and after they had washed their feet, he entertained them with a feast.

22 While they were making merry, and refreshing their bodies with meat and drink, after the labor of the journey, the men of that city, sons of Belial (that is, without yoke), came and beset the old man's house, and began to knock at the door, calling to the master of the house, and saying: Bring forth the man that came into thy house, that we may abuse him:

23 And the old man went out to them, and said: Do not so, my brethren, do not so wickedly: because this man is come into my lodging, and cease I pray you from this folly.

24 I have a maiden daughter, and this man hath a concubine, I will bring them out to you, and you may humble them, and satisfy your lust: only, I beseech you, commit not this crime against nature on the man.

25 They would not be satisfied with his words; which the man seeing, brought out his concubine to them, and abandoned her to their wickedness: and when they had abused her all the night, they let her go in the morning.

26 But the woman, at the dawning of the day, came to the door of the house, where her lord lodged, and there fell down.

27 And in the morning the man arose, and opened the door, that he might end the journey he had begun: and behold his concubine lay before the door with her hands spread on the threshold.

28 He thinking she was taking her rest, said to her: Arise, and let us be going. But as she made no answer, perceiving she was dead, he took her up, and laid her upon his ass, and returned to his house.

29 And when he was come home, he took a sword, and divided the dead body of his wife with her bones into twelve parts, and sent the pieces into all the borders of Israel.

30 And when every one had seen this, they all cried out: There was never such a thing done in Israel, from the day that our fathers came up out of Egypt, until this day: give sentence, and decree in common what ought to be done.

20:1 Then all the children of Israel went out, and gathered together as one man, from Dan to Bersabee, with the land of Galaad, to the Lord in Maspha:

2 And all the chiefs of the people, and all the tribes of Israel, met together in the assembly of the people of God, four hundred thousand footmen fit for war.

3 (Nor were the children of Benjamin ignorant that the children of Israel were come up to Maspha.) And the Levite, the husband of the woman that was killed being asked, how so great a wickedness had been committed,

4 Answered: I came into Gabaa, of Benjamin, with my wife, and there I lodged:

5 And behold the men of that city, in the night beset the house wherein I was, intending to kill me, and abused my wife with an incredible fury of lust, so that at last she died.

6 And I took her and cut her in pieces, and sent the parts into all the borders of your possession: because there never was so heinous a crime, and so great an abomination committed in Israel.

7 You are all here, O children of Israel, determine what you ought to do.

8 And all the people standing, answered as by the voice of one man: We will not return to our tents, neither shall any one of us go into his own house:

9 But this we will do in common against Gabaa:

10 We will take ten men of a hundred out of all the tribes of Israel, and a hundred out of a thousand, and a thousand out of ten thousand, to bring

victuals for the army, that we may fight against Gabaa of Benjamin, and render to it for its wickedness, what it deserveth.

11 And all Israel were gathered together against the city, as one man, with one mind, and one counsel:

12 And they sent messengers to all the tribe of Benjamin, to say to them: Why hath so great an abomination been found among you?

13 Deliver up the men of Gabaa, that have committed this heinous crime, that they may die, and the evil may be taken away out of Israel. But they would not hearken to the proposition of their brethren the children of Israel:

14 But out of all the cities which were of their lot, they gathered themselves together into Gabaa, to aid them, and to fight against the whole people of Israel.

15 And there were found of Benjamin five and twenty thousand men that drew the sword, besides the inhabitants of Gabaa,

16 Who were seven hundred most valiant men, fighting with the left hand as well as with the right: and slinging stones so sure that they could hit even a hair, and not miss by the stone's going on either side.

17 Of the men of Israel also, beside the children of Benjamin, were found four hundred thousand that drew swords and were prepared to fight.

18 And they arose and came to the house of God, that is, to Silo: and they consulted God, and said: Who shall be in our army the first to go to the battle against the children of Benjamin? And the Lord answered them: Let Juda be your leader.

19 And forthwith the children of Israel rising in the morning, camped by Gabaa:

20 And going out from thence to fight against Benjamin, began to assault the city.

21 And the children of Benjamin coming out of Gabaa slew of the children of Israel that day two and twenty thousand men.

22 Again Israel, trusting in their strength and their number, set their army in array in the same place, where they had fought before:

23 Yet so that they first went up and wept before the Lord until night: and consulted him and said: Shall I go out any more to fight against the children of Benjamin my brethren or not? And he answered them: Go up against them, and join battle.

24 And when the children of Israel went out the next day to fight against the children of Benjamin,

25 The children of Benjamin sallied forth out of the gates of Gabaa: and meeting them, made so great a slaughter of them, as to kill eighteen thousand men that drew the sword.

26 Wherefore all the children of Israel came to the house of God, and

sat and wept before the Lord: and they fasted that day till the evening, and offered to him holocausts, and victims of peace offerings,

27 And inquired of him concerning their state. At that time the ark of the covenant of the Lord was there,

28 And Phinees, the son of Eleazar, the son of Aaron, was over the house. So they consulted the Lord, and said: Shall we go out any more to fight against the children of Benjamin, our brethren, or shall we cease? And the Lord said to them: Go up, for to morrow I will deliver them into your hands.

29 And the children of Israel set ambushes round about the city of Gabaa:

30 And they drew up their army against Benjamin the third time, as they had done the first and second.

31 And the children of Benjamin boldly issued out of the city, and seeing their enemies flee, pursued them a long way, so as to wound and kill some of them, as they had done the first and second day, whilst they fled by two highways, whereof one goeth up to Bethel and the other to Gabaa, and they slew about thirty men:

32 For they thought to cut them off as they did before. But they artfully feigning a flight, designed to draw them away from the city, and by their seeming to flee, to bring them to the highways aforesaid.

33 Then all the children of Israel rising up out of the places where they were, set their army in battle array, in the place which is called Baalthamar. The ambushes also, which were about the city, began by little and little to come forth,

34 And to march from the west side of the city. And other ten thousand men chosen out of all Israel, attacked the inhabitants of the city. And the battle grew hot against the children of Benjamin: and they understood not that present death threatened them on every side.

35 And the Lord defeated them before the children of Israel, and they slew of them in that day five and twenty thousand, and one hundred, all fighting men, and that drew the sword.

36 But the children of Benjamin, when they saw themselves to be too weak, began to flee. Which the children of Israel seeing, gave them place to flee, that they might come to the ambushes that were prepared, which they had set near the city.

37 And they that were in ambush arose on a sudden out of their coverts, and whilst [the children of] Benjamin turned their backs to the slayers, went into the city, and smote it with the edge of the sword.

38 Now the children of Israel had given a sign to them, whom they had laid in ambushes, that after they had taken the city, they should make a fire:

that by the smoke rising on high, they might show that the city was taken.

39 And when the children of Israel saw this in the battle, (for the children of Benjamin thought they fled, and pursued them vigorously, killing thirty men of their army)

40 And perceived, as it were, a pillar of smoke rise up from the city; and Benjamin looking back, saw that the city was taken, and that the flames ascended on high:

41 They that before had made as if they fled, turning their faces, stood bravely against them. Which the children of Benjamin seeing, turned their backs,

42 And began to go towards the way of the desert, the enemy pursuing them thither also. And they that fired the city came also out to meet them.

43 And so it was, that they were slain on both sides by the enemies, and there was no rest of their men dying. They fell and were beaten down on the east side of the city of Gabaa.

44 And they that were slain in the same place, were eighteen thousand men, all most valiant soldiers.

45 And when they that remained of Benjamin saw this, they fled into the wilderness, and made towards the rock that is called Remmon. In that flight also, as they were straggling, and going different ways; they slew of them five thousand men. And as they went farther, they still pursued them, and slew also other two thousand.

46 And so it came to pass, that all that were slain of Benjamin, in divers places, were five and twenty thousand fighting men, most valiant for war.

47 And there remained of all the number of Benjamin only six hundred men that were able to escape, and flee to the wilderness: and they abode in the rock Remmon four months.

48 But the children of Israel returning, put all the remains of the city to the sword, both men and beasts, and all the cities and villages of Benjamin were consumed with devouring flames.

## 6. HUMILIATION AND THE LORD'S VENGEANCE

*Of all the books of the Bible, the Book of Psalms was especially influential in medieval Europe. The sixth-century Rule of Saint Benedict prescribed the reading of Psalms continuously throughout the liturgical year, and all 150 Psalms were sung over the course of each week in the Divine Office, the series of readings and prayers that monks engaged in eight times throughout the day. It is not surprising, then, that the Psalms came to be some of the most well-known texts of the medieval liturgy. The influence of the Psalms extended beyond monasteries, as early medieval bishops stressed the need for priests to understand and memorize the Psalms. Due to this degree of familiarity, coupled with the practice of memorizing the Psalms themselves, some of the vividly vengeful language found in them shows up repeatedly in medieval European texts. Vengeful imagery from the Psalms turns up especially in situations when monks or other clergy members beseeched the Lord to avenge the shame and humiliation wrought on them by their enemies.*

## a. Psalm 68

1 Unto the end, for them that shall be changed; for David.

2 Save me, O God: for the waters are come in even unto my soul.

3 I stick fast in the mire of the deep and there is no sure standing. I am come into the depth of the sea, and a tempest hath overwhelmed me.

4 I have labored with crying; my jaws are become hoarse, my eyes have failed, whilst I hope in my God.

5 They are multiplied above the hairs of my head, who hate me without cause. My enemies are grown strong who have wrongfully persecuted me: then did I pay that which I took not away.

6 O God, thou knowest my foolishness; and my offences are not hidden from thee:

7 Let not them be ashamed for me, who look for thee, O Lord, the Lord of hosts. Let them not be confounded on my account, who seek thee, O God of Israel.

8 Because for thy sake I have borne reproach; shame hath covered my face.

9 I am become a stranger to my brethren, and an alien to the sons of my mother.

10 For the zeal of thy house hath eaten me up: and the reproaches of them that reproached thee are fallen upon me.

11 And I covered my soul in fasting: and it was made a reproach to me.

12 And I made haircloth my garment: and I became a byword to them.

13 They that sat in the gate spoke against me: and they that drank wine made me their song.

14 But as for me, my prayer is to thee, O Lord; for the time of thy good pleasure, O God. In the multitude of thy mercy hear me, in the truth of thy salvation.

15 Draw me out of the mire, that I may not stick fast: deliver me from them that hate me, and out of the deep waters.

16 Let not the tempest of water drown me, nor the deep water swallow me up: and let not the pit shut her mouth upon me.

17 Hear me, O Lord, for thy mercy is kind; look upon me according to the multitude of thy tender mercies.

18 And turn not away thy face from thy servant: for I am in trouble, hear me speedily.

19 Attend to my soul, and deliver it: save me because of my enemies.

20 Thou knowest my reproach, and my confusion, and my shame.

21 In thy sight are all they that afflict me; my heart hath expected reproach and misery. And I looked for one that would grieve together with me, but there was none: and for one that would comfort me, and I found none.

22 And they gave me gall for my food, and in my thirst they gave me vinegar to drink.

23 Let their table become as a snare before them, and a recompense, and a stumbling block.

24 Let their eyes be darkened that they see not; and their back bend thou down always.

25 Pour out thy indignation upon them: and let thy wrathful anger take hold of them.

26 Let their habitation be made desolate: and let there be none to dwell in their tabernacles.

27 Because they have persecuted him whom thou hast smitten; and they have added to the grief of my wounds.

28 Add thou iniquity upon their iniquity: and let them not come into thy justice.

29 Let them be blotted out of the book of the living; and with the just let them not be written.

30 But I am poor and sorrowful: thy salvation, O God, hath set me up.

31 I will praise the name of God with a canticle: and I will magnify him with praise.

32 And it shall please God better than a young calf, that bringeth forth horns and hoofs.

33 Let the poor see and rejoice: seek ye God, and your soul shall live.

34 For the Lord hath heard the poor: and hath not despised his prisoners.

35 Let the heavens and the earth praise him; the sea, and every thing that creepeth therein.

36 For God will save Sion, and the cities of Juda shall be built up. And they shall dwell there, and acquire it by inheritance.

37 And the seed of his servants shall possess it; and they that love his name shall dwell therein.

## b. Psalm 93

1 The Lord is the God to whom revenge belongeth: the God of revenge hath acted freely.

2 Lift up thyself, thou that judgest the earth: render a reward to the proud.

3 How long shall sinners, O Lord: how long shall sinners glory?

4 Shall they utter, and speak iniquity: shall all speak who work injustice?

5 Thy people, O Lord, they have brought low: and they have afflicted thy inheritance.

6 They have slain the widow and the stranger: and they have murdered the fatherless.

7 And they have said: The Lord shall not see: neither shall the God of Jacob understand.

8 Understand, ye senseless among the people: and, you fools, be wise at last.

9 He that planted the ear, shall he not hear? or he that formed the eye, doth he not consider?

10 He that chastiseth nations, shall he not rebuke: he that teacheth man knowledge?

11 The Lord knoweth the thoughts of men, that they are vain.

12 Blessed is the man whom thou shalt instruct, O Lord: and shalt teach him out of thy law.

13 That thou mayst give him rest from the evil days: till a pit be dug for the wicked.

14 For the Lord will not cast off his people: neither will he forsake his own inheritance.

15 Until justice be turned into judgment: and they that are near it are all the upright in heart.

16 Who shall rise up for me against the evildoers? or who shall stand with me against the workers of iniquity?

17 Unless the Lord had been my helper, my soul had almost dwelt in hell.

18 If I said: My foot is moved: thy mercy, O Lord, assisted me.

19 According to the multitude of my sorrows in my heart, thy comforts have given joy to my soul.

20 Doth the seat of iniquity stick to thee, who framest labor in commandment?

21 They will hunt after the soul of the just, and will condemn innocent blood.

22 But the Lord is my refuge: and my God the help of my hope.

23 And he will render them their iniquity: and in their malice he will destroy them: the Lord our God will destroy them.

## 7. RESTRAINING VENGEFUL EMOTIONS

*Internal evidence suggests that Ecclesiasticus, or the Book of Sirach (not to be confused with Ecclesiastes), was originally written about two generations before 132 BCE. In offering restrictions on both vengeance and on vengeful emotions, the verses here (28:1–7) pick up a theme already raised by Leviticus 19. Similar ideas would later surface in the New Testament.*

1 He that seeketh to revenge himself, shall find vengeance from the Lord, and he will surely keep his sins in remembrance.

2 Forgive thy neighbor if he hath hurt thee: and then shall thy sins be forgiven to thee when thou prayest.

3 Man to man reserveth anger, and doth he seek remedy of God?

4 He hath no mercy on a man like himself, and doth he entreat for his own sins?

5 He that is but flesh, nourisheth anger, and doth he ask forgiveness of God? who shall obtain pardon for his sins?

6 Remember thy last things, and let enmity cease:

7 For corruption and death hang over in his commandments.

## 8. THE VENGEANCE OF THE MACCABEES

*The two books of Maccabees had tremendous significance in medieval sermons and commentaries concerned with vengeance. The story told in the two books purports to describe the turmoil in Judea during the second century BCE, in the turbulent wake of the short-lived reign of Alexander the Great (d. 323 BCE). The Maccabees were the brethren of the hero-figure Judas Machabeus; exiled from Jerusalem by the wicked king Antiochus, they then sought vengeance. To many authors of the High Middle Ages, the story foreshadowed the events of the Crusades and provided license to medieval writers to perceive the Crusades as an act of just vengeance for their eviction from the Holy Land. On a more general level, the idea that God gave victory in battle to the side he favored because it upheld his tenets is one that held great weight throughout the Middle Ages and is the principle behind trial by combat.*

*The following selections from 2 Maccabees tell the story of the consequences of the civil strife whipped up in Jerusalem, after King Antiochus departed into Egypt, by the evil figure of Jason. In chapter 5, a vengeful Antiochus returns to Jerusalem and commands the slaughter of its people and the plundering of the temples, prompting the flight of Judas Machabeus. Chapter 6 tells of the pollution inflicted upon Jerusalem, and of the persecution of the faithful. In chapter 8, Judas Machabeus assembles his kinsmen and friends into an army; inflamed by the defilement of Jerusalem, they fall upon and slaughter the army of the general Nicanor. Antiochus himself comes to a wretched end in chapter 9.*

5:5 Now when there was gone forth a false rumor as though Antiochus had been dead, Jason taking with him no fewer than a thousand men, suddenly assaulted the city: and though the citizens ran together to the wall, the city at length was taken, and Menelaus fled into the castle.

6 But Jason slew his countrymen without mercy, not considering that prosperity against one's own kindred is a very great evil, thinking they had been enemies, and not citizens, whom he conquered.

7 Yet he did not get the principality, but received confusion at the end, for the reward of his treachery, and fled again into the country of the Ammonites.

8 At the last, having been shut up by Aretas, the king of the Arabians, in order for his destruction, flying from city to city, hated by all men, as a forsaker of the laws and execrable, as an enemy of his country and countrymen, he was thrust out into Egypt:

9 And he that had driven many out of their country perished in a strange land, going to Lacedemon, as if for kindred sake he should have refuge there:

10 But he that had cast out many unburied, was himself cast forth both unlamented and unburied, neither having foreign burial, nor being partaker of the sepulcher of his fathers.

11 Now when these things were done, the king suspected that the Jews would forsake the alliance: whereupon departing out of Egypt with a furious mind, he took the city by force of arms,

12 And commanded the soldiers to kill, and not to spare any that came in their way, and to go up into the houses to slay.

13 Thus there was a slaughter of young and old, destruction of women and children, and killing of virgins and infants.

14 And there were slain in the space of three whole days fourscore thousand, forty thousand were made prisoners, and as many sold.

15 But this was not enough, he presumed also to enter into the temple, the most holy in all the world, Menelaus, that traitor to the laws, and to his country, being his guide.

16 And taking in his wicked hands the holy vessels, which were given by other kings and cities, for the ornament and the glory of the place, he unworthily handled and profaned them.

17 Thus Antiochus going astray in mind, did not consider that God was angry for a while, because of the sins of the inhabitants of the city: and therefore this contempt had happened to the place:

18 Otherwise had they not been involved in many sins, as Heliodorus, who was sent by King Seleucus to rob the treasury, so this man also, as soon as he had come, had been forthwith scourged, and put back from his presumption.

19 But God did not choose the people for the place's sake, but the place for the people's sake.

20 And therefore the place also itself was made partaker of the evils of the people: but afterward shall communicate in the good things thereof, and as it was forsaken in the wrath of almighty God, shall be exalted again with great glory, when the great Lord shall be reconciled.

21 So when Antiochus had taken away out of the temple a thousand and eight hundred talents [a unit of weight for gold or silver weighing about 75.6 pounds], he went back in all haste to Antioch, thinking through pride that he might now make the land navigable, and the sea passable on foot: such was the haughtiness of his mind.

22 He left also governors to afflict the people: at Jerusalem, Philip, a Phrygian by birth, but in manners more barbarous than he that set him there:

23 And in Gazarim, Andronicus and Menelaus, who bore a more heavy hand upon the citizens than the rest.

24 And whereas he was set against the Jews, he sent that hateful prince, Apollonius, with an army of two and twenty thousand men, commanding him to kill all that were of perfect age, and to sell the women and the younger sort.

25 Who, when he was come to Jerusalem, pretending peace, rested till the holy day of the sabbath: and then the Jews keeping holiday, he commanded his men to take arms.

26 And he slew all that were come forth to flee: and running through the city with armed men, he destroyed a very great multitude.

27 But Judas Machabeus, who was the tenth, had withdrawn himself into a desert place, and there lived amongst wild beasts in the mountains with his company: and they continued feeding on herbs, that they might not be partakers of the pollution.

6:1 But not long after the king sent a certain old man of Antioch, to compel the Jews to depart from the laws of their fathers and of God:

2 And to defile the temple that was in Jerusalem, and to call it the temple of Jupiter Olympius: and that in Garazim of Jupiter Hospitalis, according as they were that inhabited the place.

3 And very bad was this invasion of evils, and grievous to all.

4 For the temple was full of the riot and revellings of the Gentiles: and of

men lying with lewd women. And women thrust themselves of their accord into the holy places, and brought in things that were not lawful.

5 The altar also was filled with unlawful things, which were forbidden by the laws.

6 And neither were the sabbaths kept, nor the solemn days of the fathers observed, neither did any man plainly profess himself to be a Jew.

7 But they were led by bitter constraint on the king's birthday to the sacrifices: and when the feast of Bacchus was kept, they were compelled to go about crowned with ivy in honor of Bacchus.

8 And there went out a decree into the neighboring cities of the Gentiles, by the suggestion of the Ptolemeans [rulers of Egypt], that they also should act in like manner against the Jews, to oblige them to sacrifice:

9 And whosoever would not conform themselves to the ways of the Gentiles, should be put to death: then was misery to be seen.

10 For two women were accused to have circumcised their children: whom, when they had openly led about through the city, with the infants hanging at their breasts, they threw down headlong from the walls.

11 And others that had met together in caves that were near, and were keeping the sabbath day privately, being discovered by Philip, were burnt with fire, because they made a conscience to help themselves with their hands, by reason of the religious observance of the day.

12 Now I beseech those that shall read this book, that they be not shocked at these calamities, but that they consider the things that happened, not as being for the destruction, but for the correction of our nation.

13 For it is a token of great goodness, when sinners are not suffered to go on in their ways for a long time, but are presently punished.

14 For, not as with other nations, (whom the Lord patiently expecteth, that when the day of judgment shall come, he may punish them in the fulness of their sins:)

15 Doth he also deal with us, so as to suffer our sins to come to their height, and then take vengeance on us.

16 And therefore he never withdraweth his mercy from us: but though he chastize his people with adversity he forsaketh them not.

17 But let this suffice in a few words for a warning to the readers. And now we must come to the narration.

18 Eleazar one of the chief of the scribes, a man advanced in years, and of a comely countenance, was pressed to open his mouth to eat swine's flesh.

19 But he, choosing rather a most glorious death than a hateful life, went forward voluntarily to the torment.

*Chapter 7 describes, in similar language, the martyrdom of seven brothers and their mother.*

8:1 But Judas Machabeus, and they that were with him, went privately into the towns: and calling together their kinsmen and friends, and taking unto them such as continued in the Jews' religion, they assembled six thousand men.

2 And they called upon the Lord, that he would look upon his people that was trodden down by all and would have pity on the temple, that was defiled by the wicked:

3 That he would have pity also upon the city that was destroyed, that was ready to be made even with the ground, and would hear the voice of the blood that cried to him:

4 That he would remember also the most unjust deaths of innocent children, and the blasphemies offered to his name, and would show his indignation on this occasion.

5 Now when Machabeus had gathered a multitude, he could not be withstood by the heathens: for the wrath of the Lord was turned into mercy.

6 So coming unawares upon the towns and cities, he set them on fire, and taking possession of the most commodious places, he made no small slaughter of the enemies:

7 And especially in the nights he went upon these expeditions, and the fame of his valor was spread abroad every where.

8 Then Philip seeing that the man gained ground by little and little, and that things for the most part succeeded prosperously with him, wrote to Ptolemee, the governor of Celesyria and Phenicia, to send aid to the king's affairs.

9 And he with all speed sent Nicanor, the son of Patroclus, one of his special friends, giving him no fewer than twenty thousand armed men of different nations, to root out the whole race of the Jews, joining also with him Gorgias, a good soldier, and of great experience in matters of war.

10 And Nicanor purposed to raise for the king the tribute of two thousand talents, that was to be given to the Romans, by making so much money of the captive Jews:

11 Wherefore he sent immediately to the cities upon the sea coast, to invite men together to buy up the Jewish slaves, promising that they should have ninety slaves for one talent, not reflecting on the vengeance which was to follow him from the Almighty.

12 Now when Judas found that Nicanor was coming, he imparted to the Jews that were with him, that the enemy was at hand.

13 And some of them being afraid, and distrusting the justice of God, fled away.

14 Others sold all that they had left, and withal besought the Lord, that he would deliver them from the wicked Nicanor, who had sold them before he came near them:

15 And if not for their sakes, yet for the covenant that he had made with their fathers, and for the sake of his holy and glorious name that was invoked upon them.

16 But Machabeus calling together seven thousand that were with him, exhorted them not to be reconciled to the enemies, nor to fear the multitude of the enemies who came wrongfully against them, but to fight manfully:

17 Setting before their eyes the injury they had unjustly done the holy place, and also the injury they had done to the city, which had been shamefully abused, besides their destroying the ordinances of the fathers.

18 For, said he, they trust in their weapons, and in their boldness: but we trust in the Almighty Lord, who at a beck can utterly destroy both them that come against us, and the whole world.

19 Moreover, he put them in mind also of the helps their fathers had received from God: and how, under Sennacherib, a hundred and eighty-five thousand had been destroyed.

20 And of the battle that they had fought against the Galatians, in Babylonia; how they, being in all but six thousand, when it came to the point, and the Macedonians, their companions, were at a stand, slew a hundred and twenty thousand, because of the help they had from heaven, and for this they received many favors.

21 With these words they were greatly encouraged and disposed even to die for the laws and their country.

22 So he appointed his brethren captains over each division of his army; Simon, and Joseph, and Jonathan, giving to each one fifteen hundred men.

23 And after the holy book had been read to them by Esdras, and he had given them for a watchword, The help of God: himself leading the first band, he joined battle with Nicanor:

24 And the Almighty being their helper, they slew above nine thousand men: and having wounded and disabled the greater part of Nicanor's army, they obliged them to fly.

25 And they took the money of them that came to buy them, and they pursued them on every side.

26 But they came back for want of time: for it was the day before the sabbath: and therefore they did not continue the pursuit.

27 But when they had gathered together their arms and their spoils, they

kept the sabbath: blessing the Lord who had delivered them that day, distilling the beginning of mercy upon them.

28 Then after the sabbath they divided the spoils to the feeble and the orphans, and the widows, and the rest they took for themselves and their servants.

29 When this was done, and they had all made a common supplication, they besought the merciful Lord, to be reconciled to his servants unto the end.

30 Moreover, they slew above twenty thousand of them that were with Timotheus and Bacchides, who fought against them, and they made themselves masters of the high strong holds: and they divided amongst them many spoils, giving equal portions to the feeble, the fatherless, and the widows, yea and the aged also.

31 And when they had carefully gathered together their arms, they laid them all up in convenient places, and the residue of their spoils they carried to Jerusalem:

32 They slew also Philarches, who was with Timotheus, a wicked man, who had many ways afflicted the Jews.

33 And when they kept the feast of the victory at Jerusalem, they burnt Callisthenes, that had set fire to the holy gates, who had taken refuge in a certain house, rendering to him a worthy reward for his impieties:

34 But as for that most wicked man, Nicanor, who had brought a thousand merchants to the sale of the Jews,

35 Being, through the help of the Lord, brought down by them, of whom he had made no account, laying aside his garment of glory, fleeing through the midland country, he came alone to Antioch, being rendered very unhappy by the destruction of his army.

36 And he that had promised to levy the tribute for the Romans, by the means of the captives of Jerusalem, now professed that the Jews had God for their protector, and therefore they could not be hurt, because they followed the laws appointed by him.

9:1 At that time Antiochus returned with dishonor out of Persia.

2 For he had entered into the city called Persepolis, and attempted to rob the temple, and to oppress the city, but the multitude running together to arms, put them to flight: and so it fell out that Antiochus being put to flight, returned with disgrace.

3 Now when he was come about Ecbatana, he received the news of what had happened to Nicanor and Timotheus.

4 And swelling with anger, he thought to revenge upon the Jews the injury done by them that had put him to flight. And therefore he commanded

his chariot to be driven, without stopping in his journey, the judgment of heaven urging him forward, because he had spoken so proudly, that he would come to Jerusalem, and make it a common burying place of the Jews.

5 But the Lord, the God of Israel, that seeth all things, struck him with an incurable and an invisible plague. For as soon as he had ended these words, a dreadful pain in his bowels came upon him, and bitter torments of the inner parts.

6 And indeed very justly, seeing he had tormented the bowels of others with many and new torments, albeit he by no means ceased from his malice.

7 Moreover, being filled with pride, breathing out fire in his rage against the Jews, and commanding the matter to be hastened, it happened as he was going with violence, that he fell from the chariot, so that his limbs were much pained by a grievous bruising of the body.

8 Thus he that seemed to himself to command even the waves of the sea, being proud above the condition of man, and to weigh the heights of the mountains in a balance, now being cast down to the ground, was carried in a litter, bearing witness to the manifest power of God in himself:

9 So that worms swarmed out of the body of this man, and whilst he lived in sorrow and pain, his flesh fell off, and the filthiness of his smell was noisome to the army.

# CHAPTER TWO: THE NEW TESTAMENT

As New Testament texts took shape in the second half of the first century CE, developing Christian doctrine took the language of peace and the principle of emotional self-control found in Leviticus, Ecclesiasticus, and other Old Testament sources and made them important Christian principles. As a consequence, Old Testament themes of vengeance and hatred are largely absent in the books of the New Testament.

One simple reason for this development can be found in how early Christians defined kinship structures. The books of the Old Testament suggested that peace was a valued commodity within family groups or (according to some texts) within the entire Hebrew nation. Vengeance, in turn, was something that was directed against one's enemies outside the family unit. By imagining all humanity as one big family, early Christians eliminated the possibility of having enemies outside one's kin group and so made the language of peace operative across this newly enlarged, radically inclusive "family." In other words, Christianity did not promote a new ideology of peace so much as it created a new political anthropology.

Anthropologists describe this as a process of creating what they call "fictive kinship." A similar process also took place in Islam and is encapsulated by the idea of the umma, or the entire community of the faithful under Allah. By generating the concepts of a universal Christian family and the umma, both religions in effect extended the powerful sanctions against kin-killing (see the story of Cain and Abel, Doc. 1) that exist in any feuding society to humanity as a whole, thus eliminating any right of its members to private family vengeance. The notions of a universal Christian family or an umma were in turn related to the concept of universal citizenship that developed in the Roman Empire in the third century.

Source: The New Testament (Douay-Rheims version), trans. from the Latin Vulgate by Gregory Martin, et al. (Rheims: The English College, 1582), rev. Richard Challoner (1749–52).

## 9. PEACEMAKING AND THE TIES OF KINSHIP

The New Testament amplified the counsel of peace already found in Deuteronomy, Ecclesiasticus, and other Old Testament texts. The first extract below, from Matthew 5, is one of the most influential statements on the blessings of peace. However, the authors of the New Testament were aware that, to promote peace, it was first necessary to weaken the bonds of kinship that generated vengeance, and also to promote the idea of a universal Christian family. This is the significance of the second extract (Doc. 9b), from Matthew 10.

### a. Blessed are the peacemakers

5:9 Blessed are the peacemakers: for they shall be called the children of God.

21 You have heard that it was said to them of old: Thou shalt not kill. And whosoever shall kill, shall be in danger of the judgment.

22 But I say to you, that whosoever is angry with his brother, shall be in danger of the judgment. And whosoever shall say to his brother, *Raca* [a Hebrew term of contempt], shall be in danger of the council. And whosoever shall say, Thou fool, shall be in danger of hell fire.

23 If therefore thou offer thy gift at the altar, and there thou remember that thy brother hath anything against thee;

24 Leave there thy offering before the altar, and go first to be reconciled to thy brother, and then coming thou shalt offer thy gift.

### b. Dismantling the kin group

10:34 Do not think that I came to send peace upon earth: I came not to send peace, but the sword.

35 For I came to set a man at variance against his father, and the daughter against her mother, and the daughter in law against her mother in law.

36 And a man's enemies shall be they of his own household.

37 He that loveth father or mother more than me, is not worthy of me; and he that loveth son or daughter more than me, is not worthy of me.

## 10. HUMILITY AS VENGEANCE?

*In these verses (Romans 12:17–21), the apostle Paul restates well-known passages from Leviticus and Deuteronomy. Especially interesting is the apparent emotional vindictiveness expressed in the otherwise humble and charitable statement found in Romans 12:20. Note how Jerome (Doc. 20) chooses to interpret this passage.*

17 To no man render evil for evil, but provide good things, not only in the sight of God but also in the sight of all men.

18 If it be possible, as much as is in you, have peace with all men.

19 Revenge not yourselves, my dearly beloved; but give place unto wrath, for it is written: Revenge is mine, I will repay, saith the Lord.

20 But if the enemy be hungry, give him to eat; if he thirst, give him to drink. For, doing this, thou shalt heap coals of fire upon his head.

21 Be not overcome by evil: but overcome evil by good.

# CHAPTER THREE: ROMAN LAWS

*The legal system of the Roman Empire is often held up in contrast to the so-called Germanic law codes (see Docs. 13, 14, and 16). Roman law has a reputation for possessing an unemotional and impersonal viewpoint that is concerned, above all, with dry technicalities and otiose procedures. The Germanic law codes, promulgated by the leaders of the barbarian kingdoms that emerged from the shards of the western Roman Empire during the fifth and sixth centuries, spoke more frankly of the bloodfeud, as if they anticipated that injuries of all sorts would be met with vengeance. Specific laws identified the appropriate payments, to be made by offending parties to the victim or his or her family, that were necessary to avert the bloodfeuds.*

*Although Roman law codes did not contain similar expectations about vengeance, their creators could be deeply interested in the emotional states that generated legal actions. Some of the following selections demonstrate that Roman legislators were aware of the possibility that individuals might use the courts as a method of vengeance in order to get back at their enemies. These selections also illustrate what the emperor or the state thought about vengeance and the degree to which the exercise of force was deemed to be a monopoly of the state.*

## 11. CRIMINAL JUSTICE AND VENGEANCE IN THE THEODOSIAN CODE AND SIRMONDIAN CONSTITUTIONS

*The next few documents are from the Theodosian Code, a collection of imperial constitutions or decrees that date from the time of the Roman emperor Constantine I (r. 306–337) to the time of Theodosius II (r. 408–450). Theodosius commissioned the Code in 429, and, after its completion in 437, it was validated in the eastern part of the empire in early 438 and promulgated to the western part of the empire at the end of that year. The Theodosian Code continued to be used in the old western half of the empire even after it was superseded a century later in the remaining, eastern half by the great code of Emperor Justinian (Doc. 12). Document 11k is part of the Sirmondian Constitutions, named after their seventeenth-century discoverer, Jacques Sirmond. Issued between 333 and 425, they contain longer versions of some of the same laws as the Theodosian Code. The compilers of the Theodosian Code deliberately abbreviated laws from the Sirmondian Constitutions and either accidentally or deliberately omitted others, such as the title on sanctuary issued in 419. Accidental omission is possible since the Sirmondian Constitutions do not appear to have been gathered into a collection before the late sixth century.*

*The Theodosian Code includes penalties that vary according to social class and also suggest that injured parties were responsible for bringing a malefactor to court. Even if the injured parties did have to provide their own policing, the codes make it clear that residents of the empire ultimately had to rely on the law to provide vengeance for them. At the same time, the legal system was clearly aware of the possibility that people might use the courts unfairly in their pursuit of vengeance.*

*The claim of an imperial monopoly on legitimate vengeance is a secular counterpart to Deuteronomy 32:35, "Revenge is mine, saith the Lord" (Doc. 4b). The idea that kings and emperors, through their legal codes, could usurp God's privilege to dispense vengeance was a powerful one, for it elevated rulers to the status of God's principal representative on earth and bolstered royal claims of divine right. The royal prerogative to administer vengeance in God's name became an important component of the image of royal authority that developed in twelfth-century Europe (see, e.g., Doc. 75).*

*The laws below take the form of extracts from letters written by emperors (or, rather, an unnamed official acting in the emperor's name) to prefects and other officials in the Roman provinces. Some of the laws include interpretations added to the original text in the fifth century. The translators give two dates for a law when there is a disagreement between modern scholars.*

Source: trans. Clyde Pharr with Theresa Sherrer Davidson and Mary Brown Pharr, *The Theodosian Code and Novels and the Sirmondian Constitutions* (Princeton: Princeton University Press, 1952), pp. 100–101, 224–28, 234–40, 244–45, 255, 483–84.

## a. Accusations and inscriptions
### [Book 9, title 1]

4. Augustus [Constantine] to all Provincials [provincial officials]

If there is any person of any position, rank, or dignity whatever who believes that he is able to prove anything truthfully and clearly against any judge, count, or any of my retainers or palatines, in that any of these persons has committed some act which appears to have been done without integrity and justice, let him approach me and appeal to me unafraid and secure. I myself will hear everything; I myself will conduct an investigation; and if the charge should be proved, I myself will avenge myself. Let him speak with safety, and let him speak with a clear conscience. If he should prove the case, as I have said, I myself will avenge myself on that person who has deceived me up to this time with feigned integrity. The person, moreover, who has revealed and proved the offense I will enrich with honors as well as with material rewards. Thus may the highest divinity always be propitious to me and keep me unharmed, as I hope, with the state most happy and flourishing.

Posted on the fifteenth day before the kalends [the first day] of October at Nicomedia in the year of the consulship of Paulinus and Julianus—September 17, 325.

5. The same Augustus to Maximus, Prefect of the City.

At one time it was permitted that an accusation of crime instituted not by an inscription but by a declaration of the crime escaping from the lips in speech only would compel the accuser as well as the accused, under peril of trial, to contend for his rights as a citizen, his children, his fortunes, and, finally, for his life. It is our will, therefore, that the license and rashness of such declarations shall be abolished and a charge of crime shall be brought according to the customary form and order of inscription, that everyone shall use the ancient law in bringing criminal charges, that is, that when anger has been soothed and tranquility of mind restored by these lapses of time, they shall come to the final action with reason and counsel.

Given on the eleventh day before the kalends of June at Sirmium [Sremska Mitrovica, Serbia] – May 22. Received at Rome in the year of the seventh consulship of Constantine Augustus and the consulship of Constantius Caesar. – 326; 320 [Probably 320 based on the date of the prefect Maximus].

Interpretation: If anyone in anger should rashly accuse any person of some crime, the angry reviling must not be held as an accusation; but after space for reflection has been allowed, the accuser shall state in writing that he will prove what he said in anger. But if, perchance, he should come to his senses after his anger and perhaps should not be willing to repeat or write what he said, the person denounced shall not be held as accused of crime.

12. The same Augustuses [Valentinian and Valens] to Laodicus, Governor of Sardinia.

The right to accuse of crime must be denied accused persons until they have cleared themselves of the crimes with which they are charged. For the founders of the ancient sanctions decreed that all persons should be deprived of the right to speak invidious words against their accusers. Thus the fury of persons in jeopardy shall have no authority in the courts, for if such fury should spread too widely, not even the trial judge himself will be safe, nor will he conduct his criminal investigations in safety, if in executing the severe requirements of the law, he cannot avoid the hatred of those whom he punishes.

Given on the day before the ides of August at Carnuntum [Austria] in the year of the third consulship of Gratian Augustus and the consulship of the Most Noble Equitius. – August 12, 374; 375 [the date is uncertain. Valentinian did not depart from Gaul into Pannonia until 375].

Interpretation: The assertions against others made by persons who are accused of crime shall not be credited unless the accused persons should first prove themselves innocent, because the declaration against anyone by such defendants is dangerous and must not be admitted.

14. Emperors Gratian, Valentinian, and Theodosius Augustuses to Marinianus, Vicar of Spain.

When a person brings an action for homicide, or makes a charge of suspected homicide, he shall not prosecute such a capital case by means of a formal accusation until he has obligated himself by the bonds of the law and undertakes to conduct the controversy subject to the risk of the same punishment as the accused. Even if any person should suppose that slaves ought to be accused, torture shall not be inflicted upon the unfortunate slaves until the accuser has bound himself by the bond of inscription. For a case of criminal prosecution of slaves results in property loss and punishment for the masters.

Given on the sixth day before the kalends of June at Padua in the year of the second consulship of Merobaudes and the consulship of Saturninus. – May 27, 383.

Interpretation: When any person prosecutes another with the dangerous and capital accusation of the crime of homicide, he shall not be heard by the judges until he declares in writing that he will undergo the same punishment with which he threatens the accused; and if he should suppose that slaves belonging to others ought to be accused, he shall bind himself by a similar inscription to compensate for the punishment of innocent slaves, either by capital punishment of himself or by the forfeiture of his property.

19. Emperors Honorius and Theodosius Augustuses to the Consuls, Praetors, Tribunes of the People, and their own Senate, Greetings.

We order that the procedure formerly instituted by law for making accusations shall be maintained; that a person who is summoned to undergo the risk of a capital penalty shall not be considered immediately a defendant who could be accused formally, lest we make innocence subject to harm. But whoever it may be that brings a criminal charge, he shall come into court, indicate the name of the accused, undertake the bond of inscription, and submit to a custody similar to that of the accused, with due consideration, however, of his rank; and he shall know that the wantonness of a false accusation will not go unpunished, since by similarity of penalty vengeance is exacted of false accusers.

1. No person, however, who has confessed his own guilt under torture shall flatter himself that, by accusing another of any crime whatever, he may hope for pardon on account of the wrongs of his accomplice, or that he may

expect to be associated with a personage of higher rank by reason of mutual participation in the crime, or that by the punishment of a personal enemy he may share with him the lot of his last moments, or that he may trust that he can be saved by the efforts or privilege of a person named by him, since the authority of the ancient law does not permit those persons who have confessed their own guilt even to be questioned about the guilty knowledge of others. Therefore, when a person confesses his own crime, no one shall interrogate him about another's guilty knowledge. No one shall believe a person who is trying to escape punishment when he willingly contrives the punishment of another. We absolutely refuse credence to letters of instruction that have been secretly entrusted (Etc.)

Given on the eighth day before the ides of August at Ravenna in the year of the consulship of Asclepiodotus and Marinianus. – August 6, 423.

Interpretation: Before the execution of an inscription, no person is considered criminal; for when an inscription has been made in due order, the accused shall be received by the judge and delivered into custody along with his accuser, in such a manner, however, that the rank of the accused as well as that of the accuser shall be considered; and the judge shall cause each one to be guarded before the trial according as his hereditary status and rank permit. If those persons, however, who have confessed their own guilt under torture wish to speak about others, the judge shall not believe them, because it has been established by the law and statutes that an accused person cannot bring charges against another merely by a spontaneous declaration, and when a person has confessed that he is a criminal, his testimony shall not be credited with regard to another.

## b. The production and transfer of accused persons
## [Book 9, title 2]

5. Emperors Honorius and Theodosius Augustuses to Caecilianus, Praetorian Prefect.

Defenders, curators, magistrates, and senates of the municipalities shall not send to prison accused persons presented to them. But when any person has been apprehended in the act of robbery, in violent encounters, or in the perpetration of homicide, debauchery, rape, or adultery, and has been delivered to them by municipal legal action, after the crime has been declared by the statements of the accusers, such criminals shall immediately be dispatched, together with the accusers, under suitable escort, to a court.

Given on the twelfth day before the kalends of February at Ravenna in the year of the eighth consulship of Honorius Augustus and the third consulship of Theodosius Augustus. – January 21, 409.

## c. The Julian law on public and private violence
### [Book 9, title 10]

1. Emperor Constantine Augustus to Catullinus, Proconsul of Africa.

If any person is proved in court to have committed manifest violence, no longer shall he be punished by the exile of relegation or of deportation to an island, but he shall receive capital punishment. By the interposition of an appeal he shall not obtain suspension of the sentence which has been pronounced against him. For many crimes are included under the one term of violence: assaults and homicides are frequently discovered to have been committed when some persons attempt to employ violence and others fight back against them with indignation. Whence it is our pleasure that if, perchance, anyone should be killed, whether on the part of the possessor or of the person who has attempted to violate possession, punishment shall be inflicted on the one who attempted to employ violence and thus furnished a cause of wrongdoing to the one or the other party.

Given on the fifteenth day before the kalends of May at Sofia [Serdica] in the year of the consulship of Gallicanus and Bassus. – April 17, 317 [?]

Interpretation: A person who is convicted in court of the manifest crime of violence shall suffer capital punishment, and if condemned he shall not, by any appeal whatsoever, obtain suspension of the sentence of the judge. If, by chance, homicide should be committed by either party, the person shall be punished who made a violent entry to expel another by fighting.

2. The same Augustus to Bassus, Prefect of the City.

If any person should invade another's farm with violence, he shall suffer capital punishment. If anyone should be killed, whether on the part of the person who attempted to employ violence or of the person who repulsed injury, punishment shall be inflicted on the one who intended to eject the possessor by violence.

Given on the sixth day before the ides of March at Rome in the year of the consulship of Gallicanus and Bassus. – March 10, 317; 318.

3. The same Augustus to Bassus, Prefect of the City.

If any person should assert that a farm or any other property belongs to him and should suppose that restitution of possession is due to him legally, he shall have the right to bring a civil suit for possession or, after he has fulfilled the formalities of the law, he shall have the right to bring a criminal charge for violence, not unaware that if he should not be able to prove the crime charged, he will undergo the same sentence as that which the accused would otherwise have received. But if he should omit an appeal to the court and should employ violence against the possessor, we command that the case of violence shall be tried before all else and that in the trial it shall be determined which party employed violence and which party was the possessor who suffered violence, in order that the rights of his lost possession may be restored to the party who is proved to have been dispossessed. When the aforesaid possession has been promptly restored, the person guilty of violence, destined for a penalty not undeserved, shall be put off until the end of the whole litigation, in order that, after the principal action has been tried, if the decision should be against him, he may be deported to an island and all his goods be confiscated. But if the decision should be pronounced in favor of the person who appears to have committed violence, half of all the property involved in the litigation shall remain in his possession. The rest shall be vindicated to the account of the fisc [imperial treasury].

Posted on the day before the nones of October at Rome in the year of the fifth consulship of Constantine Augustus and the consulship of Licinius Caesar. – October 6, 319.

Interpretation: If any person should suppose that he may so accuse his adversary before the judge that he may assert that such [an] adversary has employed violence, the accuser shall be held to the proof of the accusation. But if he should not be able to prove that the person whom he had mentioned employed violence, he shall receive the same penalty as that which the person whom he charged could have received if he had been convicted. As for the rest, this law must be passed over because it is explained in the fourth book under the title, "Whence by Violence," which, however, was devised later.

4. Emperors Valentinian, Theodosius, and Arcadius Augustuses to Albinus, Prefect of the City.

When slaves are proved by the testimony of witnesses or by their own confession to have committed violence, if they committed this crime without the knowledge of their masters, we decree that they shall be surrendered and shall atone for their deeds by the supreme penalty. But if they committed the violence because of fear or the exhortation of their masters, it is clear, according to the Julian Law, that the master shall be pronounced infamous and that he cannot use as defense the dignity of his station or of his birth; but slaves who are proved to have obeyed the madness of such masters shall be sentenced to the mines. Low and infamous persons, moreover, and those who are convicted of having committed violence twice or more frequently shall be held liable to the penalty prescribed by the divine imperial constitutions. The judge must know, indeed, that he will be branded with grave infamy if he should delay or neglect to punish a crime of violence that is proved in his court, or if he should endow such crime with impunity or punish it with a milder penalty than that which we have provided.

Given on the day before the nones of March at Milan in the year of the fourth consulship of Valentinian Augustus and the consulship of the Most Noble Neoterius. – March 6, 390.

Interpretation: If slaves should confess that they have committed violence without the knowledge of their masters or should be convicted of so doing, they shall be sentenced to severe tortures and punished. But if it was at the command of their masters that they committed the crime of violence, the masters who commanded the illicit deeds shall be branded with infamy and cannot retain the dignity of their high rank or office. Slaves, moreover, who have obeyed such madness of their masters shall be cast into the mines. Judges shall not be permitted to defer or to dismiss a trial of violence or to condone such an offense; for if they should prove violence and should not punish it immediately, they shall know that they will incur peril. Persons of low rank, moreover, who are proved to have committed violence twice, or more frequently, shall be smitten in all cases by the aforesaid penalty established by the statutes.

### d. The custody of private prisons
### [Book 9, title 11]

1. Emperors Valentinian, Theodosius, and Arcadius Augustuses to Erythrius, Augustal Prefect.

If anyone hereafter should dispatch an accused person to a private prison, he shall be held guilty of high treason.

Given on the day before the kalends of May at Thessalonica in the year of the second consulship of Theodosius Augustus and the consulship of the Most Noble Cynegius. – April 30, 388.

[Interpretation:] This law does not require interpretation.

### e. The Cornelian law [81 BCE by Cornelius Sulla during his
### dictatorship] on cutthroats
### [Book 9, title 14]

2. Emperors Valentinian, Theodosius, and Arcadius Augustuses to the Provincials.

We grant to all men the unrestricted right of resistance if any soldiers or private citizens should enter their fields as nocturnal ravagers or should beset frequented roads by attacks from ambush. This right is granted to everyone

in order that whoever so deserves shall be subjected immediately to punishment, shall receive the death which he threatened, and shall incur that
danger which he intended for another. For it is better for a man to fight back
at the proper time than for him to be avenged after his death. Therefore, we
entrust the right of vengeance to you, and what is too late to punish by trial
we repress by edict. Let no man spare a soldier who should be resisted with
a weapon as a brigand.

Given on the kalends of July in the year of the consulship of Tatianus and
Symmachus. – July 1, 391.

Interpretation: Whenever anyone as a nocturnal ravager attacks either a
traveler or someone's home for the purpose of committing robbery, we grant
to those persons who sustain violence the right to resist even with arms, and
if the one who came should be killed for his rash lawlessness, the death of the
brigand himself shall be required of no one.

### f. Parricides
### [Book 9, title 15]

1. Emperor Constantine Augustus to Verinus, Vicar of Africa.

If any person should hasten the fate of a parent or a son or any person at
all of such degree of kinship that killing him is included under the title of
parricide, whether he has accomplished this secretly or openly, he shall not
be subjected to the sword or to fire or to any other customary penalty, but he
shall be sewed in a leather sack and, confined within its deadly closeness, he
shall share the companionship of serpents. As the nature of the region shall
determine, he shall be thrown into the neighboring sea or into a river, so that
while still alive he may begin to lose the enjoyment of all the elements, that
the heavens may be taken away from him while he is living and the earth,
when he is dead.

Given on the sixteenth day before the kalends of December in the year
of the fifth consulship of Licinius and the consulship of Crispus Caesar.
– November 16, 318. Received on the day before the ides of March at
Carthage in the year of the fifth consulship of Constantine Augustus and the
consulship of Licinius Caesar. – March 14, 319.

Interpretation: If any person should kill his father, mother, brother, sister,
son, daughter, or other near kinsman, all other kinds of tortures shall be
rejected, and a sack, called a *culleus,* shall be made of leather, into which he
shall be cast; then serpents shall be enclosed with him, and, if there should
not be a neighboring sea, he shall be thrown into whatever stream there may
be, so that a person condemned to such a penalty may never obtain burial.

## g. Magicians, astrologers, and all other like criminals
### [Book 9, title 16]

11. Emperors Valentinian, Theodosius, and Arcadius Augustuses to Albinus, Prefect of the City.

If anyone should hear of a person who is contaminated with the pollution of magic or if he should apprehend such a person or seize him, he shall drag him out immediately before the public and shall show the enemy of the common safety to the eyes of the courts. But if any charioteer or anyone of any other class of men should attempt to contravene this interdict or should destroy by clandestine punishment a person, even though he is clearly guilty of the evil art of magic, he shall not escape the supreme penalty, since he is subject to a double suspicion, namely, that he has secretly removed a public criminal from the severity of the law and from due investigation, in order that said criminal might not expose his associates in crime, or that perhaps he has killed his own enemy by a more atrocious plan under the pretense of avenging this crime.

Given on the seventeenth day before the kalends of September at Rome in the year of the consulship of Timasius and Promotus. – August 16, 389.

## h. The violation of tombs
### [Book 9, title 17]

2. The same Augustus [Constantius] to Limenius, Praetorian Prefect.

By the imposition of a fine we correct a deed that is customarily avenged by blood, and we so decree punishment in the future that any person who has committed the crime before the issuance of this law shall not be free from punishment. If any person, therefore, should take away columns or marble from monuments or should throw down stones for the purpose of burning them into lime, only after the time of the consulship of Dalmatius and Zenophilus, of course, he shall pay to the account of the fisc a pound of gold for each tomb thus violated, after the case has been investigated by the court of your Prudence. Those persons also shall be held liable to the same penalty who demolish a monument or diminish its ornamentation. Persons who sell to lime burners the monuments placed in their fields shall be subject to the penalty, together with those who dare to purchase such monuments; for if it is contrary to divine law for anything to be touched, it cannot be purchased without pollution. Thus one pound of gold shall be demanded of each of the two....

5. Emperor Julian Augustus to the People

Criminal audacity extends to the ashes of the dead and their consecrated mounds, although our ancestors always considered it the next thing to sacrilege even to move a stone from such places or to disturb the earth or to tear up the sod. But some men even take away from the tombs ornaments for their dining rooms and porticoes. We consider the interests of such criminals first, that they may not fall into sin by defiling the sanctity of tombs, and we prohibit such deeds, restraining them by the penalty which avenges the spirits of the dead....

Given on the day before the ides of February at Antioch in the year of the fourth consulship of Julian Augustus and the consulship of Sallustius. – February 12, 363.

## i. The rape of virgins and widows
### [Book 9, title 24]

1. Emperor Constantine Augustus to the People.

4. If any slave should report to the public courts a crime of rape passed over by connivance or disregarded by a pact, he shall be granted Latinity, or, if he is Latin, he shall be made a Roman citizen. If the parents, whom the punishment of the crime concerns especially, should show forbearance and suppress their grief, they shall be punished by deportation....

Given on the kalends of April at Aquileia in the year of the sixth consulship of Constantine Augustus and the consulship of Constantius Caesar. – April 1, 320; 326.

Interpretation: ... A person convicted of rape shall not be permitted to appeal, but he shall be punished immediately by the judge in the very beginning of the investigation. But if perhaps the ravisher should make an agreement with the parents of the girl and if the right to revenge of the parents for the crime of rape should be passed over in silence and if a slave should report this fact, he shall receive the freedom of a Latin; if he is a Latin, he shall be made a Roman citizen. Parents who come to an agreement with the ravisher in such a matter shall be condemned to exile....

## j. Malicious accusers
### [Book 9, title 39]

3. Emperors Arcadius and Honorius Augustuses to Victorius, Proconsul of Africa.

We do not permit innocent persons to be ruined by the attacks of crafty men under the pretext of false criminal accusations. If any persons should attempt such attacks, they shall know that the severity of the law will overwhelm them for the commission of such crimes.

Given on the third day before the ides of March at Milan in the year of the fourth consulship of Honorius Augustus and the consulship of Eutychianus. – March (May) 13, 398.

Interpretation: Those persons are malicious accusers who prosecute cases not pertaining to themselves without the mandate of others. Those persons are malicious accusers who attempt to renew a case when they have been defeated in a fair trial. Those persons are malicious accusers who make a demand or bring into court a matter which does not pertain to them. Those persons are malicious accusers who seek to obtain the property of others under the name of the fisc and do not permit innocent persons to remain undisturbed. Those persons are malicious accusers also who presumptuously arouse the minds of the emperors to anger by bringing false charges against some innocent person. All such persons shall be rendered infamous and driven into exile. (Here must be added from the law what persons can be malicious accusers.)

### k. Persons who flee for sanctuary to the churches [Sirmondian Constitutions, Title 13]

Emperors Honorius and Theodosius, Pious Augustuses.

It is fitting that humanity, which was known even before Our times, should temper justice. For when very many people flee from the violence of a cruel fortune and choose the protection of the defense of the churches, when they are confined therein, they suffer no less imprisonment than that which they have avoided. For at no time is an egress opened to them into the light of the vestibule. Therefore the sanctity of ecclesiastical reverence shall apply to the space of fifty paces beyond the doors of the church. If anyone should hold a person who goes forth from this place, he shall incur the criminal charge of sacrilege. For no compassion is granted to the fugitives if the free air is denied to them in their affliction.

We grant to the priest the right also to enter the courts of the prison on a mission of compassion, to heal the sick, to feed the poor, and to console the innocent; when he has investigated thoroughly and has learned the case of each person, according to law he shall direct his intervention before the competent judge. For We know, and supplications have come to Us in regard to such cases in numerous audiences, that very many persons are frequently thrust into prison in order that they may be deprived of the freedom to approach the judge; and when a rather humble person once begins to suffer imprisonment before his case is known, he is compelled to suffer the penalty of outrage. The contumacious office staff shall immediately pay to Our fisc two pounds of gold if the feral doorkeeper should exclude a priest who is caring for such sacred matters.

Given on the eleventh day before the kalends of December at Ravenna in the year of the consulship of the Most Noble Monaxius and Plinta. – November 21, 419.

## 12. CRIMINAL JUSTICE AND VENGEANCE IN JUSTINIAN'S *DIGEST*

*The Digest is a comprehensive set of passages from juristic textbooks and commentaries collected in the 530s by a team of jurists operating under the direction of Justinian (r. 527–565), emperor of the eastern Roman or Byzantine Empire. Ultimately, these passages were derived from the opinions of jurists during the High Empire, especially those – Ulpian, Alfenus, and many others – who worked under the emperor Hadrian (117–138 CE). The laws that received comment include some from the Republic (the* Lex Cornelia *[81 BCE] and the* Lex Pompeia *[55 or 52 BCE]) and the early Empire (the* Lex Julia *of 18–17 BCE). Justinian also commanded a revision, enlargement, and rearrangement of the Theodosian Code, which his scholars succeeded in producing in 529. The* Code *and the* Digest, *along with the* Novellae *(new constitutions) and* Institutes *make up the* Corpus Iuris Civilis (Body of Civil Law). *Though the* Corpus Iuris Civilis *was largely forgotten in western Europe after the sixth century, it was rediscovered by jurists and canon lawyers in the eleventh century and studied in the universities. Knowledge of the* Corpus *spread rapidly throughout western Europe, although its direct impact was less in England than it was on the continent. The* Corpus Iuris Civilis *also greatly influenced the development of canon law in the Latin Church.*

Source: rev. trans. Alan Watson, *The Digest of Justinian*, vol. 2 (Philadelphia: University of Pennsylvania Press, 1998), unpaginated.

### a. Gamblers
### [Book 11, title 5]

1. Ulpian, *Edict*, book 23: The praetor says: "If someone assaults a man on whose premises gambling is said to have taken place or causes him any damage or if anything is stolen from his home while gambling is going on, I shall not give an action. I shall punish any man who uses force for the sake of gambling according to the circumstances of the case...."

## b. Witnesses
### [Book 22, title 5]

3. Callistratus, *Cognitiones,* book 4: The reliability of witnesses must be carefully assessed. One must first inquire into their status. Are they decurions [members of a city senate] or plebians? Do they lead an honest and blameless life, or has there been some mark of disgrace? Are they well off or needy, so that they may readily act for gain? Are they enemies of those against whom they give evidence or friends of those for whom they give it? Evidence can be admitted if it is free from suspicion, because of the witness (an honest man) or the motive (not gain, favor, or enmity)....

## c. Obligations and actions
### [Book 44, title 7]

20. Alfenus, *Digest,* book 2: A slave does not usually in all cases obey the orders of his master with impunity, for instance, where the master had ordered his slave to kill a man or to commit theft against someone. Consequently, even though a slave had committed piracy on the orders of his master, an action must be brought against him after he is freed. And, therefore, whatever violent act he committed must afflict him with punishment, if the violence was not alien to a crime. But if some brawl arose from dispute and quarreling, or if some violence was committed in order to preserve a right, and no crime was constituted by these acts, then it does not behoove the praetor to allow an action against the slave when freed in respect of an act which the slave committed on the orders of his master.

## d. Criminal proceedings
### [Book 48, title 1]

2. Paul, *Praetor's Edict,* book 15: Some criminal proceedings are capital while others are not. Capital [proceedings] are those where the penalty is death or exile, which here means interdiction from fire and water, because by these penalties civil status is taken away. Other [sentences] are not properly referred to as exile but as relegation; for in them citizenship is retained. Noncapital [proceedings] are those where the penalty is a fine or some form of corporal punishment.

3. Ulpian, *Sabinus,* book 35: A public accusation lapses, should the person charged, male or female, die beforehand.

4. Paul, *Edict,* book 37: It sometimes happens that there may be a preliminary inquiry by means of a private action before a criminal trial, such as an

Aquilian action [enables a person to receive compensation from the person responsible for loss or damage to private property], an action for theft or for the removal of goods by force, or an interdict against force or for the production of a will; for in these cases matters concerning the *familia* are at issue.

5. Ulpian, *Disputations,* book 8: Someone who has been charged must clear himself and cannot bring an accusation until he has been discharged; for it is recognized in the constitutions that a charged person is cleared, not by bringing a counter charge, but by his innocence. 1. It is not certain whether he can only bring an accusation if he has actually been found not guilty, or [if he can do so] when he has undergone the penalty; for it has been laid down by our emperor and his deified father that after being found guilty a person cannot begin an accusation. I think, however, that this applies only to those who have lost citizenship or freedom. 2. It is clearly permissible for those who have initiated prosecutions before being found guilty to carry them through afterward.

## e. The Julian law on punishing adulteries
## [Book 48, title 5]

21. Papinian, *Adulteries,* book 1: A father is granted the right of killing an adulterer along with a daughter whom he has in power; no other [class of] father may lawfully do this, including a father who is a son-in-power [under the power of his own father].

22. Ulpian, *Adulterers,* book 1: (Thus, it may happen that neither a father nor a grandfather may be able to kill), nor is this unreasonable; for a man does not seem to have [anyone] in his own power if he does not have power over himself.

23. Papinian, *Adulterers,* book 1: In this statute, a natural is not distinguished from an adoptive father.

1. A father does not have a special right of accusation over a daughter who is a widow.

2. The right to kill is granted to the father in his own house, even if his daughter does not live there, or in the house of his son-in-law; the term "house" is to be taken as meaning "domicile," as in the *lex Cornelia* on *injuria* [striking or beating and home invasion].

3. However, a person who has the power to kill an adulterer is all the more able lawfully to inflict rough treatment on him.

4. The reason why it is the father and not the husband who is allowed to kill the woman and any adulterer [caught with her] is that, for the most part, the concern for family duty implicit in the title of father takes counsel for his

children; but the heat and impetuosity of a husband [too] readily jumping to a decision should be restrained.

24. Ulpian, *Adulteries,* book 1: The words of the statute "shall have caught the adulterer in his daughter" do not appear to be otiose; for the intention was that this power should be available to the father if and only if he should catch his daughter actually engaged in the crime of adultery. Labeo also approves [this interpretation], and Pomponius has written that a person caught in the actual act of love is killed. This also is what Solon and Draco say: "in the act."

25. Macer, *Criminal Proceedings,* book 1: A husband is also permitted to kill his wife's adulterer, but not, as the father is, whoever it may be; for it is provided by this statute that a husband is permitted to kill a man whom he catches in adultery with his wife in his own house (not also [in that] of his father-in-law) if the [paramour] is a pimp or if he was previously an actor or performed on the stage as a dancer or singer or if he has been condemned in criminal proceedings and is not yet restored to his former status, or if he is a freedman of the husband or wife or of the father, mother, son, or daughter of either of them (and it is of no consequence whether he was the sole property of one of them or was owned jointly with someone else) or if he is a slave.

1. It is also laid down that a husband who kills any of these is to divorce his wife without delay.

2. But it has been stated by the majority of [jurists] that it does not matter whether the husband is *sui juris* [able to manage his own legal affairs] or a son-in-power.

3. The question is asked, as regards both of them [father and husband], in terms of the sense of the statute: Is the father permitted to kill a magistrate? Again, if the daughter is of bad reputation or the wife was married contrary to the statutes, do the father and the husband nonetheless have the right [to kill her]? And what if the father or the husband is a pimp or branded with some disgrace? It will be more correct to say that [only] those who can bring an accusation under a father's or husband's right have the right to kill.

30. Ulpian, *Adulteries,* book 4: The statute has punished the *lenocinium* [serving as pimp] of a husband who after catching his wife in adultery has kept her and let the adulterer go; for he ought to have avenged himself on the man and also vented his rage on his wife, who has violated their marriage. The circumstances in which the husband is to be punished are when he cannot defend his ignorance [of the adultery] or cloak his forbearance with the pretext of disbelief; for this reason, then, the words of the statute are "[who] lets go an adulterer caught in his house," because its intention is to punish the husband who catches [the adulterer] in his actual wrongdoing....

## f. The Julian law on violent crime
## [Book 48, title 6]

1. Marcian, *Institutes*, book 14: A man is liable under the *lex Julia* on *vis publica* [a violent crime] on the grounds that he collects arms or weapons at his home or on his farm or at his country house beyond those customary for hunting or for a journey by land or sea.

3. Marcian, *Institutes*, book 14:

2. Under the same heading come those who, assembling seditiously in the most wicked manner, attack country houses and seize property with missile and hand weapons.

6. Also liable under this statute is anyone who with armed men expels someone having possession from his home, his farm, or his ship, or attacks him.

11. Paul, *Views*, book 5:

2. Persons who bear weapons for the purpose of protecting their own safety are not regarded as carrying them for the purpose of homicide.

## g. The Cornelian law on murderers and poisoners
## [Book 48, title 8]

1. Marcian, *Institutes*, book 14: Under the *lex Cornelia* on murderers and poisoners, someone is liable who kills any man or by whose malicious intent a fire is set; or who goes about with a weapon for the purpose of homicide or a theft; or who, being a magistrate or presiding over a criminal trial, arranged for someone to give false evidence so that an innocent man may be entrapped [and] condemned.

1. He also is liable who makes up [and] administers poison for the purpose of killing a man; or who with malicious intent gives false evidence so that someone may be condemned in criminal proceedings for a capital offense; or who, being a magistrate or judge of a [jury] court in a capital case, takes a bribe so that [the accused] may be found guilty under criminal law.

2. Whoever kills a man is punished without distinction as to the status of the man he killed.

3. The deified Hadrian [Roman emperor, r. 117–138 CE] wrote in a rescript [response] that he who kills a man, if he committed this act without the intention of causing death, could be acquitted; and he who did not kill a man but wounded him with the intention of killing ought to be found guilty of homicide. On this account, it should be laid down that if someone draws his sword or strikes with a weapon, he undoubtedly did so with the

intention of causing death; but if he struck someone with a key or a saucepan in the course of a brawl, although he strikes [the blow] with iron, yet it was not with the intention of killing. From this it is deduced that he who has killed a man in a brawl by accident rather than design should suffer a lighter penalty.

4. Again, the deified Hadrian wrote in a rescript that he who kills someone forcibly making a sexual assault on him or a member of his family should be discharged.

5. The deified [Antoninus] Pius wrote that a lighter penalty should be imposed on him who killed his wife caught in adultery, and ordered that a person of low rank should be exiled permanently, but that one of any standing should be relegated for a set period.

2. Ulpian, *Adulterers,* book 1: A father cannot kill his son without giving him a hearing but must accuse him before the prefect or the provincial governor.

3. Marcian, *Institutes,* book 14: Under chapter five of the same *lex Cornelia* on murderers and poisoners, someone is punished who makes, sells, or possesses a drug for the purpose of homicide....

4. Again, he is liable whose *familia,* with his knowledge, takes up arms with the intention of acquiring or recovering possession; also he who instigates a sedition; and he who conceals a shipwreck; and he who produces, or is responsible for the production of, false evidence for the entrapment of an innocent person; again, any one who castrates a man for lust or for gain is by *senatus consultum* [decree of the senate] subject to the penalty of the *lex Cornelia.*

5. The penalty of the *lex Cornelia* on murderers and prisoners is deportation to an island and forfeiture of all property. However, nowadays capital punishment is customary, except for persons of a status too high to be subject to the [modern] statutory punishment; those of lower rank are usually either crucified or thrown to the beasts while their betters are deported to an island.

6. It is lawful to kill deserters to the enemy wherever they are met with, as though they were enemies.

7. Paul, *Criminal Proceedings,* sole book: Under the *lex Cornelia,* guilty intention is presumed from the deed. But, under this law, gross negligence is not interpreted as guilty intention. Accordingly, if someone throws himself from a height and lands on another, killing him, or a pruner when throwing down a branch from a tree fails to shout a warning and kills a passer-by, punishment under this statute is not applicable.

9. Ulpian, *Edict,* book 37: If anyone kills a thief by night, he shall do so unpunished if and only if he could not have spared the man['s life] without risk to his own.

12. Modestinus, *Rules,* book 8: An infant or madman who kills a man is not liable under the *lex Cornelia,* the one being protected by the innocence of his intent, the other excused by the misfortune of his condition.

14. Callistratus, *Judicial Examinations,* book 6: The deified Hadrian wrote a rescript in the following words: "In crimes it is the intention, not the issue, to which regard is paid."

15. Ulpian, *Lex Julia et Papia,* book 8: It makes no difference whether someone kills or provides the occasion of death.

16. Modestinus, *Punishments,* book 3: Those who have committed murder of their own free will and with malicious intent, if they hold office are normally deported; if they are of inferior station, they suffer the capital penalty. This can more readily be done in the case of decurions, but in such a way that [capital punishment] takes place [only] when the emperor has first been consulted and orders it [to be carried out], unless perchance a disorder could not otherwise be quieted down.

17. Paul, *Views,* book 5: If a man dies after being struck in a brawl, one must have regard to the blows delivered by each of those who gathered together for the purpose.

## h. The Pompeian law on parricides
### [Book 48, title 9]

1. Marcian, *Institutes,* book 14: By the *lex Pompeia* on parricides it is laid down that anyone who kills his father, mother, grandfather, grandmother, brother, sister, first cousin on the father's side, first cousin on the mother's side, paternal or maternal uncle, paternal [or maternal] aunt, first cousin (male or female) by mother's sister, wife, husband, father-in-law, son-in-law, mother-in-law, [daughter-in-law], stepfather, stepson, stepdaughter, patron or patroness, or with malicious intent brings this about, shall be liable to the same penalty as that of the *lex Cornelia* on murderers. And a mother who kills her son or daughter suffers the penalty of the same statute, as does a grandfather who kills a grandson; and in addition, a person who buys poison to give to his father, even though he is unable to administer it.

2. Scaevola, *Rules,* book 4: The brother [of a parricide], who had knowledge only [not proof] and did not warn his father, was relegated, and the doctor [who supplied the drug] was put to death.

3. Marcian, *Institutes,* book 14: It must be known that first cousins are included under the *lex Pompeia,* but that others of an equal or closer degree of kindred are not similarly covered. Stepmothers and betrothed persons are left out, but are covered by the spirit of the law.

4. Marcian, *Criminal Proceedings,* book 1: since the father and mother of the

betrothed, male or female, are contained in the term "fathers-in-law" as are those engaged to one's children in the term "sons-in-law."

5. Marcian, *Institutes,* book 14: It is said that when a certain man had killed in the course of a hunt his son, who had been committing adultery with his stepmother, the deified Hadrian deported him to an island [because he acted] more [like] a brigand in killing him as the [one] with a father's right; for paternal power ought to depend on compassion, not cruelty.

6. Ulpian, *Duties of a Proconsul,* book 8: Should [only] those who kill their parents be liable to the penalty for parricide, or their accomplices also? Marcian says that the accomplices also are liable to the same penalty, and not the parricides alone. Hence, accomplices, even if outside the family, are liable to the same penalty.

7. Ulpian, *Edict,* book 29: If, with the knowledge of a creditor, money is furnished for the commission of a crime, say for the procuring of poison or for payment to bandits or assailants for the killing of a father, he who seeks [to borrow] the money and he who thus lends it, or [he] by whom it is promised, shall [all] be liable to the penalty for parricide.

8. Ulpian, *Disputations,* book 8: If someone who has been accused of parricide dies in the meantime, then if he brought about his own death, the imperial treasury must be his heir; otherwise, provided he made a will, [the heir shall] be that person whom he wished; or if he died intestate, he shall have as heirs those called by law.

9. Modestinus, *Encyclopaedia,* book 12: According to the custom of our ancestors, the punishment instituted for parricide was as follows: A parricide is flogged with blood-colored rods, then sewn up in a sack with a dog, a dunghill cock, a viper, and a monkey; then the sack is thrown into the depths of the sea. This is the procedure if the sea is close at hand; otherwise, he is thrown to the beasts, according to the constitution of the deified Hadrian.

1. Those who kill persons other than their mother, father, grandfather, or grandmother (who, as we have said above, are punished in the traditional way) shall be punished capitally or put to the extreme penalty. Truly, if anyone kills a parent in a fit of madness, he shall not be punished, as the deified brothers wrote in a rescript in the case of a man who had killed his mother in a fit of madness; for it was enough for him to be punished by the madness itself, and he must be guarded the more carefully, or even confined with chains.

10. Paul, *Penalties under All the Laws,* sole book: An accusation is always allowed against those who can be liable to the penalty for parricide.

## i. Punishment
### [Book 48, title 19]

28. Callistratus, *Judicial Examinations,* book 6:

15. The practice approved by most authorities has been to hang notorious brigands on a gallows in the place which they used to haunt, so that by the spectacle others may be deterred from the same crimes, and so that it may, when the penalty has been carried out, bring comfort to the relatives and kin of those killed in that place where the brigands committed their murders; but some have condemned these [criminals] to the beasts.

# PART II.
## THE EARLY MIDDLE AGES (400–1000)

In the wake of the Germanic invasions of the fifth and sixth centuries, the western Roman Empire was carved up into a patchwork of kingdoms ruled by different Germanic peoples, including the Franks, the Burgundians, the Lombards, the Visigoths, the Ostrogoths, and the Anglo-Saxons. Inspired, in part, by the Theodosian Code and other legacies of the Roman judicial system, the new kings of these Germanic kingdoms sponsored their own codes. The way in which laws help to define the identity of a group is part of a process called ethnogenesis, whereby formerly unrelated individuals or families come to share a set of symbols and myths, and so begin to feel themselves to be members of a people or an ethnic group. These new Germanic law codes, thus, were both practical and symbolic: practical in the sense that law courts used (or may have used) the codes, and symbolic in the sense that the new laws acted as an expression of the identity of a given people.

Historians used to associate adherence to the law and civility with the Roman world and the practice of barbaric vengeance with the victorious Germanic peoples who came after. Currently, the understanding among historians is that the Germans had little to teach the Romans about family-based vengeance. Consequently, historians now see the talk of vengeance to be found in the documents between 400 and 1000 as a comment on the generally more limited powers of kings and government in Germanic society, and on the exceptionally important role accorded to divine vengeance in Christian thought and Christian texts of the period.

# CHAPTER FOUR: CODES, CAPITULARIES, AND PENITENTIALS

*The following passages taken from the Salic law, Lombard law, and several Anglo-Saxon legal codes are all relevant for an understanding of royal perspectives on feuding and peacemaking in Europe between 500 and 950. In the process of assimilating Roman culture, many Germanic rulers sought to set out their own laws in writing, an act itself inspired by the legacy of Rome. Some laws were clearly inspired by late Roman law, while others had their roots in older Germanic customs and were expressions of ethnogenesis.*

*Many laws were designed to avert bloodfeuds by requiring injured families to receive compensation in lieu of seeking to retaliate. Compensation, or composition, was the payment of money (or a money equivalent such as cattle) to reestablish social balance after a killing or injury. In feuding societies, such actions create an imbalance of honor between two parties: the killer's honor goes up and the victim's honor (the besmirching of which is felt by his or her family) goes down. A formal system of compensation sought to negate the need for revenge by individuals or families by redressing the honor imbalance and restoring parity. Some of the passages below reveal the existence of very precise tariffs that varied according to the quality, sex, or age of the person killed or injured. Free men, for example, had a higher wergeld, or price, than slaves. Oddly enough, a free man's wergeld was sometimes less than that for a boy or for a woman of child-bearing age. What this discrepancy reveals is that boy-killing and woman-killing were seen as particularly dishonorable acts.*

*The payment of compensation was not an innovation made by kings seeking to restrain vengeance. It was a common practice in stateless Iceland in the period described by the sagas (Docs. 83 and 84) and can be found in many global societies both past and present. As such, it is important to note that compensation usually went to the victim's family and not to the king's treasury, although later laws from medieval Europe reveal that kings were gradually getting their fingers into the pie and obtaining larger and larger percentages of the payments obtained. In other words, compensations did not work like criminal fines in modern-day Western legal systems; instead, they were roughly equivalent to damages paid over to a plaintiff following a lawsuit for wrongful death or injury.*

# 13. THE LAWS OF THE SALIAN FRANKS

*The Salian Franks were a Germanic people who, in the mid-fourth century, settled within the boundaries of the former western Roman Empire, in the area of the Low Countries, and who spread out over much of northern France during the fifth century. The Salic law was compiled toward the end of the reign of Clovis (r. 481–511), the de facto founder of the Frankish kingdom, after his baptism and conversion to Catholic Christianity, and contains some of the earliest evidence we have for the payment of compensation among the Germanic peoples. That compensation was known as wergeld, or "man-price," and the law listed wergeld values in both denarii and solidi: a denarius was a small silver coin and a solidus was a larger gold coin. Both units were also used in imperial Rome and at this time there were forty denarii to the solidus (the English and French words "shilling" and "sous" are derived from solidus).*

*The Salic law was a single written code meant to supersede Roman law except in matters not covered by the Salic law, although Title 68 (Doc. 13k) was added during the sixth century. The Salic law was used throughout the ninth century in a revised and reorganized form issued by Charlemagne in 802–803, and its provisions, particularly those concerning inheritance, were influential throughout the Middle Ages. During the succession dispute over the French throne that led to the Hundred Years' War (1337–1453), the Salic law was famously interpreted as prohibiting female inheritance of royal titles or the passing of royal titles down through the female line.*

Source: trans. Katherine Fischer Drew, *The Laws of the Salian Franks* (Philadelphia: University of Pennsylvania Press, 1991), pp. 82–83, 92–94, 104–8, 121–25, 130.

## a. Concerning wounds
## [Title 17]

1. He who wounds or tries to kill another man and the blow misses him, and it is proved against him, shall be liable to pay twenty-five hundred denarii (that is, sixty-two and one-half solidi).

2. He who tries to shoot another man with a poisoned arrow and the arrow misses him, and it is proved against him, shall be liable to pay twenty-five hundred denarii (that is, sixty-two and one-half solidi).

3. He who hits another man on the head so that his blood falls to the ground, and it is proved against him, shall be liable to pay six hundred denarii (that is, fifteen solidi).

4. He who strikes another man on the head so that the brain shows, and it is proved against him, shall be liable to pay six hundred denarii (that is, fifteen solidi).

5. If the three bones that lie over the brain protrude, he shall be liable to pay twelve hundred denarii (that is, thirty solidi).

6. If the wound penetrates between the ribs or into the stomach so that it reaches the internal organs, he shall be liable to pay twelve hundred denarii (that is, thirty solidi).

7. If the wound runs continuously and never heals, he shall be liable to pay twenty-five hundred denarii (that is, sixty-two and one-half solidi). For the cost of medical attention, he shall pay three hundred sixty denarii (that is, nine solidi).

8. If a freeman strikes another freeman with a stick but the blood does not flow, for up to three blows, he shall be liable to pay three hundred sixty denarii (that is, nine solidi), that is, for each blow he shall always pay one hundred twenty denarii (that is, three solidi).

9. If the blood flows he shall pay composition as if he had wounded him with an iron weapon, that is, he shall be liable to pay six hundred denarii (that is, fifteen solidi).

10. He who strikes another three times with a closed fist shall be liable to pay three hundred sixty denarii (that is, nine solidi) – that is, he renders three solidi for each blow.

11. If a man attacks another man on the road and tries to rob him but that one evades him by flight, if it is proved against him, he shall be liable to pay twenty-five hundred denarii (that is, sixty-two and one-half solidi).

12. But if he robs him [and does not attack him] he shall be liable to pay thirty solidi [in addition to returning what he took plus a payment for the time the use of whatever was stolen was lost].

## b. Concerning disabling injuries
### [Title 29]

1. He who maims another man's hand or foot or gouges out or strikes out his eye or cuts off his ear or nose and it is proved against him shall be liable to pay four thousand denarii (that is, one hundred solidi).

2. If he has cut the hand and the hand remains hanging there, he shall be liable to pay twenty-five hundred denarii (that is, sixty-two and one-half solidi).

3. If the hand is pierced through he who did this shall be liable to pay twenty-five hundred denarii (that is, sixty-two and one-half solidi).

4. He who cuts off another man's thumb or big toe and it is proved against him shall be liable to pay two thousand denarii.

5. If the cut thumb or big toe hangs on, he who did this deed shall be liable to pay twelve hundred denarii (that is, thirty solidi).

6. He who cuts off a man's second finger [the index finger] that is used to release arrows shall be liable to pay fourteen hundred denarii (that is, thirty-five solidi).

7. He who cuts off the other remaining fingers – all three equally with one blow – shall be liable to pay eighteen hundred denarii (that is, forty-five solidi).

8. If he cuts off two of these, he shall be liable to pay thirty-five solidi.

9. If he cuts off one of them, he shall be liable to pay thirty solidi. He who cuts off a following finger [the middle] shall be liable to pay six hundred denarii (that is, fifteen solidi). If he strikes off a fourth finger, he shall be liable to pay nine solidi. If he strikes off the little finger he shall be liable to pay six hundred denarii (that is, fifteen solidi).

10. If a foot has been cut and hangs on injured, he who did this shall be liable to pay eighteen hundred denarii (that is, forty-five solidi).

11. If the foot has been struck off, he who did this shall be liable to pay twenty-five hundred denarii (that is, sixty-two and one-half solidi).

12. He who puts out another man's eye shall be liable to pay twenty-five hundred denarii (that is, sixty-two and one-half solidi).

13. He who cuts off another man's nose shall be liable to pay eighteen hundred denarii (that is, forty-five solidi).

14. He who cuts off another man's ear shall be liable to pay six hundred denarii (that is, fifteen solidi).

15. He who cuts out another man's tongue so that he is not able to speak shall be liable to pay four thousand denarii (that is, one hundred solidi).

16. He who knocks out another man's tooth shall be liable to pay six hundred denarii (that is, fifteen solidi).

17. He who castrates a freeman or cuts into his penis so that he is incapacitated shall be liable to pay one hundred solidi.

18. But if he takes the penis away entirely he shall be liable to pay eight thousand denarii (that is, two hundred solidi) in addition to nine solidi for the doctor.

### c. Concerning abusive terms
### [Title 30]

1. He who calls someone else a pederast (*cinitum*) shall be liable to pay six hundred denarii (that is, fifteen solidi).

2. He who claims that someone else is covered in dung (*concagatum*) shall be liable to pay one hundred twenty denarii (that is, three solidi).

3. He who calls a free woman or man a prostitute and cannot prove it shall be liable to pay eighteen hundred denarii (that is, forty-five solidi).

4. He who calls someone else a fox (*vulpem*) shall be liable to pay one hundred twenty denarii (that is, three solidi).

5. He who calls someone else a rabbit (*leporem*) shall be liable to pay one hundred twenty denarii (that is, three solidi).

6. The freeman who accused another man of throwing down his shield and running away, and cannot prove it, shall be liable to pay one hundred twenty denarii (that is, three solidi).

7. He who calls someone else an informer or liar and cannot prove it shall be liable to pay six hundred denarii (that is, fifteen solidi).

## d. Concerning the killing of freemen
### [Title 41]

1. He who kills a free Frank or other barbarian who lives by Salic law, and it is proved against him, shall be liable to pay eight thousand denarii (that is, two hundred solidi).

2. If he throws him into a well or holds him under water, he shall be liable to pay twenty-four thousand denarii (that is, six hundred solidi). And for concealing it, he shall be liable as we have said before.

3. If he does not conceal his crime, he shall be liable to pay eight thousand denarii (that is, two hundred solidi).

4. If he covers him over with sticks or bark or hides him with something to conceal him and it is proved against him, he shall be liable to pay twenty-four thousand denarii (that is, six hundred solidi).

5. He who kills a man who is in the king's trust (*in truste dominica*) [also known as an *antrustion*; see below] or a free woman and it is proved against him shall be liable to pay twenty-four thousand denarii (that is, six hundred solidi).

6. If he throws him [the antrustion, or king's man or vassal: e.g., a *thegn* in *Beowulf*] into the water or into a well, he shall be liable to pay seventy-two thousand denarii (that is, eighteen hundred solidi).

7. If he covers him over with sticks or bark or hides him with something to conceal him, he shall be liable to pay seventy-two thousand denarii (that is, eighteen hundred solidi).

8. He who kills a Roman who is a table companion of the king and it is proved against him shall be liable to pay twelve thousand denarii (that is, three hundred solidi).

9. If a Roman landowner who is not a table companion of the king is killed, he who is proved to have killed him shall be liable to pay four thousand denarii (that is, one hundred solidi).

10. He who kills a Roman who pays tribute and it is proved against him

shall be liable to pay twenty-five hundred denarii (that is, sixty-two and one-half solidi).

11. He who finds a freeman without hands and feet whom his enemies have left at a crossroad and kills him and it is proved against him shall be liable to pay four thousand denarii (that is, one hundred solidi).

12. He who throws a freeman into a well and that one escapes alive therefrom shall be liable to pay four thousand denarii (that is, one hundred solidi).

13. He who throws a freeman into the sea shall be liable to pay four thousand denarii (that is, one hundred solidi).

14. He who [unjustly] accuses a freeman of some crime for which he was then killed shall be liable to pay four thousand denarii (that is, one hundred solidi).

15. He who kills a free girl before she is able to bear children shall be liable to pay eight thousand denarii (that is, two hundred solidi).

16. He who kills a free woman after she begins to bear children shall be liable to pay twenty-four thousand denarii (that is, six hundred solidi).

17. He who kills her past middle age and no longer able to bear children shall be liable to pay eight thousand denarii (that is, two hundred solidi).

18. He who kills a long-haired boy [boys wore their hair long until they reached the age of twelve] shall be liable to pay twenty-four thousand denarii (that is, six hundred solidi).

19. He who kills a pregnant woman shall be liable to pay six hundred solidi.

20. He who kills an infant in its mother's womb or before it has a name shall be liable to pay one hundred solidi.

21. He who kills a freeman inside his house shall be liable to pay six hundred solidi.

## e. Concerning homicides committed by a band of men [Title 42]

1. He who with a band of men attacks a freeman in his house and kills him there shall be liable to pay twenty-four thousand denarii (that is, six hundred solidi). And if the man killed was one of the king's sworn antrustions, he who is proved to have killed him shall be liable to pay eighteen hundred solidi.

3. If the body of the dead man had received three or more blows, three of those charged who are proved to have been in that band of men shall each be required to pay as set forth above. Another three members of the band of men shall each pay thirty-six hundred denarii (that is, ninety solidi). And thirdly, three more of that band shall each of them be liable to pay eighteen hundred denarii (that is, forty-five solidi).

4. Concerning Romans or half-free men (*letis*) or servants (*pueri*) who have been killed [by a band of men], half the amount involved in the rule above shall be paid.

## f. Concerning the killing of one of a band of men
### [Title 43]

1. If at a banquet where there are four or five men present one of these is killed, those who remain must give up one of their number to be convicted or all will pay for the death of that man. This rule should be observed where there are up to seven men at a banquet.

2. If indeed there were more than seven men at that banquet, not all of them shall be held liable to punishment; but those against whom the crime is proved must pay according to this rule.

3. If a man has been killed by a band of men (*contubernio*) while he is outside of his house or making a journey or standing in a field, if he has suffered three or more wounds, then three members of that band against whom it was proved shall each pay composition for the death of that one. And if there were more members of that band against whom it was not proved, three of them shall each pay twelve hundred denarii (that is, thirty solidi), and three more from the band shall each be liable to pay six hundred denarii (that is, fifteen solidi).

## g. Concerning the *chrenecruda* (i.e., involving the kin in the payment of composition for homicide)
### [Title 58]

1. If anyone kills a man and, having given up all his property, he still does not have enough to pay the total composition, let him offer twelve oathhelpers [who will support his oath] that neither above the earth nor below the earth does he have more property than he has already given.

2. Afterwards he should enter his house and in his hand collect dust from its four corners, and then he should stand on the *duropello,* that is, on the threshold, looking into the house, and then with his left hand he should throw the earth over his shoulders onto him who is his nearest relative.

3. If his mother and brother have already paid [and the composition is still not fully paid], then he should throw the earth over the sister of his mother or her children. If there are none of these, then he should throw the earth over three from the maternal kin and three of the paternal kin who are next most nearly related.

3. If the father or mother or brother have already paid for him [and the composition is still not fully paid], then he should throw the earth over the

sister of his mother or her children; but if there are none of these, [he should throw the earth] over those three from the paternal and maternal kin who are next most nearly related.

4. And afterwards without a shirt and barefoot, with stick in hand, he should go jump over his fence [that is, abandon his house?] and those three from the maternal side shall pay half of whatever is the value of the composition or the judgment set; and those others who come from the paternal side should do the same [that is, pay the other half].

5. If any of these does not have that with which to pay his full share, let him who is poor throw the *chrenecruda* over him who has more so that he pays the entire judgment.

6. If he does not have that with which to pay the entire judgment [if he does not have that with which to pay the judgment or make the full composition], then he who has the man who committed the homicide in his surety (*sub sua fide*) should present him in court, and after presenting him in four courts, he may remove (*tollant*) his surety. And if no one exercises the surety for him by paying the composition, that is, does not pay that which would redeem him, then he shall make composition with his life [that is, become a slave to the party to whom the composition is owed].

6a. At the present time, if a man does not have enough of his own property to pay or defend himself from the law, it is fitting that everything be done from the beginning as set out above.

### h. Concerning him who wishes to remove himself from his kin group
### [Title 60]

1. He who wishes to remove himself from his kin group (*parentilla*) should go to court and in the presence of the *thunginus* [judge and debt-collector] or hundredman break four sticks of alderwood over his head and throw them in four bundles into the four corners of the court and say there that he removes himself from their oathhelping (*juramento*), from their inheritance, and from any relationship [with his kin].

2. If afterward one of his relatives dies or is killed, none of that one's inheritance or composition will belong to him.

3. If he [who removed himself from his kin group] dies or is killed, the claim for his composition or inheritance will not belong to his relatives but to the fisc [royal treasury] or to him to whom the fisc wishes to give it.

3. Likewise if he [who removed himself from his kin group] dies, no claim or inheritance of his will belong to his relatives but it will go thence with twelve oathhelpers.

## i. Concerning the composition for homicide
## [Title 62]

1. If a man who is a father is killed, his children shall collect half of the composition and those relatives who are closest to his father and to his mother shall divide the other half among them.

2. If there is no relative on one side, either the paternal or maternal, that portion of the composition will be collected by the fisc or by him to whom the fisc wishes to give it.

## j. Concerning the freeman killed while in the army
## [Title 63]

1. If a man kills a freeman in the army while in the company of his companions (*in conpanio de conpaniones suos*) and that one is not an antrustion of the king (*in truste dominica*), and he is proved to have killed him, he shall be liable to pay twenty-four thousand denarii (that is, six hundred solidi).

2. If it was an antrustion of the king who was killed, that one against whom it is proved shall be liable to pay seventy-two thousand denarii (that is, eighteen hundred solidi).

## k. On killing a freeman and the manner in which the relatives
## receive composition for his life
## [Title 68]

He who kills a freeman, and it is proved against him that he killed him, should make composition to the relatives according to law. His [the dead man's] children (*filius*) should get half the composition. Half of the rest should go to the mother [that is, the children's mother], so that one-fourth of the *wergeld* comes to her. The other one-fourth should go to the near relatives, that is, to the three nearest on his [that is, the dead man's] father's side and three on his mother's side. If the mother [that is, the wife] is not living, the relatives should divide her half of the half-*wergeld* among themselves, that is the three closest from the father's side and three from the mother's side; whoever is the closest relative of the aforementioned three shall take [two parts] and leave a third part to be divided among the other two; then he of the remaining two who is the closer relative shall take two parts of that third and leave a third part to the other relative.

# 14. THE LOMBARD LAWS

*The Lombards invaded Italy in the second half of the sixth century, in the wake of the wars between the Ostrogoths and the Byzantines. Although the wars and invasion disturbed Roman provincial administration, Lombard kings relied on Roman advisers and the Roman* civitas *(city) remained the basis for the Lombard local administration. Lombards recognized Roman law in Italy and the Romans continued to settle disputes and regulate legal transactions according to Roman law.*

*Lombard law itself owes a great deal to Roman law and the Church. The earliest known written law code of the Lombards is the edict of King Rothair (r. 636–652) from 643, which is thought to retain provisions from the pre-migration Lombard nation, though the laws were modified by experiences encountered on the migration to Italy. King Liutprand (r. 712–744) added 153 titles between 712 and 735, and later Lombard kings continued to add titles inspired by specific cases in their kingdoms until 755. This code speaks more explicitly than any other Germanic law code of how compensation functioned to avert the bloodfeud.*

Source: trans. Katherine Fischer Drew, *The Lombard Laws* (Philadelphia: University of Pennsylvania Press, 1973), pp. 61, 64–65, 73–75, 79, 87–88, 93–94, 115, 129, 149, 196–98, 204–6.

## a. Rothair's edict (643)

45. In the matter of composition for blows and injuries which are inflicted by one freeman on another freeman, composition is to be paid according to the procedure provided below and the blood feud (*faida*) shall cease.

74. In the case of all wounds and injuries mentioned above, involving freemen as they do, we have set a higher composition than did our predecessors in order that the *faida*, that is the blood feud, may be averted after receipt of the abovementioned composition, and in order that more shall not be demanded and a grudge shall not be held. So let the case be concluded and friendship remain between the parties. And if it happens that he who was struck dies from the blows within a year, then the one who struck the blow shall pay composition according to the quality of the person (*angargathungi*).

75. Concerning the death of a child in its mother's womb. If a child is accidentally killed while still in its mother's womb, and if the woman is free and lives, then her value shall be measured in accordance with her rank, and composition for the child shall be paid at half the sum at which the mother is valued. But if the mother dies, then composition must be paid for her according to her rank in addition to the payment of composition for the child killed in her womb. But thereafter the feud shall cease since the deed was done unintentionally.

138. Concerning the case of a man killed by a tree cut down by several men. If two or more men cut down a tree, and another man coming along is killed by that tree or it causes some damage, then those who were cutting the tree, however many they were, shall pay composition equally for the homicide or for the damage. In the case where one of those cutting the tree is killed by the tree, then, if there were two colleagues, half of the *wergeld* shall be assessed to the dead man and the other half shall be paid by his colleague to the relatives [of the dead man]. And if there were more than two men involved, an equal portion shall likewise be assessed to the dead man and to those who still live: each shall pay an equal share of the total *wergeld*, the feud ceasing since it happened without design.

143. Concerning the man who seeks revenge after accepting composition. If a freeman or slave is killed and composition paid for the homicide and oaths offered to avert the feud, and afterwards he who received the composition tries to avenge himself by killing a man belonging to the associates from whom he received the payment, we order that he repay the composition twofold to the relatives of the freeman or to the slave's lord. In like manner concerning him who tries to avenge himself after accepting compensation for blows or injuries, he shall restore that which he accepted in double amount. In addition, he shall pay composition, as provided above, if he has killed the man.

144. Concerning the master builders from Como (*magistri comacini*). If it happens that someone is killed by some material or by a stone falling from a house being constructed or restored, according to an agreed contract, by a master builder with his helpers, the man to whom the house belongs shall not be required to pay compensation but the master builder (*magistri comacini*) and his helpers shall pay composition for the homicide or for the damage. Since, according to the accepted agreement, the master is to be well paid, he not undeservedly should be responsible for damages.

162. If a man leaves legitimate sons and two or more natural sons, and if it happens that one of the natural sons is killed, then the legitimate brothers shall receive two-thirds of the composition for the one killed and the natural brothers shall receive the remaining one-third. Furthermore, the property of the dead man shall revert to the legitimate brothers, but not to the natural sons. We order this in order to postpone the *faida,* that is, to avert the blood feud.

188. If without the consent of her relatives a free girl or widow goes to a husband who is a freeman, then the husband who received her to wife shall pay twenty solidi as composition for the illegal intercourse (*anagrip*) and another twenty solidi to avert the feud. If she dies before he has acquired her guardianship, then the property of that woman shall revert to him who has her *mundium* [the duty to protect her] in his possession, but no liability

shall be assessed against the man who presumed to take her. The husband, however, shall lose the woman's property since he neglected to acquire her *mundium*.

189. On fornication. If a free girl or woman voluntarily has intercourse with a freeman, her relatives have the right to take vengeance on her. If it is agreed between both parties that he who fornicated with her take her to wife, he shall pay twenty solidi as composition for his offense, that is, for the illegal intercourse. If it is not agreeable that he have her to wife, then he must pay 100 solidi as composition, half to the king and half to him to whom her *mundium* belongs. If the relatives neglect this or do not wish to take vengeance on her, then the king's *gastald* [the chief administrative, judicial and military representative of the king, who presided over a *civitas* and acted as judge] or *schultheis* [royal official subordinate to the *gastald*] shall take her to the king and he shall render judgment as is pleasing to him.

190. On those who marry women betrothed to someone else. He who takes to wife, with her consent, the girl or widow betrothed to someone else, shall pay twenty solidi as composition for the illegal intercourse to the relatives of the woman or to him to whom her *mundium* belongs. He shall pay another twenty solidi to avert the feud, and then he may acquire her *mundium* at an agreed price. Moreover, he must pay him who had betrothed the woman and whom he has treated disgracefully double the amount of the marriage portion established at the time of betrothal. After the betrothed man has accepted the double payment as composition, he should be content and nothing more should be required of the surety in connection with this case.

214. He who takes to wife a free girl without the advice and consent of her relatives shall pay twenty solidi as composition for the seizure, as above, and another twenty solidi to avert the feud. Concerning her *mundium*, moreover, [let it be arranged] just as it is agreed and the law allows, provided nevertheless both man and girl are free.

326. If a horse injures a man with its hoof, or an ox injures a man with its horn, or a pig injures a man with its tusks, or if a dog bites a man – except in the case where the animal is mad as above – he whose animal it is shall pay the composition for the killing or damage, but the feud, that is the enmity, shall cease since the thing was done by a dumb animal without any intent on the part of its owner.

387. If anyone unintentionally kills a freeman, he shall pay composition according to the price at which the dead man is valued, and the feud shall not be required since it was done unintentionally.

## b. The laws of King Liutprand (713–735)

13. On the killing of freemen. If a Lombard is killed by another man (which God forbid), and according to law it is a case where composition should be paid and if he who is killed does not leave a son: although we have [earlier] established that daughters could be heirs, just as if they were boys, to all the property of their father or mother, nevertheless we decree here [in this case] that the nearest [male] relatives of him who was killed – those who can succeed him within the proper degree of relationship – shall receive that composition. For daughters, since they are of the feminine sex, are unable to raise the feud. Therefore we provide that the daughters not receive that composition, but, as we have said, the abovementioned [male] relatives [ought to have it]. If there are no near [male] relatives, then the daughters themselves shall receive half of that composition, whether there is one or more of them, and half [shall be received] by the king's treasury.

119. He who wishes to arrange a betrothal for his daughter or his sister has the right to betroth her to anyone whom he chooses, provided he is a freeman, as an earlier edict established. After he has arranged the betrothal, he may not give her to any other man as her husband within two years. If he presumes to give her to anyone else or wishes to break the betrothal agreement (*spunsalia*) he shall pay such a composition to the man to whom she was betrothed as was set out in the agreement between themselves, as provided in the earlier law; in addition he shall pay his *wergeld* as composition to the king's treasury, and the man who presumes to take her shall likewise pay his *wergeld* as composition to the treasury. If a man presumes to take a woman who is already betrothed to someone else without the consent of her father or brother, he shall pay double the marriage portion as composition to her betrothed, just as the earlier edict contains, and he shall pay his *wergeld* as composition to the king's treasury. The father or brother who did not consent in this case shall be absolved from blame.

As for the girl who presumed to do this voluntarily, if any portion of the inheritance of her relatives is due to her, she shall lose that portion: she shall receive none of the property of her relatives but those who are legally able to do so shall succeed to her share. Nor can her father or brother give or transfer any part of the inheritance to her by any means because she sinned against our people in doing this because of her desire for gain. We do this in order that enmity may cease and there may be no feud (*faida*).

If, however, God forbid, after such a betrothal agreement has been made, some hostility develops between the relatives of those betrothed and they are in enmity for any reason – such as, for example, the killing of one of their relatives

– then he who neglects to give or to take [the bride] shall pay as composition the sum which they [the prospective bridegroom and the girl's *mundwald* (the possessor of her *mundium;* the one responsible for protecting her) had agreed upon between themselves, and he shall then be absolved of further blame: because it is not good that a man should give his daughter or his sister or some other relative where hostility caused by a homicide is proven to exist.

121. He who converses shamefully with someone else's wife – that is, if he places his hands on her bosom or on some other shameful place and it is proved that the woman consented, he who commits such an evil deed shall pay his *wergeld* as composition to the woman's husband. If, however, the case is not proved but some man, suspecting another man of so treating his wife, accuses him of doing this, then he who accuses shall have the right to challenge the other man to combat or put him to the oath, as he chooses. If the woman had consented to such an illicit deed, her husband has the right to take vengeance on her or to discipline her in vindication as he wishes; nevertheless, however, she may not be killed nor may any mutilation be inflicted on her body. If perchance the man proved guilty is a freeman who does not have enough to pay the composition, then a public official shall hand him over to the woman's husband, and the husband may take vengeance on him or discipline him in vindication, but he may not kill him or inflict any mutilation on his body.

If, moreover, someone else's *aldius* or slave presumes to do this to a free woman, then his lord shall pay sixty solidi as composition to the woman's husband and hand over his person to the husband. If indeed someone else's slave or *aldius* commits such an evil deed as is stated above with the consent of his lord and it is proved that his lord consented, then the lord shall pay his own *wergeld* as composition and, moreover, the slave must also be handed over with the composition. If the case is not proved concerning the lord's consent, then the lord of that slave or *aldius* may clear himself by oath taken with his legitimate oathhelpers to the effect that he had not consented to this evil deed. He shall then be absolved and he shall carry out the provisions established above concerning his slave or *aldius*.

134. If men living in the same village are involved in a controversy over their fields or vineyards, meadow or forest, or some other property and one party of them collect themselves together for the purpose of driving their opponent forth by force from that place, and if they go and commit violence (*scandalum*) there or inflict wounds or injuries or kill the man, we decree that they shall pay composition for the wounds or injuries or for killing the man in accordance with the earlier edict which our glorious King Rothair established and which we [have supplemented] ourselves. Moreover, for their

illegal presumption in collecting themselves together thus, they shall pay twenty solidi as composition to that party who labored in the field or vine-yard or meadow or forest.

We establish this in order that no one may presume to incite or perform such evil deeds in any place and, since this case does not correspond to breach of the peace with an armed band (*arischild*) or to the banding together of rustics or to the sedition of rustics, it seems more fitting to us to regard it as the same as giving evil counsel, or plotting a death. When men, driven by their evil nature, collect themselves together and proceed against another man, they do this in order to commit some evil deed: they may even kill the man or inflict wounds or injuries upon him. Therefore, as we have said, we associate this case with that of counselling death [the penalty for which] is twenty solidi, as set forth above.

135. It has been made known to us that a certain perverse man took all of a woman's clothes while she was bathing in the river; as a result the woman was naked and everyone who walked or passed through that place considered her condition to be the result of her sinful nature. She could not, moreover, remain forever in the river and, blushing with shame, returned naked to her home. Therefore we decree that the man who presumes to do such an illicit act shall pay his *wergeld* as composition to that woman to whom he did this shameful thing. We say this because if the father or husband or near relatives of the woman had found him, they would have entered into a violent fray (*scandalum*) with him and he who was the stronger would have killed the other man. Therefore it is better that the culprit, living, should pay his *wergeld* as composition than that a feud develop over a death and produce such deeds that the eventual composition be greater still.

136. It has likewise been made known to us that a certain man has a well in his courtyard and, according to custom, it has a prop (*furca*) and lift (*tolenum*) for raising the water. Another man who came along stood under that lift and, when yet another man came to draw water from the well and incautiously released the lift, the weight came down on the man who stood under it and he was killed. The question then arose over who should pay composition for this death and it has been referred to us. It seems right to us and to our judges that the man who was killed, since he was not an animal but had the power of reason like other men, should have noticed where he stood or what weight was above his head. Therefore two-thirds of the amount of his composition shall be assessed to him [the dead man] and one-third of the amount at which he was valued according to law shall be paid as composition by the man who incautiously drew the water. He shall pay the composition to the children or to the near relatives who are the heirs of the

dead man and the case shall be ended without any feud or grievance since it was done unintentionally. Moreover, no blame should be placed on the man who owns the well because if we placed the blame on him, no one hereafter would permit other men to raise water from their wells and since all men cannot have a well, those who are poor would die and those who are traveling through would also suffer need.

## 15. CAROLINGIAN CAPITULARIES

*Capitularies are collections of legislative or administrative orders. The name is derived from the Latin word for head* (caput) *because the orders were arranged under chapter headings (little heads, or* capitula). *Royal edicts were not a Carolingian innovation, but Charlemagne was the first to use the term "capitulary" to describe an edict, and his successors continued this practice. Historians believe that the capitularies were responses to problems in areas not already covered by the Salic law, which Charlemagne reissued in 802–803 (Doc. 13). In some cases, the capitularies were instructions to the* missi, *who were the envoys or legates sent by the king throughout the kingdom to publicize the laws and make sure justice was being carried out.*

*Although kings did do their best to exert the moral authority necessary to force powerful families to accept compensation in lieu of vengeance, they were realistic about their failures, as is acknowledged in the excerpt from one capitulary of Charlemagne (Doc. 15b). The authority of the capitularies rested on the* bannus, *the right of the sovereign to command, forbid, and punish.* Bannus *can also mean a sovereign's command or, as below (Doc. 15c), the fine for disobeying such a command. The capitularies were read at a local or regional assembly and the consensus of the people was taken. Originally a formality, this ritual grew in importance as the authority of the Carolingian kings waned. The capitularies below were issued by Charlemagne (r. 768–814), his son Louis I, known to history as "the Pious" (r. 814–840), and Louis's grandson Louis II, King of Italy and emperor with his father Lothar from 850.*

*Dates given after the name of the ruler refer to the year the capitulary was issued.*

Sources: Doc. 15b, trans. D. C. Munro and revised Paul Edward Dutton, *Carolingian Civilization: A Reader*, ed. Paul Edward Dutton, 2nd ed. (Peterborough, ON: Broadview Press, 2004), pp. 76–77. Docs. 15a, 15c, 15d, ed. A. Boretius, Monumenta Germaniae Historica: Capitularia, vol. 1 (Hanover: Hahn, 1883), pp. 48, 51, 123, 281–82, 284. Trans. Kelly Gibson. Doc. 15e, ed. A. Boretius and V. Krause, Monumenta Germaniae Historica: *Capitularia*, vol. 2 (Hanover: Hahn, 1897), p. 86–87. Trans. Kelly Gibson.

### a. Sanctuary and enforcing the payment of the *wergeld*
### [Charlemagne, 779]

8. Killers and other criminals who ought to die according to the laws should not obtain impunity if they flee to a church and provisions should not be given to them there.

22. Anyone unwilling to accept the price [*wergeld*] paid to buy off vengeance should be sent to us so that we may send him where he can do the least damage. So that the damage not increase because of a man who is unwilling to submit to justice or pay the price [*wergeld*] paid to buy off vengeance, we likewise wish to send him to such a place.

### b. Making amends for homicide
### [Charlemagne, 802]

32. Murders, by which a multitude of the Christian people perishes, we command in every way to be shunned and to be forbidden; God himself forbade to his followers hatred and enmity, much more murder. For in what manner does anyone trust to placate God, who has killed his son nearest to him? In what manner truly does he, who has killed his brother, think that the Lord Christ will be propitious to him? It is a great and terrible danger also with God the Father and Christ, Lord of heaven and earth, to stir up enmities among men: it is possible to escape for some time by remaining concealed, but nevertheless by accident at some time he falls into the hands of his enemies; moreover, where is it possible to flee from God, to whom all secrets are manifest? By what rashness does anyone think to escape his anger? Wherefore, lest the people committed to us to be ruled over should perish from this evil, we have taken care to shun this by every means of discipline; because he who shall not have dreaded the wrath of God, shall find us in no way propitious or to be placated; but we wish to inflict the most severe punishment upon any one who shall have dared to murder a man. Nevertheless, lest sin should also increase, in order that the greatest enmities may not arise among Christians, when by the persuasions of the Devil murders happen, the criminal shall immediately hasten to make amends and with all celerity shall strike an accommodation for the evil done with the relatives of the murdered man. And we forbid firmly, that the relatives of the murdered man shall dare in any way to continue their enmities on account of the evil done, or shall refuse to grant peace to him who asks for it, but having given their pledges they shall receive a suitable accommodation and shall make a perpetual peace; moreover, the guilty one shall not delay to achieve an accommodation.

69

When, moreover, it shall have happened on account of sins that anyone shall have killed his brethren or his neighbor, he shall immediately submit to the penance imposed upon him, and just as his bishop arranges for him, without any ambiguity; but by God's aid he shall desire to accomplish his atonement and he shall compound for the dead man in accordance with the law, and shall make peace in every way with his relatives; and the pledge being given, let no one dare thereafter to stir up enmity against him. But if anyone shall have scorned to make the fitting accommodation, he shall be deprived of his property until we shall render our decision.

### c. Compelling peace
### [Charlemagne, 805]

5. On arms that must not be carried within our country, that is, shields and lances and breast plates. If one [bearing arms] is involved in a feud, then it should be examined which of the two [enemies] is opposed to reconciliation and they should be compelled to [make] peace, even if they are unwilling. They should be brought into our presence if they are unwilling to make peace in any other way. And if anyone after making peace kills the other, he should pay compensation for him and lose the hand which he perjured. In addition, he should pay the lord's fine [*bannus:* the fine imposed because of an offense against the public authority].

### d. Punishments for homicide
### [Louis I, 818–819]

1. On the honor of churches. If anyone kills a man in a church either from a trivial motive or without motive, he should make composition [see Doc. 13g] with his life. But if they quarrel outside and one flees from the other into a church and there kills him in self-defense, he should affirm by oath with twelve qualified oathhelpers that he killed him in self-defense, if he does not have witnesses of this deed, and then he should be compelled to pay 600 *solidi* for the benefit of the church he polluted with that homicide, in addition to our fine (*bannus*). The man killed should lie without composition and the killer should undertake penance fitting his crime according to the judgment of the canons. If his own dependent (*servus*) commits this [homicide], he should be tried by the ordeal of boiling water to determine whether he did it voluntarily or in self-defense. If his hand is harmed, he should be killed. But if it is not, his lord should pay the church according to the amount of his *wergeld*, or, if he wishes, hand him over to the same church. Concerning a dependent of the church, the

fisc, or a benefice: we wish that the first time his *wergeld* be paid and that the second time he be handed over for punishment. Nevertheless, the property of a free man condemned to death for such a crime should go to his legitimate heirs... [Reissued in 829.]

7. On preventing murders. Whoever kills a man either from a trivial motive or without motive should pay his [the deceased's] *wergeld* to the people to whom he [the deceased] is related. But on account of such insolence, he [the killer] should be sent into exile for as much time as pleases us. Nevertheless, he should not lose his property.

8. What ought not be given in payment of the *wergeld*. We wish that the things mentioned in the law be given in payment of the *wergeld*, except for a hawk and a sword (*spata*), because many times perjury is committed when these are sworn to be of a greater value than they are.

13. On limiting feuds. If anyone, compelled by necessity, committed homicide, the count in whose district the event took place should ensure that both the compensation is paid and the feud is pacified by an oath. If one party is unwilling to assent to him [the count] for this, that is, either the one who committed the homicide or the one who ought to accept the compensation, he [the count] should make the one who is disobedient to him come into our presence in order that we may send him into exile for the [amount of] time that pleases us, until he is corrected there, so that he no longer dare to be disobedient to his count and so that the damage does not thereafter increase. [Reissued in 829.]

## e. On giving aid to criminals
### [Louis II, 850]

3. We have also heard that certain men possessing houses and estates win over and form an alliance with thieves coming from elsewhere, and secretly maintain them, and give support to do crime in order to share whatever they [the thieves] obtain from this pernicious work. We judge this kind of evildoer the worst because they not only do evil deeds, but also employ the aid and kindness of others for evil deeds. Therefore, if anyone who into such suspicion in any place and if a rumor that he did these evil deeds has spread among the people, if it has not yet been made public, he should exculpate himself with twelve [oathhelpers]. But if he already has been caught in the act or found out in any way, he should immediately be captured and punished, and should suffer the penalty prescribed in the laws. If in any place a manager of the royal treasury wishes to capture either resident or vagrant thieves, and, while trying to defend himself, by chance it happens that the thief is killed,

the killer should not be punished with any legal penalty and should suffer no enmity from the family or persecution from any friend or person close to him [the thief]. And if his lord or any person close to him tries to take vengeance for this, and the public judge [*iudex*: a title given to royal officials including counts, judges, and estate managers] cannot restrain him, such a person should be brought into our presence by qualified guarantors in order that accomplices and supporters of the wicked men be moved by our reproach. Moreover, in any place where rumor has it that such men reside, there should be a sworn inquest among everyone residing nearby; those among whom this is better able to be investigated, of whatever people or status they are, should not have the power to refuse to give an oath when summoned by the count.

## 16. EARLY MEDIEVAL ENGLISH LAW

*Nominally a Roman province since Julius Caesar's conquest in 55–54 BCE, Britain had been brought firmly within the Roman ambit during the reign of Claudius (41–54 CE). When Britain was abandoned by the last Roman legions on the island in the late fourth or early fifth century, it became possible for the Anglo-Saxon peoples of northern Germany to invade or migrate to the island during the fifth and sixth centuries. Once there, they formed several kingdoms, the most prominent at first being Kent, followed by Northumbria and Mercia in the seventh and eighth centuries, then the kingdom of the West Saxons in the ninth century.*

*The legal code of King Ethelbert of Kent (Doc. 16a) was issued in 602, just after the king had accepted baptism. Documents 16b and 16c come from the later codes of the West Saxon kings Athelstan (924–939) and his half-brother Edmund (939–946), and reflect the increasing influence of Christianity and Carolingian governing practices on Anglo-Saxon law.*

Source: trans. Dorothy Whitelock, *English Historical Documents*, vol. 1 (London: Eyre & Spottiswoode, 1955), pp. 357–59, 384–85, 391–92.

### a. The laws of Ethelbert

1. The property of God and the Church [is to be paid for] with a twelve-fold compensation; a bishop's property with an eleven-fold compensation; a priest's property with a nine-fold compensation; a deacon's property with a six-fold compensation; a cleric's property with a three-fold compensation; the peace of the Church with a two-fold compensation; the peace of a meeting with a two-fold compensation.

2. If the king calls his people to him, and anyone does them injury there, [he is to pay] a two-fold compensation and 50 shillings to the king.

3. If the king is drinking at a man's home, and anyone commits any evil deed there, he is to pay two-fold compensation.

4. If a freeman steal from the king, he is to repay nine-fold.

5. If anyone kills a man in the king's estate, he is to pay 50 shillings compensation.

6. If anyone kills a freeman, [he is to pay] 50 shillings to the king as "lord-ring" [money paid to a lord for slaying a freeman].

7. If [anyone] kills the king's own smith or his messenger, he is to pay the ordinary *wergeld*.

8. The [breach of the] king's protection, 50 shillings.

9. If a freeman steals from a freeman, he is to pay three-fold, and the king is to have the fine or all the goods.

10. If anyone lies with a maiden belonging to the king, he is to pay 50 shillings compensation.

11. If it is a grinding slave, he is to pay 25 shillings compensation; [if a slave of] the third [class], 12 shillings.

12. The king's *fedesl* [fed by the king] is to be paid for with 20 shillings.

13. If anyone kills a man in a nobleman's estate, he is to pay 12 shillings compensation.

14. If anyone lies with a nobleman's serving-woman, he is to pay 20 shillings compensation.

15. The [breach of a] *ceorl's* [free peasant's] protection: six shillings.

16. If anyone lie with a *ceorl's* serving-woman, he is to pay six shillings compensation; [if] with a slave-woman of the second [class], 50 *sceattas* [small silver coins]; [if with one of] the third [class], 30 *sceattas*.

17. If a man is the first to force his way into a man's homestead, he is to pay six shillings compensation; he who enters next, three shillings; afterwards each [is to pay] a shilling.

18. If anyone provides a man with weapons, when a quarrel has arisen, and [yet] no injury results, he is to pay six shillings compensation.

19. If highway-robbery is committed, he is to pay six shillings compensation.

20. If, however, a man is killed, he is to pay 20 shillings compensation.

21. If anyone kills a man, he is to pay as an ordinary *wergeld* 100 shillings.

22. If anyone kills a man, he is to pay 20 shillings at the open grave, and within 40 days the whole *wergeld*.

23. If the slayer departs from the land, his kinsmen are to pay half the *wergeld*.

24. If anyone binds a free man, he is to pay 20 shillings compensation.

25. If anyone kills a *ceorl's* dependant, he is to pay six shillings compensation.

26. If [anyone] kills a *laet* [freedman], he is to pay for one of the highest class 80 shillings; if he kills one of the second class, he is to pay 60 shillings; if one of the third class, he is to pay 40 shillings.

27. If a freeman breaks an enclosure, he is to pay six shillings compensation.

28. If anyone seizes property inside, the man is to pay three-fold compensation.

29. If a freeman enters the enclosure, he is to pay four shillings compensation.

30. If anyone kill a man, he is to pay with his own money and unblemished goods, whatever their kind.

31. If a freeman lies with the wife of another freeman, he is to atone with his *wergeld*, and to obtain another wife with his own money, and bring her to the other's home.

32. If anyone thrusts through a true *hamseyld* [possibly a fence around a dwelling], he is to pay for it with its value.

33. If hair-pulling occur, 50 *sceattas* [are to be paid] as compensation....

## b. The laws of King Athelstan

20. If anyone fails to attend a meeting three times, he is to pay the fine for disobedience to the king; and the meeting is to be announced seven days before it is to take place.

20.1. If, however, he will not do justice nor pay the fine for disobedience, the leading men are to ride thither, all who belong to the borough, and take all that he owns and put him under surety.

20.2. If, however, anyone will not ride with his fellows, he is to pay the fine for disobedience to the king.

20.3. And it is to be announced in the meeting that everyone is to be at peace with everything with which the king will be at peace, and to refrain from theft on pain of losing his life and all that he owns.

20.4. And he who will not cease for these penalties – the leading men are to ride thither, all who belong to the borough, and take all that he owns. The king is to succeed to half, to half the men who are on that expedition. And they are to put him under surety.

20.5. If he knows no one to stand surety for him, they are to take him prisoner.

20.6. If he will not permit it, he is to be killed, unless he escapes.

20.7. If anyone wishes to avenge him or carry on a feud against any of them, he is to be at enmity with the king and all the king's friends.

20.8. If he escapes, and anyone harbors him, he is to be liable to pay his *wergeld*, unless he dares to clear himself by the [amount of the] fugitive's *wergeld*, that he did not know that he was a fugitive.

### c. From Edmund's code concerning the bloodfeud

Prologue. King Edmund informs all people, both high and low, who are in his dominion, that I have been inquiring with the advice of my councilors, both ecclesiastical and lay, first of all how I could most advance Christianity.

Prologue 1. First, then, it seemed to us all most necessary that we should keep most firmly our peace and concord among ourselves throughout my dominion.

Prologue 2. The illegal and manifold conflicts which take place among us distress me and all of us greatly. We decreed then:

1. If henceforth anyone slay a man, he is himself to bear the feud, unless he can with the aid of his friends within twelve months pay compensation at the full *wergeld*, whatever class he [the man slain] may belong to.

1.1. If, however, the kindred abandons him, and is not willing to pay compensation for him, it is then my will that all that kindred is to be exempt from the feud, except the actual slayer, if they give him neither food nor protection afterwards.

1.2. If, however, any one of his kinsmen harbors him afterwards, he is to be liable to forfeit all that he owns to the king, and to bear the feud as regards the kindred [of the man slain], because they previously abandoned him.

1.3. If, however, anyone of the other kindred takes vengeance on any man other than the actual slayer, he is to incur the hostility of the king and all his friends, and to forfeit all that he owns.

2. If anyone flees to a church or my residence, and he is attacked or molested there, those who do it are to be liable to the same penalty as is stated above.

3. And I do not wish that any fine for fighting or compensation to a lord for his man shall be remitted.

4. Further, I make it known that I will allow no resort to my court before he [the slayer] has undergone ecclesiastical penance and paid compensation to the kindred, [or] undertaken to pay it, and submitted to every legal obligation, as the bishop, in whose diocese it is, instructs him.

5. Further, I thank God and all of you who have well supported me, for

the immunity from thefts which we now have; I now trust to you, that you will support this measure so much the better as the need is greater for all of us that it shall be observed.

6. Further, we have declared concerning *mundbryce* [the violation of anyone's right of protection over others] and *hamsocn* [an attack on a homestead] that anyone who commits it after this is to forfeit all that he owns, and it is to be for the king to decide whether he may preserve his life.

7. Leading men must settle feuds: First, according to the common law the slayer must give a pledge to his advocate, and the advocate to the kinsmen, that the slayer is willing to pay compensation to the kindred.

7.1. Then afterwards it is fitting that a pledge be given to the slayer's advocate, that the slayer may approach under safe-conduct and himself pledge to pay the *wergeld*.

7.2. When he has pledged this, he is to find surety for the *wergeld*.

7.3. When that has been done, the king's *mund* [protection] is to be established: twenty-one days from that day *healsfang* [a part of the *wergeld* which went to the nearest kin] is to be paid; 21 days from then the compensation to the lord for his man; 21 days from then the first installment of the *wergeld*.

## 17. EMOTION AND SIN

*According to both the Old and New Testaments, vengeance was God's prerogative. Put differently, it was God's right alone to get angry and perform any vengeance that was needed. The Psalms (Doc. 6) indicated that frustrated victims were supposed simply to pray to God in order to have their wrongs avenged. Beginning with the early seventh-century penitentials, the Latin Church began to insist on the idea of vengeance being God's right alone. By doing so, the Church reduced the scope for legitimate expressions of anger and hatred, or, in some cases, channeled it against common enemies. These next sources provide evidence that clerical authors considered anger and hatred something rather like insanity, dementia, or the ravings of wild animals.*

*Penitential manuals, handbooks for the use of confessors that listed the penance required for various sins, emerged first and most prominently in the Celtic countries on the western edge of Europe in the sixth century. These Celtic penitentials would influence writers of both* summas *(theological treatises) and manuals of penance across Europe over the course of later centuries. Taken as a group, these manuals and treatises show the significant evolution of the intellectual history of penance in the Middle Ages. In the earlier world of the penitentials, as in the extracts from the penitentials of Theodore (written after 688), Bede (early eighth century), and Regino of Prüm (ca 906) that follow, a homicide sometimes could be treated more leniently if it was motivated by vengeance; vengeance, in short, helped to mitigate the sin. By the thirteenth century, however, this exception had disappeared (see Doc. 55).*

Source: trans. John T. McNeill and Helena M. Gamer, *Medieval Handbooks of Penance: A Translation of the Principal* Libri poenitentiales *and Selections from Related Documents* (New York: Columbia University Press, 1938), pp. 187, 224–25, 317.

## a. Penitential of Theodore
## Book 1.4. Of Manslaughter

1. If one slays a man in revenge for a relative, he shall do penance as a murderer for seven or ten years. However, if he will render to the relatives the legal price, the penance shall be lighter, that is, [it shall be shortened] by half the time.

2. If one slays a man in revenge for a brother, he shall do penance for three years. In another place it is said that he should do penance for ten years.

3. But a murderer, ten or seven years.

4. If a layman slays another with malice aforethought, if he will not lay aside his arms, he shall do penance for seven years; without flesh and wine, three years.

5. If one slays a monk or a cleric, he shall lay aside his arms and serve God, or he shall do penance for seven years. He is in the judgment of his bishop. But as for one who slays a bishop or a priest, it is for the king to give judgment in his case.

6. One who slays a man by command of his lord shall keep away from the church for forty days; and one who slays a man in public war shall do penance for forty days.

7. If through anger, he shall do penance for three years; if by accident, for one year; if by a potion or any trick, seven years or more; if as a result of a quarrel, ten years.

## b. Penitential ascribed by Albers to Bede
## Chapter 2. Of Slaughter

1. He who slays a monk or a cleric shall lay aside his weapons and serve God or do penance for seven years.

2. He who slays a layman with malice aforethought or for the possession of his inheritance, four years.

3. He who slays to avenge a brother, one year and in the two following years the three forty-day periods and the appointed days.

4. He who slays through sudden anger and a quarrel, three years.

5. He who slays by accident, one year.

6. He who slays in public warfare, forty days.

7. He who slays at the command of his master, if he is a slave, forty days: he who, being a freeman, at the command of his superior slays an innocent person, one year and for the two [years] following, the three forty-day periods and the appointed days.

8. He who by a wound in a quarrel renders a man weak or maimed shall pay for the physician and the fine for the scar, and make compensation for his work while he is recovering, and do penance for half a year. If indeed he has not the means, he shall make good these things in an entire year [of penance].

9. He who rises up to strike a man, intending to kill him, shall do penance for three weeks; if he is a cleric, three months.

10. But if he has wounded him, forty days; if he is a cleric, a whole year; but he shall also pay to the person injured, according to the severity of the wound; even if the law does not require it, he shall pay him whom he has injured, lest the injured cause scandal.

11. A mother who kills her child before the fortieth day shall do penance for one year. If it is after the child has become alive, [she shall do penance] as a murderess. But it makes a great difference whether a poor woman does it on account of the difficulty of supporting [the child] or a harlot for the sake of concealing her wickedness.

### c. The *Ecclesiastical Discipline* of Regino of Prüm

Have you committed murder either accidentally or willfully, or in the avenging of relatives, or at the command of your lord, or in public war? If you have done it willfully, you should do penance for seven years; if unintentionally or by accident, five years. If for the avenging of a relative, one year, and in the two years thereafter, the three forty-day periods and the appointed days. If in war, forty days. If you are a freeman, and at the command of your lord you have slain a slave who is innocent, one year and during two other years, three forty-day periods and the appointed days. If the slave is worthy of death, you shall do penance for forty days.

# CHAPTER FIVE:
## SERMONS, EXEGESIS, AND LETTERS

*Discussions of vengeance, anger, and hatred figure prominently in various kinds of texts produced by the early Church fathers and by early medieval clerical writers. Together with the penitential literature, these texts reveal the emergence of a consistent ecclesiastical stance against the vengeful emotions, which compared those who gave way to their base emotions to beasts (e.g., Doc. 28): a comparison that remained common in Christian moral literature for centuries to come. Certainly, where homicide was concerned, unrestrained emotions like anger were seen as being at the heart of the problem. As the ninth-century homilist Hrabanus Maurus noted, forbidding homicide alone can achieve nothing where anger exists to incite men to kill (Doc. 25).*

*Yet, as some of these documents illustrate, Christian authors were aware of the fact that vengeance could sometimes be justified. As Augustine notes (Doc. 19), vengeance was much the same thing as punishment. Thus, vengeance should be wreaked on evil-doers (e.g., Docs. 23 and 28), since the fear of judicial vengeance is what keeps one from doing evil (Doc. 22). Augustine continues that when vengeance is delivered only by God, there is no difficulty. However, medieval authors were aware that complications could arise whenever vengeance is delivered by human judges, including kings (Doc. 24), since it was possible to cloud human reason with emotion, and it is subject to ordinary human fallibility (e.g. Doc., 21).*

## 18. AUGUSTINE ON THE LEGITIMACY OF FIGHTING BACK

*Augustine (354–430), bishop of Hippo in North Africa, was the most influential of the early Church fathers. His thoughts on vengeance and killing made up an authoritative component of the approach to homicide and hatred taken by medieval penance manuals and other products of the Christian intellectual tradition. Augustine agrees with Old Testament texts in acknowledging the need for retribution but assigns to God the role of the avenger. The following tract appears in the form of a dialogue between Augustine and Evodius, an interlocutor named after Augustine's real-life friend, who debate whether God is the cause of evil. Augustine maintains that blame for any evil action rests on the person who performed it because humans have free choice of the will.*

Source: trans. Thomas Williams, *On the Free Choice of the Will* (Indianapolis: Hackett, 1993), pp. 8–10.

First, I think, we should discuss whether an attacking enemy or an ambushing murderer can be killed without any inordinate desire, for the sake of preserving one's life, liberty, or chastity.

Evodius: How can I think that people are without inordinate desire when they fight fiercely for things that they can lose against their will? Or if those things cannot be lost, what need is there to resort to killing for their sake?

Augustine: Then the law is unjust that permits a traveler to kill a highway robber in order to keep from being killed himself, or that permits anyone who can, man or woman, to kill a sexual assailant, before he or she is harmed. The law also commands a soldier to kill the enemy; and if he refuses, he is subject to penalties from his commander. Surely we will not dare to say that these laws are unjust, or rather, that they are not laws at all. For it seems to me that an unjust law is no law at all.

Evodius: I see that the law is quite secure against this sort of objection, for it permits lesser evils among the people that it governs in order to prevent greater evils. It is much better that one who plots against another's life should be killed rather than one who is defending his own life. And it is much worse for someone unwillingly to suffer a sexual assault, than for the assailant to be killed by the one he was going to assault. A soldier who kills the enemy is acting as an agent of the law, so he can easily perform his duty without inordinate desire. Furthermore, the law itself, which was established with a view to protecting the people, cannot be accused of any inordinate desire. As for the one who enacted the law, if he did so at God's command – that is, if he did what eternal justice prescribes – he could do so without any inordinate desire at all. But even if he did act out of inordinate desire, it does not follow that one must be guilty of inordinate desire in obeying the law; for a good law can be enacted by one who is not himself good. For example, suppose that someone who had gained tyrannical power accepted a bribe from some interested party to make it illegal to take a woman by force, even for marriage. The law would not be bad merely in virtue of the fact that the one who made it was unjust and corrupt. Therefore, the law that commands that enemy forces be repulsed by an equal force for the protection of the citizens can be obeyed without inordinate desire. The same can be said of all officials who by lawful order are subject to some higher power.

But as for those other men, I do not see how they can be excused, even if the law itself is just. For the law does not force them to kill; it merely leaves that in their power. They are free not to kill anyone for those things which can be lost against their will, and which they should therefore not love.

Perhaps one might doubt whether life is somehow taken from the soul when the body is slain. But if it can be taken away, it is of little value; and if it cannot, there is nothing to fear. As for chastity, who would doubt that it is located in the soul itself, since it is a virtue? So it cannot be taken away by a violent assailant. Whatever the one who is killed was going to take away is not completely in our power, so I don't understand how it can be called ours. I don't blame the law that allows such people to be killed; but I can't think of any way to defend those who do the killing.

Augustine: And I can't think why you are searching for a defense for people whom no law condemns.

Evodius: No law, perhaps, of those that are public and are read by human beings; but I suspect that they *are* condemned by a more powerful, hidden law, if indeed there is nothing that is not governed by divine providence. How can they be free of sin in the eyes of that law, when they are defiled with human blood for the sake of things that ought to be held in contempt? It seems to me, therefore, that the law written to govern the people rightly permits these killings and that divine providence avenges them. The law of the people merely institutes penalties sufficient for keeping the peace among ignorant human beings, and only to the extent that their actions can be regulated by human government. But those other faults deserve other penalties that I think Wisdom alone can repeal.

Augustine: I praise and approve your distinction, for although it is tentative and incomplete, it boldly aims at lofty heights. You think that the law that is established to rule cities allows considerable leeway, leaving many things unpunished that divine providence avenges; and rightly so. And just because that law doesn't do everything, it doesn't follow that we should disapprove of what it does do.

## 19. AUGUSTINE ON THE NEED TO AWAIT GOD'S VENGEANCE

*The* Commentary on the Psalms *was Augustine's largest exegetical work, and this commentary on Psalm 93 (Doc. 6b) is a major statement on the necessity of waiting for God to take vengeance.*

Source: trans. H. M. Wilkins, *Expositions on the Book of Psalms by Saint Augustine*, vol. 4 (Oxford: Parker, 1850), pp. 350–54. Modernized by Kelly Gibson.

7. Ver. 1. "The Lord is the God of vengeance; the God of vengeance has dealt confidently." Do you think that he does not punish? "The God of vengeance" punishes. What is, "The God of vengeance"? The God of punishments. You surely murmur because the bad are not punished: yet do not murmur, lest you be among those who are punished. That man has committed a theft,

and lives: you murmur against God, because he who stole from you does not die.... Therefore, if you want another to correct his hand, first correct your tongue: you want him correct his heart towards man, correct your heart towards God; lest by chance, when you desire the vengeance of God, if it come, it find you first. For he will come: he will come, and will judge those who continue in their wickedness, ungrateful for the prolongation of God's mercy and long-suffering, treasuring up unto themselves wrath against the day of wrath, and revelation of the righteous judgment of God, who will render to every man according to his deeds: [Rom. 2:4–6] because, "The Lord is the God of vengeance," therefore he has "dealt confidently.".... Our safety is our Savior: in him he would place the hope of all the needy and poor. And what does he say? "I will deal confidently in him." What does this mean? He will not fear, will not spare the lusts and vices of men. Truly, as a faithful physician, with the healing knife of preaching in his hand, he has cut away all our wounded parts. Therefore such as he was prophesied and preached beforehand, such was he found .... How great things then did he, of whom it is said, "He taught them as one having authority," say to them? "Woe unto you, Scribes and Pharisees, hypocrites!" [Matt. 23:13, 16]. What great things did he say to them, before their face? He feared no one. Why? Because he is the God of vengeance. For this reason he did not spare them in words so that they might remain for him to spare in judgment; because if they were unwilling to accept the healing of his word, they would afterwards incur their Judge's doom. For what purpose? Because he has said, "The Lord is the God of vengeance, the God of vengeance has dealt confidently;" that is, he has spared no man in word. He who did not spare in word when about to suffer, will he spare in judgment when about to judge? He who in his humility feared no man, will he fear any man in his glory? From his dealing thus confidently in time past, imagine how he will deal at the end of time. Murmur not then against God, who seems to spare the wicked; but be good, and perhaps for a season he may not spare you the rod so that he may in the end spare you in judgment ....

## 20. JEROME ON KINDNESS AND CRUELTY

*Jerome (ca 345–420) was born near Aquileia. Educated at Rome, he withdrew from im-*
*perial service to pursue an ascetic life. After living as a hermit in the desert of Syria for*
*four or five years, he became a priest in Antioch, served as secretary to Pope Damasus*
*from 382–85, and ended his life as abbot of a monastery in Bethlehem. Damasus*
*prompted Jerome to translate the Bible into Latin from the original languages of He-*
*brew and Greek. This famous translation, known as the Vulgate, was completed in 405*
*or 406 and was the standard translation of the Bible throughout the Middle Ages. In*
*addition, he wrote many exegetical works and undertook a number of translations. A*
*collection of his sermons, delivered between 394 and 413, have come down to us. This*
*particular sermon, a homily on Psalm 93 written around 400, includes a commentary*
*on Paul's Letter to the Romans (Doc. 10) in the New Testament.*

Source: trans. Sister Marie Liguori Ewald, *The Homilies of Saint Jerome,* vol. 2 (Washington, DC:
Catholic University of America Press, 1964), pp. 174–75, 178, 181.

"God of vengeance, Lord, God of vengeance, show yourself." He, who concealed himself for a long time and did not appear among the people, at long
last revealed himself. He, who before was unknown, afterwards triumphed
on the cross. "God of vengeance, Lord." If God is the Lord of vengeance
("Vengeance is mine; I will repay, says the Lord"), why do you seek revenge,
O man? You have the Lord as your Avenger. That is in substance what the
Apostle says: "If thy enemy is hungry, give him food; if he is thirsty, give
him drink: For by so doing thou wilt heap coals of fire upon his head." But
that does not seem like an act of kindness; rather it seems like cruelty. If I do
an enemy good only that God may do him evil, I am acting not from piety,
but from a motive of cruelty. What, then, does the Apostle mean? "If your
enemy is hungry, give him food," kind and pious words. "If he thirsts, give
him drink." Thus far it sounds like compassion. The conclusion, however:
"for by doing this you will heap coals of fire upon his head," does not seem
kind but cruel. You seem, in fact, to be giving him bread to eat and water to
drink only to torture him for all eternity. Does the Apostle really mean that:
does the preacher of mercy teach cruelty? No, it is not to be taken that way
but in another sense. If your enemy strikes you, turn to him also your other
cheek; if he does you wrong, you do him a good; for when you do that, you
are heaping coals of fire upon his head. In other words, you will purify your
enemy of sin, for your patience will conquer his cruelty. If you aim an arrow
at a stone, and the stone is hard, not only will the arrow fail to penetrate, but
it would even rebound. It is the same with your enemy; if he should strike

you and you do not retaliate, he will be conquered by your patience and you will convert him.

"How long, O Lord, shall the wicked, how long shall the wicked glory?" Human impatience does not want God to have patience. Creatures truly pitiable are we who would have God patient with us but impatient with our enemies. When we commit sin, we beg God to be patient with us; yet when somebody wrongs us, we do not expect God to be patient with him....

Do you need proof that the thoughts of men are vain?... I have an enemy with whom I must go to court, and the day of the trial is thirty days off; day and night I do nothing but prepare my defense. When I am in bed, all I do is frame answers to the charges of my enemy who is absent. My enemy is not present but my words are answering him as if he were. I rehearse in this way for days and nights. When the day of judgment arrives, however, all my carefully planned debate vanishes and I answer only what God inspires. That is precisely why the Lord says in the Gospel: "And when they bring you before the magistrate, do not be anxious how or wherewith you shall defend yourselves, or what you shall say, for the Lord will teach you in that very hour what you ought to say." "The Lord knows the thoughts of men, and that they are vain." One preoccupation alone is worthwhile and wholesome – thinking about the Lord."...

"And condemn innocent blood." There are always some who will assert that the slain would not have been slain if they had not been fornicators, or had not committed some other sin; disaster would not have overtaken this man, if he had not been a sinner. Perceive, therefore, the meaning of Holy Writ in: "And condemn innocent blood." As long as we are in this world, we endure all things together. The just man and the sinner equally suffer ship-wreck; they are equals in flesh and equals in the condition of flesh. The just and the sinner perish equally; death comes to each alike; but there are different rewards that await the just and the sinner. One goes to hell, the other is conducted into the kingdom of heaven. "And condemn innocent blood." Your conscience is sufficient for you, O just man; if you are condemned, your blood is innocent, and it will cry out to the Lord....

## 21. LAW AND THE "ACCURSED CUSTOM" OF VENGEANCE IN THEODERIC'S ITALY

*Cassiodorus (485/90–ca 580) wrote the official correspondence of the Ostrogothic rulers at Ravenna. The* Variae *included twelve books of letters, the first five of which were issued by Theoderic. At the time this letter was written, Cassiodorus was a quaestor, an administrative position which he held from 507 onward. He would later hold the titles of consul, master of the offices, and praetorian prefect. Cassiodorus edited the* Variae *in 537 after withdrawing from public life after the armies of the emperor Justinian invaded Italy as part of the Byzantine reconquest. In this extract, Theoderic notes the "accursed customs" that have arisen in his day and comments on the need for law.*

Source: trans. S. J. B. Barnish, *Selected Variae* (Liverpool: Liverpool University Press, 1992), pp. 58–59.

King Theoderic to the Illustrious Count Colosseus

... Set out, therefore, with good omens at your appointment, and girt with the honor of the illustrious belt, to Pannonia Sirmiensis, the former seat of the Goths. Defend the province entrusted to you by arms, order it by law: thus, knowing that it once happily obeyed my kindred, it may receive its former defenders with joy. You know the upright conduct by which you may commend yourself to me. Your sole means of pleasing is to imitate my actions. Cherish justice; defend innocence by virtue, so that, among the evil customs of the various peoples, you may display the justice of the Goths. They have always maintained a praiseworthy mean, since they have acquired the wisdom of the Romans, and have inherited the uprightness of the tribes. Do away with the accursed customs that have arisen: law-suits should be conducted by words rather than by weapons; to lose a case must not mean death; he who retains another's property should repay the theft, and not his life; civil accusations must not carry off more than war destroys; men should raise their shields against the enemy, not their kindred. And, lest poverty should chance to hurl a man on his death, you must nobly pay a price for such persons: you will receive a rich reward of favor from me if you can establish a civil way of life there, and a reward truly worthy of my governors, if the magistrate suffers loss to give life to a doomed man. Therefore, my customs must be implanted in savage minds, until the violent spirit grows accustomed to a decent way of life.

# 22. ISIDORE OF SEVILLE ON THE LAW OF THE TALION

*Isidore (560?–636) was bishop of Seville from ca 600. Written at the request of Visig-othic King Sisibut (r. 612–21), the* Etymologies *("Origins") is an encyclopedia designed to compile the knowledge of the ancient world. In addition to the section on laws, from which this excerpt concerning* Exodus *(Doc. 2) is drawn, the work's twenty books deal with various subjects: the liberal arts, medicine, books and offices of the Church, God, angels, saints, the Church and sects, peoples, languages, kingdoms, cities, letters, the human body, animals, the world, architecture, agriculture, gems and metals, war and gladiatorial games, clothing, ships, the home and domestic tools.*

Source: trans. Stephen A. Barney, W. J. Lewis, J. A. Beach, and Oliver Berghof, with the col-laboration of Muriel Hall, *Etymologies* (New York: Cambridge University Press, 2006), pp. 119, 124.

## 19. What a law is capable of

Every law either allows something, as "A strong man may seek reward," or it forbids, as "No one is allowed to seek marriage with a sacred virgin," or it prescribes punishment, as "Whoever has committed murder shall suffer capital punishment." Indeed, human life is regulated by the reward or punishment of law.

## 20. Why a law is enacted

Laws are enacted in order to control human audacity through the fear they arouse, and so that innocent people may be safe in the midst of reprobates, and so that even among the impious the power of doing harm may be restrained by a dreaded punishment.

## 21. What sort of law should be made

A law should be honorable, just, feasible, in agreement with nature, in agreement with the custom of the country, appropriate to the place and time, necessary, useful, and also clear, lest in its obscurity it contain something deceitful, and it should be written not for private convenience, but for the common benefit of the citizens.

24. "Compensation in kind" (*talio*) is a punishment resembling the act being punished, so that someone suffers "in such a way" (*taliter*) as he acted. This is established by nature and by law, so that: Let retribution of a similar kind fall to the one causing injury. Whence also this is said with regard to the Law of the Old Testament [Matt. 5:38]: "An eye for an eye, a tooth for a tooth." Compensation in kind is established for repaying not only injuries, but also favors, for this term is common to both injuries and favors.

## 23. POPE HONORIUS SPEAKS OF JUSTICE AS VENGEANCE

*Honorius was pope from 625–638. This letter, written by Honorius to Anatolius, the master of the armies of Naples, provides a typical example of how the concept of justice was expressed in the terms of vengeance.*

Source: *Epistolae Langobardicae collectae*, ed. Wilhelm Grundlach, Monumenta Germaniae Historica: Epistolae, vol. 3 (Berlin: Weidmann, 1892), pp. 696–97. Trans. Lori Pieper.

The bearer of the present has made supplication to us with tearful prayer, asserting that his brother was killed by a certain knight of Salernitan castle, and in addition that his property was plundered after his death. Therefore, by the very documents publicly considered authoritative by all in the matters, it is as impious as it is an offense against the statutes of laws for innocent blood shed by one committing [a crime] in no way to be avenged. Let those who are able to take vengeance and neglect to avenge it on account of convenience indeed be made known, for, if they neglect to defend innocent blood, a future and terrible judgment for the committing of such a wicked deed is to be demanded from them as participants in this crime. Therefore let your Glory, for the vindication and avenging of the deadly crime of homicide, separate the captured man from the knightly company and hasten to hand him over to be punished by the judge of the province by power of justice. But he is undoubtedly to restore the property taken away by outrageous violence from the above-mentioned suppliant, if he shall be his brother, since it is incumbent on us that the one who commits a crime might always expect and without hesitation receive punishment, and the whole group of knights is by no means to be subject to chastisement because of the homicidal contagion of one.

# 24. SMARAGDUS OF ST. MIHIEL ON RESTRAINING ROYAL ANGER

*Smaragdus (d. after 825) was abbot of the monastery of St. Mihiel, located in modern-day Lorraine, by 809. He wrote a number of theological and ascetical works, along this mirror for princes, which is one of the earliest of several produced in the ninth century. This work was written for either Charlemagne or Louis the Pious, but most likely for Louis, and perhaps either before he had come to imperial power or during the time after he had come to imperial power in 813 but had not yet been consecrated by the pope in 816. In some contemporary works (which were then adopted into the earlier historiographical tradition) Louis was seen as weak and more concerned with the church than the kingdom. More recently, it has been suggested that his rulership was influenced by the ideals of monasticism. Although written for a king, this work has several chapters in common with Smaragdus's work on monastic behavior, the* Diadem of Monks.

Source: *Smaragdi abbatis Via regia*, ed. J.-L. d'Achéry (Paris: 1661), reprinted in *Patrologia Latina* 102 (Paris: Migne, 1865), cols. 962–64. Trans. Kelly Gibson.

## 23. On not repaying evil with evil

Love [your] neighbor as yourself, with pure heart [and] sincere mind, so that you forgive and not repay evil with evil, even if he wrongs you, as it is written: "Say not: 'I will return evil': wait for the Lord and he will deliver thee" [Prov. 20:22]. Therefore, both wholeheartedly forgive the one wronging you and expect God in order to be delivered from your own wrongdoing, and do not revenge yourself upon the man who offends you. Because it is written: "He that seeketh to revenge himself, shall find vengeance from the Lord, and he will surely keep his sins in remembrance. Forgive thy neighbor if he hath hurt thee: and then shall thy sins be forgiven to thee when thou prayest" [Ecclus. (Sirach) 28:1–2]. Imitate God your good Father because you are king and son of the highest King, and forgive the neighbor's offenses so that the Lord forgive your offenses. Do to your neighbor what you wish your God to do to you: do not seek to take revenge on your neighbor lest wrongs be required of you by the avenging Lord. "Be not overcome by evil, but overcome evil by good" [Rom. 12:21]. As a man, do not do to a man what you do not wish God to do to you. In both testaments it is found written: What you do not wish to be done to you, do not do to another. Therefore, if anyone guards against doing to another what he wishes to never suffer from another, then he is on guard that he, swollen with pride, not despise his neighbor; he is on guard that he, stirred by ambition, not provoke his brother to anger; he is on guard that he not shred with the bite of jealousy. When anyone thinks about doing to another what he wishes another to do to him, without doubt he decides to render good things to bad people and better things to good people, to show mildness to the insolent, and to show the favor of kindness to the humble. He shows the way of rectitude to the errant, recalls quarrelers to peace, supplies necessities to the poor, raises the troubled with a word of consolation, and faithfully provides everything he can to neighbors.

### 24. On restraining anger .

Because man is accustomed to render vengeance to man in anger, the Apostle [Paul] forbids us to sin in anger, saying: "Be angry, and sin not. Let not the sun go down upon your anger. Give not place to the devil" [Eph. 4:26–27]. You see then, most gentle king, that a man who in anger seeks revenge against his brother makes place for the devil in his heart, and makes the true sun, who is Christ, as much as he is in him, set. And indeed, Christ is rightly understood as the sun, and the devil is understood as darkness. Sun and darkness are unable to abide together in the single chest of a man because dwelling light banishes darkness and resident darkness shuts off light. And sweetness cannot abide with bitterness, or darkness with light, or fighting with peace, or storm with calm. Therefore, most gentle king, with the Lord's help, put away anger and do not render vengeance in anger. Diligently pay attention to what the wisdom of admonishing Paul tells us. For he says: "But now put you also away all anger, indignation, and malice" [Col. 3:8]. James also says: "For the anger of man worketh not the justice of God" [James 1:20]. Solomon says: "Envy and anger shorten a man's days, and pensiveness will bring old age before the time" [Ecclus. 30:26]. Even our Lord himself, ornament and splendor of his entire Church, preacher and teacher, example and model, creator, governor and ruler, entirely removing us from fraternal anger, says: "whosoever is angry with his brother, shall be in danger of the judgment" [Matt. 5:22].

Kings must especially guard against bringing their anger to effect. With royal anger, he is not comparable to another man. About the anger of a king it is written: "As the roaring of a lion, so also is the anger of a king" [Prov. 19:12]. And again: "the wrath of a king is as messengers of death" [Prov. 16:14]. Therefore, the more powerful the anger of the king is to render vengeance, the more the most faithful kings ought to temper and avoid it. Certainly, most gentle king, if you wish to follow the Royal Way (*Via regia*) by this which we wrote, and to ascend happily to the highest and regal homeland, be gentle and mild; and if anger rushes forth, restrain it; if it seizes the mind, appease it; if it emerges in the soul, subdue it; if the frenzy of anger should beat the soul, fraternal love should subdue it, fraternal sweetness should temper anger, fraternal charity should temper animosity, fraternal love should appease indignation. For anger is a great vice: through anger wisdom is lost, through anger justice is abandoned, through anger the fellowship of love is destroyed, through anger the concord of peace is broken, through anger the law of truth is lost. The body trembles after being shaken by the sting of anger, the tongue stammers, the face becomes inflamed, the beating heart trembles, and troubled eyes grow dim. Therefore, king, so that these things not happen to you, govern all things with patience after anger is restrained, for your speech is filled with power that nobody can resist. With peace govern what must be governed, and with tranquility rule what must be ruled so that you both govern the kingdom well and justly and rejoice having eternity of your soul.

## 25. HRABANUS MAURUS'S HOMILY ON AVOIDING ANGER AND HOMICIDE

*Hrabanus (ca 780–856) was given to be a monk at Fulda by 791, when he was still a child. Around 800, he was sent to Tours to study with Alcuin (ca 735–804), one of the pioneering scholars of the Carolingian Renaissance (see Doc. 34). He returned to Fulda in 818 and was abbot from 822 to 842, governing some 600 monks there. Between 822 and 825, Hrabanus sent Latin sermons to Archbishop Haistulf of Mainz. The sermons were to be read by priests of the diocese and then preached to the people on Sundays and feast days, most likely after being translated or paraphrased into the local Germanic dialect. Hrabanus wrote sermons on all the subjects that he considered necessary for the people to know and relied heavily on extracts from the Church Fathers, including, as in the sermon below, John Cassian (ca 370–435), Gregory the Great (ca 540–604), and Alcuin. In 847 Hrabanus himself became archbishop of Mainz.*

Source: Homily 60: *De iracundia et homicidio cavendo*, ed. George Colveneer (Cologne: 1626), reprinted in *Patrologia Latina* 110 (Paris: Migne, 1852), cols. 112–14. Trans. Kelly Gibson.

Therefore, most beloved brothers, the Lord and our Savior, who teaches us mildness and patience with his word and example, completely prohibited the persistence of anger and fury in order to bring about by the teaching of the Gospel what he could not fulfill by the commandment of law. The law forbade homicide, but it did not completely eliminate the vice itself because it allowed one to become angry, which is the seed of homicide. So our redeemer, who is come not to destroy but to fulfill [cf. Matt. 5:17] the law, fulfilled with his sanction what was insufficient in law, taking away the opportunity for anger. He not only ordered us not to become angry and not kill, but even also commanded us to most patiently endure obstacles imposed by others.

For anger is a certain passion (*passio*) of the mind, which is turned into frenzy if it is not managed by reason, so that in this way man becomes powerless over his mind and does what is inappropriate. For if this [anger] settled in the heart, it removes all foresight of his own action and he will neither be able to rightly pursue a judgment of discretion nor one involving an honorable consideration of virtue, nor shall he have maturity of counsel, seeming rather to do everything through a certain recklessness. From this he spreads pride, disputes, insults, clamor, indignation, audacity, blasphemy, bloodshed, homicide, desire for vengeance, and memory of offenses. This is overcome by patience and forbearance, the intellectual reason which God plants in human minds, and remembrance of the Lord's Prayer, where it is said to God: "And forgive us our debts, as we also forgive our debtors" [Matt. 6:12].

Therefore, if we desire to obtain the whole of the divine reward, about which it is said: "Blessed are the clean of heart, for they shall see God" [Matt. 5:8]; this [anger] must not only be cut out of our actions, but also eradicated at the root from the inner reaches of the mind. For the frenzy of anger restrained in speech and not brought forth into action will not be very beneficial if God, from whom the heart's secrets are not hidden, sees that it [anger] is in the hidden places of our chest.

But like all poisonous kinds of snakes and wild animals, they remain harmless when they stay in solitude and in their lairs. Regardless, they cannot be called "harmless" from this because they do not harm anything, for this gives them a need for solitude, not a disposition of goodness. When they obtain an opportunity to harm, they immediately discharge the venom hidden inside them and reveal the savageness of their minds.

For the word of the Gospel commands that the roots rather than the fruits of vices be destroyed, which will without doubt sprout no more new growth after nourishment has been rooted out. Thus the mind will be able to remain continually in all patience and piety when these [vices] have been rooted out from the innermost parts of thoughts, not from the surface of activity and action. Anger and hatred, without which the crime of homicide can in no way be perpetrated, is therefore cut off in order that homicide not be committed. For whosoever is angry with his brother, shall be in danger of the judgment [Matt. 5:22]; whosoever hateth his brother is a murderer [1 John 3:15] in the heart where he desires to destroy the man whose blood men know that he has not shed at all with his own hand or weapon. The Lord, because he renders to everyone either a reward or a punishment not only for the effect of the deed, but also for the desire of the will and intention, pronounces him a killer from his feeling of anger.

The world's greatest preacher [Paul] verily says: "Let all bitterness, and anger, and indignation, and clamor, and blasphemy, be put away from you" [Eph. 4:31]. Indeed, a man's anger will be unable to serve the justice of God. Anger without moderation certainly lacks reason. A mild answer appeaseth wrath, but a harsh word stirreth up fury [Prov. 15:1]. "A passionate man," as Solomon says, "stirreth up strifes"; he that is patient, appeaseth those that are stirred up [Prov. 15:18]. But who will be able to hold back a spirit that is easily angered? Anger has no mercy [Prov. 27:4] and the frenzy that breaks forth knows unlimited vengeance. O man, if anger seizes you, appease it! Anger is an evil that disturbs the mind so that right counsel is lost. Anger is just and necessary when man becomes angered against his own sins and will be indignant with himself when he acts badly. The Prophet says: "Be angry, and sin not" [Ps. 4:5]. He granted what is natural [and] he took away what is a fault. Let your patience soften another's anger. Be not overcome by evil, but overcome evil by good [Rom. 12:21]. Let another's offense be your reward. Another's anger displeases you: what displeases you in another should also be displeasing in yourself. Do not pollute the tranquility of your mind with another's disruption. Do not make yourself equal to a fool, because anger rests in the breast of the foolish: if you become angry against him, there will be two evils, you and him: it were better that you be good, even though he be evil; why does the malice of another make you evil?

But what is still more serious, another prays for the enemy's death: he pursues with prayer whom he cannot pursue with a sword. The one who is cursed will still live, and nevertheless the one who curses is already considered guilty of the other's death. God orders that the enemy be loved, nevertheless God is asked to kill the enemy. Thus whoever prays in this way fights against the Creator in his prayers. Whence under the type of Judas it is said: May his prayer be turned to sin [Ps. 109:7]. For it is prayer in sin to ask for the things that he who is asked forbids. Hence Truth says: When you shall stand to pray, forgive, if you have aught in your hearts [cf. Mark 11:5].

But the enemy severely wronged us, inflicted harm, injured helpers, [and] pursued the kind: these [offenses] might be remembered if there were no sins for which we must be forgiven. And indeed our advocate composed a prayer for us in our case and the judge of the same case is the one who is advocate. Moreover, he inserted a clause into the prayer he composed, saying: "And forgive us our debts, as we also forgive our debtors." Because the judge comes who is the advocate, he who made the prayer hears it. Either we say "And forgive us our debts, etc.," without acting, and by saying this we bind ourselves further, or perhaps we leave this clause out of the prayer, and our advocate does not recognize the prayer he composed, and to himself says at once: I know what I taught, that is not the prayer I made. Therefore, what should we do, brothers, but expend the feeling of true charity to our brothers, so that just as outside our hands are kept away from feuding, inside our hearts are kept protected from hatred? For killers, as it is written, will not inherit the kingdom of God [Gal. 5:21] and, "But he that hateth his brother, is in darkness" [1 John 2:11].

First, cast out your hatred, and in this way, with God's help, you can avoid homicide. Thus you will not only not go into the exterior darkness with the creator of homicide, that is, with the devil, but you, along with the lovers of peace, will also inherit the heavenly kingdom of the Father and of the most sweet Son may the creator and restorer of our salvation, Jesus Christ our Lord, who lives and reigns with God the Father and the Holy Spirit, God in unity and perfect trinity forever and ever, deign to grant this to you and to us along with you. Amen.

## 26. EINHARD ON THE FEAR OF FAMILY VENGEANCE

*Although Einhard (ca 770–840) is most famous for his biography of Charlemagne, he also wrote the* Translation of Saints Marcellinus and Peter *(Doc. 36), a theological work entitled "On the Adoration of the Cross," and many letters. His letters, two of which appear here, offer glimpses into daily life in the Carolingian Empire. The first letter reveals how involvement in a feud could hinder one's ability to carry out day-to-day activities and fulfill one's responsibilities. The second letter provides an early medieval instance of sanctuary, a concept evident in the Old Testament (Doc. 4a), Roman law (Doc. 11k), and Carolingian capitularies (Docs. 15a and 15d), and practiced throughout the Middle Ages (Docs. 124 and 125).*

Source: trans. Paul Edward Dutton, *Charlemagne's Courtier: The Complete Einhard* (Peterborough, ON: Broadview Press, 1998), pp. 137–38.

### a. Vengeance gets in the way of military service

Einhard, a sinner, [sends his greetings] to that most revered servant of Christ, the venerable abbot, Hrabanus [of Fulda: see Doc. 25 above].

A certain man of yours by the name of Gundhart asked me to intercede on his behalf with your holiness, so that he might, without giving you offense and indeed with your approval, be given permission to avoid the military expedition that is being planned at the present time and might remain at home. He claims that he is forced to remain at home out of great need, since he has been threatened by revenge and does not dare to go on this expedition with his enemies and with those who are plotting against his life, particularly with that count whom he is ordered to accompany, for he says he is his bitterest [enemy]. Thus, he asks you not to issue an order that would place him in such great danger. He is anxious to look after the matter himself, in order to make peace with the collector of the heerban [the fine for not appearing when summoned], if he should come and compel him, without troubling you. I would not have asked you [for help] in this matter, if I had not learned for certain of this man's dire straits and the dangers [to him].

I hope that you may always be well.

### b. A request to pay composition

Einhard [wishes] eternal salvation in the Lord to my dear friend Marchrad, the distinguished deputy.

Two servants of St. Martin [of Mainz], from the village of Hedabahc, by the names of Williram and Otbert, fled to the church of Marcellinus and Peter, Christ's blessed martyrs [at Seligenstadt], because their brother had killed one of his companions. They asked to be allowed to pay the assigned *wergeld* on their brother's behalf, so that his life might be pardoned. Therefore, I ask your Kindness, as far as it is possible, to consider sparing him out of love for God and his saints, to whose church they have fled.

I hope that you always prosper in the Lord.

## 27. CHARLES THE BALD TO POPE NICHOLAS ON VENGEANCE WITHOUT VIOLENCE

*Vengeful feelings and the acts of vengeance that they led to were not always violent, especially when a feud was carried out between ecclesiastical magnates and rulers in an age where they were advised to be merciful (Doc. 24). In this letter, written by Charles the Bald (823–877) to Pope Nicholas I in 867, there is a description of the events before, during, and after Archbishop Ebbo of Rheims was stripped of his position as archbishop in 835 by Louis the Pious after Louis had regained his imperial title. Louis had been deposed as emperor in 833 by a synod at Soissons, presided over by Ebbo, and it appears that much of Louis's motivation behind Ebbo's deposition came from his desire to take revenge on Ebbo for this action.*

*These events were part of the larger strife that existed between Louis and his sons Lothar, Louis, and Pippin. Louis had planned to divide his lands among these three sons and to grant the imperial title to his oldest son, Lothar, but redistributed his lands after the birth of his fourth son, the future Charles the Bald, to provide for this additional heir. Lothar, who was presented in an exceedingly negative light in the two major contemporary histories of this dispute, Nithard's* Histories *and the* Annals of St. Bertin, *had, like his father, utilized non-violent means of removing someone who got in the way of a claim to power when he imprisoned his father Louis in the monastery of St. Medard of Soissons and imprisoned Charles in the monastery of Prüm in 833. The strife formally ended in 843 when the Treaty of Verdun divided the imperial land between Charles, Lothar, and Louis (known as the German).*

*Ebbo was restored to his see temporarily in 840, but Hincmar, who succeeded after Ebbo's deposition to the see of Rheims in 845, spent much of the 860s arguing that Ebbo had never been properly restored and thus the clerics whom Ebbo had ordained, including Wulfadus of Bourges, were never priests. In his portion of the* Annals of St. Bertin, *which he began after 861, Hincmar described the letter below as having been written in opposition to Hincmar and with the desire to silence him, and attributed its creation to Charles's forgetting of Hincmar's many years of "loyalty and work" for Charles's "honor and maintenance of the kingdom."*

Source: "Troyes, Oktober–November 867," *in Die Konzilien der karolingischen Teilreiche, 860–874,* ed. Wilfried Hartmann (Hanover: Hahn, 1998), pp. 239–42. Trans. by Kelly Gibson.

Charles, by the grace of God king and your spiritual son, to the most reverend lord and father Nicholas, highest bishop of the catholic and apostolic see, and universal pope:... You commanded that we write the truth of the matter for you and sign it with our signature. We faithfully indicate to you what we saw and know about it in order to obey your holy Paternity in all things. For none of the bishops who took part in his [Ebbo's] case now survive, except Rothadus [d. 869].

*Charles describes Ebbo's early career: born into the household of the royal fisc, he was raised in the palace of Charlemagne. He entered holy orders, served Louis the Pious, and held the position of* bibliothecarius *[librarian]. Ebbo became archbishop of Rheims [in 816] after the death of Wulfarius and the rejection of his successor, Gislemar, who could not read.*

The first time [830], when, at the devil's instigation, the people of the Franks undertook to drive from his empire the emperor appointed for them by God and crowned by the apostolic see, Ebbo remained unwaveringly faithful [to Louis], and, as was right, remained [faithful] until [Louis's] restoration. But the second [time] when all the people, at the exhortation and effort of our brother Lothar, withdrew from our father of pious memory, they placed him [Louis] into custody and carried his wife [Judith, second wife of Louis the Pious and mother of Charles the Bald] off into Italy to the city of Tortona [in 833]. They also placed me, not yet ten years old, into equal custody in the monastery of Prüm as though guilty of many crimes. Moreover, after Lothar carried off the emperor to the monastery of St. Medard of Soissons, Ebbo and almost all other bishops, some willing, some unwilling, removed the aforementioned emperor, deprived of his wife and son, all [his] followers, and his office, [who had] neither confessed nor been found guilty by anyone [a bishop must verify that charges are accurate before imposing penance], from the communion of the church. At last the clemency of compassionate God, seeing the humility of the pious emperor, touched the hearts of those whom he wished, and with his mercy inspired them to lead him from custody and restore him to imperial command. Archbishops and bishops, bringing him back from custody, humbly confessing that they had wronged him [Louis], suppliantly begged pardon from him, as was worthy, in the monastery of the most blessed martyrs Dionysius [Saint Denis], Rusticus, and Eleutherius [martyred at the same time as Dionysius]. They urged Lothar to abdicate from imperial power. Then from there he [Lothar] and those who were with him retreated from him [Louis] into other parts [of the empire]. Ebbo, after he learned of this while he was residing at Rheims, fled terrified to the city of Paris so that he might escape the wrath of the emperor by going into seclusion with a certain recluse. The emperor, hearing this because he was not far away, and sending strong and faithful messengers, ordered that he [Ebbo] be seized and placed in custody, and he entrusted the church of Rheims to the venerable abbot Fulco. Then he [Ebbo] was led to the city of Metz, where in the church of Saint Stephen, climbing up onto the pulpit (*ambo*) in the presence of everyone, he confessed that an unfair judgment had been imposed against his lord, the glorious emperor. Also there all the bishops, clergy and people honorably crowned the same most pious emperor and restored him to his former command.

Hence, again, once a general assembly was called [at Thionville, February 835], he [Louis] ordered that the aforementioned Ebbo be presented before him and, because of the injurious slanders inflicted, and with a number of bishops present [gap in the text]. The bishops, desiring to accordingly make amends to the emperor and to preserve respect for the office of bishop, convinced the emperor that Ebbo's case should be decided not in the presence of laymen but in the church. After Ebbo was deprived of all worldly aid and abandoned by all human support, looking out for an opportunity, he summoned a certain recluse named Framegaud and sent a ring by him to our mother Judith the glorious empress and tearfully begged her to have pity on him. She had given the ring to him earlier, and he was accustomed to send it whenever he was struck by any trouble. Our mother had sent the same ring to him at the moment of our birth, because he was archbishop on account of his piety and sanctity, in order that he be constantly mindful of us in his prayers. Then she, remembering and acknowledging his [Ebbo's] tearful prayers, undertook to convince the bishops who had gathered there with pious persuasion to both placate the mind of the emperor by making satisfaction and not violate divine laws by transgression, lest they, administering a punishment of severity against him who had wronged them, might perhaps seem to not render due reciprocity to God, who had mercifully freed them from such danger. For she had determined that she should, out of reverence for the office, offer no assent at all to the deposition of any bishop. And on account of this she convinced the pious emperor to no longer push for his [Ebbo's] deposition. According to the most moderate advice of the glorious empress our mother, they [the bishops] should make satisfaction to the most pious emperor and impose no punishment against Ebbo other than the one that he had [himself] issued in writing.

Hincmar, the venerable archbishop, received this valid document from the aforementioned venerable abbot Fulco, to whom the church of Rheims had been entrusted then, and sent it to you, as he reported to us. But we do not know whether it was sent to you unaltered and in its entirety. Nevertheless, we know most certainly that none of the bishops confirmed it by signing at the bottom with their own hands. For the same Ebbo, after the unavoidable reason for his crisis was ascertained, produced three witnesses, as it were, his confessors, archbishop Aiulfus [of Bourges], and bishops Modouin [of Autun] and Badaradus [of Paderborn], who, holding firm on his behalf, might declare whether it is indeed true, as Ebbo himself admitted to them, that they counseled him to retire from episcopal service. They also drew to themselves three others who saw him confessing to them: archbishop Notho [of Arles] and bishops Theuderic [of Cambrai] and Achardus [of Noyon]. After these things were finished, he was led back into custody. Moreover, after the bishops had settled these things in such a manner, the lord emperor sent letters of his dignity by Godefrid, the venerable abbot of the monastery of Saint Gregory [in Alsace], to your predecessor, the venerable pope lord Gregory [IV, d. 844], calling for his assent, if possible, in the deposition of Ebbo. He [Gregory] sent back letters of his authority by the aforementioned abbot, but what was in them is considered unknown to all bishops and all orders of our kingdom. But the skill of your sanctity through the offices of your dignity will be able to investigate what your predecessor thought. We nevertheless suppose that, if the lord emperor had had your predecessor himself as a supporter in Ebbo's deposition, he might have nominated another bishop in his place to the still vacant church, because, indeed, refusing to act with even the most temperate advice, he acted with effective shrewdness so that the effrontery inherent in reckless and venomous deeds of this kind might thenceforward be subdued, and so that the status of the church might not be undermined.

After the death of the lord emperor [Louis the Pious in 840], his guardian [the abbot of Fleury, where Ebbo had been held captive] brought the aforementioned Ebbo to our brother Lothar. Our brother reverently and kindly received him, with the bishops then assembled with him [at Ingelheim], whose advice Ebbo himself had used a little while ago in the brief document of his confession in order to make satisfaction to the emperor, and by their common consent he was restored to his ecclesiastical dignities. Moreover, while we were leaving on urgent business in parts of Aquitaine, all the clergy of the church of Rheims and the people most avidly requested him, and so at last his fellow bishops and suffragans [dependent bishops] restored him to his former see. Then everyone present received communion from him, and he gave rings and staffs and written records of their confirmation in the custom of the Gallic churches to all the suffragans who had been ordained while he was absent. Further, access to him was granted to all the communicants, and there he ordained Wulfadus and certain other sons of the church.

We briefly touched on these things concerning Ebbo's removal and restoration so that the prudence of your wisdom may decide whether they pertain to Wulfadus's deposition or not. But if anyone told your sanctity that he was canonically summoned to the synod of Soissons, and signed or presented letters of his condemnation, you should know that it is not at all true, because he was not present at that synod....

## 28. VENGEANCE FOR THE "HARD MAN"

*The Exeter Book, given to Exeter Cathedral by Bishop Leofric (d. 1072), is one of the most important manuscripts of Anglo-Saxon literature as it contains the only surviving copies of many Anglo-Saxon poems and riddles. One of its poems, "Maxims I," is an example of wisdom literature that presents an ordered view of the world where everything has its place and function and states truths thought to be as incontrovertible as those in the Bible, such as "every mouth needs food; meals must come on time," "gold is meant for giving," and "fire crumbles wood." The excerpts below reveal how vengeance fits in this worldview.*

Source: trans. S. J. A. Bradley, *Anglo-Saxon Poetry* (London: Dent, 1982), pp. 349–50.

The unbefriended man gets wolves as his comrades, beasts abounding in treachery; very often that comrade will savage him. For the grey one there has to be dread, and for the dead man a grave; it will mourn, this grey wolf, out of ravening and it will wander round the grave, but not with a dirge nor indeed will it weep for the death and destruction of men but will always wish for more.

For a wound there has to be a bandage, for a hard man vengeance; for an arrow there has to be a bow and for both alike there has to be a man as a partner. One rich gift rewards another: gold is meant for giving. God may grant belongings to prosperous people, and take them away. The hall itself must stand and grow old. A felled timber grows least; trees must necessarily spread themselves, and faith flourish, for it burgeons in the breast of the inno- cent. The renegade and reckless man, venom-hearted and faithless, over him God will not watch. Many things the ordaining Lord created, and as it was of old he bade that it should so be thenceforth…. Feuding has existed among mankind ever since earth swallowed the blood of Abel. That was no one-day strife: from it the drops of enmity splashed abroad, great wickedness among men and malice-mingled strife among many nations. His brother killed his own; but Cain kept no prerogative over murder. After that it became widely manifest that chronic strife was causing harm among men so that far abroad through the earth its inhabitants suffered a contest of arms, and devised and tempered the destructive sword.

# CHAPTER SIX: SAINTS' LIVES, CHRONICLES, AND EPICS

*In comparison with the eras preceding and following it, there are relatively few narrative sources from the early Middle Ages. The most common types are connected to the cult of the saints: these include saints' lives, accounts of the translations of relics from one place to another, and miracle collections.*

*The cult of the saints, as it developed in post-Roman Europe from the fifth century onward, was in part a creation of bishops eager to harness the threat of divine retribution in order to keep poorly defended Christian institutions and episcopal cities safe as other protections failed. Saints did not exact vengeance so much as they served as a channel for God's vengeance, as described in Deuteronomy 32:35 (Doc. 4b). God's role was seen as very much like that of a powerful relative or chieftain one would appeal to in order to have injuries avenged. In the worldview of the authors excerpted below, it was unthinkable that wicked men and women would not eventually receive their come-uppance: sometimes vengeance would arrive at the hands of their enemies or victims, and sometimes through the actions of vengeful saints. In all cases, God was behind the scenes, working through men, saints, or even diseases and natural disasters in order to punish the wicked and protect the innocent and weak, just as in 2 Maccabees (Doc. 8).*

*Many of the same sentiments that appeared in the saints' lives above also appear in the sixth-century chronicle* The History of the Franks *by Gregory of Tours. The most important source we have on the sixth-century Merovingians, Gregory's inclusion of stories that showed how political circumstances were dictated by the search for vengeance was typical for authors of chronicles and histories. Vengeance, in other words, was a significant element in the plotlines they developed. Although written in the same milieu, the more secular works included in this chapter act as a counterweight to the hagiographical evidence, for they do not typically assume that vengeance is a divine prerogative. This is the case in two other histories in our collection: Jordanes's* Gothic History *(Doc. 29) and Paul the Deacon's* History of the Lombards *(Doc. 35). In some cases, such as Liutprand of Cremona's "Tit-For-Tat" (Doc. 38), the act of writing was itself vengeance in that it conveyed to posterity a negative image of a particular ruler. Medieval writers of epics had that same reliance upon vengeance as a significant plot element, and we include here several passages from the great Anglo-Saxon epic* Beowulf *as a representative example of a different type of vengeance narrative.*

## 29. JORDANES ON VENGEANCE AND THE VANDAL WARS OF CONQUEST

*Jordanes (d. after 551), a Goth from the Balkans, was a notary to a master of the armies in the kingdom of the Ostrogothic king Theodoric. Jordanes wrote his* Gothic History, *with the purpose of justifying Gothic dominion over the Romans, some time around 550. His version was a summary, based on memory, of a lost Gothic history by Cassiodorus (see Doc. 21). He also wrote a Roman history based on a lost history by Quintus Aurelius Memmius Symmachus (d. 536). Both of Jordanes's histories were probably written at Constantinople, though the only evidence for this comes from hints within his works.*

*The following are selections from chapters 33 and 39. Chapter 33 casts the desire for vengeance as a motivating principle in the foundation legend of the Vandal kingdom in that the Roman general Boniface, charged with treason, called the Vandals to invade Africa in order to get revenge on Emperor Valentinian. Jordanes explicitly mentions the Vandal king Gaiseric's ability to sow seeds of dissension so as to manipulate enmity and other vengeful emotions among his opponents for his own benefit. Gaiseric's belief that feuding within the royal family would lead to a weakening of the Vandal kingdom is similar to that put forth by Gregory of Tours in his* History of the Franks *(see Doc. 30a). Chapter 39 contains Attila the Hun's speech to his army to encourage them as they met the combined forces of Romans, Visigoths, and Alans at the battle of Châlons in 451.*

Source: trans. Charles Christopher Mierow, *Historia Getica* (Princeton: Princeton University Press, 1915), pp. 52–53, 62–64.

33. But Gaiseric, king of the Vandals, had already been invited into Africa by Boniface, who had fallen into a dispute with the emperor Valentinian and was able to obtain revenge only by injuring the empire. So he invited them urgently and brought them across the narrow Strait of Gades, scarcely seven miles wide, which divides Africa from Spain and unites the mouth of the Tyrrhenian Sea with the waters of Ocean. Gaiseric, still famous in the city for the disaster of the Romans [the sack of Rome in 455], was a man of moderate height and lame in consequence of a fall from his horse. He was a man of deep thought and few words, holding luxury in disdain, furious in his anger, greedy for gain, shrewd in winning over the barbarians and skilled in sowing the seeds of dissension to arouse enmity. Such was he who, as we have said, came at the solicitous invitation of Boniface to the country of Africa. There he reigned for a long time, receiving authority, as they say, from God himself. Before his death he summoned the band of his sons and

ordained that there should be no strife among them because of desire for the kingdom, but that each should reign in his own rank and order as he survived the others; that is, the next younger should succeed his elder brother, and he in turn should be followed by his junior. By giving heed to this command they ruled their kingdom in happiness for the space of many years and were not disgraced by civil war, as is usual among other nations; one after the other receiving the kingdom and ruling the people in peace.

39. Now when Attila [the Hun] saw that his army was thrown into confusion by this event, he thought it best to encourage them by an extemporaneous address in this way: "Here you stand, after conquering mighty nations and subduing the world. I therefore think it foolish for me to goad you with words, as though you were men who had not been proved in action. Let a new leader or an untried army resort to that. It is not right for me to say anything common, nor ought you to listen. For what is war but your usual custom? Or what is sweeter for a brave man than to seek revenge with his own hand? It is a right of nature to glut the soul with vengeance. Let us then attack the foe eagerly; for they are ever the bolder who make the attack. Despise this union of discordant races! To defend oneself by alliance is proof of cowardice. See, even before our attack they are smitten with terror. They seek the heights, they seize the hills and, repenting too late, clamor for protection against battle in the open fields. You know how slight a matter the Roman attack is. While they are still gathering in order and forming in one line with locked shields, they are checked, I will not say by the first wound, but even by the dust of battle. Then on to the fray with stout hearts, as is your wont. Despise their battle line. Attack the Alani [the Alans, a tribe allied with the Visigoths and Romans against the Huns], smite the Visigoths! Seek swift victory in that spot where the battle rages. For when the sinews are cut the limbs soon relax, nor can a body stand when you have taken away the bones. Let your courage rise and your own fury burst forth! Now show your cunning, Huns, now your deeds of arms! Let the wounded exact in return the death of his foe; let the unwounded revel in slaughter of the enemy. No spear shall harm those who are sure to live; and those who are sure to die Fate overtakes even in peace. And finally, why should Fortune have made the Huns victorious over so many nations, unless it were to prepare them for the joy of this conflict...."

# 30. GREGORY OF TOURS ON FEUDING AND VENGEANCE

*Best known today as the author of the* History of the Franks, *Gregory of Tours (538/539–594) became bishop of Tours in 573. Born in Clermont-Ferrand, in modern-day Auvergne, he was descended from a Gallo-Roman senatorial family. For modern historians, his* History of the Franks *has become the main primary source for information about political events in the sixth-century Merovingian kingdom, as well as being a source of stories about saints, heretics, and miracles. Book one is a history of the world, as Gregory interpreted it, from the Creation to 397. The rest of the history chronicles Frankish history up to 591. Gregory also included local events, and his famous description of the enmity between Sichar and Chramnesind, two citizens of Tours, (Docs. 30e and 30f) can be read profitably in conjunction with the Salic law (Doc. 13).*

Sources: Docs. 30a–d, trans. Ernest Brehaut, *History of the Franks* (New York: Columbia University Press, 1916), pp. 105–6, 128–29, 130–31, 155; Docs. 30e-f, trans. A. C. Murray, *From Roman to Merovingian Gaul,* Readings in Medieval Civilizations and Cultures 5 (Peterborough, ON: Broadview Press, 2000), pp. 441–44.

## a. The need for kings to keep peace
### [Preface to book 5]

I am weary of relating the details of the civil wars that mightily plague the nation and kingdom of the Franks; and the worst of it is that we see in them the beginning of that time of woe which the Lord foretold: "Father shall rise against son, son against father, brother against brother, kinsman against kinsman" [cf. Matt. 10:21 and 24:7]. They should have been deterred by the examples of former kings who were slain by their enemies as soon as they were divided. How often has the very city of cities, the great capital of the whole earth, been laid low by civil war and again, when it ceased, has risen as if from the ground! Would that you too, O kings, were engaged in battles like those in which your fathers struggled, that the heathen terrified by your union might be crushed by your strength! Remember how Clovis [Merovingian king (d. 511); see Doc. 13] won your great victories, how he slew opposing kings, crushed wicked peoples and subdued their lands, and left to you complete and unchallenged dominion over them! And when he did this he had neither silver nor gold such as you now have in your treasuries. What is your object? What do you seek after? What have you not in plenty? In your homes there are luxuries in abundance, in your storehouses wine, grain and oil abound, gold and silver are piled up in your treasuries. One thing you lack: without peace you have not the grace of God. Why does one take from another? Why does one desire what another has? I beg of you, beware of this saying of the apostle: "But if ye bite and devour one another, take heed that ye be not consumed one of another" [Gal. 5:15]. Examine carefully the books of the ancients and you will see what civil wars beget. Read what Orosius writes of the Carthaginians, who says that after seven hundred years their city and country were ruined and adds: "What preserved this city so long? Union. What destroyed it after such a period? Disunion." Beware of disunion, beware of civil wars which destroy you and your people. What else is to be expected but that your army will fall and that you will be left without strength and be crushed and ruined by hostile peoples. And, king, if civil war gives you pleasure, govern that impulse which the apostle says is urgent within man, let the spirit struggle against the flesh [Gal. 5:17] and the vices fall before the virtues; and be free and serve your chief who is Christ, you who were once a fettered slave of the root of evil [1 Tim. 6:10].

## b. Sacrilege done in the church of St. Denis because of a woman [Book 5.32]

At Paris a certain woman fell under reproach, many charging that she had left her husband and was intimate with another. Then her husband's kinsmen went to her father saying: "Either make your daughter behave properly or she shall surely die, lest her wantonness lay a disgrace on our family." "I know," said the father, "that my daughter is well-behaved and the word is not true that evil men speak of her. Still, to keep the reproach from going further, I will make her innocent by my oath." And they replied, "If she is without guilt declare it on oath upon the tomb here of the blessed Denis the martyr." "I will do so," said the father. Then having made the agreement they met at the church of the Holy Martyr and the father raised his hands above the altar and swore that his daughter was not guilty. On the other hand, others on the part of the husband declared that he had committed perjury. They entered into a dispute, drew their swords and rushed on one another, and killed one another before the very altar. Now they were men advanced in years and leaders with king Chilperic. Many received sword wounds, the holy church was spattered with human blood, the doors were pierced with darts and swords and godless missiles raged as far as the very tomb. When the struggle had with difficulty been stopped, the church was put under an interdict until the whole matter should come under the king's notice. They hastened to the presence of the prince but were not received with favor. They were sent back to the bishop of the place and the order was given that if they were not found guilty of this crime they might rightly be admitted to communion. Then they atoned for their evil conduct and were taken back to the communion of the Church by Ragnemod, bishop of Paris. Not many days later the woman on being summoned to trial hanged herself.

### c. Queen Austrechild seeks an avenger
### [Book 5.35]

In these days Austrechild, wife of prince Gunthram [of Burgundy, r. 561–592], succumbed to this disease [dysentery], but before she breathed out her worthless life, seeing she could not escape, she drew deep sighs and wished to have partners in her death, intending that at her funeral there should be mourning for others. It is said that she made a request of the king in Herodian fashion saying: "I would still have had hopes of life if I had not fallen into the hands of wicked physicians; for the draughts they gave me have taken my life away perforce and have caused me swiftly to lose the light of day. And therefore I beg you let my death not go unavenged, and I conjure you with an oath to have them slain by the sword as soon as I depart from the light; so that, just as I cannot live longer, so they too shall not boast after my death, and the grief of our friends and of theirs shall be one and the same." So speaking she gave up her unhappy soul. And the king after the customary period of public mourning fulfilled her wicked order, forced by the oath to his cruel wife. He ordered the two physicians who had attended her to be slain with the sword, and the wisdom of many believes that this was not done without sin.

### d. A feud in the Jewish community
### [Book 6.17]

King Chilperic ordered many Jews to be baptized that year and received a number of them from the sacred font. Some of them however were purified in body only, not in heart, and lying to God they returned to their former perfidy so that they could be seen to observe the Sabbath as well as honor the Lord's day. But Priscus could not be influenced in any way to recognize the truth. The king was angry at him and ordered him to be put into prison, in the idea that if he did not wish to believe of his own accord he would force him to hear and believe. But Priscus offered gifts and asked for time until his son should marry a Hebrew girl at Marseilles; he promised deceitfully that he would then do what the king required. Meantime a quarrel arose between him and Phatir, one of the Jewish converts who was now a godson to the king. And when on the Sabbath Priscus clad in an orary [*orarium*: a stole worn on both shoulders by priests and on one shoulder by deacons] and carrying nothing of iron in his hand, was retiring to a secret place to fulfill the law of Moses, suddenly Phatir came upon him and slew him with the sword together with the companions who accompanied him. When they were slain Phatir fled with his men to the church of St. Julian, which was on a neighboring street. While they were there they heard that the king had granted to the master his life but ordered the men to be dragged like malefactors from the church and put to death. Then, their master being already gone, one of them drew his sword and killed his comrades and then left the church armed with his sword, but the people rushed upon him and he was cruelly killed. Phatir obtained permission and returned to Gunthram's kingdom whence he had come. But soon after he was killed by Priscus's kinsmen.

### e. Civil war among the citizens of Tours
### [Book 7.47]

At this point [585] a serious internal conflict arose among the citizens of Tours. While Sichar, son of the late John, was holding Christmas celebrations in the village of Manthelan [near Tours], with Austrighysel and other people of the district, the local priest sent round a servant to invite some people to have a drink at his place. So the servant arrived and one of the men he was inviting thought nothing of drawing a sword and striking him with it. The servant fell down dead on the spot. Sichar was connected to the priest by friendship, and as soon as he heard that the servant had been killed, he grabbed his weapons and went to the church to wait for Austrighysel. When Austrighysel heard about this, he grabbed his arms and went after Sichar. In the general commotion of the fighting that ensued when the two sides came together, Sichar was saved by some clerics and escaped to his villa, leaving behind in the priest's house money, garments, and four wounded servants. After Sichar had fled, Austrighysel attacked again, killing the servants and carrying off the gold and silver and other property.

After this the parties appeared before a tribunal of citizens. It found that Austrighysel was subject to legal penalty because he had committed homicide, killed servants, and seized property without obtaining judgment. An agreement was reached [for Austrighysel to pay compensation] and a few days later Sichar heard that the stolen property was being held by Auno, his son, and his brother Eberulf. Setting the agreement aside, Sichar, accompanied by Audinus, created a public disturbance by attacking them at night with an armed force. Sichar broke apart the quarters where they were sleeping, did in the father, brother, and son, killed slaves, and took off with property and cattle.

I was very upset when I heard news of the attack and, acting in conjunction with the count (iudex), sent a delegation with a message for the parties to come before us so that a reasonable settlement could be made and they could depart in peace without the dispute going any further.

When they arrived, and the citizens had assembled, I said, "Men, stop this criminal behavior and prevent the evil spreading further. We have already lost sons of the Church; now I fear we shall be deprived of even more of them by this quarrel. Be peacemakers, I beg of you; let whoever did wrong pay compensation out of brotherly love, so that you may be peaceable children and worthy, by God's gift, to occupy his kingdom. For he himself said, 'Blessed are the peacemakers, for they shall be called the children of God [Matt. 5:9].' Listen carefully! if anyone who is liable to a penalty has insufficient resources, Church money will be paid out on his behalf. In the meantime, let no man's soul perish."

In saying this, I offered money of the Church, but the party of Chramnesind, who had a claim for the death of his father [Auno], his brother, and his uncle, refused to accept it.

When they went away, Sichar made preparations for a journey to visit the king; with this in mind he first went to see his wife in Poitiers. While admonishing a slave at his labors, Sichar beat him with a rod. The fellow drew a sword from its baldric and without hesitation wounded his master with it. Sichar fell to the ground, but his friends ran up and caught the slave. They beat him viciously, cut off his hands and feet, and hung him up on a gibbet.

Meanwhile rumor reached Tours that Sichar was dead. When Chramnesind heard, he mustered his kinsmen and friends, and rushed to Sichar's home. He plundered it, killing some slaves and burning down all the buildings, not only Sichar's, but those of other landlords in the villa, and took off with the herds and anything he could move.

At this point the parties were brought into the city by the count and pleaded their own causes. The judges found that the side that had earlier refused compensation and then put houses to the torch should forfeit half the sum formerly awarded to it – this was done contrary to law only to ensure that they would be peaceable; as for the other side, Sichar was to pay the other half of the compensation. He paid it, the Church providing the sum that the judges had determined, and he received a notice [from Chramnesind] discharging him from future claims. Both sides took oaths to each other that neither would ever so much as mutter a word against the other.

And so the dispute came to an end.

### f. The killing of Sichar
### [Book 9.19]

The conflict among the citizens of Tours that I said above had ended arose again with renewed madness [in 588].

Sichar had struck up a great friendship with Chramnesind after having killed his relatives. They had such affection for each other that they often ate together and slept together in the same bed. One day Chramnesind had an evening dinner prepared and invited Sichar to the feast. He came and they sat down at the meal together.

Sichar got stinking drunk on wine and bragged a lot at Chramnesind's expense, until at last, so we are told, he said, "Dear brother, you owe me a great debt of gratitude for doing in your kinsmen. There's certainly no lack of gold and silver around here since you got compensation for them. If this business hadn't given you a bit of a boost, you'd now be naked and poor."

Chramnesind took Sichar's words badly and said to himself, "If I don't avenge my kinsmen's death, I should lose the name man and be called a weak woman."

He immediately extinguished the lights and split open Sichar's head with his dagger. Emitting a little cry at the end of his life, Sichar fell down dead. The servants who had come with him scattered. Chramnesind stripped the lifeless body of its clothes, hung it on a fence post and, mounting his horse, rode off to see the king [Childebert].

He entered the church and threw himself at the king's feet. "Glorious king," said Chramnesind, "I ask for my life because I have killed men who slew my kinsmen in secret and stole their property." When the details of the matter were brought to light, Brunhild [Childebert's mother] took it badly that Sichar, who was under her protection, had been killed in this way, and the queen became angry at Chramnesind. When he saw that she was against him, he went to the Vosagus district in the territory of Bourges where his kinfolk lived, because it was considered part of Guntram's kingdom.

Sichar's wife Tranquilla left her sons and her husband's property in Tours and Poitiers and went to her family in the village of Mauriopes, and there she got married again.

Sichar was about twenty years old when he died. In his life he was a foolish, drunken killer, who inflicted harm on not a few people when he was drunk. As for Chramnesind, he came back to the king, and the judgment he received was that he prove his killing of Sichar was unavoidable. This he did. But since Queen Brunhild had placed Sichar under her protection, as I have said, she ordered Chramnesind's property confiscated, but it was later restored by the *domesticus* [a palace official] Flavian. Chramnesind also went quickly to [Duke] Agino and got a letter from him protecting his person. Chramnesind's property had been granted to Agino by the queen.

[The translation of the last two sentences is uncertain.]

# 31. GREGORY OF TOURS ON GOD'S VENGEANCE

*In addition to his* History, *Gregory wrote lives of martyrs and of confessors. His collection of martyr stories was most likely set down between 585 and 588, although he could have reworked them until his death in 594.*

Source: trans. Raymond Van Dam, *Glory of the Martyrs* (Liverpool: Liverpool University Press, 1988), pp. 60, 82, 89–90, 95–96, 101–4.

## a. The vengeance of the martyr Pancratius
### [Ch. 38]

Not far from a wall of this city [of Rome] is [the tomb of] the martyr Pancratius, who is a powerful avenger against perjurers. Whenever someone who suffers from madness intends to swear a false oath at the martyr's tomb, before he approaches his tomb, or rather, after he approaches all the way to the railings that are beneath the arch where the clerics usually stand and chant the psalms, immediately either he is seized by a demon or he falls to the pavement and breathes out his spirit. In consequence, whenever a man wishes to elicit a guarantee about something from someone, he sends him nowhere else except to this church, so that he might find a true [guarantee]. For some say that although many people loiter around the churches of the apostles and of the other martyrs, they go nowhere else except the church of the blessed Pancratius for this duty [of swearing oaths]. Because his harsh punishment publicly distinguishes [oaths], either listeners believe the truth or they witness the judgment of the blessed martyr against deceit.

## b. The martyr Eugenius punishes an oathbreaker
### [Ch. 57]

... At a certain time when many people have gathered for his festival, much business takes place in the courtyard. A girl, one of the inhabitants of the region, went to a stall as if intending to buy something. When she saw an ornament she liked, she took it from the merchant. Immediately, more swiftly than words [can say], she gave the ornament to someone else and then claimed that she had not received it. But the merchant insisted: "I offered it to you with my hand, and you took it for a closer inspection." When the girl denied [the accusation], the merchant said: "If, under the influence of greed, you so persist in denying, the blessed martyr Eugenius will judge. If you take an oath before his tomb and say that you did not receive the ornament, then I will think that what I misplaced was not a loss." Promising that she could be cleared by this oath, she quickly went to the tomb. When she raised her hands to swear her oath, immediately she lost control of her limbs and became stiff. Her feet were glued to the pavement, her voice stuck in her throat, and her mouth hung open without any words. The merchant and the other people saw this, and he said: "Young girl, let the ornament that you took from me be of use to you. The punishment given by the martyr is sufficient." After saying this, he left the place. For a long time the girl was held in this pain. Finally, at the martyr's command, she spoke and openly confessed what she had wished to conceal in secret. What are you doing, o accursed greed? Why do you, female (but not male) mind, succumb to seeking after others' possessions? Why do you pierce the sturdy breastplate of the mind with the small arrow of cupidity? Why, o mankind, do you accumulate talents of rusty gold with which you will burn in hell? What is the use to you of money that will perish and that poses a threat to eternal life, according to that saying of the Lord: "What does it profit a man if he gains the whole world but suffers the loss of his life? Or what will a man exchange for his own life?" [Matt. 16:26].

## c. Divine vengeance strikes some thieves
### [Ch. 65]

At the time when Chramn [son of king Clothar, delegated to protect his father's interests in the Auvergne] came to Clermont, members of his retinue committed various crimes also in the territory of the city. Five men furtively approached the holy oratory on the estate at Yssac-la-Tourette that contained relics of Saint Saturninus. After breaking in, they stole the robes and other vessels for celebrating the liturgy. Under the cover of night they left. A priest recognized the theft. He searched among the local inhabitants but found no trace of the items that had been stolen. The thieves who had committed the crime quickly crossed into the territory of Orléans. After dividing their spoils, each accepted his portion. But as divine vengeance pursued them, soon four were killed in brawls. As the sole survivor the fifth thief claimed as his legacy the whole of their stolen goods. But once he brought everything to his house, immediately his eyes were encrusted with blood and he was blinded. Goaded by his pains and by divine inspiration he took a vow and said: "If God will notice my misery and will restore my vision, I will return what I stole to that holy place." While weeping and praying for this he received his sight. As he was traveling to Orléans he met, by God's providence, a deacon from Clermont. He handed the stolen goods to him and humbly prayed that he return them to the oratory. The deacon piously fulfilled his wish.

## d. A thief is rescued from a stern judge
### [Ch. 72]

*A blind nun finds Quintinus's body and is miraculously cured.*

In this city [St. Quintin] a thief secretly stole a priest's horse. When the priest found him, he was brought to a judge. There was no delay: the thief was arrested, bound in chains, and handed over for torture. The thief revealed his deed with his own confession and was condemned to the gallows. But the priest feared lest on account of his accusation a man lose his life. So he begged the judge that he spare his life and that the man accused of this crime be freed from this penalty. The priest said that he was satisfied with what had already been done, because after so many types of torture the thief had admitted what he had done. But no prayers could bend the severity of the judge, and he condemned the accused man to the gallows. Then the priest in tears bowed before the tomb of the holy martyr and offered a prayer of supplication. He said: "Most glorious athlete of Christ, I ask that you rescue this poor man from the hand of an unjust death, so that I might not be ashamed if this man dies as a result of my accusation. I beg you, display your power, so that by the mitigation of your gentle piety you might release the man whom human harshness could not forgive." After the priest wept and offered this prayer, the chains on the gallows broke and the accused man fell to the ground. When the judge heard of this, he was terrified and marveled at this divine miracle; but he no longer dared to harm the man.

## e. Count Gomacharius suffers God's vengeance
### [Ch. 78]

The cathedral at Agde, which rejoices in its relics of the apostle Saint Andrew, often is distinguished by glorious miracles and often exposes those who invade its possessions. Count Gomacharius [presumably appointed by the Arian Visigoths in Spain] invaded a field belonging to this cathedral. Leo, the bishop of this cathedral [some time between 506 and 567], was very upset and rushed to the count; he said: "O my son, depart from the possessions of the poor that the Lord has entrusted to my rule, lest it be harmful to you and lest you die from the tears of the needy who are accustomed to eat the produce of this field." But the count, because he was a heretic, disregarded what the bishop said and kept the field under his own control. As the day went on, he was struck with a fever. Since he suffered not only from his bodily fever but also from torment in his heart, he sent messengers to the bishop and said: "Let the bishop deign to offer a prayer on my behalf to the Lord, and I will forsake his field." After the bishop prayed, the count recovered from the illness that afflicted him. After regaining his health, he said to his servants: "What do you think these Romans are now saying? They say that I was afflicted with this fever because I had seized their field. But the fever affected me according to the nature of the human body; and since I am still alive they will not have the field." After saying this, he quickly sent a man who again seized the field. When the bishop learned of this, he went to the count and said: "Do you already regret to have done a good deed, so that you attempt again to do the opposite? I ask you, do not do this, and do not expose yourself to divine vengeance." The count said to the bishop: "Be quiet, be quiet, you decrepit man. I will have you bound with the reins to ride around the city on an ass, so that everyone who sees you might ridicule you." The bishop was silent and returned to his familiar protection [in the cathedral]. He knelt in prayer, kept vigils, and spent the entire night weeping and chanting psalms. At daybreak he went to the lamps that hung from the rafters of the cathedral, stretched out the staff that he held in his hand, and broke all the lights. He said: "No light will be lit here until God takes vengeance on his enemies and restores this field that belongs to his house." As he said this, immediately the heretic collapsed from a revived fever. When he was on the verge of death, he sent to the bishop and said: "Let the bishop pray to the Lord for me, so that I might live and restore the field and grant another similar field to his control." The bishop replied to his words: "I have already prayed to the Lord, and he has heard me." The count sent a second embassy to him, and then a third. But the bishop persisted in his one response and was not influenced to pray to the Lord for the count. When the heretic realized this, he ordered that he be placed on a wagon and brought to the bishop to beg him in person. He said: "I will restore with double restitution the field that I have unjustly taken, so that your holiness might pray for me." When the bishop refused, the count forcibly compelled him to go to the cathedral. As the bishop left to enter the cathedral, the count died. Immediately the church took back its property.

### f. The wickedness of a heretic
### [Ch. 79]

Heresy is always hostile to catholics, and wherever it can set snares it does not pass over [the opportunity]. An example is this story that rumor widely claims happened in a certain place. There was a catholic woman who had a heretical husband. When a catholic priest of our religion visited her, the woman said to her husband: "I ask of your charity that at the arrival of this priest who has deigned to visit me there might be a celebration in our house, and that we might share with him a meal prepared with the appropriate expense." Her husband agreed to do what she had asked. Then a priest of the heretics arrived, and the man said to his wife: "Today our celebration is doubled, because priests of both religions are in our house." As they sat down for the meal, the husband sat at the head [of the table] with the [heretical] priest on his right hand and put the catholic priest on his left hand. His wife sat on a stool placed at his left. The husband said to the heretical priest: "If you agree with my words, let us today mock this priest of the Romans. When the food is brought out, you hurry to bless it first. Since he will grieve and not place his hand on it, we will happily eat the food." The heretical priest replied: "I will do what you command." When the platter with the vegetables arrived, the heretical priest blessed it and was the first to put his hand on it. The woman saw this and said: "Do not do that, because I am unwilling for the catholic priest to be insulted." When other food was brought, the catholic priest took some. But the heretical priest performed the same [blessing] over the second and third courses. The fourth course was brought out, in the middle of which was a hot pan in which the food lay. The food consisted of whipped eggs mixed with a little flour and was garnished as usual with chopped dates and round olives. Before the food had even touched the table, the heretical priest lifted his hand in the way and hurried to bless it. He immediately put out his spoon and took a portion. Not knowing whether it was hot, he quickly swallowed the fiery food. Suddenly his throat was on fire and he began to burn. His stomach rumbled, he belched loudly, and he exhaled his worthless spirit. After he was taken from the feast, he was put in a tomb and covered with a pile of dirt. The priest of our religion was happy and said: "Truly God has avenged his servants." He turned to the husband who was hosting the dinner and said: "The memory of this man has perished with the sound he made, and the Lord remains in eternity. But bring something for me to eat." The husband was frightened, and after the meal he knelt at the feet of the priest and converted to the catholic faith. Along with his entire household, which this treachery had gripped, he believed. And just as his wife had requested, the celebration was multiplied.

## 32. VENGEANCE AS THE DEVIL'S WORK IN THE LIFE OF SAINT SADALBERGA

*Sadalberga (ca 605–670) was abbess of Laon. She had been born into a pious aristocratic family that was committed to the Irish monastic system and was involved in the re-evangelization of the French countryside during the conversion period. Her brother was Saint Bodo, bishop of Toul, and two of her five children (Anstrude and Baldwin) became saints. The text below was reputedly composed in the late seventh century, at the request of Anstrude, although Bruno Krusch, who edited the text in the early twentieth century, believed that it was composed during the ninth century.*

Source: trans. Jo Ann McNamara and John E. Halborg, with E. Gordon Whatley, *Sainted Women of the Dark Ages* (Durham and London: Duke University Press, 1992), pp. 187–88.

16. From ancient times – which many still remember, for there are those still living here who saw these crimes – worship of the ancient serpent cruelly flourished in this city and he used his cunning arts to sport with the rustic louts and stupid men. For it is written of him: "He injures by a thousand arts." Under a form of idolatrous baptism, he claimed them for his own. In ancient times, they derived "idol" from *ludo,* sport. Accordingly, the devil disported himself in their midst and many murders were perpetrated. And this most nefarious demon plied his crafty arts so that if a man were hurt in some way by his neighbor, he would cause his innocent relatives by consanguinity or affinity to shed torrents of blood. Thus over time, increments of evil accumulated through the abominable custom and the wicked robber [the devil] claimed the miserable city for his own, entangled in his net. But the omnipotent Lord, merciful in all things, who will have all men to be saved, and to come unto knowledge of the truth, looked kindly at the creatures in his keeping and uprooted the sacrilege and wicked crimes of the past from the city.

## 33. SAINT AMANDUS RESCUES A MAN FROM JUDICIAL VENGEANCE

*Saint Amandus (d. ca 675) was born near Nantes and, after leaving home to serve God on an island, spent time in Tours and Bourges. Consecrated as bishop without a fixed see, he did missionary work in Flanders, in Carinthia along the Danube, and in Gascony. Before leaving for Gascony, he unhappily served as bishop of Maastricht for about three years. He founded a monastery at Elnon, near Tournai, of which he was abbot during the last years of his life. The idea that God's justice could overturn the rulings of secular justice was a recurring hagiographic trope throughout the early and high Middle Ages. This episode from the* Life of Saint Amandus, *composed in the late eighth or early ninth century, is possibly based on an earlier life written before or during the late eighth century that survives only in fragmentary form.*

Source: *Vita Amandi,* ed. B. Krusch, Monumenta Germaniae Historica: Scriptores rerum Merovingicarum, vol. 5 (Hanover: Hahn, 1910), pp. 438–39. Trans. Kelly Gibson.

14. We also thought it worthwhile to add to this page what we learned from a venerable man, the priest called Bonus, who attested that he had been present when this deed was done.

A certain count of Frankish birth named Dotto sat as ordered to settle legal disputes with a large multitude of assembled Franks. At once execution-ers (*lictores*) presented a certain defendant (*reus*) before him. The entire crowd shouted that the man deserved death. Cruelly injured and vigorously beaten, [he was] half dead even now. When Dotto decreed that they ought to hang him on the gallows, the man of God Amandus came and began to demand with resolute requests that he consider it worthy to allow the man to live. But, since he [Dotto] was savage and crueler than any beast, he could not convince him. In the end, the officials (*ministri* and *apparitores*) hanged the thief on the gallows and he breathed his last breath.

While Dotto, surrounded by a crowd of people, was returning home, Amandus, the holy man of the Lord, swiftly ran to the gallows and found the man already dead. After he was taken down from the gallows, he [Amandus] had the man brought to the little cell in which he [Amandus] was accustomed to intimately pray. After the brothers had left the cell, he leaned in prayer over the limbs of the dead man and poured forth tears and prayers for a very long time until, by God's command, the soul returned to the body and he began to speak with the man of God.

When the time of Matins [the morning office of prayer] was approaching and the brothers were called together, he [Amandus] ordered that water be brought. They [the brothers] thought that it was to wash the body for burial, as is the custom. When they entered the cell, they suddenly saw the same man, whom they had left dead, healthy and uninjured, sitting and speak-ing with the man of God [Amandus]. They began to wonder exceedingly because they saw alive the man whom they had left dead a little earlier. Then the man of the Lord Amandus began to most vigorously implore them to never reveal to anyone this [deed], which the Lord deigned to work through him, asserting that it is not to be ascribed to his own power but to the mercy of the Lord, who deigns to be present everywhere for those who put their trust in him. And thus after washing the entire body, and scars, he restored flesh to flesh in such a way that no evidence of the blows suffered earlier was visible on his body, and, sending him home this way, he restored him to his relatives unharmed.

## 34. SAINT WILLIBRORD FORGOES VENGEANCE AND ANGER

*A luminary at the court of Charlemagne, Alcuin (d. 804) was from Northumberland and was educated at York, in northern England. After meeting Charlemagne in 781 he was invited to join Charlemagne's court, where he became a leading figure in the Caro-lingian Renaissance. From 796 until his death, Alcuin was the abbot of St. Martin's at*

*Tours. He wrote biblical exegeses, treatises against the heresy of Adoptionism, a work on the Trinity, manuals on the liberal arts, correspondence, and poems. He supervised the production of Bibles written in clear script and his preference for the Vulgate made it the standard translation of the Bible in the West. In addition to his account of the life of the Frisian missionary Willibrord (ca 658–739), which he perhaps based on an earlier biography that is now lost, Alcuin produced an abbreviated account of the life of Saint Martin of Tours and revised and expanded earlier biographies of Saint Richarius and Saint Vedastus. Alcuin, who stated at the beginning of the* Life of Saint Willibrord *that he succeeded to possession of the chapel founded by Willibrord's father, was related to Saint Willibrord.*

Source: trans. C. H. Talbot, *Soldiers of Christ: Saints and Saints' Lives from Late Antiquity and the Early Middle Ages,* ed. Thomas F.X. Noble and Thomas Head (University Park: Pennsylvania State University Press, 1995), pp. 201–2.

Many miracles were also wrought by divine power through his servant. While the ministry of preaching the Gospel is to be preferred to the working of miracles and the showing of signs, yet, because such miracles are recorded as having been performed, I think mention of them ought not to be suppressed; and so that glory may be given to God who vouchsafed them, I will insert them into this narrative, and in this way what we know to have been achieved in former times may not be lost to future ages. Thus, when the venerable man, according to his custom, was on one of his missionary journeys he came to a village called Walcheren, where an idol of the ancient superstition remained. When the man of God, moved by zeal, smashed it to pieces before the eyes of the custodian, the latter, seething with anger, in a sudden fit of passion struck the priest of Christ on the head with a sword as if to avenge the insult paid to his god. But, as God was protecting his servant, the murderous blow did him no harm. On seeing this, Willibrord's companions rushed forward to kill the wicked man for his audacity. The man of God good-naturedly delivered the culprit from their hands and allowed him to go free. The same day, however, he [the custodian] was seized and possessed by the devil and three days later he ended his wretched life in misery. And thus, because the man of God followed the Lord's command and was unwilling to avenge the wrongs done to him, he was vindicated all the more by the Lord himself, just as he had said regarding the wrongs which the wicked inflicted upon his saints: "Vengeance is mine, I will repay, says the Lord" [Rom. 12:19].

# 35. *HISTORY OF THE LOMBARDS* BY PAUL THE DEACON

*Paul the Deacon (ca 720–ca 800) came from a noble Lombard family. He was educated, in all probability, at the Lombard court of Pavia, and he later was the tutor for the daughter of Lombard king Desiderius (r. 756–774). Around 781, Paul paid a visit to Charlemagne on behalf of his brother Arichis, who had been implicated in a revolt at Friuli in 776; this led to an invitation to remain at Charlemagne's court, which he accepted, and he stayed until some time around 785.*

*Paul wrote the* History of the Lombards *during the last years of his life, which he spent at the great Montecassino monastery. The work is an incomplete history in six books that covers events to the death of Liutprand in 744. This end date, conveniently, allowed Paul to avoid discussion of the Carolingian takeover of Lombard Italy or his brother's Fruilian revolt. The* History *includes a number of conventional stories involving vengeance and emotion; the two excerpted below, which took place ca 543 and 572, are typical.*

Sources: Doc. 35a, trans. William Dudley Foulke, *History of the Langobards* (Philadelphia: University of Pennsylvania Department of History, 1906), pp. 44–45; Doc. 35b, *Historia Langobardorum*, ed. L. Bethmann and G. Waitz, Monumenta Germaniae Historica: Scriptores rerum Langobardicarum et Italicarum saec. VI-IX (Hanover: Hahn, 1878), pp. 87–90. Trans. Lori Pieper.

## a. King Turisind prevents vengeance
### [Book 1.4]

When he heard these things from his father, Alboin, taking only forty young men with him, journeyed to Turisind, king of the Gepidae, with whom he had before waged war, and intimated the cause in which he had come. And the king, receiving him kindly, invited him to his table and placed him on his right hand where Turismod, his former son, had been wont to sit. In the meantime, while the various dishes were made ready, Turisind, reflecting that his son had sat there only a little while before, and recalling to mind the death of his child and beholding his slayer present and sitting in his place, drawing deep sighs, could not contain himself, but at last his grief broke forth in utterance. "This place," he says, "is dear to me, but the person who sits in it is grievous enough to my sight." Then another son of the king who was present, aroused by his father's speech, began to provoke the Lombards with insults declaring (because they wore white bandages from their calves down) that they were like mares with white feet up to the legs, saying: "The mares that you take after have white fetlocks." Then one of the Lombards thus answered these things: "Go to the field of Asfeld and there you can find by experience beyond a doubt how stoutly those you call mares succeed in kicking; there the bones of your brother are scattered in the midst of the meadows like those of a vile beast." When they heard these things, the Gepidae, unable to bear the tumult of their passions, were violently stirred in anger and strove to avenge the open insult. The Lombards on the other side, ready for the fray, all laid their hands on the hilts of their swords. The king leaping forth from the table thrust himself into their midst and restrained his people from anger and strife, threatening first to punish him who first engaged in fight, saying that it is a victory not pleasing to God when any one kills a guest in his own house. Thus at last the quarrel having been allayed, they now finished the banquet with joyful spirits. And Turisind, taking up the arms of Turismod his son, delivered them to Alboin and sent him back in peace and safety to his father's kingdom. Alboin having returned to his father, was made from that time his table companion. And when he joyfully partook with his father of the royal delicacies, he related in order all the things which had happened to him among the Gepidae in the palace of Turisind. Those who were present were astonished and applauded the boldness of Alboin nor did they less extol in their praises the most honorable behavior of Turisind.

### b. Rosemunda avenges her father
### [Book 2.28–30]

[Alboin], who afterwards reigned as king in Italy for three years and six months, was killed by a trap made by his wife. This was the cause of his death. When he had sat at a banquet in Verona, more cheerful than was proper, with a drinking cup that he had made from the head of King Cunimund, his father-in-law, he had caused wine to be given to the queen to drink and invited her to drink happily with her father. So that this might not seem impossible to anyone, I speak the truth in Christ: I saw this drinking cup on a certain feast day as Prince Ratchis showed it to his guests, holding it in his hand. Wherefore Rosemunda, when she became aware of the matter, conceived deep sorrow in her heart. Not being able to restrain it, her heart burned to murder her husband so as to avenge her father's corpse, and she quickly formed a plan with Helmechis, who was the king's scilpor, that is, his armor-bearer, and foster-brother, for him to kill the king. He urged the queen to associate Peredeo, who was a very strong man, with them in this plan. When Peredeo did not want to give his consent to such great wickedness, though the queen urged him, she substituted herself at night in the bed of her wardrobe girl, with whom Peredeo was accustomed to have unlawful intercourse. Peredeo, unaware of the matter, came there and lay with the queen. When the wicked deed had been perpetrated, she asked him who he thought her to be, and he gave the name of her friend, whom he thought her to be. The queen said, "Not at all as you think, but I am Rosemunda. Certainly now Peredeo, you have now done such a thing that either you must kill Alboin or he will slay you with his sword." Then he understood the wrong that he had done: he who had not wanted to do so voluntarily was in this way forced to give his consent to the death of the king. When Alboin had gone to sleep at midday, Rosemunda ordered that there be a great silence in the palace, and taking away all other arms, she strongly fastened his broad, two-edged sword to the head of the bed, so that it could not be taken or removed from its sheath. According to the plan, Peredeo introduced the killer Helmechis, more cruel than any beast. Alboin immediately awakened from sleep, and, understanding the evil that was threatening, quickly reached for his broad, two-edged sword, which since it was tightly bound, he was not able to remove. Grasping the footstool, he defended himself with it for some time. But oh, alas, this man, most warlike and of the greatest boldness, could in no way prevail against the enemy and was killed like one of the weak, perishing by a plan of his little hussy of a wife, he who was most renowned in war for so many massacres of his enemies. His body was buried with the greatest weeping and lamenting of the Lombards, under a certain flight of steps, which was adjoining the palace. He was of tall stature and in his whole body fit for waging war. When Giselpert, who had been duke of Verona, opened this tomb in our days, he removed his sword and whatever ornaments of his that he found. Because of this, with the usual vanity among ignorant people, he boasted that he had seen Alboin.

Therefore, when Alboin was dead, Helmechis attempted to invade his kingdom. But by no means was he able to, because the Lombards, very greatly sorrowing over his death, tried to kill him. And immediately Rosemunda ordered Longinus, the Prefect of Ravenna, to quickly arrange a ship, in which he might pick them up. Longinus, made happy by such a message, quickly arranged the ship in which Helmechis entered with Rosemunda, now his wife, fleeing at night. And taking with them Albsuinda, the king's daughter, and all the treasure of the Lombards, they quickly arrived in Ravenna. Then Longinus the prefect began to urge Rosemunda to kill Helmechis and join with him in marriage. She, ready for all wickedness, then desired to become the lady of Ravenna, and gave her assent to perpetrating so great a crime. Helmechis was washing himself in the bath, and when he came out to her from the bath, he drank a cup of poison, which they insisted was for his health. When he realized that he had drunk a cup of death, drawing his sword over Rosamunda, he forced her to drink what was left. And so by the judgment of Almighty God, the most unjust killers perished at one moment.

After they were thus killed, Longinus the prefect sent Albsuinda with the treasure of the Lombards to the emperor in Constantinople. Some say that Peredeo also came to Ravenna with Helmechis and Rosemunda, and from there went with Albsuinda to Constantinople and there killed a lion of astounding size in the popular theater before the emperor. As they say, so that something malicious might not be attempted in the royal city, since he was a strong man, his eyes were torn out by order of the emperor. After some time he prepared two knives for himself, which were hidden in both of his sleeves, headed for the palace, and promised certain things for the utility of Augustus [the emperor], if he might be admitted to speak with him. Augustus sent to meet him two patricians familiar to him, who listened to his words. When they came to Peredeo, he approached them, as though to say something to them in secret, and wounded them severely with the swords which he had hidden in both hands, so that they immediately fell on the ground and died. Thus that most strong man, in one way not unlike Samson, was avenged for his injuries; and in exchange for the light of his two eyes, he did away with two men very useful to the emperor.

## 36. EINHARD ON THE PEACE INSPIRED BY THE RELICS OF SAINTS MARCELLINUS AND PETER

*Einhard (ca 770–840) was born near the Main River in Germany and was educated at the nearby monastery of Fulda before leaving to join Charlemagne's court in 791–792. In 815, Louis the Pious granted Einhard the properties of Michelstadt and Mulinheim, located in the same region where Einhard spent his early years (today Hesse). Einhard's* Translation *(ca 830) describes how he acquired the relics of Saints Marcellinus and Peter, martyred during the reign of the emperor Diocletian, from the catacombs of Rome for his church at Michelstadt. The saints were not happy at Michelstadt and, through visions and miracles, requested to be moved. The miracle below, one of many in Einhard's work, occurred after the relics arrived in Mulinheim, their final resting place, located on the Main river about twenty-five miles north of Michelstadt. The miracle demonstrated the saints' happiness with their new home, which came to be known as Seligenstadt ("city of the saints") after the relic translation, as well as the general validity and efficacy of the relics, which was Einhard's goal in recording the story of the translation and the miracles that followed.*

Source: trans. Paul Edward Dutton, *Charlemagne's Courtier: The Complete Einhard* (Peterborough, ON: Broadview Press, 1998), pp. 89–90.

After that we began our journey and, thanks to the merits of the saints, we came at last on the sixth day, with the Lord's help, to the village of Mulin-heim [Seligenstadt], where I had left the sacred ashes of the blessed martyrs when I had departed for court [in January]. I must report how much joy and happiness the arrival of those relics brought to the people living along [our] route, but it cannot be related or described in all its richness. Nevertheless, I must try to describe it, so that it not seem that something that brought forth so much praise of God was buried in silence because of my laziness. To begin with, I am anxious to report what I and many others remember having seen after we left the palace. A stream called the Wurm [which flows into the Ruhr] lies about two miles from the palace of Aachen and has a bridge across it. When we reached it, we stopped for a short time so that the crowd that had followed us all the way from the palace and now wanted to turn back might have an opportunity to pray. One of the men who was praying there approached the relics with another man and, turning to his companion, said, "For the love and honor of this saint, I release you from the debt you know you owe me." For he owed him, as that man admitted, half a pound of silver. Likewise, another man led a companion by the hand to the relics, and said, "You killed my father and for that reason we have been enemies. But now, for the love and honor of God and this saint, I want to end our feud and to make and enter into an agreement with you that henceforth we shall maintain a lasting friendship between us. Let this saint be a witness to the reconciliation we have promised each other and let him punish the first person tempted to destroy this peace."

9. At this point the crowd that had left the palace with us, after adoring and kissing the sacred relics and after shedding many tears, which they could not restrain because everyone was filled with so much joy, returned home....

## 37. SAINT GERALD OF AURILLAC SEEKS PEACE WITH HIS ENEMIES

*Saint Gerald, who died in 909, was a Carolingian noble who lived such a monastic life that he refused to marry the sister of William, duke of Aquitaine, preferring to remain chaste. Odo of Cluny, Gerald's biographer, likely drew on his own experiences when describing aspects of Gerald's noble life. Odo was born near Le Mans around 879 and was brought up at the court of William of Aquitaine, who was also the founder of Cluny. Odo became a canon at Tours and, around 909, became a monk at Baume, where he would take charge of the monastery school. Odo became abbot of Cluny in 927, and died in 942. In addition to his biography of Gerald, Odo also wrote moral*

*essays, sermons, an epic on the Redemption (the Occupatio), and twelve choral an-*
*tiphons. Odo's* Life of Saint Gerald *(ca 920) can be seen as a depiction of the ideal*
*behavior of an earthly magnate.*

Source: trans. Gerard Sitwell, *Soldiers of Christ: Saints and Saints' Lives from Late Antiquity and the
Early Middle Ages,* ed. Thomas F. X. Noble and Thomas Head (University Park: Pennsylvania
State University Press, 1995), pp. 301–3.

After the death of his parents, when he attained full power over his property,
Gerald was not puffed up, as youths often are who boast of their grown-up
mastery, nor did he change the modesty that was springing up in his heart.
His power of ruling increased, but the humble mind did not grow haughty.
He was compelled to be occupied in administering and watching over things
that, as I have said, came to him by hereditary right, and to leave that peace of
heart, which he had to some extent tasted, to take up the weariness of earthly
business. He could scarcely bear to leave the inner solitude of his heart, and he
returned to it as soon as he could. But while he seemed to fall headlong from
the heights of contemplation to the occupations of earth, as the chamois in its
fall saves itself from death by its horns, so, turning to the divine love and the
meditation of Holy Scripture he escaped the ruin of spiritual death. Inspired,
as I think, by the very spirit of David, in his fervor he gave no sleep to his
eyes, until freed from daily activities he might find within himself a place for
the Lord and exulting in it secretly he "tasted the kindness of the Lord" [1
Pet. 2:3]. Perchance Christ, the rock, poured forth rivers of oil for him, in accordance with the saying of Job [Job 29:6], lest many waters should be able to
extinguish in him the light of charity. Dragged down to earth, he yearned for
this spiritual refreshment, but his household and dependants demanded that
he should break into his repose and give himself to the service of others.

He admitted these gnawing cares unwillingly for the sake of the complaints
of those who had recourse to him. For his dependants pleaded querulously,
saying: "Why should a great man suffer violence from persons of low degree
who lay waste his property?" adding that, when these discovered that he did
not wish to take vengeance they devoured the more greedily that which was
rightfully his. It would be more holy and honest that he should recognize the
right of armed force, that he should unsheathe the sword against his enemies,
that he should restrain the boldness of the violent; it would be better that
the bold should be suppressed by force of arms than that the undefended
districts should be unjustly oppressed by them. When Gerald heard this he
was moved, not by the attack made on him but by reason, to have mercy and
to give help. Committing himself entirely to the will of God and the divine
mercy, he sought only how he might visit the fatherless and widows and

"keep oneself unstained from the world" [Ja. 1:27] according to the precept of the apostle.

He therefore exerted himself to repress the insolence of the violent, taking care in the first place to promise peace and most easy reconciliation to his enemies. And he did this by taking care, that either he should overcome evil by good, or if his enemies would not come to terms, he should have in God's eyes the greater right on his side. And sometimes indeed he soothed them and reduced them to peace. When insatiable malice poured scorn on peaceful men, showing severity of heart, he broke the teeth of the wicked, that, according to the saying of Job, he might "make [them] drop the prey from [their] jaws" [Job 29:17]. He was not incited by the desire for revenge, as is the case with many, or led on by love of praise from the multitude, but by love of the poor, who were not able to protect themselves. He acted in this way lest, if he became sluggish through an indolent patience, he should seem to have neglected the precept to care for the poor. He ordered the poor man to be saved and the needy to be freed from the hand of the sinner. Rightly, therefore, he did not allow the sinner to prevail. But sometimes when the unavoidable necessity of fighting lay on him, he commanded his men in imperious tones, to fight with the backs of their swords and with their spears reversed. This would have been ridiculous to the enemy if Gerald, strengthened by divine power, had not been invincible to them. And it would have seemed useless to his own men, if they had not learned by experience that Gerald, who was carried away by his piety in the very moment of battle, had not always been invincible. When therefore they saw that he triumphed by a new kind of fighting that was mingled with piety, they changed their scorn to admiration, and sure of victory they readily fulfilled his commands. For it was a thing unheard of that he or the soldiers who fought under him were not victorious. But this also is certain, that he himself never wounded anybody, nor was wounded by anyone. For Christ, as it is written, was at his side [cf. Ps. 118:6], who seeing the desire of his heart, saw that for love of him he was so well disposed that he had no wish to assail the persons of the enemy, but only to check their audacity. Let no one be worried because a just man sometimes made use of fighting, which seems incompatible with religion. No one who has judged his cause impartially will be able to show that the glory of Gerald is clouded by this. For some of the fathers, and of these the most holy and most patient, when the cause of justice demanded, valiantly took up arms against their adversaries, as Abraham, who destroyed a great multitude of the enemy to rescue his nephew and King David who sent his forces even against his own son. Gerald did not fight invading the property of others, but defending his own, or rather his people's rights, knowing that the rhinoceros, that is, any powerful man, is to be bound with a thong that he may break the clods of the valley, that is, the oppressors of the lowly. For as the apostle says, the judge "does not bear the sword in vain, for he is the servant of God to execute his wrath" [Rom. 13:4]. It was lawful, therefore, for a layman to carry the sword in battle that he might protect defenseless people, as the harmless flock from evening wolves according to the saying of Scripture [cf. Acts 20:29], and that he might restrain by arms or by the law those whom ecclesiastical censure was not able to subdue. It does not darken his glory, then, that he fought for the cause of God, for whom the whole world fights against the unwise. Rather is it to his praise that he always won openly without the help of deceit or ambushes, and nevertheless was so protected by God, that, as I said before, he never stained his sword with human blood. Hereafter, let him who by his example shall take up arms against his enemies, seek also by his example not his own but the common good. For you may see some who for love of praise or gain boldly put themselves in danger, gladly sustain the evils of the world for the sake of the world, and while they encounter its bitterness lose the joys, so to speak, which they were seeking. But of these it is another story. The work of Gerald shines forth, because it sprang from simplicity of heart.

## 38. LIUTPRAND OF CREMONA'S "TIT-FOR-TAT"

*Liutprand of Cremona (ca 922 to ca 972) was a member of a prominent Pavian family. As a young man, he entered the service of Berengar, then ruler of northern Italy, and was sent by Berengar on an embassy to Constantinople in 949. Liutprand, who allied himself with Otto I, became bishop of Cremona after Otto I overthrew Berengar in 961. Pope John XII had supported Otto, whom he crowned emperor in 962, but after subsequently plotting against Otto with Berengar, the pope stood trial and was deposed in 963. Liutprand took part in this assembly in Rome and, in 968, was sent to Constantinople to arrange a marriage between the emperor's daughter and Otto's son. His work* Antapodosis *or "Tit-for-Tat" (written ca 950) describes events from 888–949.*

Source: trans. F. A. Wright, *The Works of Liudprand of Cremona* (London: Routledge, 1930), p. 109.

1. I do not doubt, reverend father, that the title of this work causes you some surprise. You say perhaps: "Since it sets forth the deeds of illustrious men, why is it called *Antapodosis* [Tit-for-Tat]." My answer is this: The aim and object of this work is to reveal, declare and stigmatize the doings of this Berengar, who now is not king but rather despot of Italy, and his wife Willa, who because

of her boundless tyranny is rightly called a second Jezebel, and because of her insatiable greed for plunder a Lamia vampire. Such shafts of falsehood, such extravagance of robbery, such efforts of wickedness have they gratuitously used against me and my household, my kinsmen and dependents, as neither tongue avails to express nor pen to record. Let this present page then be to them antapodosis, that is, repayment. In return for the troubles I have endured I will unveil to present and future generations their infamous sacrilege, that is, the abominable impiety of which they have been guilty. But my book will also be repayment for the benefits conferred upon me by men of sanctity and repute. Of all those whose deeds are recorded, or are worth recording, in history, there are few or none – except only this accursed Berengar of course – for whose kindness the fathers and sons of my family have not to render hearty thanks. Finally, that this book has been written *en captivité,* that is, in my captivity and sojourning abroad, my present exile shows....

## 39. HEROIC VENGEANCE

*The famous Anglo-Saxon epic* Beowulf *is preserved in a single manuscript which dates from ca 1000. The action of the epic revolves around a feud: Grendel, a monster descended from Cain, repeatedly attacks the hall of the Geat lord Hrothgar out of jealousy over the hall's magnificence; Beowulf slays Grendel; Grendel's mother attacks the hall to avenge her son; Beowulf then kills Grendel's mother. The backstory of* Beowulf *is also driven by feud. Hrothgar had paid to settle a feud involving Beowulf's father, and so expected Beowulf to return that favor "out of obligations to friendship's bond" (lines 457–72) by coming to defend the hall from Grendel. A poem within the poem about Finn, a king of the Frisians who, despite his marriage to the sister of the king of the Danes, attacked visiting Danes and was later killed in revenge (lines 1068–1159), illustrates how the back-and-forth nature of vengeance gave structure to stories that were of great entertainment value. Below are three commentaries on feud from* Beowulf: *a digression on the operation of feud, a speech, and a song.*

Source: trans. R. M. Liuzza, *Beowulf: A New Verse Translation,* (Peterborough, ON: Broadview Press, 2000), pp. 94–96, 114–16, 127–30.

### a. Grendel's mother pursues vengeance
### [Verses 1328–1398]

As a nobleman should be,
always excellent, so Aeschere was!
In Heorot he was slain by the hand

of a restless death-spirit; I do not know
where that ghoul went, gloating with its carcass,
rejoicing in its feast. She avenged that feud
in which you killed Grendel yesterday evening
in your violent way with a crushing vice-grip,
for he had diminished and destroyed my people
for far too long. He fell in battle,
it cost him his life, and now has come another
mighty evil marauder who means
to avenge her kin, and too far has carried out her revenge,
as it may seem to many a thane
whose spirit groans for his treasure-giver,
a hard heart's distress – now that hand lies dead
which was wont to give you all good things.
    I have heard countrymen and hall-counselors
among my people report this:
they have seen two such creatures,
great march-stalkers holding the moors,
alien spirits. The second of them,
as far as they could discern most clearly,
had the shape of a woman; the other, misshapen,
marched the exile's path in the form of a man,
except that he was larger than any other;
in bygone days he was called 'Grendel'
by the local folk. They knew no father,
whether before him had been begotten
any more mysterious spirits. That murky land
they hold, wolf-haunted slopes, windy headlands,
awful fenpaths, where the upland torrents
plunge downward under the dark crags,
the flood underground. It is not far hence
– measured in miles – that the mere stands;
over it hangs a grove hoar-frosted,
a firm-rooted wood looming over the water.
Every night one can see there an awesome wonder,
fire on the water. There lives none so wise
or bold that he can fathom its abyss.
Though the heath-stepper beset by hounds,
the strong-horned hart, might seek the forest,
pursued from afar, he will sooner lose
his life on the shore than save his head

and go in the lake – it is no good place!
The clashing waves climb up from there
dark to the clouds, when the wind drives
the violent storms, until the sky itself droops,
the heavens groan. Now once again all help
depends on you alone. You do not yet know
this fearful place, where you might find
the sinful creature – seek it if you dare!
I will reward you with ancient riches
for that feud, as I did before,
with twisted gold, if you return alive."
    Beowulf spoke, son of Ecgtheow:
"Sorrow not, wise one! It is always better
to avenge one's friend than to mourn overmuch.
Each of us shall abide the end
of this world's life; let him who can
bring about fame before death – that is best
for the unliving man after he is gone.
Arise, kingdom's guard, let us quickly go
and inspect the path of Grendel's kin.
I promise you this: he will find no protection –
not in the belly of the earth nor the bottom of the sea,
nor the mountain groves – let him go where he will!
For today you must endure patiently
all your woes, as I expect you will."
The old man leapt up, thanked the Lord,
the mighty God, for that man's speech.

### b. Beowulf vaunts his vengeance
### [Verses 1999–2069]

Beowulf spoke, son of Ecgtheow:
"It is no mystery to many men,
my lord Hygelac – the great meeting,
what a time of great struggle Grendel and I
had in that place where he made so many
sorrows for the victory-Scyldings,
life-long misery – I avenged them all,
so that none of Grendel's tribe needs to boast
anywhere on earth of that uproar at dawn,
whoever lives longest of that loathsome kind,

enveloped in foul evil. First I came there
to the ring-hall to greet Hrothgar;
quickly the famous kinsman of Healfdene,
once he knew of my intentions,
assigned me a seat with his own sons.
That troop was in delight; never in my life
have I seen among hall-sitters, under heaven's vault,
a more joyous feast. At times the famous queen,
bond of peace to nations, passed through the hall,
urged on her young sons; often she gave
twisted rings before she took her seat.
At times before the hall-thanes the daughter of Hrothgar
bore the ale-cup to the earls in the back –
Freawaru, I heard the men in the hall
call her, when the studded treasure-cup
was passed among them. She is promised,
young, gold-adorned, to the gracious son of Froda;
the ruler of the Scyldings has arranged this,
the kingdom's shepherd, and approves the counsel
that he should settle his share of feud and slaughter
with this young woman. But seldom anywhere
after the death of a prince does the deadly spear rest
for even a brief while, though the bride be good!
    It may, perhaps, displease the Heathobards' prince,
and every retainer among his tribe,
when across the floor, following that woman, goes
a noble son of the Danes, received with honors;
on him glitters an ancestral heirloom,
hard, ring-adorned, once a Heathobard treasure
as long as they were able to wield their weapons.
And then in that deadly shield-play they undid
their beloved comrades and their own lives.
Then an old spear-bearer speaks over his beer,
who sees that ring-hilt and remembers all
the spear-deaths of men – his spirit is grim –
begins, sad-minded, to test the mettle
of a young thane with his innermost thoughts,
to awaken war, and says these words:
"Can you, my friend, recognize that sword,
which your father bore into battle
in his final adventure beneath the helmet,

that dear iron, when the Danes struck him,
ruled the field of slaughter after the rout of heroes,
when Withergyld fell – those valiant Scyldings?
Now here some son or other of his slayer
walks across this floor, struts in his finery,
brags of the murder and bears that treasure
which ought, by right, to belong to you."

    He urges and reminds him on every occasion
with cruel words, until the time comes
that Freawaru's thane, for his father's deeds,
sleeps, bloodstained from the bite of a sword,
forfeits his life; from there the other
escapes alive, for he knows the land well.
Then on both sides the sworn oaths of earls
will be broken, once bitter violent hate
wells up in Ingeld, and his wife-love
grows cooler after his surging cares.
Thus I expect that the Heathobards' part
in the Danish alliance is not without deceit,
nor their friendship fast.

### c. A sinful crime
### [Verses 2425–2509]

Beowulf spoke, the son of Ecgtheow:
"In my youth I survived many storms of battle,
times of strife – I still remember them all.
I was seven years old when the prince of treasures,
friend to his people, took me from my father;
Hrethel the king held me and kept me,
gave me gems and feasts, remembered our kinship.
I was no more hated to him while he lived
– a man in his stronghold – than any of his sons,
Herebeald and Haethcyn and my own Hygelac.
For the eldest, undeservedly,
a death-bed was made by the deeds of a kinsman,
after Haethcyn with his horn bow
struck down his own dear lord with an arrow –
he missed his mark and murdered his kinsman,
one brother to the other with a bloody shaft.
That was a fight beyond settling, a sinful crime,

shattering the heart; yet it had to be
that a nobleman lost his life unavenged.
 So it is sad for an old man
to live to see his young son
ride on the gallows – then let him recount a story,
a sorry song, when his son hangs
of comfort only to the ravens, and he cannot,
though old and wise, offer him any help.
Each and every morning calls to mind
his son's passing away; he will not care
to wait for any other heir or offspring
in his fortress, when the first one has
tasted evil deeds and fell death.
He looks sorrowfully on his son's dwelling,
the deserted wine-hall, the windswept home
bereft of joy – the riders sleep,
heroes in their graves; there is no harp-music,
no laughter in the court, as there had been long before.
He takes to his couch and keens a lament
all alone for his lost one; all too vast to him
seem the fields and townships.
 So the protector of the Weders
bore surging in his breast heartfelt sorrows
for Herebeald. He could not in any way
make amends for the feud with his murderer,
but neither could he hate that warrior
for his hostile deeds, though he was not dear to him.
Then with the sorrow which befell him too sorely,
he gave up man's joys, chose God's light;
he left to his children his land and strongholds –
as a blessed man does – when he departed this life.
 Then there was strife between Swedes and Geats,
a quarrel in common across the wide water,
hard hostility after Hrethel died,
until the sons of Ongentheow
were bold and warlike, wanted no peace
over the sea, but around the Hill of Sorrows
they carried out a terrible and devious campaign.
My friends and kinsmen got revenge for those
feuds and evils – as it is said –
although one of them paid for it with his own life,

a hard bargain; that battle was fatal
for Haethcyn, king of the Geats.
Then, I've heard, the next morning, one kinsman
avenged the other with the sword's edge,
when Ongentheow attacked Eofor;
his battle-helm slipped, the old Scylfing
staggered, corpse-pale; Eofor's hand recalled
his fill of feuds, and did not withhold the fatal blow.
I have paid in battle for the precious treasures
he gave me, as was granted to me,
with a gleaming sword; he gave me land,
a joyous home. He had no need
to have to go seeking among the Gifthas
or the Spear-Danes or the Swedes
for a worse warrior, or buy one with his wealth;
always on foot I would go before him,
alone in the front line – and all my life
I will wage war, while this sword endures,
which before and since has served me well,
since I slew Daeghrefn, champion of the Hugas,
with my bare hands in front of the whole army.
He could not carry off to the Frisian king
that battle-armor and that breast-adornment,
but there in the field the standard-bearer fell,
a nobleman in his strength; no blade was his slayer
but my warlike grip broke his beating heart,
cracked his bone-house. Now the blade's edge,
hand and hard sword, shall fight for the hoard."

# CHAPTER SEVEN: FORMULARIES, CHARTERS, AND JUDGMENTS

*Several kinds of records relevant to the actual practice and prevention of vengeance have survived from the early Middle Ages. Medieval formularies were "fill-in-the-blank"-style documents that allowed notaries to draw up binding charters or contracts quickly and easily. The appearance of these handbooks in the mid-seventh century perhaps indicates a shortage of trained notaries in the Merovingian kingdom, although they continued to be used into the ninth century. Charters and judgments, in turn, were like deeds or contracts; they were drawn up when two parties reached an agreement or when a decision on some matter was issued. They helped to provide proof of a transaction in situations, as in the examples below, where a disagreement had broken out.*

*Together, these documents reveal the methods of early medieval legal procedure and its players, and attest to the important role that written documents played in dispute settlement. Although Marculf's formulary included a template for documenting the peace made with the victim's family after a murder, the surviving Merovingian and Lombard judgments, as well as those that survive from the Carolingian era, concern land disputes rather than violent crimes. It is possible, however, that these judgments concerning land, often made in favor of a church, may have been the only documents of this type to survive. Churches and monasteries, where nearly all surviving early medieval manuscripts were held, kept these judgments (and occasionally created them) to serve their interests.*

## 40. PROMISE FOR PEACE AFTER A MURDER

*The form below is part of Marculf's formulary. This particular formulary has been dated to the mid-seventh century, based on Marculf's mention in the prologue of Landericus, who was bishop of Paris from 650 to 656. Historians believe that Marculf was a monk in Landericus's diocese, and most probably one at the Abbey of St. Denis, just north of the city of Paris.*

Source: *Marculfi formularum libri duo,* ed. and French trans. Alf Uddholm (Uppsala: Eranos, 1962), pp. 242–43. Trans. Kelly Gibson.

### Book 2, no. 18

A promise not to take revenge for a homicide committed, if the two parties will make peace with each other:

From N. to his brother, lord N. Since, at the devil's instigation, you killed our brother N., which you should not have done, you could have risked your life if priests and distinguished men, whose names are attached below, had not intervened and recalled us to the concord of peace. We have dropped this claim against you with the *festuca* [symbolic staff used in legal transactions, going back to Roman manumission ceremonies; grasping the *festuca* made an agreement binding] on the condition that you give me so much money in a friendly settlement for this deed, and you have now discharged the debt by means of a promise to pay [*wadium*: something given by the debtor to the creditor giving the creditor the right to seize property if the debtor fails to pay]. Therefore, in accordance with our agreement, it pleased us to write for you this letter of promise not to take revenge so that you, being entirely free from concern and absolved, no longer fear any opposition or harm from me, my heirs, his heirs, judicial powers, or anyone because of the death of our brother. And if I myself or some of my heirs or anyone wishes to trouble you because of this, and I do not prevent it, we shall pay you, with the fisc in charge of collecting it, double what you gave to us; and not everything that one claims can be restored, but this letter of promise not to take revenge made by me should remain valid.

# 41. AN ORDERLY MEROVINGIAN JUDGMENT

*The surviving* placita, *or judgments made by a king, were concerned with inheritance and land disputes, rather than with violent physical crimes. These sorts of quarrels were usually between a church or monastery and an heir of a donor who questioned the church's right to the land, as in this case involving the monastery of St. Denis. This example of a Merovingian judgment was issued in November of either 659 or 660 by the Merovingian king Clothar III (r. 657–673). It is the oldest placitum to survive in its original, seventh-century form and is on papyrus, which, following Roman practice, was still imported and used in the Merovingian kingdom at the time. However, as will be seen in Doc. 90, it is important to note that, of the many Merovingian documents that survive as parchment copies from later centuries, some are actually forgeries that were composed in later centuries.*

*Although a good bit of the text for this document is lost, enough survives to illustrate both the orderly nature of Merovingian dispute settlement and the kinds of written records the legal decisions relied on.*

Source: ed. T. Kölzer, based on C. Brühl with M. Hartmann and A. Stieldorf, Monumenta Germaniae Historica: Die Urkunden der Merovinger, vol. 1 (Hanover: Hahn, 2001), pp. 240–41. Trans. Kelly Gibson.

[No. 93]

Clothar, king of the Franks [Intitulation: the king in whose name the *placitum* was issued].

We were sitting to decide and settle by just judgment. There came advocates of the monastery of our own special patron lord Dionysius [Saint Denis], where the precious [saint] himself rests in body, and Ingober [perhaps Ingoberga or Ingoberta: suffix unknown, text missing] to whom the above-mentioned woman responded that she had a charter of agreement [proving] that Ermelenus her husband had bestowed those villas to him. But on the other side, the advocates [text missing] and the aforementioned bishop then present [in court] showed the precarial grant [*precaria:* a grant allowing use of land for a certain period of time] made by the woman. When [the grant] was read, it was ascertained that the woman concerning the entire [text missing; likely "estate" immediately follows] and the estate of the same had made to Ermelenus. But the advocates of the aforementioned basilica showed the deed of sale and precarial grant made by Ermelenus for his brother Chagliberctius [text missing] he had written concerning his entire estate, and then they showed those [documents] to be read out and they contended that those two parts of the aforementioned villas of Thorigné and [text missing] was able to claim for his dominion the entirety of the aforementioned villas and their appurtenances. Therefore, we, together with our magnates, saw it fit to judge that those two parts of the aforementioned villas [text missing] and the illustrious man Chadoloadus, count of our palace [palace official who helped with judicial, military, or administrative matters, including reporting the outcome of a trial to the king] reported that this case is recognized to have been set out in this way and investigated in order and settled. We order that those two parts of the aforementioned villas belong to lord Dionysius, that [his] advocates should hold the awarded property for all time, and that the dispute between them about this should be forever put to rest.

Tetbert recognized.

Given ... November ... in the third year of our rule ... in the name of the Lord, happily.

## 42. LOMBARD RECORD OF JUDGMENT AT PAVIA

*This* notitia, *a record of court proceedings dating from 762, illustrates the process of dispute settlement in Lombard Italy. Like most disputes in the surviving judgments, it is concerned with a rightful inheritance to land. Proof of rightful ownership depended both on written documents and adherence to the Germanic practices that made a trans-action legally binding. The two practices mentioned during the dispute are* garethinx, *where an item is formally handed over, possibly conducted among a group of men holding lances, and in any case in front of witnesses, and* launichild, *the giving of a small sum of money or an object as a promise of a full payment, which worked much like a modern deposit.*

Source: *Notitia iudicati*, ed. Luigi Schiaparelli, *Codice diplomatico Longobardo 2,* Fonti per la storia d'Italia 63 (Rome: Dall'istituto storico Italiano, 1933), pp. 109–12. Trans. Kelly Gibson.

## [No. 163]

In the name of the Lord. When, by the order of the most excellent lord King Desiderius, we, Giselpert of Verona [see Doc. 35b], Bussio the mayor of the palace, and Assiulf the gastald [the chief administrative, judicial and military representative of the king, who presided over a *civitas* and acted as judge], had sat with illustrious men in the holy palace at Ticino, Tasso, an armed retainer (*gasindius*) of the lord king of the city of Pistoia, who was handling the case of Rotrude, and Alpert from the city of Pisa, came before us.

Tasso said: "You, Alpert, took possession of your late brother Auripert's property against the natural order of things because in his will your brother founded a hospital (*xenodochium*) for the maintenance and relief of the poor and ordered that it ought to be managed and directed without negligence by the bishop of the city of Pisa, and if he [the bishop] neglects it, that it be man-aged by Rotrude herself; therefore, as I said, none of this property belongs to you, and you ought to submit to justice and cede the property to us."

Alpert responded: "Nothing prevents me [from holding the property even] if Auripert himself made a will concerning his goods and the hospital because, as you see in the copy of the charter of agreement which Auripert had made with me, if one of us dies without legitimate sons, one of us ought to succeed the other. Because Auripert died without sons, I ought to succeed him."

Tasso replied against him: "It does not prevent me [from holding the property] because you do not have the original of the copies which you show, and, neither done through *thinx* [abbreviation of *garethinx*] nor through *launichild,* it would not have been able to stand even if you had the original. See the copy of the will of Auripert: since he will lavish his property on the poor, we ought to stand by the law."

Again asserting against him, Alpert [said]: "If that copy ought not to stand according to the laws, Tasso, how do you wish to confirm the copy of the will?"

Tasso again responded against him: "The copy ought to stand because the will had been made and confirmed by the charter of the lord king Aistulf."

Then when we, the aforementioned judges, had heard all of their arguments, we had the copy of Auripert's will read to us, in which it was read that he had ordered that there be a hospital from his property managed by Rotrude, that she have license and use of his movable property on the day of his death to give for his soul, and that forty men be freed. At the same time, we had the copy of the agreement which Alpert showed read to us. And when we investigated the case through the documents and arguments of both parties, it seemed right to us that the will that the late Auripert had made for the salvation of his soul ought to stand and the hospital be just as he had ordered, and that the opposing party [Alpert] not in any way have the hospital or anything he claims because his charter, notwithstanding that it was only a copy and he did not have the original, should in no way stand because it had not been done through either *garethinx* or *launichild*, as is written in the text of the laws [Liutprand]. Moreover, when we assembled in the presence of the aforementioned ruler, we reported everything in order to him about their trial and what the documents contained. It pleased his piety that we had rightly given judgment, and the ruler said to us that he had seen that will and by his request Lord Aistulf had confirmed it through his charter. We prompted the notary Leontace to make this record (*notitia*) of how it was set out and settled in our presence.

And I, Peter, wrote by his dictation, in the sixth and third year [respectively] of our lords kings Desiderius and Adelchis in the name of God, in the fifteenth indiction; happily.

Sign[ed] with the hand of Giselpert, who gave this judgment.

Sign[ed] with the hand of Bussio, mayor of the palace, who gave this judgment.

Sign[ed] with the hand of Assiulf, gastald, who gave this judgment.

# PART III.
# THE HIGH MIDDLE AGES (1000-1250)

The eleventh century was a great century of monastic and papal reform and of territorial lordship. It saw the beginnings, too, of the territorial expansion of Europe, the Crusades, and other movements that affected every aspect of life over the next two hundred and fifty years, the period that has come to be known as the High Middle Ages. Medieval attitudes towards violence and violent acts also shifted as part of a larger transformation in theology and Christology that began to depict the Lord as a figure of peace and mercy, rather than one of vengeance, and his Son as suffering and pitiable rather than imperturbable and powerful. Christian authors intensified their condemnation of all actions that they chose to characterize as "violence," and in the process increased the prominence of the ideology of peace. Although never absent from biblical, patristic, and Carolingian political thought, the ideology of peace gained importance during the High Middle Ages, as measured by the growing number of peace acts produced in the eleventh century and beyond.

Over the course of the eleventh century, what previously had been scattered clerical diatribes against violence developed into a clearly enunciated rhetoric. Against the wound of violence, clerics proposed the balm of peacemaking, later a theme of tremendous significance in the rhetoric of the great mendicant preachers. This new rhetoric found its greatest expression in the peace movements known to historians as the peace and truce of God. However, the desire to promote the internal peace of Christendom encouraged, perhaps inevitably, the idea that violence could be exported and used against external enemies, an idea that came into circulation a half century before the conflict that later came to be known as the First Crusade (1096–99). According to this logic, violence against Christians was diabolical and an offense to Christ's passion; just war against Muslims and pagans, by contrast, was holy.

By the late twelfth century, challenges to the practice and legitimacy of private vengeance were also being enacted by the rulers of the newly emerging kingdoms and city-states of high medieval Europe. Like their predecessors, these new powers were inclined to condemn any private quarrel, regarding such actions as an offense to the majesty of the ruler or the commonwealth. As states and rulers claimed the right and the obligation to take vengeance against malefactors, individual subjects found that their own right of vengeance, including their right to accept compensation for injuries, was slowly being withdrawn. As a wide variety of contemporary sources, from law codes to judicial inquiries, clearly demonstrate, however, it took a long time for this process to unfold. Many people throughout the High and later Middle Ages, and not only members of the nobility, continued to practice vengeance or retaliation of one sort or another despite the costs. Many jurisdictions, moreover, continued to authorize private vengeance either tacitly or explicitly, illustrating the uneven nature of the trends in question.

# CHAPTER EIGHT: THE EFFORT TO
# REGULATE VIOLENCE AND EMOTION

*Copious legislation concerning vengeance and emotions like anger and hatred was gen-*
*erated both by ecclesiastical and secular bodies during the High Middle Ages. Ecclesias-*
*tical regulation continued to develop and expand upon the negative attitudes expressed*
*toward vengeful emotion set forth in the penitential literature of earlier centuries (see*
*Doc. 17). Territorial lords, including bishops, kings, and counts, also got into the game*
*by creating peace acts or other laws aimed at restricting incidents of violence in their*
*territories.*

*As is usually the case, these laws and acts are statements of how men and women*
*in the Middle Ages thought things ought to be, and not how things were. Historians*
*have argued that some of the important peace acts generated at the great Peace councils*
*(see, e.g., Docs. 43 and 47–49), which aimed to defend churches and other ecclesiastical*
*property, were created during ongoing feuds or enmities between secular lords and castel-*
*lans. There is little evidence that the resulting peace acts had much, if any, effect on the*
*behavior of warring parties, at least in the short run. The same is true for the growing*
*body of penitential literature, which had little if any success in regulating or restraining*
*emotions like anger and hatred. The continuing insistence on preserving the right of*
*ecclesiastical sanctuary (Doc. 49), whereby killers were allowed to seek sanctuary in*
*churches from their bloodthirsty enemies, is a tacit acknowledgment of the persistence of*
*vengeance-based killings.*

## 43. THE PEACE OF GOD IN CHARROUX

*The Council of Charroux (989) was one of the earliest recorded peace councils. The*
*movement known to historians as the "peace and truce of God" began in Aquitaine*
*(as at Charroux) and Septimania during the late tenth century, and later spread to*
*Burgundy and other regions.*

Source: trans. Oliver J. Thatcher and Edgar H. McNeal, *A Source Book for Mediaeval History*
(New York: Scribners, 1905), p. 412.

Following the example of my predecessors, I Gunbald, archbishop of Bordeaux, called together the bishops of my diocese in a synod at Charroux, ...
and we, assembled there in the name of God, made the following decrees.
1) Anathema [formal curse] against those who break into churches. If anyone
breaks into or robs a church, he shall be anathema unless he makes satisfaction. 2) Anathema against those who rob the poor. If anyone robs a peasant

or any other poor person of a sheep, ox, ass, cow, goat, or pig, he shall be anathema unless he makes satisfaction. 3) Anathema against those who injure clergymen. If anyone attacks, seizes, or beats a priest, deacon, or any other clergyman, who is not bearing arms (shield, sword, coat of mail, or helmet), but is going along peacefully or staying in the house, the sacrilegious person shall be excommunicated and cut off from the Church, unless he makes satisfaction, or unless the bishop discovers that the clergyman brought it upon himself by his own fault.

## 44. PENANCE FOR HOMICIDE IN THE *DECRETUM* OF BURCHARD OF WORMS

*Born around 965 and consecrated bishop of Worms in 1000, Burchard (d. 1025) was one of the most influential bishops of his time. He successfully asserted his episcopal authority in the secular affairs of his diocese while building new churches, forming new parishes, and disciplining his clergy. The* Decretum *(1008–12), one of the earliest collections of canon law, was especially influential in the eleventh and twelfth centuries.*

Source: *Patrologia Latina* 140 (Paris: Migne, 1880 [1549]), cols. 763–78. Trans. Daniel Lord Smail.

### [Book 6]

This book treats homicides committed both intentionally and not intentionally, parricides, fratricides, those who kill their legitimate wives and their elders, and the killing of clerics, and it shows which penance ought to be imposed for each of these types of homicide.

1. If anyone shall have committed homicide of his own free will, it behooves him, according to the decrees of Pope Miltiades [r. 311–314] and the statutes of the council of Tribur, to do a penance such as this. (From the council at Tribur [895], ch. 4.) First, he should not be allowed to enter the church for the first forty days; let him go about with bare feet and employ no means of transportation. Let him wear woolen clothing without leg coverings; let him not bear arms; and he shall eat nothing for these forty days apart from some bread and salt, and let him drink pure water. And let him have no fellowship with other Christians, nor let him share food and drink with any other penitent, until the forty days are fulfilled. No one else may partake of the food that he eats. Out of consideration for the condition of his body or illness, he may eat fruit, greens, or vegetables only as seems appropriate.

5. (From the council at the city of Thionville, ch. 3.) In the council of the

city of Thionville, in which thirty-two bishops took part, Haistulf of Mainz, the archbishop [see Doc. 25], with his suffragans [dependent bishops]; Hetti, the archbishop of Trier, with his suffragans; and Ebbo, the archbishop of Rheims [see Doc. 27], with his suffragans, along with the representatives of the other bishops of Gaul and Germany, by reason of the excessive presumption of certain tyrants raving against the priests of the Lord, and on account of the event which recently took place in the Basque country in which the bishop John was killed in a shameful and unheard way, it was decreed that, in unison and with humble devotion, they beseech the prince, if it be pleasing to his piety, [to rule] that an injury inflicted on Christ's priests be adjudged fully according to the statutes of the synod.

In the judgment of the bishops this too would be pleasing if, out of all, the matter could be settled according to their power, that is, that they be smitten with canonical judgment, namely they who, putting off the fear of the Lord, presume to attack his ministers. If indeed it be pleasing to his piety – according to the rulings of previous kings, in which their foresight mercifully recommended that certain sums of money for the offenses be given for the consolation of the holy Church – that the aforementioned matters be settled according to the judgment of the bishops, by means of the money fine conceded by the emperors to the bishops and by means of penance, if his piety might deign to agree, then it would be pleasing to them to be settled in this way. If anyone shall have insulted a subdeacon, or wounded or injured him, and he should recover, he shall do penance for five Lenten periods, not including the rest of the years, and for his composition fine he shall settle in the amount of 300 shillings, and let him settle with the bishop through the episcopal penalties. But if the victim shall have died, the killer shall do penance for each of the aforesaid Lenten periods along with the following years, and pay 400 shillings, with a triple composition, and let him settle with the bishop for a threefold episcopal penalty. If he shall have insulted a deacon, he shall do penance for each of the abovementioned Lenten periods, along with the following years, and pay 400 shillings, with a triple composition, and let him settle with the bishop for the episcopal penalties. If, however, the victim has died, the killer should do penance for each of the six Lenten periods mentioned above, and pay 600 shillings with a triple composition, and let him settle with the bishop for a triple episcopal penalty. If he shall have insulted and punished a priest, let him do penance for six Lenten periods without the subsequent years, and pay 600 shillings with triple composition, and settle for a triple episcopal penalty. If the victim shall have died, a penance of twelve years shall be imposed on him according to the canons, and he shall pay 900 shillings with a triple composition, and let him settle for a triple episcopal penalty. If he shall have plotted against a bishop, seized him, or in any way dishonored him, he shall do penance for ten Lenten periods with the following years, and he shall settle a triple composition on the murdered priest. If, however, the victim shall have been killed by chance and not intentionally, the killer shall do penance for homicide by the judgment of the provincial bishops. If he shall have killed him deliberately, however, let him not eat meat nor drink wine for all the days of his life; he shall put aside military service, and let him remain perpetually without expectation of marriage. Haistulf, the archbishop of Mainz, said: "If it be pleasing to kings and to their vassals, we would ask that it be approved and signed." And it was approved, and signed, both by the king, and by all the rest.

8. On the killing of priests. (From the council of Worms, ch. 3.) He who shall have killed a priest intentionally, let him not eat meat nor drink wine for all the days of his life. He shall fast until evening, apart from holidays and Sundays; he shall not bear arms, nor mount a horse, nor enter a church for five years, but let him remain outside the gates of the church. After five years, he may enter the church, but in the meantime let him not take communion, but remain among the audience. When twelve years have passed, however, permission to take communion shall be granted to him, and permission to ride shall be allowed. But let him continue with the remaining obligations three days out of every week, so that he might deserve to be purified more thoroughly.

9. On priests deposed, and then killed. (From the council of Tours, ch. 3.) It was made known to us that certain people, who at one time called themselves priests, and afterward were degraded for their sins [defrocked], were slaughtered while they were traveling through various places, seeking the approval of the saints by doing penance. We deny every ecclesiastical dignity to killers of this kind, until they have paid a worthy penance for their evil deed according to the judgment of the bishops, because they ought to do penance more weightily than other homicides do.

10. Concerning priests without a long outer garment who are killed. (From the council of Tribur, where King Arnulf was present, ch. 26.) Priests ought not go about unless they are dressed in a long outer garment or *orarium* [a stole worn on both shoulders by priests]. And if they are despoiled or wounded or killed while on the road while not wearing a long outer garment, they shall be redeemed by a simple correction. If they are dressed in a long outer garment, then a threefold correction.

11. Concerning a murdered priest, to whom his composition is to be paid. (From the same council.) The composition for a murdered priest is paid to the bishop of his parish; it is paid, in other words, so that the bishop might allot half his *wergeld* for the business of the church to which he pertained, and distribute the other half appropriately in his charitable works, since no

one among us seems to be his closer heir than the one who brought him to the Lord.

12. Concerning those who shall have committed a homicide through plots. (From the council of Nantes, ch. 2.) If anyone intentionally and through plots shall have killed a man, let him submit to the yoke of penance. And if this act is well known publicly, if he is a layman, then let him be separated from the communion of prayers for five years. After five years let him be received again in the communion of prayers, but let him not offer nor approach the body of the Lord. Persisting in this state for fourteen years, then he may be received to full communion with oblations.

## 45. THE LAWS OF THE FAMILY OF ST. PETER

*Burchard was not only a bishop; like many bishops in the area of what is now modern-day Germany, he was also a territorial lord who sought to govern his land. In Burchard's writings, therefore, we can see how ecclesiastical and moral regulation work in tandem with practical regulation. The "family of St. Peter" was Burchard's term for the Christians who lived in his diocese and were subject to his rule. In providing humiliating corporal punishments for killers, Burchard was going beyond what early medieval rulers normally felt comfortable legislating. We cannot know whether Burchard's judges actually enacted these punishments; we do know that they were an important statement about how Burchard felt justice ought to be done.*

Source: *Constitutiónes et Acta Publica Imperatorem et Regum*, ed. Ludwicus Weiland, Monumenta Germaniae Historica: Legum Sectio IV, vol. 1 (Hanover: Hahn, 1893), pp. 640–44. Trans. Lori Pieper.

In the name of the Holy and Undivided Trinity. I, Burchard of Worms, bishop of the church, on account of the constant lamentations of the poor and the numerous plots of many people, who, like dogs were tearing to pieces the family of St. Peter, imposing different laws on them and oppressing those who are weaker by their judgments, with the advice of the clergy and the knights and of the whole family, have given orders to write these laws, so that some advocate or viscount or ministerial or among them some other long-winded person of the above-mentioned family might not be able to introduce anything new, but that one and the same law might be common to all, the rich and poor, previously written down before their eyes.

8. If anyone with others, whom he shall bring in with him, commits an injustice against anyone from his community, the law of the family shall be that he only, along with his men, shall reconcile himself by one satisfaction and each of the others is to reconcile himself by his own satisfaction.

9. The law of the family shall be: that five pounds from the *wergeld* of a man of the fisc are to be paid to the treasury and two and a half pounds are to go to his friends.

18. The law of the family shall be: that each person, with his companion, is to swear with one hand: if it shall be on account of a feud, with seven companions, and similarly with the bishop.

20. If anyone in the city of Worms shall kill an associate by a duel, he is to pay as security sixty shillings, if he shall die in a duel outside the city, but within the family, he is to pay triple composition as justice to the one he shall have fought for the battle unjustly fought, he is to pay the penalty to the bishop, and to the advocate he is to give twenty shillings; or he is to lose his skin and hair.

23. The law of the family shall be: if one of them shall enter the house of another with arms in his hand and shall carry off his daughter by violence, he is to restore to her father or guardian, threefold for each one, all the clothes in which she had been dressed when she was raped, and for each part of the clothing he is to pay as composition a penalty to the bishop, lastly, he is to hand her over to her father, for his threefold satisfaction, along with the penalty of the bishop, and since he shall be unable to have her legitimately according to the canonical precept, he is to pay twelve shields to that man's friends, and as many lances, and one pound in pennies for reconciliation.

27. And the law shall be: that if someone shall strike someone in the city, so that he falls to the ground dead, he is to pay a composition of sixty shillings for penalty to the bishop; if, however, he shall strike someone with his fist or a lightweight whip that is called a *bluathra,* and he does not die, he is to pay a composition of only five shillings.

28. The law shall be: if someone in the city unsheathes his sword to kill someone or shall draw bow and place arrow to the string or extend a lance to wound someone, he is to pay a composition of sixty shillings.

30. On account of the homicide however, which used to be committed almost daily within the family of St. Peter in a monstrous way – because one used to attack another in an insane rage, often for nothing or through drunkenness or for pride, so that in the course of one year thirty-five servants of St. Peter without fault have been killed by the servants of the same church, and the killers themselves have gloried in it and have become swollen up with pride from it, rather than show any penitence – consequently, on account of that greatest detriment to our church with the advice of our faithful, we decree that this correction be made: that if anyone from the family shall kill his companion without necessity, that is without the necessity that the victim

wished to kill him or if the victim was a thief and he was defending himself and his goods, but if without these above-mentioned things, we decree that his skin and hair are to be taken from him and he is to be burned on both jaws with an iron for this deed, and he is to pay *wergeld* and he is to make peace in the usual way with the next of kin of the victim, and the next of kin are to be forced to accept this. But if the next of kin of the victim wish to prosecute the next of kin of the killer, if anyone of the next of kin shall be able to expurgate themselves of having contributed advice and deeds by an oath, they are to have firm and perpetual peace with the next of kin of the victim. If, however, the next of kin of the victim decide to scorn this constitution and the above-mentioned people prepare ambushes, but harm nothing, except that they lie in wait, they are to lose their skin and hair without burning. But if someone of them shall kill or wound out of contempt, they are to lose their skin and hair and are to suffer the above-mentioned burning. But if the killer escapes and he cannot be caught, whatever he has is to be collected for the fisc, and his next of kin, if they are blameless, are to have a firm peace. If however the killer shall not escape but shall wish to defend his innocence with the next of kin of the person killed by a duel and he shall win, he is to pay the *wergeld* and make peace with the next of kin. If however none of the next of kin of the person killed wish to fight with the killer, he is to purge himself with boiling water before the bishop and is to pay the *wergeld* and make peace with the next of kin, and they are to be bound to accept it. If however on account of the fear of this constitution, they go to another family and enrage them against their own companions, and if there is no one who dares to fight a duel against someone of theirs, all are to expurgate themselves before the bishop, and if anyone shall be defeated, he is to suffer those things that have been written above. If anyone however from the family in the city without the above-mentioned necessities shall kill someone from the family, he is to lose his skin and hair, and is to suffer burning in the above-mentioned way, and he is to pay the penalty and pay the *wergeld* and make peace with the next of kin and they are to be bound to accept it. If however someone from a separate family cultivates the land of St. Peter and he shall have such presumption, and that is, if he shall kill someone from our family without the necessity described above, he is either to suffer the above-mentioned things or lose our land, and he is to have the ambushes of the family and the advocate. If however our servant, who is on our manor, or our ministerial dares to presume such a thing, we decree that it is to be in our power, with the advice of our faithful, to decide how such presumption is to be avenged.

31. If anyone from the family shall fight with his fellow about any kind of thing, whether about fields or vineyards or dependants or money, if it can be discerned from both sides with witnesses of both sides without an oath, we praise it; but so that perjury might be avoided, we wish that their witnesses be presented from both sides, and so they are to have consenting witnesses as it were free: and from the above-mentioned two sides, two witnesses are to be chosen to fight and they are to decide the dispute by a duel; and the one, whom the victor shall kill, shall lose, and his witness is to suffer such things for false witness, as if he has taken the oath.

# 46. THE PENITENTIAL OF BURCHARD OF WORMS

*This penitential (ca 1025) provides a glimpse into Burchard's understanding of how killings within the "family of St. Peter" (see Doc. 45) could have been the product of family-based vengeance. The distinction between intentional and unintentional killings made in early penitentials is one that continued to be significant for Burchard.*

Source: ed. F. W. H. Wasserschleben, *Die Bussordnungen der abendländischen Kirche* (Graz: Akademische Druck- und Verlagsanstalt, 1958), p. 632. Trans. Daniel Lord Smail.

7. Have you committed a homicide so as to avenge kinfolk? If you have done so, you shall do penance for forty days, which they call *carrina,* together with the seven subsequent years, since the Lord said "Vengeance is mine."

8. If you have committed a homicide unintentionally, such that in your anger you wanted to strike someone but not kill him, yet you did kill, you shall do forty days penance, that is the *carrina,* and the seven following years. But the first, third, and fifth day and the sabbath you may redeem by means of pennies, that is to say the price of one penny or the feeding of three paupers. The remaining days ought to be observed, however, for the seven years, just as was prescribed for homicides willfully committed.

# 47. TRUCE OF GOD IN ARLES

*The truce of God made by the archbishop of Arles in southern France was one of many such acts of peace that were produced in the wake of the important late tenth-century peace councils such as Charroux (see Doc. 43). The following document is a record of the truce of God from Arles, written some time between 1035 and 1041. It is more detailed than that of Charroux and includes a clear statement of how it was considered normal to be in a state of enmity with others. An important passage (see paragraph 5 below) also prescribes a form of penitential exile for homicide.*

Source: trans. Oliver J. Thatcher and Edgar H. McNeal, *A Source Book for Mediaeval History* (New York: Scribners, 1905), pp. 414–16.

In the name of God, the omnipotent Father, Son, and Holy Spirit. Reginbald, archbishop of Arles, with Benedict, bishop of Avignon, Nithard, bishop of Nice, the venerable abbot Odilo [of Cluny], and all the bishops, abbots, and other clergy of Gaul, to all the archbishops, bishops, and clergy of Italy, grace and peace from God, the omnipotent Father, who is, was, and shall be.

1. For the salvation of your souls, we beseech all you who fear God and believe in him and have been redeemed by his blood, to follow the footsteps of God, and to keep peace one with another, that you may obtain eternal peace and quiet with him.

2. This is the peace or truce of God which we have received from heaven through the inspiration of God, and we beseech you to accept it and observe it even as we have done; namely, that all Christians, friends and enemies, neighbors and strangers, should keep true and lasting peace one with another from vespers on Wednesday to sunrise on Monday, so that during these four days and five nights, all persons may have peace, and, trusting in this peace, may go about their business without fear of their enemies.

3. All who keep the peace and truce of God shall be absolved of their sins by God, the omnipotent Father, and his son Jesus Christ, and the Holy Spirit, and by Saint Mary with the choir of virgins, and Saint Michael with the choir of angels, and Saint Peter with all the saints and all the faithful, now and forever.

4. Those who have promised to observe the truce and have willfully violated it, shall be excommunicated by God the omnipotent Father, and his son Jesus Christ, and the Holy Spirit, from the communion of all the saints of God, shall be accursed and despised here and in the future world, shall be damned with Dathan and Abiram and with Judas who betrayed his Lord, and shall be overwhelmed in the depths of hell, as was Pharaoh in the midst of the sea, unless they make such satisfaction as is described in the following:

5. If anyone has killed another on the days of the truce of God, he shall be exiled and driven from the land and shall make a pilgrimage to Jerusalem, spending his exile there. If anyone has violated the truce of God in any other way, he shall suffer the penalty prescribed by the secular laws and shall do double the penance prescribed by the canons.

6. We believe it is just that we should suffer both secular and spiritual punishment if we break the promise which we have made to keep the peace.

For we believe that this peace was given to us from heaven by God; for before God gave it to his people, there was nothing good done among us. The Lord's Day was not kept, but all kinds of labor were performed on it.

7. We have vowed and dedicated these four days to God: Thursday, because it is the day of his ascension; Friday, because it is the day of his passion; Saturday, because it is the day in which he was in the tomb; and Sunday, because it is the day of his resurrection; on that day no labor shall be done and no one shall be in fear of his enemy.

8. By the power given to us by God through the apostles, we bless and absolve all who keep the peace and truce of God; we excommunicate, curse, anathematize, and exclude from the holy mother Church all who violate it.

9. If anyone shall punish violators of this decree and of the truce of God, he shall not be held guilty of a crime, but shall go and come freely with the blessing of all Christians, as a defender of the cause of God. But if anything has been stolen on other days, and the owner finds it on one of the days of the truce, he shall not be restrained from recovering it, lest thereby an advantage should be given to the thief.

10. In addition, brothers, we request that you observe the day on which the peace and truce was established by us, keeping it in the name of the holy Trinity. Drive all thieves out of your country, and curse and excommunicate them in the name of all the saints.

11. Offer your tithes and the first fruits of your labors to God, and bring offerings from your goods to the churches for the souls of the living and the dead, that God may free you from all evils in this world, and after this life bring you to the kingdom of heaven, through him who lives and reigns with God the Father and the Holy Spirit, forever and ever. Amen.

## 48. A COMITAL PEACE ASSEMBLY OF BARCELONA

*The counts of Barcelona, like many secular rulers, were aggressive in their pursuit of the new fashion for legislating peace. Certain passages from this text, written in 1064, are good examples of the spatial restrictions on violence found in some early medieval law codes.*

Source: trans. Donald Kagay, *The Usatges of Barcelona* (Philadelphia: University of Pennsylvania Press, 1994), pp. 103–5.

In the year of our Lord 1064, a confirmation of the peace or pact of the Lord was made by the bishops, namely, Berenguer of Barcelona, Guillem of

Ausona, and Berenguer of Gerona as well as the abbots, the religious clerics of each order at Barcelona in the church of the see of the Holy Cross by the order of the princes, the Lord Ramón and Lady Almodis of Barcelona, with the assent and acclamation of the magnates of their land and other God-fearing Christians.

1. Indeed, by the constitution of the aforesaid bishops and princes, it was enacted that from this day hereafter no person of either sex shall violate or invade either a church or dwellings which are or will be within a circle of thirty paces [one hundred and fifty feet] around the church except the bishop or canons to whom this church is subject on account of its rent or to eject an excommunicated person from it. Yet we do not place under this protection those churches in which fortifications are built. Indeed, we order that those churches in which robbers or thieves put booty or stolen goods or from which they leave or to which they return while committing offenses, shall be unmolested until charges concerning the offense are preferred before the church's own bishop or before the see of Barcelona. If however, these robbers or thieves do not want to undergo justice according to the order of the bishop or canons of the see of Barcelona or postpone it, then by the authority of the bishop of the aforesaid see and the canons, let this church be considered without immunity. Moreover, let one who otherwise violates a church or attacks whatever is within a circle of thirty paces around it make restitution with the sum of six hundred sous for the sacrilege and let him be subject to excommunication until he shall suitably make compensation.

2. Likewise it was resolved that no person shall assault clerks who are not bearing arms, monks, nuns, and other women or those traveling with bishops if they are not bearing arms. Indeed, let no person violate a community of canons or monks or steal anything from there.

3. Likewise the aforesaid bishops and princes confirmed that no person in this bishopric of Barcelona shall make plunder of horses or their foals, male or female mules, cattle, male or female asses, sheep, or goats. Indeed, let no man burn or destroy the dwellings of peasants or clergy who are not bearing arms except for those properties in which knights live. Let no person dare seize or distrain a male or female villager or extort money from them. Let no one burn or cut standing crops, cut down an olive tree, or remove their fruits. Indeed let no one pour out another's wine.

4. Moreover, whoever violates this peace which we have proclaimed and does not make compensation with the sum of the fine within fifteen days to the person against whom he violated it, let him make double compensation if the fifteen days have passed.

5. Moreover, the aforesaid bishops strongly confirmed the pact of the Lord, which the people call *treuga* [truce]; namely, from the first day of the Advent

of the Lord to the octave of the Epiphany of the Lord and from the Monday preceding Ash Wednesday to the first Monday after the octave of Pentecost Sunday and in the three vigils as well as the feasts of Holy Mary, indeed the vigils and feasts of the Twelve Apostles and also the vigils and feasts of the martyrs Saint Eulalia and Saint Cugat of Barcelona and also the vigils of the two feasts of Christmas and the Holy Cross. We also placed these feasts with their vigils; namely, those of Saint John the Baptist, Saint Lawrence, Saint Michael the Archangel, Saint Martin, and All Saints Day under this observance of religion. And they similarly placed under such an observance the vigils of the same [All Saints Day] and fast days of the four seasons.

6. The aforesaid bishops not only confirmed that the aforesaid feast days are in the truce of the Lord but also they ordered all the following [days] to be observed until the rising of the sun of the next day.

7. If, however, anyone commits a crime against another during the aforesaid truce, let him make double compensation and then let him amend the truce of the Lord by the judgment of cold water in the see of the Holy Cross.

8. Moreover, if anyone deliberately kills a man during this truce, it was resolved by the consent of all Christians that after making the compensation for homicide he shall be condemned to exile for all the days of his life or confined in a monastery after having assumed the monastic habit.

9. The aforesaid bishops and princes ruled that the aforesaid pact of the Lord shall be rigorously kept and observed by all accompanying them in the upcoming expedition or by those remaining here in this land during the entire period of this expedition until thirty days after their return. Thus it was established that none of these persons, whether those going or remaining, shall dare to wrong any other faithful person or in any of his possessions. But if he does so, let him pay double compensation for the wrongdoing and be deprived forever of Christian communion until suitable compensation shall be made by him.

10. Moreover, the aforesaid bishops and princes thus ejected from the communion of the Church and Christianity those perverse men who capture Christians to sell them to pagans [Muslims] or act for the damage of Christianity so if anyone should come upon them, he need not consider them under the [protection of] the truce of the Lord.

## 49. THE TRUCE OF GOD IN COLOGNE

*The peace and truce of God produced at Cologne in 1083 is an especially rich expression of the expectations of the peace movement. Like many previous peace acts, it includes provisions for the exile, rather than the execution, of murderers, a practice that remained the norm in many regions of Europe through the later Middle Ages. The sanction of excommunication was inflicted on those who resisted the peace, suggesting how moral regulation could be and was brought to bear on practical regulation. The importance of ecclesiastical sanctuary was also strongly defended.*

Source: trans. Dana C. Munro, *Urban and the Crusaders* (Philadelphia: University of Pennsylvania Department of History, 1895), pp. 9–12.

Inasmuch as in our own times the Church, through its members, has been extraordinarily afflicted by tribulations and difficulties, so that tranquility and peace were wholly despaired of, we have endeavored by God's help to aid it, suffering so many burdens and perils. And by the advice of our faithful subjects we have at length provided this remedy, so that we might to some extent re-establish, on certain days at least, the peace which, because of our sins, we could not make enduring. Accordingly we have enacted and set forth the following: having called together our parishioners to a legally summoned council, which was held at Cologne, the chief city of our province, in the church of St. Peter, in the 1083rd year of our Lord's Incarnation, in the sixth indiction, on the twelfth day before the Kalends of May, after arranging other business, we have caused to be read in public what we proposed to do in this matter. After this had been for some time fully discussed "pro and con" by all, it was unanimously agreed upon, both the clergy and the people consenting, and we declared in what manner and during what parts of the year it ought to be observed: namely, that from the first day of the Advent of our Lord through Epiphany, and from the beginning of Septuagesima [the third Sunday before Lent] to the eighth day after Pentecost and through that whole day, and throughout the year on every Sunday, Friday and Saturday, and on the fast days of the four seasons, and on the eve and the day of all the apostles, and on all days canonically set apart – or which shall in the future be set apart – for fasts or feasts, this decree of peace shall be observed; so that both those who travel and those who remain at home may enjoy security and the most entire peace, so that no one may commit murder, arson, robbery or assault, no one may injure another with a sword, club or any kind of weapon, and so that no one irritated by any wrong, from the Advent of our Lord to the eighth day after Epiphany, and from Septuagesima to the eighth day after Pentecost, may presume to carry arms, shield, sword or lance, or moreover any kind of armor. On the remaining days indeed, namely, on Sundays, Fridays, apostles' days and the vigils of the apostles, and on every day set aside, or to be set aside, for fasts or feasts, bearing arms shall be legal, but on this condition, that no injury shall be done in any way to any one. If it shall be necessary for any one in the time of the decreed peace – that is, from the Advent of our Lord to the eighth day after Epiphany, and from Septuagesima to the eighth day after Pentecost – to go from one bishopric into another in which the peace is not observed, he may bear arms, but on the condition that he shall not injure any one, except in self-defense if he is attacked; and when he returns into our diocese he shall immediately lay aside his arms. If it shall happen that any castle is besieged during the days which are included within the peace the besiegers shall cease from attack unless they are set upon by the besieged and compelled to beat the latter back.

And in order that this statute of peace should not be violated by any one rashly or with impunity, a penalty was fixed by the common consent of all; if a free man or noble violates it, that is, commits homicide or wounds any one or is at fault in any manner whatever, he shall be expelled from our territory, without any indulgence on account of the payment of money or the intercession of friends, and his heirs shall take all his property; if he holds a fief, the lord to whom it belongs shall receive it again. Moreover, if it is learned that his heirs after his expulsion have furnished him any support or aid, and if they are convicted of it, the estate shall be taken from them and given to the king. But if they wish to clear themselves of the charge against them, they shall take oath with twelve, who are equally free or equally noble. If a slave kills a man, he shall be beheaded; if he wounds a man, he shall lose a hand; if he does an injury in any other way with his fist or a club, or by striking with a stone, he shall be shorn and flogged. If, however, he is accused and wishes to prove his innocence, he shall clear himself by the ordeal of cold water, but he must himself be put into the water and no one else in his place; if, however, fearing the sentence decreed against him, he flees, he shall be under a perpetual excommunication; and if he is known to be in any place, letters shall be sent thither, in which it shall be announced to all that he is excommunicate, and that it is unlawful for any one to associate with him. In the case of boys who have not yet completed their twelfth year, the hand ought not to be cut off; but only in the case of those who are twelve years or more of age. Nevertheless if boys fight, they shall be whipped and deterred from fighting.

It is not an infringement of the peace, if any one orders his delinquent slave, pupil, or any one in any way under his charge to be chastised with rods or cudgels. It is also an exception to this constitution of peace, if the Lord King publicly orders an expedition to attack the enemies of the kingdom or is pleased to hold a council to judge the enemies of justice. The peace is not violated if, during the time, the duke or other counts, advocates or their substitutes hold courts and inflict punishment legally on thieves, robbers and other criminals.

The statute of this imperial peace is especially enacted for the security of those engaged in feuds; but after the end of the peace, they are not to dare to rob and plunder in the villages and houses, because the laws and penalties enacted before the institution of the peace are still legally valid to restrain them from crime, moreover because robbers and highwaymen are excluded from this divine peace and indeed from any peace.

If any one attempts to oppose this pious institution and is unwilling to promise peace to God with the others or to observe it, no priest in our diocese shall presume to say a mass for him or shall take any care for his salvation; if he is sick, no Christian shall dare to visit him; on his death-bed he shall not receive the Eucharist, unless he repents. The supreme authority of the peace promised to God and commonly extolled by all will be so great that it will be observed not only in our times, but forever among our posterity, because if any one shall presume to infringe, destroy or violate it, either now or ages hence, at the end of the world, he is irrevocably excommunicated by us.

The infliction of the above mentioned penalties on the violators of the peace is not more in the power of the counts, centenaries or officials, than in that of the whole people in common; and they are to be especially careful not to show friendship or hatred or do anything contrary to justice in punishing, and not to conceal the crimes, if they can be hidden, but to bring them to light. No one is to receive money for the release of those taken in fault, or to attempt to aid the guilty by any favor of any kind, because whoever does this incurs the intolerable damnation of his soul; and all the faithful ought to remember that this peace has not been promised to men, but to God, and therefore must be observed so much the more rigidly and firmly. Wherefore we exhort all in Christ to guard inviolably this necessary contract of peace, and if any one hereafter presumes to violate it, let him be damned by the ban of irrevocable excommunication and by the anathema of eternal perdition.

In the churches, however, and in the cemeteries of the churches, honor and reverence are to be paid to God, so that if any robber or thief flees thither, he is by no means to be killed or seized, but he is to remain there until by urgent hunger he is compelled to surrender. If any person presumes to furnish arms or food to the criminal or to aid him in flight, the same penalty shall be inflicted on him as on the criminal. Moreover, by our ban we interdict laymen from punishing the transgressions of the clergy and those living under this order; but if seized in open crime, they shall be handed over to their bishop. In cases in which laymen are to be executed, the clergy are to be degraded; in cases in which laymen are to be mutilated, the clergy are to be suspended from office, and with the consent of the laymen they are to suffer frequent fasts and floggings until they atone.

## 50. PEACE OF THE LAND IN MAINZ

*The German kings of the Holy Roman Empire produced numerous acts mandating peace that were known collectively as* Landfrieden, *or "landpeaces"; this one is from Mainz, and was issued in 1103.*

Source: trans. Oliver J. Thatcher and Edgar H. McNeal, *A Source Book for Mediaeval History* (New York: Scribners, 1905), p. 419. Modernized by Kelly Gibson.

In the year of the incarnation of our Lord 1103, the emperor Henry established this peace at Mainz, and he and the archbishops and bishops signed it with their own signatures. The son of the king and the nobles of the whole kingdom, dukes, margraves, counts, and many others, swore to observe it. Duke Welf, Duke Bertholf, and Duke Frederick swore to keep the peace from that day to four years from the next Pentecost. They swore to keep peace with churches, clergy, monks, merchants, women, and Jews. This is the form of the oath which they swore:

No one shall attack the house of another or waste it with fire, or seize another for ransom, or strike, wound, or slay another. If anyone does any of these things he shall lose his eyes or his hand, and the one who defends him shall suffer the same penalty. If the violator flees into a castle, the castle shall be besieged for three days by those who have sworn to keep the peace, and if the violator is not given up it shall be destroyed. If the offender flees from justice out of the country, his lord shall take away his fief, if he has one, and his relatives shall take his patrimony. If anyone steals anything worth five solidi or more, he shall lose his eyes or his hand. If anyone steals anything worth less than five solidi, he shall be made to restore the theft, and shall lose his hair and be beaten with rods; if he has committed this smaller theft three times, he shall lose his eyes or his hand. If you shall meet your enemy on the road and can injure him, do so; but if he escapes to the house or castle of anyone, you shall let him remain there unharmed.

## 51. THE LAWS OF HENRY I OF ENGLAND

*Shortly after Henry I (1068–1135) came to the throne of England in 1100, he sponsored a compilation of existing English law. These laws contained detailed compensation values for injuries.*

Source: trans. L. J. Downer, *Leges Henrici Primi* (Oxford: Clarendon Press, 1972), pp. 183, 221, 273–75.

### a. The payment of compensation
### [Section 59]

4. With respect to money which has been pledged in order to deal with the question of settlement or continued bloodfeud, the appointed day or the plea concerning the killing of bloodfeud enemies must not be deferred (unless a duty to the king of military service prevents attendance or some question of sickness or other appropriate genuine excuse occurs), and after that a firm, established, and undivided peace shall stand between them.

### b. Rules for determining who should bear the feud
### [Section 88]

9. If anyone asks another that he join him in his work, and while there that other is killed by his employer's enemies, he shall pay compensation for him, he, that is, by whose encouragement and furtherance the slain man came into the place of death; he shall clear himself of the charge of being cognizant of it or of being in agreement in any respect, if he is accused, and he shall do this by an oath equal in value to the *wergeld*.

9a. If however he can prove that the slain man came with him unasked, then if any of the accused's enemies kill him and he (the deceased) is not connected by consanguinity or blood relationship with him (the accused), it is just that the slayers shall make amends in accordance with their wrongdoing, and vengeance shall be taken against them by relatives and lords or they shall pay compensation in the matter.

9b. For vengeance is not to be taken, in these matters, against a person's men or servants.

10. Any person may aid his lord without incurring a *wite* [fine] if anyone attacks him, as we have said before; however due consideration shall be given to the matter in all cases.

11. If a person, having resisted his enemy beyond what the law sanctions,

has inflicted death or injury on anyone or has been responsible for anything of the kind, so that death appears to have resulted while he was enforcing what was due to him, vengeance is not to be taken indiscriminately on all relatives, either paternal or maternal, whether connected with the slayer or the slain.

11a. For in the case of every payment of *wergeld* for a slaying, two parts are the responsibility of the paternal kindred, and one third part is the responsibility of the maternal kin.

11b. There is one *wergeld* or revenge-slaying appropriate for a thegn, and another for a villein, as we have said before.

11c. If any have done otherwise than they are entitled, the relatives of the dead man shall demand the surplus of the *wergeld* or retributory vengeance, as well as against the kindred in general as against the closer relatives.

12. It is written in the laws of King Edmund [939–946, see Doc. 16c]: I myself and all of us are greatly displeased by the unlawful and manifold disputes which exist between us.

12a. If anyone henceforth slays a man, he himself shall bear the feud for the slaying, unless with the help of his kinsmen he makes payment within twelve months of the full amount of the *wergeld*, according to whatever the slain man's rank is.

12b. If then his kindred abandon him and will not pay compensation for him, it is my wish that all the kindred shall be free from the feud except the wrongdoer alone, if they thereafter provide him with neither food nor protection.

12c. If any of his kindred afterwards harbors him, he shall forfeit all his possessions to the king, and shall bear the feud against the slain man's kindred, because previously the slayer's kindred had disclaimed him.

12d. If anyone from the other kindred takes vengeance on any person other than the wrongdoer himself, he shall be an enemy of the king and of all his kindred.

13. If anyone because of the existence of a feud or for some other reason wishes to withdraw from his kindred and abjures them and cuts himself off from association with them and any right of inheritance and all relationship with them, and if anyone of his relatives whom he has renounced subsequently dies or is slain, no part of the inheritance or *wergeld* shall fall to him.

13a. If however he himself dies or is slain, his inheritance or *wergeld* shall lawfully accrue to his sons or his lords.

## c. Unintentional killings
### [Section 90]

1. If anyone, while he is endeavouring to separate persons fighting among themselves, is killed, though innocent, either intentionally or through the negligence of the disputants, the one who slew him shall pay amends for him, even though he did not start the quarrel.

2. If anyone suffers any injury or mischief through the sudden discharge of a bow or *ballista* or because of a mantrap, erected for the capture of wolves or some other animal, the person who set it up shall pay amends.

3. If anyone digs a well or cistern or opens up one previously made and something falls in so that it suffers death or injury, he shall provide something of equal value to compensate, but may keep for himself the thing killed or injured.

6. If a tree kills anyone while he is engaged on a common task with another, the tree shall be handed over to the kindred of the man who is killed, on condition that it is removed from the district within thirty days; otherwise it shall go to the person who owns the wood.

6a. We assert the same about anything made by a man's hand: if a man has been killed in this way, he shall not be paid for unless anyone appropriates to his own use the thing which is the cause of the killing; in that case he shall be adjudged guilty but without obligation to pay the fine.

6b. But there shall be some difference of result depending on whether someone asked the man who is skilled to join him in the task, or whether he came of his own volition, whether he was working for pecuniary reward or without payment, whether he falls by accident or is thrown down by someone; it makes a difference also whether the task is being done jointly for their lord or is a joint operation of the persons themselves or is being done for someone else.

7. If a man falls from a tree or some man-made structure on to someone else so that as a result the latter dies or is injured, if he can prove that he was unable to avoid this, he shall in accordance with ancient ordinances be held blameless.

7a. Or if anyone stubbornly and against the opinion of all takes it upon himself to exact vengeance or demand *wergeld*, he shall if he wishes climb up and in similar fashion cast himself down on the person responsible.

8. If anyone's hand has misdirected a missile so that while intending to kill one person he slays another, he shall pay compensation just the same.

11. There are very many kinds of misfortune which occur by accident rather than by design and which should be dealt with by the application of mercy rather than by formal judgment.

11a. For it is a rule of law that a person who unwittingly commits a wrong shall wittingly make amends.

11b. In circumstances in which a man cannot lawfully swear that a person was not through his agency further from life or nearer to death, he shall pay appropriate compensation, according to the facts of the case.

11c. Among these circumstances are the following cases: if anyone, by the dispatch of another, is the cause of his death while on the errand; if anyone sends for a person and the latter is killed while coming; if anyone, when summoned to a place by a person, suffers death there; if anyone's weapons kill a person when they have been laid on the spot by the one who owns them; if anyone throws them down, whether the person who has been killed or someone else, and they cause harm; if anyone, on being summoned to a place, is transfixed on someone's weapons wherever they have been laid; if anyone frightens or stirs a person so that in falling from a horse or something else he suffers some harm; if anyone, being brought to witness a public exhibition of a wild beast or a madman, incurs some injury at their hands; if anyone entrusts a horse or other thing to a person and thence some harm befalls him; if a person's horse, when goaded or struck under the tail by someone, runs into anyone else.

11d. In these and similar cases where a man intends one thing and something else results (where what is actually done is the subject of the accusation, and not the intention) the judges shall for preference fix a compensation determined on grounds of compassion and intended to repair any violation of honor, as appropriate to the circumstances.

### d. Dealing with slayers
### [Section 92]

3b. If the slayer has been killed by the relatives of the murdered man before being handed over, so that he cannot in fact be handed over as a person amenable to justice, or if he is captured after seven days have passed, he shall contribute nothing to the payment of the fine.

15. With respect to an offender who has either confessed or is of manifest guilt, the proper course is to hand him over to the relatives of the slain man so that he may experience the mercy of those to whom he displayed none.

15a. If the slain man has no relatives the king shall apply his justice to the case.

## 52. THE USATGES OF BARCELONA

*The* Usatges, *a term meaning customs or laws, were issued by the comital court of Count Ramon Berenguer IV of Barcelona (1131–62). They drew on feudal practice, peace and truce documents, and Roman and Visigothic law. The influence of the growing body of penitential literature is particularly strong in the* Usatges, *where considerable attention was paid to the emotions, and particularly to anger. See items 14, 17, 80 in particular, and item B6 especially, which the translator notes was derived in large part from the works of Ivo, Gratian, and other works of canon law. Other* usatges *in the document demonstrate princely interest in the regulation of the exercise of vengeance-taking.*

Source: trans. Donald J. Kagay, *The Usatges of Barcelona: The Fundamental Law of Catalonia* (Philadelphia: University of Pennsylvania Press, 1994), pp. 77–79, 82–85, 89, 96–97, 100.

14. If one, in anger, strikes any type of blow to another's body, let him give a single sou [shilling, *solidus*] for each blow which does not show [leave a bruise]. For those which do, let him give two sous apiece. And if there is bloodshed from these, five sous; for the breaking of a bone in the body, fifty sous. If in angrily assaulting and dragging down another, one makes blood flow from mouth or nostrils, let him give to him twenty sous in compensation.

16. If one spits in another's face, let him make compensation of twenty sous to him or suffer his retaliation.

17. If one criminally slanders another and does not want to or cannot prove this about him, either let him swear an oath to him that he uttered this slander in anger and not from the truth which he then knew or let him make as much compensation to him [the victim] as he lost by this slander as if it had been the truth if the slandered wished that the slanderer should purge himself on oath concerning it.

58. Likewise, they ruled that all men, noble and ignoble alike, even though they might be mortal enemies, shall be safe for all time day and night and observe a sound truce and true peace from Montcada to Castelldefels from the hill of Finistrel to that of Gavara and from the hill of Erola to the valley of Vitraria and within twelve leagues out to sea. And if anyone disobeys this order in any way, let him make double compensation for the wrong and dishonor which he has done and pay the prince a hundred golden ounces for the violation of his ban [that is, his judicial authority].

61.... Let the truce and promise not to take violent action which the princes have ordered to be in effect between enemies be rigorously observed, even though these enemies have not confirmed to him the approval of the same truce. Let no one dare violate the protection which the prince makes in person, through his messenger, *sagio* [counselor], or by his seal unless he first prefers charges with the prince in accordance with the custom of his court.

71. By the authority and request of all their nobles, the oft-mentioned princes R[amón Berenguer] and A[lmodis] decreed that all men, noble and ignoble alike, going to, staying with, or returning from the ruler shall have the [protection] of the peace and truce for the whole time, day and night. They shall be unmolested by all their enemies, along with all their fiefs and property as well as all men holding their fiefs, residing on them, or laboring in their service, along with everything which these persons hold and possess, continually until they return to their homes. And if anyone harms anything of theirs or inflicts any damage or commits a crime against them, from that day, he may consider his ties to the ruler broken. And if he suffers any wrong because of this, let no compensation be made him in any way. And let he who disobeys the prince's commands and, for any reason, does any wrong to those placed under this protection or to their possessions, make restitution eleven times over under the constraint of the ruler for all the wrongs which he has committed and everything he has stolen or carried off to those persons against whom he committed these violent acts and afterwards let him make compensation to the ruler for the dishonor he has done him with his own property and by the swearing of an oath with his own hands.

72. They also ruled that, once complaints were made by both sides, if the parties involved in a case afterwards enter into homage, an oath of fealty, or even a pact of friendship by an exchange of good faith and if the aforesaid suits were not maintained, they shall be perpetually null and void and considered terminated.

73. Indeed, let none of the magnates – namely, the viscounts, *comitores* [knights], or *vasvassores* [vassals] – hereafter presume in any way to either punish criminals (that is, to hang them for justice) or to build a new castle against the prince, or hold his fortification under siege or wage war with siege engines which are vulgarly called *fundibula, goza,* and *gata* [trebuchets] since this is a great dishonor to the rulers. But if a person does this, let him abandon or destroy the castle or give it back to the prince without any lessening of its value if he had captured it, immediately after being so demanded by the prince. And by the distraint of the prince, let him make double compensation for all offenses he has committed there to the person against whom he committed them. And if he captures knights and other vassals there, let him release and return them to the prince. Indeed, let him afterwards make compensation to him for the dishonor which he has done him in this matter with his property or fief by swearing an oath with his own hands but he is not bound to make any further compensation to him. Thus the exercise of this distraint is conceded to none but the rulers.

Since the rendering of justice in regard to criminals – namely, concerning murderers, adulterers, sorcerers, robbers, rapists, traitors, and other men – is granted only to the rulers, thus let them render justice as it seems fit to them: by cutting off hands and feet, putting out eyes, keeping men in prison for a long time and, ultimately, in hanging their bodies if necessary.

In regard to women, let the rulers render justice: by cutting off their noses, lips, ears, and breasts, and by burning them at the stake if necessary. And since a land cannot live without justice, therefore it is granted to the rulers to render justice. And just as it is granted to them to render justice, thus it is permissible for them to release and pardon whomever they please.

74. Let all offenses committed during the truce of the Lord always be doubly compensated, except for those persons who are ejected from the peace and truce of the Lord.

75. Let a truce given between friends and enemies be observed and maintained without deceit for all time. Indeed, if, God forbid! it is violated in any way, let simple restitution be made.

77. If one suffers any wrong, and, before he seeks vengeance for it, consequently seeks justice and if the malefactor promises to render justice to him and he [the victim], refusing it, afterwards commits another crime, first let him make compensation for the wrong which he has committed and afterwards let him then receive justice from the malefactor from whom justice must then be rendered him. But if the malefactor resists justice and he afterwards suffers any wrong, let no compensation be made him in any way.

78. Likewise, the aforesaid princes decreed that rulers shall confirm and maintain for all time the peace and truce of the Lord, and act to have it confirmed and maintained by the magnates and knights of the land, as well as all men living in their country. And if anyone violates the peace and truce of the Lord in any way, he must make restitution according to the judgment of the bishops.

79. If anyone has vassals who, without his order or consent, commit any wrong to another and he promises to render justice between them and the other parties and he wishes to post a surety so that he should act to render justice and if he who has suffered the crime does not want to receive justice and thereafter commits some crime to any of the vassals, first, let him make restitution just as it was judged for the crime he has committed and then let him receive justice from the lord for his vassals just as a lord is bound to render it for them. Thus just as a reprisal committed because of a deprivation of justice must in no way remain in effect, so compensation shall not be made.

80. If a person has any grievance against another and summons him to render justice, and he, for the fear of God, nor by an order of a judge, nor by the advice of relatives and friends, wants to render justice to the plaintiff

and the plaintiff, moved by anger, steals his chattels, burns down his houses, destroys his standing crops, vines, and trees, and then at any times afterwards the defendant comes to justice, first, let him make restitution for any damage he has done to the plaintiff and for the profit which he might have garnered from the plaintiff's possessions, and then let the plaintiff give back any of the defendant's possessions he might have. But indeed if any of these possessions were consumed, let him restore as much profit as he garnered to the present time and afterwards let the defendant render justice to the plaintiff, as is obligatory and fitting for him to do.

81. If anyone is proven guilty and convicted of homicide, let him come into the custody of the deceased's next-of-kin and their lord. If he does not want to or cannot render justice, they can do what they wish with him, short of his death.

82. Concerning the compensation for all men who were killed, their sons or relatives, from whom a legitimate succession is fitting for the claim of inheritance, could charge the defendant or murderer, and undoubtedly have the right to take vengeance on him. But if they do this, let them have the compensation for homicide just as it was decreed to be done concerning defendants or murderers according to the laws or the customs of their land.

95. When a peasant suffers injury to the body or damage to his property or fief, let him in no way dare take vengeance or settle the dispute but as soon as he suffers the wrong, then let him make an end to this matter in accordance with his lord's command.

123. The judgments of the court and the rules of customary law must be freely accepted and observed, since they were only issued because of the severity of the law, in that, everybody can file suit according to the law but not everyone can carry out all compensation in accordance with the laws which judge that homicide is to be compensated by three hundred golden *solidi* which is worth four thousand fine silver sous; the putting out of an eye, by a hundred; the cutting off a hand, by a hundred; of a foot, by a hundred; and the same for other members of [the] body. Of course, they judge all men equally and indeed rule noting [relations] between vassal and lord. Since these things must be done or were done in accordance with the rules of customary law, the aforesaid princes ruled that all judgments shall be rendered according to the rules of customary law, and when the rules of customary law are not sufficient, let the laws, the ruling of the prince, and the judgment of his court be reverted to.

124. If anyone lies in ambush during the truce of God, or arranges for an ambush within the fief or the boundaries of his enemy's castle and commits a crime through this ambush on the day after the truce ends, he therefore must make compensation as if he had done it during the truce of the Lord.

125. The above-mentioned princes ruled that everyone shall wait for his adversary until the third hour of the day. Indeed, then if he so wishes, let him take possession of the pledges and consider this failure to appear to be a deprivation of justice if the adversary himself who has failed to come to the tribunal does not consider himself to be without deceit. And if he does retain them, he may not demand the suit's adjudication through his advocate. This is not so between vassals and their lords – it seems fitting that vassals wait for their lords until the ninth hour [3 PM].

B6. Those who were enemies the day before or shortly before cannot be plaintiffs or witnesses so that they, in anger, should not desire to cause harm or take vengeance. There an unobstructed, uninfluenced, and believable will of the plaintiffs and witnesses must be sought. Let those who seem capable of being commanded by the parties for whom they appear as witnesses not be considered credible witnesses.

## 53. RULES FOR TRIAL BY COMBAT IN BRESCIA

*This July 1158 decree of the assembly at Brescia, in northern Italy, ordered trial by combat as the means of resolving a murder case. Earlier in the Middle Ages, trial by combat had been used to settle property-based claims, such as for charges of theft of property worth over six solidi and disputes over whether a charter was false (see Doc. 87). Over the course of the twelfth century, all types of judicial ordeals became increasingly common throughout Europe. Although the practice of the judicial ordeal was banned at the Fourth Lateran Council in 1215, trial by combat persisted for several centuries, especially in aristocratic circles.*

*The rules for trial by combat found in the Brescia document also exemplify attempts by the Church to regulate violence through a legal procedure built around the recognition of the strength of ties of family and friendship.*

Source: *Conventus Brixiae*, ed. G. Pertz, Monumenta Germaniae Historica: Legum, vol. 2 (Hanover: Hahn, 1837), p. 107–8. Trans. Kelly Gibson.

3. If anyone commits homicide and is convicted by someone close to the slain or by a friend or a companion by means of two true witnesses who are not blood relations of the slain, he shall suffer capital punishment. But if witnesses are lacking and the slayer wishes to exculpate himself by oath, a close friend of the slain can challenge him to a duel.

... Archbishops, bishops, and abbots, after giving their right hands, confirmed this truce for themselves and vowed that violators of the peace must be punished with the severity of the pontifical office.

## 54. THE PENITENTIAL OF ALAIN OF LILLE

*The penitential written by Alain of Lille (1125/30–1203) was a manual designed for use by confessors of the laity, rather than for other religious. He dedicated it to Henri de Sully, archbishop of Bourges and a great helper in the pope's reforms. Educated at Chartres and a teacher at Paris (ca 1150–ca 1185) and afterwards at Montpellier, Alain was a poet, theologian, and preacher. It is likely that he wrote his penitential while he was in southern France to take part in fighting against the Cathar heresy in the region (ca between 1191 and 1199). For this work, he collected some of the important statements made by previous authors of penitentials and made them available in a convenient volume.*

Source: ed. Jean Longère, *Liber poenitentialis,* vol. 2 (Louvain: Éditions Nauwelaerts, 1965), pp. 55–59. Trans. Daniel Lord Smail.

[Book 2, chapters 14–20]

From the *decretum* of Pope Miltiades. In the Council of Tribur, fourth chapter. Concerning voluntary homicide.

It is to be seen what were the divisions of the ancient form of making amends, and how, according to modern times and according to the state of the sinners, some part of that severity might be remitted. We read in the penitentials that if anyone shall have committed homicide voluntarily, and not for some necessary purpose, nor while in an army, but through his own desire so that he might elevate himself above his station, he shall do penance for forty days in a row, which in the vernacular is called *carentia* [privation], so that, according to custom, he might do penance on bread and water and observe, for the following seven years, as follows.

The first year after those forty days, he ought to abstain completely from wine, mead, sweet wine, beer and from *moras* [a type of drink], and from meat and blood, and from cheese and all oily fishes, except on those feast days in the bishopric where he remains [which] are celebrated by the whole population. If he is engaged in some great travel, or is involved at the royal court or has some illness, he may be allowed to redeem the third and fifth day and the sabbath for one penny or the price of one penny or in feeding three paupers. In other words, he might partake of one thing from the three mentioned above, that is to say, he might either drink wine, or mead, or sweet wine, or beer. After he gets home, however, or is restored to health, he shall no longer have the ability to redeem. Once the whole year is complete, let him be brought back to church and let the kiss of peace be granted to him.

In the second and third year, he shall fast in the similar fashion, except that he has the ability to redeem the third and fifth day and the sabbath for the price named above. Let him faithfully observe all the rest, as listed at the outset.

For each of the four remaining years, he ought to fast for three forty-day periods on legitimate holidays. The first before Easter, like other Christians; the next before the birth of Saint John the Baptist, and if anything is left over, let it be fulfilled afterward; the third before the birth of our Lord; let him abstain from wine, mead, sweet wine, beer, from blood and cheese and oily fishes during these days.

After the four years mentioned above, he may take on the third and fifth day and the sabbath whatever he wishes. He can now, moreover, redeem the second and fourth day, as above. He must always fast on bread and water on the sixth day and, having completed all this, let him take holy communion with this purpose, that he never be without penance for as long as he shall live, but instead do penance on bread and water every sixth day for his whole life. And if he wishes to redeem, let him have the ability to redeem for one penny, or the price of one penny, or by feeding three paupers. We allow him thus, following mercy and according to the penalty of the canons, since the holy canons order it.

From the council of Nantes. Concerning a homicide which is done for money.

If anyone shall have committed a homicide through effort and greed, let him give up the world and be enrolled in a monastery of monks, where he might serve God obediently.

From the Penitential of Theodore. Concerning homicide which is done for vengeance. Has he committed a homicide so as to avenge kinfolk? If he does so, let him do penance for forty days, since the Lord says: Vengeance is mine, I shall take revenge.

From the Council of Nantes. Concerning he who wished to wound but not kill someone but nevertheless killed. If he did the homicide without wishing to do so, so that in anger he wished to strike someone and not kill but nevertheless killed, let him do penance for forty days on bread and water and observe the seven following years in the manner described above. But on the first, third, and fifth day and on the sabbath he is able to redeem [his penance], each one for a single penny, or for feeding three paupers. Let him observe the remaining six years, however, as was described for homicides willfully committed.

From the Council of Paris. Concerning he who was defending himself from enemies and killed an innocent man. If anyone shall not have committed a homicide willfully but instead shall have killed an innocent and simple bystander while resisting a violent attack and acting with force, let him do grave penance up to the end of his life. Nevertheless, if he fulfills the penance well, the viaticum of communion shall not be denied to him at his end.

From the Council of Tours. Concerning he who, having lost his mind, kills a man. If any raving man shall have killed anyone, if he returns to a healthy mind, there ought to be imposed upon him a penance that is lighter than on one who commits such a thing in sound mind. Although penance ought to be imposed on him, since the illness is believed to have been the cause of the sin, the penance that is to be imposed ought to be that much lighter than that imposed on he who has killed someone while of sound mind, as the difference that can be discerned between health and sane and between rational and irrational.

From the Council of Vienne and at Verberie concerning those who are fighting with one man and he is killed by them. If a number of men shall have fought against one man and he shall have died from these wounds, whoever sprung the trap on him is to be judged according to the statutes of the canons as a homicide. The rest of those who attacked him, wishing to kill him, shall do penance in a similar fashion. They who were neither attacking, nor inflicting any injury, nor aiding by advice or assistance, but nevertheless were present, are free from punishment.

# 55. THE PENITENTIAL OF ROBERT OF FLAMBOROUGH

*Robert was a regular canon in the abbey of St. Victor in Paris; originally, he was probably from Flamborough in Yorkshire. This penitential (1208–13) was the first manual for confessors to incorporate the emerging collections and practice of canon law into its stipulations and penalties. In the section below, concerning homicide committed for the sake of vengeance, compare the penance assigned by Robert to those listed in the earlier medieval penitentials (Doc. 17) and Alain of Lille's (Doc. 54).*

Source: ed. J. J. Francis Firth, *Liber Poenitentialis: A Critical Edition with Introduction and Notes* (Toronto: Pontifical Institute of Mediaeval Studies, 1971), pp. 223–27. Trans. Daniel Lord Smail.

### 5.2.8. On Simple Homicides

260. If anyone through his own passion shall have willfully committed a homicide, let him do penance in this way. First, so that he might have leave to enter into church, let him walk barefooted for the next forty days, and

let him not be brought by any means of conveyance; he shall wear woolen garments with no leg coverings; he may not bear arms, and let him partake of nothing for these forty days apart from some bread and salt, and he shall drink unmixed water; and he shall not take communion with other Christians nor food or drink with another penitent before the forty days are complete. No one else may consume the food that he eats. Taking into account the condition of his body or illness, he may be allowed some fruit or greens or vegetables among the other things, whatever seems right; and from canonical authority it shall be entirely forbidden to him that he join with any female during this time, nor shall he approach his own wife, nor may he sleep with any man. Let him attend the church before whose doors he wept for his sin; and let him not go about from place to place, but stay in one place for these forty days. But in situations where he might meet up with men lying in ambush along his path, let his penance be deferred by the bishop until peace has been granted by his enemies. And if he is held back by an illness such that he cannot do penance, let the penance be deferred until he is restored to health. If, however, he is held back by a long sickness, it is in the hands of the bishop to decide the question of how the matter and the infirmity ought to be handled. Once the forty days have been completed, cleansed with water, he shall take up his clothing and his shoes again and trim his hair.

261. For the first year after the forty days, let him abstain for the entire year from wine, mead and honeyed beer, from meat and cheese and oily fishes, apart from the holy days which are celebrated by the entire population in that bishopric, unless perchance he shall be engaged in a long journey or the royal army or held back by a sickness. In this case, he shall be allowed to buy back every third day, fifth day, and the sabbath by means of a penny or a pennyworth or by feeding three paupers, so, to be precise, he may enjoy one of three things, namely, wine or mead or beer. After he returns to his house or is restored to health, he shall no longer have the ability to buy back. Once the year is complete, let him be brought to church and let the kiss of peace be granted to him.

In the second and third year he shall fast in a similar fashion, unless he has the power to buy back the third and fifth day and the sabbath by means of a payment wherever he is. He shall faithfully observe all the others as in the first year. For each of the four years which remain, he must fast for three Lents and legitimate days. During these four years, let him take whatever he might desire on the third and fifth day and the sabbath. The second and fourth day he can buy back for the said price. The sixth day he shall always observe by means of bread and water. Once these are completed, let him take holy communion with the understanding that he should not be without penance for as long as he lives, but for his entire life he shall do penance every sixth day. If he should wish to buy it back, however, let him have that power in the manner described above, and this according to mercy, not according to canonical measure, since the canons require thus: if anyone shall have committed this [crime] through effort or desire, let him abandon the world and enter a monastery and there let him serve God continuously.

262. Just as the seven years of public penance are divided up in this way, so in fact the question of where penances are divided up in public are not found, but it is simply said regarding penance: "Let him do penance for forty days on bread and water and for the seven following years," not at any rate on bread and water as in the first forty days, but instead just as their division can be found here or there or in some other authentic document.

263. If anyone shall have killed a man deliberately and by means of plots, let him submit to continual penance. And if this action was publicly observed, if he is a layman, let him be removed from the communion of prayers for five years; after five years, however, let him receive the communion of prayers, but let him neither offer nor touch the body of the Lord; having suffered in this condition for fourteen years, then let him be received to full communion with oblations.

If anyone shall have committed homicide deliberately, let him always lie before the door of the church, and take communion at the end of his life. If, however, he shall not have committed a homicide deliberately, but for some other reason, the first canon required him to do penance for seven years, a second ordered five.

If anyone shall have committed homicide willfully, and, not violently resisting but instead acting with force, he shall have killed an innocent man of simple status, he shall do weighty penance until the end of his life; but nevertheless, if he completes the penance well, at his death the viaticum shall not be denied to him.

5.2.10. Concerning those who publicly kill a penitent. If anyone in public shall have killed a man doing penance, let him do penance doubly for a homicide willfully committed, and let him not take communion except at the end.

5.2.11. Concerning a homicide done for the sake of vengeance. He who shall have killed a man to avenge a brother or other kinfolk, let him do penance thus as for a homicide willfully committed, since Truth itself says: Vengeance is mine and I shall retaliate.

5.2.12. Concerning a homicide not committed willfully. If anyone by chance shall have perpetrated a homicide not willingly, let him do penance for forty days on bread and water. With these done, he shall be excluded from the prayer of the faithful for the space of two years, nor shall he take communion nor offer it. After two years, he shall be taken back into the communion of prayer; he may offer communion [that is, a priest may do so] but may not take it. After a period of five years, he shall be received to full communion. Let the manner of his abstention from food rest in the judgment of the priest.

## 56. GENERAL CONSTITUTION CONCERNING JUDGMENTS AND KEEPING THE PEACE

*Emperor Frederick II (1212–50) was one of the great rulers of the Holy Roman Empire. Frederick's general constitution, printed below, is typical of the kinds of orders sent out in the dozens and hundreds by thirteenth-century kings and rulers throughout Europe. A noteworthy feature of this act from 1234, and one shared by the genre, is the declaration that those who neglected to follow the commands of the ruler risked incurring his anger.*

Source: ed. G. Pertz, Monumenta Germaniae Historica: Legum, vol. 2 (Hanover: Hahn, 1837), pp. 301–2. Trans. Daniel Lord Smail.

An order concerning the preservation of peace. Frederick, by the grace of God emperor of the Romans, eternal Augustus, and king of Sicily, sends his favor and every good thing to all the archbishops, bishops, abbots, dukes, nobles, freemen, and *ministeriales* [unfree knights in the service of the king] appointed in the realm. You should doubtless be aware and in no way doubt that, if your lands are in an evil state, and there is a disturbance in your regions, as we have heard, that this is displeasing to us in every way, and we intend to apply all the efforts of which we are capable so that it may be corrected in the best possible manner. For this reason, we order you, so as to maintain our favor, to swear to a firm peace within four weeks at the court being held at Frankfurt, including both the wealthy and the poor from among our subjects, and they should also swear and preserve the peace. To this we attentively add and command that whosoever shall not have sworn, and neglects to fulfill our order, should be aware that he has incurred our anger. And we also wish this, that those who have contempt for our order be called openly into our presence at the next meeting to be held of the court.

# CHAPTER NINE: SERMONS AND LEARNED COMMENTARY ON ANGER AND VENGEANCE

*In the eleventh century, the norms of Christian piety began to be collated into great col-
lections of canon law (see Doc. 44) and academic treatises, including Thomas Aquinas's
influential* Summa Theologiae *(Doc. 67). To those who did this work, however, it was
not enough merely to collect and systematize these norms. A major goal of the Church,
in the wake of the ecclesiastical reform movement of the eleventh century, was to transmit
established, accepted religious norms to the laity by means of sermons and* exempla. *The
idea of peace and emotional restraint was an especially noteworthy element of these sermons. The growing chorus of writers creating treatises and sermons on the importance of
these ideas and attitudes, of course, does not reflect the actual influence such exhortations
might have had in actually changing the behaviour of the general population.*

## 57. AELFRIC'S SERMON ON ANGER AND PEACE

*Aelfric (955–1020) was trained at Winchester's Old Minster under Bishop Aethelwold
(r. 963–984), who had replaced the secular clergy at Winchester's Old Minster with
Benedictine monks. Like his teacher, Aelfric adhered to the ideals of this monastic
reform movement. Around 987, he went to Cerne Abbey in Dorset, where he issued
eighty English homilies in two sets (990–994). Each set runs through the whole year,
providing homilies for Sundays and the general feast days of the year, though not every
Sunday has a homily – there are only ten homilies for the twenty-seven Sundays after
Pentecost. Aelfric names Augustine, Jerome, Bede, Gregory the Great, Smaragdus,
and Haymo of Halberstadt as his sources, most of whom we have already encountered
in this volume.*

*The particular sermon below, written for the seventh Sunday after Pentecost, took
Matthew 5:20–22 (see Doc. 9a) as its text.*

Source: trans. Carmen Acevedo Butcher, *God of Mercy: Aelfric's Sermons and Theology* (Macon,
GA: Mercer University Press, 2006), pp. 134–37.

Moses's law commanded the scribes and Pharisees to love their friend and hate
their enemy. But while he was here in this world, the Savior commanded us
to always love our friend and every Christian person without pretense, and
also – because of God's love – to love our enemy, so our righteousness would
be greater than theirs. Remember, we are destined to enjoy the heavenly life,
if we are obedient to God's commands with works....

"You have heard the commands God gave long ago to the Israelites under Moses's law, saying these things to them: 'Don't kill. Whoever kills a person will be subject to a judge's sentence.' I tell you, however, that whoever is now angry with his own brother will be subject to judgment." At that Judgment the nature of a person's offense is determined, and often someone who previously had been considered guilty will be declared innocent there. And good will can pacify a person's unexpected anger, and also wisdom can arrest it more easily than a person can make amends if he kills someone he is angry with. Lawful judgment is prescribed for both anger and for murder. But a person's penance is lighter if the one he is angry with is still alive. Even if a person is angry, his anger will heal, as the latter part of this Gospel tells us, so we can be reconciled to the person whom we offended earlier.

"Whoever speaks an insult to his brother will be subject to judgment." Here now are two things, anger and insult. And judgment is prescribed for these two things, so by means of deliberation an offender will be sentenced to punishment and will suffer for them both. But sometimes a guilty person escapes, as the interpreter [Augustine] tells us in Latin.

"And whoever calls him a foolish person will be in danger of punishment in the tormenting fire of the world to come." Here are now three things, and therefore greater punishment: anger, insult, and disdain. And as the book tells us, these things must be purified in the future punishment, unless a person voluntarily makes amends for them. Here in this world a person can make amends for much greater sins and can appease the Savior, so he does not need to suffer in the life to come. Through his prophet, God said he will have mercy on every person who turns from his sins to him and does penance with groaning. Afterwards that person's sins will not be in God's memory....

Let us now learn the Savior's remedy. Let us see how here in this world we can heal the evil words we have said against someone we have provoked. "If you offer God any sacrifice at his altar, and then you remember your brother has something against you, set your sacrifice down before the altar, and first go quickly to your brother and be reconciled to him. And when you come again, offer your sacrifice." The Savior said again in another place: "When you stand at your prayers, then forgive in your hearts all the people who have sinned against you, so the heavenly Father may forgive your sins. And unless you forgive, God will not forgive you."

When our brother has something against us, if we injured him or did him wrong, then we must act according to our Lord's teaching and determine to be reconciled to our brother, that Christian person, without pretense, so God himself can gladly receive our gift. Before that reconciliation and before we have peace in a truthful heart, God would have been unwilling to receive anything from us. If any person injures us or wrongs us, we must forgive it, as the Savior said, so our sins can be forgiven us.

Our sacrifices are the holy prayers we offer God and the alms we give to help the poor, and every thing we do as praise to our Lord. These are all God's sacrifices, and we should offer them with good will, so they will be acceptable and pleasing to God, who always loves peace, and always judges all people with gentleness.

Concerning this, the psalmist sang these words to God, *Adiutor meus, tibi [p]sallam*, etc. [Ps. 58:18]. That is in English: "You are my Helper, and I sing to You. You are my Protector, my own true God, and my Mercy." God commanded him to have mercy because God himself is merciful, and in countless ways God helps anyone who with singleness of mind always puts their trust in our Lord.

To whom is glory and honor forever. Amen.

## 58. WULFSTAN'S "SERMON OF THE WOLF" ON THE EVILS OF HIS DAY

*Wulfstan (d. 1023) was bishop of London from 996 to 1002, and then became archbishop of York and of Worcester from 1002 to 1016. He wrote a work of political theory concerned with the duties of the different ranks of society, the "Institutes of Polity," and, after 1008, composed much of the legislation of the English kings Aethelred and Canute. He wrote numerous homilies, of which this one, written in 1014, is the most famous. Here, as in most Christian sources of the time, Wulfstan saw the Viking raids that had been savaging England both as God's retribution against those who had wronged him with their sinful life and as a warning to correct ways before the Last Judgment.*

Source: trans. Michael Swanton, *Anglo-Saxon Prose* (London: Dent, 1975), pp. 118–20.

Beloved men, recognize what the truth is: this world is in haste and it is drawing near the end, and therefore the longer it is the worse it will get in the world. And it needs must thus become very much worse as a result of the people's sins prior to the advent of Antichrist; and then, indeed, it will be terrible and cruel throughout the world. Understand properly also that for many years now the Devil has led this nation too far astray, and that there has been little loyalty among men although they spoke fair, and too many wrongs have prevailed in the land. And there were never many men who sought a remedy as diligently as they should; but daily they added one evil to another, and embarked on many wrongs and unlawful acts, all too commonly throughout this whole nation. And on that account, we have also suffered many injuries and insults. And if we are to expect any remedy then we must deserve better of God than we have done hitherto. Because we have earned the miseries which oppress us by great demerit, we must obtain the cure from God, if it is to improve henceforth by very great merit. Indeed, we know full well that a great breach requires a great repair and a great conflagration no little water if one is to quench the fire at all. And the necessity is great for every man henceforth to observe God's law diligently and pay God's dues properly.... But it is true what I say; there is need of a remedy, because ... the laws of the people have deteriorated all too much....

For it is clear and evident in us all that we have hitherto more often transgressed than we have atoned, and therefore many things fall upon this nation. For long now, nothing has prospered here or elsewhere, but in every region there has been devastation and famine, burning and bloodshed over and again. And stealing and slaughter, plague and pestilence, murrain and disease, slander and hatred, and the plundering of robbers have damaged us very severely ... wherefore for many years now, so it seems, there have been in this country many injustices and unsteady loyalties among men everywhere. Now very often kinsman will not protect a kinsman any more than a stranger, nor a father his son, nor sometimes a son his own father, nor one brother another. Nor has any of us regulated his life just as he ought, neither clerics according to rule, nor laymen according to the law. But all too frequently, we have made lust a law to us, and have kept neither the teachings nor the laws of God or man just as we ought; nor has anyone intended loyally towards another as justly as he ought, but almost all men have betrayed and injured others by word and deed; and in any case, almost all men wrongfully stab others in the back with shameful attack; let him do more if he can. For there are here in the land great disloyalties towards God and towards the state, and there are also many here in the country who are betrayers of their lords in various ways.... And they have destroyed too many godfathers and godchildren widely throughout this nation, as well as too many other innocent people who have been all too commonly slain....

... Many are forsworn and greatly perjured, and pledges are broken over and again; and it is evident in this nation that the wrath of God violently oppresses us, let him realize it who can.

And indeed, how can more shame befall men through the wrath of God than frequently does us on account of our own deeds? If any slave escape from his lord, and, leaving Christendom, becomes a Viking, and after that it happens that an armed encounter occurs between thegn and slave; if the slave should slay the thegn outright he will lie without payment to any of his family; and if the thegn should slay outright the slave whom he previously owned, he will pay the price of a thegn. Over-cowardly laws and shameful tributes are, through the wrath of God, common among us, understand it who can; and many misfortunes befall this nation over and again.... And often ten or twelve, one after another, will disgracefully insult the thegn's wife, and sometimes his daughter or near kinswoman, while he who considered himself proud and powerful and brave enough before that happened, looks on.... But all the disgrace we often suffer we repay with honor to those who bring shame on us....

## 59. PETER DAMIAN ON RESTRAINING ANGER

*Peter Damian (ca 1007–72) was one of the leading figures in the papal reform movement of the eleventh century. Born in Ravenna, he studied at Faenza and Parma and later took the sobriquet "Damian" in honor of the brother who had provided for his education. From 1035 onward, he lived a life of extreme austerity in the hermitage at Fonte Avella. After being chosen prior of Fonte Avella around 1043, he began founding new monasteries and reforming old ones, eventually becoming cardinal of Ostia in 1057. He was famous for preaching against the worldliness of the clergy, and also against the practice of simony (the buying or selling of religious offices, indulgences, or pardons), as seen in "On Restraining Anger" below. His other surviving writings include 180 letters, saints' lives, a defense of the validity of sacraments given by priests guilty of simony, and an attack against homosexuality. He also wrote a dialogue between an advocate of the king and a defender of the Roman Church in order to encourage the synod that met at Augsburg in 1062 to declare the legitimacy of Pope Alexander II, who had been elected by a council called by the imperial court of Henry IV.*

*"On Restraining Anger" is an important and forceful warning to Damian's listeners on how vengeful emotions can cause the loss of reason. What also makes this excerpt interesting is his understanding of the nature of the Christian sacrament: that is, that its original purpose is to restore peace. Damian wrote "On Restraining Anger" for Bishop V. (who is otherwise unknown), who had recently recovered from an illness. Perhaps in the hope that the bishop be more receptive to advice after having been at risk of death, Peter apparently took this opportunity to urge the bishop to restrain his anger.*

Source: De frenenda ira et simultatibus exstirpandis, *Patrologia Latina* 145 (Paris: Migne, 1867), cols. 654–56. Trans. Daniel Lord Smail.

## 5. That anger makes man insane

So you see how it is that anger makes a man insane, for while he is doing whatever impatience suggests, he offers food for mockery to those who ridicule him. Through every vice which is perpetrated by men, of course, the venom of the ancient enemy has various ways to suffuse a miserable heart. In the curse of wrath, truly, the serpent strikes at all his own entrails; vomiting, it pours out every bitterness of gall. In such a way it makes a prudent man witless, a reasonable man wild, and renders insane a man who is innately clever. Indeed, wrath sends the wretched into exile, and compels them, like demons, to act crazily. Certainly, whatever is altogether prohibited to all Christians, ought to be especially shunned by priests. For truth teaches all the faithful in common that whosoever is in a state of disagreement should forsake his gift before the altar and dare not to offer it before he is reconciled to his brother for any injury [Matt. 5:24]. Since this is so, a priest ought to be much more willing to do likewise, that is to say he who will offer not a pile of metal, not a pearl liable to decay, especially not a handful of grain fields, but the sacrament of the life-giving eucharist! And since from the very beginning that unique sacrifice is offered on behalf of enemies, as the Apostle bears witness by saying "Although we were enemies, we were reconciled to God through the death of his son" [Rom. 5:10], with what attitude toward so terrifying a sacrament, with what audacity of rashness does he dare to approach the feast of the heavenly table, if, while he is celebrating the mystery of reconciliation, he scorns to be reconciled with his own brother? A man in a state of enmity offers the host, which dissolves enmities; lacking peace, he approaches the mystery of peace. For it is better for the sinner to renounce the sacrifice than to offer the glorious host; and it is more pleasing to God for the sinner to renounce the holocaust of good will than to offer the sacrament of a strange offering.

Whence, not idly do we believe that if anything is set in place by these words, it is spread about through an account celebrated by not a few people. A certain man, it is said, killed a man more powerful than him. Following the customs of the age, not the principles of the Holy Gospel, he then suffered many troublesome attacks by the man's son, that is to say, the avenger of the dead father, who exhaled massacres of men and sucked back in the booty of frequent robberies. Caught by the murderer in these difficult straits, accordingly, he resolved to approach the emperor on his road, in case he could perchance find solace for his many calamities. Having ascertained this, the avenger of his father's blood came in pursuit and followed him energetically, either to bind him by the law of the tribunes or to crush him suddenly with swords. At the time, the emperor was in Germany. And so, since the killer was marching along carelessly, advancing without haste, and since the one pursuing him was hurrying along at all speed, finally it happened that, drawing near to each other, they were brought face to face with each other. Yet he who was guilty of homicide was accompanied by scarcely four or five followers, and since the son of the slain man was in contrast surrounded by nearly thirty servants in arms, the killer urged his men to run away. Seeing that he himself could not get away from the hands of those persecuting him, he begged for the protection of the soul, and took sanctuary in the shelter of humility. Throwing away his weapons, his arms extended in the manner of the cross, he fell down upon the ground, and awaited either the pardon of compassionate men or the blows of assailants. But he who was now the victor, staying his hand out of reverence for the cross, held back; beyond that, he forbade that he be smitten by anyone. In the end, making a sound peace in honor of the holy life-giving cross, he not only restored the man's life, but even remitted the injury of his father's death.

With this victory achieved through honor, he emerged as the victor not so much of another as of himself, and, as I would grant, a conqueror not so much over an enemy as over his own heart. He went to the royal court, since it was not far off: but as soon as he entered the church to pray, there happened a thing wondrous and astonishing beyond measure, for the image of the Savior, visibly expressed on the cross, was seen to salute him three times by inclining its head.

O, how glorious and worthy of heralds, that he should deserve to be received reverently by the author of mercy, he who thanks to his own reverence foreswore to avenge himself; and to receive the honor of salvation from him for whom he set aside a vengeance incompatible with salvation. Hearing this, the emperor immediately received him honorably and with kindly feelings, as he deserved, and liberally heaped upon him an abundance of gifts. O, if that man exercised the duty of the priestly order, how confidently could he approach God bearing the gift! On the contrary, whosoever piles up the confusions of anger or hatred in his heart, and anticipates the moment of vengeful retribution, how perniciously, how harmfully does he approach the sacred altars! Men, indeed, abandon to the flames that which is given to us for the increase of consolation.

# 60. A LETTER BY PETER DAMIAN ON THE VENGEANCE OF SPIRITUAL LEADERS

*Peter Damian wrote this letter in early 1062, from his cell at Fonte Avella, to Olderic, the bishop of Fermo. The schism in the Church caused by the election of the antipope Honorius II (see Doc. 59), among other crises of the time, are mentioned in the letter to indicate Damian's feeling that the world was nearing an end. The schism also allowed him to raise the question of whether bishops and abbots should be allowed to take up arms to defend their property. This source can be read in conjunction with the 1098 judgment that describes a champion engaging in trial by combat on behalf of a church in a land dispute (Doc. 87).*

Source: trans. Owen J. Blum, *Peter Damian, Letters 61–90* (Washington, DC: Catholic University of America Press, 1992), pp. 303–8.

[Letter 87]

... But since amid such evils that insolently occur in our day, with violent men seizing our very churches and invading the lands and other properties dedicated to sacred use, some raise the question whether spiritual leaders should not seek revenge and, like laymen, repay evil for evil. For there are many who, as soon as violence is used against them, at once rush out and declare war, gather their armed men, and thus punish their enemies more severely, perhaps, than they themselves were injured. But to me this seems to be quite absurd, that the very priests of the Lord should attempt to carry out the very thing they forbid their people to do, and to assert in deed what they attack in word. For what is more certainly contrary to Christian Law than repaying injury with injury? Where, I ask, are all the proclamations of Scripture? Where are the Lord's own words: "When a man takes what is yours, do not demand it back?" [Luke 6:30, with wide variation from the Vulgate]. And if we are not allowed to take back the very things that were stolen from us, how it is permissible in their regard to seek revenge and to inflict wounds in retribution? There is also this in Scripture: "If someone slaps you on the right cheek, turn and offer him your left. If he makes you go one mile, go with him two. If he takes away your shirt, let him have your coat as well" [cf. Matt. 5:39–41].

But perhaps someone will object that these rules are for laymen and not for bishops, that is, that the heads of churches must preach such things, but not observe them. Yet even a fool would have such ideas, since the Lord says, "If a man sets aside even the least of the Law's demands, and teaches others to do the same, he will have the lowest place in the kingdom of heaven, whereas anyone who keeps the Law, and teaches others so, will stand high in the kingdom of Heaven" [cf. Matt. 5:19]. Therefore, a bishop who would attain a high position in the kingdom of heaven should lead the way for his people, so that what he prescribes in word for those who follow him, he should first fulfill in living deeds. And so, to avoid every occasion for misunderstanding, as the first among all the Church's priests he should not say, "Lord, how often should a brother forgive a brother if he goes on wronging him?" But rather, speaking as one who has assumed the burden of all other priests, he should say, "Lord, how often am I to forgive my brother if he goes on wronging me?" [Matt. 18:21–22]. And when the reply comes back that he should forgive "seventy times seven times," there can be no doubt that this universal command must also be observed by bishops. On the evidence of Luke the evangelist we learn that, when the Lord was on his way to Jerusalem, the disciples set out and went into a Samaritan village to make arrangements for him [cf. Luke 9:52]. But when the Samaritans would not have them, James and John were angry and, letting human nature have its way, they said, "Lord, may we call down fire from heaven to burn them up, as Elijah did?" [Luke 9:54; cf. 2 Kings 1:10–12]. But he turned and rebuked them: "You do not know," he said, "to what spirit you belong; for the Son of Man did not come to destroy men's lives but to save them" [Luke 9:55–56]. And then he continued thus: "And when they went on to another village," as if he were saying, not in so many words, but by his actions, "Do not seek revenge" [Rom. 12:19]; or rather, what he himself said, "when you are persecuted in one town, take refuge in another" [Matt. 10:23].

Evidently, our savior's earthly life, no less than his preaching, is for us the gospel and his proposal for the direction in which our life should progress. And so, just as he overcame all obstacles of a world gone mad, not by threats of dire punishment but by the insuperable majesty of his resolute patience, he taught us in this way to bear quietly this rabid world, rather than to take up arms or to answer him who harms us with injuries. This is especially so, since within the *imperium* [the sphere of secular authority] and the *sacerdotium* [the sphere of the priestly order] we must distinguish functions that are proper to each, so that the king may employ secular arms, while the bishop should buckle on the sword of the spirit, which is the word of God [cf. Eph. 6:17]. For Paul says of the secular prince, "It is not for nothing that he holds the power of the sword, for he is God's agent of punishment, for retribution on the offender" [Rom. 13:4]. Because King Uzziah usurped the priestly office he was afflicted with leprosy [cf. 2 Chron. 26:19–21], and what price will a bishop pay if he takes up arms, which is a function that belongs to laymen? Indeed, we may say that even before the preaching of the gospel, David lived according to evangelical principles, since we find him sparing not only Shimei and Saul, but many other enemies. To this I might add further examples from the other holy Fathers, if I were not certain that these and other cases are much better known to you than they are to me.

Clearly, who is not aware how indecently confusing it would be for the Church brazenly to do the very thing against which it inveighs and, while preaching patience to others, to react against those who do her harm with unbridled anger?...

[On charity and patience]. Armed with these virtues, the founding apostles built Holy Church and with their help, its champions, the holy martyrs, triumphantly suffered various kinds of death. If, therefore, it is never permitted to take up arms in defense of the faith by which the universal Church lives, how may armored hosts revel in bloodshed for the sake of earthly and transitory possessions of the Church? Moreover, if when holy men prevailed, they never killed heretics and idolators, but instead refused to flee death at their hands for the sake of the Catholic faith, how can a Christian wage war against a Christian over the loss of trivial things, since he is not unaware that the other was also redeemed by the blood of Christ?

The event that I now relate came to my attention as having happened in Gaul. A grave dispute over lands occurred between an abbot and a certain most powerful secular lord. After the supporters of each had engaged in protracted quarrels and threats, both sides at length decided to fight it out. The secular prince, indeed, after gathering his troops, entered the field of battle, drew up his lines, and arranged his forces. With a vigorous harangue he fired up his men to fight bravely. The place was dense with swords and red with shields, and the clamor of shouting men grew more intense. The threatening clash of armed men was frightening as they unsheathed their weapons, and only the attack by the opposing side was awaited by excited men prepared to engage. But the abbot, placing his hope not in the earthly weapons but in him who had won man's salvation, forbade all those who had come to fight for him to enter the fray. Advancing, with only his monks mounted on horses, he ordered them to cover their heads with their cowls and so, under the banner of the cross, came to the site of battle with his monks covered and corseted with the arms of faith. When his opponent, as he had hoped, saw nothing of weapons but beheld something like a heavenly and angelic array approaching, such a dreadful fear of God gripped him and all his men that, dismounting from their horses, they at once threw down their arms, prostrated themselves humbly on the ground, and begged to be forgiven. It was thus that the abbot gained victory and fame, not by trusting in neighing horses and flashing swords, but only by virtue of the power of God.

... Do we ever hear of any of the saints who had recourse to war? Therefore, let secular law or the decisions of episcopal councils decide ecclesiastical cases, so that what should be handled by judicial tribunals or judged by the decisions of the bishops, to our shame, not be adjudicated in trial by battle....

## 61. WILLIAM OF MALMESBURY ON THE CONSEQUENCES OF RESISTING PEACE

*This excerpt is taken from William of Malmesbury's* Life of Wulfstan of Worcester, *written shortly after 1126, and illustrates the fate of five brothers who angrily refused to make peace with the killer of their brother.*

Source: trans. R. C. van Caenegem, *English Lawsuits from William I to Richard I,* vol. 1 (London: The Selden Society, 1990), pp. 110–12.

At the invitation of the most reverend abbot [of Gloucester, Wulfstan] returned to that town and consecrated a church. There was a vast crowd, which as usual was hoping for remission of penitence and attached particularly great importance to the blessing of the bishop. Although rather reticent, he was inclined to rejoice as he saw the crowd gathering in God's service with a fervor comparable to the surge of floodwater. He did not withhold the torrent of his eloquence from those who were thirsting for it, but infused it lavishly with his charity. His sermon filled a good part of the day, as he told them abundantly what he knew to be the most important thing to hold. I mean peace, than which nothing is sweeter to hear, nothing more desirable to search for and finally nothing better to be found by mortals; peace which should be the beginning of human salvation and its end, and is as it were the extreme limit of God's commands. It was sung by an angelic choir on the threshold of redemption, it was given by the Lord to his disciples as he was preparing for crucifixion and was restored to them as a triumphal gift on his resurrection. All this the bishop explained to the crowd, and therefore he necessarily had to use examples. But since I speak to literate people, what I have to say is too well known to need explanation by examples. Many who previously resisted all efforts at reconciliation were on that day persuaded to consent to pacification. People encouraged each other and if anyone thought he had to resist, the bishop was consulted. A certain William, nicknamed the bold, lacked the confidence to bring his quarrels into the open. He had killed a man by accident and not on purpose and he could in no way buy the friendship of the relations of the killed man nor at any price obtain their forgiveness. The reverend abbot had often tried to bring about an accord between them, but all his attempts had been in vain. There were five brothers who were so furious and uttered such threats for the death of their brother that they could frighten away anyone. Who would not lose heart if he saw so many mature, strong and bold men rise up as one group? They were brought before the bishop who asked them to forgive the wrong, but they refused utterly and violently. They added to their deed some words that were no milder, that is, that they would rather be altogether excommunicated than give up the revenge of the death of their brother. Thereupon the bishop wearing his episcopal insignia threw himself before their feet hoping to obtain full satisfaction. As he was lying on the ground, he repeated his prayers promising the benefit of masses and other advantages, in Worcester as well as Gloucester, to the dead man. In no way influenced by such humility, they rejected all conciliation. Such was their sorrow for the death of their brother that they lost all humanity. How great was the fury that spurned the holy old man, who was lying in the dust before them and whom the angels themselves, I think, would have revered! Divine injury was added to his contempt and his pontifical dress was trodden under foot by human arrogance. Hence, as the bishop made little headway by using blandishments, he fought the sickness of their stubborn attitude with a more severe remedy, maintaining that it was easy to distinguish the sons of God from the sons of the devil. If we believe the truth, since we believe him who said: "blessed are the peacemakers, for they shall be called the children of God" [Matt. 5:9], it is evident that they who resist peace are sons of the devil, for whose works one does, his son one is called.

The people shouted that this was so and was what they wanted, and they heaped abuse upon those who showed contempt [for the bishop]. The malediction of the people was followed immediately by divine vengeance, for one of the brothers, the most violent, went mad. He rolled around on the ground, biting the soil and scratching it with his fingers, foaming abundantly at the mouth and as his limbs were steaming in an unheard manner he infested the air with a horrible stench. What courage do you think was left to the others when they saw this? Their pride left them, their insolence disappeared, their arrogance withered away. You should also have seen them cherish what they had spurned, offer peace, implore mercy. Fright had forced them into reverence, compassion with their brother had led them to humility. For they were afraid that their bad deed would be punished in the same way as his, they were all equally involved. The sight of these events moved the bishop to clemency and immediately after mass he restored health to the patient and security to the others and established peace between them all.

## 62. POPE URBAN II URGES VENGEANCE ON THE ENEMIES OF CHRISTENDOM IN ROBERT THE MONK'S *HISTORY OF JERUSALEM*

*Robert the Monk included this speech in his* Historia Hierosolymitana (History of Jerusalem). *This is one of four accounts of the famous speech delivered by Pope Urban II at Clermont, France, in 1095 that initiated the armed pilgrimage to the Holy Land that later came to be known as the First Crusade. The element of the speech especially relevant for the study of vengeance is Urban's understanding that war against the infidel was a device that could minimize feuds among Christians.*

Source: trans. Dana C. Munro, *Urban and the Crusaders* (Philadelphia: The Department of History of the University of Pennsylvania, 1895), pp. 5–8.

Oh, race of Franks, race from across the mountains, race chosen and beloved by God – as shines forth in very many of your works – set apart from all nations by the situation of your country, as well as by your catholic faith and the honor of the holy church! To you our discourse is addressed and for you our exhortation is intended. We wish you to know what a grievous cause has led us to your country, what peril threatening you and all the faithful has brought us.

From the confines of Jerusalem and the city of Constantinople a horrible tale has gone forth and very frequently has been brought to our ears, namely, that a race from the kingdom of the Persians, an accursed race, a race utterly alienated from God, a generation forsooth which has not directed its heart and has not entrusted its spirit to God, has invaded the lands of those Christians and has depopulated them by the sword, pillage and fire; it has led away a part of the captives into its own country, and a part it has destroyed by cruel tortures; it has either entirely destroyed the churches of God or appropriated them for the rites of its own religion. They destroy the altars, after having defiled them with their uncleanness. They circumcise the Christians, and the blood of the circumcision they either spread upon the altars or pour into the vases of the baptismal font. When they wish to torture people by a base death, they perforate their navels, and dragging forth the extremity of the intestines, bind it to a stake; then with flogging they lead the victim around until the viscera having gushed forth the victim falls prostrate upon the ground. Others they bind to a post and pierce with arrows. Others they compel to extend their necks and then, attacking them with naked swords, attempt to cut through the neck with a single blow. What shall I say of the abominable rape of the women? To speak of it is worse than to be silent. The kingdom of the Greeks is now dismembered by them and deprived of territory so vast in extent that it cannot be traversed in a march of two months. On whom therefore is the labor of avenging these wrongs and of recovering this territory incumbent, if not upon you? You, upon whom above other nations God has conferred remarkable glory in arms, great courage, bodily activity, and strength to humble the hairy scalp of those who resist you.

Let the deeds of your ancestors move you and incite your minds to manly achievements; the glory and greatness of king Charles the Great [Charlemagne], and of his son Louis, and of your other kings, who have destroyed the kingdoms of the pagans, and have extended in these lands the territory of the holy Church. Let the holy sepulcher of the Lord our Savior, which is possessed by unclean nations, especially incite you, and the holy places which are now treated with ignominy and irreverently polluted with their filthiness. Oh, most valiant soldiers and descendants of invincible ancestors, be not degenerate, but recall the valor of your progenitors.

But if you are hindered by love of children, parents and wives, remember what the Lord says in the Gospel, "He that loveth father or mother more than me, is not worthy of me" [Matt. 10:37]. "Every one that hath forsaken houses, or brethren, or sisters, or father, or mother, or wife, or children, or lands for my name's sake shall receive an hundred-fold and shall inherit everlasting life." Let none of your possessions detain you, no solicitude for your family affairs, since this land which you inhabit, shut in on all sides by the seas and surrounded by the mountain peaks, is too narrow for your large population; nor does it abound in wealth; and it furnishes scarcely food enough for its cultivators. Hence it is that you murder and devour one another, that you wage war, and that frequently you perish by mutual wounds. Let therefore hatred depart from among you, let your quarrels end, let wars cease, and let all dissensions and controversies slumber. Enter upon the road to the Holy Sepulcher; wrest that land from the wicked race, and subject it to yourselves. That land which as the Scripture says "floweth with milk and honey," was given by God into the possession of the children of Israel.

Jerusalem is the navel of the world; the land is fruitful above others, like another paradise of delights. This the Redeemer of the human race has made illustrious by his advent, has beautified by residence, has consecrated by suffering, has redeemed by death, has glorified by burial. This royal city, therefore, situated at the center of the world, is now held captive by his enemies, and is in subjection to those who do not know God, to the worship of the heathens. She seeks therefore and desires to be liberated, and does not cease to implore you to come to her aid. From you especially she asks succor, because, as we have already said, God has conferred upon you above all nations great glory in arms. Accordingly undertake this journey for the remission of your sins, with the assurance of the imperishable glory of the kingdom of heaven.

When Pope Urban had said these and very many similar things in his urbane discourse, he so influenced to one purpose the desires of all who were present, that they cried out, "It is the will of God! It is the will of God!" When the venerable Roman pontiff heard that, with eyes uplifted to heaven he gave thanks to God and, with his hand commanding silence, said:

Most beloved brethren, today is manifest in you what the Lord says in the Gospel, "Where two or three are gathered together in my name there am I in the midst of them" [Matt. 18:20]. Unless the Lord God had been present in your spirits, all of you would not have uttered the same cry. For, although the cry issued from numerous mouths, yet the origin of the cry was one. Therefore I say to you that God, who implanted this in your breasts, has drawn it forth from you. Let this then be your war-cry in combats, because this word is given to you by God. When an armed attack is made upon the enemy, let this one cry be raised by all the soldiers of God: It is the will of God! It is the will of God!

And we do not command or advise that the old or feeble, or those unfit for bearing arms, undertake this journey; nor ought women to set out at all, without their husbands or brothers or legal guardians. For such are more of a hindrance than aid, more of a burden than advantage. Let the rich aid the needy; and according to their wealth, let them take with them experienced soldiers. The priests and clerks of any order are not to go without the consent of their bishop; for this journey would profit them nothing if they went without permission of these. Also, it is not fitting that laymen should enter upon the pilgrimage without the blessing of their priests.

Whoever, therefore, shall determine upon this holy pilgrimage and shall make his vow to God to that effect and shall offer himself to him as a living sacrifice, holy, acceptable unto God, shall wear the sign of the cross of the Lord on his forehead or on his breast. When, truly, having fulfilled his vow he wishes to return, let him place the cross on his back between his shoulders. Such, indeed, by the two-fold action will fulfill the precept of the Lord, as he commands in the Gospel, "He that takes not his cross and follows after me, is not worthy of me" [Matt. 10:38].

# 63. AN ACCOUNT OF THE SPEECH OF POPE URBAN II BY FULCHER OF CHARTRES

*Fulcher (ca 1059–ca 1127) was one of the major chroniclers of the First Crusade. He accompanied the crusaders to the Middle East, and later lived in the Latin principalities of Antioch, Edessa, and Tripoli, and in the kingdom of Jerusalem, until his death there around 1127. The chronicle does not mention Fulcher as taking part in the fighting, so we can assume he was in holy orders by then, and was probably ordained before 1096.*

Source: trans. Frances Rita Ryan, *A History of the Expedition to Jerusalem 1095–1127* (Knoxville: University of Tennessee Press, 1969), reprinted in Patrick J. Geary, ed. *Readings in Medieval History*, 3rd ed. (Peterborough, ON: Broadview Press, 2003), pp. 407–9.

Here Beginneth the First Book Concerning the Deeds of the Franks, Pilgrims to Jerusalem

## a. The council held at Clermont

1. In the year 1095 after the Incarnation of Our Lord, while Henry [IV] the so-called emperor was reigning in Germany and King Philip in France, evils of all kinds multiplied throughout Europe because of vacillating faith. Pope Urban II then ruled in the city of Rome. He was a man admirable in life and habits who strove prudently and vigorously to raise the status of Holy Church ever higher and higher.

2. Moreover he saw the faith of Christendom excessively trampled upon by all, by the clergy as well as by the laity, and peace totally disregarded, for the princes of the lands were incessantly at war quarreling with someone or other. He saw that people stole worldly goods from one another, that many captives were taken unjustly and were most barbarously cast into foul prisons and ransomed for excessive prices, or tormented there by three evils, namely hunger, thirst and cold, and secretly put to death, that holy places were violated, monasteries and villas consumed by fire, nothing mortal spared, and things human and divine held in derision.

3. When he heard that the interior part of Romania had been occupied by the Turks and the Christians subdued by a ferociously destructive invasion, Urban, greatly moved by compassionate piety and by the prompting of God's love, crossed the mountains and descended into Gaul and caused a council to be assembled in Auvergne at Clermont, as the city is called. This council, appropriately announced by messengers in all directions, consisted of 310 members, bishops as well as abbots carrying the crozier.

4. On the appointed day Urban gathered them around himself and in an eloquent address carefully made known the purpose of the meeting. In the sorrowing voice of a suffering Church he told of its great tribulation. He delivered an elaborate sermon concerning the many raging tempests of this world in which the faith had been degraded as was said above.

5. Then as a suppliant he exhorted all to resume the powers of their faith and arouse in themselves a fierce determination to overcome the machinations of the devil, and to try fully to restore Holy Church, cruelly weakened by the wicked, to its honorable status as of old.

### b. The decree of Urban in the same council

11. "Whoever shall have seized a bishop, let him be accursed. Whoever shall have seized monks or priests or nuns, and their servants, or pilgrims and traders, and despoiled them, let him be accursed. Let thieves and burners of houses, and their accomplices, be banished from the Church and excommunicated."

12. "'Thereafter we must consider especially,' said Gregory, 'how severely punished will be he who steals from another, if he is infernally damned for not being generous with his own possessions.' For so it happened to the rich man in the familiar Gospel story [Luke 16:19–31]. He was not punished for stealing from another, but because having received wealth he used it badly."

13. "By these evils it has been said, dearest brethren, that you have seen the world disturbed for a long time and particularly in some parts of your own provinces as we have been told. Perhaps due to your own weakness in administering justice scarcely anyone dares to travel on the road with hope of safety for fear of seizure by robbers by day or thieves by night, by force or wicked craft, indoors or out."

14. "Wherefore the truce commonly so-called, which was long ago established by the holy fathers, should be renewed. I earnestly admonish each of you to strictly enforce it in your own diocese. But if anyone, smitten by greed or pride, willingly infringes this truce, let him be anathema by virtue of the authority of God and by sanction of the decrees of this council."

### c. Urban's exhortation concerning a pilgrimage to Jerusalem

1. When these and many other matters were satisfactorily settled, all those present, clergy and people alike, spontaneously gave thanks to God for the words of the Lord Pope Urban and promised him faithfully that his decrees would be well kept. But the pope added at once that another tribulation not

less but greater than that already mentioned, even of the worst nature, was besetting Christianity from another part of the world.

2. He said, "Since, oh sons of God, you have promised him to keep peace among yourselves and to faithfully sustain the rights of Holy Church more sincerely than before, there still remains for you, newly aroused by Godly correction, an urgent task which belongs to both you and God, in which you can show the strength of your good will. For you must hasten to carry aid to your brethren dwelling in the East, who need your help for which they have often entreated."

3. "For the Turks, a Persian people, have attacked them, as many of you already know, and have advanced as far into Roman territory as that part of the Mediterranean which is called the Arm of Saint George. They have seized more and more of the lands of the Christians, have already defeated them in seven times as many battles, killed or captured many people, have destroyed churches, and have devastated the kingdom of God. If you allow them to continue much longer they will conquer God's faithful people much more extensively."

4. "Wherefore with earnest prayer I, not I, but God exhorts you as heralds of Christ to repeatedly urge men of all ranks whatsoever, knights as well as foot-soldiers, rich and poor, to hasten to exterminate this vile race from our lands and to aid the Christian inhabitants in time."

5. "I address those present; I proclaim it to those absent; moreover Christ commands it. For all those going thither there will be remission of sins if they come to the end of this fettered life while either marching by land or crossing by sea, or in fighting the pagans. This I grant to all who go, through the power vested in me by God."

6. "Oh what a disgrace if a race so despicable, degenerate, and enslaved by demons should thus overcome a people endowed with faith in Almighty God and resplendent in the name of Christ! Oh what reproaches will be charged against you by the Lord himself if you have not helped those who are counted like yourselves of the Christian faith!"

7. "Let those," he said, "who are accustomed to wantonly wage private war against the faithful march upon the infidels in a war which should be begun now and be finished in victory. Let those who have long been robbers now be soldiers of Christ. Let those who once fought against brothers and relatives now rightfully fight against barbarians. Let those who have been hirelings for a few pieces of silver [Matt. 27:3] now attain an eternal reward. Let those who have been exhausting themselves to the detriment of body and soul now labor for a double glory. Yea on the one hand will be the sad and the poor, on the other the joyous and the wealthy; here the enemies of the Lord, there his friends."

8. "Let nothing delay those who are going to go. Let them settle their affairs, collect money, and when winter has ended and spring has come, zealously undertake the journey under the guidance of the Lord."

## 64. A SERMON BY SAINT FRANCIS ON HATRED AND PEACE

*As a young man, Francis (ca 1181/2–1226) worked in his father's business in Assisi as a cloth merchant until he was twenty years old. While fighting with his city against Perugia, he was taken prisoner and held captive for over a year. After he was released, he set off to join in battle against Frederick II, but was directed by a vision to return to Assisi, where he stopped living the life that was usual for a well-to-do young man and became increasingly devout. While on pilgrimage to Rome around 1205, he exchanged his clothes with a beggar and begged for alms himself for a day. Around 1208 he put on a long dark garment and went out to preach. When he had gained twelve followers, he wrote a rule for them, which Pope Innocent III approved in 1209, and so was founded the Franciscan order. The Franciscan and Dominican orders (the Dominicans were founded by Saint Dominic in 1216), as they emerged in the early thirteenth century, were called mendicant or "begging" orders. Members of the orders, who delivered sermons on the Christian faith to the laity, quickly became involved in the papacy's ongoing battle against heresy. Franciscans and Dominicans also played an important role in papal inquisitions against suspected enemies of the faith. An important theme of mendicant sermons centered on the values of peacemaking, and members of both orders were also commonly involved in arbitration and peacemaking efforts as a natural outgrowth of their preaching activity. The following sermon, delivered at Bologna in 1222, was included in the* Historia Salonitarum *of Thomas, archdeacon of Split, in what is now Croatia.*

Source: trans. Paul Oligny, *Writings and Early Biographies: English Omnibus of the Sources for the Life of Saint Francis*, ed. Marion A. Habig (Chicago: Franciscan Herald Press, 1973), pp. 1601–02.

1. In that year [1222], I [Thomas] was residing in the Studium of Bologna; on the feast of the Assumption, I saw Saint Francis preach in the public square in front of the public palace. Almost the entire city had assembled there. The theme of his sermon was: "Angels, men and demons." He spoke so well and with such sterling clarity on these three classes of spiritual and rational beings that the way in which this untutored man developed his subject aroused even among the scholars in the audience an admiration that knew no bounds. Yet, his discourses did not belong to the great genre of sacred eloquence: rather

they were harangues. In reality, throughout his discourse he spoke of the duty of putting an end to hatreds and of arranging a new treaty of peace. He was wearing a ragged habit; his whole person seemed insignificant; he did not have an attractive face. But God conferred so much power on his words that they brought back peace in many a seignorial family torn apart until then by old, cruel, and furious hatreds even to the point of assassinations. The people showed him as much respect as they did devotion; men and women flocked to him; it was a question of who would at least touch the fringe of his clothing or who would tear off a piece of his poor habit.

## 65. THE WOLF OF GUBBIO

*The story of the wolf of Gubbio is in the form of an* exemplum, *a vivid little tale used in a sermon to deliver a moral lesson. One of the stories that came to be told about Saint Francis of Assisi, the story of the wolf of Gubbio can be read as an allegory of peacemaking. The ability of a saint to tame a wild animal is common in the hagiographical tradition.*

Source: trans. T. W. Arnold, *The Little Flowers of Saint Francis of Assisi* (London: Florence Press, 1909), pp. 67–72. Modernized by Kelly Gibson.

Of the miracle which Saint Francis performed when he converted the wolf of Gubbio

At the time when Saint Francis lived in the city of Gubbio there appeared in the neighborhood an enormous wolf, terrible and ferocious, which devoured not only animals but even men also. All the citizens stood in great terror because he had approached the city many times, and all carried arms when they went out of the city as though they were going to battle. Yet despite all this, if anyone met the wolf alone he could not defend himself against him. And for fear of this wolf it had come to such a pass that no one had the courage to go out of the city. Therefore Saint Francis had compassion on the men of the place and desired to go out to this wolf, although all the citizens together counseled him not to do so. Making the sign of the most holy cross, he went out into the fields with his companions, all his confidence resting in God. The others hesitated to go any further, but Saint Francis went to the place where the wolf was.

And behold! Seeing the many citizens who had come out to witness the miracle, the wolf went at Saint Francis with open mouth. And when he had come near, Saint Francis made on him the sign of the most holy cross, and called him to him, saying: "Come along, Brother Wolf, I command on the part of Christ that you do no harm, neither to me nor to anyone." And O wonder! Immediately, when Saint Francis had made the holy sign, the terrible wolf shut his mouth, ceased to run, and did as he was commanded, coming gently as a lamb, and lay down to rest at the feet of Saint Francis. Then Saint Francis spoke to him: "Brother Wolf, you have done much damage in these parts, and many evil deeds, ravaging and killing the creatures of God without his permission; and not only killing and devouring the cattle, but having the audacity to destroy men made in the image of God, for which you deserve to be hung upon the gallows like a convict, as being a thief and the worst of murderers. All the people cry out and murmur because of you, and the whole neighborhood is hostile to you. But, Brother Wolf, I would make peace between them and you, so that you offend no more, and they shall pardon all your past offenses, and neither men nor dogs shall persecute you anymore."

At these words, the wolf, by the motions of his body and his tail and his eyes and by inclining his head, showed that he accepted what Saint Francis had said, and was ready to observe it. Then Saint Francis said again: "Brother Wolf, since it pleases you to make and to keep this peace, I promise that I shall have food given to you continually by the men of this place as long as you shall live, so that you suffer no more hunger, for I know well that it is hunger which made you do all this evil. But since I have obtained this grace for you, I desire, Brother Wolf, that you promise me to never again harm man or beast; do you promise me this?"

And the wolf by inclining his head made evident signs that he promised. And Saint Francis said to him: "Brother Wolf, I need your pledge that you will keep this promise, without which I cannot trust you." And when Saint Francis held out his hand to receive his pledge, the wolf immediately lifted up his right paw and gently placed it in the hand of Saint Francis, thus giving him such pledge of faith as he was able.

Then Saint Francis said: "Brother Wolf, I command you in the name of Jesus Christ that you come now with me, without hesitation; let us go and confirm this peace in the name of God." And the wolf obediently went with him like a mild and gentle lamb, which the citizens saw, and marveled greatly.

And immediately the news spread over the whole city, and all the people, men and women, great and small, young and old, thronged to the piazza to see the wolf with Saint Francis. And when all the people had gathered together, Saint Francis got up to preach, telling them amongst other things how it was on account of sin that God permitted such calamities, and also pestilences. "Much more terrible," he said, "are the flames of hell which the damned will have to endure eternally, than the fangs of the wolf which cannot destroy more than the body. How much more then are the jaws of hell to be feared, when we see so many held in terror by the jaws of a little animal! Turn therefore, beloved, to God, and do worthy penance for your sins, and God will deliver you now from the fires of hell."

When the sermon ended, Saint Francis said: "Listen, my brothers: Brother Wolf, who is here before you, has promised, and has pledged me his faith to make peace with you, and never to offend again in anything; and you will promise to give him every day what is necessary; and I make myself surety for him, that he will faithfully observe the treaty of peace." Then all the people promised with one voice to feed him continually. And Saint Francis, before them all, said to the wolf: "And you, Brother Wolf, do you promise to observe and to keep the treaty of peace that you will not offend either man or beast, or any creature?" And the wolf knelt down and inclined his head, and by gentle movements of his body and his tail and his ears, showed as well as he could that he was willing to keep all that he had promised them. Then said Saint Francis said: "Brother Wolf, I desire that as you have pledged your faith to this promise outside the gates, you will pledge your faith again before all the people, and not deceive me in the promise and guarantee which I have given for you." Then the wolf, lifting up his right paw, placed it in the hand of Saint Francis.

While this and the rest that had been told above was taking place, there was such joy and admiration amongst all the people, both through devotion to the saint and through the novelty of the miracle, and also on account of the peace made with the wolf, that all began to cry to heaven, praising and blessing God for sending them Saint Francis, who by his merits had delivered them from the jaws of the cruel beast. And after this, the said wolf lived two years in Gubbio. He went sociably into the houses, going from door to door without doing harm to anyone or anyone doing harm to him, and was continually entertained by the people. And thus, as he went through fields and lanes no dog ever barked at him. Finally, after two years, Brother Wolf died of old age. At this the citizens grieved much, for while he went so gently about the town they remembered the virtue and sanctity of Saint Francis.

## 66. ALBERTANUS OF BRESCIA ON THE COST OF PURSUING PRIVATE WAR

*Albertanus of Brescia, a layman and judge, first shows up in the historical record in April 1226. Commander of the Italian fortress of Gavardo in August 1238, Albertanus was taken prisoner when the fortress was captured by the Holy Roman Emperor,*

*Frederick II, and was imprisoned in Cremona, an event that inaugurated his writing career. This work, written in 1246 for Albertanus's son, Joannes, included an argument to the effect that vengeance was a costly proposition and therefore not a good path for an injured party to follow. Exhortations against hatred and vengeance were traditionally based on Scripture; the economic perspective favored by Albertanus gave the campaign against vengeance a whole new dimension. Albertanus's stance, ultimately, was derived from the Roman intellectual heritage, not from that of Christianity. The treatise was written as a dialogue between Melibeus, the would-be avenger, and his wife Prudence, and later became the basis for Chaucer's* Tale of Melibe. *The word* guerra, *translated here as "private war," can be taken as a synonym for bloodfeud.*

Source: *Liber consolationis et consilii*, ed. Thor Sundby (London: N. Trübner, 1873), pp.102–103. Trans. Louis Hamilton.

## 46. On the evil of private war

[Lady Prudence, wife of Lord Melibeus is speaking.]

By my judgment, power and even wealth in no way suffice for the costs of private war. As a certain philosopher has said, "No one is able to be made wealthy enough in war." Since to the extent that people are wealthy and would persevere in a private war, they should lose either their riches or the war, or perhaps both together and their life. If they are poor they cannot in any way sustain a private war; if they possess much wealth, they will have many more costs. For as with all men who are sinning, the greater the sinner, the more infamous his sin; as Martial says: "The more famous the man, the more infamous the crime." Thus in private war a person is made poor, and the greater the man, the greater his costs. If by chance he should lose the war, he will be subjected to an even greater calamity. As the saying goes, "Calamity destroys the high-born more easily." And in Lucan it is said: "envious of a succession of disasters." And Martial has said: "The higher one ascends, the more lowly is he brought down from the heights." And not only is wealth lost through private war, but even the love of God and paradise and present life and friends are greatly lost and even destroyed through the adverse fortune of war, from which all the aforementioned evils follow, and which hurls straight to hell the souls of men along with the body. Out of love of God and fear of so many evils, you ought to avoid private war as much as you can.

# 67. THOMAS AQUINAS ON HOMICIDE, VENGEANCE, AND ANGER

*Thomas Aquinas (ca 1225–74) was born to a noble family near Aquino, in the kingdom of Naples. At age five he was given to the monastery of Montecassino, but was later sent to the University of Naples after the Holy Roman Emperor Frederick II occupied the abbey in 1239. While in Naples, Aquinas became a Dominican over the protests of his own family. On his way to Paris so that he would be out of reach of his family, he was seized north of Rome by his brothers and held for two years in his family's castle. Aquinas eventually gained his freedom and began his theological studies at the Dominican priory at the University of Paris and continued his studies with Albertus Magnus at the University of Cologne. He returned to Paris to lecture, became a master of theology in 1256, and then served as lector (reader) in Dominican houses in Italy from 1259 until 1268, when he returned to Paris.*

*These extracts are taken from the* Summa Theologiae, *which Aquinas began in 1265 while directing a Dominican* studium *(house of studies) at Santa Sabina in Rome. In Paris, while holding one of the Dominican chairs of theology from 1268 until 1272, he finished the second part. In 1272 he returned to Italy, where he completed the third part. Although originally designed as a handbook for friars not bound for university study, it is one of the greatest works of the thirteenth-century intellectual movement known as scholasticism.*

Source: Doc. 67a, trans. Fathers of the English Dominican Province, *The Summa Theologica of Saint Thomas Aquinas,* 2nd rev. ed. (London: Baker, 1918), pp. 197–201, 208–10; Docs. 67b-c, trans. Fathers of the English Dominican Province, *The Summa Theologica of Saint Thomas Aquinas* (London: Burns, Oates, and Washbourne Ltd., 1921), pp. 64–75, 158, 190–206.

## a. Question 64: Homicide

Second Article. Whether it is lawful to kill sinners?

We proceed thus to the Second Article: –

Objection 1: It seems that it is not lawful to kill men who have sinned. For our Lord in the parable [Matt. 13] forbade the uprooting of the cockle which denotes wicked men according to a gloss [a commentary]. Now whatever is forbidden by God is a sin. Therefore, it is a sin to kill a sinner.

Obj. 2. Further, human justice is conformed to divine justice. Now according to divine justice sinners are kept back for repentance, according to Ezekiel 33:11: I desire not the death of the wicked, but that the wicked turn from his way and live? Therefore it seems altogether unjust to kill sinners.

Obj. 3. Further, it is not lawful, for any good end whatever, to do that which is evil in itself, according to Augustine and the Philosopher [Aristotle].

Now to kill a man is evil in itself, since we are bound to have charity towards all men, and we wish our friends to live and to be, according to Ethic. 9. Therefore it is nowise lawful to kill a man who has sinned.

On the contrary, it is written [Exod. 12:18]: Wizards thou shalt not suffer to live; and [Ps. 100:8]: In the morning I put to death all the wicked of the land.

I answer that, as stated above, it is lawful to kill dumb animals, in so far as they are naturally directed to man's use, as the imperfect is directed to the perfect. Now every part is directed to the whole, as imperfect to perfect, wherefore every part is naturally for the sake of the whole. For this reason we observe that if the health of the whole body demands the excision of a member, through its being decayed or infectious to the other members, it will be both praiseworthy and advantageous to have it cut away. Now every individual person is compared to the whole community, as part to whole. Therefore if a man be dangerous and infectious to the community, on account of some sin, it is praiseworthy and advantageous that he be killed in order to safeguard the common good, since a little leaven corrupteth the whole lump [1 Cor. 5:6].

Reply Obj. 1. Our Lord commanded them to forbear from uprooting the cockle in order to spare the wheat, that is, the good. This occurs when the wicked cannot be slain without the good being killed with them, either because the wicked lie hidden among the good, or because they have many followers, so that they cannot be killed without danger to the good, as Augustine says. Wherefore our Lord teaches that we should rather allow the wicked to live, and that vengeance is to be delayed until the last judgment, rather than that the good be put to death together with the wicked. When however, the good incur no danger, but rather are protected and saved by the slaying of the wicked, then the latter may be lawfully put to death.

Reply Obj. 2. According to the order of his wisdom, God sometimes slays sinners forthwith in order to deliver the good, whereas sometimes he allows them time to repent, according as he knows what is expedient for his elect. This also does human justice imitate according to its powers; for it puts to death those who are dangerous to others, while it allows time for repentance to those who sin without grievously harming others.

Reply Obj. 3. By sinning man departs from the order of reason, and consequently falls away from the dignity of his manhood, in so far as he is naturally free, and exists for himself, and he falls into the slavish state of the beasts, by being disposed of according as he is useful to others. This is expressed in Psalm 48:21: Man, when he was in honor, did not understand; he hath been compared to senseless beasts, and made like to them, and Proverbs 11:29: The fool shall serve the wise. Hence, although it be evil in itself to kill a man so long as he preserve his dignity, yet it may be good to kill a man who has sinned, even as it is to kill a beast. For a bad man is worse than a beast, and is more harmful, as the Philosopher states.

Third Article. Whether it is lawful for a private individual to kill a man who has sinned?

We proceed thus to the Third Article: –

Objection 1: It seems that it is lawful for a private individual to kill a man who has sinned. For nothing unlawful is commanded in the divine law. Yet, on account of the sin of the molten calf, Moses commanded [Exod. 32:27]: Let every man kill his brother, and friend, and neighbor. Therefore it is lawful for private individuals to kill a sinner.

Obj. 2. Further, as stated above, man, on account of sin, is compared to the beasts. Now it is lawful for any private individual to kill a wild beast, especially if it be harmful. Therefore for the same reason, it is lawful for any private individual to kill a man who has sinned.

Obj. 3. Further, a man, though a private individual, deserves praise for doing what is useful for the common good. Now the slaying of evildoers is useful for the common good, as stated above. Therefore it is deserving of praise if even private individuals kill evildoers.

On the contrary, Augustine says: A man who, without exercising public authority, kills an evildoer, shall be judged guilty of murder, and all the more, since he has dared to usurp a power which God has not given him.

I answer that, as stated above, it is lawful to kill an evildoer in so far as it is directed to the welfare of the whole community, so that it belongs to him alone who has charge of the community's welfare. Thus it belongs to a physician to cut off a decayed limb, when he has been entrusted with the care of the health of the whole body. Now the care of the common good is entrusted to persons of rank having public authority: wherefore they alone, and not private individuals, can lawfully put evildoers to death.

Reply Obj. 1. The person by whose authority a thing is done really does the thing, as Dionysius declares. Hence according to Augustine, he slays not who owes his service to one who commands him, even as a sword is merely the instrument to him that wields it. Wherefore those who, at the Lord's command, slew their neighbors and friends, would seem not to have done this themselves, but rather he by whose authority they acted thus, just as a soldier slays the foe by the authority of his sovereign, and the executioner slays the robber by the authority of the judge.

Reply Obj. 2. A beast is by nature distinct from man, wherefore in the case of a wild beast, there is no need for an authority to kill it; whereas, in the case of domestic animals, such authority is required, not for their sake, but on account of the owner's loss. On the other hand a man who has sinned is not by nature distinct from good men; hence a public authority is requisite in order to condemn him to death for the common good.

Reply Obj. 3. It is lawful for any private individual to do anything for the common good, provided it harm nobody: but if it be harmful to some other, it cannot be done, except by virtue of the judgment of the person to whom it pertains to decide what is to be taken from the parts for the welfare of the whole.

Seventh Article: Whether it is lawful to kill a man in self-defense?

We proceed thus to the Seventh Article: –

Objection 1. It seems that nobody may lawfully kill a man in self-defense. For Augustine says to Publicola [one of Augustine's correspondents]: I do not agree with the opinion that one may kill a man lest one be killed by him; unless one be a soldier, or exercise a public office, so that one does it not for oneself but for others, having the power to do so, provided it be in keeping with one's person. Now he who kills a man in self-defense, kills him lest he be killed by him. Therefore this would seem to be unlawful.

Obj. 2. Further, he says: How are they free from sin in sight of divine providence, who are guilty of taking a man's life for the sake of these contemptible things? Now among contemptible things he reckons those which men may forfeit unwillingly, as appears from the context: and the chief of these is the life of the body. Therefore it is unlawful for any man to take another's life for the sake of the life of his own body.

Obj. 3. Further, Pope Nicholas I [r. 858–67, see Doc. 27] says in the Decretals: Concerning the clerics about whom you have consulted us, those, namely, who have killed a pagan in self-defense, as to whether, after making amends by repenting, they may return to their former state, or rise to a higher degree; know that in no case is it lawful for them to kill any man under any circumstances whatever. Now clerics and laymen are alike bound to observe the moral precepts. Therefore neither is it lawful for laymen to kill anyone in self-defense.

Obj. 4. Further, murder is a more grievous sin than fornication or adultery. Now nobody may lawfully commit simple fornication or adultery or any other mortal sin in order to save his own life; since the spiritual life is to be preferred to the life of the body. Therefore no man may lawfully take another's life in self-defense in order to save his own life.

Obj. 5. Further, if the tree be evil, so is the fruit, according to Matthew 7:17. Now self-defense itself seems to be unlawful, according to Romans 12:19: Not defending [Douay: revenging] yourselves, my dearly beloved. Therefore its result, which is the slaying of a man, is also unlawful.

On the contrary, it is written [Exod. 12:2]: If [a thief] be found breaking into a house or undermining it, and be wounded so as to die; he that slew him shall not be guilty of blood. Now it is much more lawful to defend one's life than one's house. Therefore neither is a man guilty of murder if he kill another in defense of his own life.

I answer that, nothing hinders one act from having two effects, only one of which is intended, while the other is beside the intention. Now moral acts take their species according to what is intended, and not according to what is beside the intention, since this is accidental as explained above. Accordingly the act of self-defense may have two effects, one is the saving of one's life, the other is the slaying of the aggressor. Therefore this act, since one's intention is to save one's own life, is not unlawful, seeing that it is natural to everything to keep itself in being, as far as possible. And yet, though proceeding from a good intention, an act may be rendered unlawful, if it be out of proportion to the end. Wherefore if a man, in self-defense, uses more than necessary violence, it will be unlawful: whereas if he repel force with moderation his defense will be lawful, because according to the jurists, it is lawful to repel force by force, provided one does not exceed the limits of a blameless defense. Nor is it necessary for salvation that a man omit the act of moderate self-defense in order to avoid killing the other man, since one is bound to take more care of one's own life than of another's. But as it is unlawful to take a man's life, except for the public authority acting for the common good, as stated above, it is not lawful for a man to intend killing a man in self-defense, except for such as have public authority, who while intending to kill a man in self-defense, refer this to the public good, as in the case of a soldier fighting against the foe, and in the minster of the judge struggling with robbers, although even these sin if they be moved by private animosity.

Reply Obj. 1. The words quoted from Augustine refer to the case when one man intends to kill another to save himself from death. The passage quoted in the Second Objection is to be understood in the same sense. Hence he says pointedly, for the sake of these things, whereby he indicates the intention. This suffices for the Reply to the Second Objection.

Reply Obj. 3. Irregularity results from the act though sinless of taking a man's life, as appears in the case of a judge who justly condemns a man to death. For this reason a cleric, though he kill a man in self-defense, is irregular, albeit he intends not to kill him, but to defend himself.

Reply Obj. 4. The act of fornication or adultery is not necessarily directed to the preservation of one's own life, as is the act whence sometimes results the taking of a man's life.

Reply Obj. 5. The defense forbidden in this passage is that which comes from revengeful spite. Hence a gloss says: Not defending yourselves, – that is, not striking your enemy back.

## b. Question 108: Vengeance

We must now consider vengeance, under which head there are four points of inquiry: 1. Whether vengeance is lawful? 2. Whether it is a special virtue? 3. Of the manner of taking vengeance: 4. On whom should vengeance be taken?

First Article. Whether vengeance is lawful?

We proceed thus to the First Article: –

Objection 1. It seems that vengeance is not lawful. For whoever usurps what is God's sins. But vengeance belongs to God, for it is written [Deut. 32:35 and Rom. 12:19]: Revenge [belongs] to me, and I will repay. Therefore all vengeance is unlawful.

Obj. 2. Further, he that takes vengeance on a man does not bear with him. But we ought to bear with the wicked, for a gloss on Canticles 2:2, as the lily among the thorns, says: He is not a good man that cannot bear with a wicked one. Therefore we should not take vengeance on the wicked.

Obj. 3. Further, vengeance is taken by inflicting punishment, which is the cause of servile fear. But the New Law is not a law of fear, but of love, as Augustine states. Therefore at least in the New Testament all vengeance is unlawful.

Obj. 4. Further, a man is said to avenge himself when he takes revenge for wrongs inflicted on himself. But, seemingly, it is unlawful even for a judge to punish those who have wronged him: for [John] Chrysostom says: Let us learn after Christ's example to bear our own wrongs with magnanimity, yet not to suffer God's wrongs, not even by listening to them. Therefore vengeance seems to be unlawful.

Obj. 5. Further, the sin of a multitude is more harmful than the sin of only one: for it is written [Ecclus. 26:5–7]: Of three things my heart hath been afraid ... the accusation of a city, and the gathering together of the people, and a false calumny. But vengeance should not be taken on the sin of a multitude, for a gloss on Matthew 13:29–30, Lest perhaps ... you root up the wheat ... suffer both to grow, says that a multitude should not be excommunicated, nor should the sovereign. Neither therefore is any other vengeance lawful.

On the contrary, we should look to God for nothing save what is good and lawful. But we are to look to God for vengeance on his enemies: for it is written [Luke 18:7]: Will not God revenge his elect who cry to him day and night? as if to say: He will indeed. Therefore vengeance is not essentially evil and unlawful.

I answer that, vengeance consists in the infliction of a penal evil on one who has sinned. Accordingly, in the matter of vengeance, we must consider the mind of the avenger. For if his intention is directed chiefly to the evil of the person on whom he takes vengeance, and rests there, then his vengeance is altogether unlawful: because to take pleasure in another's evil belongs to hatred, which is contrary to the charity whereby we are bound to love all men. Nor is it an excuse that he intends the evil of one who has unjustly inflicted evil on him, as neither is a man excused for hating one that hates him: for a man may not sin against another just because the latter has already sinned against him, since this is to be overcome by evil, which was forbidden by the Apostle, who says [Rom. 12:21]: Be not overcome by evil, but overcome evil by good.

If, however, the avenger's intention be directed chiefly to some good, to be obtained by means of the punishment of the person who has sinned (for instance that the sinner may amend, or at least that he may be restrained and others be not disturbed, that justice may be upheld, and God honored), then vengeance may be lawful, provided other due circumstances be observed.

Reply Obj. 1. He who takes vengeance on the wicked in keeping with his rank and position does not usurp what belongs to God, but makes use of the power granted him by God. For it is written [Rom. 13:4] of the earthly prince that he is God's minister, and avenger to execute wrath upon him that doeth evil. If, however, a man takes vengeance outside the order of divine appointment, he usurps what is God's and therefore sins.

Reply Obj. 2. The good bear with the wicked by enduring patiently, and in due manner, the wrongs they themselves receive from them: but they do not bear with them so as to endure the wrongs they inflict on God and their neighbor. For Chrysostom says: It is praiseworthy to be patient under our own wrongs, but to overlook God's wrongs is most wicked.

Reply Obj. 3. The law of the Gospel is the law of love, and therefore those who do good out of love, and who alone properly belong to the Gospel, ought not to be terrorized by means of punishment, but only those who are not moved by love to do good, and who, though they belong to the Church outwardly, do not belong to it in merit.

Reply Obj. 4. Sometimes a wrong done to a person reflects on God and the Church: and then it is the duty of that person to avenge the wrong. For example, Elias made fire descend on those who were come to seize him [4 Kings 1]; likewise Eliseus cursed the boys that mocked him [4 Kings 2]; and Pope Sylverius excommunicated those who sent him into exile. But in so far as the wrong inflicted on a man affects his person, he should bear it patiently if this be expedient. For these precepts of patience are to be understood as referring to preparedness of the mind, as Augustine states.

Reply Obj. 5. When the whole multitude sins, vengeance must be taken on them, either in respect of the whole multitude – thus the Egyptians were drowned in the Red Sea while they were pursuing the children of Israel

[Exod. 14], and the people of Sodom were entirely destroyed [Gen. 19] – or as regards part of the multitude, as may be seen in the punishment of those who worshipped the calf.

Sometimes, however, if there is hope of many making amends, the severity of vengeance should be brought to bear on a few of the principals, whose punishment fills the rest with fear; thus the Lord [Num. 25] commanded the princes of the people to be hanged for the sin of the multitude.

On the other hand, if it is not the whole but only a part of the multitude that has sinned, then if the guilty can be separated from the innocent, vengeance should be wrought on them: provided, however, that this can be done without scandal to others; else the multitude should be spared and severity forgone. The same applies to the sovereign, whom the multitude follow. For his sin should be borne with, if it cannot be punished without scandal to the multitude: unless indeed his sin were such, that it would do more harm to the multitude, either spiritually or temporally, than would the scandal that was feared to arise from his punishment.

Second Article: Whether Vengeance is a Special Virtue?

We proceed thus to the Second Article: –

Objection 1. It seems that vengeance is not a special and distinct virtue. For just as the good are rewarded for their good deeds, so are the wicked punished for their evil deeds. Now the rewarding of the good does not belong to a special virtue, but is an act of commutative justice. Therefore in the same way vengeance should not be accounted a special virtue.

Obj. 2. Further, there is no need to appoint a special virtue for an act to which a man is sufficiently disposed by the other virtues. Now man is sufficiently disposed by the virtues of fortitude or zeal to avenge evil. Therefore vengeance should not be reckoned a special virtue.

Obj. 3. Further, there is a special vice opposed to every special virtue. But seemingly no special vice is opposed to vengeance. Therefore it is not a special virtue.

On the contrary, Tully [Cicero] reckons it a part of justice.

I answer that, as the Philosopher states, aptitude to virtue is in us by nature, but the complement of virtue is in us through habituation or some other cause. Hence it is evident that virtues perfect us so that we follow in due manner our natural inclinations, which belong to the natural right. Wherefore to every definite natural inclination there corresponds a special virtue. Now there is a special inclination of nature to remove harm, for which reason animals have the irascible power distinct from the concupiscible. Man resists harm by defending himself against wrongs, lest they be inflicted on him, or he avenges those which have already been inflicted on him, with the intention, not of harming, but of removing the harm done. And this belongs to vengeance, for Tully says that by vengeance we resist force, or wrong, and in general whatever is obscure [that is, derogatory], either by self-defense or by avenging it. Therefore vengeance is a special virtue.

Reply Obj. 1. Just as repayment of a legal debt belongs to commutative justice, and as repayment of a moral debt, arising from the bestowal of a particular favor, belongs to the virtue of gratitude, so too the punishment of sins, so far as it is the concern of public justice, is an act of commutative justice; while so far as it is concerned in defending the rights of the individual by whom a wrong is resisted, it belongs to the virtue of revenge.

Reply Obj. 2. Fortitude disposes to vengeance by removing an obstacle thereto, namely, fear of an imminent danger. Zeal, as denoting the fervor of love, signifies the primary root of vengeance, in so far as a man avenges the wrong done to God and his neighbor, because charity makes him regard them as his own. Now every act of virtue proceeds from charity as its root, since, according to Gregory [the Great], there are no green leaves on the bough of good works, unless charity be the root.

Reply Obj. 3. Two vices are opposed to vengeance: one by way of excess, namely, the sin of cruelty or brutality, which exceeds the measure in punishing: while the other is a vice by way of deficiency and consists in being remiss in punishing, wherefore it is written [Prov. 13:24]: He that spareth the rod hateth his son. But the virtue of vengeance consists in observing the due measure of vengeance with regard to all the circumstances.

Third Article. Whether vengeance should be wrought by means of punishments customary among men?

We proceed thus to the Third Article: –

Objection 1. It seems that vengeance should not be wrought by means of punishments customary among men. For to put a man to death is to uproot him. But our Lord forbade [Matt. 13:29] the uprooting of the cockle, whereby the children of the wicked one are signified. Therefore sinners should not be put to death.

Obj. 2. Further, all who sin mortally seem to be deserving of the same punishment. Therefore if some who sin mortally are punished with death, it seems that all such persons should be punished with death: and this is evidently false.

Obj. 3. Further, to punish a man publicly for his sin seems to publish his sin: and this would seem to have a harmful effect on the multitude, since the example of sin is taken by them as an occasion for sin. Therefore it seems that the punishment of death should not be inflicted for a sin.

On the contrary, these punishments are fixed by the divine law as appears from what we have said above.

I answer that, vengeance is lawful and virtuous so far as it tends to the prevention of evil. Now some who are not influenced by motive of virtue are prevented from committing sin, through fear of losing those things which they love more than those they obtain by sinning, else fear would be no restraint to sin. Consequently vengeance for sin should be taken by depriving a man of what he loves most. Now the things which man loves most are life, bodily safety, his own freedom, and external goods such as riches, his country, and his good name. Wherefore, according to Augustine's reckoning, Tully writes that the laws recognize eight kinds of punishment: namely, death, whereby man is deprived of life; stripes, retaliation, or the loss of eye for eye, whereby man forfeits his bodily safety; slavery, and imprisonment, whereby he is deprived of freedom; exile, whereby he is banished from his country; fines, whereby he is mulcted [fined] in his riches; ignominy, whereby he loses his good name.

Reply Obj. 1. Our Lord forbids the uprooting of the cockle, when there is fear lest the wheat be uprooted together with it. But sometimes the wicked can be uprooted by death, not only without danger, but even with great profit, to the good. Wherefore in such a case the punishment of death may be inflicted on sinners.

Reply Obj. 2. All who sin mortally are deserving of eternal death, as regards future retribution, which is in accordance with the truth of the divine judgment. But the punishments of this life are more of a medicinal character; wherefore the punishment of death is inflicted on those sins alone which conduce to the grave undoing of others.

Reply Obj. 3. The very fact that the punishment, whether of death or of any kind that is fearsome to man, is made known at the same time as the sin, makes man's will averse to sin: because the fear of punishment is greater than the enticement of the example of sin.

Fourth Article. Whether vengeance should be taken on those who have sinned involuntarily?

We proceed thus to the Fourth Article: –

Objection 1. It seems that vengeance should be taken on those who have sinned involuntarily. For the will of one man does not follow from the will of another. Yet one man is punished for another, according to Exodus 20:5, I am [the lord thy] God [mighty,] jealous, visiting the iniquity of the fathers upon the children, unto the third and fourth generation. Thus for the sin of Cham, his son Chanaan was cursed [Gen. 9:25], and for the sin of Giezi, his descendants were struck with leprosy [4 Kings 5]. Again the blood of Christ lays the descendents of the Jews under the ban of punishment, for they said [Matt. 27:25]: His blood be upon us and upon our children. Moreover, we read [Josh. 7] that the people of Israel were delivered into the hands of their enemies for the sin of Achan, and that the same people were overthrown by the Philistines on account of the sin of the sons of Heli [1 Kings 4]. Therefore a person is to be punished without having deserved it voluntarily.

Obj. 2. Further, nothing is voluntary except what is in a man's power. But sometimes a man is punished for what is not in his power; thus a man is removed from the administration of the Church on account of being infected with leprosy; and a Church ceases to be an episcopal see on account of the depravity or evil deeds of the people. Therefore vengeance is taken not only for voluntary sins.

Obj. 3. Further, ignorance makes an act involuntary. Now vengeance is sometimes taken on the ignorant. Thus the children of the people of Sodom, though they were in invincible ignorance, perished with their parents [Gen. 19]. Again, for the sin of Dathan and Abiron their children were swallowed up together with them [Num. 16]. Moreover, dumb animals, which are devoid of reason, were commanded to be slain on account of the sin of the Amalekites [1 Kings 15]. Therefore vengeance is sometimes taken on those who have deserved it involuntarily.

Obj. 4. Further, compulsion is most opposed to voluntariness. But a man does not escape the debt of punishment through being compelled by fear to commit a sin. Therefore vengance is sometimes taken on those who have deserved it involuntarily.

Obj. 5. Further, Ambrose says on Luke 5 that this ship, in which Judas was, was in distress; wherefore Peter, who was calm in the security of his own merits, was in distress about those of others. But Peter did not will the sin of Judas. Therefore a person is sometimes punished without having voluntarily deserved it.

On the contrary, punishment is due to sin. But every sin is voluntary according to Augustine. Therefore vengeance should be taken only to those who have deserved it voluntarily.

I answer that, punishment may be considered in two ways. First, under the aspect of punishment, and in this way punishment is not due save for sin, because by means of punishment the equality of justice is restored, in so far as he who by sinning has exceeded in following his own will suffers something that is contrary to his will. Wherefore, since every sin is voluntary, not excluding original sin, as stated above, it follows that no one is punished in this way, except for something done voluntarily.

Secondly, punishment may be considered as a medicine, not only healing the past sin, but also preserving from future sin, or conducing to some good, and in this way a person is sometimes punished without any fault of his own, yet not without cause.

It must, however, be observed that a medicine never removes a greater good in order to promote a lesser; thus the medicine of the body never blinds the eye, in order to repair the heel: yet sometimes it is harmful in lesser things that it may be helpful in things of greater consequence. And since spiritual goods are of the greatest consequence, while temporal goods are least important, sometimes a person is punished in his temporal goods without any fault of his own. Such are many of the punishments inflicted by God in this present life for our humiliation or probation. But no one is punished in spiritual goods without any fault on his part, neither in this nor in the future life, because in the latter punishment is not medicinal, but a result of spiritual condemnation.

Reply Obj. 1. A man is never condemned to a spiritual punishment for another man's sin, because spiritual punishment affects the soul, in respect of which each man is master of himself. But sometimes a man is condemned to punishment in temporal matters for the sin of another, and this for three reasons. First, because one man may be the temporal goods of another, and so he may be punished in punishment of the latter: thus children, as to the body, are a belonging of their father, and slaves are a possession of their master. Secondly, when one person's sin is transmitted to another, either by imitation, as children copy the sins of their parents, and slaves the sins of their masters, so as to sin with greater daring; or by way of merit, as the sinful subjects merit a sinful superior, according to Job 34:30: Who maketh a man that is a hypocrite to reign for the sins of the people? Hence the people of Israel were punished for David's sin in numbering the people [2 Kings 24]. This may also happen through some kind of consent or connivance: thus sometimes even the good are punished in temporal matters together with the wicked, for not having condemned their sins, as Augustine says. Thirdly, in order to mark the unity of human fellowship, whereby one man is bound to be solicitous for another, lest he sin; and in order to inculcate horror of sin, seeing that the punishment of one affects all, as though all were one body, as Augustine says in speaking of the sin of Achan [Josh. 7:1–26]. The saying of the Lord, visiting the iniquity of the fathers upon the children unto the third and fourth generation, seems to belong to mercy rather than to severity, since he does not take vengeance forthwith, but waits for some future time, in order that the descendants at least may mend their ways; yet should the wickedness of the descendants increase, it becomes almost necessary to take vengeance on them.

Reply Obj. 2. As Augustine states, human judgment should conform to the divine judgment, when this is manifest, and God condemns men spiritually for their own sins. But human judgment cannot be conformed to God's hidden judgments, whereby he punishes certain persons in temporal matters without any fault of theirs, since man is unable to grasp the reasons of these judgments, so as to know what is expedient for each individual. Wherefore according to human judgment a man should never be condemned without fault of his own to an inflictive punishment, such as death, mutilation or flogging. But a man may be condemned, even according to human judgment, to a punishment of forfeiture, even without any fault on his part, but not without cause: and this in three ways.

First, through a person becoming, without any fault of his, disqualified for having or acquiring a certain good: thus for being infected with leprosy a man is removed from the administration of a church: and for bigamy, or through pronouncing a death sentence a man is hindered from receiving sacred orders.

Secondly, because the particular good that he forfeits is not his own but common property: thus that an episcopal see be attached to a certain church belongs to the good of the whole city, and not only to the good of the clerics.

Thirdly, because the good of one person may depend on the good of another: thus in the crime of high treason a son loses his inheritance through the sin of his parent.

Reply Obj. 3. By the judgment of God children are punished in temporal matters together with their parents, both because they are a possession of their parents, so that their parents are punished also in their person, and because this is for their good lest, should they be spared, they might imitate the sins of their parents, and thus deserve to be punished still more severely.

Vengeance is wrought on dumb animals and any other irrational creatures, because in this way their owners are punished; and also in horror of sin.

Reply Obj. 4. An act done through compulsion of fear is not involuntary simply, but has an admixture of voluntariness, as stated above.

Reply Obj. 5. The other apostles were distressed about the sin of Judas, in the same way as the multitude is punished for the sin of one, in condemnation of unity, as stated above.

## c. Question 158: Anger

We must next consider the contrary vices: 1. Anger that is opposed to meekness; 2. Cruelty that is opposed to clemency.

Concerning anger there are eight points of inquiry: 1. Whether it is lawful to be angry? 2. Whether anger is a sin? 3. Whether it is a mortal sin? 4. hether it is the most grievous of sins? 5. Of its species. 6. Whether anger is a capital vice? 7. Of its daughters. 8. Whether it has a contrary vice?

First Article: Whether it is lawful to be angry?

We proceed thus to the First Article: –

Objection 1: It seems that it is unlawful to be angry. For Jerome in his exposition on Matthew 5:22, whosoever is angry with his brother, etc., says: Some codices add 'without cause.' However, in the genuine codices the sentence is unqualified, and anger is forbidden altogether. Therefore it is nowise lawful to be angry.

Obj. 2: Further, according to Dionysius: The soul's evil is to be without reason. Now anger is always without reason: for the Philosopher says that anger does not listen perfectly to reason; and Gregory says that when anger beats the tranquil surface of the soul, it mangles and rends it by its riot; and Cassian says: From whatever cause it arises the angry passion boils over and blinds the eye of the mind. Therefore it is always evil to be angry.

Obj. 3: Further, anger is the desire for vengeance according to a gloss on Leviticus 19:17: Thou shalt not hate thy brother in thy heart. Now it would seem unlawful to desire vengeance, since this should be left to God, according to Deuteronomy 32:35: Revenge is mine. Therefore it would seem that to be angry is always an evil.

Obj. 4: Further, all that makes us depart from likeness to God is evil. Now anger always makes us depart from likeness to God, since God judges with tranquility according to Wisdom 12:18. Therefore to be angry is always an evil.

On the contrary, Chrysostom says: He that is angry without cause, shall be in danger; but he that is angry with cause, shall not be in danger, for without anger, teaching will be useless, judgment unstable, crimes unchecked. Therefore to be angry is not always an evil.

I answer that, properly speaking anger is a passion of the sensitive appetite, and gives its name to the irascible power, as stated above when we were treating of the passions. Now with regard to the passions of the soul, it is to be observed that evil may be found in them in two ways. First by reason of the passion's very species, which is derived from the passion's object. Thus envy, in respect of its species, denotes an evil, since it is displeasure at another's good, and such displeasure is in itself contrary to reason: wherefore, as the Philosopher remarks, the very mention of envy denotes something evil. Now this does not apply to anger, which is the desire for revenge, since revenge may be desired both well and ill. Secondly, evil is found in a passion in respect of the passion's quantity, that is in respect of its excess of deficiency; and thus evil may be found in anger, when, to wit, one is angry, more or less than right reason demands. But if one is angry in accordance with right reason, one's anger is deserving of praise.

Reply Obj. 1. The Stoics designated anger and all the other passions as emotions opposed to the order of reason; and accordingly they deemed anger and all other passions to be evil, as stated above when we were treating of the passions. It is in this sense that Jerome considers anger; for he speaks of the anger whereby one is angry with one's neighbor, with the intent of doing him a wrong. But, according to the Peripatetics, to whose opinion Augustine inclines, anger and the other passions of the soul are movements of the sensitive appetite, whether they be moderated or not, according to reason: and in this sense anger is not always evil.

Reply Obj. 3. It is unlawful to desire vengeance considered as evil to the man who is to be punished, but it is praiseworthy to desire vengeance as a corrective of vice and for the good of justice; and to this the sensitive appetite can tend, in so far as it is moved thereto by the reason: and when revenge is taken in accordance with the order of judgment, it is God's work, since he who has power to punish is God's minister, as stated in Romans 13:4.

Second Article:

I answer that ... a passion of the sensitive appetite is good in so far as it is regulated by reason, whereas it is evil if it set the order of reason aside. Now the order of reason, in regard to anger, may be considered in relation to two things. First, in relation to the appetible object to which anger tends, and that is revenge. Wherefore if one desire revenge to be taken in accordance with the order of reason, the desire of anger is praiseworthy, and is called zealous anger. On the other hand, if one desire the taking of vengeance in any way whatever contrary to the order of reason, for instance if he desire the punishment of one who has not deserved it, or beyond his deserts, or again contrary to the order prescribed by law, or not for the due end, namely the maintaining of justice and the correction of defaults, then the desire of anger will be sinful, and this is called sinful anger....

# CHAPTER TEN: SAINTS' LIVES, CHRONICLES, AND EPICS

*The depth and variety of the narrative sources that have survived from the High Middle Ages onward has made it possible for modern readers to explore the language of vengeance from the perspectives of clerics, kings, and nobles, and even from those of commoners like the farmer-stockbreeders of Iceland. In general, saints' lives from approximately the tenth century onward show an increased emphasis on the role of the saint in the making of peace, while miracles of divine vengeance were minimized accordingly, though they do not disappear altogether. At the same time, secular rulers began to apply the theory that they possessed a divine prerogative to wreak vengeance on the wicked (see Docs. 69 and 75). Conversely, the establishment of royal prerogatives concerning vengeance led to restrictions on the rights of freemen to pursue their own vengeance and compensation, as is stated eloquently in the opening lines of the* Laxdaela Saga *(Doc. 83).*

## 68. RODULPHUS GLABER ON THE TRUCE OF GOD

*Rodulphus Glaber (ca 985–ca 1047) was born in Burgundy and entered a monastery, possibly St. Germanus of Auxerre, when he was twelve. From 1015 to 1030, he served as the chronicler of William of Volpiano, abbot of St. Benignus of Dijon, and filled the same post at the monastery of Cluny, under the abbot Odilo, from 1030 to 1035. He then returned to Auxerre, where he continued to work on his history until his death, some time around 1047. He saw the "renewal of peace" as part of a wider movement of religious revival in which lay people would go to ceremonies centered upon the display and veneration of saints' relics.*

Source: trans. Richard Landes, *The Peace of God: Social Violence and Religious Response in France around the Year 1000*, ed. Thomas Head and Richard Landes (Ithaca: Cornell University Press, 1992), p. 342.

5.1.15. It happened about that time [1041] that, by the inspiration of divine grace, a pact was confirmed starting in Aquitaine and then gradually spreading throughout Gaul; according to this men agreed, through both love and fear of the Lord, that from Wednesday evening to dawn the following Monday no man might presume to steal by force from another, or take vengeance on an enemy or even take a pledge from an oathtaker. Whoever broke this public decree should either die or be driven from his own country and the company of Christians. It further unanimously pleased all that this should be called, in the vulgar tongue, the truce of God (*treuga Dei*), since it was upheld not only by human sanctions but also by oft-displayed divine terrors.

Various raging fools in their audacity did not fear to break the pact, and immediately divine retribution or the avenging human sword appeared. This happened so often in so many places that I cannot record individual instances. This was only just. For just as Sunday is considered holy in recollection of the resurrection of our Lord (and called the octave), so the fifth, sixth, and seventh days, out of reverence for the supper and passion of our Lord, should be free of iniquitous deeds.

5.1.16. And it happened that while this statute was, as we have said, strictly observed throughout almost all of Gaul, the people of Neustria refused to adopt it.

*Glaber details the devastation of the war between Henry I and the sons of Odo of Blois.*

Then, by a hidden judgment of God, divine vengeance rained furiously upon that people. A deadly fever consumed many people, as many from the magnates as from the middling and the least of people. It spared some, indeed, with an arm or a leg amputated, to serve as examples for future generations. And then the people of almost the entire world endured a famine for lack of wine and wheat.

## 69. HOW THE EMPEROR CONRAD PACIFIED HIS REALM, ACCORDING TO WIPO

*Conrad II, born in 990, ruled as Holy Roman Emperor from 1024 to 1039. Wipo, the author of* The Deeds of Conrad *(1040–46), was a native of the Swabian part of Burgundy, and served until his death in 1046 as priest and chaplain to Conrad II and his successor, Henry III.*

Source: trans. Theodor E. Mommsen and Karl F. Morrison, *Imperial Lives and Letters of the Eleventh Century* (New York: Columbia University Press, 1962), pp. 75–87.

### 18. Of the wicked lord Thasselgard

At that time in Italy, there was a certain wicked lord called Thasselgard, who had committed many crimes in the kingdom in the time of Emperor Henry. But by seaside retreats and other fortifications, which he kept immeasurably safe, he had been able to evade the pursuit of Caesar Henry. Noble though he was by descent, he was despicable in person, reprehensible in habits, a great predator of churches and widows. The Emperor Conrad hunted him down most diligently and arranged ambushes for him on all sides and in every way. [At last] when he wanted to flee from one of his castles to another, he was captured by soldiers of Caesar.

When the emperor heard this, he hastened with such great speed that he traversed almost one hundred Latin miles [a Latin mile was roughly equivalent to the modern mile] in a day and a night. For he thought that he might escape again in his accustomed way. When the emperor arrived, the wicked lord was presented to him. When he saw him, the emperor is reputed to have said, "Is this not that lion which has devoured the game of Italy? By the Holy Cross of the Lord, such a lion will eat no more of my bread." Thus he said, and, with the other princes of the kingdom sitting in judgment, he straightaway ordered that he be hanged on a gallows. After he had been hanged, peace and security, which had long lain hidden, emerged at once through all that province.

### 19. On the conspiracy of certain Germans

In the meantime, while the emperor was staying in Italy, great malice, many plans, many factions arose among the Germans against the emperor, though to no avail. To begin with the lesser and to come to the greater: a certain count in Swabia, named Welf, rich in estates, powerful in arms, and Bruno, bishop of Augsburg, clashed between themselves and produced many evils in the kingdom through their lootings and burnings. Finally, the aforesaid count invaded Augsburg itself, despoiled the treasury of the bishop, and laid waste the whole city. Later, under the constraint of the emperor, he restored everything and made amends to the bishop.

Cuono, duke of Worms, cousin of the emperor, who was neither faithful to the emperor nor, on the other hand, very harmful to him, remained quiet for the time being. Frederick, duke of the Lotharingians, stepfather of the aforesaid Cuono, was prevented by his own death from acting as an enemy of the emperor.

Ernst, duke of Alamannia, stepson of Emperor Conrad, only lately exalted by him with benefices and gifts, deserted him and, at the instigation of the Devil, promoted a rebellion again. By the advice of certain of his vassals, he devastated the province of Alsace and laid desolate castles of Count Hugo, who was a relative of the emperor. After that, he assembled a great army of young men, invaded Burgundy, and began to fortify a certain island above castle Solothurn with breastworks and ramparts. But because Rudolf, king of the Burgundians, was afraid to harbor an enemy of the emperor, he forbade the undertaking to him. After [Ernst] had returned from there, he fortified a certain castle above Zürich and incurred no ordinary condemnation by the fatherland, by harassing to a very great degree the church of Reichenau and the abbey of St. Gall. With law and justice thus set aside, he stood fast in his iniquitous endeavors until the return of the emperor.

### 20. Where Duke Ernst surrendered himself again

After peace had been confirmed through all Italy, Emperor Conrad returned to Alamannia in great prosperity and began to take counsel about those who had betrayed the fatherland, holding an assembly of the royal household with his vassals in Augsburg. Coming thence to the town which is called Ulm, he held there a publicly announced assembly.

Duke Ernst did not come here with a suppliant vow. But relying on the great number of the best of his vassals whom he had with him, [he came] in order that he might either make peace with Caesar according to his own taste or leave from there [unimpeded] by virtue of his own power. And when an assembly with his own men had been held, he first reminded them of their sworn promise of fealty [to him]; then he exhorted them not to desert him, lest they lose their honor. [He added] that it would not be seemly for them to be mindless of the fact that in their ancestral histories the Alamanni had always borne witness of good faith and steadfastness toward their lords and that, if they were faithful to him, there would be rewards for themselves and glory and honor for their posterity.

To these words of his, two counts, Frederick and Anselm, responded for the others in this fashion:

"We do not wish to deny that we promised fealty to you firmly against all except him who gave us to you. If we were slaves of our king and emperor, subjected by him to your jurisdiction, it would not be permissible for us to separate ourselves from you. But now, since we are free, and hold our king and emperor the supreme defender of our liberty on earth, as soon as we desert him, we lose our liberty, which no good man, as someone says, loses save with his life. Since this is so, we are willing to obey whatever honorable and just requirement you make of us. If, however, you will something which is contrary to this, we shall return freely into that position whence we came under certain conditions to you."

After hearing these remarks, the duke realized that he was abandoned by his own men and therefore rendered himself to the emperor without any negotiated agreement. Caesar made him go into exile in Saxony to a certain crag which is called Gibichenstein [Giebichenstein], so that, confined there, he might desist from any further rebellion once and for all.

### 21. That the King of Burgundy came to meet the Emperor at Basel

The emperor, traversing Alamannia, received in surrender all who had been rebels against him and cast down their bulwarks. Going through to Basel, he talked to Rudolf, king of Burgundy, who came to meet him there outside the city at a village which is called Muttenz. And after a familiar discussion, the emperor took the king with him into the city. When peace had been confirmed between them – the empress Gisela mediating in all these matters – and the kingdom of Burgundy had been given over to the emperor with the same sort of agreement as that by which it had been given earlier to his predecessor, Emperor Henry, the king [Rudolf], enriched again with gifts, returned with his own men into Burgundy.

But the emperor, descending by the Rhine, came into Franconia, and there Duke Cuono, his cousin, formerly a rebel, gave himself up. The emperor confined him for some time under light guard, and after his bulwarks had been destroyed – the best which he had – he received him into favor and restored his full honor to him. Shortly after, Adalbero, duke of the Istrians or Carinthians, convicted of lese majesty, was exiled with his sons by the emperor, and that Cuono just mentioned received from the emperor his [Adalbero's] dukedom, which the father of this very Cuono is said to have had once. So Duke Cuono, as long as he lived, remained faithful and one who strove well for the emperor and also for his son, King Henry....

### 25. How Duke Ernst received his Dukedom and lost it at once

In the year of the Lord 1030, Emperor Conrad celebrated Easter at Ingelheim. There Ernst, the above-mentioned duke of Alamannia, released from custody, received his dukedom, on the condition that, with all his men, he would pursue as an enemy of the commonwealth Wezelo, his vassal, who had disturbed the kingdom with many factious intrigues, and that he confirm with a solemn vow that he was going to do it. When the duke was unwilling to do this, he was adjudged a state enemy of the emperor, and, with the complete loss of his dukedom, he withdrew from that place with a few men. The emperor gave the dukedom of Alamannia to Herman, the younger brother of this same Ernst, and commended him to Warmann, bishop of Constance. But, by the common counsel of all the princes of the realm, the emperor had the same Ernst and all those resisting justice and peace excommunicated by the bishops and ordered their possessions to be sequestered by the state. The empress Gisela herself—a thing pitiable to recount, but laudable to do — holding her ill-advised son in less esteem than her wise husband, gave publicly official assurance that, whatever happened to him [Ernst; Gisela's son from a previous marriage and Conrad's step-son], she would indulge no vindictiveness or animosity because of this affair.

## 26. That the Emperor came upon the Hungarians with his army

At this same time, many dissensions arose between the Pannonian nation and the Bavarians, through the fault of the Bavarians. And, as a result, King Stephan of Hungary made many incursions and raids in the realm of the Norici (that is, of the Bavarians). Disturbed on this account, Emperor Conrad came upon the Hungarians with a great army. But King Stephan, whose forces were entirely insufficient to meet the emperor, relied solely on the guardianship of the Lord, which he sought with prayers and fasts proclaimed through his whole realm. Since the emperor was not able to enter a kingdom so fortified with rivers and forests, he returned, after he had sufficiently avenged his injury with lootings and burnings on the borders of the kingdom; and it was his wish at a more opportune time to complete the things he had begun. His son, King Henry, however, still a young boy entrusted to the care of Eigilbert, bishop of Freising, received a legation of King Stephan which asked for peace; and solely with the counsel of the princes of the realm, and without his father's knowledge, he granted the favor of reconciliation. Acting justly and wisely, he received in friendship the king who had been wrongly wronged and who sought favor voluntarily.

## 27. That Duke Ernst sought aid from Count Odo

Meanwhile, when this was going on, the aforesaid Ernst, deprived of the dignity of his dukedom, contemplating many things, attempting many things to the end that he might resist the emperor, spent his great labors in vain. After he had gotten together his vassal Wezelo and a few others, he went into Latin Francia [France] to Count Odo, his relative. For the mother of Odo and the mother of Empress Gisela had been sisters. But this man from whom he sought counsel and aid — whether he did not want or did not dare to — gave him no succor against the emperor.

## 28. How Duke Ernst perished

Duke Ernst, having turned back, came again into Alamannia. There he stayed in the safest places, and he lived by petty brigandage in a certain wilderness which is called the Black Forest. Finally, when he was hemmed in on all sides by the soldiery of Caesar, some persons who favored the emperor, by means of ambushes laid in the pastures, took away the best horses which the duke and all his men had. After the horses in which he had placed great reliance had been lost, the duke, no longer caring about anything, did not know what to do in such perturbation. But after he had collected everywhere horses of whatever sort he could get, he left the forest with all the men whom he had then, considering it better to die with honor than to live in shame. And when they had come to woodlands in that region of Alamannia which is called Baar, they saw a deserted camp which their enemies had occupied the night prior. Straightway, they realized that ambushes were prepared for them. For Manegold, a vassal of the emperor, holding a great fief of the abbey of Reichenau, had been placed on guard by the emperor and Warmann, bishop of Constance (who then governed Alamannia in the stead of Duke Herman), lest Duke Ernst make raids to plunder or pillage in the region. At once, Duke Ernst and his followers became all too cheerful, thinking that they were swiftly to avenge their wrongs upon their enemies; and taking to the road, they began to pursue their pursuers. With the same intent, Count Manegold and those who were with him advanced here and there and diligently observed the maneuvers of the duke. With this occasion given on each side, they were so deployed in relation to each other that the one could see and accost the other. There were, however, many more knights on the side of Manegold than on the side of the duke.

Without holding back, all who had come together fought bitterly; those on the side of the duke, aroused by wrath, ferocity, boldness; those on the other side, driven on by desire for glory, for reward. Those who were with the duke, since they thought nothing of life, all hastened to destruction. The duke, since he spared no one, found no one in this battle sparing him, and after being wounded by many, at length he fell dead. There fell Count Wezilo, the vassal of the duke on whose account all these things occurred. The noble men Adalbert and Werin, and many others, were slain there. On the other side, Count Manegold himself, author of this melée, fell and many others with him. The body of Duke Ernst was brought away to Constance, and after an indulgence from the episcopal power had been obtained first [which was necessary] because of his excommunication, he was entombed in the church of St. Mary. The body of Manegold was buried in Reichenau.

This battle, forever most pitiable, occurred on the XV of the kalends of September. When it was reported to the emperor, he is reputed to have said, "Rarely will rabid dogs [live to] multiply with offspring."

## 70. ADAM OF BREMEN ON THE ATTACKS OF BISHOP ADALBERT'S ENEMIES

*Very little is known about Adam of Bremen (ca 1040–ca 1081), who merely identified himself as a canon named "A" in his work. Helmold (see Doc. 78), who drew on this work in his own chronicle, called this work's author "Adam." Adam was born in east Franconia and probably received an education at Bamberg. He came to Bremen in 1066 or 1067, possibly at the invitation of Bishop Adalbert, and was soon made a canon of the cathedral chapter there. Before 1069 he (or another Adam) had been placed in charge of the cathedral school.*

*The following excerpt comes from book 3 of Adam's* History of the Archbishops of Hamburg-Bremen *(written 1072–76) and concerns the episcopate of Adalbert (1043–72). Adalbert had been influential at court during the minority of the Holy Roman Emperor Henry IV, but Adalbert's enemies compelled Henry to dismiss him in 1066. These same enemies that Adalbert had made while trying to increase the power of Bremen then invaded his archbishopric, which is the subject of this extract. Adam blamed Adalbert's excessive involvement in court politics for the decline of the see of Bremen. Adalbert was recalled by Henry and regained part of his property in 1069, but foreign invasion (pagan Wends destroyed Hamburg in 1071–72) would soon trouble his archbishopric.*

Source: trans. Francis J. Tschan, *History of the Archbishops of Hamburg-Bremen* (New York: Columbia University Press, 1959), pp. 148–51, 154–56.

Of these the most hostile both to him and to our Church were Duke Bernhard and his sons. Their envy, enmity, and hatred, likewise also their plottings, reproaches, and calumnies drew the archbishop headlong to make all those offensive remarks of which we have spoken above and made him as it were insane, as long as he appeared to be less than they and yielded to them. Still he gave way at times of his own accord because of his priestly office, wishing to overcome ill will with kindness and to render good for evil. But he labored in vain, as all his efforts to mend his ill-tied friendship with the dukes came to naught in every respect.

Baffled, finally, by the harassments of his persecutors and embittered by sorrow over his afflictions, he more than once cried out with Elijah: "Lord God, [they have] thrown down thy altars, they have slain thy prophets...and

I alone am left, and they seek my life, to take it away." As for how unjustly our bishop suffered such things, it is enough to give here one example from which it can be seen that the friendship he maintained with the envious was of no use.

Spurred on by avarice, the duke moved against the Frisians because they did not pay the tribute they owed. He came into Frisia accompanied by the archbishop, who went only for the sake of reconciling the mutinous folk with the duke. And since the duke was fond of Mammon, he demanded the total sum of the duty, and when he could in no wise be placated with seven hundred marks of silver, the people forthwith became barbarous and furiously enraged and "... rushed on the sword for freedom's sake" [Vergil, *Aeneid*, 8.648]. Many of our men were then wounded, the rest saved themselves by flight. The camps of the duke and the archbishop were sacked. The Church lost much treasure there. Still the loyalty of friendship tested in danger gained us nothing with the duke and his followers, nor did it restrain them from their determination to persecute the Church. They say that the duke, apprehensive of the future, often declared with a sigh that his sons were by the fates destined to destroy the Church of Bremen. For in a dream he saw bears and boars, then stags, and last of all hares going out of his chambers into the church. "The bears and boars," he said, "were our fathers, armed in their fortitude as with teeth. My brother and I are the stags, fitted out only with horns. But our sons are the hares, of moderate strength and timid. For them I fear that in attacking the Church they will incur divine vengeance." With the solemn charge of the fear of God, therefore, he forewarned them not to plan anything impious against the church and its pastor; to injure either her or him is perilous, because an assault on them falls ultimately upon Christ. These injunctions fell on deaf ears. Now let us see how vengeance immediately pursues the sinners.

Bernhard, the duke of the Saxons, died in the seventeenth year of our archbishop. Ever since the days of the elder Lievizo [d. 1013; a former arch-bishop of Hamburg], for forty years, indeed, he had vigorously administered the affairs of the Slavs and the Nordalbingians [a Saxon people] and our own. After his death his sons Ordulf and Hermann received their father's inheri-tance, which boded ill for the Church at Bremen. For they were mindful of the ancient though concealed hatred which their fathers had borne against that church and made up their minds that vengeance was now openly to be wrought on the bishop and the whole vassalage of the church. Indeed, while his father still lived, Duke Ordulf, attended by a hostile multitude, devastated, first, the bishopric of Bremen in Frisia and blinded the vassals of the church; then he ordered others, even legates sent to him to sue for peace, to be publicly whipped and shorn; lastly, he in every way assailed, plundered, struck, and insulted the church and its ministers. Although the bishop was, as he ought to be, fired with ecclesiastical zeal at this treatment and visited the sword of anathema upon those who contemned him, and even referred the dispute to the royal court, he met with nothing but derision. For, as they say, the king [Henry IV], a mere boy, was at first also treated with derision by our counts. Accommodating himself to circumstances, therefore, the archbishop is said to have adopted Count Hermann as a vassal in order to part the oath-bound brothers from each other. The archbishop made use of his knightly service at the time when he, as the king's tutor and chief counselor, set out on an expedition into Hungary, leaving the archbishop of Cologne to oversee the affairs of the kingdom. On having restored to his throne Solomon, whom Béla had expelled, our archbishop returned victorious from Hungary with the boy king.

Then Count Hermann hoped for and solicited a large fief, which the bishop would not grant him. Immediately beside himself with rage, he moved against Bremen with a large army. There he seized everything that came to hand, sparing only the church. All the herds of oxen and horses were taken as spoil. Going in like manner through the entire diocese, he left the men of the Church naked and in want. At that time, too, all the strongholds which the bishop, foreseeing the future, had built in different places were laid level with the ground.

At that time the archbishop held the first place at court. When his charge against the count was heard, the latter was banished in accord with a decision of the palace, but after a year was pardoned through the king's clemency. Then the same Count Hermann and his brother, Duke Ordulf, made satisfaction to the Church for their offense by presenting it with fifty hides of land, and the land rested for a few days.

Distressed at the desolation of the church at Bremen, the king at that time sent it for consolation nearly a hundred vestments besides silver vessels, likewise books, candlesticks, and censers adorned with gold. These are the gifts that the king sent for refurnishing Hamburg....

... At this time our metropolitan is also said to have contemplated the renewal of a kind of golden age in his consulate, by extirpating from the city of God all who work iniquity, evidently those especially who had laid hands on the king or had plundered the churches. Since nearly all the bishops and princes of the realm were afflicted with guilty consciences, they were unanimous in their hatred and conspired to destroy him so that the rest should not be imperiled. They all met together therefore, at Tribur and, since they had the support of the king's presence, drove our archbishop from court as if he were a magician and seducer. So much was his hand "against all men, and all men's hands against him" [Gen. 16:12] that the end of the controversy reached the point of bloodshed.

Now, when our dukes heard that the archbishop had been expelled from the senatorial order, they were filled with great joy and thought that the time to take vengeance on him was also at hand, to deprive him of his bishopric altogether, declaring, "Raze it, even to the foundation thereof," and cut him "off out of the land of the living." Thus, many were their plots, many their taunts against the archbishop, who, because he had no safer place, stayed then in Bremen as if he were besieged and hemmed in by a watchful enemy. Although all the duke's vassals derided the pastor and the church and the people and the sanctuary, still Magnus raged more than all the others and boasted that the taming of the rebel church had been at length reserved for him.

And so the duke's son, Magnus, collected a multitude of brigands and undertook to attack the church, not in the manner in which his forebears had operated but by attacking the person of the pastor of the church. Evidently to put an end to the long drawn-out contest he sought either to maim the bishop in his members or utterly to destroy him. The latter, nevertheless, did not lack craft in protecting himself, but he got absolutely no aid from his vassals. As he was at that time hard pressed by Duke Magnus, the archbishop secretly fled by night to Goslar and stayed there half a year in the security of his estate of Lochtum. His stronghold and revenues were plundered by the enemy. Caught in this distressful noose, the archbishop concluded what was in truth an ignominious but necessary alliance with his oppressor, thus turning his enemy into his vassal. The archbishop presented him in benefice with over a thousand hides of church lands — on the condition, to be sure, that Magnus was without all subterfuge to revindicate and defend the rights of the church to the counties of Frisia, of which Bernhard retained one and Egbert another against the bishop's will.

## 71. THE CATTLE RAID OF COOLEY

*Written in the early twelfth century, the* Táin Bó Cúalnge *is part of the Ulster Cycle of Irish heroic sagas. A collection of stories set in iron-age Ireland, the events of the Táin take place between the second and the first centuries BCE, before the arrival of the Romans and Christians. In the saga, four of Ireland's provinces are ruled by King Ailill and Queen Medb of Connacht. They are in a state of enmity with Conchobor of Ulster, whose province is defended by his nephew, the seventeen-year-old hero Cú Chulainn. Fergus, Cú Chulainn's foster father, is the leader of a group of Ulstermen who have joined forces with Medb. After Ailill and Medb argue over who is wealthier,*

*Medb raids Ulster to take the bull Donn Cúalnge. The following excerpt, from the beginning of the "story proper," comes from the* Book of Leinster *(Recension 2), which is a unified narrative based on earlier versions and oral tradition written by an anonymous monk in the early twelfth century.*

Source: trans. Cecile O'Rahilly, *Táin Bó Cúalnge from the Book of Leinster* (Dublin: Dublin Institute for Advanced Studies, 1984), pp. 171–92.

The four great provinces of Ireland came the next day eastwards over Cruinn, that is, [the] mountain [called Cruinn]. Cú Chulainn went ahead of them. He met the charioteer of Órlám, the son of Ailill and Medb who was at Tamlachta Órláim to the north of Disert Lochad, cutting chariot poles from a holly-tree in the wood. "Well, Láeg," said Cú Chulainn, "boldly do the Ulstermen behave if it is they who are thus cutting down the wood in front of the men of Ireland. And do you stay here for a little while until I find out who is cutting down the wood in this manner." Then Cú Chulainn went on and came upon the charioteer. "What are you doing here, lad?" asked Cú Chulainn. "I am cutting the chariot poles from a holly-tree here," said the driver, "for our chariots broke yesterday hunting that famous deer, Cú Chulainn. And by your valor, warrior, come to my help, lest that famous Cú Chulainn come upon me." "Take your choice, lad," said Cú Chulainn, "either to gather the poles or to strip them." "I shall gather them for it is easier." Cú Chulainn began to strip the poles, and he would draw them between his toes and between his fingers against their bends and knots until he made them smooth and polished and slippery and trimmed. He would make them so smooth that a fly could not stay on them by the time he cast them from him. Then the charioteer looks at him. "Indeed it seems to me that it was not a labor befitting you that I imposed on you. Who are you?" asked the driver. "I am the famous Cú Chulainn of whom you spoke just now." "Woe is me!" cried the charioteer, "for that am I done for." "I shall not slay you, lad," said Cú Chulainn, "for I do not wound charioteers or messengers or men unarmed. And where is your master anyway?" "Over yonder on the mound," said the charioteer. "Go to him and warn him to be on his guard, for if we meet, he will fall at my hands." Then the charioteer went to his master, and swiftly as the charioteer went, more swiftly still went Cú Chulainn and struck off Órlám's head. And he raised the head aloft and displayed it to the men of Ireland.

Then came the three Meic Árach on to the ford at Aid Ciannacht to meet with Cú Chulainn. Lon and Ualu and Díliu were their names; Mes Lir and Mes Laig and Mes Lethair were the names of their charioteers. They came to encounter Cú Chulainn because they deemed excessive what he had done against them the previous day, namely, killing the two sons of Nera mac Nuatair meic Thacáin at Áth Gabla and killing Órlám, the son of Ailill and Medb, as well and displaying his head to the men of Ireland. [They came then] that they might kill Cú Chulainn in the same way and bear away his head as a trophy. They went to the wood and cut three rods of white hazel [to put] in the hands of their charioteers so that all six of them together might fight with Cú Chulainn. Cú Chulainn attacked them and cut off their six heads. Thus fell Meic Árach by the hand of Cú Chulainn.

There came also Lethan on to his ford on the Níth in the district of Conaille Muirtheimne, to fight with Cú Chulainn. He attacked him on the ford. Áth Carpait was the name of the ford where they reached it, for their chariots had been broken in the fighting at the ford. Mulchi fell on the hill between the two fords, whence it is still called Gúalu Mulchi. Then Cú Chulainn and Lethan met, and Lethan fell by the hand of Cú Chulainn who cut off his head from his trunk on the ford, but he left it with it, that is, he left his head with his body. Whence the name of the ford ever since is Áth Lethan in the district of Conaille Muirtheimne.

*The four provinces ravage the plains of Mag mBreg and Mag Muirtheimne. Cú Chulainn kills one of Medb's handmaids, thinking it is Medb, along with a hundred of her men.*

That night the men of the four great provinces of Ireland came and encamped in Druim Én in the district of Conaille Muirthemne, and Cú Chulainn took up his position close beside them at Ferta in Lerga. And that night Cú Chulainn waved and brandished and shook his weapons so that a hundred warriors among the host died of fright and fear and dread of Cú Chulainn. Medb told Fiachu mac Fir Aba of the Ulstermen to go and parley with Cú Chulainn and to offer him terms. "What terms would be offered him?" asked Fiachu mac Fir Aba. "Not hard to say," answered Medb. "He shall be compensated for the damage done to Ulstermen that he may be paid as the men of Ireland best adjudge. He shall have entertainment at all times in Crúachu and wine and mead shall be served to him, and he shall come into my service and into the service of Ailill for that is more advantageous for him than to be in the service of the petty lord with whom he now is." – And that is the most scornful and insulting speech that was made on the Foray of Cúailnge, namely, to call Conchobor, the finest king of a province in Ireland, a petty lord.

Then came Fiachu mac Fir Aba to parley with Cú Chulainn. Cú Chulainn welcomed him. "I trust that welcome." "You may well trust it." "To parley with you have I come from Medb." "What [terms] did you bring?" [The terms are presented as above.] "No, indeed," said Cú Chulainn. "I would not exchange my mother's brother for another king." "Come early tomorrow to Glenn Fochaíne to a meeting with Medb and Fergus." ...[At the meeting] Medb began to address Cú Chulainn and chanted a lay:

"Cú Chulainn renowned in song, ward off from us your sling. Your fierce famed fighting has overcome us and confused us."

"Medb from Múr mac Mágach, I am no inglorious coward. As long as I live I shall not yield to you the driving of the herd of Cúailnge."

"If you would accept from us, O triumphant Hound of Cúailnge, half your cows and half your womenfolk, you will get them from us through fear of you."

"Since I, by virtue of those I have slain, am the veteran who guards Ulster, I shall accept no terms until I am given every milch cow, every woman of the Gael."

"Too greatly do you boast, after slaughtering our nobles, that we should keep guard on the best of our steeds, the best of our possessions, all because of one man."

"O daughter of Eochu Find Fáil, I am no good in such a contention. Though I am a warrior – clear omen! – my counsels are few."

"No reproach to you is what you say, many-retinued son of Deichtere. The terms are such as will bring fame to you, O triumphant Cú Chulainn."

After that lay: Cú Chulainn accepted none of the terms that Medb asked of him. In that manner they parted in the glen and each side withdrew equally angry.

*The men of the four provinces camp for three nights.*

And every night until the bright hour of sunrise on the morrow, Cú Chulainn used to kill a hundred of their warriors. "Not long will our hosts last in this manner," said Medb, "if Cú Chulainn kill a hundred of our men every night. Why do we not offer him terms and why do we not parley with him?" "What terms are those?" asked Ailill. " Let him be offered those of the cattle that have milk and those of the captives who are base-born, and let him cease to ply his sling on the men of Ireland and let him allow the hosts at least to sleep."

*Mac Roth goes to offer these terms to Cú Chulainn and returns.*

I found a surly, angry, fearsome, fierce fellow between Focháin and the sea. I do not know if he is the famed Cú Chulainn." "Did he accept those terms?" "He did not indeed." And Mac Roth told them the reason why he did not accept. "It was Cú Chulainn to whom you spoke," said Fergus.

"Let other terms be taken to him," said Medb. "What terms?" asked Ailill. "All the dry kine of the herds, all the noble among the captives, and let him cease to ply his sling on the hosts for not pleasant is the thunderfeat he performs against them every evening."

*Cú Chulainn rejects these as well. He will only accept combat with one man of the army of the peoples of Ireland each day. Medb agrees to these terms, and Cú Chulainn begins to kill the men one by one. Cú Chulainn sends Láeg to find out who will attack next.*

Then Láeg went back to Cú Chulainn, crestfallen, sad, joyless and mournful. "Crestfallen, sad, joyless and mournful my friend Láeg comes to me," said Cú Chulainn. "It means that one of my fosterbrothers comes to attack me." – For Cú Chulainn disliked more that a warrior of the same training as himself should come to him rather than some other warrior. – "Good now, friend Láeg," said Cú Chulainn, "who comes to attack me today?" "The curse of his intimacy and brotherhood, of his familiarity and friendship be upon him! It is your very own fosterbrother, Fer Báeth mac Fir Bend. He was taken just now into Medb's tent. The girl was placed at his side, and it is she who pours goblets for him. It is she who kisses him with every drink, it is she who serves his meal. Not for all and sundry does Medb intend the liquor which is served to Fer Báeth. Only fifty wagon-loads of it were brought to the camp."

Fer Báeth waited not until morning but went at once to renounce his friendship with Cú Chulainn. Cú Chulainn adjured him by their friendship and intimacy and brotherhood, but Fer Báeth did not consent to relinquish the combat. Cú Chulainn left him in anger, and trampled a sharp shoot of holly into the sole of his foot so that it injured alike flesh and bone and skin. Cú Chulainn tore out the holly shoot by the roots and cast it over his shoulder after Fer Báeth, and he cared not whether it reached him or not. The holly shoot hit Fer Báeth in the depression at the nape of his neck and went out through his mouth on to the ground, and thus Fer Báeth died.

*Cú Chulainn again sends Láeg to ask Lugaid who will attack next. Lugaid will speak to Cú Chulainn.*

His two horses were harnessed for Lugaid and his chariot was yoked to them. He came to meet Cú Chulainn and a conversation took place between them. Then said Lugaid: "They are urging a brother of mine to come and fight with you, a foolish youth, rough, uncouth, but strong and stubborn, and he is sent to fight you so that when he falls by you, I may go to avenge his death on you, but I shall never do so. And by the friendship that is between us both, do not kill my brother. Yet I swear, that even if you all but kill him, I grant you leave to do so, for it is in despite of me that he goes against you." Then Cú Chulainn went back and Lugaid went to the camp.


## 72. FEUD BETWEEN BISHOP GAUDRY AND BARON GÉRARD IN THE *AUTOBIOGRAPHY* OF GUIBERT OF NOGENT

*Guibert (ca 1053/65–ca 1125) was abbot of Nogent, near Laon, from 1104 to sometime around 1125. His* Autobiography *(1125), in addition to describing his childhood, recounts his time as a monk at Fly, his life as abbot of Nogent, and the affairs of the commune of Laon, as in the extract below. Guibert believed that the troubles at Laon were due to the errors of the bishops of Laon, starting with Bishop Adalbero's love of wealth and betrayal of his lord, Charles of Lorraine, in 991. Adalbero was followed by a series of bishops criticized for their greed, bribery, desire for fame, failure to guard the rights of the church, simony, and lust. With his account of Bishop Gaudry (elected in 1106) below, Guibert added involvement in murder to this list. The events below begin around 1109, about three years after Gaudry's ordination.*

Source: trans. J. F. Benton, *Self and Society in Medieval France: The Memoirs of Guibert of Nogent* (New York: Harper and Row, 1970), pp. 157–74.


[Book 3]


5. About three years after his ordination, the bishop [Gaudry] gave the following sign, as it were, to his time. One of the barons of the city was the castellan of the nunnery, named Gérard, a man of great power. Although in appearance he was short in stature and lean of body, he had so lively a mind and tongue and such energy in the pursuit of war that he compelled the provinces of Soissons, Laon, and Noyon to fear him, and won the respect of a great many men. Although he was known far and wide as one of sterling character, sometimes he made biting jests in filthy language against those about him, but never against people of good character. He therefore took it upon himself both to speak ill in private and to show open displeasure against that countess [Sybille, wife of Enguerrand of Boves] to whom some reference was made before. In doing this he acted in a very wrongheaded manner, because he was attacking Enguerrand, this woman's consort, who

had with his great wealth advanced Gérard's fortunes. Before taking a wife, Gérard himself had been too intimate with the woman of whom we are speaking [Sybille]. After he had been her lover for some time, when he married he reined in his lasciviousness. Then the women, too, began to attack one another with foul words. They were mutually aware of their earlier looseness, and the more they knew of each other's secrets, the fouler was their abuse. The countess was enraged against the other woman's husband [Gérard] because she had been jilted by him, and against his wife because she knew that the woman frequently abused her with twisted words. Being more venomous than any serpent, her determination to ruin the man grew greater every day.

Because God puts a stumbling block in the way of those who sin willfully, an opportunity for destroying Gérard suddenly occurred in an outbreak of enmity between him and Bishop Gaudry. Gérard said unsuitable things about the bishop and his associates, which the bishop endured silently but not patiently. After plotting with his own people and almost all the leading nobles of the city for the death of Gérard, and after exchanging with them mutual oaths of assistance, to which certain wealthy women were also parties, Bishop Gaudry left the matter in the hands of his fellow-conspirators and went on a journey to St. Peter's at Rome. He was led there by the basest designs, not to seek the Apostle, as Thou knowest, O God, but so that through his absence he might seem uninvolved in such a crime. Setting out about Martinmas, he arrived at Rome and stayed there for a while until he learned of the accomplishment of the death of the man he hated, for the less Gérard was hated by all good people, the more hateful he was to the evil.

The deed was done in the following manner. On Friday in the week of Epiphany, in the morning while the light was still faint, Gérard rose from his bed to go to the cathedral of Notre-Dame. When one of the nobles bound by that oath came up to him, he told him about a dream he had the night before, which he said had frightened him thoroughly. He vividly dreamed that two bears were tearing out of his body either his liver or his lungs, I am not sure which.

Alas Gérard had had the misfortune not to receive the sacrament for the following reason. A monk living at Barisis St. Amand had undertaken to teach the French language to two little boys who could speak only the Germanic tongue. Now, Barisis with the manors attached to it was under Gérard's protection. Seeing that the boys had fine manners and knowing they were not of mean birth, he seized them and held them for ransom. The mother of the boys sent with the sum agreed upon a fur cloak made of ermine and called a mantle.

Dressed in this mantle over a robe of Tyrian purple, he went on horseback with some of his knights to the church. After entering, he stopped before the image of the crucified Lord, his followers dispersed here and there among the various altars to the saints, and the servants of the conspirators kept an eye on them. Word was then sent to the household of the bishop in the episcopal palace that Gérard of Quierzy (as he was called, since he was lord of that castle) had come to the church to pray. Carrying their swords under their cloaks, the bishop's brother Rorigon and others went through the vaulted ambulatory to the place where he was praying. He was stationed at the foot of a column, called a pillar, a few columns away from the pulpit, at about the middle of the church. While the morning was still dark and there were few people to be seen in the great church, they seized the man from behind as he prayed. He was praying with the fastening of his cloak thrown behind and his hands clasped on his breast. Seizing the cloak from behind, one of them held him in it like a sack so that he could not easily move his hands. When the bishop's steward had seized him in this fashion, he said, "You are taken." With his usual fierceness, Gérard turned his eye round on him (for he had only one) and looking at him said, "Get out of here, you dirty lecher!" But the steward said to Rorigon, "Strike!" and, drawing his sword with his left hand, he wounded him between the nose and the brow. Knowing he was done for, Gérard said, "Take me wherever you want." Then as they stabbed at him repeatedly and pressed him hard, in desperation he cried out with all his strength, "Holy Mary, aid me!" Saying this, he fell in extreme suffering.

The two archdeacons of the church, Gautier and Guy, were in this conspiracy with the bishop. Guy was also the treasurer, and had a house on the other side of the church. From this house, there soon rushed out two servants, who ran up to him and took part in the murder. For by that sacrilegious oath it had been agreed that if those of the bishop's palace took the first step, helpers should immediately come forth from that house. When they had slashed his throat and his legs and given him other wounds, and he was groaning in the nave of the church in his last agonies, a few of the clergy who were then in the choir and some poor women who were going around to pray murmured against them, but half dead with fear, they did not dare to cry out openly. When the murder had been committed, the two carefully picked knights returned to the bishop's palace, and with them, along with the archdeacons, were gathered the nobles of the city, thus betraying their own treason.

At this the royal *prévôt* [provost], a very capable man named Ivo, summoned the king's men and the burghers of the abbey of St. Jean, of which Gérard had been the guardian. They attacked the houses of those who had taken the oath to the conspiracy, plundering and burning and driving them out of the city. The archdeacons and the nobles accompanied the murderers of Gérard everywhere, making a display of their fealty to the absent bishop.

6. The bishop remained at Rome, as if he enjoyed the presence of the apostolic lord, while he listened with eager expectation for some pleasing news to reach him from French parts. At last the fulfillment of his wishes was announced, and the lord pope became aware that a great crime had been done in a great church. The bishop had an interview with the pope and by flattering presents warded off suspicion of this infamy. And so, more pleased than ever, Gaudry left Rome.

Since the church had been outraged by that wicked act and needed purification, a messenger was sent to Hubert, the bishop of Senlis, who had recently lost his power on a charge of simony, summoning him to do that work. At the assembly of the clergy and people, I was requested by Master Anselm, the dean of the church, and by the canons to preach to the people on the calamity that had occurred. The following is the general sense of that address:

"Save me, O God, for the waters are come in even unto my soul. I stick fast in the mine of the deep and there is no sure standing" [Ps. 68:2–3]. If you have had evil of some sort up to this point, now the sword has come even unto my soul. You are sunk in the mire of the deep, since as the just deserts of your sins, you had fallen into the extreme evil of utter despair. Amid such things there is no sure standing, because the honor and power of those to whom you should have recourse in peril – that is, your rulers and nobles – are fallen. Though your bodies were sometimes hard pressed by your hatreds of one another, yet the soul was untouched, since the church, where the desire of salvation remained, rejoiced that it flourished inwardly without any stain. The waters and the sword come in even unto the soul when tribulations and discords penetrate and pollute the sanctity of the inner refuge. How do you, who are ignorant of spiritual things, think that place can obtain any reverence from you when a man cannot say his prayers there in safety? Behold, God has 'sent upon us the wrath of his indignation: indignation and wrath and trouble, which he sent by evil angels' [Ps. 77:49]. There is a wrath of indignation, wrath conceived out of indignation. Indignation, as you know, is less than wrath. Was not God indignant with the transgressions of your sins, when outside your city you often permitted plunder, burning, and killing? Was he not wrathful when strife from without was brought within this city and civil discord became active in our midst, when with mutual provocations lords moved against burghers, and burghers against lords, and when with improper hostility abbots' men were angered at bishops' men, and bishops' men against abbots' men? But because indignation and wrath brought no amendment from you, at last he brought down tribulation on your stubborn minds. It was not simply any church that was defiled with Christian blood, not anywhere that the beginning of war brought force into the church and destroyed the refugees, but malignant passion conceived with criminal deliberation butchered a man in prayer before the image of Christ hanging on the Cross, not in simply any church, I say, but in the most flourishing of the churches of Gaul, one whose fame has traveled far beyond the Latin world. And who was the man? Was he not one admired for his illustrious birth, whose feats of arms, so remarkable in a man small in size but of lofty soul, made him famous throughout France? Therefore the place, the crime, and the shame will be talked about everywhere. If, then, in your souls, in your innermost hearts, you are not in fear at this mournful moment, if you have no compunction for such dishonor done to a sacred place, be assured that without doubt God will make a way for a path to his anger; that is, to your utter destruction, he will openly spread abroad his hidden anger. And how can you think that God will spare the corralling of cattle – that is, of your bodies – when because of your obstinacy in sin he did not spare souls from death? Since divine vengeance with its deadly advance comes on against us step by step, be sure that unless you show yourselves amended under God's scourge, you will fall into a far worse state through those civil conflicts that are arising among you."

Responding to the request of the clergy and the wish of the people, and weaving together these and other remarks, I declared that the murderers of that noble man, their backers in that outrage, and their confederates ought to be excommunicated by Bishop Hubert, who was reconciling the church, and not less those who had defended or harbored them. And when their excommunication had been pronounced by all of us, the church was duly reconciled. Meanwhile this sentence of anathema was carried to the ears of the archdeacons and nobles, who had withdrawn from the community of the city. Because of the sermon which I preached and the excommunication that was pronounced, all those who had been cut off from the church turned their hatred against me. Archdeacon Gautier in particular was in a frenzy of rage against me. There was indeed terrible thundering to be heard, but out of it, by God's will, no lightning came. In secret they were against me, openly they showed respect. Let me now return to what I have left out.

Armed with bulls and papal rescripts [rulings], the lord bishop returned from Rome. After the murder of Gérard, since the king believed without doubt that the bishop was privy to the crime, which under color of absence he sought to conceal, he ordered that all the bishop's palace should be despoiled of grain, wine, and meat. While he was still in Rome, the bishop was aware of the plundering and the cause of it. And so letters were sent to the king, who had determined that he should be kept out of his see and had deprived him of his property, and other letters were dispatched by him to his fellow-bishops and to the abbots of his own and other dioceses. As we have said before, the bridge over the Ailette was on the boundary between the dioceses of Laon and Soissons, and so those archdeacons and nobles whom we had just excommunicated hastened to meet him there when he first set foot on the soil of his diocese. He received them with such loving kisses and embraces that he did not deign to pay a visit to the church of Notre-Dame, which by God's will we serve, although that was the first in his bishopric to which he came, but close to it he had a long talk with those who he thought were the only ones faithful to him. Leaving there, he was entertained at Coucy with all his following.

When I knew this, since I had greatly feared such conduct on his part, I refrained entirely from seeing or saluting him. After three days, if I am not mistaken, he let the madness which he inwardly felt against me seem outwardly to be lulled (for his satellites had bitterly attacked me before him with regard to the aforesaid events), and he ordered me to come to him. When I had presented myself there and had seen his house full of excommunicated men and murderers, I was enraged. He accused me of striving for his exclusion from the church, showing me the pope's letters. I promised what help I could, falsely, as Thou knowest, O God, and not from my heart. For I saw that he was truly in evil communication with those whom his own church had excommunicated and who had so greatly defiled it, since Enguerrand of Coucy was sitting beside him, and he was cherished by the countess, who had sharpened the swords of the two murderers with her own tongue the day before Gérard was killed. Since he was shut out of the city by the king's orders, with exceedingly rash boldness he threatened to enter it with the help of other knights in the city, and declared he would do by force of arms what would scarcely be possible for the imperial Caesars. He collected a troop of knights and spent large sums of what he had accumulated by evil means, but, as was usual with him, without anything coming of it. At length, after gaining nothing but ridicule with so many auxiliaries, with the help of intermediaries and a huge bribe he made terms with King Louis, the son of King Philip, for himself and his accomplices in the murder of Gérard, that is, the nobles of the city and both the archdeacons.

After entering the city, he held a conventicle at St. Nicolas-aux-Bois, and during the mass which he celebrated there, he declared he was about to excommunicate those who had injured the goods of the conspirators after Gérard was killed and had then left the city. When I heard him say this, whispering in the ear of a fellow-abbot sitting next to me, I said, "Do listen to this absurd twist. He ought to excommunicate those who polluted his church with such a horrible crime, whereas he revenges himself on those who inflicted a just punishment on the murderers." The bishop was afraid of everyone with a good conscience, and when he saw me muttering, he thought I was speaking of him. "What are you saying, lord abbot?" he asked. Then Archdeacon Gautier, putting himself forward before he had permission to speak, said, "Go on, lord, with what you had begun. The lord abbot was speaking of other things."

And so he excommunicated those who had harmed the band of sacrilegious slaughterers, an act that was execrated by clergy and people. For a long time the whole city and diocese were embittered against the bishop because he put off for so long excommunication of the murderers of Gérard. At last, seeing himself suspected and almost cursed by everyone, he did excommunicate the guilty men and their accomplices. Moreover, since he had promised much money to the royal courtiers who had helped him and the accomplices of the assassins with the king, when he then began to draw back from his promises, who shall say what taunts he heard in public? None of those who were his accomplices dared to enter the king's court until with much silver and gold they had redeemed their doomed heads from the death threatening them. And yet he could not be accused by the church when it was known that he was excused by the Apostolic See.

7. ... After this sworn association of mutual aid among the clergy, nobles, and people had been established, the bishop returned with much wealth from England. Angered at those responsible for this innovation, for a long time he kept away from the city. But at last a quarrel full of honor and glory began between him and Gautier the archdeacon, his accomplice. The archdeacon made very unbecoming remarks about his bishop concerning the death of Gérard. I do not know what the bishop did with others on this matter, but I do know that he complained to me about Gautier, saying, "Lord abbot, if Gautier should happen to bring up any charges against me at some council, would you take it without offense? At the time when you left your monks and retired to Fly, didn't he openly flatter you but secretly raise up discord against you, publicly taking your side but privately stirring me up against you?" Talking like this, he inveigled me to oppose that dangerous man, conscious of the very great weight of the charges against him, and fearful and suspicious of universal condemnation.

Although he said that he was moved by relentless wrath against those who had sworn an oath to the association and those who were the principals in the transaction, in the end his high-sounding words were suddenly quieted by the offer of a great heap of silver and gold. Then he swore that he would maintain the rights of the commune, following the terms of the charters of the city of Noyon and the town of St. Quentin. The king, too, was induced to confirm the same thing by oath with a bribe from the people.

O my God, who can describe the controversy that broke out when, after accepting so many gifts from the people, they then took oaths to overturn what they had sworn; that is, when they tried to return the serfs to their former condition after once freeing them from the yoke of their exactions? The hatred of the bishop and the nobles for the burghers was indeed implacable, and as he was not strong enough to crush the freedom of the French, following the fashion of Normandy and England, the pastor remained inactive, forgetful of his sacred calling through his insatiable greed. Whenever one of the people was brought into a court of law, he was judged not on his condition in the eyes of God but, if I may put it this way, on his bargaining power, and he was drained of his substance to the last penny.

Since the taking of gifts is commonly attended by the subversion of all justice, the coiners of the currency, knowing that if they did wrong in their office they could save themselves by paying money, corrupted the coinage with so much base metal that because of this many people were reduced to poverty. As they made their coins of the cheapest bronze, which in a moment by certain dishonest practices they made brighter than silver, the attention of the foolish people was shamefully deceived, and, giving up their goods of great or little value, they got in exchange nothing but the most debased dross. The lord bishop's acceptance of this practice was well rewarded, and thus not only within the diocese of Laon but in all directions the ruin of many was hastened. When he was deservedly powerless to uphold or improve the value of his own currency, which he had wickedly debased, he instituted halfpence of Amiens, also very debased, to be current in the city for some time. And when he could by no means keep them going, he struck a contemporary impression on which he had stamped a pastoral staff to represent himself. This was received with such secret laughter and scorn that it had even less value than the debased coinage.

However, since on the issue of each of these new coins a proclamation was made that no one should laugh at the dreadful designs, there were a great many opportunities to accuse the people of speaking evil of the bishop's ordinances, and hence they could exact all sorts of heavy fines. Moreover, a monk named Thierry, who had the most shameful reputation in every respect, imported very large quantities of silver from Flanders and from Tournai, of which he was native. Bring it all down to the very debased money of Laon, he scattered it all over the surrounding province. By appealing to the greed of the rich people of the province with his hateful presents and by bringing in lies, perjury, and poverty, he robbed the country of truth, justice, and wealth. No enemy action, no plundering, no burning has ever hurt the province more since the Roman walls contained the ancient and thoroughly respected mint of the city.

Since

> Sooner or later long-hidden sin
> Forces its way through the veil of decency.
> Glistening things cannot be concealed,
> And as bright light pierces glass,
> So sin shows through the countenance,

what the bishop had done to Gérard, secretly and as if he were not responsible, he did some time afterward to another Gérard, giving manifest proof of his cruelty. This Gérard was some sort of rural officer or manorial bailiff of the peasants who belonged to him. The bishop considered him a particular enemy because Gérard inclined toward the most evil man of all we know in this generation, Thomas, the reputed son of that Enguerrand with whom we dealt before. The bishop seized this Gérard and threw him into a prison in the episcopal palace, and then at night had his African man put out his eyes. By this deed he brought open shame upon himself, and the old story of what he had done to the first Gérard was dug out again, both clergy and people being aware that a canon of the Council of Toledo, if I am not mistaken, forbade bishops, priests, and clerks to execute or pass a sentence of death or mutilation. The news of this also angered the king. I do not know whether the story reached the Apostolic See, but I do know that the pope suspended him from his office, and I believe he did it for no other reason. To make matters worse, during his suspension he dedicated a church. Therefore he went to Rome, softened the lord pope with gifts once again, and was sent back to us with his authority restored. And so, seeing that masters and subjects were by act and will partners in wickedness, God could no longer restrain his judgment and at last permitted the malice that had been conceived to break out into open rage. When one is driven headlong by pride, through the vengeance of God he is completely shattered by a dreadful fall.

Calling together the nobles and certain of the clergy in the last days of Lent in the most holy Passiontide of our Lord, the bishop determined to attack the commune, to which he had sworn and had with presents induced the king to swear. He had summoned the king to that pious duty, and on the day before Good Friday – that is, on Maundy Thursday – he instructed the king and all his people to break their oaths, after first placing his own neck in that noose. As I said before, this was the day on which his predecessor

Bishop Ascelin had betrayed his king. On the very day when he should have performed that most glorious of all episcopal duties, the consecration of the oil and the absolution of the people from their sins, he was not even seen to enter the church. He was intriguing with the king's courtiers so that after the sworn association was destroyed the king would restore the laws of the city to their former state. But the burghers, fearing their overthrow, promised the king and his courtiers four hundred pounds, and possibly more. In reply, the bishop begged the nobles to go with him to interview the king, and they promised on their part seven hundred pounds. King Louis, Philip's son, was a remarkable person who seemed well-suited for royal majesty, mighty in arms, intolerant toward sloth in business, of dauntless courage in adversity; although in other respects he was a good man, in this matter he was most unjust and paid too much attention to worthless persons debased by greed. This redounded to his own great loss and blame and the ruin of many, which certainly happened here and elsewhere.

When the king's desire was turned, as I said, toward the larger promise and he ruled against God, the oaths of the bishop and the nobles were voided without any regard for honor or the sacred season. Because of the turmoil with which he had so unjustly struck the people, that night the king was afraid to sleep outside the bishop's palace, although he had the right to compulsory lodging elsewhere. Very early the next morning the king departed, and the bishop promised the nobles they need have no fear about the agreement to pay so much money, informing them that he would himself pay whatever they had promised. "And if I do not fulfill my promise," he said, "hand me over to the king's prison until I pay it off."

After the bonds of the association were broken, such rage, such amazement seized the burghers that all the craftsmen abandoned their jobs, and the stalls of the tanners and cobblers were closed and nothing was exposed for sale by the innkeepers and chapmen, who expected to have nothing left when the lords began plundering. For at once the property of such individuals was calculated by the bishop and nobles, and the amount any man was known to have given to establish the commune was demanded of him to pay for its annulment.

These events took place on the Parasceve, which means preparations. On Holy Saturday, when they should have been preparing to receive the Body and Blood of the Lord, they were actually preparing only for murder and perjury. To be brief, all the efforts of the bishop and the nobles in these days were reserved for fleecing their inferiors. But those inferiors were no longer merely angry, but were goaded into an animal rage. Binding themselves by mutual oaths, they conspired for the death, or rather the murder, of the bishop and his accomplices. They say that forty took the oath. Their great undertaking could not be kept completely secret, and when it came to the attention of Master Anselm toward evening of Holy Saturday, he sent word to the bishop, who was retiring to rest, not to go out to the service of matins, knowing that if he did he would be killed. With excessive pride the bishop stupidly said, "Nonsense, I'm not likely to die at the hands of such people." But although he scorned them orally, he did not dare to go out for matins and to enter the church.

The next day, as he followed the clergy in procession, he ordered the people of his household and all the knights to come behind him carrying short swords under their garments. During this procession when a little disorder began to arise, as often happens in a crowd, one of the burghers came out of the church and thought the time had come for the murder to which they were sworn. He then began to cry out in a loud voice, as if he were signaling, "Commune, Commune!" over and over again. Because it was a feast day, this was easily stopped, yet it brought suspicion on the opposition. And so, when the service of the mass was over, the bishop summoned a great number of peasants from the episcopal manors and manned the towers of the cathedral and ordered them to guard his palace, although they hated him almost as much, since they knew that the piles of money which he had promised the king must be drained from their own purses.

On Easter Monday it is the custom for the clergy to assemble at the abbey of St. Vincent. Since the conspirators knew they had been anticipated the day before, they had decided to act on this and they would have done so if they had not seen that all the nobles were with the bishop. They did find one of the nobles in the outskirts of the city, a harmless man who had recently married a young cousin of mine, a girl of modest character. But they were unwilling to attack him, fearing to put others on their guard.

Coming through to Tuesday and feeling more secure, the bishop dismissed those men whom he had put in the towers and palace to protect him and whom he had to feed there from his own resources. On Wednesday I went to him because through his disorders he had robbed me of my grain supply and of some legs of pork, called *bacons* in French. When I requested him to relieve the city of these great disturbances, he replied, "What do you think they can do with their riots? If Jean, my Moor, were to take by the nose the most powerful man among them, he would not even dare to grunt. For just now I have compelled them to renounce what they call their commune for as long as I live." I said something, and then, seeing the man was overcome with arrogance, I stopped. But before I left the city, because of his instability we quarreled with mutual recriminations. Although he was warned by many of the imminent peril, he took no notice of anyone.

## 73. *THE MURDER OF CHARLES THE GOOD* BY GALBERT OF BRUGES

*Galbert of Bruges (d. 1134) was a Flemish notary and chronicler who worked in the service of Charles the Good, count of Flanders. This is an extract of his famous account of the murder of Charles on 2 March 1127 by members of the Erembald clan led by Bertulf, an important official known as the provost of Bruges. The Erembalds, according to the account, were men of peasant stock who had risen up to become one of the leading families of the region. They became enemies of the count when Charles sought to reduce them to their former condition of servitude. According to Galbert, the events leading up to the murder of the count originated in the feud pitting Bertulf and his nephews against a man named Thancmar. This account provides a valuable description of how feuding parties undertook acts of vengeance.*

Source: trans. James Bruce Ross, *The Murder of Charles the Good Count of Flanders by Galbert of Bruges,* rev. ed. (New York: Harper and Row, 1967), pp. 102–19.

### 9. Private war breaks out between Borsiard and Thancmar, 1127

When strife and conflict broke out between his [that is, Bertulf's] nephews and those of Thancmar, whose side the count justly favored, the provost was delighted because it gave him an opportunity to betray the count, for he had called to the aid of his nephews all the knights of our region, using money, influence, and persuasion. They besieged Thancmar on all sides in the place where he had entrenched himself, and finally with a considerable force strongly attacked those within. Breaking the bolts of the gates, they cut down the orchards and hedges of their enemies. Though the provost did not take part and acted as if he had done nothing, he actually did everything by direction and deception. He pretended in public that he was full of good will and told his enemies that he grieved to see his nephews engaged in so much strife and killing, although he himself had incited them to all these crimes. In that conflict many on both sides fell on that day wounded or dead. When the provost had learned that this fight was going on, he himself went to the carpenters who were working in the cloister of the brothers and ordered that their tools, that is, their axes, should be taken to that place for use in cutting down the tower and orchards and houses of his enemies. Then he sent around to various houses in the town to collect axes which were quickly taken to that place. And when in the night his nephews had returned with five hundred knights and squires and innumerable footsoldiers, he took them into the cloister and refectory of the brothers where he entertained them all with various kinds of food and drink and was very happy and boastful about the outcome.

237

And while he was harassing his enemies in this way, spending a great deal in support of those who were helping his nephews, first the squires and then the knights began to plunder the peasants, even seizing and devouring the flocks and cattle of the country people. The nephews of the provost were forcibly seizing the belongings of the peasants and appropriating them for their own use. But none of the counts from the beginning of the realm had allowed such pillaging to go on in the realm, because great slaughter and conflict come to pass in this way.

### 10. The count takes measures against the nephews of Bertulf, 27–28 February 1127, and returns to Bruges

When the country people heard that the count had come to Ypres, about two hundred of them went to him secretly and at night, and kneeling at his feet begged him for his customary paternal help. They entreated him to order their goods to be returned to them, that is, their flocks and herds, clothes and silver, and all the other furniture of their houses which the nephews of the provost had seized together with those who had fought with them continuously in that attack and siege. After listening solemnly to the complaints of those appealing to him, the count summoned his counselors, and even many who were related to the provost, asking them by what punishment and with what degree of severity justice should deal with this crime. They advised him to burn down Borsiard's house without delay because he had plundered the peasants of the count; and therefore strongly urged him to destroy that house because as long as it stood, so long would Borsiard indulge in fighting and pillaging and even killing, and would continue to lay waste the region. And so the count, acting on this advice, went and burned the house and destroyed the place to its foundations. Then that Borsiard and the provost and their accomplices were beside themselves with anxiety both because in this act the count had clearly lent aid and comfort to their enemies and because the count was daily disquieting them about their servile status and trying in every way to establish his rights over them.

After burning the house the count went on to Bruges. When he had settled down in his house, his close advisers came to him and warned him, saying that the nephews of the provost would betray him because now they could claim as pretext the burning of the house, although even if the count had not done this they were going to betray him anyway. After the count had eaten, mediators came and appealed to him on behalf of the provost and his nephews, begging the count to turn his wrath from them and to receive them mercifully back into his friendship. But the count replied that he would act justly and mercifully toward them if they would henceforth give up their fighting and pillaging; and he assured them, moreover, that he would certainly compensate Borsiard with a house that was even better. He swore, however, that as long as he was count, Borsiard should never again have any property in that place where the house had been burned up, because as long as he lived there near Thancmar he would never do anything but fight and feud with his enemies and pillage and slaughter the people.

The mediators, some of whom were aware of the treachery, did not bother the count very much about the reconciliation, and since the servants were going about offering wine they asked the count to have better wine brought in. When they had drunk this, they kept on asking to be served again still more abundantly, as drinkers usually do, so that when they had finally received the very last grant from the count they could go off as if to bed. And by the order of the count everyone present was abundantly served with wine until, after receiving the final grant, they departed.

### 11. The Erembalds seal the plot against the count, during the night of 1 March 1127

Then Isaac and Borsiard, William of Wervik, Ingran, and their accomplices, after receiving the assent of the provost, made haste to carry out what they were about to do, by the necessity of divine ordination, through free will. For immediately those who had been mediators and intercessors between the count and the kinsmen of the provost went to the provost's house and made known the count's response, that is, that they had not been able to secure any mercy either for the nephews or their supporters, and that the count would treat them only as the opinion of the leading men of the land had determined in strict justice. Then the provost and his nephews withdrew into an inner room and summoned those whom they wanted. While the provost guarded the door, they gave their right hands to each other as a pledge that they would betray the count, and they summoned the young Robert to join in the crime, urging him to pledge by his hand that he would share with them what they were about to do and what they had pledged by their hands. But the noble young man forewarned by the virtue of his soul and perceiving the gravity of what they were urging upon him, resisted them, not wishing to be drawn unwittingly into their compact until he could find out what it was they had bound themselves to do; and while they were pressing him, he turned away and hurried toward the door. But Isaac and William and the others called out to the provost guarding the door not to let Robert leave until by the pressure of his authority Robert should do what they had demanded. The young man, quickly influenced by the flattery and threats of the provost, came back and gave his hand on their terms, not knowing what he was supposed to do with them, and, as soon as he was pledged to the traitors he inquired what he had done. They said: "We have now sworn to betray that Count Charles who is working for our ruin in every way and is hastening to claim us as his serfs, and you must carry out this treachery with us, both in word and in deed."

Then the young man, struck with terror and dissolved in tears, cried out: "God forbid that we should betray one who is our lord and the count of the fatherland. Believe me, if you do not give this up, I shall go and openly reveal your treachery to the count and to everyone, and, God willing, I shall never lend aid and counsel to this pact!"

But they forcibly detained him as he tried to flee from them, saying:

"Listen, friend, we were only pretending to you that we were in earnest about that treachery so that we could try out whether you want to stay by us in a certain serious matter; for there is something we have concealed from you up to this point, in which you are bound to us by faith and compact, which we shall tell you about in good time."

And so turning it off as a joke, they concealed their treachery.

Now each one of them left the room and went off to his own place. When Isaac had finally reached home, he pretended to go to bed, for he was awaiting the silence of the night, but soon he remounted his horse and returned to the castle. After stopping at Borsiard's lodgings and summoning him and the others whom he wanted, they went secretly to another lodging, that of the knight, Walter. As soon as they had entered, they put out the fire that was burning in the house so that those who had been awakened in the house should not find out from the light of the fire who they were and what sort of business they were carrying on at that time of night, contrary to custom. Then, safe in the darkness, they took counsel about the act of treason to be done as soon as dawn came, choosing for this crime the boldest and rashest members of Borsiard's household, and they promised them rich rewards. To the knights who would kill the count they offered four marks and to the servingmen who would do the same, two marks, and they bound themselves by this most iniquitous compact. Then Isaac returned to his home about daybreak, after he had put heart into them by his counsel and made them ready for such a great crime.

### 12. Borsiard and his accomplices slay the count on 2 March 1127; the news spreads

Therefore when day had dawned, so dark and foggy that you could not distinguish anything a spear's length away, Borsiard secretly sent several serfs out into courtyard of the count to watch for his entrance into the church. The count had arisen very early and had made offerings to the poor in his own house, as he was accustomed to do, and so was on his way to church. But as his chaplains reported, the night before, when he had settled down in bed to go to sleep, he was troubled by a kind of anxious wakefulness; perplexed and disturbed in mind, he was so disquieted by the many things on his mind that he seemed quite exhausted, even to himself, now lying on one side, now sitting up again on the bed. And when he had set out on his way toward the church of St. Donatian, the serfs who had been watching for his exit ran back and told the traitors that the count had gone up into the gallery of the church with a few companions. Then that raging Borsiard and his knights and servants, all with drawn swords beneath their cloaks, followed the count into the same gallery, dividing into two groups so that not one of those whom they wished to kill could escape from the gallery by either way, and behold they saw the count prostrate before the altar, on a low stool, where he was chanting psalms to God and at the same time devoutly offering prayers and giving out pennies to the poor.

Now it should be known what a noble man and distinguished ruler those impious and inhuman serfs betrayed! His ancestors were among the best and most powerful rulers who from the beginning of the Holy Church had flourished in France, or Flanders, or Denmark, or under the Roman Empire. From their stock the pious count was born in our time and grew up from boyhood to perfect manhood, never departing from the noble habits of his royal ancestors or their natural integrity of life. And before he became count, after performing many notable and distinguished deeds, he took the road of holy pilgrimage to Jerusalem. After crossing the depths of the sea and suffering many perils and wounds for the love of Christ, he at last fulfilled his vow and with great joy reached Jerusalem. Here he also fought strenuously against the enemies of the Christian faith. And so, after reverently adoring the sepulcher of the Lord, he returned home. In the hardship and want of this pilgrimage the pious servant of the Lord learned, as he often related when he was count, in what extreme poverty the poor labor, and with what pride the rich are exalted, and finally with what misery the whole world is affected. And so he made it his habit to stoop to the needy, and to be strong in adversity, not puffed up in prosperity; and as the Psalmist teaches, "The king's strength loves judgment," he ruled the county according to the judgment of the barons and responsible men.

When the life of such a glorious prince had undergone martyrdom, the people of all lands mourned him greatly, shocked by the infamy of his betrayal. Marvelous to tell, although the count was killed in the castle of Bruges on the morning of one day, that is, the fourth day of the week, the news of this impious death shocked the citizens of London, which is in England, on the second day afterwards about the first hour; and towards evening of the same second day it disturbed the people of Laon who live far away from us in France. We learned this through our students who at that time were studying in Laon, as we also learned it from our merchants who were busy carrying on their business on that very day in London. For no one could have spanned these intervals of time or space so quickly either by horse or by ship!

## 13. Bertulf's past: his ambition, pride, and simony

It was ordained by God that bold and arrogant descendants of Bertulf's ancestors should be left behind to carry out the crime of treachery. The others, prevented by death, were influential men in the fatherland in their lifetime, persons of eminence and of great wealth, but the provost passed his life among the clergy, extremely severe and not a little proud. For it was his habit when someone whom he knew perfectly well came into his presence, to dissemble, in his pride, and to ask disdainfully of those sitting near him, who that could be, and then only, if it pleased him, would he greet the newcomer. When he had sold a canonical prebend [living] to someone he would invest him with it not by canonical election but rather by force, for not one of his canons dared to oppose him either openly or secretly. In the house of the brothers in the church of St. Donatian the canons had formerly been deeply religious men and perfectly educated, that is, at the beginning of the provostship of this most arrogant prelate. Restraining his pride, they had held him in check by advice and by Catholic doctrine so that he could not undertake anything unseemly in the church. But after they went to sleep in the Lord, the provost, left to himself, set in motion anything that pleased him and toward which the force of his pride impelled him. And so when he became head of his family, he tried to advance beyond everyone in the fatherland his nephews who were well brought up and finally girded with the sword of knighthood. Trying to make their reputation known everywhere, he armed his kinsmen for strife and discord; and he found enemies for them to fight in order to make it known to everyone that he and his nephews were so powerful and strong that no one in the realm could resist them or prevail against them. Finally, accused in the presence of the count of servile status, and affronted by the efforts of the count himself to prove that he and all his lineage were servile, he tried, as we have said, to resist servitude by every course and device and to preserve his usurped liberty with all his might. And when, steadfast in his determination, he could not succeed otherwise, he himself, with his kinsmen, carried through the treachery, which he had long refused to consider, with frightful consequences involving both his own kinsmen and the peers of the realm.

### 14. Omens and predictions of the crime; the character of
Galbert's work

But the most pious Lord thought fit to recall his own by the terror of omens, for in our vicinity bloody water appeared in the ditches, as a sign of future bloodshed. They could have been called back from their crime by this if their hardened hearts had not already entered into a conspiracy for betraying the count. They often asked themselves, if they killed the count, who would avenge him? But they did not know what they were saying, for "who," an infinite word, meant an infinite number of persons, who cannot be reckoned in a definite figure; the fact is that the king of France with a numerous army and also the barons of our land with an infinite multitude came to avenge the death of the most pious count! Not even yet has the unhappy consequence of this utterance reached an end, for as time goes on they do not cease to avenge the death of the count upon all the suspect and the guilty and those who have fled in all directions and gone into exile. And so we, the inhabitants of the land of Flanders, who mourn the death of such a great count and prince, ever mindful of his life, beg, admonish, and beseech you, after hearing the true and reliable account of his life and death (that is, whoever shall have heard it), to pray earnestly for the eternal glory of the life of his soul and his everlasting blessedness with the saints. In this account of his passion, the reader will find the subject divided by days and the events of those days, up to the vengeance, related at the end of this little work, which God alone wrought against those barons of the land whom he has exterminated from this world by the punishment of death, those by whose aid and counsel the treachery was begun and carried through to the end.

### 15. The murder of Count Charles, Tuesday, 2 March 1127

In the year one thousand one hundred and twenty-seven, on the sixth day before the Nones of March, on the second day, that is, after the beginning of the same month, when two days of the second week of Lent had elapsed, and the fourth day was subsequently to dawn, on the fifth Concurrent, and the sixth Epact, about dawn, the count at Bruges was kneeling in prayer in order to hear the early mass in the church of St. Donatian, the former archbishop of Rheims. Following his pious custom he was giving out alms to the poor, with his eyes fixed on reading the psalms, and his right hand outstretched to bestow alms; for his chaplain who attended to this duty had placed near the count many pennies which he was distributing to the poor while in the position of prayer.

The office of the first hour was completed and also the response of the third hour, when "Our Father" is said, and when the count, according to custom, was praying, reading aloud obligingly; then at last, after so many plans and oaths and pacts among themselves, those wretched traitors, already murderers at heart, slew the count, who was struck down with swords and run through again and again, while he was praying devoutly and giving alms, humbly kneeling before the Divine Majesty. And so God gave the palm of the martyrs to the count, the course of whose good life was washed clean in the rivulets of his blood and brought to an end in good works. In the final moment of life and at the onset of death, he had most nobly lifted his countenance and his royal hands to heaven, as well as he could amid so many blows and thrusts of the swordsmen; and so he surrendered his spirit to the Lord of all and offered himself as a morning sacrifice to God. But the bloody body of such a great man and prince lay there alone, without the veneration of his people and the due reverence of his servants. Whosoever has heard the circumstances of his death has mourned in tears his pitiable death and has commended to God such a great and lamented prince, brought to an end by the fate of the martyrs.

## 74. PETER ABELARD'S "STORY OF MY ADVERSITIES"

*Peter Abelard (ca 1079–ca 1144) was a scholastic philosopher and theologian who had a brilliant but troubled career. He described his misfortunes to a friend in a letter written in 1132, with the hope that his story would bring comfort. From this letter, we learn of his decision to give up the military life expected for an eldest son in order to learn dialectic in Paris and of his rise to prominence as a renowned teacher. He also writes of his fall, as his treatise on the Trinity was declared heretical and he suffered at the hands of his enemies, which he attributed to the jealousy of other men that increased as his reputation grew.*

*He is most famous for his passionate relationship with Heloise, a young woman whose uncle had hired Abelard as her teacher. Although this work was written as a personal letter of consolation, it is known to have reached Heloise, who became abbess of the Paraclete after Abelard founded it in 1131, and it was perhaps intended for wider circulation in order to gain sympathy and pave the way for Abelard's return to teaching.*

Source: trans. J. T. Muckle, *The Story of Abelard's Adversities: A Translation with Notes of the Historia Calamitatum*, 2nd ed. (Toronto: Pontifical Institute of Mediaeval Studies, 1964), pp. 37–39.

And so when the infant [Peter and Heloise's son, Astrolabe] was born we entrusted it to my sister and returned secretly to Paris. After a few days, we spent a night in a secret vigil of prayer in a church and early on the following day we were joined by the nuptial blessing in the presence of her uncle and some of his and our friends. We straightway separated and left secretly. After that we saw each other only rarely and then on the quiet, hiding by dissimulation what we had done.

But her uncle and the members of his household seeking solace for his disgrace began to make our marriage public and thereby to break the word they had given regarding it. Heloise on her part cursed and swore that it was a lie. Her uncle became strongly aroused and kept heaping abuse upon her. When I found this out, I sent her to the convent of nuns in a town near Paris called Argenteuil where as a young girl she had been brought up and received instruction. I had a religious habit, all except the veil, made for her and had her vested in it.

When her uncle and his kinsmen heard of this they considered that now I had fooled them and that by making her a nun I wanted easily to get rid of her. They became strongly incensed against me and formed a conspiracy. One night when I was sound asleep in an inner room of my lodgings, by bribing my attendant they wrought vengeance upon me in a cruel and shameful manner and one which the world with great astonishment abhorred, namely, they cut off the organs by which I had committed the deed which they deplored. They immediately fled but two of them were caught and had their eyes put out and were castrated; one of these was my servant already mentioned who while in my service was brought by greed to betray me.

When morning came, the whole city flocked to me and it is hard, yes impossible, to describe the astonishment which stunned them, the wailing they uttered, the shouting which irritated me and the moaning which upset me. The clerics and especially my students by their excessive lamentation and wailing pained me so that I endured more from their expressions of sympathy than from the suffering caused by the mutilation. I felt the embarrassment more than the wound and the shame was harder to bear than the pain. I fell to thinking how great had been my renown and in how easy and base a way this had been brought low and utterly destroyed; how by a just judgment of God I had been afflicted in that part of my body by which I had sinned; how just was the betrayal by which he whom I had first betrayed paid me back; how my rivals would extol such a fair retribution; how great would be the sorrow and lasting grief which my mutilation would cause my parents and friends; with what speed the news of this extraordinary mark of disgrace would spread throughout the world; what course could I follow; how could I face the public to be pointed at by all with a finger of scorn, to be insulted by every tongue and to become a monstrosity and a spectacle to all the world.

## 75. THE DEEDS OF LOUIS THE FAT BY SUGER OF ST. DENIS

*A man of humble origin, Suger (ca 1081–1151) entered the abbey of St. Denis around 1091, where he was educated along with King Louis VI, known as "the Fat" (1081–1137). Suger was active in abbey affairs from 1106 on, and became provost of Berneval in 1107 and Toury in 1109. The king sent him to the papal curia and, as he was returning from visiting Pope Callistus II in 1122, he was elected abbot of St. Denis. He was an influential adviser to French kings and an active administrator of his monastery's lands. He earned the title "father of the country" for acting as regent while Louis VII was on crusade. Among other activities, he supervised the building of the cathedral at St. Denis, wrote a description of the new church, and produced a work about monastic government.*

Source: trans. Richard Cusimano and John Moorhead, *The Deeds of Louis the Fat* (Washington, DC: Catholic University of America Press, 1992), pp. 84–93, 106–9.

### a. How Louis destroyed the castle of Le Puiset after he captured Hugh

Just as very tasty fruit from a fruitful tree reproduces its fragrant taste if a shoot is transplanted or branches are grafted, in the same way evil and wickedness, qualities that should have been rooted out, continued to sprout forth and produced one man out of the branch of many wretched men. He was like a snake amid eels, which torments and stirs them up and enjoys the taste of its own sort of bitterness, as if it were absinthe. Hugh of Le Puiset was of such a kind, a wretched man, made rich only by virtue of his own tyranny and that of his ancestors. He succeeded his uncle Guy in the lordship of Le Puiset, for his father had taken up arms with amazing pride and had gone early on the expedition to Jerusalem. And Hugh proved to be a worthless shoot who took after his father with every kind of evil, but "those whom his father beat with whips, he, more despicable than his parent, beat with scorpions."

Elated for having gone unpunished while he brutally tyrannized needy churches and monasteries, Hugh had reached the stage where "the workers of evil have fallen; they were cast out and could not stand" [Ps. 36:12]. Since he did not think much of either the king of the universe or the king of the French, he attacked the most noble countess of Chartres and her son

Theobald, a very handsome youth and valiant warrior. He ravaged their land all the way to Chartres, delivering it over to plunder and fires. When they could, the noble countess and her son fought back; but their efforts were too little and too late for them to avenge themselves. They hardly ever or never approached within eight or ten miles of Le Puiset. So limitless was Hugh's daring, so cogent was the force of his powerful pride that, although few loved him, many came to his service. And although many strove to defend him, a large number of them longed for his destruction, for he was more feared than loved.

Count Theobald came to see that he could accomplish little against Hugh through his own efforts but much through those of the king. So, accompanied by his very noble mother, who had always served the king nobly, he hurried into the royal presence and begged the king with many pleas to give aid, showing how he had merited it for his great service. He related some of the dishonorable deeds done by Hugh, his father, grandfather, and ancestors, saying: "As befits your royal majesty, lord king, remember the dishonor and shame inflicted on your father Philip by Hugh's grandfather, a man detestable for breaking his sworn word. He drove him away from Le Puiset in disgrace when he was striving to avenge the many crimes that had been committed. With the scornful contempt typical of a very wretched family and a seditious faction, Hugh's grandfather chased your father's host all the way back to Orléans. He dishonored the captured count of Nevers, Lancelin of Beaugency, nearly one hundred knights, and, what had never been heard of before, even some bishops, by throwing them into his prison."

Continuing his reproaches, Count Theobald went on to discuss the purpose and the origin of the castle of Le Puiset, which had been built not too long ago by the venerable queen Constance in the middle of the land of the saints for its protection. He explained how Hugh's grandfather had afterward taken it all for himself and left nothing for the king but villainy. Now, if he wished, the king could easily avenge the insults done him and his father by overthrowing the castle and disinheriting Hugh, for the large host from Chartres, Blois, and Chateaudun, which usually helped Hugh oppose the king, would now not only desert him but stand against him. He could end the persecution of the churches, the plunderings of the poor, and the ungodly hardships endured by widows and orphans whenever Hugh ravaged the land of the saints and its cultivators. But if the king did not choose to punish the wrongs done to him personally and to those who deserved well of him, then he himself should share the blame for them.

Feeling the force of numerous complaints like these, the king set a day for taking counsel about them. We met at Melun where many archbishops, bishops, clerics, and monks flocked together, for Hugh had been more rapacious than a wolf in devouring their lands. They cried out and threw themselves down at the feet of the king, against his will. They begged him to keep that greedy robber Hugh in check and snatch away from the jaw of the dragon their prebends, which the generosity of previous kings had granted the servants of God in the Beauce, a land fertile in grain. They prayed that he spare no effort in setting free the lands of the priests which, in a like way, were the only ones freed from the burdens imposed by Pharaoh. They pleaded that the king, as the representative of God, render free the part that belonged to God, whose image he maintained and kept alive in his own person.

The king received their petition favorably and took appropriate action. The prelates of the Church, namely the archbishop of Sens, the bishop of Orléans, and the venerable Ivo of Chartres, departed. Ivo had formerly been held in prison when he had been locked up by force in that very same castle for many days. With the consent of Abbot Adam, our predecessor of good memory, the king sent me back to Toury, a profitable estate in the Beauce belonging to St. Denis, where I was in charge. It was fertile in grain but in no way fortified. While he summoned Hugh to court to answer these charges, he ordered me to equip the estate and strengthen it with a force of his and our knights as best I could. He wanted me to keep Hugh from destroying it by fire, for he planned to reinforce it and then attack the castle from it, as his father had done.

With the help of God, we filled the estate with a good supply of knights and foot soldiers in a very short time. Then, after judgment was rendered against Hugh when he failed to appear in court, the king came to us at Toury with a great host and demanded back from Hugh the castle whose possession he had lost in the verdict. And, when Hugh refused to depart, he did not delay. He quickly attacked the castle, directed his host of knights and foot soldiers against it, and brought to bear different kinds of crossbow, bow, "shield, sword, and war." What a sight to behold. Arrows were raining down, sparks of fire were flashing from countless blows atop gleaming helmets, and shields were being pierced and broken with amazing speed. The enemy were pushed back through the gate into the castle; but once inside they hurled down from the ramparts and the palisade a surprising volley of missiles on our men, which even the boldest among them found almost unbearable. By dismantling roof timbers and throwing down the beams, the enemy began driving our men back, but they did not succeed, for the royal forces called upon their own valiant strength of body and spirit and fought bitterly against their foes. When their shields had been broken, they crouched behind shingles from the roof, doors, anything made of wood, and pushed against the gate. We had also loaded wagons with great piles of dry wood, greased with fat and lard, which would make them quickly burst into flames

— a fitting end for the excommunicated within, who were devils through and through. A brave band of our men, taking cover behind these great heaps of wood, set the wagons up against the gate. They planned to turn them into a fire that no one could extinguish.

While our side took risks struggling to set the wagons afire, and theirs to put them out, Count Theobald led a great host of knights and foot soldiers in an attack against the castle from a different side, namely the one facing Chartres. Mindful of the wrongs he had suffered, the count hurried into battle, encouraging his men to climb up the steep slope of the embankment. But he lost heart when they fell back down again with even greater haste; to be precise, they tumbled down in a heap. He saw those whom he had urged to bend forward and creep up carefully plunge back down again on their backs recklessly. He did his best to find out whether they had breathed their last under the shower of rocks falling upon them. The knights who were defending and circling the castle on swift horses came unexpectedly upon the men clinging to the palisade with their hands and cut them down. They slaughtered them and sent them to the ground with thuds, from the top of the wall to the very bottom of the ditch.

With the hands of our men broken and their knees buckling, our attack had almost come to a standstill when almighty God willed that this great and just revenge be credited entirely to his powerful, or rather almighty, hand. From the general levies of the land that were present, God awakened the firm and courageous spirit of a bald priest; and, contrary to what men could believe, it became possible for him to do what had been impossible for an armed count and his followers. Carrying a flimsy shingle, which left his front exposed, he swiftly climbed all the way up and reached the palisade. Once there, he hid beneath the coverings fitted to it and took them down little by little. Glad to find no hindrance to his labor, he gave a signal for help to the others who had been hanging back and taking a rest in the field. When they saw an unarmed priest bravely tearing down the enclosures, they surged forward with their weapons and began striking the palisade with their axes and whatever iron tools they had. They hacked it down and destroyed it; and, what was an amazing sign of heaven's judgment, as if the walls of a second Jericho had fallen, the hosts of the king and the count entered at the very same hour through the chopped-down enclosures. A large number of Hugh's men could find no place to escape the assaults of their enemies, who were rushing in from all sides. They were quickly surrounded and forcefully struck down.

Hugh himself was among the survivors, but seeing that the interior wall of the castle would not give him enough protection, he took himself off to the motte and the wooden tower on top of it. He cowered there before the menacing lances of the pursuing host, and the man who had been beaten down surrendered without delay. Taken prisoner along with his men in his own residence, he was shackled with horrible chains and soon learned what a fall such great pride prepares.

Having won this victory, the king led away his noble captives, prey that suited his royal majesty. He ordered that all the castle's furnishings and costly things be appropriated, and that the castle itself be burned down; but the tower alone he delayed burning for a few days. Count Theobald had failed to remember the great advantage he had gained, which he would never have gained by himself, and devised a scheme to widen his borders by erecting a castle on an estate called Allaines, in the lordship of Le Puiset, which he held in fief from the king. But when the king would in no way approve of his action, the count offered to provide evidence through Andrew of Baudement, steward of his land, that they had made an agreement on this point. The king in return offered to support his case that he had never made such an agreement, by clear evidence and by the law of the duel, through Anselm, his seneschal, in any safe place chosen by the combatants. The valiant men in question frequently demanded that the court be convened for this battle, but nothing ever came of it.

After the castle of Le Puiset had been totally demolished and Hugh imprisoned in the tower of Château-Landon, Count Theobald, relying on support from his eminent uncle Henry [I], the English king, made war with his accomplices against King Louis. Count Theobald threw the land into confusion, drew his barons into his party with promises and gifts, and jealously plotted every sort of harm for the state. The king, however, being an adept knight, repeatedly sought to take revenge on him and despoiled his land in the company of many other barons, especially his uncle, Count Robert of Flanders, whom he had called to his side. Count Robert was a remarkable man who had initially won great renown among Christians and Saracens for his skill as a warrior during the expedition to Jerusalem.

One day, when the king had brought his host to the city of Meaux to move against the count, he caught sight of the man and flew into a rage. He rushed against him and his men, and did not hesitate to pursue them as they fled back across the bridge.

With help from the swords of Count Robert and other magnates of the kingdom, he struck them down and drove into the water men who were already jumping in of their own free will. What a sight! This warrior was swinging arms as powerful as Hector's and launching attacks worthy of a giant on top of that trembling bridge, and no one was able to hinder him. Despite heavy resistance he strove to seize the town right at its very dangerous approach, and not even the barrier of the great river Marne would have stopped him if a closed gate on the other side of the river had not stood in his way.

Equal was the renown for valor the king won in a distinguished action when he moved the host out of Lagny and turned his forces against the knights who were coming to encounter him on a plain covered with beautiful grass near Pomponne. Under a hail of blows he forced them to beat a swift retreat, but the narrow approach to a nearby bridge became a dreadful prospect for them as they fled. Some feared for their lives like cowards, but nevertheless they did not fear to risk death by jumping into the river. Others rushed for the bridge, trampled each other under foot and, casting aside their weapons, became more dangerous to themselves than to their enemies. Only one man reached the bridge, even though all of them had the same desire at the same time. This disorderly knocking into one another threw them into confusion; and the more they hurried the more they were delayed. So it happened that the first found themselves last and the last first. But the entrance to the bridge was enclosed by a ditch that gave them some protection, as it allowed the king's knights to pursue them only in single file. Although many of them tried, even at heavy cost to themselves, only a few were able to reach the bridge. When these gained entrance in whatever way they could, more often than not the great crowd of our men and theirs threw them into confusion. Knocked to their knees unwillingly, they leapt back to their feet, causing others to be bumped down. The king and his men gave chase and hemmed them in amid much slaughter. Those he came up against he wiped out, and he wiped them out as much by the blow of his sword as by the very fierce charge of his horse, sending them splashing into the river Marne. The unarmed were light and managed to float, but those in hauberks were encumbered by their weight and went under for a first time. Dragged out by helpful companions before they sank three times, they did not escape the shame of a second baptism, if one could call it that.

Tormenting the count with troubles like these, the king laid waste his lands everywhere, in Brie and in the countryside of Chartres; and it did not matter whether the count was more present than absent or more absent than present. Frightened by the slim numbers and inactivity of his men, the count became skillful in luring the king's barons away from him. He enticed them with gifts and promises, giving them hope that their various complaints would be satisfied before he would make peace with the king.

Among those who joined him were Pagan of Montjay and Lancelin of Bulles, the lord of Dammartin; their lands, located like a crossroads, allowed anyone who would make trouble for Paris to approach in safety. For the same reason Count Theobald lured to his side Ralph of Beaugency, whose wife was the daughter of Hugh the Great and first cousin to the king. Prompted by a great deal of worry, for as the proverb says, "the prod speeds the old woman along," the count put the useful before the honorable and shamefully coupled his noble sister in an incestuous marriage to Milo of Montlhéry, whom we mentioned above when the king gave back his castle.

By so doing the count made it difficult to travel about and, as it were, placed the old alarming storms and wars in the very center of France. With Milo on his side, Count Theobald secretly won over that man's relatives, Guy of Rochefort and Hugh of Crécy, the lord of Châteaufort; and he would have opened up the countryside around Paris and Etampes to hostilities if a force of knights had not prevented it. A wide area of approach to Paris and Senlis now lay open to Count Theobald and the men of Brie, as well as to his uncle, Hugh of Troyes, and the men of Troyes on this side of the Seine, and to Milo on the other side; the ability to bring aid to each other was thus taken away from the inhabitants of the land. A similar thing happened to the residents of Orléans when the men of Chartres, Châteaudun, and Brie met no opposition and shut them in with help from Ralph of Beaugency. The king was maneuvering often enough at their rear but the abundant resources of both England and Normandy allowed him no rest when the illustrious king Henry expended all his effort and all his energy in raiding his land. He was hit so hard by these attacks that it seemed "as if the rivers threatened … to withdraw all their waters from the sea."

## b. The overthrow of Thomas of Marle's castles at Crécy and Nouvion

By their powerful right arm and by virtue of the office they have sworn to uphold, kings put down insolent tyrants whenever they see them inciting wars, taking pleasure in endless plunder, persecuting the poor, and destroying churches. Kings put a stop to their wanton behavior, which kindles even greater insanity in them if left unbridled. They become like evil spirits who prefer to slaughter those whom they fear to lose and favor by all means possible those whom they hope to keep, adding fuel to the flames which will then devour them with much greater pain.

Such a person was the most accursed Thomas of Marle. While King Louis was occupied with the wars just mentioned and many others, Thomas ravaged the countryside around Laon, Reims, and Amiens; and the devil helped him succeed, for the success of fools generally leads them to perdition. He devoured and destroyed everything like a wolf gone mad, and fear of ecclesiastical punishment did not compel him to spare the clergy nor any feeling of humanity the people. He slaughtered all, ruined all, and even grabbed two prosperous estates from the convent of nuns of St. John of Laon. He fortified the very formidable castles of Crécy and Nouvion with a marvelous rampart and lofty towers, as if they were his own. And changing them into a lair of dragons and a den of thieves, he cruelly handed over nearly the whole land to pillaging and fires.

Worn down by the unbearable trouble caused by this man, the Gallic Church sat at Beauvais in a general council. It hoped to proceed with an initial judgment and publish a sentence of condemnation against the enemies of its true spouse, Jesus Christ, for the countless complaints of the churches and the miseries of the poor and the orphaned cried out for action. Cono, the venerable legate of the holy Roman Church and bishop of Palestrina, took up the sword of the blessed Peter and struck down Thomas's tyranny with a general anathema. Although Thomas was not present, he stripped him of his knightly status and, in accordance with the judgment of all, deposed him from every honor as a wicked, ill-famed enemy of the Christian name.

The woeful plea of this great council persuaded the king, and he quickly set his forces into motion against Thomas. Accompanied by the clergy to whom he was always humbly attached, he turned off the road toward the well-fortified castle of Crécy. Helped by his powerful band of armed men, or rather by the hand of God, he abruptly seized the castle and captured its very strong tower as if it were simply the hut of a peasant. Having startled those criminals, he piously slaughtered the impious, cutting them down without mercy because he found them to be merciless. What a sight! The castle was burning with such a hellish fire that everyone quickly concluded, "The whole world will fight for him against these madmen."

Having won this victory, the king quickly followed up his successes, and he was heading for the other castle, called Nouvion, when a man came up and informed him: "My lord king and serene highness, be aware that the men lingering in that miserable castle are awful wretches. Hell is the only place they are fit to be. The time you ordered that the commune of Laon be done away with, they are the ones, I tell you, who set fire to the city and the noble church of the Mother of the Lord and many others as well. They made martyrs of nearly all the nobles of the city to punish them for their true fealty when they tried hard to bring help to their lord the bishop. Bishop Gaudry himself, the venerable defender of the church, they killed with great cruelty, not fearing to lay hands on the Lord's anointed [see Doc. 72]. Having cut off the finger that held his bishop's ring, they left his naked body in the square as food for beasts and birds of prey. Then with their wicked seducer, Thomas himself, they struggled to seize your tower and separate you from your property."

Stirred to action once again, the king attacked the evil castle and smashed to pieces its hellish places of punishment and sacrilege. He set free the innocent and punished the guilty severely, he alone avenging the crimes committed by many. Thirsting for justice he ordered that any of those wretched murderers whom he ran across be fixed to a gibbet and left as common food for the insatiable appetite of kites, crows, and vultures. In this way he taught what those deserve who do not fear to lay hand on the Lord's anointed.

After he had leveled those unlawful castles and restored the estates to St. John's, he returned to the city of Amiens and laid siege to its tower. It was held by Adam, a tyrant who was laying waste the churches and the entire neighborhood. The king penned up the tower's defenders in a tight siege for nearly two years before he finally forced them to surrender. He captured the tower, and having captured it he demolished it down to its foundations, and having demolished it he restored welcome peace to the land. Thus he fulfilled the office of a king who "does not carry his sword in vain"; and he disinherited forever that most vile Thomas and his heirs from the lordship of the city.

## 76. THE VENGEANCE OF KINGS IN GEOFFREY OF MONMOUTH'S *HISTORY OF THE KINGS OF BRITAIN*

*Geoffrey (ca 1100–54) was bishop of St. Asaph in Wales. This work of imaginary history traces the history of Britain from its mythical founder Brutus, the great-grandson of the Greek hero Aeneas, to the Welsh king Cadwaladr of Gwynedd in the seventh century CE. The* History *was most famous for its account of Merlin and King Arthur.*

Source: trans. Sebastian Evans, *Histories of the Kings of Britain* (London: Dent, 1904), pp. 189–92, 256–57. Modernized by Kelly Gibson.

### a. The vengeance of the sons of Constantine
### [8.1–3]

When Merlin had made these and many other prophecies, all the bystanders were stricken with amazement at his words, although they could not understand the full meaning. Vortigern, marveling more than the others, praised the young man's wit as much as the predictions themselves. For that age had produced no one who had said such things when in his presence. Accordingly, wanting to learn what would bring his own death, he asked the young man to tell him what he knew about it. To this Merlin said:

"Flee from the fire of the sons of Constantine, if you can! Even now they are fitting forth their ships – even now they are leaving the coasts of Brittany behind and spreading their sails upon the deep. They will head for the island of Britain and invade upon the Saxons. They will subdue that accursed people, but first they will imprison you in a tower and burn you! To your own ruin you betrayed their father and invited the Saxons into the island. You invited them as your bodyguard, but they have come over as your executioners. Two deaths await you, but it is not clear which one you will escape first. On the one side, the Saxons will lay waste to your kingdom and will seek to bring about your death. On the other, the two brothers Aurelius [Ambrosius] and Uther Pendragon will enter into your land seeking to avenge their father's [Constantine's] death upon you. Seek out refuge if you can. Tomorrow they will land in Totnes. The faces of the Saxons shall be red with blood: Hengist shall be slain, and thereafter Aurelius Ambrosius shall be crowned king. He shall give peace unto the nations: he shall restore the churches, yet he shall die of poison. His brother Uther Pendragon shall succeed him, and his days shall likewise be cut short by poison. Your own descendants will be present at this black betrayal, and then the Boar of Cornwall will devour them!"

Aurelius Ambrosius and his brother, with ten thousand warriors, came ashore immediately when the next day dawned. When the news of their coming was announced abroad, the Britons who had been scattered with such slaughter gathered together again, and strengthened by the comradeship of their fellow-countrymen, were more cheerful than they had been recently. They called the clergy together, anointed Aurelius as king, and did homage to him according to custom. But when they advised attacking the Saxons, the king dissuaded them, interested first of all in pursuing Vortigern, for he took the treachery that had been done against his father to heart so grievously that he thought of nothing other than first of all avenging him. Accordingly, desiring to fulfill his purpose, he marched his army into Wales and headed toward the castle of Ganarew where Vortigen had fled for refuge. This castle was in the country of Archenfield, upon the river Wye on the mountain that is called Doward. When Ambrosius had come there, remembering the treason done against his father and brother, he spoke to Eldol, duke of Gloucester, saying: "See now, noble duke, whether the walls of this city are strong enough to protect me from burying the point of my sword in Vortigern's bowels. For he deserved violent death, and I think that you know how much he deserved it. O most impious of men, worthy to die in unspeakable torment! First, he betrayed my father Constantine, who had delivered him and his country from the ravages of the Picts; then Constans, my brother, whom he raised to be king, only to destroy him; then, when he had branded himself by his own treacheries, he thrust his heathens in amongst the freemen of the land in order to exterminate all who loyally abided by their fealty to me. Yet by God's permission he has now fallen unaware into the trap that he had laid for his faithful. For when the Saxons found out about his evil deeds, they thrust him from the kingdom, for which no one should be sorry. Yet, I think, all men may well feel great sorrow that this accursed people whom this accursed man has invited here have slaughtered my noble freemen, have laid waste to my fruitful country, have destroyed the holy churches and nearly done away with all Christianity from sea to sea. Now, therefore, my fellow-countrymen, go like men and wreak your vengeance first of all upon the one who wrought all these evil deeds! Then let us turn our arms against the enemies that surround us, and save the country from being swallowed up in their insatiable mouth!" Immediately, they brought their engines of all kinds into play and strove their best to breach the walls, but when all else failed, they set the place on fire. Finding fuel, the fire spread, blazing up until it had burned up the tower with Vortigern inside. When the report of this reached Hengist and his Saxons he was struck with dread, for he feared the prowess of Aurelius.

## b. The speech of Augusel
### [9.18]

When Hoel had ended his speech, Augusel, King of Scotland, went on to declare what he thought in this way: "From the moment that I understood my lord to have this opinion, such gladness entered into my heart that I cannot describe at present. For in all our past campaigns that we have fought against kings so many and so mighty, all that we have done seems like nothing to me as long as the Romans and the Germans remain unharmed, and we do not revenge like men the slaughter they have formerly inflicted upon our fellow-countrymen. But now that we are allowed to meet them in battle, I rejoice with exceedingly great joy, and yearn with desire for the day when we shall meet. I thirst for their blood as I would for a well-spring after being forbidden to drink for three days. O may I see tomorrow! How sweet will the wounds be whether I give them or receive! When the right hand deals with right hand. Yes, death itself will be sweet, so I may suffer it in avenging our fathers, in safeguarding our freedom, in exalting our king! Let us fall upon these half men, and falling upon them, tread them under foot, so that when we have conquered them we may spoil them of their honors and enjoy the victory we have won. I will add two thousand horsemen to our army, in addition to those on foot."

# 77. THE BLOODFEUD OF MEINGOLD AND ALBRIC

*The* Life of Count Meingold *is the story of the feud between Meingold and his brother-in-law, Duke Albric. Below is an episode from the beginning of the feud that would lead to Meingold's "martyrdom" in 892, when blood relations of Judge Ingelfrid killed him in the monastery of Retel (along the Moselle River) while he was on pilgrimage. The* Life of Count Meingold *was written during the second half of the twelfth century, likely at Huy, in modern-day Belgium, in connection with the translation of his relics there (ca 1172–89). The work confuses Meingold, count of Huy, with Megingoz, count in Wormsgau. Scholars consider this work to be a "romance" created from tradition and knowledge of historical events and figures. The work is therefore more informative about twelfth-century ideas than about ninth-century ones.*

Source: *Vita Meingoldi comitis,* ed. O. Holder-Egger, Monumenta Germaniae Historica: Scriptores rerum Germanicarum, vol. 15.1 (Hanover: Hahn, 1887), pp. 559–60. Trans. Kelly Gibson.

*When Meingold married Geila, he gained control of properties that had belonged to Count William of Huy, Geila's first husband, and to Duke Albric, Geila's brother (or, according to other sources, father). Meingold restored the estates that had suffered from neglect when tenants had abandoned them in fear or had been destroyed by attack during a dispute between William and Albric.*

8. Hence Duke Albric's impious thoughts and persistent fury again broke out. Neither a reverent sister [Geila] nor only nephew [Liethard] nor laws could turn him towards the path of rectitude. Moreover, so that he add greater and stronger power to his armed forces, he joined with Duke Baldwin, who was called by the corrupt name Bevin, in order to rise up against and utterly destroy Meingold and his goods with a band of knights. The Eighth Day of the Lord's Nativity [January 1] came, when the due rent was to be paid on Meingold's best estate. Anticipating, Albric came there with Duke Baldwin and on the same holy day he took the rents, burned the estate, and carried off captured farmers and spoils. But Meingold, unaware of this and not thinking at all about misfortune, was going along without a care to his estate when he heard the shouts of the captives, the roars of animals, and the voices of those dividing the spoils as they returned. After he carefully assessed the evidence of the facts, with justice helping him and with the violation of the solemn day hindering them, he attacked them with a powerful band. He killed Duke Baldwin and many men, captured even more, and put Albric to flight. As the victor, after rescuing his own men from their hands, he restored to the same

estate what had been snatched away. This gave rise to a serious commotion in the land because Duke Baldwin was survived by four sons and Albric made his nephew Liethard break with Meingold [who had raised him] with gifts and promises.

9. Emperor Arnulf took counsel [*consilium*: the obligatory counsel a vassal owed his lord] about this event with honest and reverent nobles of the kingdom and approached Albric and the four sons of Duke Baldwin through honorable mediators with a humble request and the offering of many things. As humbly and as devotedly as he was able, relinquishing imperial right, he worked to restore peace so that, if in such business he exceeded the proper limits of power, the love of his nephew [Meingold, whose mother was Arnulf's sister] could not be called a harm of the empire. Albric, the four sons of Duke Baldwin, his nephew Liuthard (whom he had snatched away from Meingold, the man who had honorably brought him up), and Judge Ingelfrid heaped against Meingold threats, assaults, treachery, and attacks on the estates. Meingold, with his nephew Richard [supposedly the son of Meingold's sister Adheliz and Oswald, king of Northumbria] and strong knights, did not send out his armed forces but, fortifying the strongholds, he endured and hid, and for the killing of the nobles he humbly offered through Palatine counted what they deserved by right of law and even more besides. Therefore, King Arnulf [of Carinthia, king of the East Franks 887–899 and Holy Roman Emperor 896–899], with [Meingold's] humility ever before him, came to imperial judgment with the agreement of the nobles and, summoning Meingold and his enemies to his seat at Metz, held a general assembly. To sum up, for point one, he dealt with reconciliation for the homicide and, for this business, he offered the adversaries, on Meingold's behalf, more than [what] justice and law [prescribed]. But they, obdurate of mind and insisting at length on his death, did not welcome the things of peace. Finally, after the Palatine counts had, at the admonition of the emperor, agreed on one sentence, date, and place, Albric and his accomplices praised the king for this case since there would be a promise on both sides not to take revenge in the future.

10. Therefore, Meingold and Albric retreated from the emperor's court to their own [courts], going on the same path but without the same intention. With every fiber of his being Meingold strove for the reconciliation of enemies, and Albric and his men thirsted for Meingold's death in their souls. Accordingly, Meingold still repeated words of humble petition, and like a strong lion, confident of [his] pure conscience, he offered himself to Albric and the sons of Duke Baldwin for judgment or concord in his [Albric's] house. Judge Ingelfrid, speaking to Albric alone, advised that he agree to judgment

on the day and place, because, skilled in law, he could entrap and condemn Meingold to death by interrupting [Meingold's] response. Therefore, on the appointed day, Meingold with his nephew Richard came to Albric's house where the sons of Duke Baldwin and Judge Ingelfrid also were. They [Meingold and Richard] left their horses with their squires in the fenced areas of the field and with swords entered the palace, where a multitude of noble leading men were sitting all around....

11. Duke Albric charged Meingold with the death of Duke Baldwin. He [Meingold], wisely answering just how it had happened, fell at the feet of the sons sitting there and offered for their decision the options of *harmscar* [a dishonoring punishment given to knights that required them to walk with their horse's saddle on their back along a defined path], homage (*hominium*), and compensation. But Judge Ingelfrid, one of those who, sitting in the gate [*porta*: place of judgment], do not judge justly for a foreigner, orphan, or widow, entirely dedicated himself to hostile vengeance, and imputing that Meingold is a foreigner from abroad, judged that Meingold should suffer capital punishment because of this. But he [Meingold] thought and by reason of noble birth denied Ingelfrid's judgment since a duel has been proposed. Ingelfrid, out of disregard for the laws and now taking his own life in [his] hands, hit him [Meingold] upon the head with a staff with premeditation in order that the sons of Duke Baldwin and others rush against him [Meingold] at one onset. But because everyone did not have the same intention [some of the men hoped Meingold would escape, others did not], many men intermixed themselves to soften the attack. Richard, Meingold's nephew, powerfully charges forth and cut off Ingelfrid's head with a sword.

12. Therefore, while the others are running around and entangled, Meingold and Richard rushed from the hall and, mounting their horses in a manly way, made a quick and successful journey to safety. In fact, his noble and reverent wife Geila had looked out for Meingold by dissuading him from going to the home of her brother, Duke Albric. Knowing his [Albric's] ferocity and treachery, she frequently insisted to him [Meingold] that if there were opportunity, he would kill [her] second [husband] just as [he killed] her first husband. Therefore, during that journey [to Albric's house] she appealed to divine clemency with pious works for his successful return. Because these were mercifully heard, she welcomed him home after he had been rescued from death.

## 78. HARIULF ON THE SWEET WORDS OF ARNULF OF SOISSONS

*After pursuing the military career expected of the nobility, Arnulf (d. 1087) became a monk and then abbot of the monastery of St. Médard at Soissons. In 1081, he was acclaimed bishop of Soissons, but, after being prevented from entering the city by a man who claimed to hold the office at the request of the king, Arnulf based himself outside of the city. It was during his time as bishop that he undertook his peacemaking mission, and it has been argued that it was Arnulf's status as an outsider that helped him succeed as peacemaker. He then founded a monastery at Oudenbourg in Flanders, where he was buried. Hariulf, who wrote the longer of the two versions of the* Life of Saint Arnulf *written shortly after Arnulf's death, finished his adaptation in 1114.*

Source: *Ex vita Arnulfi episcopi Suessionensis auctore Hariulfo*, ed. O. Holder-Egger, Monumenta Germaniae Historica: Scriptores rerum Germanicarum, vol. 15.2 (Hanover: Hahn, 1888), pp. 887–88. Trans. Kelly Gibson.

14. At that time throughout certain, more exactly all, places in Flanders, daily homicides and an insatiable shedding of human blood had disturbed the peace and quiet of the entire region. Because of this, a great multitude of the nobility intensely requested and got the bishop [Arnulf] of the lord to visit the places where the most savage cruelty raged and to somehow remind the ignorant and bloodthirsty minds of the people of Flanders of the good of peace and concord. The man [Arnulf], feeling in his spirit that this [is] pleasing in the eyes of God and, as is written [above], knowing that he ought to come to this place by divine command and the intervention of the blessed apostle Peter, assented all the more swiftly to their requests the more certainly he saw all these things being worked out by God. Thus, surrounded by a crowd of nobles and magnates, he came to the town of Bruges, and from there into the interior of Flanders to the village of Oudenbourg. In these places there was so much madness of killing and frenzy of avenging that they considered it a pleasure to be incessantly splattered with human blood and thought it cowardly and shameful to cease feuding for even one day. Hardly a father spared his son, a son his father, a brother his brother, or a nephew his maternal or paternal uncle. In fact, a paternal uncle handed over his nephew to be killed for a small offense. But the man of the lord Arnulf, with the word of sweetly flowing preaching and examples (*exempla*) of exceptional piety, tamed their diabolical madness and raging destruction in a wondrous way at Bruges, at Furnes, and at Oudenbourg, and, although very laboriously, he made the hearts of the bloodthirsty well disposed to the way of concord. By

being insistent, preaching opportunely and ruthlessly, and frequently prostrating himself at their feet, all enmity was finally put to rest and the most hostile enemies were joined together closely in firm friendship.

## 79. *CHRONICLE OF THE SLAVS* BY HELMOLD OF BOSAU

*Born in Harz, in the region of Saxony in central Germany, Helmold (ca 1120–ca 1177) studied in Brunswick starting around 1140, and lived in Holstein from 1156 until his death sometime after 1177. This work addresses the Christianization of the Slavic people who lived in an area between the lower Elbe River and the Baltic Sea (now part of modern Germany) from the days of Charlemagne to the time of the chronicle's writing. Until the year 1066, Helmold's account relies on the work of Adam of Bremen (see Doc. 70).*

Source: trans. Francis J. Tschan, *Chronicle of the Slavs* (New York: Octagon Books, 1966), pp. 90–93, 154–58, 178–80.

### a. The story of Gottschalk
### [1.19–20]

19. The Persecution of Gottschalk

In those days there was a firm peace in Slavia because Conrad who succeeded the pious Henry in the Empire wore down the Winithi in successive wars. Nevertheless, the Christian religion and the service of the house of God made little headway, since it was hindered by the avarice of the duke and of the Saxons, who in their rapacity let nothing remain either for the churches or for the priests. The chiefs of the Slavs were Anadrag and Gneus, and a third Udo, a bad Christian. On this account and also because of his cruelty he was suddenly stabbed by a Saxon deserter. His son named Gottschalk was being instructed in the learned disciplines at Lüneburg. When he heard of his father's death he rejected the faith along with his studies and, crossing the river, came to the tribe of the Winithi. Having brought together a multitude of robbers, he smote, out of vengeance for his father, the whole land of the Nordalbingians. Such slaughter did he perpetrate on the Christian people that his cruelty exceeded all measure. Nothing in the land of the Holzatians and of the Sturmarians and of those who are called Ditmarshians escaped his hands, except those well-known fortified places, Itzehoe and Bökelnburg. Thither certain armed men had betaken themselves with their women and children and the goods that had escaped pillage. One day, however, as the said chieftain coursed like a robber through field and thicket and saw what had at one time been a country teeming with men and churches reduced to a waste solitude, he shuddered at the work of his own savagery and "it grieved him at his heart." He deliberated how at length to stay his hands from their nefarious undertakings. He therefore presently withdrew from his associates and, going out as if into ambush, unexpectedly came upon a Saxon who was a Christian. And when the latter fled from the armed man as he approached from a distance, Gottschalk raised his voice and exhorted him to stop, swore even that he would do him no harm. When the timid man took courage and paused, Gottschalk began to inquire of him who he was and what news he had. "I am," said he, "a poor man born in Holzatia. Daily we get sinister reports that that prince of the Slavs, Gottschalk, is bringing many evils upon our people and country and that he longs to slake his cruel thirst with our blood. It were time, indeed, that God, the vindicator, should avenge our injuries."

Gottschalk answered him: "You seriously arraign that man, the prince of the Slavs. Yet he has, in very truth, brought many afflictions upon your land and people. A splendid avenger of his father's murder is he. But I am the man about whom we are now speaking and I have come to talk with you. I am sorry that I have done God and the worshipers of Christ so much wrong and I earnestly desire to return to the favor of those on whom I am beginning to realize I have unjustly inflicted such enormities. Heed, then, my words and go back to your people. Tell them to send trustworthy men to a designated place that they may secretly treat with me about an alliance and a covenant of peace. This done, I shall deliver into their hands that whole band of robbers with whom I am engaged more from necessity than from choice." And with these words he set for him the place and the time.

When the man came to the stronghold in which the Saxon survivors were staying in great trepidation, he made known to the elders the saying that was hid and urged them by all means to send men to the place fixed for the conference. But they, thinking it a trick rife with guile, did not heed him.

And so some days later that prince was captured by the duke and was thrown into chains, as if he had been a robber chieftain. The duke, however, reckoned that a man so brave and warlike would be useful to him. He entered into an alliance with Gottschalk and permitted him to depart honorably laden with gifts. On being dismissed, the prince went to the king of the Danes, Cnut, and remained with him many days and years, winning for himself glory by his valor in various warlike deeds in Normandy and in England. Wherefore, also, was he honored with the hand of the king's daughter.

20. The Faith of Gottschalk

After the death of King Cnut, Gottschalk went back to the land of his fathers. Finding that his heritage had been seized by certain usurpers, he determined to fight and, since victory was his, he got back his possessions in their entirety with the principate. He at once directed his mind to winning glory and honor for himself before the Lord and strove to rouse the Slavic peoples, who still lived forgetful of the Christian religion which they had held of old, that they might receive the grace of faith and take thought for the well being of the Church. And the work of God so prospered in his hands that a countless multitude of pagans thronged to receive the grace of baptism. Throughout the whole country of the Wagiri and even in that of the Polabi and Abodrites the churches which had been demolished of old were rebuilt. The call went out into all the lands for priests and ministers of the Word, who were to instruct the untutored pagans in the teachings of the faith. The faithful, therefore, rejoiced over the increase of the new plantation and it came to pass that his territories abounded in churches, and the churches in priests. Now the Kicini and the Circipani and all the tribes who lived along the Peene River also received the grace of faith. This is that Peene River at the mouth of which is located the city of Demmin. Thither the limits of the diocese of Oldenburg at one time extended.

All the Slavic peoples who pertained to the cure of Oldenburg devoutly kept the Christian faith all the time that Gottschalk lived. This very devout man is said to have been inflamed with such zeal for the divine religion that he himself often made discourse in church in exhortation of the people, because he wished to make clearer in the Slavic language matters which were abstrusely preached by the bishops and the priests. Surely in all Slavia there has never arisen anyone mightier or anyone so fervent in the Christian religion. If a longer life had been granted him, he would have disposed all the pagans to embrace Christianity, since he converted nearly a third of those who had under his grandfather, Mistivoi, relapsed into paganism. Then were also founded in several cities communities of holy men who lived according to canonical rule; also communities of monks and of nuns, as those who saw the several houses in Lübeck, Oldenburg, Ratzeburg, Lenzen, and in other cities bear witness. In Mecklenburg, which is the foremost city of the Abodrites, there are said in fact to have been three communities of those who served God.

## b. The murder of Cnut
### [1.50–51]

50. Nicholas

About this time it happened that Cnut, the king of the Abodrites, went to Schleswig to hold a diet with his uncle Nicholas. When the people had come to the conference and the older king, clothed in royal robes, had seated himself on the throne, Cnut sat down opposite him, likewise wearing a crown, that of the kingdom of the Abodrites, and attended by a line of followers. But when his uncle, the king, saw his nephew in royal attire and that he neither stood up before him nor gave him the customary kiss, he pretended not to notice the slight and went over to greet him with a kiss. The latter met him half way and conducted himself throughout as the equal of his uncle both in rank and in dignity. This behavior drew on Cnut deadly hatred. For Magnus, the son of Nicholas, who was present with his mother at this spectacle, burned with an incredible rage when she said to him: "Do you see how your cousin has assumed the scepter and now reigns? Consider him, therefore, a public enemy who has not scrupled to arrogate to himself the royal title though your father is still alive. If you let this go on unnoticed very long and do not kill him, you may be sure that he will deprive you both of life and of the kingdom."

Urged on by these words Magnus began to evolve insidious plans to kill Cnut. When King Nicholas became aware of these designs he called together all the princes of the realm and took pains to bring the estranged youths together. As their dissension, then, turned toward peace, both parties swore to a pact. But this agreement, which was considered fast by Cnut, was besmirched with guile by Magnus. As soon as he had with feigned constancy sounded Cnut's disposition and thought it free of every suspicion of evil, Magnus asked Cnut to meet him in a private conference. Cnut's wife advised him not to go because she feared he would be ensnared; she was at the same time also troubled over what she had seen in a dream the night before. Nevertheless the trustful man could not be detained. He went as he had agreed to the place of the conference, accompanied by only four men. Magnus was there with the same number of men and with an embrace kissed his cousin, whereupon they sat down to transact their business. Without delay an ambuscade rose out of its hiding place and, striking down Cnut, killed him and dismembered his body, passionately thirsting to satisfy its ferocity even on his corpse. And from that day tumults and domestic wars were multiplied in Denmark. Of these some mention must be made in the following record, for the reason that they affected the country of the Nordalbingians very much. On hearing the bad news, the emperor Lothar and his consort,

Richenza, were not a little saddened because there had fallen a man most intimately attached by friendship to the empire. With a formidable army Lothar came to that well-known wall, the Dinewerch, near the stronghold of Schleswig for the purpose of avenging the calamitous death of that excellent man, Cnut. Magnus had taken up a position opposite him with an immense army of Danes to defend his country. But because he was terrified by the valor of the German knighthood he purchased immunity from the Caesar with an immense sum of gold and vassalage.

51. Eric

Therefore, when Eric, Cnut's brother born of a concubine, saw that the Caesar's wrath was cooled, he began to arm in order to avenge his brother's blood. Hastening over land and sea, he brought together a multitude of Danes who execrated the impious death of Cnut. He assumed the title of king and attacked Magnus in battle after battle, but he was overcome and put to flight. Hence, Eric was also called Hasenvoth, that is, harefoot, because of these continual fleeings. Expelled at length from Denmark, he took refuge in the city of Schleswig. The inhabitants, mindful of the favors which Cnut had bestowed on them, received him and were ready for his sake to suffer death and destruction. Thereupon, Nicholas and his son Magnus ordered all the Danish people to war on Schleswig, and the siege became endless. When the lake which adjoins the city was frozen over and was therefore traversable, they stormed the city by land and by sea. Then the people of Schleswig sent messengers to Count Adolph, offering him a hundred marks if he would come with the Nordalbingian people to the assistance of the city. But Magnus offered just as much if he should hold back from the war. Uncertain what to do, the count consulted the elders of the province. They advised that he ought to go to the assistance of the city for the reason that they often got merchandise from it. When Count Adolph, therefore, had assembled an army, he crossed the Eider River, but it seemed to him that he should wait a little until the whole army could come together and that he should then proceed with considered caution into the enemy country. But the populace, eager for booty, could not be held back. They went forward with such speed that when the first came to the Dyavel woods, the last had hardly reached the Eider River.

As soon as Magnus heard of the count's approach, he picked from his force a thousand mail-clad men and advanced to meet the army which had come from Holzatia and joined battle with them. The count was put to flight and the Nordalbingian people were dealt a very great blow. However, the count and as many as had escaped from the battle retreated across the Eider to safety. After he had thus achieved victory, Magnus returned to the siege, but his efforts were in vain because he became master neither of the city nor of the enemy. With the passing of winter the siege also fell off, and Eric slipped away to the coastal region of Scania, complaining everywhere about the death of his innocent brother and about his own misfortunes. On hearing that Eric was in the field, Magnus at the approach of summer led an expedition of innumerable ships against Scania. Although attended by only a small number of the inhabitants, Eric took up a position opposite him. The Scanians alone withstood all the Danes. As Magnus was pressing his forces into conflict on the holy day of Pentecost, the reverend bishops said to him: "Render the God of heaven glory and hallow this great feast. Rest today. You may fight tomorrow." But he scorned their admonitions and proceeded to battle. Eric also "brought forth his host and met him with a mighty power." That day Magnus fell and the whole force of the Danes was defeated and utterly destroyed by the men of Scania. By this victory Eric was made famous and a new name was invented for him: he was called Eric Emun, that is, the memorable. Nicholas, the elder king, now escaped by ship and came to Schleswig where he was struck down by the men of the city for the favor of the victor.

Thus, the Lord avenged the blood of Cnut slain by Magnus, the violator of the oath he had sworn. Eric then ruled in Denmark and had by a concubine, Thunna, a son named Svein. Cnut also had a son, the noble Waldemar, and Magnus, too, had begotten a son Cnut. This royal progeny was left to the Danish people that they might be exercised by them, so they would not lose their skill in war and sometime become effeminate. Only for their civil wars are the Danes distinguished.

## 80. EMOTIONS AMONG THE MILITARY ARISTOCRACY IN *RAOUL OF CAMBRAI*

Raoul de Cambrai *was one of the greatest of a group of twelfth-century French epics centered on the theme of the "rebellious vassal." Raoul, the protagonist, had been unjustly disinherited by the evil machinations of the emperor Louis, and, aided by his uncle Guerri the Red, sought to avenge his shame on those who supplanted him in his rightful fief. Rather than being the work of one identifiable poet, the poem was written in stages by three anonymous authors over the course of the twelfth century. Supposedly based on historical events (much embellished in the retelling) that took place during the reign of Louis the Pious, it takes aim, indirectly, at the ambitions of the French kings to centralize their power (see Doc. 75). The excerpts below – which begin as Guerri, in conversation with the emperor, realizes that his nephew has been disinherited – illustrate the authors' sensitivity to the emotions that could spur noblemen to action.*

Source: trans. Jessie Crosland, revised Richard Abels, *Raoul of Cambrai*. Available at *http://www. deremilitari.org/resources/sources/cambrai.htm*. Accessed 8 September 2007.

32. The white-bearded Guerri speaks: "By my faith, sire, I will not lie to you. My nephew has served you now for a long time and he will get nothing from his friends if you do not recompense his services. Restore to him at least the fief of Cambrésis, the land of the hardy knight Taillefer." "It is not in my power," replied the king; "the knight of Le Mans has it with my glove as pledge. This arrangement grieves my heart; many a time have I repented of it since, but it was done on the advice of my barons." Then said the red knight, "This is ill treatment. I challenge it, by Saint Geri!" Quickly he strode forth from the room and came to the palace in an evil humor. Raoul of Cambrai was playing chess like a man who expects no evil tidings. Guerri saw him there and seized him by the arm with such force that he tore his fur mantle. "Son of a whore," he called to him, but the words were false, "miserable coward, what are you doing playing here? I tell you for a fact, you haven't enough land of your own to rub down an old pack horse on." Raoul heard these words and sprang to his feet; he spoke so loudly that the palace resounded, and many a noble knight in the hall heard him as he cried, "Who takes it from me? I think him very foolhardy." Guerri replied: "The king himself. How he must hold you in disgrace, he who ought to be upholding us and warranting your land!" Raoul heard his words, and all his blood boiled. Two knights brought up at his father's court heard the noise and the clamor and placed themselves at his disposal straightway; and Bernier served them all with wine. Full speed they came before the king and their words did not fall to the ground. Raoul spoke with Guerri the Red standing at his side.

33. Raoul, full of anger, spoke thus: "Just emperor, by Saint Amant I swear that I have served you ever since I carried arms and you have never given me as much as a bezant [that is, penny] for it. Now at least give me the glove as a pledge that I may hold my own land as my valiant father held it before me." "I cannot grant it," replied the king; "I have given it to the knight of Le Mans, and for all the wealth of Milan I would not take it from him." Guerri listened, then he shouted: "I will fight for it first, armed and on horseback, against that mercenary Gibouin of Le Mans." Guerri called Raoul a coward and a recreant. "By the apostle whom the penitents seek, if now you do not take possession of your land, this very day or tomorrow before the sun sets, neither I nor any of my men will ever aid you again." What Raoul now said, the words from which he would never retreat, would cause the bloody death of many a baron: "Just emperor, I tell you all this. First, everyone knows that the land of the father ought by right to pass to the child. By Saint Amant, everyone, both small and great, will heap scorn

upon me, if I do nothing about the shame of another man holding my land. By God who made the firmament, if ever I find that mercenary of Le Mans, no ordinary death shall he die by my sword." The king was heavy at heart when he heard these words.

34. The knight of Le Mans was sitting at a table in the palace. He heard these threats and was filled with fear. He put on his cloak of ermine and came to the king: "Just emperor," said he, "now am I in a sorry plight. You gave me Cambrésis, near Artois; and now you cannot guarantee the possession of it to me. Here now is this arrogant Count Raoul with his fine armor and weapons (he is your nephew, as the Frenchmen know well), and Guerri the Red, his loyal friend. I have no friend so good in all this land who would be worth anything to me against these two. I have served you long with my Viennese blade, and never have I obtained as much as a penny for it. I shall go forth on my good Norwegian steed poorer than I came, and the Alamans and the Germans, the men of Burgundy, of Normandy and France will all talk of it, that all my service will not have earned me a penny." Sorrow filled the heart of King Louis. He beckoned Raoul to him with his embroidered glove and said: "Fair nephew, by God, the giver of laws, I pray you let him hold it for another two or three years on such terms as I will tell you: if any count dies between here and Vermandois, or between Aix-la-Chapelle [Aachen] and Senlis, or from Monloon to Orléans, you shall inherit the rights and the land. You shall not lose a fraction of a penny by the exchange." Raoul listened and did not hesitate: at the advice of Guerri of Artois he accepted the pledge – it was by reason of it that he lay cold in death at last.

35. Count Raoul called Guerri to speak of the matter. "Uncle," said he, "I regard you as my friend. I will accept this gift, you will not be let down." For his father's fief he began a great conflict that was to be fatal to many a baron in the end. Then they demanded hostages from King Louis; and the king listened to bad advice and allowed Raoul to choose them from some of the highest-born in the land. Forty hostages swore and pledged their word to them, but they were bitterly to regret it. Lohier the king gave them, and Anceis; Gociaume was amongst them and Gerard and Gerin, Herbert of the Maine and Geoffroy of Anjou, Henry of Troyes and the young Gerard who held Senlis on the Beauvoisin side. Together with them the king gave them Galeran and Gaudin and then Berart, who held Quercy as his fief. Count Raoul acted in no ignoble fashion; he brought the sacred objects to the marble palace – precious relics of Saint Firmin, Saint Peter, and Saint Augustine, and the king swore without the aid of any priest that, when the time came, he would give him the possessions of the first count who should die between the Loire and the Rhine.

36. Furthermore the king gave him Oliver, Garnier and Poncon, and then in addition Amaury and Droon, Richer the aged and Foucon, Berenger and his uncle Samson. These were the hostages that the king gave to Raoul. In the castle, in the king's presence, they took an oath that they would support the other hostages and stand surety that if any count should die from Orléans to Soissons, from Monloon to Aix-la-Chapelle, Raoul should have his lands forthwith. Raoul was in the right, we can truly say, but the emperor acted like a felon when he granted to his nephew such land as would cause so many knights to lose their lives. Raoul was wise, we tell you truly to demand hostages in abundance....

39. Hostages he had now; as many as he wanted, and for some time things remained thus – for a year and fifteen days, to my knowledge. Raoul returned to Cambrai, and during the time of which I have been speaking, Herbert, a powerful count, died; he was a loyal man and wise and had a great many friends. All Vermandois was his territory, also Roie, Péronne, Origny, Ribemont, St. Quentin and Clairy. A man born with so many friends is fortunate indeed! Raoul heard of his death and bestirred himself. He quickly mounted his steed and summoned those who had pledged themselves in this matter. His uncle Guerri the Red of Arras accompanied him and with them rode a hundred and forty men all finely clothed in fur. He rode straight without stopping to demand from King Louis the fatal gift. Raoul was in his right, as I have told you, and it was the king of St. Denis who was in the wrong. When the king is bad many a loyal man suffers for it. The barons arrived at the court at Paris and dismounted beneath the olive trees. Then they went up the palace steps and demanded to see the king. They found King Louis sitting upon his throne; he looked and saw all these nobles coming, headed by the eager Raoul. "Salutations to the great king Louis," said he, "on behalf of God who suffered on the cross." The emperor replied slowly: "May God, who made paradise, protect you, nephew!"

40. Raoul, the noble baron, spoke: "Just emperor. I desire to speak only to you; I am your nephew and you must not act unfairly toward me. I have heard of the death of Herbert, who used to hold and protect Vermandois. Now invest me at once with his land, for thus you swore that you would do, and you pledged it to me by hostages." "I cannot, nephew," said the noble Louis. "This noble count of whom you speak has four praise-worthy sons, than whom no better knights can be found. If now I handed their land over to you, every right-minded person would blame me for it and I could not summon them to my court, for they would refuse to serve or honor me. Besides, I tell you, I have no desire to disinherit them. I do not wish to vex four men on account of one." Raoul listened and thought he would go mad.

He cannot think, he is so enraged, but he turns away in a fury and does not stop till he reaches his palace and finds the hostages waiting there, whereupon he calls them to him upon their oath.

41. Count Raoul was very angry. He called upon Droon and Geoffroy the Bold of Anjou, who was much dismayed at the news, Herbert of the Maine and Gerard and Henry, Samson and the aged Bernard. "Come forward, barons, I pray you, as you have pledged and sworn to do. Tomorrow at daybreak I summon you upon your oath to my castle and, by Saint Geri, you will be filled with despair." Geoffroy shuddered when he heard these words and said, "Friend, why do you alarm me thus?" "I will tell you," replied Raoul. "Herbert who owned Origny and St. Quentin, Péronne and Clairy, Ham and Roie, Nesle and Falvéy, is dead. Do you think that I have been invested with this rich fief? I tell you no, for the emperor has failed toward me completely." And the barons all replied: "Give us time: for we will go to Louis and learn from his own lips how he means to protect us." "I grant it, by my faith," said Raoul, and Bernier goes to the palace and all the hostages go straightway to the king. Geoffroy speaks first and implores the mercy of the king: "Just emperor, we are in an evil plight, why have you given us as hostages to this devil, the greatest felon that ever wore a hauberk? Herbert, the best of barons, is dead, and Raoul wishes to be invested with the whole of his fief."

42. Geoffroy the Bold spoke again: "Just emperor, you committed great folly when you gave your nephew such a heritage, and the rights and title to someone else's land. Count Herbert is dead who conducted himself as a great baron. Raoul is in the right; the outrage is yours. You will have to invest him with it – we are the hostages to your promise." "God," said the king, "it nearly makes me mad to think that four men should lose their heritage on account of one! By the one who caused the statue to speak, I swear this gift will turn out to be his undoing. Unless this is resolved by some marriage settlement, there will be grief in many a noble home."

43. The king speaks, and he is sad at heart: "Come here, fair nephew Raoul. I give you the glove, but the land is yours on such terms as I shall tell you: namely, that neither I nor my men will act as guarantors." "I ask for nothing better," Raoul replies. But Bernier heard his words and leapt up, and he speaks out so that all can hear: "The sons of Herbert are valiant knights, rich and possessed of many friends and never will they suffer any loss through you." The Frenchmen in the palace, both old and young, talk of the matter, and they say: "The boy Raoul has the mind of a man. He is demanding a fair exchange for his father's land. The king is stirring up a great war which will bring a sad heart to many a fair lady."

## 81. THE HATRED OF KRIEMHILD AND BRUNHILD IN *THE NIBELUNGENLIED*

*Written in Bavaria by an unknown poet around 1200, this famous poem is actually two old heroic tales combined into an unbroken epic sequence. The first story tells the tale of the murder of the hero Siegfried, and the second relates how his wife, Kriemhild, sister of King Gunther, avenged her husband. The excerpt below describes the quarrel between Kriemhild and her sister-in-law, King Gunther's consort Queen Brunhild, that began the feud that led to Siegfried's murder.*

Source: trans. Daniel B. Shumway, *The Nibelungenlied* (New York: Houghton-Mifflin Co., 1909), pp. 112–19. Modernized by Kelly Gibson.

[Lines 814–1072]

The ladies both grew extraordinarily angry. Then Lady Kriemhild spoke [to Brunhild]: "This must now happen: since you have called my husband your liegeman [vassal], the men of the two kings must see today whether I dare walk to church ahead of the queen. You must see today that I am noble and free and that my husband is worthier than yours; nor will I be reproached for it. You shall notice today how your liegewoman goes to court in the presence of the knights of the Burgundian land. I myself shall be more distinguished than any queen was known to be, who ever wore a crown." Great hate then arose between the ladies.

Then Brunhild answered: "If you are not a liegewoman of mine, then you and your ladies must separate yourselves from my entourage when we go to church."

To this Kriemhild replied: "You can trust that will be done."

"Now get ready, my maids," spoke Siegfried's wife. "I must be here without reproach. Let it be seen today that you have rich garments. Brunhild shall willingly deny what she has here avoided."

Without needing much of a command, they sought rich robes and many women and maids dressed themselves well. Then the wife of the noble king went forth with her entourage. Fair Kriemhild, too, was well dressed and had 43 maidens with her, whom she had brought to the Rhine. They wore bright clothes made in Arabia, and thus the well-dressed maids went to the minster. All of Siegfried's men waited for them in front of the house. The people marveled when the queens were seen to walk separately, not together as before. From this many a warrior later suffered dire distress. In front of the minster stood Gunther's wife, while many good knights flirted with the lovely ladies they saw there.

Then came the Lady Kriemhild with a large and noble entourage. Whatever kind of clothes the daughters of noble knights have ever worn were nothing compared with her retinue. She was so rich in goods that she had more than the wives of thirty kings. Men had never seen such costly dresses as those her well-dressed maidens wore. Kriemhild had only done it to anger Brunhild. They met in front of the spacious minster. In her great hate the mistress of the house in an evil way ordered Kriemhild to wait: "No wife of a vassal should ever walk before the queen."

Then Kriemhild angrily spoke: "It would be well for you if you could have kept quiet." You have disgraced yourself. How might a vassal's mistress ever be the wife of any king?"

"Who are you calling a mistress?" spoke the queen.

"That I call you," said Kriemhild. "Your body was first caressed by Siegfried, my dear husband. Certainly, it was not my brother who won your virginity. Where could your wits have wandered? It was an evil trick. Why did you let him love you, if he is your vassal? I hear you complain without good reason."

Brunhild swore, "Gunther shall hear of this."

"What is that to me?" said Kriemhild. "Your pride has betrayed you. With words you have claimed me for your service. It will always make me sad, but I shall no longer be your faithful friend."

Then Brunhild wept. Kriemhild delayed no longer and entered the minster with her entourage before the queen. Thus there arose great hatred, from which bright eyes grew dim and moist.

No matter what men did or sang to God's service there, the time seemed far too long for Brunhild because she was sad of heart and mood. Many a brave knight and good man must later rue this day. Brunhild with her ladies now went forth and stopped before the minster. She thought: "Kriemhild must tell me more of what she, a clever woman, has so loudly charged. If Siegfried has boasted of this, it will cost him his life."

Now the noble Kriemhild came with many a valiant liegeman. Lady Brunhild spoke: "Stand still a while. You have declared me for a mistress, which you must now prove. Know that through your speech, I have fared poorly."

Then spoke the Lady Kriemhild: "You should have let me pass. I'll prove it by the ring of gold I have upon my hand, and which my lover brought me when he first lay at your side."

Brunhild had never seen so horrible a day. She spoke: "This costly hoop of gold was stolen from me, and has been wrongly hidden from me for a long time. I'll find out yet who has taken it from me."

Both ladies now had fallen into grievous wrath.

Kriemhild replied: "I'll not be called a thief. You would have done better to have held your peace and cherished your honor. I'll prove by the girdle which I wear about my waist that I do not lie. Certainly, my Siegfried became your lord."

She wore the cord of silk of Nineveh, set with precious stones; in truth it was fair enough. When Brunhild saw it, she began to weep. Gunther and all the Burgundian men must now learn of this.

Then spoke the queen: "Tell the prince of the Rhineland to come here. I will let him hear how his sister has mocked me. She said here openly that I am Siegfried's wife."

The king came with knights, and when he saw his love weeping, how gently he spoke: "Please tell me, dear lady, who has done you wrong?"

She answered to the king: "I must stand unhappy; your sister would willingly take away all my honor. She swears that Siegfried, her husband, has had me as his mistress."

Said King Gunther: "Then has she done wrong."

"She wears my girdle, which I have lost, and my ring of ruddy gold. It makes me wish that I was never born, unless you clear me of this very great shame, for that I'll serve you forever."

King Gunther spoke: "Have him come here. He must tell us if he has boasted of this, or he must make denial, the hero of the Netherlands." Kriemhild's love was fetched at once.

When Siegfried saw the angry women (he knew not of the tale), how quickly he spoke: "I want to know why these ladies weep and why the king has had me fetched."

Then King Gunther spoke: "It makes me regretful. My Lady Brunhild has told me here a tale, that you have boasted you were the first to clasp her lovely body in your arms; this Lady Kriemhild, your wife, says."

Then spoke Lord Siegfried: "And she shall regret that she has told this tale and I'll clear myself with solemn oaths in front of all your men that I have not told her this."

The king of the Rhineland said: "Let that be seen. The oath you offer, given now, shall free you of all false charges."

They ordered the proud Burgundians to form a ring. Siegfried, the bold, stretched out his hand for the oath; then spoke the mighty king: "Your great innocence is so well known to me that I will free you from what my sister accuses you and say that you have never done this thing."

Siegfried replied: "If my wife gets anything out of Brunhild's sadness, it will surely cause me boundless grief."

Then the strong and good knights gazed upon each other. "One should train women," spoke again Siegfried, the knight, "to leave haughty words unsaid. Forbid it to your wife, and I'll do the same to mine. In truth, I am ashamed of her lack of courtesy."

Many fair ladies were parted by the speech. Brunhild mourned so much that it moved King Gunther's men to pity. Then Hagen of Troneg came to his lady. He found her weeping, and asked what grief she had. She then told him the tale. On the spot he vowed that he would be happy only if Kriemhild's lord regretted it. Ortwin and Gernot joined their conversation and these heroes urged Siegfried's death. Giselher, the son of the noble Uta, came too. When he heard the talk, he spoke the truth: "You trusty knights, why do you do this? Siegfried has not deserved such hate that he should lose his life. Certainly women often grow angry over little things."

"Shall we then raise cuckolds?" answered Hagen; "Such good knights would gain only little honor from that. Because he has boasted of my liege lady, I would rather die than to have Siegfried continue living."

Then the king himself spoke: "He has shown us nothing but love and honor, so let him live. What does it matter if I now should hate the knight? He was always faithful to us and did so willingly."

Knight Ortwin of Metz then spoke: "His great prowess shall not give him anything. If my lord permits, I'll do him every evil."

So without cause the heroes had declared a feud against him. None followed in this, except that Hagen always advised King Gunther that he would rule many royal lands if Siegfried no longer lived. At this the king grew sad, so they let it drop.

Jousting was seen once more. O what stout shafts they splintered before the minster in the presence of Siegfried's wife, even down to the hall! Enough of Gunther's men were now angry. The king spoke: "Let this murderous rage be, he is born to our honor and to our joy. Then, too, the amazingly bold man is so fierce of strength, that none should match him."

"No, not he," spoke Hagen then, "You may well keep still; I think I will secretly make him regret Brunhild's tears. Certainly, Hagen has broken with him for all time."

Then spoke King Gunther: "How might that happen?"

To this Hagen answered: "I'll let you hear. We'll order messengers, unknown to anyone here, to ride into our land and declare war upon us openly. Then you'll tell your guests that you and your men will take the field. When that is done, he will vow to serve you then and from this he shall lose his life, and I learn the tale from the bold knight's wife."

The king wrongly followed his liegeman Hagen. These chosen knights planned greater faithlessness than anyone had ever seen. From two women's quarreling full many a hero lost his life.

# 82. *PARZIVAL* BY WOLFRAM VON ESCHENBACH

*The grail romance* Parzival *(ca 1200) is the first work by Wolfram von Eschenbach, who wrote it in what is now Bavaria. The Grail Kingdom has been seen as an analog of the Holy Roman Empire, with the Grail symbolizing the imperial crown. Two families that figure in the romance, those of Mazadan and Titurel, mirror the Guelfs and Ghibellines, Italian factions whose conflicts deeply marked Italy in the thirteenth century (see Doc. 108 and Doc. 112).*

Source: trans. Jessie L. Weston, *Parzival: A Knightly Epic* (New York: Stechert, 1912), pp. 61–65. Modernized by Kelly Gibson.

[Lines 388–510]

"King Irot was my father, slain by King Lot of old.
Call me King Gramoflanz, and such valor my heart knows
That, because of evil done me, I will fight with only one foe,
Knight Gawain, of him I have heard such fame
That I am ready with him to fight, and vengeance from him claim.
For Gawain's father was treasonous when my father in fair greeting he
     slew,
Good cause for my anger I have and the words that I speak are true.
Now King Lot is dead, and Gawain's fame above all knights of the
     Round Table stands high
And I still yearn for the day of our combat to draw nigh."
Then King Lot's son said fearlessly, "Would it please your lady still,
If indeed she is your lady, and you speak of her father ill,
And judge him of false treason, and wish her brother to slay?
Then indeed she must be a false maiden if she does not mourn your
     deeds always!
If a true daughter and sister she were, for the two she would surely speak,
And forbid you from wreaking your hatred on kinsmen so near, I think.
I believe, if your true love's father his loyalty has broken,
You as kinsman should avenge the evil about the dead spoken!
His son will not fear to do so, and I think little he'll care
Whether in his need he finds small aid from the love of his sister fair.
He, himself, will be pledge for his father, and his sin be upon my head,
For Sir King, I am Gawain, and you war not with the dead!
But I, to free him from such shame, what honor be mine or fame,
In combat I will give to the scourging before you slander my father's
     name!"

Said the king, "Are you he whom I hated with hatred as yet unstilled?
For my soul with both joy and sorrow your valor has filled.
That at last I may fight with you is one thing in you that pleases me,
And I tell you that great honor in this you have won from me,
Since I vowed to fight with you alone – And our fame shall grow great
    always,
If many a lovely lady we bring to behold the fray.
For I can bring fifteen hundred, and you are of a fair host king
At Château Merveil; and on your side your uncle can others bring
From the land that he rules, King Arthur, and Lover its name shall be,
And the city is Bems by the Korka, as known to you it shall be.
There he lies now with his vassals, and here can make his way,
In eight days, with great joy; so I ask you to meet me the sixteenth day,
When I come, for my wrong's avenging, to Ioflanz upon the plain,
And the pay for this garland's plucking there I shall from your hand
    gain!"
Then King Gramoflanz begged Gawain to ride unto Rosche Sabbin,
"For nearer, I think, than the city no way over the flood you'll win!"
But said the gallant Gawain, "I will back even as before I came,
But in all else your will I'll follow." Then they swore them by their fair
    fame
That with many a knight and lady at Ioflanz they would meet for strife
On the chosen day, and alone there would battle for death or life.
And in this way Gawain parted for awhile from the noble knight,
And joyful he turned his bridle, and the wreath adorned his helmet so
    bright.
And he did not slow his steed, but spurred it to the edge of the gulf once
    more,
Nor did Gringuljet miss his footing, but he sprang the chasm over,
And he fell not again, the hero – Then the lady she turned her rein
As he sprang to the ground to tighten the girths of his steed again,
And swiftly to give him welcome, I believe, she to earth did spring,
And low at his feet she cast herself, and she spoke, "such need did I bring
Upon you, Sir Knight, as I knew well was more than your worth might
    ask,
And yet have I felt such sorrow, for the sorrow of this your task,
And the service that you have done me, as I deem she alone does know
Who loves in truth, and, faithfully, weeps over her lover's woe!"
Then he said, "Is this truth, and your greeting be not falsehood in
    friendly guise,
Then you honor yourself, Lady! For in this shall I be so wise

That I know a knight's shield claims honor, and you did against
  knighthood sin,
For so high it stands that I think from no man does he mocking win,
Who as true knight has ever borne him – This, Lady, I must say,
Whoever had looked upon me had known me as knight always,
Yet when you first saw my face my knighthood you would refuse,
But henceforth that may rest – Take this garland I won at your will for
  you,
But I bid you henceforth beware that never your beauty bright
Shall again in such ways mislead you to dishonor a gallant knight,
For I know, before such scorn and mocking again at your hand I bore,
Your love you should give to another, I would ask for it no more!"
Then she spoke as she wept greatly, that lady so sweet and fair,
"Sir Knight, did I tell you the woe that my heart does bear,
You would own my sorrow fully – If I shall discourteous be,
Then he whom I wrong may forgive me of true heart with forgiveness
  free.
For no man can rob me of such joy as the joy that I lost awhile
In that knight of all knights the bravest, Eidegast, who knew nothing of
  guile!
So brave and so fair my true love, his fame was as sunlight's ray,
And for honor he strove so truly that all others, in this his day,
Both here and afar, born of woman, admitted that his praise stood high
Over that of all men, and no glory might ever with his glory vie.
A fountain of virtue forever upspringing, his gallant youth,
And falsehood never shamed his honor nor darkened the light of truth.
Into light he came forth from the darkness, and his honor aloft he bore,
That none who spoke word of treason might reach to it evermore.
Planted from the root in a true heart it waxed and it spread exceedingly,
Until he rose over all men as Saturn high over the planets holds sway.
And true as the one-horned marvel, since the truth I am happy to tell,
The knight of my love and desiring – for whose fate maids may weep
  full well,
Through its virtue I believe it dies – And I was as his heart,
And he was my body! Ah! woe is me, that I must from such true love
  part!
And King Gramoflanz, he slew him, the knight you just now did see,
And the bough you have brought me from the tree of his ward shall be.
Sir Knight, if I did badly entreat you, I did it for this alone,
I would prove if your heart were steadfast, and my love might to you
  atone.

I know well my words did wound you, yet they were just to prove you
    meant,
And I pray you, of this your goodness, be your anger with pity blended,
And forgive me the wrong I did you. I have found you both brave and
    true,
As gold that is tried in the furnace shines forth from the flame anew,
So, I think, your courage shines. He, for whose harm I brought you
    here,
As I thought before, and I think still, his valor has cost me dear."
Said Gawain, "If death spare me awhile, such lesson I'll read the king
That will put an end to his pride, and his life in peril bring.
My faith as a knight I have pledged him, hereafter, a little space,
To meet him in knightly combat, nor our manhood shall we disgrace.
And here I forgive you, Lady, and if you will not disdain
My counsel so rough, I'll tell you how you may honor gain,
What shall befit you well as a woman, nor in anything shall unfitting be,
Here we two are alone, I beg you show favor and grace to me!"
But she said, "In an armored arm like this I seldom warmly lay;
Yet would I not strive against you, you shall on a fitting day
Win reward for your service – Your sorrow will I bemoan,
Until your wounds are healed and all thoughts of your trouble be away
    flown;
To Château Merveil I'll ride with you." "Now grows my joy indeed!"
Said the hero, desirous of love, and he lifted her on her steed,
And closely clung his arm around her: it was more than she deemed him
    worth
When first by the spring she saw him, and mocked him with bitter
    mirth.
Then joyful Gawain he rode there; yet the lady wept always,
And he mourned with her woe, and he asked her the cause of her grief
    to say,
And in God's Name cease from weeping! Then she said, "I must mourn,
    Sir Knight,
Because of the man that slew the knight I love in fight;
That deed brought sorrow to my heart, though nothing but delight had
    I known
When Eidegast's love rejoiced me; yet I was not so overthrown
But since then I might seek his mischief, whatever the cost might be,
And many fierce jousts have been ridden that were aimed at his life by
    me.

And here, I think, you can help me get revenge on him, my foe,
And repay me for this great sorrow that my heart will forever know."

## 83. HARALD'S NORWAY AND THE FLIGHT TO ICELAND IN THE *LAXDAELA SAGA*

*Although the saga literature of Iceland describes events that took place as early as the ninth and tenth centuries, the so-called "family" sagas were not set into writing until the thirteenth century, when the kings of Norway were beginning to press their claims to suzerainty or lordship over Iceland. King Hakon of Norway made good on these claims in 1262, and Iceland was considered part of the Norwegian kingdom until 1536. The sagas were set down, in short, at a time when the farmer-stockbreeders of Iceland were growing increasingly aware of Norwegian royal claims and perhaps feared for their diminishing capacity to negotiate, independently of the king, the compensation due for a fallen kinsman.*

Source: trans. Muriel A. C. Press, *Laxdaela Saga* (London: Dent, 1899), pp. 2–3. Modernized by Kelly Gibson.

2. In Ketill's last days the power of King Harald the Fairhaired arose in such a way that no folkland king or other great men could thrive in the land unless he alone ruled what title should be theirs. When Ketill heard that King Harald intended to give him the same choice as other men of might – namely, not only to put up with his kinsmen being left unatoned, but also to be made a hireling – he called together a meeting of his kinsmen, and began his speech in this way: "You all know what dealings there have been between me and King Harald, which there is no need to set forth; for it is a greater need for us to take counsel about the troubles that now are in store for us. I have true news of King Harald's enmity toward us, and it seems to me that we cannot trust that quarter. It seems to me that there are two choices left for us, either to flee the land or to be slaughtered each in his own seat. Now, as for me, my will is rather to endure the same death that my kinsmen suffer, but I would not lead you by my willfulness into so great a trouble, for I know the temper of my kinsmen and friends, that you would not desert me, even though it would be some trial of manhood to follow me." Bjorn, the son of Ketill, answered: "I will make my wishes known at once. I will follow the example of noble men, and flee this land. For I deem myself no greater a man by enduring King Harald's enslavement at home that may chase me away from my own possessions or may result in my death at their hands." At this there was made a good cheer, and they all thought it was spoken bravely. This counsel then was settled, that they should

leave the country, for the sons of Ketill urged it much, and no one spoke against it. Bjorn and Helgi wished to go to Iceland, for they said they had heard much pleasing news about it. They had been told that there was good land to be had there, and no need to pay money for it; they said there was plenty of whale and salmon and other fishing all the year round there. But Ketill said, "Into that fishing place I shall never come in my old age." So Ketill then told his mind, saying his desire was rather to go west over the sea, for there there was a chance of getting a good livelihood. He knew lands there wide about, for there he had raided far and wide.

## 84. THE STORY OF A FEUD IN *NJAL'S SAGA*

*Njal's Saga (1280) tells the story of a long-running and complex set of intertwining feuds between several different households. This excerpt traces one of the feuds, but it is necessary to read the entire saga to appreciate how the author(s) wove feuding into the narrative.*

Source: trans. George Webbe Dasent, *The Story of Burnt Njal* (New York: Dutton, 1900), pp. 38–65. Modernized by Kelly Gibson.

35. Now it was the custom between Gunnar and Njal to each make the other a feast, alternating each winter, for friendship's sake; and it was Gunnar's turn to go feast at Njal's. So Gunnar and Hallgerda set off for Bergthorsknoll, and when they got there Helgi and his wife were not at home. Njal gave Gunnar and his wife a hearty welcome, and when they had been there a little while, Helgi came home with Thorhalla his wife. Then Bergthora went up to the bench, and Thorhalla with her, and Bergthora said to Hallgerda, "You must give place to this woman."

She answered, "I will give place to no one, for I will not be driven into the corner for any one."

"I shall rule here," said Bergthora. After that Thorhalla sat down, and Bergthora went around the table with water to wash the guests' hands. Then Hallgerda took hold of Bergthora's hand, and said, "There's not much to choose, though, between you two. You have hangnails on every finger, and Njal is beardless."

"That's true," says Bergthora, "yet neither of us finds fault with the other for it; but Thorwald, your husband, was not beardless, and yet you plotted his death."

Then Hallgerda said, "It stands me in little stead to have the bravest man in Iceland if you do not avenge this, Gunnar!"

He sprang up and strode across away from the board, and said, "Home I will go, and it would be more appropriate for you to wrangle with those of your own household, and not under other men's roofs; but as for Njal, I owe him for much honor, and I will never be goaded by you like a fool."

After that they set off home.

"Remember Bergthora," said Hallgerda, "we shall meet again."

Bergthora said she would not be better off for that. Gunnar said nothing at all, but went home to Lithend, and was there at home all winter. And now the summer was running on toward the Althing [the annual assembly].

36. Gunnar rode away to the Thing, but before he rode from home he said to Hallgerda, "Be good now while I am away, and show none of your ill temper in anything involving my friends."

"The trolls take your friends," says Hallgerda.

So Gunnar rode to the Thing, and saw it was not good to come to words with her. Njal rode to the Thing with all his sons.

Now what happened at home must be told. Njal and Gunnar owned a wood in common at Redslip; they had not shared the wood, but each chopped in it as he needed, and neither said a word to the other about that. Hallgerda's overseer's name was Kol; he had been with her long, and was one of the worst of men. There was a man named Swart; he was Njal's and Bergthora's housecarle [servant]; they were very fond of him. Now Bergthora told him that he must go up into Redslip and chop wood; but she said, "I will get men to bring home the wood."

He said he would do the work she set him to do; and so he went up into Redslip, and was to be there a week.

Some drifters came to Lithend from the east across Markfleet, and said that Swart had been in Redslip, and chopped wood, and done a lot of work.

"So," says Hallgerda, "Bergthora must mean to rob me in many things, but I'll take care that he does not chop again."

Rannveig, Gunnar's mother, heard that, and said, "There have been good housewives before now, though they never set their hearts on manslaughter."

Now the night wore away, and early next morning Hallgerda came to speak to Kol, and said, "I have thought of some work for you"; and with that she put weapons into his hands, and went on to say, "Go to Redslip; there you will find Swart."

"What shall I do to him?" he says.

"You need to ask yourself that when you are the worst of men?" she says.

"You must kill him."

"I can get that done," he says, "but it is more likely that I will lose my own life for it."

"Everything grows big in your eyes," she says, "and you behave ill to say this after I have spoken up for you in everything. I must get another man to do this if you do not dare."

He took the axe, and was very angry, and takes a horse that Gunnar owned, and rides now until he comes east of Markfleet. There he got off and waited in the wood until they had carried down the firewood, and Swart was left alone behind. Then Kol sprang on him, and said, "More people can chop great strokes than you alone"; and so he struck the axe on his head, and dealt him his death-blow, and rides home afterwards, and tells Hallgerda of the slaying.

She said, "I shall take such good care of you that no harm shall come to you."

"Maybe so," says he, "but I dreamed the opposite while I slept before I did the deed."

Now they come up into the wood, and find Swart slain, and bring him home. Hallgerda sent a man to Gunnar at the Thing to tell him of the slaying. Gunnar at first said nothing bad about Hallgerda to the messenger, and at first men did not know whether he thought well or ill of it. A little after he stood up, he asked his men to go with him: they did so, and went to Njal's booth. Gunnar sent a man to fetch Njal, and begged him to come out. Njal went out at once, and he and Gunnar began talking, and Gunnar said, "I have to tell you of the slaying of a man, and my wife and my servant Kol were those who did it; but Swart, your housecarle, fell before them."

Njal was silent while he told him the whole story. Then Njal spoke, "You must be careful not to let her have her way in everything."

Gunnar said, "You shall settle the terms yourself."

Njal spoke again, "It will be hard work for you to atone for all Hallgerda's mischief; and somewhere else there will be a broader trail to follow than this which we both now have a share in, and yet, even here much will be lost before all is well; and we shall need to bear in mind the friendly words that passed between us before; and something tells me that you will come out of it well, but still you will be greatly tested."

Then Njal took the award into his own hands from Gunnar, and said, "I will not push this matter to the extreme; you shall pay twelve ounces of silver; but I will add this to my award, that if anything happens from our homestead for which you have to give an award, you will not be less easy in your terms."

Gunnar paid up the money out of hand, and rode home afterwards. Njal, too, came home from the Thing with his sons. Bergthora saw the money, and said, "This is very justly settled; but even as much money shall be paid for Kol as time goes on."

Gunnar came home from the Thing and blamed Hallgerda. She said, "better men lay unatoned in many places." Gunnar said, "she might have her way in beginning a quarrel, but how the matter is to be settled rests with me."

Hallgerda was forever chattering of Swart's slaying, and Bergthora didn't like it. Once Njal and her sons went up to Thorolfsfell to see about the house-keeping there, but that same day this thing happened when Bergthora was out of doors: she sees a man ride up to the house on a black horse. She stayed there and did not go in, for she did not know the man. That man had a spear in his hand, and was girded with a short sword. She asked this man his name.

"Atli is my name," says he.

She asked from where he came.

"I am an Eastfirther," he says.

"Where are you going?" she says.

"I am a homeless man," says he, "and I thought to see Njal and Skarphedinn, and ask if they would take me in."

"What work is handiest to you?" says she.

"I am a man used to field-work," he says, "and many other things come very easily to me; but I will not hide from you that I am a man of hard temper, and it has been many a man's lot before now to bind up wounds at my hand."

"I do not blame you," she says, "though you are no wimp."

Atli said, "Do you have any voice in things here?"

"I am Njal's wife," she says, "and I have as much to say to our housefolk as he."

"Will you take me in then?" says he.

"I will give you your choice of that," says she. "If you will do all the work that I set before you, though I wish to send you where a man's life is at stake."

"You must have so many men at your service," says he, "that you will not need me for such work."

"That I will settle as I please," she says.

"We will strike a bargain on these terms," says he.

Then she took him into the household. Njal and his sons came home and asked Bergthora who that man might be.

"He is your housecarle," she says, "and I took him in." Then she went on to say he was not sluggish at work.

"He will be a great worker enough, I daresay," says Njal, "but I do not know whether he will be such a good worker."

Skarphedinn was good to Atli.

Njal and his sons ride to the Thing in the course of the summer; Gunnar was also at the Thing.

Njal took out a purse of money.

"What money is that, father?"

"Here is the money that Gunnar paid me for our housecarle last summer."

"That will come to stand you in some stead," says Skarphedinn, who smiled as he spoke.

37. Now we must take up the story and say that Atli asked Bergthora what work he should do that day.

"I have thought of some work for you," she says; "you shall go and look for Kol until you find him; for now you shall slay him this very day, if you will do my will."

"This work is well fitted," says Atli, "for we both are bad fellows; but still I will put myself out for him so that one of us shall die."

"May you fare well," she says, "and you shall not do this deed for nothing."

He took his weapons and his horse, and rode up to Fleetlithe, and there met men who were coming down from Lithend. They were at home east in the Mark. They asked Atli where he meant to go. He said he was riding to look for an old horse. They said that was a small errand for such a workman, "but still it would be better to ask those who have been about last night."

"Who are they?" he asks.

"Killer-Kol," they say, "Hallgerda's housecarle, left the fold just now, and has been awake all night."

"I do not know whether I dare to meet him," says Atli, "he is bad-tempered, and maybe I shall let another's wound be my warning."

"Beneath the brows you look like no coward," they said, and showed him where Kol was.

Then he spurred his horse and rides fast, and when he meets Kol, Atli said to him, "Do the pack-saddle bands go well?"

"That's no business of yours, worthless fellow, nor of anyone else from where you come."

Atli said, "You have something behind that is earnest work, but that is to die."

After that Atli thrust at him with his spear, and struck him about his middle. Kol swept at him with his axe, but missed him, and fell off his horse, and died at once.

Atli rode until he met some of Hallgerda's workmen, and said, "Go up to the horse there, and look to Kol, for he has fallen off, and is dead."

"Have you slain him?" say they.

"Well, it will seem to Hallgerda as though he has not fallen by his own hand."

After that Atli rode home and told Bergthora; she thanked him for this deed, and for the words which he had spoken about it.

"I do not know," says he, "what Njal will think of this."

"He will take it well upon his hands," she says, "and I will tell you one thing as a token of it, that he has carried away with him to the Thing the price of that servant which we took last spring, and that money will now serve for Kol; but though peace be made you must still watch yourself, for Hallgerda will keep no peace."

"Will you send a man to Njal to tell him of the slaying?"

"I will not," she says, "I would like it better if Kol were unatoned."

Then they stopped talking about it.

Hallgerda was told of Kol's slaying, and of the words that Atli had said. She said Atli should be paid off for them. She sent a man to the Thing to tell Gunnar of Kol's slaying; he answered little or nothing, and sent a man to tell Njal. He too made no answer, but Skarphedinn said, "Servants are braver than before; they used to fly at each other and fight, and no one saw much harm in that; but now they will do nothing but kill," and as he said this he smiled.

Njal pulled down the purse of money which hung up in the booth, and went out: his sons went with him to Gunnar's booth.

Skarphedinn said to a man who was in the doorway of the booth, "Tell Gunnar that my father wants to see him."

He did so, and Gunnar went out at once and gave Njal a hearty welcome. After that they began to talk.

"It is wrong," says Njal, "that my wife should have broken the peace and let your housecarle be slain."

"She shall not be blamed for that," says Gunnar.

"Settle the award yourself," says Njal.

"So I will do," says Gunnar, "and I value those two men at an even price, Swart and Kol. You shall pay me twelve ounces in silver."

Njal took the purse of money and handed it to Gunnar. Gunnar knew the money, and saw it was the same that he had paid Njal. Njal went away to his booth, and they were just as good friends as before. When Njal came home, he blamed Bergthora; but she said she would never give way to Hallgerda. Hallgerda was very angry with Gunnar because he had made peace for Kol's slaying. Gunnar told her he would never break with Njal or his sons, and she flew into a great rage; but Gunnar paid no attention to that, and so they sat for that year, and nothing noteworthy happened.

38. Next spring Njal said to Atli, "I wish that you would move to the east firths, so that Hallgerda may not put an end to your life."

"I am not afraid of that," says Atli, "and I will willingly stay at home if I have the choice."

"Still that is less wise," says Njal.

"I think it better to lose my life in your house than to change my master; but this I will beg of you, if I am slain, that a servant's price not be paid for me."

"You shall be atoned for as a free man; but perhaps Bergthora will make you a promise which she will fulfill, that revenge, man for man, shall be taken for you."

Then he made up his mind to be a hired servant there.

Now it must be told of Hallgerda that she sent a man west to Bearfirth, to fetch Brynjolf the Unruly, her kinsman. He was a base son of Swan, and he was one of the worst of men. Gunnar knew nothing about it. Hallgerda said he was well fitted to be a servant. So Brynjolf came from the west, and Gunnar asked what he was to do there. He said he was going to stay there.

"You will not better our household," says Gunnar, "after what has been told of you, but I will not turn away any of the kinsmen Hallgerda wishes to be with her."

Gunnar said little, but was not unkind to him, and so things went on until the Thing. Gunnar rides to the Thing and Kolskegg rides too, and when they came to the Thing they and Njal met, for he and his sons were at the Thing, and all went well with Gunnar and them.

Bergthora said to Atli, "Go up into Thorolfsfell and work there a week."

So he went there, and was there on the sly, and burnt charcoal in the wood.

Hallgerda said to Brynjolf, "I have been told Atli is not at home, and he must be winning work on Thorolfsfell."

"What do you think that he is likeliest working at?" says he.

"At something in the wood," she says.

"What shall I do to him?" he asks.

"You shall kill him," says she.

He was rather slow in answering her, and Hallgerda said, "It would grow less in Thiostolf's eyes to kill Atli, if he were alive."

"You shall have no need to goad me on much more," he says, and then he seized his weapons, and takes his horse and mounts, and rides to Thorolfsfell.

There he saw a great cloud of coal smoke east of the homestead, so he rides there, and gets off his horse and ties him up, but he goes where the smoke was thickest. Then he sees where the charcoal pit is, and a man stands by it. He saw that he had thrust his spear in the ground by him. Brynjolf goes along with the smoke right up to him, but he was eager at his work, and didn't see him. Brynjolf gave him a stroke on the head with his axe, and he turned so quickly around that Brynjolf dropped the axe, and Atli grasped the spear, and hurled it after him. Then Brynjolf cast himself down on the ground, but the spear flew away over him.

"Lucky for you that I was not ready for you," says Atli, "but now Hallgerda will be very pleased, for you will tell her of my death; but it is a comfort to know that you will have the same fate soon; but come now take your axe which has been here."

He never answered him, nor did he take the axe before he was dead. Then he rode up to the house on Thorolfsfell, and told of the slaying, and after that rode home and told Hallgerda. She sent men to Bergthorsknoll, and let them tell Bergthora that now Kol's slaying was paid for.

After that Hallgerda sent a man to the Thing to tell Gunnar of Atli's killing.

Gunnar stood up, and Kolskegg with him, and Kolskegg said, "Hallgerda's kinsmen will be unthrifty to you."

Then they go to see Njal, and Gunnar said, "I have to tell you of Atli's killing." He told him also who slew him, and went on, "And now I will bid you atonement for the deed, and you shall make the award yourself."

Njal said, "We two have always intended to never come to strife about anything; but still I cannot make him out a servant."

Gunnar said that was all right, and stretched out his hand.

Njal named his witnesses, and they made peace on those terms.

Skarphedinn said, "Hallgerda does not let our housecarles die of old age."

Gunnar said, "Your mother will take care that blow goes for blow between the houses."

"Yes," says Njal, "there will be enough of that work."

After that Njal fixed the price at a hundred in silver, but Gunnar paid it down at once. Many who stood by said that the award was high; Gunnar got angry, and said that a full atonement was often paid for those who were no worthier than Atli. With that they rode home from the Thing.

Bergthora said to Njal when she saw the money, "You think you have fulfilled your promise, but now my promise is still behind."

"There is no need that you should fulfill it," says Njal.

"No," says she, "you have guessed it would be so; and so it shall be."

Hallgerda said to Gunnar, "Have you paid a hundred in silver for Atli's slaying, and made him a free man?"

"He was free before," says Gunnar, "and besides, I will not make Njal's household outlaws who have forfeited their rights."

"There's no difference between you," she said, "for both of you are so soft."

"That's as things prove," says he.

Then Gunnar was for a long time very short with her, until she gave way to him; and now all was still for the rest of that year; in the spring Njal did not increase his household, and now men ride to the Thing around summer.

39. There was a man named Thord, he was surnamed Freedmanson. Sigtrygg was his father's name, and he had been the freedman of Asgerd, and he was drowned in Markfleet. That was why Thord was with Njal afterwards. He was a tall man and strong, and he had fostered all Njal's sons. He had set his heart on Gudfinna Thorolf's daughter, Njal's kinswoman; she was house-keeper at home there, and was then with child.

Now Bergthora came to talk with Thord Freedmanson; she said, "You shall go to kill Brynjolf, Hallgerda's kinsman."

"I am no man-slayer," he says, "but still I will do whatever you will."

"This is my will," she says.

After that he went up to Lithend, and made them call Hallgerda out, and asked where Brynjolf might be.

"What's your will with him," she says.

"I want him to tell me where he has hidden Atli's body; I have heard that he has buried it badly."

She pointed to him and said he was down in Acretongue.

"Take heed," says Thord, "that the same thing does not befall him as befell Atli."

"You are no man-slayer," she says, "and so nothing will come of it even if you two do meet."

"Never have I seen man's blood, nor do I know how I should feel if I did," he says, and gallops out of the "town" and down to Acretongue.

Rannveig, Gunnar's mother, had heard their talk.

"You goad his mind a lot, Hallgerda," she says, "but I think him a daunt-less man, and your kinsman will find that out."

Thord and Brynjolf met on the beaten path; and Thord said, "Be careful, Brynjolf, for I will do no ignoble man's deed by you."

Brynjolf rode at Thord, and struck at him with his axe. Thord struck at him at the same time with his axe, and chopped the handle in half just above Brynjolf's hands, and then immediately chopped at him a second time, and struck him on the collar-bone, and the blow went straight into his trunk. Then he fell from his horse and was dead on the spot.

Thord met Hallgerda's herdsman, and announced the slaying as done by his hand, and said where he lay, and ordered him to tell Hallgerda of the slaying. After that he rode home to Bergthorsknoll, and told Bergthora of the slaying, and other people too.

"Good luck for your hands," she said.

The herdsman told Hallgerda of the slaying; she was curt about it, and said much ill would come of it, if she has her way.

40. Now news of this comes to the Thing, and Njal made them tell him the tale three times, and then he said, "More men now become man-slayers than I expected."

Skarphedinn spoke, "That man, though, must have been doubly doomed," he says, "who lost his life by our foster-father's hand, who has never seen man's blood. And many would think that we brothers would rather have done this deed with the turn of temper that we have."

"You will have little time," says Njal, "before the same befalls you; but need will drive you to it."

Then they went to meet Gunnar, and told him of the slaying. Gunnar spoke and said that was little loss, "but yet he was a free man."

Njal offered to make peace at once, and Gunnar said yes, and he was to settle the terms himself. He made his award there and then, and set it at one hundred in silver. Njal paid down the money on the spot, and they were at peace after that.

41. There was a man whose name was Sigmund. He was the son of Lambi, the son of Sighvat the Red. He was a great voyager, and an attractive and a courteous man; tall too, and strong. He was a man of proud spirit, and a good poet, and well trained in most feats of strength. He was noisy and boisterous, and given to jibes and mocking. He landed east in Homfirth. Skiolld was the name of his fellow-traveler; he was a Swedish man, and bad to deal with. They took horse and rode from the east out of Hornfirth, and did not draw bridle before they came to Lithend, in the Fleetlithe. Gunnar gave them a hearty welcome, for the bonds of kinship were close between them. Gunnar begged Sigmund to stay there that winter, and Sigmund said he would take the offer if Skiolld his fellow might be there too.

"Well, I have been so told about him," said Gunnar, "that he does not improve your temper; but as it is, you rather need to have it bettered. This, too, is a bad house to stay at, and I would just give both of you a bit of advice, my kinsman, not to fire up at the goading of my wife Hallgerda; for she takes much in hand that is far from my will."

"His hands are clean who warns another," says Sigmund.

"Then mind the advice given you," says Gunnar, "certainly you will be greatly tested; go along always with me, and depend on my counsel."

After that they were in Gunnar's company. Hallgerda was good to Sigmund; and it soon came about that things grew so warm that she loaded him with money, and treated him no worse than her own husband; and many talked about that, and did not know what lay under it.

One day Hallgerda said to Gunnar, "It is not good to be content with that hundred in silver which you took for my kinsman Brynjolf. I shall avenge him if I may," she says.

Gunnar said he had no intention to exchange words with her, and went away. He met Kolskegg, and said to him, "Go and see Njal; and tell him that Thord must watch out for himself although peace has been made, for I think that there is faithlessness somewhere."

He rode off and told Njal, but Njal told Thord, and Kolskegg rode home, and Njal thanked them for their faithfulness.

Once upon a time Njal and Thord were out in the "town"; a male goat would go up and down in the "town," and no one was allowed to drive him away. Then Thord spoke and said, "Well, this is a wondrous thing!"

"What is it that you see that seems after a wondrous fashion?" says Njal.

"I think the goat lies here in the hollow, and he is all one gore of blood."

Njal said that there was no goat there, nor anything else.

"What is it then?" says Thord.

"You must be a doomed man," says Njal, "and you must have seen your spirit twin that follows you, and now watch out for yourself."

"That will stand me in no stead," says Thord, "if I am doomed for death."

Then Hallgerda came to talk with Thrain Sigfus's son, and said, "I would consider you my son-in-law indeed," she says, "if you slay Thord Freedmanson."

"I will not do that," he says, "for then I shall have the wrath of my kinsman Gunnar; and besides, great things hang on this deed, for this slaying would soon be avenged."

"Who will avenge it?" she asks; "is it the beardless carle?"

"Not so," says he, "his sons will avenge it."

After that they talked long and low, and no man knew what counsel they took together.

Once it happened that Gunnar was not at home, but those companions were. Thrain had come in from Gritwater, and then he and they and Hallgerda sat out of doors and talked. Then Hallgerda said, "You have two brothers in arms, Sigmund and Skiolld, who promised to slay Thord Freedmanson; but Thrain you have promised me that you would stand by them when they did the deed."

They all acknowledged that they had given her this promise.

"Now I will advise you on how to do it," she says: "You shall ride east into Homfirth after your goods, and come home round the beginning of the Thing, but if you are at home before it begins, Gunnar will want you to ride to the Thing with him. Njal will be at the Thing and his sons and Gunnar, but then you two shall slay Thord."

They all agreed that this plan should be carried out. After that they rushed them east to the Firth, and Gunnar was not aware of what they were doing, and Gunnar rode to the Thing. Njal sent Thord Freedmanson away east under Eyjafell, and ordered him to stay there one night. So he went east, but he could not get back from the east because the river had risen so high that it could not be crossed on horseback. Njal waited for him one night because he had wanted him to ride with him; and Njal said to Bregthora that she must send Thord to the Thing as soon as he came home. Two nights after, Thord came from the east, and Bergthora told him that he must ride to the Thing, "But first you shall ride up into Thorolfsfell and see about the farm there, and do not be there longer than one or two nights."

42. Then Sigmund came from the east with those companions. Hallgerda told them that Thord was at home, but that he was to ride immediately to the Thing after a few nights. "Now you will have a fair chance at him," she says, "but if this goes off, you will never get near him." Men came to Lithend from Thorolfsfell, and told Hallgerda that Thord was there. Hallgerda went to Thrain Sigfus's son, and his companions, and said to him, "Now Thord is on Thorolfsfell, and now your best plan is to attack him and kill him as he goes home."

"That we will do," says Sigmund. So they went out, and took their weapons and horses and rode on the way to meet him. Sigmund said to Thrain, "Now you shall have nothing to do with it; for we do not need all of us."

"Very well, so I will," says he.

Then Thord rode up to them a little while after, and Sigmund said to him, "Give yourself up," he says, "for now you shall die."

"That shall not be," says Thord, "unless you engage in single combat with me."

"That shall not be either," says Sigmund; "we will make the most of our numbers; but it is not strange that Skarphedinn is strong, for it is said that a fourth of a foster-child's strength comes from the foster-father.

"You will feel the force of that," says Thord, "for Skarphedinn will avenge me."

After that they fall into him, and he breaks a spear of each of them, so well did he guard himself. Then Skiolld cut off his hand, and he still kept them off with his other hand for some time, until Sigmund thrust him through. Then he fell dead to earth. They put turf and stones over him; and Thrain said, "We have done a bad deed, and Njal's sons will not take this slaying well when they hear of it."

They ride home and tell Hallgerda. She was glad to hear of the slaying, but Rannveig, Gunnar's mother, said, "It is said 'the hand's joy in the blow is but a short while,' and so it will be here; but still Gunnar will set you free from this matter. But if Hallgerda makes you take another fly in your mouth, then that will be your undoing."

Hallgerda sent a man to Bergthorsknoll, to tell of the slaying, and another man to the Thing, to tell it to Gunnar. Bergthora said she would not fight against Hallgerda with ill words about such a matter; "That," she said, "would be no revenge for so great a quarrel."

43. But when the messenger came to the Thing to tell Gunnar of the slaying, then Gunnar said, "This has happened ill, and no tidings could come to my ears which I should think worse; but yet we will now go at once and see Njal. I still hope he may take it well, though he be greatly tried."

So they went to see Njal, and called him to come out and talk to them. He went out at once to meet Gunnar, and they talked, nor were there any more men present at first than Kolskegg.

"I have difficult news to tell you," says Gunnar; "the slaying of Thord Freedmanson, and I wish to offer you self-judgment for the slaying."

Njal held his peace for a while, and then said, "That is well offered, and I will take it; but it is to be expected that I shall have blame from my wife or from my sons for that, for it will upset them much; but still I will run the risk, for I know that I have to deal with a good man and true; nor do I wish that any breach should arise in our friendship on my part."

"Will you let your sons be present?" says Gunnar.

"I will not," says Njal, "for they will not break the peace which I make, but if they stand by while we make it they will not work well together with us."

"So it shall be," says Gunnar. "You alone will see to it."

Then they shook one another by the hand, and made peace well and quickly.

Then Njal said, "The award that I make is two hundred in silver, and you will think that is a lot."

"I do not think it is too much," says Gunnar, and went home to his booth.

Njal's sons came home, and Skarphedinn asked from where that great sum of money came, which his father held in his hand.

Njal said, "I tell you of your foster-father's Thord's slaying, and we two, Gunnar and I, have now made peace in the matter, and he has paid an atonement for him as for two men."

"Who slew him?" says Skarphedinn.

"Sigmund and Skiolld, but Thrain was standing near too," says Njal.

"They thought they had need of much strength," says Skarphedinn, and sang a song:

> "Bold in deeds of bravery,
> Burdeners of ocean's steeds,
> Strength enough it seems they needed
> All to slay a single man;
> When shall we our hands uplift?
> We who brandish burnished steel –
> Famous men once reddened weapons,
> When? if now we sit quiet?"

"Yes! when shall the day come when we shall lift our hands?"

"That will not be long off," says Njal, "and then you shall not be hindered; but still, I think, it is very important that you keep this peace that I have made."

"Then we will not break it," says Skarphedinn, "but if anything arises between us, we will bear in mind the old feud."

"Then I will ask you to spare no one," says Njal.

44. Now men ride home from the Thing; and when Gunnar came home, he said to Sigmund, "You are a more unlucky man than I thought, who turns your good gifts to your own ill. But still I have made peace for you with Njal and his sons; and now, take care that you do not let another fly come into your mouth. You are not at all like me, you go about with jibes and jeers, with scorn and mocking; but that is not my turn of mind. That is why you get along so well with Hallgerda, because you two have minds more alike."

Gunnar scolded him a long time, and he answered him well, and said he would follow his advice more in the future than he had followed it so far. Gunnar told him then they might get along together. Gunnar and Njal kept up their friendship though the rest of their people saw little of one another. It happened once that some drifter women came to Lithend from Bergth- orsknoll; they were great gossips and rather spiteful tongued. Hallgerda had a room, and sat often in it, and there sat with her daughter Thorgerda, and there too were Thrain and Sigmund, and a crowd of women. Gunnar was not there, nor Kolskegg. These drifter women went into the room, and Hallg- erda greeted them, and made space for them; then she asked them for news, but they had none to tell. Hallgerda asked where they had been overnight; they said at Bergthorsknoll.

"What was Njal doing?" she says.

"He was hard at work sitting still," they said.

"What were Njal's sons doing?" she says; "they think themselves men at any rate."

"Tall men they are in growth," they say, "but so far they are all untried; Skarphedinn whetted an axe, Gim fitted a spearhead to the shaft, Helgi riv- eted a hilt on a sword, Hauskuld strengthened the handle of a shield."

"They must be bent on some great deed," says Hallgerda.

"We do not know that," they say.

"What were Njal's housecarles doing?" she asks.

"We don't know what some of them were doing, but one was carting dung up the hill-side."

"What good was there in doing that?" she asks.

"He said it made the hay swathes better there than anywhere else," they reply. "Now Njal is witless," says Hallgerda, "though he knows how to give counsel on everything."

"How so?" they ask.

"I will only bring forward what is true to prove it," says she; "why doesn't he make them cart dung over his beard so that he may be like other men? Let us call him 'the Beardless Carle': but his sons we will call 'Dung-beardlings'; and now please do give us a verse about them, Sigmund, and let us get some good by your gift of song."

"I am quite ready to do that," says he, and sang these verses:

> "Lady proud with hawk in hand,
> Please, why should dungbeard boys,
> Deprived of reason, dare to hammer
> Handle fast on battle shield?
> For these lads of loathly feature –
> Lady scattering swanbath's beams –
> Shaft not shun this ditty shameful

Which I shape upon them now.
He the beardless carle shall listen
While I lash him with abuse,
Loon at whom our stomachs sicken,
Soon shall bear these words of scorn;
Far too nice for such base fellows
Is the name my bounty gives,
Even my muse her help refuses,
Making mirth of dungbeard boys.
Here I find a nickname fitting
For those noisome dungbeard boys, –
Loath am I to break my bargain
Linked with such a noble man –
Knit we all our taunts together –
Known to me is mind of man –
Call we now with outburst common,
Him, that boor, the beardless carle."

"You are a jewel indeed," says Hallgerda; "how yielding you are to what I ask!"

Just then Gunnar came in. He had been standing outside the door of the room, and heard all the words that had passed. They were in a great fright when they saw him come in, and then all were silent, but before there had been bursts of laughter.

Gunnar was very angry, and said to Sigmund, "You are a foolish man, and one that cannot keep to good advice, and you revile Njal's sons, and Njal himself who is most worthy of all; and this you do in spite of what you have already done. Know this will be your death. But if any man repeats these words that you have spoken, or these verses that you have made, that man shall be sent away at once, and have my wrath as well."

But they were all so afraid of him that no one dared to repeat those words. After that he went away, but the drifter women talked among themselves, and said that they would get a reward from Bergthora if they told her all this.

Then they went afterwards and took Bergthora aside and told her the whole story of their own free will.

Bergthora spoke and said, when men sat down to the board, "Gifts have been given to all of you, father and sons, and you will be no true men unless you repay them somehow."

"What gifts are these?" asks Skarphedinn.

Big insult on women's [handwritten note in left margin]

"You, my sons," says Bergthora, "have got one gift between you all. You are nicknamed 'Dungbeardlings,' but my husband 'the Beardless Carle.'"

"Ours is no woman's nature," says Skarphedinn, "that we should fly into a rage at every little thing."

"And yet Gunnar was angry for your sakes," says she, "and he is thought to be good-tempered. But if you do not take vengeance for this wrong, you will avenge no shame."

"The woman, our mother, thinks this fine sport," says Skarphedinn, and smiled scornfully as he spoke, but still the sweat burst out upon his brow, and red flecks came over his cheeks, but that was not usual. Grim was silent and bit his lip. Helgi made no sign, and he never said a word. Hauskuld went off with Bergthora; she came into the room again, and fretted and foamed much.

Njal spoke and said, "'Slow and sure,' says the proverb, mistress! and so it is with many things, though they try men's tempers, that there are always two sides to a story, even when vengeance is taken."

But even when Njal had come into his bed, he heard an axe against the panel ring loudly, but there was another bed closet, and there the shields were hung up, and he sees that they are away. He said, "Who has taken down our shields?"

"Your sons went out with them," says Bergthora.

Njal pulled his shoes on his feet, and went out at once, and around to the other side of the house, and sees that they were taking their course right up the slope; he said, "Where are you going, Skarphedinn?"

"To look after your sheep," he answers.

"You would not then be armed," said Njal, "if you meant that, and your errand must be something else."

Then Skarphedinn sang a song,

> "Squanderer of hoarded wealth,
> Some there are that own rich treasure,
> Ore of sea that clasps the earth,
> And yet care to count their sheep;
> Those who forge sharp songs of mocking,
> Death songs, scarcely can possess
> Sense of sheep that trim the grass;
> Such as these I seek in fight";

and said afterwards, "We shall fish for salmon, father."

"It would be well then if it turned out so that the prey does not get away from you."

They went their way, but Njal went to his bed, and he said to Bergthora,

"All your sons were out of doors with arms, and now you must have goaded them to do something."

"I will give them my heartfelt thanks," said Bergthora, "if they tell me of the slaying of Sigmund."

45. Now they, Njal's sons, go up to Fleetlithe, and were that night under the Lithe, and when the day began to break, they came near to Lithend. That same morning both Sigmund and Skiolld rose up and meant to go to the studhorses; they had bits with them, and caught the horses that were in the "town" and rode away on them. They found the studhorses between two brooks. Skarphedinn saw them because Sigmund was in bright clothing. Skarphedinn said, "See the red elf over there?" They looked that way, and said they saw him.

Skarphedinn spoke again: "You, Hauskuld, shall have nothing to do with it, for you will often be sent about alone without due notice; but I mean to take Sigmund for myself; I think that is like a man; but Grim and Helgi, they shall try to slay Skiolld."

Hauskuld sat him down, but they went until they came up to them. Skarphedinn said to Sigmund, "Take your weapons and defend yourself; that is more necessary now than making mocking songs about me and my brothers."

Sigmund took up his weapons, but Skarphedinn waited. Skiolld turned against Grim and Helgi, and they fell hotly to fight. Sigmund had a helmet on his head, and a shield at his side, and was armed with a sword, his spear was in his hand; now he turns against Skarphedinn, and thrusts at once at him with his spear, and the thrust came on his shield. Skarphedinn dashes the spearhaft in two, and lifts up his axe and chops at Sigmund, and cleaves his shield down to below the handle. Sigmund drew his sword and cut at Skarphedinn, and the sword cuts into his shield, so that it stuck fast. Skarphedinn gave the shield such a quick twist, that Sigmund let go his sword. Then Skarphedinn chops at Sigmund with his axe; the "Ogress of War." Sigmund had on a breastplate, the axe came on his shoulder. Skarphedinn cleft the shoulder-blade right through, and at the same time pulled the axe toward him. Sigmund fell down on both knees, but sprang up again at once.

"You have swung low to me already," says Skarphedinn, "but still you shall fall upon your mother's bosom before we part."

"That is ill, then," says Sigmund.

Skarphedinn gave him a blow on his helmet, and after that dealt Sigmund his death-blow.

Grim cut off Skiolld's foot at the ankle-joint, but Helgi thrust him through with his spear, and he got his death there and then.

Skarphedinn saw Hallgerda's shepherd, just as he had chopped off Sigmund's head; he handed the head to the shepherd, and ordered him to take it to Hallgerda, and said she would know whether that head had made jeering songs about them, and with that he sang a song –

> "Here! this head shall you, that heap
> Hoards from ocean-caverns won,
> Bear to Hallgerda with my greeting,
> She that hurries men to fight;
> Sure am I, O firewood splitter!
> That the spendthrift there knows it well,
> And will answer if it ever
> Uttered mocking songs about us."

The shepherd casts the head down as soon as they parted, for he dared not do so while they were watching him. They went along until they met some men down by Markfleet, and told them the news. Skarphedinn gave himself up as the slayer of Sigmund and Grim and Helgi as the slayers of Skiolld; then they went home and told Njal the news. He answers them, "Good luck to your hands. Here no self-judgment will come to pass as things stand."

Now we must take up the story, and say that the shepherd came home to Lithend. He told Hallgerda the news.

"Skarphedinn put Sigmund's head into my hands," he says, "and ordered me to bring it to you; but I dared not do it, for I did not know how you would like that."

"It was wrong that you did not do that," she says; "I would have brought it to Gunnar, and then he would have avenged his kinsman, or have to bear every man's blame."

After that she went to Gunnar and said, "I tell you of your kinsman Sigmund's slaying: Skarphedinn slew him, and wanted them to bring me the head."

"Just what might be expected to befall him," says Gunnar, "for ill speech brings ill luck, and both you and Skarphedinn have often done one another spiteful turns."

Then Gunnar went away; he let no steps be taken toward a suit for manslaughter, and did nothing about it. Hallgerda often put him in mind of it, and kept saying that Sigmund had fallen unatoned. Gunnar paid no attention to that.

Now three Things passed, at each of which men thought that he would follow up the suit; then a tough situation came on Gunnar's hands, which he knew not how to set right, and then he rode to find Njal. He gave Gunnar a hearty welcome. Gunnar said to Njal, "I have come to seek a bit of good advice about a tough situation."

"You are worthy of it," says Njal, and gave him advice on what to do. Then Gunnar stood up and thanked him. Njal then spoke, and said, taking Gunnar by the hand, "For a long time your kinsman Sigmund has been unatoned."

"He was long ago atoned," says Gunnar, "but still I will not fling back the honor offered me."

Gunnar had never spoken an ill word of Njal's sons. Njal would have nothing else than that Gunnar should make his own award in the matter. He awarded two hundred in silver, but let Skiolld fall without a price. They paid down all the money at once.

Gunnar declared their atonement at the Thingskala Thing, when most men were present, and attached great importance to the way in which Njal and his sons had behaved; he told too those bad words which cost Sigmund his life, and no man was to repeat them or sing the verses, but if any sung them, the man who uttered them was to fall without atonement.

Both Gunnar and Njal gave each other their words that no such matters should ever happen that they would not settle among themselves; and this pledge was well kept ever after, and they were always friends.

# CHAPTER ELEVEN: PEACE CHARTERS AND OATHS

*Documents that relate to the practice of vengeance are more commonly found dating from the High Middle Ages on than from the early Middle Ages. The main reason for the significant increase in the number of surviving relevant documents after 1250 is that this is the period during which the systematic practice of keeping fiscal and judicial registers began. Numerous charters and other sources from the High Middle Ages record the formal act of peacemaking between two formerly hostile parties, illustrating the degree to which vengeance was practiced in the period. Included among the documents here are samples of such charters.*

## 85. PEACE OATH PROPOSED BY BISHOP WARIN OF BEAUVAIS TO KING ROBERT THE PIOUS

*This formula from France, dated 1023, illustrates the kind of oath that parties were expected to swear after having been caught breaking the peace.*

Source: trans. Richard Landes, Vatican, Reg. lat. 566, fol. 38v, *The Peace of God: Social Violence and Religious Response in France around the Year 1000*, ed. Thomas Head and Richard Landes (Ithaca: Cornell University Press, 1992), pp. 332–34.

I will not invade a church for any reason. Nor will I invade the storehouses on the premises of a church because of its protected status, unless to catch [someone who has committed] a homicide, or a wrongdoer who broke this peace, or a horse. But if I invade a storehouse for such a reason, I will, to my knowledge, take out nothing more than that wrongdoer or his equipment. I will not assault an unarmed cleric or monk, nor anyone walking with him who is not carrying a spear or a shield, nor will I seize their horse unless they are committing a crime or unless it is in recompense for a crime for which they would not make amends, fifteen days after my warning. I will not seize bulls, cows, pigs, sheep, lambs, goats, asses or the burden they bear, mares, or their untamed colts.

I will not seize villeins of either sex, or sergeants or merchants, or their coins, or hold them for ransom, or ruin them with exactions on account of their lord's war, or whip them for their possessions. I will not exact by extortion mules and horses, male and female, and colts pasturing in the fields from the first of March to All Souls' Day, unless I should find them doing damage to me. I will not burn or destroy houses unless I find an enemy horseman or thief within, and unless they are joined to a real castle. I will not cut down or uproot the vineyards of another, or harvest them for reasons of war, unless it is on my land, or what, to' my knowledge, ought to be my land. I will not destroy a mill, or seize the grain that is in it, unless I am on a cavalcade, or with the host, or it is on my land.

I will not, to my knowledge, harbor or assist an admitted and notorious public robber. And that man who will break this peace knowingly, I will not protect him after I learn of it, and if he did it unknowingly and came to me for protection, either I will make amends for him, or I will make him make amends within fifteen days after I have been informed, or I will deny him my protection.

I will not attack merchants or pilgrims or take their possessions unless they commit crimes. I will not kill the animals of villeins except for my consumption or that of my men. I will not plunder a villein or take his property at the perfidious instigation of his lord. I will not assault noble women in the absence of their husbands, or those who travel with them, unless I should find them committing misdeeds against me; and the same holds for widows and nuns. I will not take wine from those who carry it in carts or take their oxen. I will not capture hunters or take their horses or dogs, unless, as it is said, I find them doing me damage. And from those who will have sworn this [oath] and keep it in my regard – with the exception of lands that are mine by freehold or benefice or by delegation, and except when building or besieging a castle, or when I am in the host of the king or our bishops, or on cavalcade – I will accept only what I need for subsistence, and I will take nothing home with me except horseshoes, and I will not break into the protected areas of churches while on the aforementioned military expeditions, unless they refuse to sell me what I need to live.

From the beginning of Lent until the end of Easter, I will not assault unarmed horsemen or take their possessions, and if a villein should do damage to another villein or horseman, before I seize him, first I will make complaints about him and await fifteen days for satisfaction before punishing him, but no more than the law allows.

The above-written was sworn in these words. You heard this, King Robert, just as recorded in this brief text, and as I, Bishop Warin, in this last hour set forth and just as those present now heard and understood. Thus I expect from my part against those who swear this oath now and will swear it between now and the feast of Saint John next June, and from the festival for six years, with the exception of royal war....

# 86. HENRY II SETTLES A FEUD ON MONASTIC LAND

*The Holy Roman Emperor Henry II (973–1024), a leading supporter of the Church reform movement, was the last of the Saxon emperors of Germany. This charter, dated to 1024, sought to redress grievances and offer punishments for the feud between the people living under the lordship of the monasteries of Fulda and Hersfeld.*

Source: trans. Boyd H. Hill, Jr., *Medieval Monarchy in Action: The German Empire from Henry I to Henry IV* (London: George Allen and Unwin, 1972), pp. 190–92.

In the name of the holy and indivisible Trinity. Henry, by God's grace emperor augustus of the Romans. To all the faithful present and future we desire it to be noted how constant complaint has alarmed us on account of the numerous and frequent disputes between the family of Fulda and that of Hersfeld, which now have grown so bad that there have even been innumerable homicides committed between them, and hence the greatest possible damage has been suffered by both churches.

Therefore, in order that such boldness of so great presumption should not remain any longer between the two families without a fitting revenge, we have drawn up a decree in the form of this diploma upon the advice and consent of both abbots, Richard of Fulda and Arnold of Hersfeld, as follows:

First of all injustice which has remained uncompensated for a long time on both sides is to be fully corrected by the advocates and provosts of each place.

And henceforth if any member of the family of either church should pursue and assail any servant of Saint Boniface or Saint Wigbert, and through bold daring with an armed band should break into either his courtyard or his house in order to kill or plunder, and if he should either run away or if he were not perchance at home or if [the victim] gets free from that power or attack somehow or other, let the skin and hair of whoever was a leader or principal of this bold invasion be removed, and, moreover, let him be scratched and burned well on both cheeks with a white hot iron, and let his henchmen be deprived of skin and hair.

However, if the victim is killed there, then all those who took part in this murder or invasion are to undergo the punishments stated above. And if he who is killed and those who do the killing are from the family of one and the same church, they must each pay the *wergeld* of the slain man and everything owed, just as they have done so far, to their own church.

If, however, he who is killed is from one family and the murderers are from another, the author of the homicide alone shall pay the *wergeld* for the others.

And if someone is slain in whatever place from one or the other family, unless he who committed the murder has witnesses worthy of credit or is able to prove by means of a white-hot iron that he did it because he could not otherwise have escaped alive from the attack of the other, he is to undergo the said punishment. On the other hand, if he can prove this, nothing may be allowed except what the same church has legally held up to now.

The advocate in whose jurisdiction this has taken place is faithfully to carry out this decree with the knowledge of both abbots and in the presence of their commissioners. And if the advocate, corrupted by a bribe or motivated by pity, should seek to avoid this decree by any sort of trickery, he will lose our grace and the advocacy, unless he dares to swear on the holy relics that he can nowhere apprehend the murderer or intruder; and still he should apprehend him as soon as possible.

And if the advocate in whose area this took place could not or would not apprehend the criminal, let the faithful of the other abbot apprehend him if they can and present him to the commissioners of both abbots to carry out the aforesaid punishment.

And in the case of chamberlains and butlers and other honored servants of both abbots, we have decided that if any of them should do such a thing, he should undergo the aforesaid punishment according to the will of the abbot or else pay ten pounds of *denarii*.

And I desire this and strongly command in order that no one should dare to renew the dispute which has been clearly and legally defined once and for all.

But if the aforesaid abbots wish to nullify this decree, each is to pay me or my successor two pounds of gold; and yet they may not carry out their impulse.

And in order that this regulation may remain stable and unshaken, we have ordered this diploma to be marked with the impression of our seal.

Sign of Lord Henry, most invincible august emperor of the Romans.

Ulrich, chancellor, verified it for Archchaplain Aribo.

Given in the year of our Lord's Incarnation 1024, in the twenty-second year of the reign of Henry, emperor augustus, in the eleventh year of his empire, the seventh year of the indiction; given the seventh day before the ides of March; carried out under favorable auspices at Bamberg.

# 87. ATTEMPTED SETTLEMENT BY COMBAT

*Although previous royal charters, as well as the laws of Justinian, were invoked during this 1098 hearing over a land dispute from northern Italy, the judges and the defending party preferred to use trial by combat as the means to come to a resolution. The battle itself, however, was declared an unfair fight and the disagreement over land between a group of men and an abbot remained unsettled.*

Source: ed. Cesare Manaresi, *I placiti del "Regnum Italiae,"* Fonti per la storia d'Italia 97 (Rome: Nella sede dell'instituto palazzo Borromini, 1960), pp. 432–34. Trans. Kelly Gibson.

July 5, 1098, Garfagnolo.

We decided to briefly make known in writing what is needed about the dispute between the abbot of the monastery of Saint Prosper of Reggio and the men said to be from Vaglie so that it is more firmly committed to memory for posterity.

With his advocate, the abbot made a claim before Judge Ubaldo of Carpineti that men from Vaglie unjustly held certain pieces of land in the estate (*curtis*) of Nasseto that rightfully belonged to the church of St. Prosper. After Judge Ubaldo examined this question with great diligence and it was settled by the oath of three men of the estate of Nasseto, he returned the possession to the church, as is read in the record of the court proceedings (*notitia*).

After this, the men from Vaglie went to Countess Matilda and said that they were unjustly dispossessed. Therefore, the countess sent Judge Bono of Nonantola and ordered Judge Ubaldo to [with Bono] investigate the truth and order both parties to prepare for battle.

When the parties were gathered for this in the presence of the aforementioned judges, the abbot immediately showed royal charters of Charles and Otto in which it is clearly recognized that the property belongs to the church according to the church's charters. Moreover, the advocates of the abbot showed the law of the most serene emperor Justinian in which it is written that those who receive anything from the treasury or from the imperial household are immediately safe whether cleansed by expiatory rites or brought to agreement, as is plainly clear in Justinian's *Code* and *Institutions*. The aforementioned judges absolutely rejected [these and] many other excellent arguments and said that they [the litigants] will in no way do anything but battle. Although the party of the church was unwilling, they made an appeal and a war-wager under the penalty of ten Lucchese pounds.

On the appointed day, when the champions were ready for battle, the party of the church had such great humility that all the property in dispute was conceded on behalf of the party of the church to their opponents, according to the judgment of the countess's legates. The opponents absolutely refused this. After the champions were gathered for battle [but] before they began the battle, the champion of the men of Vaglie cast a feminine glove (*wantonem*) decorated with various colors above the head of the champion of the church as an evil gesture, which the laws absolutely prohibit and punish. Nobody fell during the fight, but, while they grabbed and butchered each other with [their] hands, a multitude of men of the party of those from Vaglie surrounded the champion of the church and seized him, though he escaped from their hands and like a man demanded battle when he returned to the field. They advanced and again violently took hold of him and beat him most cruelly. Although smallest in number, the party of the church wished to help him, yet by seeking recompense nearly everyone was beaten and wounded and scarcely escaped. After all these things happened in the order that is read above, a controversy arose: the party of men from Vaglie said that they had won in battle and the party of the church asserted that they were in no way defeated. The champion of the party of the church said that he was by no means conquered and, like a man and most prudently, he wished to fight. And Judge Ubaldo, under whose guidance the battle had been arranged, said that the dispute was not decided by this battle and remains in doubt. For this reason the judges gave no opinion. This case happened in the presence of judges Ubaldo and Bono, advocates Alberto and Ubaldino, Heriberto the advocate of the aforementioned church, Giberto Carbone and Frogerio and others: Adegerio and Ugo, sons of the late Manfredo of Gruppo; Gottefredo of Rosano; Sigefredus Sigezone and Ildeberto of Reggio; Sigezone and Giberto, sons of *Bibentisaquam;* Rozone of Pievepelago; Ingebaldo; Mazolino and his son; Rodulfo of Pugliano and his brother; Bitenengo of Bundolo; and Mainfredo of Villula; and many others. In the 198th year after the incarnation of our Lord Jesus Christ, the third nones of July, in the seventh indiction, in the village called Garfagnolo.

## 88. GRANT TO THE NORMAN BISHOPS OF FINES DUE FROM BREACHES OF THE TRUCE OF GOD

*This grant, describing the procedure for assessing the guilt of those who violate the Truce of God, was given by King Stephen of England (b. 1096), who reigned from 1135 to 1154. Stephen's reign, following the death of his uncle King Henry I, was a time of civil war (generally called "the anarchy") because the legitimacy of his succession was challenged by Henry's daughter, Matilda. Given early in Stephen's reign (1136–39), this grant upholding a previous grant made by Henry I can perhaps be viewed as a demonstration of continuity with the previous reign, which may have been a way of presenting Stephen as Henry's legitimate heir.*

Source: ed. H. A. Cronne and R. H. C. Davis, *Regesta regum Anglo-Normannorum 1066–1154*, vol. 3 (Oxford: Clarendon, 1968), pp. 224–25. Trans. Kelly Gibson.

## [No. 609]

Stephen, by the grace of God king of the English and duke of the Normans, greets Archbishop Hugo of Rouen, and bishops, abbots, counts, barons, viscounts, and everyone dwelling in Normandy now and in the future. Because the most high is ruler in the kingdom of men and he will give that [kingdom] to whom he wishes for his honor and my salvation, with the advice and assent of the princes and my faithful, I decreed and confirmed that all episcopal and synodal rights are given to you, Archbishop Hugo, and to your successors and all bishops of Normandy. Concerning those who break the truce of God and in the truce of the Lord kill men, I decreed in a way that upholds the command of my uncle, King Henry. If anyone wishes to duel to prove the guilt of one who kills during the truce of the Lord, that duel will be at my court (*curia*). If the slayer is convicted, the bishop in whose diocese he broke the truce of God will first have his fine, that is, nine pounds from the property of the convicted, collected by my justice. If the property of the convicted is not enough to make those nine pounds, the bishop will have it all, however much less is there. Nothing will be taken for my benefit from the property of the convicted before the bishop has his entire fine. If there is no man who wishes to duel to prove the guilt of one who kills during the truce of God, then the slayer, summoned by church officials, will absolve himself by the manifest proof of judgment of either water or of fire. If he is convicted, then the bishops' fine should be collected by my justice as written above. Moreover, if the breaker of the truce of God is unwilling to undergo the ordeal, the bishop will similarly have his fine, collected by my justice. If a slayer who flees makes peace with me afterwards, his fine for my peace will not be taken from the bishop, but he will render it [the fine] to the bishop or make satisfaction for it with him. Finally, I, who ought to obey God first, condemn all the disobedient and declare that they must be punished with both the severity of the sword and with episcopal censure. With witnesses Henry, bishop of Winchester, Bernard, bishop of Saint David's, Robert, bishop of Bath, William the Hammer, and G. de Pommeraye. At Witham [either Witham, Essex, or Wytham, Berkshire].

# 89. A CATALAN PEACE SETTLEMENT

*This charter from 1137 records a peace settlement reached between Count Ramón Be-*
*renguer IV of Barcelona and Count Ponç Hug I of Empuries, a town in Catalonia,*
*on 5 March 1137.*

Source: trans. Donald Kagay, *The Usatges of Barcelona: The Fundamental Law of Catalonia* (Philadelphia: University of Pennsylvania Press, 1994), pp. 112–14.

In the one-hundred-and-thirty-seventh year of the Incarnation of the Lord
after the millennium, a spontaneous peace and amicable settlement was made
between the venerable Count Ramón of Barcelona and Count Ponç Hug of
Empuries concerning the very many disputes, offenses, and infractions of the
truce and peace and fealty on account of which they often complained to one
another. Indeed first the aforesaid Count Ponç agreed to serve faithfully his
lord Count Ramón and maintain the charter of agreement and abandonment
of claims which his father Count Hug [II] of Empuries made to the church
of Gerona and its bishops and canons concerning the fief which the church
of Gerona has or ought to have in Castilion and within its boundaries. And
he agreed to the same count along with the parishioners of each sex of the
church of Castilion that they shall not prevent the provost of the church of
Gerona in any way from working, holding, or exchanging these lands whenever and wherever he wishes. Likewise, the aforementioned Count Ponç,
with a spontaneous assent and voluntary decision, agreed with him [Ramón]
that he would totally destroy, eradicate, and remove settlers from the castle
of Charmez. And the aforementioned count of Barcelona agreed to remove
settlers from and to totally destroy the castle of Rocaberti under the aforesaid
voluntary decision and spontaneous assent of the count of Empuries, and
that the aforesaid Count Ponç on no occasion or for no reason shall be annoyed with the aforesaid count of Barcelona because of the destruction of the
aforesaid castles. Further that the aforesaid castles shall in no way be rebuilt
by the aforesaid Count Ponç or by any counsel or deceit of his without
the voluntary permission of the aforementioned Count Ponç. Let there be
a secure peace without deceit between Ramón de Peralta and his brother
Aimeric and the aforesaid Count Ponç. And let them render homage to him
[Ponç] and draw out his coinage in Perelada and let them conserve the coinage in Perelada and let this circulate at six dinars for each libra [pound] for
the fief of the aforesaid Count Ponç. Concerning the disputes of the Viscount
of Castellnou and the aforementioned Count Ponç, it was decreed that after
a pledge was redeemed, the count of Barcelona shall place such peaceful
men [arbiters] there as to make a firm peace between them. Moreover, I, the

aforesaid Count Ponç, agree to maintain, observe, and fulfill all the things written above under homage and fealty to you Count [Ramón] as my lord and to put an end to all those things by which I harmed you in word or deed; and attend to all this by faith without deceit.

[There follows a pact by which Ramón Berenguer IV grants castles and revenues held by Ponç Hug I's father in return for his homage and fealty].

## 90. A TWELFTH-CENTURY FORGED DONATION OF KING DAGOBERT III

*This charter granting territory to Schuttern Abbey, supposedly issued by the Merovingian king Dagobert III on 5 November 707 at the request of Bishop Arbogast of Strasbourg, is a twelfth-century forgery. Unlike authentic Merovingian charters of donation, this document gives the king the responsibility to punish those who violate the agreement.*

Source: ed. T. Kölzer, based on C. Brühl with M. Hartmann and A. Stieldorf, Monumenta Germaniae Historica: Die Urkunden der Merovinger, vol. 1 (Hanover: Hahn, 2001), pp. 411–12. Trans. Kelly Gibson.

In the name of the holy and indivisible Trinity, Dagobert, by divine clemency august emperor of the Romans. If we strive to enrich the venerable places of the churches of God with the benefit of any gift, we do not hesitate at all to make it for the remedy of our soul. Therefore, the diligence of all the faithful of God and of us, now and in the future, will know that at the advice of our beloved venerable Arbogast, bishop of Strasbourg, to a certain monastery called *Offonisuuilare* [Schuttern], which was built in honor of the holy mother of God and of the holy apostles Peter and Paul, we concede and grant and completely transfer from our right and dominion to its right and dominion, for the remedy of our soul and [the souls] of our predecessors, through this, our imperial charter, one estate (*curtim*) in the village called *Herleichesheim* [Herrlisheim], located in the territory of the bishopric of Basel, with everything belonging to it: fenced areas, open spaces, duties and revenues, [lands] claimed or unclaimed, cultivated and uncultivated, meadows, pastures, forests, bodies of water and watercourses, dependents (*mancipia*) of both sexes, with all appurtenances belonging to the same properties which are able in any way to be named, on the condition that the abbot of the same monastery and his successors have from the same charter of donation the power to do whatever they please for the use of the monastery, free from the objection of all men of the kingdom. In addition, with the consultation of our faithful, we order that the abbot and brothers of the aforementioned monastery serving the Lord there should possess [this] by our strongest authority, so that no public judge [*iudex*: a title given to royal officials including counts, judges, and estate managers] or any person, superior or subordinate, dare to do anything unjust in the churches or villages (*villas*), places, [or] fields of the same monastery, or dare to strip off by force or irrationally disturb the men, free and unfree (*servi*), of that monastery. Moreover, if any haughty man shall be tempted to unjustly claim for himself the possessions of the same monastery, which are known to be scattered in the territory of the aforementioned bishopric, or neglects to pay the rents due for the support of the brothers, let it be declared loudly in the court we have frequently made mention of and let justice be demanded, and let him be severely corrected by the abbot and the abbot's guardian (*defensor*) according to a law of the people of this sort, lest he dare such things ever again. But if he seems incorrigible and disobedient to them, his obstinacy should be reported to the governance of the kingdom in order that vengeance be taken on him and the others have fear. And so that this imperial donation of ours remains stable and unshaken, we ordered that this imperial charter be marked with the imprint of our seal, corroborating with our own hand.

Given the nones of November in the year of the incarnation 705, in the ninth indiction, and in the eleventh year of the reign of the most glorious king Dagobert. Done at Strasbourg, happily in the name of God, Amen.

## 91. A PEACE TREATY FROM AVIGNON

*This charter from 1226 illustrates how peace treaties could involve the entire population of a city.*

Source: ed. M. A. de Maulde, *Coutumes et règlements de la république d'Avignon au treizième siècle* (Paris: L. Larose, 1879), pp. 246–48. Trans. Lori Pieper.

### The concord made by the lord bishop among the citizens
of Avignon

Let it be known to all men present and well as future who will see the present page, that in the year of the Lord 1226, that is the nones of February, Lord Spino of Surrexina being podesta [governor] in the city of Avignon, on whom all most excellent gift and every perfect offering is from on high, descending from the father of lights, the discord and war, which had arisen and progressed between the people of Avignon at the instigation of the cunning of Satan, to the honor of the holy and undivided Trinity, has been put to sleep and pacified with the attendance of the Holy Spirit.

Since indeed on the occasion of the aforesaid discord, on account of the rule of the late podesta, many knights and burgesses of the aforesaid city went out, the general counsel and the heads of the guilds gathered together in the principal church of Blessed Mary on the feast of the virgin Saint Agatha, the patron of the confraternity, and for themselves and for the whole city of Avignon who remained within the city at the time of the discord, tearfully on their bended knees they asked the knights and others who went out of the same city that they might kindly allow the aforesaid city to be under the rule of the podesta for ten years, and that thus a stable and perpetual concord might be established among all the people of Avignon. They responded as wisely as kindly about this to them that they would generously grant what they asked from them. Now, however, that this kind of matter might be settled among the aforesaid by consultation and amicably, at last it pleased everyone that a meeting be convoked at the episcopal residence and there all the aforesaid things would be treated. There, the signal having been given by the sound of the bell and by the herald likewise, for the citizens to immediately gather together from throughout the city, and for the knights and others who went out of the city to tell of their former feeling of love and faith, [and] for them, with devout humility and humble devotion, to entrust [themselves] to the decision of those who remained within the city; likewise they and theirs conceding to the same, as liberally as gladly, the possession of the office of podesta for ten years, as they asked. Since [this] party desired to be gracious to the other party in all things, they received the aforesaid knights and the others into their trust, putting themselves and theirs with all their property at their disposal and good pleasure. And so with matters being thus, it was the unanimous will of all the aforesaid people, standing and promising before the relics of Blessed Mary, that a stable peace and concord might be preserved among them in this way: that is, that all the aforesaid and individuals over fourteen years of age might swear bodily on the holy Gospels that they would preserve, swear and defend themselves and one another against all men who might injure or wish to injure them, and that the said knights and burgesses of Avignon and all those on their side who went out of the city might preserve, aid and defend the persons and the property of the knights and all the upright men and of each individual who remained within the city of Avignon [and] the persons of all and each of the knights who went out of the city, and all the property of those, wherever they might be, [who were] against the city of Avignon, and completely outside all its power and all its laws. Therefore immediately in the same place, the aforesaid knights and burgesses who went out of the city and all the others of their side put away and ended, with pure and spontaneous affection, all of the bad will, rancor of mind, hatred, injury, enmity and iniquity that they used to have against all those or any of those who remained within the city of Avignon by reason of the action of the podesta or by reason of the war recently past, or injury given to them in some way within the city of Avignon or outside it, or by reason of some injury said or caused to them at the time of the beginning of the war up to the present day, saving and holding back this: that the lord Spinus the podesta, or another man, or other men, with the consent of both parties, shall arrange concerning the damage caused to both according to the plenitude of power granted to the same lord podesta both by those who went out of the city and those who remained within the city. This same forgiveness and ending of the hatred, rancor of mind, injury, bad will, and enmity was made in the exact same way by all those who remained within the city to all those who went out of the same city. And so that all the above-mentioned knights and others of their party who went out of the city might keep and observe the aforesaid peace and concord in good faith, they gave to the knights and all the upright men and individuals who remained within the city, and the side of those who remained similarly [gave] in turn to those who went out, God Almighty and his glorious Virgin Mother and all the angels and archangels and saints of God as pledges for themselves.

However, they mutually added to themselves this penalty: that is that if any knight or anyone of the other side shall break or violate the aforesaid peace by committing homicide, he is to be expelled from the city of Avignon and from all its district in perpetual exile: thus if he cannot be caught; but if he can be caught he is to be condemned to the death of the gallows with due measure, and all his goods are to be put up for public sale. If however he shall be wanting for money, the malefactor is to make good the damage and in addition, fourfold damage to that suffered, and he is to give to the commune by way of penalty 1000 shillings for such an assault. If however, such a transgressor shall not have the means to pay, if he can be caught, he is to lose one of his limbs according to the will of the podesta or another rector who for the time shall be in the above-mentioned city. If however he cannot be caught, he is to be exiled in perpetuity. These things were done in the city of Avignon in the episcopal court; as witnesses were present: Master Fulco and Willelmus Amelius, canon of Avignon; Bertold de Auriolo and Petrus, clerics of the church of Avignon; brother Willelmus, trustee in charge of material concerns of the church of Cavallice; Rostagnus Montorosus, Pontius de Ponte Meylloretus, Ugo de Ponte Meilloretus, Bertoldus de Remolinis, [and] Petrus Bermundus, notary. And I, Petrus de Cavomonte, public notary of Avignon, was present, along with all the above mentioned; [and] by the command of both parties and by the authority and consent of Lord Jacobus Bonivicinus, at that time vicar in the city of Avignon, and of Lord Jacobus de Osa, judge in the same city, I have written the present instrument, signed it and sealed it with the seal of the commune of Avignon.

# PART IV.
## THE LATER MIDDLE AGES (1250–1500)

*The number and variety of sources available from the later Middle Ages are considerably richer than from earlier in the medieval period, though much of the wealth takes the form of unedited manuscripts and archival material kept in registers, a great part of which has yet to be studied closely. The selections in this section provide a tiny sampling of the material available. Many of these documents have been translated here for the first time; they include selections from Italian municipal statutes, several mendicant sermons, miracle stories, and several lawsuits and peace acts from the city of Marseille. The laws and statutes are frequently at odds with one another; alongside flat condemnations of homicide and vengeance, one can find – in the* Customs of Beauvaisis, *for example – sets of rules governing how noble families may proceed in their pursuit of personal vengeance.*

*Many of the documents in Part IV are records of the actual practices, rather than of the ideals, of medieval populations. What they suggest is that vengeance, despite being a behavior that was officially condemned by the emerging kingdoms and states of the period as well as by the Church, was a relatively normal and tolerated practice throughout the period.*

# CHAPTER TWELVE: MUNICIPAL, TERRITORIAL, AND ROYAL LAWS CONCERNING VENGEANCE AND MURDER

*By the thirteenth century, kings, cities, and other sovereign entities were busily setting down legal codes and statutes aimed at regulating, and even criminalizing, homicide and vengeance. Many of these codes took inspiration from the* Corpus Iuris Civilis *of Justinian, in which the mere act of creating books of statutes was believed to be an act of sovereign majesty. By all appearances, these emerging states, like the Roman and Carolingian empires before them, were attempting to develop a monopoly on the legitimate exercise of force within their territorial boundaries, a feature that sociologists have suggested is an essential component of a modern state. All injuries, in principle, were considered injuries to the body politic, and hence it was up to the state, not private parties, to pursue redress. The passage on homicide in the* Laws and Customs of England *(Doc. 92) is a classic statement of this centralizing interest, which is also found in the perpetual Peace of the Land declared by Maximilian I in 1495 (Doc. 103). Thirteenth-century law codes from other regions, including France, Germany, and Spain, however, indicate that feuds remained perfectly legal as long as they followed rules that were collected and set down in customaries or law codes. In the case of the* Customs of Beauvaisis *(Doc. 96), the right to private warfare was restricted to the nobility, an indication of how military aristocrats considered this right a privilege of their estate.*

*Municipal law codes from Mediterranean Europe (Docs. 97–102) typically forbade homicide and sometimes prescribed harsh penalties. A careful reading of some statutes, however, will reveal that the framers were aware that killers typically escaped into self-imposed exile, and the text of the statutes often shows more interest in defining the act of peacemaking that was supposed to bring concord between feuding families and permit the reintegration of the killer.*

## 92. HOMICIDE IN THE *LAWS AND CUSTOMS OF ENGLAND*

The Laws and Customs of England, *a collection of English royal laws, was initially set down during the 1220s. Later, it was revised under the guidance of a royal justice named Henry of Bracton (d. 1268), with other officials working with him, between 1230 and 1260. Influenced by Roman jurisprudence, the* Laws *helped to define English common law, which was the law common to the entire kingdom of England, and so superseded all local laws and customs. The categorical definition of homicide as a breach of the king's peace, and hence a crime, theoretically precluded any room for legitimate pursuit of vengeance in England, though historians have shown that vengeance killings remained relatively common.*

Source: trans. Samuel E. Thorne, *Bracton on the Laws and Customs of England,* vol. 2 (Cambridge Mass.: Belknap, 1968), pp. 340–44.

## The crime of homicide and the divisions into which it falls

Among other crimes there is a capital crime [called homicide], which partly concerns the king, whose peace is broken, and partly the private individual who is slain wickedly and in breach of the king's peace. Hence we must see what it is and why it is so called, its various kinds, and the punishment imposed. Homicide is the slaying of man by man. If it is done by an ox, a dog or some thing it will not properly be termed homicide. For it is called "homicide" from "homo" and "caedo, caedis," "man-killing," so to speak. There are several kinds of homicide, for one is spiritual, the other corporal, but of spiritual homicide we have nothing to say here at the moment. Corporal homicide is where a man is slain bodily, and this is committed in two ways: by word or by deed. By word in three ways, that is, by precept, by counsel, and by denial or restraint. By deed in four ways, that is, in the administration of justice, of necessity, by chance and by intention. In the administration of justice, as when a judge or officer kills one lawfully found guilty. But it is homicide if done out of malice or from pleasure in the shedding of human blood [and] though the accused is lawfully slain, he who does the act commits a mortal sin because of his evil purpose. But if it is done from a love of justice, the judge does not sin in condemning him to death, nor in ordering an officer to slay him, nor does the officer sin if when sent by the judge he kills the condemned man. But both sin if they act in this way when proper legal procedures have not been observed. Of necessity, and here we must distinguish whether the necessity was avoidable or not; if avoidable and he could escape without slaying, he will then be guilty of homicide; if unavoidable, since he kills without premeditated hatred but with sorrow of heart, in order to save himself and his family, since he could not otherwise escape [danger], he is not liable to the penalty for homicide. By chance, as by misadventure, when one throws a stone at a bird or elsewhere and another passing by unexpectedly is struck and dies, or fells a tree and another is accidentally crushed beneath its fall and the like. But here we must distinguish whether he has been engaged in a proper or an improper act. Improper, as where one has thrown a stone toward a place where men are accustomed to pass, or while one is chasing a horse or ox someone is trampled by the horse or ox and the like, here liability is imputed to him. But if he was engaged in a lawful act, as where a master has flogged a pupil as a disciplinary measure, or if [another is killed] when one was unloading hay from a cart or cutting down a tree and the like, and if he employed all the care he could, that is, by looking about him and shouting out, not too tardily or in too low a voice but in good time and loudly, so that if there was anyone there, or approaching the place, he might flee and save himself, or in the case of the master by not exceeding mean and measure in the flogging of his pupil, liability is not imputed to him. But if he was engaged in a lawful act and did not employ due care, liability will be attributed to him. By intention, as where one in anger or hatred or for the sake of gain, deliberately and in premeditated assault, has killed another wickedly and feloniously and in breach of the king's peace. Homicide of this kind is sometimes done in the sight of many bystanders, sometimes in secret, out of the sight of all, so that who the slayer is cannot be ascertained; homicide of that kind may be termed murder, as will be explained below. The punishment for homicide is of two kinds [since homicides are of two kinds], namely, spiritual and corporal. The spiritual is discharged by penance. One slays another in two ways, sometimes by word, sometimes by deed: by word, as where one dissuades another and by such dissuasion restrains him from doing the good he intended when he wished to rescue someone from death; thus in an indirect way he commits homicide. The punishment for homicide committed by deed varies; for homicide committed in doing justice, with a proper and lawful intention, no punishment is to be inflicted. If one strikes a pregnant woman or gives her poison in order to procure an abortion, if the fetus is already formed or quickened, especially if it is quickened, he commits homicide. Several may be guilty of homicide just as one may be, as where several have quarreled among themselves in some dispute and one of them is slain; [if] it does not appear by whom nor by whose blow it was done all may be called homicides, those who struck, those who with evil intent held while he was struck, and those who came with the intention of slaying though they struck no blow. Also those who neither slew nor had any intention of slaying but came to lend counsel and aid to the slayers, sometimes even though their [the slayers'] violence is repulsed. Not only is he who strikes and slays liable, but he who orders him to strike and slay, for since they are not free of guilt, they ought not to be free of punishment; nor ought he to be free who, though he could rescue a man from death, failed to do so. Homicide also occurs in war, and we must then ascertain whether the war is just or unjust. If it is unjust he who kills will be liable; if just, as a war in defense of the patria, he will not, unless he acts with evil intent.

Of the office of coroners

[Wherever men are found dead, which may] sometimes be in the houses of a town, or the streets, sometimes outside the town in fields or woods, or when a homicide occurs, it is the business of the coroners to make diligent inquiry with respect to such and if they have been slain, as to the slayer, when he is unknown, and therefore, as soon as they have their order from the bailiff of the lord king or from the responsible men of the district, they ought to go to those who have been slain or wounded or drowned or have met untimely deaths, [or] to where there has been housebreaking [or] where it is reported that treasure has been found, at once and without delay to the place where the dead man has been found, and on their arrival there to order four, five or six of the neighboring vills to come before them at once and by their oath hold an inquest. When they are required [to hold an inquest] on a slain man, [they must inquire].

### Of inquests: where he was slain

First of all, where he was slain, in a house or in the fields. [If in a house or] at a wake, or in a tavern or at a gathering of some sort, they must then inquire who were then present, and which of them, man or woman, adult or child, were in any way the cause of that deed, and which of those were guilty as principals and which as accessories, counselors or instigators. A careful inquiry having been made, let as many as the inquest has found guilty in any of the aforesaid ways be arrested at once, if they are present or can be found elsewhere, and handed over to the sheriff and clapped into jail. Also let those the inquest has found [to have been] in the house or [at the gatherings] where the dead man was slain, though they are not guilty of any wrongdoing, be attached until the coming of the justices and the names of their pledges entered on the coroners' rolls.

### Of attaching the guilty

Nor are they to be released on finding pledges without the special order of the lord king, an inquest having first been taken as to whether they are appealed through hate and spite or by a genuine appeal. A writ for making an inquest of this kind ought to be granted gratis, as may be seen in the charter of liberties. The inquest is not to be taken as to anyone, only as to those who are in prison.

### If [the slain man is found] in fields or woods

If the dead man is found in fields or woods let those who found him be attached, whether men or women, of whatever age, whether the dead man was slain where he was found or elsewhere. If he was not slain there, as may be ascertained by presumptions, often, if he has wounds, by the flow of blood, the traces left by the malefactors are to be promptly and immediately discovered and followed, by pursuing the tracks of a cart, the hoof-marks of horses, the footprints of men or in some other way, according as that may best and most efficiently be done.

### If the slain man is known or unknown

Let inquiry also be made into whether the dead man is known or a stranger, and where he lodged that night, and depending upon what is discovered let his hosts, male and female, and the entire household found in the house in which he lodged be attached [or imprisoned].

### If the slayer has taken to flight

If because of such slain men someone has taken to flight, as to whom there is some suspicion of guilt, let the coroners go at once to his house and carefully inquire into his chattels and the corn in his barn, even though he is a villein, and if he is a free man, how much free land he has and what it is worth, and whether there is a crop growing on it or not. And when they have made such inquiry let them cause the corn and the chattels to be appraised at a price at which they may quickly be sold, the free land at what it is worth a year, and let them hand everything over to the township to answer for the value before the justices, saving the service due to the lords of the fee. And after inquiry has thus been made into all these matters let the bodies of the slain be buried. If they are buried prior to the said inquest and the coroners' view the entire township will be amerced.

### Of those who are drowned

If an inquest is to be made as to those who have been drowned or crushed by misadventure, or have met untimely deaths in some other way, it ought to be done in the same way. Inquiry must be made as to who were present when the said persons were drowned, crushed, or died without warning, and then let the bodies of those deceased, no matter how they died, be viewed, naked and uncovered, in order to ascertain whether it is a matter of felony or misadventure, as that may be inferred from external signs, as where open wounds are found or bruises which have not broken the skin, as where they have been strangled, which may be inferred from the mark of the impress of the rope around the neck. [If] by some wound discovered on the body, the coroners ought to proceed to an inquest in the manner described above and to make attachments of persons or property according as the male factors have or have not been found they ought to attach, until the coming of the justices, all those who were of the company when the said misadventure occurred. If there were none, then the finder. Let the boats from which such persons have been drowned be appraised, and any other things which are the cause of death and are deodands [forfeited goods] for the king, [that is] if he has been drowned in fresh water, not in the sea, where neither the ship nor, if the ship has broken up, its timber, will be deodands, because all will belong to their owners, if they are alive, as their chattels. Nor are there deodands arising from misadventure at sea, nor is there wreck, nor is there a murderfine as to those slain or drowned at sea.

## 93. FROM THE *SACHSENSPIEGEL*

*The* Sachsenspiegel, *or* "The Saxon Mirror," *was a compilation in a single volume of Germanic customary law that was roughly contemporaneous with Bracton's* Laws and Customs of England. *The* Sachsenspiegel *was not the product of the German emperors. It was commissioned by Count Hoyer von Falkenstein, bailiff of Quedlinburg, and compiled by a Saxon judge and knight named Eike von Repgowe (1180/90–after 1233). Originally written in Latin between 1221 and 1224, the version that still survives today is a Low German translation made at some point between 1224 and 1227. Most historians feel that the presence and influence of the* Sachsenspiegel *slowed down the pace at which Roman law eventually came into use in Germany. Like the French customaries (see Docs. 94 and 96), the* Sachsenspiegel *includes provisions governing how legitimate feuds ought to be declared.*

Source: trans. Maria Dobozy, *The Saxon Mirror: A "Sachsenspiegel" of the Fourteenth Century* (Philadelphia: University of Pennsylvania Press, 1999), pp. 44–45, 82, 86–90, 94–95, 96–98, 105, 117–19, 123, 128–29, 177–78.

### a. The imperial landpeace of Mainz

The emperor promulgated this law in Mainz with the support of the princes.

We establish and decree by the power of our imperial authority and in conjunction with the loyal men of the realm: If a son expels his father by force from his castle or any other property, or attacks it by burning or robbing, or allies himself with his father's enemies securing the alliance by word of honor or oath when the aim is to damage the father's reputation or ruin him, and if his father convicts him [with an oath] on the relics before the judge and is helped by two oathhelpers of indisputable integrity and full legal capacity, then the son shall be stripped of all property held in fief and in free ownership, all movable property and all inheritance from father and mother forever so that neither the father nor a judge will ever be able to help him recover any rights to such property. Any son who plots against his father's life or viciously attacks him, wounding or imprisoning him or laying him in any type of bonds that one would call imprisonment, and is convicted for it as previously stated, forfeits his legal rights and privileges forever and may never regain them. All those whom the father names as witnesses to the judge regarding any of the causes described previously will not be disqualified on grounds of feudal loyalty or for any other reason when they reveal the truth to the father. Whoever is not willing to do this will be ordered to do so by the judge unless he swears on the relics to the judge that he knows nothing of it....

This law is concerned with preventing anyone from taking revenge himself. We establish and decree that a person may not exact revenge for whatever damage he suffers before he brings his complaint to the judge and follows the legal process through to the end as is lawful unless the dispute has progressed to where he must defend his life and property with arms. Whosoever takes revenge in any other manner than here described shall repay twofold whatever harm he causes, and whatever damage he himself incurs shall be lost to him, and he will never be allowed to make any claims for compensation. However, if someone does bring charges as described above but is not given a hearing, then he must resort to declaring a feud against his enemies. This he must do in daylight. From the day he declares the feud, he will not do the other party any injury either to person or property for four days so that he has three entire days of peace. The person thus challenged must likewise refrain from doing harm to the challenger's person and property for four days. And if this rule is broken by one party, then the other will go to his judge and bring charges against the malefactor. Thereupon the judge or his deputy shall summon him to court. If the accused cannot clear himself on the relics with seven men having full legal capacity, he is stripped of all legal rights and privileges forever so that he may never regain them....

Regarding feuds. When two parties are feuding with each other, and one party or both has a protective escort, and one of them attacks the other's men and harms them, then if he is lawfully conceived, he will be sentenced as a highway robber.

... If a person breaks the peace against another after the two parties had sworn the peace with a handshake, and the plaintiff proves it with an oath on the relics with two additional men having full legal capacity before the judge who had witnessed the peace agreement, the judge will then place the person who broke the peace in royal outlawry. The judge must never allow the malefactor to recover his legal rights without the plaintiff's permission, otherwise the judge forfeits his hand for it. But if the breach of peace was homicide, then a kinsman of the deceased will bring charges for the deed and prosecute the perpetrator as described earlier. And if he is convicted with an oath, he will never be released from outlawry except through death. And he shall have no legal rights or protection. However, if the person who agreed to the peace with a handshake does not admit truthfully that the peace was broken against the plaintiff, the judge will command him by the emperor's grace to aid the litigant in achieving justice unless he swears on the relics that he knows nothing of it. If he fails to do this claiming vassal fealty or any other excuse, he forfeits his hand to the emperor.

... Should a person drive an outlaw away or attack him, no one may come to his aid. But if someone is proved to have protected an outlaw knowingly, he bears the same culpability and is sentenced like an outlaw. If an outlaw comes into town, he may not be allowed to remain. And if someone does him evil, no one may hinder it.

### b. Trial by combat
### [Book 1]

50. If a wounded man challenges the person who wounded him to a judgment by combat and is not able to complete the duel for weakness of body and has no guardian who is willing to fight in his stead, one shall postpone the date [of the duel] until he is able to fight for himself. Further, if someone wounds or kills another and brings him bound before the court and wants to prosecute him for violating the peace but does not complete the procedure, then he shall be indicted by the court for the injustice he did to that person. Even if a man is a minstrel or illegitimate of birth, he is nevertheless not the legal equal of a robber or a thief, so it is not possible to bring a case against him using a champion.

63. Whoever wants to challenge his peer to trial by combat must ask the judge for permission to seize the offender he sees there in order to stand trial. If the judge rules that he may do so, then he will ask where he should seize him so that it may help him to his rights. The following ruling is then given: he may seize him by the neck opening with propriety. Once he has seized and released him with permission, then he must make known to the accused why he has seized him. He may do so immediately, if he so wishes, or hold consultation regarding it. Then he must bring formal charges that the offender has violated the peace against him either on the king's road or in the village [and describe] the manner in which he acted against him. This is

the way he must bring charges. If he then also accuses the man of wounding him and using force against him and can prove it, then he must exhibit the wound or, if it has healed, the scar. Then he may bring further charges that the accused has robbed his goods and taken so much that it is not unjustified to challenge him to trial by battle. It is necessary to bring suit at the same time for these three criminal charges. If one withholds one of them, he has lost his combat. He shall state the following: "I myself saw this person and raised the hue and cry. If he admits this, then I accept it, and if he does not, then I shall prosecute him with all the rights that the people within this jurisdiction accord me or the *Schöffen* [judge] deem when the court convenes under the king's jurisdiction." After that the accused shall request security, and it shall be granted. However, the plaintiff may correct his charges before the security is granted. Once the security is given, the defendant offers his proof of innocence, which consists of a cleansing oath and a legal duel if the accuser challenged him to a rightful settlement and if it is so, as I suppose, that the accuser is able to fight in spite of his injury. Any man may refuse a challenge from someone of lesser birth, but if the challenger is of higher birth, then the lesser-born man may not refuse him. A man may refuse a duel if he is challenged after the noon hour unless the proceedings began earlier. The judge must also supply the defendant with a sword and shield should he need them. A man may refuse a duel with family members if they are related to each other by swearing with six others on the relics that they are so closely related that they may not lawfully do battle. The judge shall designate two deputies, one to each person who will fight, in order to ensure that they arm themselves according to proper custom. They may wear as much linen and leather they wish; head and feet are bare in front; only thin gloves are worn on the hands. [They may have] an unsheathed sword in their hand and one or two on their belt, according to preference; in the other hand [is] a round shield of wood or leather only, with the exception of the boss, which can be of iron. A coat without sleeves is worn over the armor. Order shall be maintained in the enclosed combat ring on pain of death so that no one may interfere with their duel. To each fighter the judge shall assign a deputy to carry his pole. These men shall not hamper the fighters in any way. But if one of the combatants falls, the deputy shall place the pole between them, or if one is wounded or asks for the pole. He may not do this of his own accord but only when he receives permission. After the combat ring is made secure, the fighters shall request to enter it for judgment, and the judge shall give them permission to do so. Next they break the tip of the scabbard once they have permission from the judge. Both should step fully armed before the judge and swear – the one that the accusation made against the defendant has been truthfully made, and the other that he is not guilty – so that God may stand by them in combat. When the opponents first face each other, it is necessary to align them so that neither is at a disadvantage by having the sun in his eyes. If the defendant is convicted, then he shall be sentenced, but if he prevails, he shall go free with a court fine and a compensation payment. The plaintiff enters the circle first. If the other tarries too long, the judge must send the bailiff with two *Schöffen* to the house in which he is arming himself to summon him. This shall be done a second and a third time. If he does not come at the third summons, the plaintiff stands up and offers to fight. He swings two blows and makes one thrust into the wind. With that act, he convicts the defendant for the charges as he had spoken them. The judge shall then sentence him as if he had been convicted by the combat.

67. If a person presses charges against someone for a criminal offense, the accused shall be summoned three times, each of a fortnight, but if one brings charges against a man of *Schöffen* rank, he shall be summoned three times as well, but each of a six-week period, under the king's jurisdiction and to the official court location. Whoever does not appear at the third scheduled hearing shall be placed in limited outlawry. On no other grounds shall anyone outlaw a man except for crimes that are punishable by loss of life or hand.

68. However, when one person bludgeons another so that the wounded spots swell, or beats another black-and-blue without breaking the skin, and if the injured person brings charges to the judge, or to the bailiff, or to the village headman and villagers and proves it right away as a fresh crime, and if the accused does not appear by the time of the regular court session to defend himself or to make restitution according to law, then he shall be outlawed. A man can challenge another to combat with black-and-blue injuries lacking lacerations, or with scars, or with the words leading to a challenge. A man can even kill or permanently disable another without breaking the skin, be it by beating, shoving or punching, throwing, or in many other ways. In these cases, the perpetrator forfeits his life or his hand for it and draws limited outlawry upon himself. Regardless of the liability for which a man has been outlawed, if he is caught in limited outlawry and brought before the court, the penalty is death if he is convicted of the deed and of the outlawry. But if he releases himself from limited outlawry and comes before the court uncaptured, he can be restored to his rights as if he had never before been outlawed.

## c. Penalties for crime
### [Book 2]

10. An outlaw may be apprehended during peace days, but one may not make any determination about him unless it concerns a red-handed deed. In court, no one is required to give a surety higher than his *wergeld* unless it

concerns a debt that he admits or that has already been determined against him in court. On peace days one may not swear anything but the peace [to someone] or against a man caught red-handed. Anyone who transgresses the peace on peace days is unprotected by the peace law. Likewise, the church and churchyard do not protect anyone for a deed committed there. The judge may certainly preside over any complaint on a peace day except a felony; the judge shall instruct the accused to come at the appropriate time to admit and make compensation, or to deny the complaint.

14. Now hear about criminal acts [and] the penalties that apply. A thief shall be hanged. If one day a theft occurs in a village amounting to less than three shillings in value, then the village headman shall try the case the same day. The theft carries the penalty of flogging and shorn hair. The sentence can be redeemed with a fine of three shillings, but the thief suffers impaired legal capacity. This is the village headman's highest jurisdiction. If the case is carried over to the day after the charges had been made, then he may no longer preside. He may also preside over greater amounts of money and other types of movable goods. The same penalty applies to the use of false measures and weights, and fraudulent vending in cases where someone has been able to win a conviction.

All murderers, those who take by force a plow or [something from] a mill or a church or churchyard, as well as traitors and murderous arsonists, and all those who use their deputation to their own advantage shall be broken on the wheel. One who beats or abducts a man, or robs, or commits arson (with the exception of murderous arson), or rapes a woman or girl and violates the peace shall be beheaded. So too must one behead anyone who is caught in adultery. If those who possess or protect articles acquired through theft or robbery, or those who aid the perpetrators are convicted, then they shall be sentenced to the same penalty as thieves and robbers. A Christian man or woman who is without faith and practices magic or mixes potions and is convicted must be burned on the pyre. A judge who does not sentence a person for a crime draws upon himself the same penalty that is applied to the perpetrator. In addition, no one is required to attend the court of a judge or support him as law requires as long as he himself refuses to carry out the law.

15. If a man slays another in self-defense and cannot remain with him in order to bring him before the court and be judged because he fears for his life, then he may come without the dead man. If he does this and admits the deed before anyone brings a charge, and offers to fulfill his legal duty, one may not condemn him to death. The judgment should grant the highest court fine in pennies permissible within the customary range to the judge, and *wergeld* to the family of the deceased. The relatives are to be summoned to receive their money at the next court session, and at the second and the third. If they still

do not appear, the slayer shall keep the *wergeld* until they bring an action to claim it, and he shall be given immunity. No one may bring a suit against him that requires a death sentence since he offered himself for justice before anyone brought charges. However, if one brings the slain man unburied to court to make a formal complaint against the slayer, he must prove his case against the dead man or answer for his own deed with his life.

17. Each man shall provide guaranty to his lord and his agnatic relation in cases of manslaughter or [assault resulting in] injury or permanent disability. If someone is convicted of wounding or permanently injuring another, his hand shall be cut off. If a man is convicted of a criminal act in trial by combat, it costs him his life. For every compensation fine, the tariff is levied according to each man's legal status determined by his birth unless he has forfeited it [through misdeed]. When the bailiff pays a court fine to the judge for failure to fulfill his legal duty, he suffers the penalty of the king's *malder,* that is, thirty-two lashes with a green oak rod two ells long [an ell was roughly the length of an arm]. A man is to be compensated when he suffers permanent injury to any one [of the following]: the mouth, nose, eyes, tongue, ears, his sexual organs, hands, or feet. One must pay him a compensation that is half of his established *wergeld*. Each finger and each toe carries its own specific tariff based on a tenth part of the person's *wergeld* according to his birth. Regardless of how many injuries a man receives during a single violent act, he is to be indemnified once with half of his *wergeld* if he does not die. As may times as a person injures a disabled person in a different part of the body, that many times shall he compensate that person with half his *wergeld* individually for each injury. Whenever one person strikes another without breaking the skin, or calls someone a liar, he must pay that person compensation according to his birth. If someone is injured by another in a body part that has already been redressed by the court, even if it is severed completely, he may sue for no higher compensation than his composition tariff.

40. If someone's dog or breeding boar or ox or whatever kind of beast kills or injures a person or an animal, his owner shall make compensation for the harm according to the proper *wergeld* or value if he takes the beast into his care after the damage occurred. However, if he turns it out, refuses it shelter in house or barn, and gives it no food or water, then he is not responsible for the damage. In that case the injured party can initiate a legal action for the animal [as compensation] for the damage. Under no circumstances does the judge ever lose his court fine when an animal causes damage. Harm of whatever kind done by a man's horse or livestock while under the supervision of his servant or others of his household shall be paid by the person in whose care it was. If that person flees, and the horses or oxen and cart are found with evidence of the deed on them, and it is proven with an oath,

then the owner of the animal and cart must pay indemnity if he cannot clear himself. He must pay the value of the horse or other draft animal and the cart which has been taken into custody, or he must forfeit the animal, and the other person keeps it in compensation for the damages. If a man allows his hogs or geese, which can not be confiscated, to feed on his neighbor's grain or another's crops, and then that man sets his dogs on them, and they bite the animals, wounding or killing them, he pays no penalty.

### d. Legal procedures
### [Book 3]

1. No one shall raze a village building by reason of any type of crime unless a girl or woman has been raped in it or brought into it after the rape. It shall be condemned or cleared legally. Once a judgment has been laid down, then even if a person comes forward to clear [the building], he receives no compensation for it, because he did not clear it before the court reached its judgment. All living creatures present at the rape shall be beheaded. All those responding to the hue and cry [shall] seize the victim and the attacker. They suffer no penalty for bringing the accused to court even if he is not convicted.

8. It is said that castles and princes need no peace that can be broken because castles have fortifications, and princes travel with armed defenders. But that is not so. Anyone who pledges peace to the princes and is bound in loyalty to it will be tried and sentenced if he violates it.

12. When one person brings a claim against another, and that second person brings suit against the first one, then the first plaintiff does not have to answer the claim of the second until the second plaintiff has been cleared of liability in the first suit. If several people press charges against a man, he does not have to respond to the others before he is cleared of the first charge. If the case continues to the next day, he may not give surety except for his *wergeld* even if the charges are numerous.

13. If a man is charged with a crime in court when he is not present, and a date for a hearing is set, then if the plaintiff meets the defendant before that date, he may certainly detain him according to law based on his accusation until the accused provides surety that he will appear. [This procedure is allowed] because the judge provides protection for the plaintiff and not for the defendant who is summoned into his presence.

36. If one man challenges another to a trial by combat in a court of law, and the court rules to postpone the complaint until the next day, then peaceful conduct is imposed on both parties. And if this peace pledge is broken, the offender must pay compensation before any lawful combat [can be held]. But if the offender is caught in flagrante, he is judged according to law.

48. A man may not press charges against more than one person for a single wound, but he may charge several people for aiding and abetting the perpetrator. When someone takes something belonging to another by force or by mistake, he shall return it with a compensation fine or swear that he is not able to return it. [If he cannot return it,] he shall reimburse the owner according to the terms the owner demands unless the debtor reduces the estimated value with his oath. Singing birds, hunting falcons, greyhounds, chasing hounds, and trackers are replaced in kind with animals that are equally good when one swears this on the relics. When someone kills the kind of animal we normally eat that belongs to another, either intentionally or not, he must make restitution in the amount of the fixed *wergeld*. If he wounds it, he reimburses the owner with half [the tariff] without a fine, and in addition, the owner also keeps his animal.

49. However, whoever willfully kills or lames the kind of animal that is not eaten, he must [pay] the full money tariff and punitive damages; if he injures it in the eye, he pays half [the tariff]. But if a man is responsible for the unintentional death or injury of an animal and confirms it with an oath, he pays restitution without a fine as discussed earlier.

50. When a person's dog goes into the fields, he shall be kept on a leash so that he does no one any harm, but if it does do damage, that person whom the dog follows out into the fields shall make restitution, or if he himself is not able to pay, then his master shall do so.

52. Now hear about the *wergeld* of birds and animals....

## 94. GUARANTEES OF PEACE IN THE CUSTOMS OF TOURAINE AND ANJOU

*As we saw in the two preceding documents, royal or comital officials in many regions were compiling collections of customary law during the thirteenth century for reasons that were partly practical and partly symbolic. The drive to compile such customs was particularly well developed in France, where officials sponsored by Louis IX collected numerous customaries, called Etablissements, including those of Touraine and Anjou (ca 1246).*

Source: trans. F. R. P. Akehurst, *The Etablissements de Saint Louis: Thirteenth-Century Law Texts from Tours, Orléans, and Paris* (Philadelphia: University of Pennsylvania Press, 1996), pp. 24–25, 28–29.

30. On fights. A man who kills another in a fight and can show a wound which the other inflicted on him before he killed him will not be hanged

by a judgment, except in one instance, which is that if a member of the dead man's family appealed against him for the death of the person and accused him of having killed the person without having been struck or wounded by him, and he claimed that the dead man had commanded him and appointed him to prove it and argue it, the other man could say that he did not believe that the dead man had given him the command and the appointment; and at that point a battle could be ordered by a judgment. And if either man was sixty years old, he could have another replace him [in the battle], but he would have to swear he was that old. And the person defeated in the battle would be hanged.

31. On requesting a guaranteed peace in the secular court, and on broken truces. If it happened that a man was on his guard against another and he appeared before the judge to obtain a guaranteed peace, the judge should obtain the guaranteed peace for him, since he is asking for it; and he must make the person he is complaining of promise or swear that neither he nor his family will do any harm to him or his family. And if after this he did him some harm, and it could be proved against him, he would be hanged; for this is called a broken truce, which is one of the greatest treacheries there is. And the baron has jurisdiction of this matter.

And if he did not want to give a guaranteed peace, and the judge admonished him and said to him: "I forbid you to go away until you have given him this guaranteed peace"; and if he went away after the judge had forbidden it, and someone burned down one of the other person's houses, or spoiled his vines or killed him, he would be as guilty as if he had committed the action.

41. On threats and refusing to give a guaranteed peace before the judge, and on requesting [a guaranteed peace] from the sovereign, maintaining the rights of the parties. If in the presence of a judge a man threatened to do another man harm, to his person or his property, and the latter requested a guaranteed peace, and the other replied: "I will take counsel," and the judge said to him: "Do not go away until you have given him a guaranteed peace"; and he went away, when this had been said and the prohibition stated, without giving a guaranteed peace; and the second man's house was burned; and the man who did not want to give him a guaranteed peace had not yet done so, he would be proved guilty and found guilty just as if he had truly done it. Or if somebody killed the person who was seeking the guaranteed peace, and the other was accused in court, who had refused to give the guaranteed peace in the court of the king, or in a baron's court, or that of any other man who had the power to administer justice in his lands, then he would be as guilty as if he had performed the act; and he could be arrested by law, even if he had done nothing; and he would have deserved to be punished. For this

reason no one should refuse a safe truce before a judge. (And if somebody is in fear, he should come before a judge and request a guaranteed peace, according to written law in the *Code, De hiis qui ad Ecclesiam confugiunt*, 1. *Denunciamus, in fine.*)

## 95. THE LAW OF HOMICIDE IN THE *FUERO REAL*

*The* Fuero Real *(1252–55) was created by King Alfonso X of Castile to be used by new cities and towns as a template for their law codes. The code was influenced by Roman and canon law, and was perhaps inspired by the desire to make Castilian municipal statutes more uniform. Since greater royal power was resisted both by members of the nobility and by the towns, the king sometimes had to confirm the existing* fueros *(laws) and other urban privileges within his realm, but the* Fuero Real *was made available after 1255 to towns that were granted charters after that date. The word* omizillo, *mentioned in the text below, referred both to the act of homicide and to the monetary penalty for homicide. It also could indicate the kind of enmity, especially between families, that was often aroused by a homicide or some other injury.*

Source: ed. Gonzalo Martínez Diez, with José Manuel Ruiz Ascencio and César Hernández Alonso, *Leyes de Alfonso X,* vol. 2, *Fuero Real* (Avila: Fundación Sánchez Albornoz, 1988), pp. 464–68. Trans. Nina Melechen.

### [Book 4, title 17]
### Title concerning the *omizillos*

1. Every man who kills another knowingly should die for it, unless he thus kills his known enemy; or [is] defending himself; or if he finds him lying with his wife, wherever he finds him; or if he finds him in his house lying with his daughter or with his sister; or if he finds him carrying off a raped woman in order to lie with her or with whom he has already lain; and [*sic*] if he kills a thief who he finds at night in his house, stealing or breaking in; or if he finds him fleeing with the stolen goods; or if he intends to keep him in bonds; or if he finds him attacking his own [property] and does not want to give it up; or if he kills him by chance, not intending to kill him nor having previous ill-will against him; or if he kills him supporting his lord whom he came to kill or whom they [*sic*] wish to kill, or his father or son or grandfather or brother or another man whom he must revenge because of lineage; or if he kills in such another way that they can show that he killed him rightfully.

2. Every man who kills another treacherously or perfidiously should be dragged along the ground for it and hanged, and the king should have all the traitor's property, and from the property of the perfidious man the king should have half and his heirs half; and if he kills him in another unrightful manner they should hang him, and his heirs should inherit all his property, and he should not pay the *omizillo*.

3. Every man whom they find dead [or] beaten black and blue in any house and they do not know who killed him, the resident of the house should be held responsible for showing who killed him; if [he does] not, he should be held responsible for the death except for the right to defend himself if he can.

4. If that one who unrightfully kills another flees so that they are not able to catch him to do justice for it, the city magistrates or the other justices of the king should take 500 *sueldos* [*solidi* or shillings] from his property for the *omizillo*, and when they are able to catch him should do justice for it; and every other man who kills his enemy, even if he has challenged him rightfully, if he kills him before the king or the magistrates of the place have declared him to be an enemy, should pay 500 *sueldos* for the *omizillo* and remain as an enemy of his relatives, and there should be no other penalty from the king nor from his representative; and if he kills him after they have declared him an enemy there should not be any penalty. And if there are many killers, they should not pay more than one *omizillo;* and from each payment of *omizillo* the king should have three-fifths and the relatives two.

5. If any man falls from a wall or from another place or if another pushes him, and he falls on another and kills the one he falls on, there should not be a penalty nor any harm; but that one who pushed him, if he did it from rage or ill-will, should pay the *omizillo,* and there should be no other penalty.

6. When two men are fighting, and one intends to injure the other or [*sic*] by chance kills some other man, the magistrate must learn which of them began the fight; and that one who began it should pay the *omizillo,* and that one who killed him by chance should pay a half *omizillo;* and if he does not die of the wound, he who gave it to him should pay half a fine and he who began it should pay the whole; and these fines should be divided as the law commands and there should be no other penalty because neither of them intended to do it.

7. If some man, not out of evil but mocking, dashes his horse in the road or in a populated street, or plays ball or hockey or quoits or another similar thing, or [*sic*] by chance kills some man, he should pay the *omizillo* and there should be no other penalty, for although he did not intend to kill him he cannot be blameless, because he was playing in a place where he should not

have; and if he does any of these things outside of the populated area and kills someone by chance as is aforesaid, and [*sic*] there should not be any penalty. And if someone throws a javelin publicly and with bells (*sonages*) in the road or in a populated street on a feast day, as well as on Easter or Saint John's Day, or at a wedding, or at the arrival of the king or of the queen, or in another manner similar to these, and by chance kills a man, he should not be held responsible for the *omizillo;* and if he did not prove the bells, the killer should pay the *omizillo* and there should not be another penalty.

8. Whatever artisan takes an apprentice to teach his craft and, punishing him or training him, injures him with an injury such as he ought to, as with a belt or with a palm or with a thin lash or with another light thing, and from those injuries he by chance dies, should not be held responsible for the *omizillo;* and if he injures him with stick or with stone or with iron or with another thing that he should not, and he dies of it, he should be held responsible for the death. And we order this same thing if in this manner he gives him some wound, for he can not excuse himself from guilt because he gave the injury as he should not have done.

9. Whoever chops down a tree or knocks down a wall or another similar thing, should be held responsible for telling those who are around to look out; and if he has said it and they did not want to guard themselves and the tree or the wall falls and kills [someone] or causes another wound, he should not be held responsible for the death nor for damage that came therefrom; and if he did not say it before he chopped it down or knocked it over, he should be held responsible for the death or for the wound; and if he killed or wounded an old or sick or sleeping man who could not be on guard although they [*sic*] wanted to, he should be held responsible for the death or for the wound; and if he kills or wounds a herd animal or other animal, he should pay its owner for it and the dead or wounded animal should belong to the one who did the damage.

## 96. PROCEDURES FOR PRIVATE WAR IN THE *CUSTOMS OF BEAUVAISIS*

*The descriptions of "private war" and of peacemaking found in this famous French customary by Philippe de Beaumanoir (1283) show, in great detail, how vengeance and peacemaking were thoroughly worked into local law, for a time. The right to pursue vengeance according to the rules laid out in these passages was, in theory, restricted to the nobility.*

Source: trans. F. R. P. Akehurst, *The* Coutumes de Beauvaisis *of Philippe de Beaumanoir* (Philadelphia: University of Pennsylvania Press, 1992), pp. 610–26.

Here begins the fifty-ninth chapter of this book, which speaks of [private] wars, how wars come about, and how wars are ended.

1667. Since we have spoken in various places of wars, we want everyone to know that war cannot be made between two full brothers, born of one father and one mother, for any dispute which there is between them, even if one had struck or injured the other, for neither has a lineage which is not as close to the other brother as to himself. And anyone who is as close in lineage to the one party as to the other who are principal combatants of this war should not get involved in this war. Thus if two brothers have a dispute and one commits an offense against the other, the offender cannot use as a defense the right of war, nor can anyone of his lineage who wants to aid him against his brother, as might happen to those who prefer one to the other; thus when such a dispute arises the lord should punish the one who commits an offense against the other and do justice in the dispute.

1668. If it happens that various of my relatives are at war and I am as close in lineage to the one as to the other, and I do not join in the war on the one side or the other, and one of the parties does harm to me because he believes that I prefer the other party, he cannot use as a defense the right of war. Instead he should be dealt with according to the offense. But it would be otherwise if I went to the aid of, or in the company of, one of the armed parties, or if I lent him my arms or my horses or my house, to assist him and to do harm to the other. For in such a case I would join the war by my act, so that if harm came to me afterwards from the adverse party, even if that party was as close to me in lineage as the other party, he could raise as a defense the right of war. And by this you can see that people can join a war who lend aid to those who are making war, even if they did not belong from the point of view of lineage.

1669. Although we have said that war cannot be made between two full brothers of one father and one mother, if they were not brothers except by the mother or by the father, then war could very well be made between them according to custom, for each would have a lineage which did not belong to the other; so that if they were brothers by their father but not by their mother, the lineage that each one had through his mother would not belong to the other brother and for this reason they would be able to engage in war with each other. However, although custom allows these wars in the Beauvais region, between gentlemen, for a *casus belli* [justification to go to war], the count (or the king if the count will not) can require the parties to make peace with each other or to make a truce; but they must do without a guaranteed peace (*asseurement*) unless one of the parties requests it. And likewise when there is a war between those who are of the same lineage, the lord should make great efforts to end the war, for otherwise the lineage might be destroyed, since each one in the war would be opposing his closest relative, whereby sometimes one cousin kills another.

1670. War can arise in various ways, for example by deeds or by words. War arises by words when one party threatens the other with insults or bodily harm (*a fere vilenie ou anui de son cors*), or when he defies him or his people; and it arises by deeds when a mutual combat in anger (*chaude mellee*) arises between gentlemen. And it must be understood that when war arises through fact, those who are present at the fact are at war as soon as the fact is completed; but the lineages of the one party and the other do not enter the war until forty days after the fact. If war begins by threats or by defiance, those who have defied each other or threatened each other begin to be at war from then on. But it is true that because very sharp practice could occur in such a case, for example, if someone had made ready to act before he had threatened or defied another person, and then, at the time of the fact, he threatened or defied the other person, he could not use that threat or that defiance as a defense. Therefore the gentleman who threatens or defies must abstain from fighting until the person who has been defied can put himself in a position of defense, or otherwise he has no excuse for the offense, and must be punished if he commits an offense.

1671. According to our custom war cannot begin between commoners (*gens de pooste*) or between townsmen. Therefore if threats or defiance or fights begin between them, they must be dealt with according to the offense, and they cannot claim a right of war. And if it should happen that someone had killed another person's father, and the son, after the first act, killed the person who had killed his father, he would be tried for homicide, unless it should happen that the person who had killed his father was under banishment, because of offenses for which he did not dare come to court to await a hearing (*atendre droit*); for in such case leave is given to the family to arrest those who have committed an offense toward them, after they have been banished, either dead or alive. And if they take them alive, they must surrender them to the lord for him to deal with them according to the crime and according to the banishment. And they may not kill them at the time of arrest unless they defend themselves. And if they defend themselves, so that they cannot take them alive, but must kill them, they must immediately go to the judge and make a report, and once the truth is known they should not be accused of anything.

1672. Now let's see whether, if a threat or defiance or a fight commences between a gentleman on the one side and a commoner or a townsman on the other, there can be war between them; for no one but gentlemen can make war, as we have said. Therefore we say that war cannot be made between

commoners and gentlemen, for if the gentleman made war on the townsman or commoners, and townsmen or commoners could not make war on
gentlemen, they would soon be dead or in terrible trouble (*mal bailli*). Therefore when such a case arises when the townsmen or commoners request a
guaranteed peace, they should have it; and if they do not want it or deign
to ask for it and they have committed an offense toward the gentlemen and
the gentlemen take vengeance on them, the gentlemen cannot be accused of
anything; and if it is the gentlemen who have committed an offense toward
the townsmen or the commoners, and afterwards they do not deign to ask
for peace or guaranteed peace, the townsmen or the commoners cannot for
this reason take vengeance for the offense, for then it would seem as if they
could make war, which they cannot do. For this reason when a gentleman
commits an offense toward a townsman or a commoner, the latter must seek
justice through the courts, not by war.

1673. Although gentlemen can make war according to our customs, the
judge should not for that reason refrain from taking steps on his own initia-
tive (*de son office*) to set right the first offense, for if a gentleman kills or does
bodily harm to another gentleman, without open war between them, and the
families on both sides want to turn this into a war without having resort to
a judge, the judge should not for this reason refrain from doing everything
in his power to arrest the offenders and to try them according to the offense.
For those who commit such offenses do not offend only against their adverse
party or their adverse party's family, but also against the lord, who has to
protect them and discipline (*justicier*) them. For we see nevertheless that when
some crime of homicide or bodily harm or other serious crime is committed
and peace is made between the families of both parties, nevertheless it is appropriate that the party be pursued by the lord such as the king or the baron
in whose jurisdiction the parties are. For another lord cannot make or permit
such a peace, and for this reason it is clear that those who commit these serious crimes are not only committing offenses against their adverse party or his
family but against the lord as we have said above.

1674. The gentleman who has committed a *casus belli* against another
gentleman, or who has threatened or defied him, must know that as soon as
he has done one of these things he is at war; for the person who threatens
or defies another one with death in war must know that he himself is at war
even though the person whom he defied did not send back any defiance.
And for this reason it is said that "Whoever threatens another or defies him
should be on his guard," for a person who wants to commit an offense against
another should not feel entirely secure in his person. And this is what we also
say about an act which is a *casus belli*.

VENGEANCE IN MEDIEVAL EUROPE: A READER

1675. If someone wants to make war on another through his words, he must not make them ambiguous or secret, but so clear and so evident that the person to whom the words are spoken or sent knows that he must be on his guard, and if a person acted otherwise it would be treachery (*traïsons*). And if defiance is announced to someone, it must be announced by people who can testify to it [to having done so] if there is a need, as to the place and time. And the same thing is true when someone wants to accuse another of doing some harm (*fere vilenie*) with premeditation and without defiance, for in such a case there is a need to prove the defiance as a defense to an accusation of treachery.

1676. We have explained above in this chapter how war is made according to our custom. Now let us say how war ends, for it may end in various ways.

1677. The first of the ways in which war ends is when peace is made by the agreement of the parties, for after the keeping of the peace is promised (*creantee*) or covenanted, all those who were at war (in the war in which the peace was made) must be at peace with each other; and if anyone breaks this peace and is convicted, he is to be hanged.

1678. If peace is made between the parties who are at war, it is not necessary for the whole family of each party to be there when peace is made or promised. Rather it is sufficient if peace is made or agreed between those who were the leaders of the war (*chief de la guerre*), and if there are people in the family who do not want to consent to the peace which is made and agreed between the principal combatants of the war (*chevetaigne de la guerre*), they must make it known that people must be on their guard against them, because they do not want to be a part of that peace. And if they do not make this announcement, and they harm the adversaries who thought they were at peace with them, they can be sued for breaching the peace and they cannot use as a defense that they did not know about the peace, or say that they did not agree with the peace; for when peace is made between the chief parties (*chevetaignes*) in the war, it must exist between all the lineages of the one party and the other, except those who say or send word that they do not want to be part of that peace.

1679. When peace is made between those who are chiefs of some war (*chevetaigne d'aucune guerre*) and some people of one family or the other do not want to be in that peace and instead say or send word that people must be on their guard against them, none of those who agree to the peace and none of those who did not make the announcement that people had to be on their guard against them may give aid or comfort to those that remain at war, for they could be accused of breaching the peace (*pes brisiee*). And after they have

[once] assented to the peace by act or by word they cannot go back on this but they must keep the peace. And since we have said that those who have assented to the peace in word or by deed cannot renounce this, nor announce that others should be on their guard against them, it is right that we should declare how a person consents to the peace by both deed and word, or by deed without word, or by word without deed.

1680. It should be known that a person consents to the peace both by deed and by word who drinks and eats and speaks and keeps company (*tient compaignie*) with a person who used to be among his enemies. Therefore after he has done this, if he does or procures shame or annoyance (*honte ou anui*) to that person, he can be accused of treachery and breaching the peace. And those who are in the peace by their words without deed are those who at the peacemaking, and in front of good people or a judge, said that they are bound by the peace and that they want peace. Those who are in the peace by deed without words are those who are in the family of the principal combatant and have made no announcement of defiance but rather go around without arms among those who used to be their enemies, for they show by their deeds that no one should be afraid of them. And I explain these three manners of [making] peace so that people may know who is breaking them, for such persons can be accused of treachery and breaching the peace.

1681. The second way in which a private war ends is by giving of a guaranteed peace (*asseurement*), for example when the lord obliges the principal parties (*les parties chevetaignes*) to give guarantees to each other (*asseurer li uns l'autre*). And although the peace which is made by the families and the peace which is made by a judge is a good and strong and binding peace, nevertheless the binding of peace by guarantees (*asseurement*) is stronger; and we will speak of this in a chapter which comes after this one which discusses truces and the giving of a guaranteed peace [Chapter 60].

1682. The third way in which war ends is when the parties plead in court by wager of battle concerning the action because of which they were, or could have been, at war. For you must not seek vengeance on your enemy by war and by going to court at the same time. Therefore when there is a suit in court on the dispute because of which the war occurred, the lord should take the war into his hands and prevent the parties from doing harm to each other and then give judgment on what is pleaded in his court.

1683. The fourth manner in which war ends is when punishment is meted out by the judge for the offense which caused the war, for example, when a man is killed and those who killed him and were guilty of his death are arrested by the judge and drawn and hanged. In such a case, the family of the dead man must not maintain a war against the relatives of those who committed the offense; for when the crime is punished (*vengiés*), the family of the dead person should count themselves as properly satisfied (*bien paié*) and they should not keep up a war against those who had no guilt in the offense.

1684. By what is said about war in this chapter it can be seen that gentlemen are at war because of the actions of their family even if they were not present at the action, but only when forty days have elapsed after the fact. However, if anyone wants to take himself out of the war, he can do so in one way, which is to summon his enemies before the judge and force them to appear and after, when they have appeared, in their presence and in front of the judge, he must ask that he should not be considered at war, inasmuch as he is a person who is prepared to reject those who committed the offense. When the rejection has been made of those who were guilty of the offense, the lord should give him a guaranteed peace individually, and the oath that he must make must be to swear that he has no guilt in the offense which was the reason for the war, and that he will give neither aid nor help to those that he may know to have been guilty, nor to any of those of his lineage who want to continue the war to the detriment of the family of the person against whom the offense was committed. And after he has made this oath, if the adverse party does not wish to make a formal accusation against him as guilty of this offense, he must be left and must remain in peace as an individual (*en sa persone*), as is said above.

1685. If any one has taken himself out of the war in the manner stated above, he must be careful not to go against his oath; for if he gives aid or companionship in arms (*compagnie a armes*) or lends horses or armor or houses, or he causes them to be lent, he puts himself back in the war by his act, and if harm comes to him then it is right and proper, for at the very least he is a perjurer. And if the adverse party wants, he can consider him at war like the others, and if he prefers he can accuse him in front of the judge of having broken his oath; and if he is proved or found guilty, he has deserved a long prison term and his lord can impose any fine he wants. But it would be different if he had, after the announcement, beaten or struck or wounded any of those whom he had requested to consider him out of the war, and for whom he rejected his relatives who were keeping up the war and those who were guilty of the offense, for in this case, he would be as liable to be hanged as those who break a guaranteed peace.

1686. It used to be that you could take vengeance by right of war as far as the seventh degree of kinship, and that was not surprising at that time because marriage could not be made up to the seventh degree; but now that marriage can be made up to the fourth degree of kinship, war cannot be made on a person who is more distant than the fourth degree of kinship, for in all these cases kinship ends as soon as it is so distant that a marriage can be made, except for redeeming land (*rescousse d'eritage*), for you can still buy back land up to the seventh degree by reason of kinship. So, according to what is said above, it can be known that those who attack because of their private war persons beyond the fourth degree of kinship from those who were guilty of the action by which the war began cannot use as a defense that they did so because of the right of war. But instead they must be brought to justice according to the offense as if there were no war at all.

1687. It would be different if a person, who was distant in kinship up to the fifth or sixth or seventh degree, entered the war either by deed or by word along with those of whose family he was, for then he could be counted at war just like the others, and that would be true also for a person who was completely a stranger who, on either side, had never belonged nor did belong [to the family]; for a person who loves one of the parties who are at war, to the point where he gives him his aid and his company against his enemies, puts himself into the war even though he does not belong to that family, excepting the mercenaries which people pay to be on their side in a war: for these mercenaries, as long as they are of assistance to one of the parties, are in the war, but when they have left, because their term of service has ended, or because they wish to, or because they are no longer wanted, they are out of the war. Therefore if harm were done to them after they had left, no excuse could be found in the right of war. And what we have said about mercenaries, we also say about those who have to give aid by reason of suzerainty, as it is proper that vassals who hold fiefs or tenants holding tenancies from them (*li ost qui tienent d'aus ostises*) and serfs give aid to their lords when they are at war, even though they do not belong to their family. Therefore as long as they are supporting their lords they can be counted as at war, and as soon as they have left they are out of the war and you should not make war on them for having done their duty towards their lords.

1688. Certain persons are exempt from wars, even though they are part of the natural family of those who are at war, such as clerks, and those who have entered religion, and women and minor children and bastards – unless they join the war by their acts – and those who have been placed in or sent to leper-houses or hospitals. All such persons must be out of danger of war carried on by their families. And if anyone attacks them, his action cannot be excused by right of war.

1689. And there are even other persons who must not be accounted at war because of the war of their relatives, such as those who, when the quarrel began, were on a journey overseas or some distant pilgrimage, or sent to foreign countries by the king or for the common good. For if such people were at war for the quarrels which arose when they were out of the country, then they could be killed wherever they were, or on the way out or back, without their knowing anything about the war, which would be a terrible thing and a great danger for those who go on journeys to distant lands; and it would be a poor and dishonest vengeance on the part of those who took their vengeance in this manner, and it would not be vengeance, but treachery.

Here ends the chapter on war.

Here begins the sixtieth chapter of this book, which speaks of truces and guaranteed peace (*asseurement*), and of who can be excluded from them, and of the danger of breaking truces and guaranteed peace.

1690. It is true that we have spoken in the chapter before this one of wars which can occur according to the custom of our district (*païs*). And it is right that in this chapter following after we should speak of truces and guaranteed peace because a truce is a thing which gives protection from private war for the time that it lasts and a guaranteed peace creates a confirmed peace for ever by the force of law. And we will speak of the difference that there is between truces and guaranteed peace, and how they should be made, and what sort of people can be excluded from them, and how those who break truces and guaranteed peace are to be punished.

1691. It is the custom in the county of Clermont that if commoners have harmed each other as it were by a serious crime (*de fet aparent*) and one of the parties asks the other in court for a truce, he does not get it, but rather the judge will make a full guarantee of peace if the parties do not make peace between them; for commoners cannot, according to custom, carry on a war, and between people who cannot make war on each other there is no possibility of a truce.

1692. Jehan, who was a gentlemen, sued Pierre, who was a gentleman, saying that he and Pierre had had a fight and blows had been struck, for which reason he requested his sovereign's truce (*trives par souverain*), as a person who was in fear. To this Pierre replied, that he did not want to give a truce, since in respect of the act in question he was in a state of friends' armistice (*astenance...par amis*), and he was willing to prolong this friends' armistice any time it should be asked. And upon this they requested a judgment on the question of whether Jehan would have his sovereign's truce.

1693. It was found in the opinion that, according to the custom, Jehan would not have his truce, but that the sovereign would oblige Pierre to extend his friends' armistice any time that he showed signs of not keeping it. And it was also said that, when a war has begun between gentlemen, the party who wants to be safe may seek this by one of three different methods, whichever he pleases: either by friends' armistice, or a truce (through family or through the court), or a guaranteed peace. And once he had chosen one of these methods, he could not abandon it to pursue one of the other methods.

1694. There is a great difference between truce and guaranteed peace, for a truce lasts for a specified time, and a guaranteed peace lasts for ever. And again, when someone breaks a truce, only those who break the truce are accused, and when a guaranteed peace is broken, both those who break it and also the person who made the guarantee are accused, even though it is openly known that the person who made the guarantee was not part of the act of breaking it; for a guaranteed peace has such force that the person who gives a guarantee takes responsibility thereby for his whole lineage, except for those that he can properly exclude, for there are certain persons he can exclude when he gives the guarantee, and if they are not excepted, then they are all included.

1695. Those who can be excluded by custom are those who are living in distant lands outside the kingdom, concerning whom there is no hope of their speedy return. But if it happens that they are excluded and they do come back, the person who gave the guarantee must warn the person to whom he gave it to be on his guard that people have come back to the district who were out of the guarantee; and if he does not so inform him, and they remain forty days in the district, and then after the forty days they break the guaranteed peace, then the person who gave the guarantee is held responsible; and if he does make it known, the person to whom the guarantee was given must force them through the sovereign to be in the guarantee, and if he does not force them they are in the guarantee by custom when they have been in the district for forty days. But if the person who gave the guarantee can do nothing to make them want to abstain from harming the person to whom the guarantee was made, he must so inform the person to whom he gave the guarantee, and also the sovereign, and swear on the saints that he cannot make them do it; and then the judge must arrest them if they can be found, and keep them in prison until they have joined the guarantee. And if they are not found, if they are commoners, they must be summoned three times to come fifteen days later to the provost's court; and if they do not come in that time, at the end of the third period it must be announced that they must come to the next judge's assize on a guaranteed peace matter, and if they do not come to the assize they must be banished. If they are gentlemen, and have come back from outside the country in the manner described above, they must be arrested without delay, if they can be found; and if they run away so that they cannot be found, then a great many guards must be placed on their property, if they have any, and they must be called three times to appear fifteen days later in the provost's court on the sovereign's business (*au droit du souverain*); and if they do not appear, they must be called at three subsequent assizes when there are at least forty days between assizes; and if they do not come by that last assize, they must be banished. Truces between gentlemen, whether friends' truces or those given by a judge, must be handled in the same way as described above.

1696. The second kind of persons who can be excluded from truces or guaranteed peace are those who were banished before the guaranteed peace was made; but if they are recalled and absolved from banishment by the will of the sovereign, so that they come back into the district, they must be treated in the manner described above concerning guaranteed peace.

1697. The third kind of persons who can be excluded from truces and guaranteed peace are bastards, for by our custom a bastard has no lineage; and this is clear, for my relatives at the fourth degree would inherit my estate if I had no closer relative than my bastard son. But nevertheless, since bastards are moved by natural love to give aid to their relatives, those who give truces or guarantee peace must name them at the time of giving the truce or guaranteeing the peace, so that those to whom the truce or the guaranteed peace is given know whom they should beware of; and if he does not exclude them from the guarantee, the person who gives the guarantee is to blame; but in the case of truces, as I said before, only the person who actually commits the offense is accused.

1698. If these three kinds of people described above are summoned to court to give a guaranteed peace or a truce, and they let the time run until they are banished, and then they are arrested after the banishment, they have deserved a long prison term and their fine is at the sovereign's discretion, whether they are gentlemen or commoners. And when they have paid the fine to the lord and they are out of prison, they are to give their word on the guaranteed peace (or the truce, if they were summoned for a truce). But it is different for those who are summoned on suspicion of serious crime, of which they have been accused, for example murder, or treachery, or homicide, or rape, or arson or willful damage to property, or escaping from prison – in other words whenever someone is arrested for any crime for which the punishment is death if he were found guilty – or larceny, for if anyone is summoned for one of the cases described above and waits so long that he is banished by the custom of the area and he is caught after the banishment, in that case he has lost his life and his property and he is dealt with as if he had committed to the common knowledge the crime for which he was summoned.

1699. When any *casus belli* occurs between gentlemen who can make war, if there is a death, the truce or guaranteed peace must be requested from the closest relative of the deceased, provided he is fifteen or more years old; and if he refuses because he does not want to give a truce or guaranteed peace, the count must summon him to court at fifteen-day intervals. And nevertheless, because of the danger that there is in delay, the count should send guards to the person from whom the truce or guaranteed peace is requested, and double them each day, so that the person appears in court to avoid loss; if he does not want to come, whether to avoid loss or for anything else, and he has been summoned three times to appear fifteen days later in the provost's court and then to three assizes, if he does not appear, he must be banished; and after he is banished, the truce or guaranteed peace can be requested of the nearest relative after him. But because of the danger of delay, when they refuse, the count can and should take the quarrel into his own hands and forbid them on pain of life and property to do harm to each other. And if they do harm to each other in spite of the count's prohibition, if there is a death, all those who were present at the offense fall into the count's discretion as to life and property; and if there is an action without death, such as an injury or a battery, the fine of each person who is guilty of the offense is sixty pounds to the count.

1700. If there is a fight between gentlemen in which no one is killed, but there is injury or battery, and someone wants to request a truce or guaranteed peace, the person must ask it of those to whom the action was done, and he cannot ask it of anyone else in the family until the person to whom the action was done has been banished in the manner stated above.

1701. It often happens that there is a fight or a quarrel or a threat, between gentlemen or between commoners, and then each party is so proud that he will not condescend to ask for a truce or guaranteed peace; but because of the statute of good King Louis, that does not mean that there should be nothing done; rather each person who holds directly from the king, such as the count of Clermont, and the other barons, when they know that there is some action or threat between parties, and the latter do not condescend to request truce or guaranteed peace, they should have the parties arrested and force them to give a truce if they are gentlemen; and if they are commoners, they must be compelled to give a formal guaranteed peace; and if they flee, so that they cannot be arrested, the escapees must be forced by guards [namely, placed on their property] and summoned and even eventually banished, in the manner stated above.

1702. There used to be a very bad custom concerning private wars in the kingdom of France, for when some case of death arose, or of injury or battery, the person to whom this harm had been done looked for one of the relatives of those who had done the wrong to them, and who lived far away from the place where the injury had been done, so that they know nothing about the injury, and then they went there, riding night and day, and as soon as they found him, they killed him or injured him, or beat him, or did whatever they wanted to him, as it was possible for them to do to a person who was not on his guard and did not know that anyone who belonged to his lineage had done them any wrong. And because of the great danger which arose because of this, good King Philippe [III] made a law which says that, when some harm has been done, those who are present at the action must be on their guard directly after the action and they have no truce until it has been made by a judge or by their family; but all those in the lineage of either party who were not present at the action have by the king's law forty days of truce, and then after the forty days they are in the war; and because of these forty days people in the family have time to know what is happening to their lineage, so that they can make ready either to make war or to seek a guaranteed peace, a truce, or [simply to make] peace.

1703. If some action occurs by reason of which it is appropriate for those who were present at the action to be at war, and there are some men of their lineage who join with them to help them, for example if they consort with them in arms, or they protect them in their houses, such people are in the war as soon as they begin to help them in their war, and they have no benefit of the forty-days' truce described above, for it is clearly evident that they know very well about the action when they undertake to make war along with those who were present at the action.

1704. When someone who has been the victim of an offense takes revenge on some of those who were not present at the action within the forty days that they have a truce according to the above-mentioned law, it should not be called vengeance but treachery; and for this reason, those who in this way do harm to those who are under a truce must be dealt with: if there is a death they must be drawn and hanged and lose all their property; if there is only a battery, they should receive a long prison term and the fine is at the discretion of the lord who holds directly from the king, for it is not right that any lord below the one who holds directly from the king should receive the fine for a broken truce which is confirmed by the sovereign; rather, the fine and cognizance of the offense belong to the count.

1705. It often happens that some families are in a state of truce or guaranteed peace with each other, and yet it happens that some new dispute arises among some of those in the family so that by this new action there is a fight or some *casus belli* (*fet aparant*). Now let's see if a truce or guaranteed peace is broken in such a case. And we say no, for to accuse someone of a broken truce or guaranteed peace, the offense by which the truce or guaranteed peace is broken must derive from the first offense by reason of which the truce or guaranteed peace was given, so that those who are defendants cannot claim that there is some new action. And in this case the judge must take great care to discover what was the first action for which the truce or guaranteed peace was given and what was the later action by which they hoped to have a defense to the accusation of having broken the truce or guaranteed peace. And if the judge sees that the latest incident took place because of the first, he should proceed in such a case as if it were a broken truce or guaranteed peace. But if the action is so new that it cannot be shown that it derived from the first action, but rather it is clear that the quarrel arose between the parties because of a new action, then there should be no punishment of this action for a broken truce or guaranteed peace; instead, punishment should be made according to the action as if there never had been any truce or guaranteed peace.

·1706. What we have said about a new action which arises between those who were under a truce or guaranteed peace, we mean to apply [only] to those persons of a lineage on either side who did not swear to the truce or guaranteed peace; for as for those who formally (*droitement*) gave a truce or guaranteed peace, if they fight again afterwards, they cannot have the defense of a new incident. So that if there is any contention between them, they must seek justice through law or custom; and if they fight or if there is some other *casus belli,* the person who began the action must be tried for broken truce or broken guaranteed peace, but the person who defends himself should not be accused of anything, since any person who is attacked is permitted to defend himself to avoid danger of death or bodily harm.

1707. Pierre and Jehan had fought each other and there was a *casus belli* and each was so proud that he did not condescend to request truce or guaranteed peace or to make a complaint about the action. We learned of the action: we arrested them and wanted them to make a formal (*droit*) guaranteed peace, and each party declared that he was not obliged to make peace when neither party requested it, and they asked us to hold a hearing. And at their request we called for a judgment on the question of whether there should be a guaranteed peace between them.

1708. And it was judged that when we learned of the *casus belli* we could and should keep the parties imprisoned until a guaranteed peace was given, or a good and certain peace [established] by the assent of the parties, for much harm can be avoided in this manner and all princes and barons should, by exercising judicial control (*en justiçant*), prevent such evils as might otherwise occur.

Here ends the chapter on truce and guaranteed peace.

## 97. THE STATUTE OF HOMICIDE OF MARSEILLE, FRANCE

*Although most of Mediterranean Europe effectively adopted Roman law from the twelfth century onward, the law as practiced allowed for a kind of common law valid throughout the continent (ius commune) as well as local laws (iura propria). The statutes of the French Mediterranean seaport of Marseille, first set down around 1252 and later revised, were local laws heavily influenced by the trend toward the making of municipal statutes that began in Italy in the twelfth century.*

Source: ed. and trans. Régine Pernoud, *Les statuts municipaux de Marseille* (Monaco: Archives du Palaise, 1949), p. 178. Trans. Daniel Lord Smail.

### 5.25. How Homicides May Be Punished

Since it is a matter of great importance to the republic that crimes not go unpunished, and especially homicides committed illicitly, by the authority of this statute we ordain...that if anyone shall have assaulted or wounded or mortally injured anyone else in Marseille or its territory...[and] if perchance the man who did such things shall have fled from Marseille...at no subsequent point in time may the criminal in any way be allowed or permitted to return to Marseille or its suburbs unless he shall have first made composition for the crime with four or five of the closest relatives of the murdered or dead man, and at the same time unless he, or another in his place, shall have first paid the fine assessed to him for the act or crime by the rector or councilmen or the Commune of Marseille.... Similarly, if the murderer shall be found or can be found anywhere within Marseille or its territory, then he shall be captured by the rector or by the councilmen of Marseille, or by others acting for them, by force if necessary, and then the rector and councilors shall do with him what they think ought to be done....

## 98. FROM THE STATUTES OF ACQUI, ITALY

*The cities of late medieval and Renaissance Italy issued an extraordinary number of municipal law codes; of the approximately ten thousand manuscripts that are extant, most have not been edited. All were deeply influenced by Roman law, but there is enough variance in them to show how local circumstances, including a desire on the part of cities to be distinctive, often overrode Roman legal categories. Compare, for example, the type of execution proposed in this passage from the statutes of Acqui (a one-hundred-pound fine or decapitation) with that proposed in the statutes of Apricale*

*(Doc. 99) (burial alive under the body of the victim).*

*Once set down, statutes were subject to continuous revision. The sampling here and in the following documents includes a spectrum of possible responses to a homicide or wounding. Many statutes took pains to include provisions governing how the court should proceed if the offender should flee the city and take exile in the countryside, and records of actual court cases show that flight was indeed the norm. In cases where the offender had fled the city, statutes typically required that a peace between the rival parties be made before the offender could return or "be restored" to the city. The following set of statutes is from 1277.*

Source: ed. Giuseppe Fornarese, *Statuta Vetera Civitatis Aquis* (Bologna: Forni Editore, 1971), pp. 21–26. Trans. Lori Pieper and Daniel Lord Smail.

## 27. On striking without blood

If a citizen strikes a blow while assaulting someone living in the city, male or female, and blood does not flow, or if he gives a slap, or pulls the person by the hair, or shoves wrongfully so that he falls, the offender shall pay a penalty of 60 shillings. If the victim does not fall down, the offender shall pay a penalty of 20 shillings just for the shoving. And if he commits any of these things against a consul or judge, he shall give a triple penalty; if against a scribe who holds a communal office, double. He who beats a public prostitute shall pay a penalty of ten shillings, unless he breaks a bone, in which case, he is to pay a penalty of 20 shillings. If an exiled person or a fugitive, during an assault, strikes a citizen, male or female, or does one of the things mentioned in this chapter, he is to pay a penalty twice that which a citizen pays for striking another citizen, and if any citizen strikes a fugitive or exiled person, he shall pay a penalty of 20 shillings. If, however, the citizen strikes in defending himself, he is not held to pay the penalty. We say the same about an assault, whether the assault is committed by a citizen or by a fugitive, but if there is doubt about who began it, it is to be investigated by the law, through the swearing of an oath by the offender; but if the truth of the matter cannot be discerned, it is to be settled by the judgment of the podesta. If he does this to his wife, to any children or nephews or grandchildren living with him, to a mistress – a woman, that is to say, who does not have a husband – or a wage-laborer...he should not be held to pay the fine. And if a guardian or caretaker, or a relative, in giving correction, strikes another relative, or another person close to him, he is not held to the penalty, nor for a female servant in any way. If there shall be several brothers or blood relatives of the first degree in the same house, they are not held to the penalty if they fight among themselves, which is understood to be all those staying and living in a house, provided that they are related to each other by some relationship or affinity. Women are held to pay a third part of these penalties, and for those less than fourteen years of age, it is to be decided by decision of the consul.

### 28. On striking with bloodshed

If a citizen commits an assault against a citizen living in the city, male or female, striking with a spear, knife, falchion, or other iron sword, or a rock or a piece of wood, and if blood flows from the wound, he is to pay a penalty of 100 shillings. If a wounded citizen was defending himself, he is not held to pay the penalty. If any offender with forethought strikes a citizen with a knife, falchion, or other iron sword or a piece of wood, and blood flows from the wound, he is to pay a penalty of 10 pounds. Anyone who caused or commanded that the said fighting come to pass is to suffer the same penalty, as well as anyone who gave advice, and this penalty is to be paid, if it was fought in the daytime; but at night, double, since he did this furtively and by lying in wait.

Concerning these matters, minors of fourteen years are to be adjudged by a decision of the consul, which cannot exceed a third part of the fines listed in this chapter. Women are held to pay a third part of these penalties, as is contained in the chapter. Anyone who does not have the means to pay the fine is to be exiled and his goods are to be thrown open to the public, and he who is the first to take over his estate is to pay the penalty given to the offender. If an offender chooses not to pay, he is to suffer the same penalty of degradation and publication.... If he tilled them prior to the crime, the fruits of his labor having been harvested, he is to abandon them, assigning a part to the lord of the commune. Nor is the offender to stay in the city, unless he pays the penalty, and for each aggression or vengeance delivered, he is held to pay the fine contained and defined in this chapter. Also, if anyone with forethought and lying in wait strikes and wounds a citizen and is unable to pay the penalty, he is to lose a foot or a hand. Also, if a citizen strikes a foreigner, he is to pay a fine of up to 60 shillings, or as much as the foreigner would pay if he were to strike a citizen of Acqui on his land. If, however, the outsider who is struck had previously laid hands on the citizen who struck him, the offender is not held to pay the penalty, unless an accord had earlier been made between the two.

He who, in striking, disfigures a limb, or renders it useless by cutting it off or damaging it, is to pay a penalty of 25 pounds. Anyone who causes or commands that it be done is to undergo the same penalty, along with anyone who gave counsel and aid in the act. If these things are done at night, he is to pay a double penalty. Those less than fourteen years of age are to be adjudged by a decision of the consul and the decision of the consul cannot exceed a third part of the penalty named in this chapter. Women are held to the third part of these penalties. Whosoever does not have enough movable goods to pay the fine, let his immovable goods be given to the commune up to the amount of the fine. Anyone who does not have the means to pay the penalty in coin and who can be caught shall lose a foot or a hand, and this is to be understood to concern the striking and cutting off of limbs. Otherwise, he is to be exiled and he is not to return unless the penalty is paid. If he does things to the rector or a judge or a knight, he is to pay a triple penalty; to a scribe, double. If, however, a fugitive or an exile offends anything contained above in this chapter, he is to pay double the penalty paid by a citizen for a citizen, and more if it should seem fitting to the council. Everyone is required to attack him and capture him and present him to the podesta. Anyone who brings him back to the city and gives him counsel and help shall pay the same penalty that the outsider must pay, and the outsider, if he can be caught, is to be held in prison, and he is to be held there until he can satisfy those things which are contained in the aforesaid chapter. If anyone shall shed blood without assault his punishment is to be according to the decision of the consuls.

29. On the killing of human beings

If a citizen, God forbid, in committing an assault kills a citizen living in this city, he is to pay a penalty of 100 pounds; otherwise he is to lose his head. If he cannot be caught, he is to be exiled as above, and if he has committed any of the things listed in the chapter concerning blows in the presence of the podesta or in a great church or in the square before the church, the cemetery, the market or in the bath or the area around the bath or the square there – by the square of the bath we mean that which is defined by the Chapter of the bath [that is, the officials in charge], and by the square of the church we mean from the church up to the corner of the Avenas and to the corner of the oven of the canons – he is to pay a double penalty, and if he does not have the cash or cannot pay it, he is to be punished by having his head cut off, if he can be caught. If he cannot be caught, he is to be exiled, and he is not to return unless the penalty is paid and concord is made with the friends of the dead man, with his father, son, brother, blood relative of the first degree, the second degree, father-in-law, brother-in-law, relative, or with the greater part of them, and his property is to be laid waste and put up to public sale if he does not pay; and even if he does pay, he is to be expelled from the city, unless an accord can be made with the dead man's friends and relatives as above. For each occasion on which he returns to the city, he is to pay a penalty of

10 pounds, unless he did so by permission of the rector. If a citizen kills an outsider, he is to pay a fine of up to 25 pounds, and more or less depending on how much he, the outsider, would have paid in his own land if he killed a foreigner. If anyone has struck another citizen in his house, he is to pay a double penalty as above except for homicides. If, however, it is doubtful that he was the aggressor, it is to be proven by combat, if the truth of the matter cannot be discerned otherwise; and this by the friends of the deceased, if they wish to prove it.

He who kills a man in secret, and sure proof can be had, and the dead man's friends have this proof and wish to prove it, they can do so through combat. The same goes for those who ordered it to be done and whoever gave help or advice, this is said if the commune has sure proof. Also, he who breaks a peace after the peace has been made and commits homicide is to pay a double fine. The same goes for any blow given after a peace has been made, as is contained in the chapter on blows; otherwise, he is to be banished as above. Whoever is unable to pay this penalty from his movable goods, let his immovable property be taken as above, and the one who causes it or orders it to be done, and who gave advice and aid, is to undergo the same penalty. And if he shall do any of these things to the podesta or judge or a knight, he is to pay a triple penalty; and concerning other officials of the commune, the treasurer and the scribe, they pay double. And if he who strikes or wounds or kills any fugitive or exile who is not staying in Acqui with his family, and does this outside the city of Acqui, or outside the territory of Acqui, he is not to be held to the fine in any way, if the killer is punished in the place of the crime. Otherwise, he is to be held to pay the fine as if he had committed the said crime within the effective power of Acqui.

## 99. FROM THE STATUTES OF APRICALE, ITALY

*This extract comes from the earliest recension of the statutes of Apricale, made in 1267.*

Source: ed. Nino Lamboglia, *Gli antichi statuti di Apricale (1267–1430)* (Bordighera: Istituto Internazionale di Studi Liguri, Museo Bicknell, 1986), p. 21. Trans. Lori Pieper.

### 7. About homicide committed on any person

Anyone who shall commit homicide on any man or woman of Apricale, wherever the said homicide is committed, if the killer can be caught, he is to be punished corporally in this way: the killer is to be put in a pit under the dead person and covered with earth in such a way that he dies. If he cannot be caught, the penalty shall be 20 Genoese pounds. One half goes to the court and the other half to the heirs of the dead person. The house of the killer is to be demolished to its foundation, and the whole timber is to be burnt. If he is a fugitive in perpetuity, he is not to be restored again to the city unless the heirs of the dead man are willing, or unless the killer committed the crime in self-defense.... In this case, no punishment is required of him.

## 100. FROM THE STATUTES OF SAONE, ITALY

*The "I" in this text refers to the* podesta, *or governor, of the city who had to swear to uphold the statutes of the city he governed. The statutes are from 1345.*

Source: ed. Laura Balletto, *Statuta antiquissima Saone* (1345), vol. 2 (Bordighera: Istituto Internazionale di Studi Liguri, Museo Bicknell, 1971), pp. 7–8. Trans. Lori Pieper.

Here Begins the Second Book on Crimes

### 1. On blows struck that cause death

If any person, who is fourteen years old or above, strikes or has struck another person, and he dies from it, unless the offender was defending himself, or defending some person or persons, neighbors or relatives or sons-in-law or fathers-in-law, and unless it shall have been a matter of children who are playing at battle who are less than fourteen, I swear that, if I can catch him, I will have him hung and killed or have his head cut off. If I cannot catch him, I swear that I will destroy his goods or have them destroyed and dispersed. And what shall remain after the destruction, I will give to the heirs of the person who was killed to keep as their own, and in addition I will exile the offender from Saone and its district in perpetuity, wherever he shall have committed the crime, so that he is never to be restored to the city nor removed from the ban, with his tenement [property] left to the podesta or rector who comes after me, who should look after it, and the tenement should be left to all of the subsequent podestas or rectors. In addition, I will have it proclaimed that no one is to give him shelter or sustenance. After he has been outlawed, if anyone should shelter the offender or give him any sustenance at any point during my period of governance, I shall fine him 20 pounds for each time that he does this and it becomes known to me, if I can obtain as much from his goods. If I cannot, I will lay waste to it or I shall have property up to the amount of 20 pounds destroyed, if I can find goods of this value, or I will destroy or have destroyed all that he shall have if he does not have property worth twenty pounds.

## 2. On blows struck without death

Also, if any person fourteen years old or above shall strike with premeditation or have struck any person with a knife or iron object or sword so that he does not die from it, unless this shall happen in a riot or in his defense, I will take from him, for every blow, twenty-five pounds, if I can obtain so much of his goods, if blood shall flow from the said blow. If someone shall strike another in the face and blood shall flow from the wound, he is to pay fifty pounds. But if blood does not flow from it, I shall take from him five pounds and no more. And if such striking shall be done on account of which or from which the member is lost, I shall take from the one who struck such a blow a hundred pounds and no more. And, if he is not able to pay the said penalty himself or another for him, I shall have cut from him the same limb as the victim lost, if I can catch him. If I cannot catch him I shall destroy or have destroyed all of his goods that I can find, and in addition I shall exile him from Saone and its effective power so that he is not to be restored or removed from exile until he shall pay the said penalty; and, if I am able to catch him and he does not have the means to pay the said penalty, I shall have him placed in prison, nor will I permit him to come out until he has paid the said penalty. Except that, if they shall be in agreement within fifteen days after this takes place, I will take from him who struck the blow half of the above-mentioned penalty and no more. If they are relatives up to the third degree, or father-in-law or relative or son-in-law and they are in agreement within fifteen days, I shall take no penalty from him in consequence.

# 101. FROM THE STATUTES OF CUNEO, ITALY

*These statutes are from 1380.*

Source: ed. Piero Camilla, *Corpus statutorum comunis Cunei 1380,* Biblioteca della società per gli studi storici archeologici e artistici della provincia di Cuneo (Cuneo: Stabiliment o tipografica, 1970), pp. 219–21. Trans. Lori Pieper.

## 423. On blows struck with a sword

Also it is to be declared that if anyone strikes someone with a sword, with wrathful intent, and causes blood to flow, if in the shinbone or hipbone, foot or hand, he is to pay as penalty five pounds of Asti. And if the victim was struck in other parts, the culprits are to pay as penalty twenty-five pounds of Asti. And if he throws a stone but does not hit anyone, he is to pay a penalty of sixty shillings of Asti, if he is over twenty. And if from twenty years down to fourteen, twenty shillings of Asti. And if below fourteen, he pays nothing for the penalty, unless he causes any blood to flow from the nose, in these two cases he is to pay as penalty five pounds of Asti and no more. A staff or club are not to be considered arms. If, however, he causes blood to flow, he is to pay as penalty sixty shillings of Asti. And if from the said blows anyone has a broken bone or a cut, he shall pay double the amount for the aforesaid penalty. And if the victim of any of the said blows loses a limb or any part of a limb, the offender shall pay as penalty fifty pounds of Asti. Teeth and fingers are not to be considered limbs, except for the thumb, for which twenty-five pounds of Asti is to be paid as penalty. But if from any of the blows struck the victim loses a tooth or one finger or several, he is to pay for each tooth and for each finger lost ten pounds of Asti. And if the offender cannot pay the aforesaid penalties of blows or insults, if he commits an offense without a sword, or if with a sword and blood does not flow, or flows but there is no broken bone, he is to be beaten from the Karante gate up to the Burgi gate. But if he attacks with a sword and there is a broken bone or if the victim shall lose a limb, he is to lose a foot or hand of his choice. A sword is to be understood as everything that is contained in the appellation of arms except for the staff or club as above. If, however, any person or persons commits the offense in the presence of lords, vicar, or judge of Cuneo or under the portico of the court of Cuneo, he is to pay double the said penalty, in the decision of the lords, vicars and judges, after the nature of the persons and of the deed have been inspected. And if anyone commits the aforesaid on the person of a scoundrel or prostitute, he cannot be condemned beyond sixty shillings of Asti or less in the decision of the lords, vicars and judges, after the nature of the person and the deed have been inspected. And in addition to all these penalties, the vicar of the lord and the judge of Cuneo are required, without any dispute or evasion, to have the expenses of the doctors and other damages paid to the victim by the offender, according to what seems good to the same lord vicar or judge, if they shall be requested to do so. But the aforesaid penalties are not to be incurred by the one who does the aforesaid things in his defense or the defense of his property with moderation, without fault, as a guardian, or who does the aforesaid things with the intention of punishing someone or breaking up a fight. The penalties, each and every one, are to be paid by the decision of the judge, according to the nature of the persons and the deed. So that it may not be excessive, however, they may lower it with cause, according to what seems good to the judge.

## 424. On blows struck among relatives

Also let it be decreed that if any person from Cuneo or the district, in word or deed, shall offend personally any of his children or brothers or sisters or blood-relations of the first degree, or those who are within the same degree or are related to him within the said degree, or anyone with whom he is staying for a loaf of bread and a glass of wine, the court of Cuneo neither can nor should inquire into such a crime or offense or carry out any trial unless he is or was caused to be denounced or accused by the person offended by this deed as it shall be caused to be written by the said person denouncing or accusing with an oath in the books of the court. With this exception: if the blow struck or offense is such that from it the victim has a broken bone or disabled limb, then the court can inquire into and punish such a crime, provided that the offender is not to be condemned when it is initiated without denunciation or accusation, except in the middle of the banns or penalties in which he should be condemned if he committed the said injury or offense on another person. And this chapter is not to claim for itself a place in homicide.

## 425. On homicide

Also let it be established that whoever kills another human being from Cuneo or its district is to die if he can be caught. If, however, he cannot be caught, the vicar of the lord and the judge are required to take a hundred pounds of Asti from the goods and property of the killer by way of punishment and penalty, if he shall be a person not possessing goods beyond a thousand pounds. And if he shall be a person who possesses goods beyond the sum of a thousand pounds of Asti, he is to pay for the penalty two hundred pounds of Asti. The offender also has to pay the same amount to the children of the victim. And if the victim does not have daughters or sons, this penalty is to be given to the parents, that is, to the father and mother of the victim. And if the parents themselves have died, it is to be given to the brother or brothers if there are several, and the offender is to be expelled in perpetuity from the place of Cuneo and its district, unless he did this in self-defense. Anyone may kill the said fugitive without punishment or penalty. The fugitive may remain anywhere he shall have agreed upon with the friends of the victim, that is with the father, children and brothers, paternal uncles and [maternal] uncles, and with nephews, blood brothers and sisters, and those of second degree, and with the court of Cuneo. And nevertheless, he is to pay the sum of money given above. And if anyone, through error, or accidentally without a fight, kills anyone, and it was clearly an accident, he is not to bear or undergo any penalty inflicted on his property or his body on account of this. And where it says "relatives," this is to be understood as being from the paternal, not the maternal, line.

### 426. On exiles and fugitives

Also it is declared that if anyone from Cuneo or the jurisdiction of Cuneo flees or becomes a fugitive for any offense, he neither can nor should be restored to the city even when the penalty for the crime has been paid, unless he first comes to an agreement with his victim or with the victim's heirs. And the lord vicar or the judge is required to make the announcement in the aforesaid villages. And the one who has been expelled or exiled from Cuneo is to be expelled and exiled from all the villages who pay dues of fodder to Cuneo and the commune of Cuneo such that he is under no circumstances to be welcomed in the aforesaid villages. And if anyone from the aforesaid villages brings back any fugitive or banned person of Cuneo, from wherever he may be, or if he is welcomed in the said village after the announcement has been made by the same lord vicar or the judge by the advice of the said village, the village must pay whatever penalty was assessed against the exiled person or else turn him over as a captive into the power of the lord vicar of the judge of the court of Cuneo.

## 102. FROM THE STATUTES OF CELLE, ITALY

*Statutes continued to be produced for Italian communes throughout the later Middle Ages; these are from 1414.*

Source: ed. Maddalena Cerisola, *Gli statuti di Celle (1414)* (Bordighera: Istituto Internazionale di Studi Liguri, Museo Bicknell, 1971), pp. 110–12. Trans. Lori Pieper and Daniel Lord Smail.

### 129. On insult, striking, and homicides

If any person, fifteen years or older, of the jurisdiction of Celle or from elsewhere, commits an assault with premeditation and strikes any person in the head or another part of the body with a stick, a boot or a foot, a stone, or in any other way on any part of the body – except for that which is contained in the chapter under the heading of striking a person with the hands and so on – and blood shall flow from the victim's head, the offender is to be condemned for each and every blow to a fine of 10 pounds of Saone, unless the offender comes to an accord with the victim within fifteen days, counting from the day of the commission of the blow. In this case he is to be condemned only to 5 pounds of the said money.... If he strikes below the head with shedding of blood, the offender is to be condemned to 5 pounds, unless he comes to an accord with the victim within fifteen days counting from the day of the assault. In that case he is to be condemned only to 3 pounds. But if blood does not flow, he is to be condemned to 3 pounds, unless he comes to an accord with the victim within the fifteen days, then in this case he is only to be condemned to 2 pounds. If any person shall direct a blow in anger against another person, using a blade, a sword, or another iron weapon, and he does not hit his target, he is to be condemned, for each and every attempt, to 3 pounds, unless the parties come to an accord within eight days, in which case he is only to be condemned to 2 pounds. And if anyone shall draw a sword or blade – except for that which is contained in another chapter under the heading of the punishment for drawing a sword etc. – even if he does not strike a blow, he is to be condemned, each and every time, to 2 pounds, unless the parties come to an accord within eight days, in which case he is to be condemned only to 20 shillings [1 pound]. And if any person shall strike another with a blade, a sword, a lance or another iron weapon, either by day or by night, with the shedding of blood: if in the head, he is to be condemned, for each and every blow, to 25 pounds, unless the offender comes to an accord with the victim within eight days, counting from the day of the assault, in which case he is to be condemned only to 5 pounds. And if not in the head, but in another part of the body, with the shedding of blood, he is to be condemned to 10 pounds, unless the offender comes to an accord with the victim within eight days, in which case he is to be condemned only to 3 pounds. And if the offender cannot pay the fine or a portion of it, the podesta or rector [the governor of the city] is required to lay waste to the movable or immovable property of the offender, for an amount double the size of the fine if the offender has enough property. If he does not, then he is to be considered banished until he pays the penalty to the commune as has been said above. And if the offender is within the legal power of his father (filius familias), the podesta should take this vengeance only on the portion of the paternal goods that would have come to the son were the father to have died intestate. And if, because of the blow, the offender shall have caused the loss of any limb struck in this way with a blade, a sword, a lance or any other iron weapon, the fine will be 50 pounds, and if he refuses to pay or cannot pay the fine, let him be held in the jail for two months. Two-thirds of the fine should go to the victim and the remaining third to the commune of Celle. And if, at the end of the two months, the offender still refuses to pay the 50 pounds, then the podesta should amputate the same limb as was lost by the victim. If the victim should die – let us hope otherwise – the offender shall lose his head, such that he himself dies, unless he can prove that it was done in his own defense. If he reaches an accord within eight days, he is to be condemned only to 25 pounds and in restitution of any expenses which the victim might have paid [that is, before his death].

## 103. THE PERPETUAL PEACE OF THE LAND PROCLAIMED BY MAXIMILIAN I

*The Holy Roman Emperor Maximilian (1459–1519) was a member of the Habsburg ruling dynasty; he was known for his efforts on behalf of imperial reform, of which this landpeace, issued on 7 August 1495, was a part.*

Source: ed. Wilhelm Altmann and Ernst Bernheim, *Ausgewählte Urkunden zur Erläuterung der Verfassungsgeschichte Deutschlands im Mittelalter,* 5th ed. (Berlin: Weidmann, 1920), pp. 283–87. Trans. Susanne Pohl.

[131 (110)]

1. From the time of the publication of this peace, no one, no matter of what rank or position, shall carry on a feud against another, or make war on him, or rob, seize, attack, or besiege him, or aid anyone else to do so. And no one shall attack, seize, burn, or in any other way damage any castle, city, market town, fortress, village, farmhouse, or group of houses, or in any way aid others to do such things. No one shall receive those who do such things into his house, or protect them, or give them anything to eat or drink. But if anyone has a ground for complaint against another, he shall summon him before the court. For the command is now given that all such matters must hereafter be tried before the supreme court.

2. We hereby forbid all feuds and private wars throughout the whole empire.

3. All, of whatever rank or position, who disobey this command, shall, in addition to other punishments, be put under the imperial ban, and anyone may attack their person or their property without thereby breaking the peace. All their charters and rights shall be revoked, and their fiefs shall be forfeited to their lord. And so long as the guilty one lives, the said lord shall not be bound to restore it to him or to his heirs.

4. In case this peace is broken and violence is done to anyone, whether elector, prince, prelate, count, lord, knight, city or anyone else no matter of what rank or position, secular or ecclesiastical, and the guilty ones are not known, but suspicion rests on anyone, those who were injured may make

complaint against the suspected ones, and summon them, and compel them to clear themselves by oath of the crimes of which they are suspected. If any of the suspected ones refuse to clear themselves in this way, or refuse to come at the appointed time, they shall be considered guilty of having broken the peace, and they shall be proceeded against in accordance with the terms of this document. But the one who summons them shall give them a safe-conduct to come and to return to their homes. If it is impossible to deliver the summons to them in person, it shall be posted in a few places which they are known to frequent. If, contrary to this peace, anyone is attacked or robbed, all those who are present and see it, or learn of it in any way, shall take action against the offender with as much earnestness and promptness as if it concerned them alone.

5. No one shall in any way aid or protect such peace-breakers, or permit them to remain in his territory or lands, but he shall seize them and begin proceedings against them and give aid to anyone who makes complaint against them....

6. If such peace-breakers have such protection or are so strong that the state must interfere and make a campaign against them, or if anyone who is not a member of the peace breaks the peace or aids those who have broken it, charges shall be made by the injured, or by the presiding judge of the supreme court, to us or to our representatives and to the annual diet [imperial assembly], and aid shall be sent at once to those who have been attacked. If through war or anything else it is impossible to hold the diet, we give the presiding judge of the supreme court the authority to call us and the members of the diet together in any place where we, or our representatives, can meet and take whatever measures are necessary. But nevertheless the presiding judge and the whole court shall not cease to prosecute all such peace-breakers with all the legal means possible.

7. There are many mercenaries in the land who are not in the service of anyone, or who do not long remain in the service of those who hire them, or their masters do not control them as they should, but they go riding about the country seeking to take advantage of people and to rob. We therefore decree that such men shall no longer be tolerated in the empire, and wherever they are found they shall be seized and examined and severely punished for their evil deeds, and all that they have shall be taken from them, and they shall give security for their good conduct by oath and bondsmen.

8. If any clergyman breaks this peace, the bishop who has jurisdiction over him shall compel him to make good the damage which he has done, and his property shall be taken for this purpose. If the bishops are negligent in this matter, we put them as well as the peace-breakers under the ban and deprive

them of the protection of the empire, and we will in no way defend them or protect them in their evil doing. But they may clear themselves of suspicion in the same way as laymen.

9. During this peace no one shall make an agreement or treaty with another which shall in any way conflict with this peace. We hereby annul all the articles of such agreements or treaties which are contrary to this peace, but the rest of such agreements or treaties shall remain in force. This peace is not intended to interfere in any way with existing treaties. Without the consent of those who have been injured we will not free from the ban anyone who has through an offense against the peace been proscribed, unless he clears himself in a legal way.

10. We command you...to observe this peace in all points, and to compel all your officials and subjects to observe it, if you wish to avoid the punishments of the imperial law and our heavy disfavor.

11. We hereby annul all grants, privileges, etc., which have been granted by us or our predecessors, which in any way conflict with this peace.

12. This peace is not intended to annul any of the laws of the empire or commands which have already been issued but rather to strengthen them and to command that all men shall hereafter observe them.

# CHAPTER THIRTEEN: ECCLESIASTICAL AND SECULAR COMMENTARY ON PEACE AND THE RESTRAINT OF EMOTIONS

*By the later Middle Ages, the ecclesiastical assault on the emotions that led to vengeance, including envy, anger, and hatred, was in full swing. The authors of manuals for preachers, such as the* Fasciculus Morum *(Doc. 104), wrote of the need to "bridle" the sinful desires. The desire for vengeance, in this model, was as much a sin as sexual desire, gluttony, or avarice, and had to be regulated in much the same way. On a more practical level, the great preachers of the age, including Vincent Ferrer (Doc. 105) and Bernardino of Siena (Doc. 107), gave sermons on the need for peace between neighbors, and to that end counseled interior peace and self-restraint. Historians, following the work of the sociologist Norbert Elias, have described the bridling of emotions as part of a larger "civilizing process," though questions remain about what, exactly, this process was. Contemporaries were aware of the contradiction that emotions like anger and hatred were not intrinsically negative, and Leonardo Bruni pointed out (Doc. 106) that there are many contexts in which emotions like anger move people in good ways. By the same token, peace and fellowship are not intrinsically good, since there can be peace among thieves (Doc. 105).*

## 104. THE NATURE OF WRATH ACCORDING TO A PREACHER'S MANUAL

*The* Fasciculus Morum *(lit. a "small bundle of morals") is a treatise on the seven deadly sins and remedies for them that was written by an unknown Franciscan author in England in the early fourteenth century. It was intended to be a preacher's manual, which functioned as a guide to help preachers convey Christian truths in a language easy to understand by general parishioners.*

Source: trans. Siegfried Wenzel, Fasciculus Morum: *A Fourteenth-Century Preacher's Handbook* (University Park: Pennsylvania State University Press, 1989), pp. 117–33.

### 2.1 The Nature of Wrath

Since a cruel mother usually gives birth to a savage daughter, in this second part we deal with wrath, as the chief daughter of that wicked mother, pride. Its main character is to be quickly inflamed, and it can never be mitigated until it has spent itself by totally venting its irascibility, just as a fire that is given dry sticks is easily kindled and cannot stop of itself until all the sticks are burnt. Therefore I plan to deal with wrath in the following way: to see first what its nature is, second what evil consequences its wickedness has, third what its members are, and fourth why it should be totally condemned.

Concerning the first point we must know that according to Gregory, in book 5 of his *Morals,* wrath is sometimes considered as zeal and sometimes as a vice. The former occurs when one's mind is disturbed on account of some evil; according to the Psalm: "Be angry and sin not" [Ps. 4:5]. But the kind of wrath which is a sin, with which we are dealing here, is according to Augustine "the unbridled desire always to get vengeance and never to have pity," as we saw above in the example of fire.

### 2.2 The Evil Consequences of Wrath

Concerning the evil consequences which its wickedness has, we must know first that the soul, which is the image of God in man, is destroyed by it, just as turbulent water does not hold the shape of a reflection in the same way as clear and still water does. Whence we read in *The Lives of the Fathers* about a desert father who put a denarius in a bowl full of clear water, and as he saw its image he said to his brother: "Thus does the image of God appear in tranquil hearts." After saying that he moved the water, and the image of the denarius disappeared, and he said: "Thus is the image of God destroyed in troubled hearts." Second, wrath obstructs God's grace from flowing into the soul, as turbulent air obstructs the brightness and radiance of the sun. Therefore, Gregory says in book 5 of *Moralia in Job*: "Through wrath the light of truth is lost, for when anger injects the darkness of confusion into the mind, God withholds from it the ray of his knowledge."

The third evil is that wrath makes a person who suffers from it a member of the devil. Jeremiah 6[:23]: "He is cruel and will take no pity." Against such a person Augustine says: "He deserves no mercy who denies it to his neighbor." Those people may rightly be said to be worse than the devil; for the devil, who instigates evil, remembers sins as long as they are being committed; but when they are wiped away through penance, he forgets them altogether, and Christ forgives them in his grace. As an example we have the case of a person of whom Blessed Gregory reports that, after he had sworn fealty to the devil and had received his marks in his hand, when he later on felt remorse and confessed and received his penance, the marks disappeared and the devil no longer recognized him as his own. Ezekiel 18[:21]: "If the wicked does penance, I will not remember all his iniquities, says the Lord." Much less, then, will the devil remember them. For the devils return evil for evil in like measure and cannot give punishment beyond what is deserved, nor can they punish one person for the sins of another. But wrathful people, in truth, return a thousand words for one, and for one blow in the face they thrust deadly weapons into the body, and not just into the one alone who gave the blow, but they try to destroy his entire offspring if they can. Thus it is evident that they are worse than the devil. On this we have the following saying in verse: Anger blocks our mind from seeing what is true.

### 2.3 The Members of Wrath

Concerning its members we should know that there are two in particular, namely hate and revenge. For many people today cannot take their revenge with material weapons and therefore retain hatred through hardened anger in their hearts. But notice that there are two kinds of wrath, one virtuous, the other a vice. Of the first Augustine says: "Just anger is not devoid of either justice or knowledge, namely, when you neither hate men because of their vices, nor love vices because of human beings. For it is right for us to hate evil in wicked men yet to love the created human being, so that the created being should not be condemned because of his vice, nor should a vice be loved for the sake of man's nature." And elsewhere he says: "Men should be loved in such a way that one does not love their mistakes; for it is one thing to love what has been created in them, another to hate what they do." And again: "No sinner, insofar as he is a sinner, must be loved; but every human being, insofar as he is human, must be loved for God's sake, but God for himself."

Of the evil and vicious kind of wrath, however, Augustine says likewise in a sermon: "If it is not permitted to be angry with one's brother without cause, or to call him 'racha' or 'fool,' much less is it right to nurse hatred whereby one turns hatred into indignation," for such hatred makes a man like the devil. There is a natural hatred between men and snakes, as there is between horses and griffins, wolves and dogs; whence God said to the serpent, in Genesis 3[:15]: "I will put enmity between you and the woman." Therefore, anyone who hates a human being has the nature of the serpent, and by this he becomes like the devil, who has been cursed; and thus a person who hates is cursed by God together with the serpent. Such anger and hatred may therefore be indicated by the wind of which Job 1[:19] speaks: it "came from the side of the desert and shook the four corners of the house, and it fell upon the children." Thus when anger and hatred come upon the house of our soul, they overthrow its four affects, that is, the four virtues, and destroy whatever good comes to life in it, because no good is of any value without charity.

The second member of wrath is revenge. Whoever practices that against his neighbor both unjustly and beyond due measure (which even the devil does not do, as has been said), seems to be not human but a wild beast. Therefore [John] Chrysostom speaks of Herod as follows: "When a wild beast is wounded by someone, out of its natural defensive fierceness it makes its natural cruelty twice as painful, and, as it were, blind with fury no longer looks for the one who has wounded it but instead tears to pieces whoever comes into its sight, be it man or another animal, as if it were the cause of its wound; so did Herod vent his wrath on innocent children when he had been fooled by the Magi."

Such people are like the juniper, whose nature it is, according to Isidore [bishop of Seville, d. 636, see Doc. 22], *Etymologies,* book 17, chapter 7, to keep a fire alive for a year if the glowing coals are covered with its own ashes. Surely, the same is true of many people who keep the fire of wrath alive under the ashes or the cover of their own wickedness and who through many years still wait for an opportunity to take vengeance. Such people are commonly confounded in their own wrath, as is shown typologically in Exodus [14:6–31] by Pharaoh, who unjustly persecuted the children of Israel and drowned with his army in the Red Sea; similarly by Samson, who, when he was tricked by the Philistines, craved vengeance and killed himself with the others, according to Judges [16:28–30]; and similarly by Haman, who was hanged on the gallows he had prepared for Mordecai, Esther 7[:10].

Such an unruly desire for vengeance easily makes a wrathful man like a magnet, which by its nature attracts iron, and the more magnetic it is, the greater is its attractive power. Augustine in *The City of God,* book 21, chapter 10, says he once saw a magnet held underneath a silver bowl, and the magnet, in wonderful fashion, attracted a piece of iron that was placed in the silver bowl. Spiritually speaking, by the magnet I understand anger, by the iron, revenge, for iron is usually interpreted as symbolizing revenge; wrath draws iron, because through wrath lances, swords, and all kinds of weapons are drawn out. And thus wrath is the ground for all such things, and the more wrathful a person is and the more powerful, the more iron he attracts. For we see that a count attracts more lances and armor than a baron, and a baron more than a knight, and so on. But it sometimes happens as it does in the instance reported by Augustine, according to the nature of this stone: if a simple citizen has offended some magnate, whether rightly or wrongly, but then asks him for grace and sends him gifts and presents, he certainly covers that magnet as it were with a silver bowl, so that such a lord may not draw his iron in vengeance against him. But it sometimes happens that there is a diabolical magnet under the bowl which moves the stone, that is, a great scoundrel who is counselor to that lord and who always instigates him to evil, saying that if *he* were in the lord's place, he would not for all those gifts and presents refrain from taking revenge; and in this way he attracts the iron despite the silver bowl. Therefore I fear that I can say the words of Deuteronomy 8[:9]: "Such is the land whose stone is iron."

Such people are also like another stone called "asbestos," which, once it has been ignited, can never be extinguished. In similar fashion, such wrathful people in our days do not forgive any offense without taking revenge.

### 2.4 How to Detest Wrath

In the fourth place, it remains to show why wrath should be totally rejected: because it goes directly against God's commandment and his will when he calls out and says, "Be merciful as your Father is merciful." Whence Bernard [of Clairvaux, d. 1153] declares: "It is easier to count the stars of heaven, the fish in the sea, and the leaves of the forests, than for you to appraise God's mercy, for according to the Psalmist, 'his mercies are above all his works.'" God's mercy receives into his grace any sinners that ask from their heart for his forgiveness, as is seen in Thais, the prostitute: on account of her beauty many men lost their possessions, many shed their blood, many lost their lives; yet when she was led to remorse and penance, she obtained mercy and grace. Notice also the story about the knight who on Good Friday forgave another knight the death of his father, out of love for him who died on that day for all mankind. When the two knights went together to worship the cross and bring their offerings, the Crucified detached his arms and embraced the one who had acted so mercifully, and he then heard a voice speaking of forgiveness. The same is true of Blessed Paul, of Magdalene, of the Good Thief, and of others. Therefore, in commenting on the verse "I do not want the death of the sinner," Bernard says: "Whatever plight may lead you to penance, neither the number of your sins nor the wickedness of your life nor the short time you have to do good bars you from God's forgiveness, as long as you have true contrition of heart, confession of mouth, and satisfaction in deed." Whence Bernard says in the same place: "O good Jesus, you did not turn in horror from the thief who confessed, the sinful woman who wept, the woman of Canaan who implored you, the adulteress who was caught, your disciple Peter when he denied you, or Paul, who persecuted the Church, or the ruthless men who crucified you. How then should I despair of your mercy?" – as if he were saying, not at all; for "there is greater joy in heaven over one sinner who repents," and so forth.

But notice that this divine mercy, so sweet and benign, has two very evil squires: on one hand, presumption or sinning with confidence that stems from overly relying on God's mercy; on the other hand, despair of receiving forgiveness for one's sins.

Against the former, that is, sinning with overconfidence, the Lord says in Isaiah 36[:5]: "In whom do you trust," add: overly in your sin, "that you are revolted from me?" Similarly Proverbs 10[:28]: "The hope of the godless will perish." Three kinds of people follow this vice. First, hypocrites, who trust most wickedly in outward show; Job 8[:13–14]: "The hope of the hypocrite shall perish, it shall not please him in his heart, for his trust shall be like spiderwebs." Second, the proud follow that vice, on account of their strength and power, against whom is written in Amos 6[:1]: "Woe to those who trust in Mount Satnaria," that is, in high estate and arrogance, or riches and wealth, as covetous and greedy men do. Third, lechers follow it in their carnal lust, against whom is written in Jeremiah 17[:5]: "Cursed is the man who trusts in man and makes flesh his arm," that is, who desires carnal pleasures. Let us therefore beware of thus sinning in confidence of God's mercy. God's attitude toward sinners is similar to the relationship between the eagle and the crow. The crow pursues the eagle, who is king of the birds, but the latter pays no heed in his great-heartedness and courtesy. When the crow sees that, it becomes even more daring and pursues him, until the eagle gets too tired and annoyed and finally catches the crow with violence and tears it to pieces. Thus will Christ likewise kill sinners in the end if they do not give up their wicked confidence while they sin. There is another story about such a person who confidently sinned in lechery. When he was taken to task by some holy churchman, he answered: "God has died for me as well as for you; therefore he won't damn me any more than he will you. So, I trust so much in his mercy that as long as I can say these three words 'Have mercy, Lord' before I die, I shall be saved." It happened that one day when he crossed a bridge and began to reel off backwards, he forgot his three words and instead said: "Devil take it." Thus it is clear that one must not sin in presumption, by trusting in God's mercy and believing that one will receive it whether one has lived well or not because God will not lose or condemn what he has redeemed. The latter is certainly true insofar as it depends on God, yet anyone who sins in this way loses and condemns himself. Therefore, whoever wishes to have true hope and trust must first reflect on the sins he has committed and correct them, and then apply himself to doing good and continue in this. For against the presumptuous is said in Ecclesiasticus 5[:4]: "Do not say, 'I have sinned,'" etc. And later [Ecclus. 5:5–9]: "Do not add sin upon sin, saying, 'God's mercy is great, he will have mercy on the multitude of my sins,'" rather, "do not delay to turn to him and do not defer from day to day, for his wrath shall come on a sudden, and in the time of vengeance he will destroy you."

So that you may neither lose heart nor be overconfident, but instead have true hope and trust, it is necessary to reflect carefully on the three parts of prudence: first on the past, remembering what evil you have done, what good you have left undone, and how few good things you have accomplished; second on the present, paying attention that you do not fall, doing the good you have not done, and making restitution; and third on the future, looking out that you do not slide back into what is forbidden or give up the good you have begun.

And we should further notice that, just as we must not be overconfident of God's mercy, as has been shown, we must likewise in no way despair of it. For Augustine says: "Sin with despair will of necessity forego salvation." According to Ambrose [d. 397], a man sins more gravely by despairing than by committing an evil. And Jerome, in his commentary on the Psalms, says that Judas offended God more when he hanged himself than when he betrayed him. Therefore it is said in Proverbs 24[:10]: "Do not despair on the day of distress." And Bernard comments on the verse [Gen. 4:13] "My iniquity is greater," etc., from Genesis, as follows:

"You lie, Cain, because in comparison with the savior's mercy the malice of any man is like a spark of fire in the middle of the sea."

Notice that this sin usually comes from three causes. First from faintheartedness, when a sinner thinks of the punishment that is due to his sins, such as doing seven years of penance for a mortal sin and the like; when he sees or hears that, the sinner loses heart, and in this torpor and despair does not take up his penance. Second, it comes from the gravity of the sin itself, as from a sin against nature. And third it comes from the difficulty of avoiding a sin one commits out of habit, because according to the Philosopher [Aristotle], "habit is our second nature." This was well prefigured in I Kings 23[:26], where it is said that "David despaired of fleeing from the face of Saul, because he and his men encompassed David like a crown." Saul stands for the devil, and his men for evil thoughts which encompass David, that is, the sinner's soul, so that it may seem to him that he cannot evade them through penance, and then he despairs, according to Job 7[:16]: "I have despaired, I shall not live any longer," that is to say, I shall hardly receive the reward of mercy and of penance.

Let us not do thus, but rather withstand the devil and his temptations, and God will help us according to the lines:

> Cease, and I forgive;
> Fight, and I help;
> Win, and I crown you.

Proverbs 3[:25–26] says: "Be not afraid of sudden fear, nor of the power of the wicked falling upon you, for the Lord will be with you as a strong helper." Behold the following story. Diascorides [an ancient Greek physician, d. ca 90 CE] reports about the Trinity that once there were two noble and strong civil lawyers. One of them used his physical strength on whores and other follies, and his learning in unjust lawsuits. As both were asleep one night, it happened that the Heavenly Father appeared to the one who had thus foolishly spent the gifts he had received from God and said to him: "Get up and come to your judgment. You have sinned against me whose mark is power. You have badly misused the strength I have given you. You shall be condemned." When the lawyer heard this, he gave a horrified cry so that he woke his companion. When the latter asked him what was the matter, he told him all. But his companion comforted him and said: "Don't pay any attention to nocturnal visions and such illusions!" And they went back to sleep. Then Christ, the Son of God, appeared to him and said, as the Father had done: "Get up, prepare yourself for your judgment. You have likewise sinned against me who am the Father's wisdom, by badly misusing in unjust lawsuits the wisdom you have received from me; and therefore you shall be condemned." Again the lawyer woke up in terror and cried out even more horrified than he was earlier. His companion asked: "And what is it now?" And he told him all that he had seen from the Son of God. Since his companion could not talk him out of his despair, yet knowing in his prudence that he would not be condemned in spite of these visions, he then put the following case to him: "Imagine that three men jointly own an inheritance in equal shares, so that no one could sell it without the other two, nor could two of them do so without the third. If one or two of them wanted to do that, would not the law be openly against them?" He answered that this was so indeed. Then his companion said: "Thus it is in your case. The Father, the Son, and the Holy Spirit hold joint ownership of the heavenly inheritance, with equal right and power. If therefore the Father or the Son wanted to take it from you for which you were given a claim in baptism, by the power of Christ's blood, they certainly could not do so without the consent of the Holy Spirit. Therefore, even though the Father and the Son may want to take it from you, because as they say you have misused the Father's power that you were given as well as the Son's wisdom, wait till the Holy Spirit comes, to whom belong clemency and goodness. And when he comes, implore him at once that because of his great clemency he may help you to achieve mercy between the Father and the Son and to restore yourself, by promising him that you will amend your life. If you do that, I give you my pledge that you will gain your blessed inheritance." By this saying the lawyer was comforted in his mind.

Therefore prepare yourself, O sinner, to ask for his mercy and do not despair, for you will find him more ready to give than you are to ask. It takes much to offend God, but little to make peace with him; Wisdom 6[:7]: "To him that is little, mercy is granted." "Ask and you shall receive." Whence we read in [Geoffrey of Monmouth's] *The Deeds of the Britons* [see Doc. 76] that there was a king in this realm called Cassibelanus, who had a relative by the name of Androgeus. Between them was a very great enmity on account of the death of some squire, as history tells us. This enmity grew so great that it destroyed nearly all the lands in Kent, that is, all the people, by fire and sword. Then it happened that Julius Caesar was gravely moved against the king and kindly disposed toward his relative Androgeus, and he fought against the king and forced him to flee. When the latter saw that he could not withstand Caesar and was in fear of his power and attack, he sent letters to his kinsman on whom he had inflicted so many evils and asked for his mercy and good grace in recognition that he was his relative, and begged him further to make peace between himself and the emperor. When Androgeus had seen and read the letters, he replied to the messenger: "One rightly should not fear a prince who in time of war is mild like a lamb and in peace fierce like a lion." Then he added: "Although he has deserved no grace or mercy from me whatsoever, I will yet try to reconcile him with Caesar if I can. I am satisfied, for the injury he has done to me, that the king in his own land is humbly begging for my grace." And thus he made peace between the emperor and the king. Morally speaking, these two relatives are the Son of God and man, between whom there was great enmity and ever will be as long as man gives in to sin, for in that case man pursues the Son of God so much that, if it were in his power, he would crucify him again; for if one does that for which the Son of God has died, namely sin, one hands the Son over to death and crucifies him again in as much as lies in one's power, according to Hebrews 6[:6]: "Crucifying the Son of God again in themselves." By this we cause the greatest offense to the highest emperor, our heavenly Father. What then is to be done? Indeed, it is necessary that such a sinner ask his relative, Christ, for grace and mercy. And if he has done so, he should not distrust that the grace he has asked for with humble heart might not be reckoned sufficient retribution before God, and that God might not remit his sin. With this, Christ will reestablish peace between the emperor, his heavenly Father, and the sinner.

Therefore, if you fear his vengeance, flee to his mercy, as a certain knight did who was condemned to death by the Roman emperor on account of his guilt. When the knight heard this, he appealed, and as the emperor wondered to whom he might be appealing since there was no one higher than himself on earth, the knight answered: "Every emperor and king must of necessity have not only a throne of justice but also a throne of mercy. Therefore, if I am condemned in the throne of justice, I appeal to the throne of mercy, which is the higher place and virtue in a prince." Hearing this, the emperor said: "You have appealed to mercy, and mercy will free you from death." It will of necessity be likewise with Christ our emperor, whose eyes, according to the Psalmist, "are on those who fear him and on those who hope for his mercy." Whence Augustine says: "What more merciful word is there to hear for the sinner who is condemned to eternal punishments and has nothing whereby he may save himself, than God the Father's saying: 'Take my Only-begotten Son and give him for yourself' and likewise the Son's saying: 'Take me and save yourself,' etc." Therefore, the Apostle says in his letter to Titus, 3[:5]: "Not by the works of justice which we have done, but according to his mercy he has saved us."

## 105. A SERMON ON PEACE BY VINCENT FERRER

*Vincent Ferrer (1350–1419) was born in Valencia, Spain, and entered the Dominican Order in 1367. He taught theology at the cathedral school in Valencia from 1385 to 1390, and worked in the curia of Cardinal Pedro de Luna from 1394 to 1398. From 1399 until his death, he toured Europe as a preacher, and usually did so along with followers who heard confessions, gave instruction, and led processions of flagellants (groups of men and women who whipped themselves). This sermon was composed between 1399 and 1419.*

Source: Sermon 184 for Fferia Viª, ed. Gret Schib, *Sermons*, vol. 6 (Barcelona: Barcino, 1988), pp. 19–21. Trans. Jennifer Speed.

Today I will preach to you about the peace that we must have in this world, if we wish to have the peace of Jesus Christ. Now, the holy prophet Zachariah, prophesying the coming of Jesus Christ, said this, "Behold, your God comes to you as just," that is, according to himself, "and savior," according to us, "and he will speak peace to all the nations" [Zech. 9:9–10]. And then, it was at the nativity when the angels sang, "Glory to God in the highest, and peace on earth to all men of good will" [Luke 2:14]. After greeting them, "Peace be with you." For this reason Saint Paul said, "He is truly your peace" [Eph. 2:14–17]. And especially by the peace of the Apostles, saying "My peace I give to you" [John 14:27]. Also, [Paul] said to them, "Whatever house you enter, first say: 'Peace upon this house,' and if there is a man of peace there, your peace will rest upon him. If not, it will return to you" [Luke 10:6]. Afterwards, at the Resurrection, when he appeared, he said, "Peace be with you. It is I" [Luke 24:36]. And you see here, the prophecy is fulfilled truly and completely, and the theme, you see, speaks of this peace. But why did Christ say "Peace be with you" three times?

First, on account of the Jews, so that the Apostles would not be afraid of them. And for this reason, Christ said to them "Peace be with you." Afterwards, he said to them another time "Peace be with you" on account of the doubt which they had about his truly having risen. Afterwards, on account of Saint Thomas who did not believe it, and for that Christ said, "Peace be with you." Those three peace offerings may signify that the person who wants to come to the paradise of God should have three kinds of peace: the first, interior peace within oneself; the second, exterior peace with one's neighbor; and the third, a superior peace from almighty God.

The first peace is interior, within oneself. Now, how must we see this peace? Now you may know that the self is already at war by nature, because the flesh battles the soul, and this war is in the natural world, for the angels do not have this opposition. Accordingly, David said [to God], [you] "who makes your angels spirits, and your ministers a burning flame" [Ps. 103:4]. And he said that they are the flame of fire, and for that reason they resemble God. You see, then, how they are not at war with themselves. After them, there are other creatures that do not have even a little bit of this substance [purity]. After them, there are creatures that are entirely substance, etc. On account of the war that we have by nature, interior peace is necessary. And how will we have it? I say to you, when two men have mortal combat, you see that they may not reach an end except in one of two ways: either by agreement or by submission. No one has agreement except when both men are in accord with a single will, submission if one man is more powerful than the other. In that case, the less powerful one has to submit to that which the other man wishes. And you see that he makes the peace by submission and not by agreement; it displeases him, for he does it out of fear.

We have to arouse ourselves to do this. Even more you see that we cannot make peace with God by agreement. And to that end, Saint Paul said, "Interiorly, I rejoice in the law of my God" [Rom. 7:22]. It is better to do it by submission. And how? By fasting, by alms, by prayers, etc. There are many more who do not feel this opposition, this battle, by which the soul is subject to the flesh. For that reason, such peace is not good. To that, Saint Bernard said, "It is neither fitting for the lady to serve nor for the servant to rule." How shall we understand this? If there is a maidservant in a house, and she does not wish to do that which she must, rather she wants the lady of the house to do it, then the maidservant is acting like a lady. I tell you it is this: the lady is the soul, the maidservant is the flesh. And when you, man, do that which the flesh orders, you wish to be the lady, and the soul is the maidservant. And for this, many people are condemned. And call to mind the parable about the king who married his daughter to the knight [from a previous passage].

The second peace is exterior, with one's neighbor. And the reason is this, as the philosopher [Aristotle] said: "Man is sociable by nature." Accordingly, man forms a household with his companions and they make a congregation, and in that way they have this mystery of exterior peace. As Saint Paul said, "With holiness may you remain in peace" [cf. Heb. 12:14]. Thieves have peace among themselves, but it is not that peace from holiness, for holiness must be in gathering together people of good works; even more, that peace must be between father and mother and sons and daughters, loving one another from the heart. Also, we must have peace with our enemies. And how? Do not seek vengeance for yourselves. And in nature you see how the beasts of the desert have made peace, on account of friendship.

The third peace is superior, from God, that is, having peace with the Lord, for it is a terrible thing to be at war with God. And you see how we may have it, that is, by keeping the commandments with submission. And you see, as God said to Job, "Submit yourself to it," [Job 22:21] that is, that he should consent himself to do the will of God, and by that, honor the commandments. And like a city that has peace with the king, which does his will, you yourself will have peace with God, if you observe these four things: the first, faithfulness of heart; the second, not to swear on the Lord's name; the third, to keep holy the day of the Lord; and the fourth, to obey the commandments of the Lord's spouse, the Church.

## 106. LAUDABLE ANGER IN LEONARDO BRUNI'S *HANDBOOK OF MORAL PHILOSOPHY*

*Leonardo Bruni (ca 1370–1444) was born at Arezzo, in Tuscany. He went to Florence around 1384, where he studied rhetoric, law, and Greek. Influenced by the humanist circle around Florentine chancellor Coluccio Salutati, he absorbed classical scholarship, became involved in politics, and, in 1415, began writing a history of the Florentine people. This next excerpt is from Bruni's Handbook of Moral Philosophy (1425), and the text begins toward the end of a Socratic discussion between the author and his interlocutor.*

Source: *Isagogicon moralis disciplinae*, ed. Hans Baron, *Leonardo Bruni Aretino, Humanistisch-Philosophische Schriften mit einer Chronologie seiner Werke und Briefe* (Leipzig: Teubner, 1928), pp. 32–34. Trans. Louis Hamilton.

"The rest of the virtues which you have mentioned," he said, "so far seem rightly to be considered means. I wonder if gentleness, however, ought to be considered a mean. For, indeed, if we accept this, then we will also confess that a certain kind of anger is laudable. For myself, to be honest, I hesitate to admit this. If you don't mind my interrupting, I'll try to describe why I'm so unsure."

"It's your decision," I replied, "as this discourse was begun for your benefit, not mine."

"I do not think anger laudable in any way," he said. "But if it is not praiseworthy, it cannot be a virtue, since all virtue is praiseworthy. Virtue describes excellence or preeminence. Really, there is nothing at all which people do better enraged than without anger. Now, right reason, which does not exist without virtue, requires a sedate and a serene mind. Anger, in truth, so disturbs and excites that it twists and bends not only the good judgment of the mind but also the praiseworthy condition of the body. Wild eyes, trembling limbs, garbled, half-formed words, convulsions, stupid pronouncements – these things, I would submit to your peace, seem to me to belong more to madness than to virtue. It is, therefore, completely absurd to say that right reason rules the virtues and yet at the same time to acknowledge that anger, which turns us away from right reason, can be considered among the virtues, to believe that someone could be capable of preserving composure in his public affairs if he cannot preserve composure within himself.

"Moreover, wise men testify most aptly to what I have just said. We can find many books written against anger. Indeed, who would write against tranquility? Nobody has up until now, as far as I know. Thus, we find, since it would be laudable not to become enraged, to become enraged is a vice. But if it is established that anger is never praiseworthy, it follows that its mean ought never be praised, but, rather, every internal disturbance of the mind, of this kind, ought to be condemned."

Then I said: "I am not unaware that this is usually said by those who argued against the Peripatetics [a school of philosophy in ancient Greece]. Nevertheless, a person's feelings are important. You ask if I approve of an explosive temper and inordinate violence. Indeed I do not; I detest it. What is more foolish? What is more like madness? You ask if I would approve a tranquil and slothful temperament at all times? Again, these lead to vice and I find them reprehensible.

"Now, I put it to you: If your servant was beating up one of your parents or raping your virgin daughter, should you watch this calmly? Or would it be better if there arose in you some feeling for putting a stop to it? Piety herself and Reason would respond, 'You are reprehensible if you do not feel indignation at such an abuse of your parent or daughter and are not moved by an all-consuming desire for vengeance.' I ask you, what ought a son to do, seeing such an indignant abuse of one of his parents? I wonder: would he maintain the same expression, the same state of mind? Wouldn't he be moved by such abuse of those nearest and dearest to him? And who would not detest such a person or find him reprehensible? So it is that a certain kind of anger is praiseworthy and not to be angered is to be considered vice. That person who is so obtuse and negligent as to neither grieve nor be upset when country, parents, siblings, or others whom we ought to hold most dearly suffers abuse, seems insensitive and unreasonable.

"Nor was it very sensible to say, as you did, that there is nothing people don't do better without anger. As for your claim that no one has ever written anything against tranquility, you seem to me to be ignoring Aristotle, who strongly condemns sloth and tranquility. Therefore, since you compare the quick-tempered man to a maniac, so I would compare the dissolute and slothful to an imbecile who seems neither to feel nor care nor to be affected by anything."

## 107. SERMON ON THE IMPORTANCE OF PEACE BY BERNARDINO OF SIENA

*Bernardino of Siena (1380–1444) became a Franciscan friar at the age of twenty-two, and was based at the Church of St. Francis during the time he preached in Siena. Later on, he was elected Vicar General of the Friars of the Strict Observance in Italy, an order within the Franciscan movement. The following excerpt is taken from Bernardino's 1427 sermon on Psalm 133:1: "Behold how good and how pleasant it is for brethren to dwell together in unity," which concerns King David's search for peacefulness on earth. Bernardino uses the Latin version of the psalm, as well as many Latin quotations from Scripture, as a starting point in his effort to urge the inhabitants of Siena to make peace with their fellow citizens and within their own households. His three-part analysis of the psalm concludes with the notion that a life centered on peace is the best life that can be led.*

Source: ed. Carlo Delcorno, *Prediche Volgari sul Campo di Siena 1427*, vol. 2 (Milan: Rusconi, 1989), pp. 1254–61. Trans. Laura K. Morreale.

Saturday I will preach in the Franciscans' Square: tomorrow I will preach there, and Sunday, as a farewell, I will also preach there. Tomorrow I will preach to you about the glory of eternal life, and Sunday I will preach to you about what the Holy Spirit engenders within us. Let us return home.

First we have where it says "Behold how good," which is the request; then "and how pleasant it is," the illustration; then, "for brethren to dwell together in unity," [Ps. 133:1] the challenge. The first part, the request: "Behold how good." This peace is such a useful thing! It is such a sweet thing, that even the word "peace" gives a sweetness to the lips. Look at the opposite, and say "war." It is such a vulgar thing, and gives such harshness, that it forces the mouth to scowl. You see, you painted it at the top of your city hall, so that when you see Peace pictured, it is a joy. And it is gloomy to see War pictured on the other side. Do you remember when God waged war against the creatures of the world, those whom he had made? He killed all of the creatures of the world, except those who were in the ark, and he saved those ones so they would grow and multiply and glorify him. And Noah did not know that God would make peace with human nature again, for he sent out a dove, and it was God's will that it should return to the ark with the olive branch in its mouth, demonstrating that he had made peace with them on account of Noah's humility. And so those who are sinful are always against God, and those who humble themselves are always with God. And so I tell you, I tell you on God's behalf, that no one should be so stubborn as to not wish to forgive, but with perfect humility, should bow his head for love of his creator. And this is what Paul said to the Romans in chapter 12: "If it be possible, as much as lieth in you, live peaceably with all men" [Matt. 12:18]. If it is possible, my children, work to be at peace with everyone. It is as though he is saying, "Never wish to be the cause of war, hate, or enmity; rather, be a source of peace, love, and harmony."

You wonder whether this is possible. Do you remember the one about the son who wanted to go off to study, and who said to his father, "Oh, my father, I request your leave so that I may go off to study the sciences and the virtues." And the father, because he knew that hate and hostility were terrible things, said to him, "My son, if you would like me to give you permission to go and study, I would like you to promise me that there will never be problems between you and anyone around you." The son responded, "My father, I promise you there will never be any problems on my account." And the father said, "No, no, I do not want you to go; go then, put your horse back in the stable." And the son said, "Oh, my father, why do you not want me to go?" "Do you know why?" said the father, "Because you are not fit for this. You will not obey me in what I have directed you to do. You say that you will not have problems with anyone, with you as the cause of the problem. But I want you to have no disputes originating from you or from anyone else." And for this word alone, he did not allow him to go off to study.

I say the same to you, citizens; wish for no disagreements and no conflicts. If you see that conflict arises from someone else, make sure that you do not perpetuate it. Swallow, swallow everything. Do not keep every word in your mouth, but act as if you had the throat of a goose. If you want to go around looking for who did this thing, and who did the other, you are searching for hostility and hate; do not do this, I say. But moreover, you should ask your eyes, which like to see things that can cause hurt and hate in your soul; if you go looking for it, you will find more evil than you would ever wish to find. Whoever goes looking for evil is actually in need of finding it; if you look for hatred, you will find it, even from God. If you look for enmity, you will find it, even from God. And yet, every time you go after this, you are always going from bad to worse. When you see something that disturbs you, leave it be; do not go about to investigate (asking, "How did this happen?"

and "How was it done?"). Do just as if you had thrown it away, over your shoulder. You should know how to get along and converse with good people, evil people, those worse than that, and even the worst kind of people. You should get along together, and not wish to ruin each other, but to love each other. And if no one close to you wants war, you will not want it either. Run from it; do so that you are always among those who search for peace, amid other people, in your own soul, and in God's soul. Do so that every thought, every act, every deed, all is centered on peace. And then, as in the teachings of David, "Petition for things that are for peace" [Ps. 122:6], pray to God for your city, that it may always remain in peace and unity.

Do you want me to tell you what I believe is really needed? Prayer! Because the way things are, I do not believe that you will be able to avoid war, just as he who does not eat will not be able to escape hunger. And this alone will occur, because among you there is neither peace nor unity: you all do not get along with each other. I will go off, and it will be painful to me; if something else happens, do not think ill of me, for I have made this clear to you. I tell you, this is something that will provoke God's anger. Do you all remember the saying in the fourteenth chapter of John, delivered by Christ's own mouth? Settle your mind on what he says: "Peace I leave with you, my peace I give unto you: not as the world giveth, give I unto you. Let not your heart be troubled" [John 14:27]. I leave you my peace, I give you my peace; not the peace the world gives, which means being at peace with one another; for not everyone can achieve this kind of peace – this peace is what I leave for you to accomplish. The other kind of peace is what people keep within themselves, within their hearts; this is the kind I give to you, and it is a gift of great value, so I want you never to wage war against anyone else, and if you want me to remain with you always, I want you to have this kind of peace. Where there is war, God is never there. Do you think God will be in your home, when you have war and discord there? Certainly not. He only wants to abide where there is peace, harmony, and tranquility. "The peace I give you," says the Lord, "cannot be taken away from you by anyone, but the peace of the world will often be wanting." And in Isaiah: "And his place is in peace: and his abode in Sion" [Ps. 76:3]. His place is in peace, and his dwelling in tranquility. And then think about how it is in your home; how you see division in your homes among fathers, mothers, brothers and children, and I say, "This is not the dwelling place of the Lord."

I know of so many people who are at war, wives with their husbands, and husbands with their wives; and also among many others, who I believe have collections of writings, memories, and issues that exist between citizens, pitting one against the other. And although I cannot make peace in each individual case, we can speak in generalities, and through my words we can come to an individual and a general peace. Oh, my citizens, embrace each other once more; whoever has been injured, forgive, for the love of God, and in this way you will demonstrate that you wish your city well. You have the example of Christ's life; he always said, "Peace." You will find nothing as tenderly recommended as peace. This is the request.

Let us look at the second part, the illustration of the request, where it says, "and how pleasant it is." Our Lord was always an example of peace and unity when he lived on earth, for he wished to demonstrate just how pleasing peace was in his eyes. For when he came down and became flesh in Mary's womb, there were twelve years of peace and unity throughout the world; this was before he was incarnated. And then when he became flesh, the angels in heaven sang this beautiful song, "Glory to God in the highest: and on earth peace to men of good will" [Luke 2:14]. Glory to God in the highest, he is born to the world, and peace be on earth to all men of good intention. And the Lord always demonstrated that if someone wants God's grace and, ultimately, his glory, he has only to follow the example given by the king of peace.

My dear citizens, I preach peace to you, I recommend peace. Oh, to you who are of good will, do not pull back, but follow this peace for the love of him who has suggested it to you. Let there always be perfect love and perfect charity within you. Would you like to know why I kept this sermon about peace until the end? Because only after having first seen the sins which you commit, and pointing out the pains which the Lord takes for those who remain unmoved, can I give these words to stir your hearts and lead you to bend to those who caused injury, and to make peace with them. Whoever remains hard-hearted, their deeds remain evil. In this way, they do not appreciate or heed God's commandments. "For wisdom will not enter into a malicious soul, nor dwell in a body subdued by sin" [Wis. 1:4]. Neither the malicious nor the evil-spirited will come to know peace, for although they know it is a useful and holy thing, they do not wish to hear about it because of their malice. But for those who follow God, it will always grow and mature, because those who heed the reasoning and the advice of the Church doctors, and the will of God and what the holy Church commands, who willingly come to listen to sermons such as these, and who willingly apply them, know that our words are holy and good and useful to those who are numbered among God's chosen ones. Would you like to see how the Lord always instructed his followers to employ the virtue of peace? Didn't he say to his disciples, "When you come into a house, greet it, saying 'Peace to this house'" [Matt. 10:12]. When you enter into a house make sure that the first thing you do is to say, "Peace be in this house." Saint Francis teaches us to do the same.

You have seen that before God became flesh there was peace throughout the world. You have also seen that when he was born, the angels sang this sweet song of peace. Now let us see it in his words. He lived among his apostles and whenever there was a circumstance that led to difficulties among them, he always made peace between them, illustrating what a beautiful thing peace is. Thus, whenever he saw any quarrel arise among them, he would always rub it out; so you can see that peace, above all other virtues, is the most pleasing to God. Let us now look at his death to see how he dedicated himself to continuously proclaiming peace, and devoted himself to renouncing and banishing war and discord when he was on the cross. "There (upon the cross) brake he the arrows of the bow, the shield, and the sword, and the battle" [Ps. 76:4]. With peace, he conquered all temptation, with the bow of living a righteous life, with the shield always on the defensive, with a blade from the right hand and from the left, and in the battles with the Pharisees, the Scribes, the Judges, the high priests, and the tyrants. He was always victorious, in every way, because he never fell into sin, either in thought or in deed. But, every act that he performed was entirely perfect, providing us with an example. And he did this as he finished his life, bowing his head when he commended his spirit to the Father, illustrating in this act a sign of love and peace, almost saying, "Learn, my children, that those of you who would like to follow the life I have led, in each and every way in all that you do, and at all times, you should make sure to overcome the temptation the devil offers you. You can see how much humiliation I endured during my time, so that there would never be a risk that I would harm my soul, but I always remained calm and at peace; at my home, the home of the Lord, there always has been, and will be, pure peace." What a mystery! You know, when the temple of Solomon was built in Jerusalem, "there was neither hammer nor axe, nor any tool of iron heard in the house when it was in building" [3 Kings 6:7]. No noise was made, neither with hammers, tongs, axes, nor the other tools with which it was made, which provides and illustrates a sign that in the temple of God, there is nothing but peace, so that throughout Christ's life, until his death, you could always see this peace. In the same way, after his death, when he appeared to the disciples, his words were always "*Pax vobis:* peace be with you." Within him, one could see nothing more pleasing than this peace. He always said, "Peace, peace, peace." You have seen then the first two parts; now let us look at the third.

In the third part, we see the challenge of peace, "for brethren to dwell together in unity," and about this I will say very little....

# CHAPTER FOURTEEN:
## SAINTS' LIVES, CHRONICLES, AND EPICS

*The later Middle Ages was a particularly fertile time for writers of narrative sources on vengeance. The documents selected for this chapter provide especially vivid examples of how notions and practices of both vengeance and peacemaking were conceived and put into effect. Like the sermons of Vincent Ferrer and Bernardino of Siena in the previous chapter, the narrative sources below provide indirect confirmation that vengeance remained a societal concern in later medieval Europe, despite the prohibitions against killing found in secular laws of the period (see Ch. 12) and in the moral condemnations of unbridled emotions that were also made at this time (Ch. 13).*

*Despite these condemnations and prohibitions, political processes in some cities like Florence (Doc. 112) actually promoted vengeance-taking on a larger scale. As political parties emerged, it is likely that feuding families aligned themselves with larger factions so as to gain the resources and allies necessary to pursue their own vendettas. Tit-for-tat vengeance, to modern observers, looks like a never-ending process that will inevitably dissolve into anarchy. However, narrative sources from the period (e.g., Doc. 116) speak of the yearning for peace in the midst of vendetta and extol saints and other intermediaries who were able to guide vengeful parties into a peaceful state of mind (Docs. 108 and 110). It remained possible and even necessary for God to exact vengeance, of course (Docs. 109 and 114).*

## 108. AMBROSE SANSEDONI'S PREACHING OF PEACE AROUSES ENMITY

*Born to a noble family on 16 April 1220, Ambrose was entrusted to a poor woman of Porta Romana after his birth, possibly because of his deformed limbs. He was miraculously cured after a year in St. Maddalena, the first church of the Dominicans, and he consequently became a Dominican in 1237. After studying at Siena, he continued his education in Paris and Cologne. Out of humility, he refused the title of Master of Theology after feeling called to a more apostolic mission of preaching and peacemaking. This Life was composed shortly after his death in 1287 by four of Ambrose's contemporaries, Gisbertus, Recuperatus, Aldobrandinus, and Oldradus, at the request of Pope Honorius IV.*

Source: *Vita quam conscripserunt Fr. Gisbertus, Alexandrinus; Recuperatus de Petramala, Aretinus; Aldobrandinus Paparonus, Oldradus Bis-dominus, Senenses, Ordinis Praedicatorum, de mandato*

*D. Honorii IV Pontificis Maximi, Acta Sanctorum Martii,* vol. 3 (Paris: Victor Palmé, 1865), col. 191. Trans. Kelly Gibson.

The servant of God even showed the greatest humility in face of the abuse and persecution he suffered from vicious men and disturbers of the peace which he desired to bring about. Many splendid examples (*exempla*) of this kind were seen. For sake of brevity, we will report one of these. A certain great man who painfully tolerated the way of life of the man [Ambrose], especially in regard to a certain peace that was supposed to be set up amid a few public disagreements, was trying to turn him [Ambrose] away from his holy intentions with threats and terrors, saying: "You are a false man, a seducer and deceiver of the Christian people, filled with ambition and vainglory. You deserve every punishment that I will give to you if you do not give up these undertakings." The holy man, humbly responding to him, said: "God the king is called peaceful. Therefore, every person of faith should desire peace with [his] neighbor. Indeed, no shred of peace is given except to those who most freely concede peace to another. However much effort I make, I do it not by myself, but following his [God's] pleasure which holds sway within me. Now, if you are disturbed by my message, I seek pardon: I beg God, who knows the thoughts of men and is the most just judge (*retributor*) of good and bad deeds, to grant pardon for ill-phrased words and to refrain from attributing this sin to you, and if I am worthy of any punishment whatsoever, I will receive it freely in remission of my sins."

That man was cruel and ferocious by nature; he had within him absolutely no fear of God but was filled instead with anger and vengeance; he had no desire for peace but instead loved quarrels. Yet although he had been inflamed in this way against the servant of God, nevertheless, as he listened to the words of the man of God, he immediately said, lying prostrate on the ground: "Forgive me, servant of God, and pray for me, so that he concede true peace to me: also I will be ready for peace with you." The holy man did not allow the man to lie prostrate in his presence. Immediately raising him from the ground, he kissed him, and, praying to God to forgive the man, he urged him to continue in fear of the Lord. Afterwards he became a God-fearing man and a devoted Christian, the best living. Moreover, the blessed man with great ease restored peace to the best effect. O how great and beneficial such an example was, by which in a brief space of time many peaces between princes and counts, especially between Guelfs and Ghibellines [political factions: see Doc. 112], were made with the servant of God Ambrose himself mediating.

Blessed Ambrose in his preaching said that vengeance is the sin of idolatry because vengeance belongs to God alone: whence a man taking vengeance seizes what belongs to God, and, therefore, one who takes vengeance ought to suffer greatly and do penance. From this conclusion, he inferred that great sin attaches to subordinates who aspire ambitiously to those things which rightfully pertain to their superiors.

The wondrous example of a certain man who had resolved to take vengeance must not be passed over in silence. In the city of Siena there was a certain man, greatly hardened against peace and the forgiveness of wrongs, who was unable to be moved to make peace by the admonition and persuasion of the man of God. To this end, the holy man was trying to induce him to beg God to inspire him to make peace, if it seemed better to him. The hard man refused to do this. The blessed man said: "I will pray for you." However, the man, fully burning for vengeance, said: "I do not care whether anyone prays for me." But the pious father, filled with charity, prayed to God: "Lord Jesus Christ, through the great providence and care which you continually have for the human race, I beg that you use your power to intervene in the vengeance that is being sought, and reserve [it] for yourself so that everyone might learn that the punishment of offenders belongs to you alone and so that feeling might not get in the way of the ruling of your indescribable justice."

Preaching publicly, he taught the people this prayer and urged them to say it for anyone who remains resolutely opposed to the forgiveness of wrongs. At nearly the same hour that the holy man said the prayer, the obstinate man, with his friends and relatives, was warning that they should absolutely not make peace and should in no way listen to blessed Ambrose. Rather, [he was] inciting them to vengeance. Nevertheless, the prayer of the just man was of such effectiveness that the hard man suddenly became remorseful, and, reflecting in his mind about the blessed man's persuasive reasons in favor of peace, disposed himself entirely to make peace with enemies. Moreover, grieving over the manner of the sin of his obstinacy, for two days he remained without eating practically anything and sleeping for less than a night. Conferring with friends and urging them to peace, they came together to the man of God and asked him to make peace between them and give pardon for their error. The blessed man was made exceedingly happy by this and, giving thanks to God, made peace between them with great ease.

# 109. THE VENGEFUL MIRACLES OF SAINT BRIDGET OF SWEDEN

*Bridget (1303–73) was the daughter of the governor of Upland in Sweden. She married at age fourteen and had eight children, one of whom also became a saint. In 1335, she was summoned to be the lady-in-waiting to Queen Blanche of Namur, wife of Magnus II. Guided by the revelations from God she had experienced since childhood, she urged the king and queen to reform their lives, but found them and their courtiers resistant to her efforts. Her advice on governing the kingdom met with more success, according to her Life, which reports that she prevented the king from imposing unjust taxes. After leaving the court, Bridget and her husband, who died in 1344, lived as penitents at the Cistercian monastery at Alvastra. In 1346, she founded a double monastery for sixty nuns and twenty-five monks on Lake Vattern. Three years later, she went to Rome for approval of her order, which was given in 1370 by Pope Urban V. She did not return to Sweden, but instead was directed by God to make pilgrimages throughout Italy and to Jerusalem. She died in Rome upon her return.*

Source: *Appendix de miraculis S. Birgittae, Acta Sanctorum Octobris*, vol. 4 (Paris: Victor Palmé, 1866), cols. 534–35. Trans. Daniel Lord Smail.

In the city of Leipzig a certain master painter, Henry by name, used to speak often to the learned regarding the holiness of the blessed Bridget, and used to say many things from her books of celestial revelations for the love that he bore for her. On one occasion, one of the learned said to him indignantly: "Unless you leave off speaking of this new heresy and the books of that old woman, I will have you conveyed to the flames." What he proposed to do, he subsequently did to him, so that on the following day, in the morning, Henry had to appear before the magistrates. And so the said painter beseeched a certain cleric, a devotee of the blessed Bridget, Walter by name, for wise advice in this matter; indeed, he feared for his life. This man, comforting him, persuaded him to continue in his devotion toward God and Saint Bridget, having no doubts concerning their support. And this priest, with another master of his named Johannes Torto, willingly agreed to entreat the Lord for this same man for his devotion to Saint Bridget, which was done. When morning came, Henry appeared before the court in an anxious mind, and suffered rigorous questioning with a view to punishing him as a convicted heretic. But through the prayers of Saint Bridget, for whom he contended, imbued with the holy spirit, that simple and illiterate layman put forth the greatness of God so efficiently that the enemies of his soul, who were speaking in the case, were not able to overcome him. Not long afterward, God, the lord of vengeance, exacted vengeance on the principle mover of this to-do. For, going healthy to bed, he perished at night, struck by a fatal illness, and his body instantly putrefied with so great a stench and horror that no one dared approach him, and at the touch of the hands the flesh slid in pieces from his bones. The hired gravediggers eventually carried his miserable corpse to the grave; affirming that if they had known the depth of the so powerful stench in the body, even if they had doubled their price, they would have scarcely laid hands on it.

A short while after these events, a certain learned member of the Order of Friars Minor [Franciscans], who was traveling toward Stolpa to visit his friends, acquired the aforesaid lord Walter as a traveling companion. When he had spoken of Saint Bridget and her divine revelations along the splendid journey, the learned man, not upholding sound doctrine, said: "Cease talking about that old woman, and her frivolous superstitions and new heresies." When they had entered Stolpa he took a bath and then enjoyed a memorable feast with his friends. Going to bed upstairs, he was cast down by a divine blow, and expired forthwith.

A certain highly learned member of the Order of Preachers was inflamed against the revelations of Saint Bridget, to the point where he openly said they ought to be burned, and called the people of her cult "lulardos" [Lollards] and "beguttas" [Beguines]. Another master of the secular clergy offered Saint Bridget's books of celestial revelation to him, so that by reading them he might be changed for the better. But this healthy advice having been spurned, he added: "I fear that the Lord Jesus will avenge himself and his saint on you by means of divine vengeance, since you have so pertinaciously fought against this saint." And when they separated, immediately the hand of the Lord took violent action against this man, and his body was infected more and more by so great a leprosy that no convent of his brothers dared to eat, drink, or converse with him, or offer him any aid. For as long as he should travel the road of universal flesh, let God look kindly upon him. How perilous it is to disparage Saint Bridget, or through audacious boldness to go against the revelations made to her, is made clear by the above. Verses 90 and 92 of chapter six of the Book of Revelations show how divine justice vigorously avenges pride by these doings. Let God, the triune and the one, protect us from pride.

## 110. SAINT CATHERINE OF SIENA AS PEACEMAKER

*Catherine, born around 1347, was the twenty-third of twenty-five children in the family of a Sienese dyer. At age sixteen, she joined the Dominican Order of Penance (later known as the Third Order) and lived at home in seclusion for three years until she had*

*a vision that told her to devote herself to caring for the poor and sick and converting*
*sinners. She is known to have acted as a mediator between warring factions in and*
*around Siena, as well as in the conflict between Florence and the Holy See, before her*
*death in 1380, indicating she had a remarkable amount of influence for a woman of her*
*time. This* Life *was written by Raymond of Capua in 1380.*

Source: trans. George Lamb, *The Life of St. Catherine of Siena* (New York: P. J. Kennedy and
Sons, 1960), pp. 212–15.

There was living in Siena a certain Nanni di Ser Vanni, a man well known
in worldly circles and so artful that he would have tricked God himself if he
could. He suffered from one of the city's worst characteristics; he was quite
incapable of keeping the peace with anyone and was always starting private
feuds – setting traps for people and then pretending to know nothing about
it. Someone had been killed in one of these feuds and the guilty parties were
keeping a wary eye on Nanni, for they knew how cunning he was. They had
tried several times to get people to get him to make his peace with them, but
Nanni's only response was to say that he never even thought of such things
and that he was a man of peace; but he was the real obstacle to peace because
he wanted to take his revenge when he felt like it.

When Catherine heard of this, she tried to get him to herself to talk to
and so bring this unfortunate affair to an end, but Nanni avoided her as the
snake avoids the charmer. In the end a holy man, a certain Friar William of
England, of the Order of the Hermits of Saint Augustine, spoke to him, and
got him to promise to go and see the virgin and listen to what she had to say;
but he would not promise to do anything she told him. However, he kept his
word and went to Catherine's house when I happened to be there, but he did
not find her at home because she was out doing good to other souls.

While I was waiting for her, someone came and told me that Nanni was
at the door wanting to speak to Catherine. I was glad to hear this, knowing
how much the holy virgin wanted to see him, and I hurried down to tell
him that the virgin was out and asked him to come in and wait for her. To
encourage him I took him into her own austere little room; but it was not
long before he began to grow impatient and said, "I promised Friar William
to come here and listen to this lady, but seeing [as] she's out and I'm a busy
man I can't waste any more time. Please make my apologies to her and tell
her that I have a lot of other things to attend to."

Seeing this and sad at the virgin's absence, I began to talk to him about the
peace mentioned above, but he at once broke in. "See here," he said, "you are
a priest and a friar, and this religious woman is supposed to be a great saint, so
I mustn't tell lies to you and I will tell you the whole truth; but don't imagine

that that means that I have any intention of doing what you want me to do. It is true, I do stay in the background and disturb the peace now and again, and it is true that in this case the whole thing would die down if I wanted it to; but that is not my idea at all, and it is no use preaching to me about it because I shall never agree with you, never. Let it be enough for you that I have told you what I have never told to another living soul, and don't bother me again!" I tried to answer him but he would not listen to a word I said.

At that moment God willed that the virgin should return home from doing good. The sight of her took Nanni aback and I was filled with joy. She greeted this man of the world with heavenly charity, then sat down and asked him why he had come. Nanni repeated word for word what he had said to me, insisting that he had no intention of mending his ways. Then the holy virgin began to point out the mortal peril he was in, and gradually she went after him, using words now biting, now sweet; but like a deaf adder he kept the ears of his heart tight shut against her. Realizing this, the virgin began to pray silently to herself and to ask for divine aid.

I saw what she was doing and turned to him, and, hoping for help from heaven, I began to talk, and by so doing kept him from going away. After a short while he said, "I don't want to be such a villain as to refuse you anything. I must go. I have four feuds; as to one of them [here he gave details], you can do what you like about it." Having said this he got up and made to go, but as he did so he exclaimed, "My God, how contented I feel in my soul from having said I shall make peace!" And he went on, "Lord God, what power is this that draws and holds me? I cannot go away and I cannot say no. Who has taken my liberty from me? What is it stopping me?" And with this he burst into tears. "I own myself beaten," he said, "I cannot breathe." He fell on his knees and said, weeping, "Most holy virgin, I will do as you say, not only as regards the enemy I told you about but with all the others too. I realize that the Devil has held me enchained; now I want to do anything you suggest. Tell me how I can save my soul from the Devil's clutches."

At these words the holy virgin, who had gone into ecstasy while she was praying, returned to her senses, thanked the Lord, and said, "O beloved brother, have you at last by the grace of God realized the mortal peril you are in? I talked to you, and you would not pay any attention; I spoke to the Lord, and he at once heard my prayer. So do penance for your sins, if you do not want to run into some new tribulation." To cut a long story short, Nanni with great grief confessed all his sins to me; through the virgin he was reconciled with all his enemies, and, following my advice, he was also reconciled with the most high whom he had for so long offended.

A few days after Nanni had confessed, he was arrested by the Sienese authorities and put in prison. Finally a rumor spread that he was to be beheaded.

When this news came to my ears I went in a state of great perturbation to Catherine and said to her, "Do you see? When this man was serving the Devil everything went well for him; now that he has returned to God, heaven and earth turn against him. Mother, I am afraid that this tender young shoot may be uprooted by this tempest and end up in desperation. Pray to the Lord for him! Protect him by your prayers during the time of his adversity, as with your prayers you saved him from the Devil!"

She answered, "Why are you getting so upset about him, when you should be pleased? If the Lord afflicts him with temporal punishments, you can be sure that he has forgiven him his eternal ones. According to the Savior, the world first loved its own, but when he went out from the world, the world began to hate him. At first the Lord had destined this man for eternal punishment, but now in his mercy he has changed this into temporal punishment. Do not be afraid that he will give way to despair: he who saved him from the Devil will free him from prison too."

And it happened as she said. As a matter of fact Nanni was released from prison within a few days, though he had to suffer considerable loss of temporal goods. But the virgin was delighted about this, for she said, "The Lord has cleansed him of the poison that was infecting him."

Subsequently he was subjected to illnesses, and his devotion increased. By public deed he made a gift to the holy virgin of a magnificent castle of his about two miles out from Siena, so that she could use it as a women's convent. Under special license from Pope Gregory XI of holy memory, granted when I and all her other sons and daughters were present, she began to build a wall round it and turn it into a convent, calling it "Holy Mary, Queen of the Angels." The Supreme Pontiff's representative there was Friar Giovanni of the order of Saint William of the monastery of St. Antimo, which I believe lies in the diocese of Chiusi.

The transformation of this man's way of life was made by the most high through Catherine, as I hereby testify. I was Nanni's confessor for a long time and I know that at least during the time of our acquaintance he did all he could to amend his life.

## III. VENGEANCE AND PEACE IN THE *LIFE OF COLA DI RIENZO*

*Cola di Rienzo (Nicola, son of Lorenzo) was born in Rome around 1313 and died in 1354. His political activity is said to have been driven by a desire to avenge the death of a younger brother who was accidentally killed in the streets of Rome when he got caught up in a battle between the warring Colonna and Orsini factions. Cola did seek to restore Rome to order, but never himself mentioned this incident. In 1347, he effected a revolution: he addressed the people of Rome, was accepted as tribune (in ancient Rome the ruler who represented the people), and published a series of laws. Although his authority was accepted by all classes, not just those who, like him, came from a humble background, he made enemies with the emperor and the pope when he attempted to unify Italy, with Rome as the capital. Although he defeated the forces authorized by the pope to take him into custody, he abdicated at the end of 1347 and lived in a monastery until 1350. By 1354 he had regained power in Rome, but lost it very quickly by ordering a number of executions that were seen by the Romans as arbitrary. He was, subsequently, killed by a mob. This extract is from chapter nine of the* Life.

Source: trans. John Wright, *The Life of Cola di Rienzo* (Toronto: Pontifical Institute of Medi-aeval Studies, 1975), p. 46–47.

For these things the tribune established the House of Justice and Peace and set up in it the banner of Saint Paul, on which the naked sword and the palm of victory were depicted, and assigned to it the most just plebeians, who were in charge of peace, the good men who were the peacemakers. This was the procedure followed there: two enemies came in and gave guarantees of making peace; then, when the nature of the injury had been established, the man who had done it suffered just what he had done to the victim. Then they kissed each other on the mouth, and the offended man gave complete peace. A man had blinded another in one eye; he came and was led up the steps of the Campidoglio and knelt there. The man who had been deprived of an eye came; the malefactor wept and prayed in God's name that he pardon him. Then he stretched out his face for him to draw out his eye, if he wanted to. The second man did not blind him, but was moved by pity; he forgave him his injury. Civil suits were likewise settled promptly.

At this time a horrible fear entered the minds of robbers, murderers, male-factors, adulterers, and every person of evil repute. Every infamous person left the city surreptitiously, and the criminals fled secretly; they were afraid that they would be seized in their own houses and dragged off to punish-ment. So the guilty ones fled beyond the boundaries of the Roman coun-tryside. They looked to no one for protection; they left their houses, fields, vineyards, wives, and children. Then the forests began to flourish because no robbers were found in them. Then the oxen began to plough; the pilgrims began to seek out the sanctuaries; the merchants began to travel and go about their business.

## 112. DINO COMPAGNI ON THE FLORENTINE FACTIONS

*Dino Compagni (ca 1260–1324) was a successful Florentine merchant, six times consul of the silk guild, and a leader in establishing the Priors of the Guilds, the leaders of Florence under the Guelfs. The Guelf party was the Italian political faction usually associated with the papal cause; their enemies, as seen in previous documents, were the Ghibellines, who were linked to the imperial cause. By 1300, the Guelf party itself, victorious in battle over their Ghibelline rivals, had split into two smaller parties, the Blacks, who remained associated with papal interests, and the Whites, who opposed papal influence. In 1293, Compagni served as the city's standard-bearer of justice, in which he became the official responsible for enforcing city laws. Just two years later, however, he experienced five years without any involvement in politics when his friend Giano della Bella was exiled. Della Bella had been blamed for inciting a popular riot when he did not prevent people from killing a man believed to be guilty, but allowed him to go free. In 1300, Compagni returned to public life first as advisor to the guild priors and then as a guild prior again.*

*Compagni began to write his* Chronicle of Florence, *which covers the history of Florence from 1280 to 1312, after 1310, when it began to appear that his party, the White Guelfs, was going to return to power. Compagni believed that Henry of Luxembourg, the new Holy Roman Emperor, would bring peace as well as punish citizens of Florence for their sins. This extract is from the beginning of Book 2 and describes events that took place in 1301.*

Source: trans. Daniel E. Bornstein, *Dino Compagni's Chronicle of Florence* (Philadelphia: University of Pennsylvania Press, 1974), pp. 33–36.

### [Book 2, chs. 1–5]

1. Arise, wicked citizens full of discord: grab sword and torch with your own hands and spread your wicked deeds. Unveil your iniquitous desires and your worst intentions. Why delay any longer? Go and reduce to ruins the beauties of your city. Spill the blood of your brothers, strip yourselves of faith and love, deny one another aid and support. Sow your lies, which will fill the granaries of your children. Do as did Sulla in the city of Rome. Yet all the evils that Sulla achieved in ten years, Marius avenged in a few days: do you believe that God's justice has faltered since then? Even the justice of this world demands an eye for an eye. Look at your ancestors: did they win merit through discord? Yet now you sell the honors which they acquired. Do not delay, wretches: more is consumed in one day of war than is gained in many years of peace, and a small spark can destroy a great realm.

2. The citizens of Florence, divided like this [into Black and White Guelfs], began to slander one another throughout the neighboring cities and in Pope Boniface's court at Rome, spreading false information. And words falsely spoken did more damage to Florence than the points of swords. They worked on the pope, telling him that the city would return to the hands of the Ghibellines and become a bastion for the Colonna [one of the most powerful families in Rome and enemies of Pope Boniface], and they reinforced these lies with a great deal of money. The pope was persuaded to break the power of the Florentines, and so he promised to aid the Black Guelfs with the great power of Charles of Valois, of the royal house of France, who had set out from France to oppose Frederick of Aragon in Sicily. The pope wrote that he wanted messer Charles to make peace in Tuscany, opposing those who had rebelled against the Church. This commission of peacemaker had a very good name, but its purpose was just the opposite, for the pope's aim was to bring down the Whites and raise up the Blacks, and make the Whites enemies of the royal house of France and of the Church.

3. Since messer Charles had already arrived at Bologna, the Blacks of Florence sent ambassadors to deliver this message: "My lord, have mercy for God's sake. We are the Guelfs of Florence, faithful servants of the king of France. For God's sake, look out for yourself and your men, for our city is ruled by Ghibellines."

After the ambassadors of the Blacks had left, the Whites arrived with the greatest reverence and gave messer Charles many gifts, as if he were their lord. But the malicious words carried more weight with messer Charles than the true ones, for to him saying "watch where you're going" seemed a greater sign of friendship than did gifts. He was advised to come by way of Pistoia, so that he might fall out with the Pistoiese. The Pistoiese wondered why he should take that route, and out of fear they guarded the city gates with hidden weapons and men. Then the sowers of discord said to messer Charles: "My lord, do not enter Pistoia, for they will take you prisoner. They have armed the city secretly, and they are very bold men and enemies of the house of France." And they filled him with such fear that he bypassed Pistoia and followed a little rivulet, thus displaying his hostility to the city. And this fulfilled the prophecy of an ancient peasant, who long ago had said: "From the west along the Ombroncello will come a lord who will do great things. Because of his coming, beasts of burden will walk on the peaks of Pistoia's towers."

4. Without entering Florence, messer Charles traveled on to the papal court in Rome. There he was greatly aroused and many suspicions were planted in his mind. This lord did not understand the Tuscans or their malice. Messer Muciatto Franzesi, a very wicked knight, small in stature but great in spirit, knew full well the malice behind the words said to his lord;

but because he too was corrupt he confirmed everything that was said by the sowers of discord who surrounded messer Charles every day.

The White Guelfs had ambassadors at the papal court of Rome together with the Sienese, but they were not sound men. Some of them were actually harmful: one such person was messer Ubaldino Malavolti, a Sienese jurist and a man full of cavilings, who stopped on the journey to demand the return of certain jurisdictions belonging to a castle which the Florentines held, saying that they pertained to him. And he so delayed the journey of his companions that they did not arrive in time.

When the ambassadors did arrive in Rome, the pope received them privately in his chambers and said to them in secret: "Why are you so obstinate? Humble yourselves to me. I can truthfully say that I have no intention other than to make peace among you. Let two of you return home, and they shall have my blessing if they see to it that my will is obeyed."

5. At that time new *signori* were elected in Florence, more or less unanimously by both parties. They were good men who were not suspect and the *popolo minuto* placed great hope in them. So too did the White Party, because the new *signori* were free of arrogance and supporters of unity and they wished to apportion the offices fairly, saying: "This is the final remedy."

Their enemies also took hope from them, for they knew the new signori to be weak and peace-loving men, and believed they could easily delude them with the semblance of peace.

These *signori* who took office on October 15, 1301 were: *Dino lists seven names, including himself and the Standard-bearer of Justice.* When their names were drawn, they went to Santa Croce, for their predecessors' turn in office was not finished. The Black Guelfs immediately arranged to go visit them in groups of four or six at a time. They said: "Lords, you are good men and our city needs such men. You can see the discord of your fellow citizens: it is up to you to pacify them, or the city will perish. You are the ones who have the authority; and to help you exercise it we offer you our goods and persons, in good and loyal spirit." I, Dino, replied by commission of my companions, and said: "Dear and faithful citizens, we willingly accept your offers and would like to begin to put them to use. We ask you to counsel us and set your minds to it, so that our city can be calmed." And so we wasted time, since we did not dare to shut the doors and stop listening to these citizens – even though we distrusted such false promises and thought that they were cloaking their malice with lying words.

We sought to make peace with them when we should have been sharpening our swords. And we began with the captains of the Guelf Party, messer Manetto Scali and messer Neri Giandonati, saying to them: "Honorable captains, put everything else aside. Leave it, and work only to bring peace to the party of the Church, and we will put our office entirely at your disposal in any way you desire."

The captains left very happy and in good spirits, and they began to persuade men and speak compassionate words. The Blacks, hearing this, at once called this malice and treason and they began to flee from these words.

Messer Manetto Scali was so courageous that he tried to arrange peace between the Cerchi and the Spini; and this was held to be treason. The people who sided with the Cerchi became timid because of this: "We do not need to trouble ourselves since peace is coming." And all the while their enemies planned to bring their malice to fruition. No preparation was made for battle, since for many reasons the Whites could think of nothing but achieving concord. The first reason was love of the Guelf Party and unwillingness to share the offices of the city with the Ghibellines. The second reason was that even though there was nothing but discord, the injuries were not yet so widespread that concord could not be restored if they shared the offices evenly [between the Guelf factions]. But the Blacks thought that those who had made enemies could not escape vengeance unless the Cerchi and their followers were destroyed; and the Cerchi power was so great that they could hardly do this without destroying the city.

## 113. TRIAL BY COMBAT IN FROISSART'S *CHRONICLES*

*Jean Froissart (ca 1335–1404) was a native of Valenciennes, in France, who moved between England and the continent. His famous chronicle, which covers the years 1325 to 1401, is one of the most vivid extant accounts of the Hundred Years' War between France and England, and documents with care the culture and behavior of the military aristocracy of the age. The parts up to 1361 were drawn from a similar work by Jean le Bel; the remainder of the chronicle was based largely upon eyewitness accounts. This excerpt describes a trial by combat (see also Docs. 53, 87, and 93b), which may be seen as a kind of highly stylized feud contained within a formal legal setting.*

Source: trans. Thomas Johnes, *The Chronicles of England, France, Spain, Etc. by Sir John Froissart* (New York: E.P. Dutton, 1906), pp. 364–67.

About this time there was much said in France respecting a duel which was to be fought at Paris, for life or death. I will relate the cause of the duel as I was informed respecting it. It chanced that Sir John de Carogne, a knight of the household of Peter, Count d'Alençon, took it into his head that he should gain glory if he went on a voyage to the Holy Land; he therefore took leave of his lord and of his wife, who was then a young and handsome lady, and whom he left in his castle of Argenteuil, on the borders of Perche. The lady remained with her household in the castle, living for some time most respectably. Now it happened (this is the matter of quarrel) that the devil entered into the body of James le Gris, also a squire of the household of the Count d'Alençon, and induced him to commit a crime, for which he afterwards paid dearly. He cast his thoughts on the lady of Sir John de Carogne, and one day paid her a visit at her castle. The servants made a most handsome entertainment for him, and the lady, thinking no evil, received him with pleasure, led him to her apartment, and showed him many of her works; James, fully intent upon accomplishing his wicked design, begged the lady to conduct him to the dungeon, as his visit was partly to examine it. She instantly complied, and as she had the fullest confidence in his honor, took none of her attendants with her. As soon as they had entered this alone, James fastened the door, and when he had succeeded in his brutal purpose, he made his escape from the castle, leaving the lady bathed in tears. She determined to say nothing of what had happened to those in the castle, but to await her husband's return.

At length the Lord de Carogne came back from his journey, and was joyfully received by his lady and household. When night came Sir John went to bed, but his lady excused herself; and on his kindly pressing her to come to him, she walked pensively up and down the chamber; and at last, throwing herself on her knees at the bedside of her husband, bitterly bewailed the insult she had suffered. The Lord de Carogne would not for some time believe it, but she urged it so strongly, that he said, "Certainly, lady, if the matter has passed as you say, I forgive you; but the squire shall die."

On the morrow Sir John sent messengers with letters to his friends, and the nearest relatives of his wife, desiring them to come instantly to Argenteuil; on their arrival the lady related most minutely everything that had taken place during her husband's absence, and it was agreed that the Count d'Alençon should be informed of it. The count, who loved much James le Gris, was not inclined to believe what the lady had said. James boldly denied the charge, and by means of the household of the count, proved that he had been seen in the castle at four o'clock in the morning; the count said that he was in his bed-chamber at nine o'clock, and he argued that it was quite impossible for any one to have ridden twenty-three leagues and back again, and do what he was charged with, in four hours and a half. He said the lady must have dreamed it, and commanded that henceforth all should be buried in oblivion, and that under pain of incurring his displeasure, nothing further should be done in the business. Sir John being a man of courage, and having full confidence in his wife, would not submit to this, but appealed to the parliament at Paris. James le Gris was summoned, the cause lasted upwards of a year, and could not in any way be compromised. The count conceived a great hatred against the Lord de Carogne, and would have had him put to death if he had not placed himself under the protection of the parliament. As no other evidence could be produced against James le Gris than the lady herself, the parliament at last judged that the matter should be decided in the tilt-yard, by a duel for life or death. The knight, the squire, and the lady, were instantly put under arrest, until the day of the mortal combat, which by order of parliament was fixed for the ensuing Monday. On hearing of this duel the king declared he would be present at it, and the dukes of Berry, Burgundy, Bourbon, and the constable of France, expressed their wish to be there; it was therefore agreed that the day should be deferred.

The king kept the feast of the Calends at Arras, and on his return to Paris shortly after, lists were made for the champions in the place of Saint Catherine, behind the Temple; and in order to have a good view of the combat, the lords had scaffolds erected for them on one side. The crowd of people was truly wonderful. The two champions entered the lists armed at all points, and each was seated in a chair opposite the other. The count de St. Pol directed Sir John de Carogne, and the retainers of the Count d'Alençon, James le Gris. On the knight entering the field he went to his lady, who was covered with black, and seated on a chair, and said to her, "Lady, from your accusation, and in your quarrel, I am thus adventuring my life to combat James le Gris; you know whether my cause be loyal and true." "My lord," she replied, "it is so; you may fight securely, for your cause is good." The lady remained seated, making fervent prayers to God and the Virgin, entreating that she might gain the victory according to her right. Her affliction was great, for her life depended on the event: should her husband lose the victory she would be burnt and he would be hanged. I know not whether she ever repented having pushed matters to such peril; however, it was now too late, she must abide the event.

The two champions then advanced opposite each other, when they mounted their horses, and made a handsome appearance, for they were both expert men-at-arms. Their first course was run without harm to either. After the tilting they dismounted, and made ready to continue the fight. They behaved with great courage. At the first onset Sir John de Carogne was slightly wounded in the thigh, notwithstanding which he fought so desperately that he struck his adversary down, and thrusting his sword through his body, caused instant death. Upon this he demanded of the spectators, whether he had done his duty; when all replied that he had. The body of James le Gris was delivered to the hangman, who dragged it to Montfaucon, and hanged it there. Sir John approached the king and fell on his knees; the king made him rise, and ordered 1,000 francs to be paid him immediately; he also retained him in his household, with a pension of 200 livres a year, which he received as long as he lived. Sir John, after thanking the king and his lords, went up to his lady and kissed her; after which they went together to make their offerings in the church of Notre-Dame, and then returned home.

## 114. *THE VENGEANCE OF OUR LORD*

*In the early Middle Ages, there were countless stories of God and his saints avenging themselves against those who had done them wrong. These stories include tales of vengeance taken against Jews for violence done to Christians. Gregory of Tours, for example, told the story of a Jewish boy whose father threw him in a furnace as punishment for taking communion; the boy was protected from the fire by Mary and Jesus. As this story was retold into the late Middle Ages, the miracle took on a darker tone as the father came to be thrown into the furnace himself, in retribution. The twelfth century also gave rise to the* Miracles *of William of Norwich, which recounted the martyrdom of a young boy at the hands of Jews and the vengeance that the saint then took against them.*

*The theme of vengeance taken by Christians against the Jews for their part in the crucifixion of Jesus had been a common theme in Europe since the eleventh century. A major version of this theme can be found in an immensely popular text, "The Vengeance of Our Lord," which took the form of both epics and plays and appeared in Old English, French, Latin, and other languages. The Latin version first appeared in a ninth-century manuscript that originated at St. Omer, in France. The story was carried to England in the eleventh century, where it formed the basis for an Old English translation. A fifteenth-century mystery play based on the theme of God's vengeance on the Jews was one of the most popular of its genre. The version of the story excerpted here, originally written in French, tells the story of how the Roman emperor Vespasian, after being miraculously cured by Saint Veronica's kerchief, wanted to convert to Christianity. To illustrate his commitment to his new faith, Vespasian brought about the destruction of Jerusalem and the killing or enslavement of its Jewish population by way of vengeance for Christ's death. The story was set down in the late fourteenth century and was shaped by some of the preoccupations of that period, notably worries about famine. The theme of the story suggests how vengeance directed against enemies, imagined or real, could serve as a political device for binding a people together.*

Source: ed. Alvin E. Ford, *La Vengeance de Nostre-Seigneur: The Old and Middle French Prose Versions. The Version of Japheth* (Toronto: Pontifical Institute of Mediaeval Studies, 1984), pp. 68–72, 83–86, 91–98, 133–36, 158–87, 194–202. Trans. Kathleen M. M. Smail.

## a. Vespasian seeks a cure for leprosy

13. At the time when Gaius, the seneschal, arrived [in Rome], the emperor had sent for the princes of his country and of his empire, and he had kings, dukes, princes, counts, viscounts, barons and knights. And thus all the nobility of his sea and empire was there. And they came for the reason that the emperor wanted to crown Titus, his son, because he himself was so disfigured and so agitated because he could no longer govern his empire, so it occurred to him that he ought to crown his son the following day. And then the seneschal came before the emperor all happy and greeted him and the emperor greeted him back. And without delay the emperor asked him if he had found any thing by which he might be healed. And Gaius said to him: "Sire, make yourself happy and prepare a feast and give thanks to God, for I have found a holy woman who has the face of the Holy Prophet on a woven cloth, by which she was immediately healed of what she had. And she too was all leprous. And Sire, if you but believe in Jesus Christ and adore him as the true and all powerful God that he is, and if you should put all your faith in him, you will be healed just as soon. But if you do not believe in him, you cannot be healed but will languish all your days." Then the emperor said: "I well believe what you are telling me. And if it pleases Jesus Christ to do as much for me, from his grace, I will avenge his death if he should deign to give me health. Now, have this woman come to me and tell her to bring this cloth in as dignified a way as is appropriate." "Sire," said the seneschal, "tomorrow when all the barony is assembled, I will have the woman come before you, in the presence of all, so that they may see the miracle and believe in Jesus Christ. And then you can crown your son." And the emperor said that it was well said and that it was pleasing to him and that it would be done to God's pleasure.

*After being healed, Vespasian crowned his son Titus. He tried to reward Veronica, but she refused everything, and offered the reward to Clement, a disciple of Jesus, to take whatever he wished on her behalf.*

19. And Clement said to him: "I want nothing from you other than that you be baptized and have your people baptized and believe in the faith of Jesus Christ who did so much for you out of mercy, for you know well that he is God the all powerful."

20. And then the emperor said to him: "Friend, I want you to be the apostle [successor to Saint Peter] and head of all Christianity and I want you to preach and have preached through all my land the holy faith of Jesus

Christ. And every person who wishes to convert, it will please me well, but know that I will not myself be baptized until I have avenged the death of the Holy Prophet. And I promise you that immediately upon my return, if it pleases God that I return, I will be baptized and have all my people baptized. And thus I will go off in a short while to Jerusalem to avenge the death of Jesus Christ because he met his death wrongly and without cause." Then the emperor elevated Clement and made him an apostle and had a church built, with an altar, founded for Saint Simeon [St. Peter's in Rome]. On the altar he put the woven cloth of Veronica on two rods where the face of Jesus Christ was. And in this church he arranged for a font for baptizing all those who would want baptism, and the holy Clement baptized Veronica without mentioning her name. And then he preached to the people many times near Neron [a part of Rome]. And many were baptized because of his sermons.

### b. Jaffet, a friendly Jew, joins Vespasian

*Vespasian gathers men and supplies and sails to Acre, and the people hand the city over to the emperor.*

23. And when the emperor, Titus, and all their contingent were refreshed in that place, they went and lay siege to a castle between Acre and Jerusalem which is called Caffe [Jaffa or Haifa]. When the Jews of the castle saw so many people encamped around their castle, they were ready to surrender willingly if the emperor would have mercy on them. And when the [besieging] hosts were in their tents, our Lord sent such a great snow and such great wind that one could barely keep oneself in the camp. The castle was well constructed and well outfitted because [of the way in which] the lord of the castle, a holy man and a good Jewish knight, had had it built. He had been born in Nazareth and was also a first cousin of the noble Joseph who put Jesus Christ in the sepulcher, and he was named Jaffet of Caffe. His advice was to go to the emperor seeking mercy, but the emperor refused to grant them mercy. After a short while the emperor seized the castle and had all the Jews killed except for Jaffet, who hid himself for three days with a group of men, nine in all, in a grotto that he had below the surface. When they realized that they were just about to die of hunger, they arranged it so that between them, they would kill one another with knives so that they would die there. They all did it thus except for Jaffet and one of his cousins who had refused to agree to this. When the seven Jews were dead, Jaffet said to his cousin: "I was lord of this castle and thus I was esteemed a most holy man. Cousin, it would be great madness were we to die here. Let us instead leave here because we cannot survive and so let us go boldly to the emperor and

plead for mercy from him, and if we make ourselves known he will not kill us when he learns who I am.

24. Then the emperor had the castle knocked down and the trenches filled. Jaffet and his cousin left the place where they had been and went along to the emperor and knelt before him. And Jaffet said to the emperor: "Sire, I was lord of this castle that you have knocked down and I heard that you have come to avenge the death of Jesus Christ who was wrongly made to suffer in Jerusalem. And also I have heard it said that you come to destroy Jerusalem because she [the city] consented [to Christ's suffering]. Sire, know that this Holy Prophet was very much my friend, so much so that a cousin of mine, who is named Joseph of Arimathea, took him down from the cross and put him in his tomb. And know, Sire, that if you want to take Jerusalem, we will be of good service to you and give good counsel also, because [the city] will be hard to take. So we beg, Sire, that you have mercy on us, and if it be pleasing to God, we will give you good and loyal counsel." Then the emperor took mercy on them and they begged that someone give them something to eat. And then they told how they had been hidden in the grotto. And when they had eaten, the emperor had them come before him and asked if they believed in the Holy Prophet. And they told him yes. And then the emperor said to them: "I want you to be a part of my private council from now on."

25. Then Vespasian and Titus, his son, were advised to go ahead to Jerusalem with all their forces. And then it came about as Saint Luke the evangelist recounts, who says that when Jesus Christ drew near to Jerusalem, he cried over her and said: "O city, if you knew what would become of you, you would cry, for you know not the days of your visitation, for you will be besieged and attacked on all sides, and not one stone will be left atop another. And the sons who are with you will be destroyed" [Luke 19:42–44].

### c. A battle miracle

*The army comes to Jerusalem and Vespasian demands surrender from Pilate, the governor. On the advice of Archelan, son of Herod, Pilate refuses and battle is joined.*

42. When they had come to where the hosts of Pilate were, it was about nine in the morning, and Pilate's forces were not yet all out of Jerusalem. When they were all out and the battle was joined, they [the two sides] came together and struck one another with such a great force of lances on shields and other armor that three thousand of Pilate's troops and eight hundred of the emperor's men died in the first onslaught. And so the battle carried on until about three in the afternoon. Then when the first engagement was completed, they drew apart to rest. After they had rested sufficiently, they returned

to the field and began to strike one another so harshly that at the end, three thousand and seven hundred of Pilate's men and twelve hundred on the side of the emperor were dead. And the battle continued until sundown.

43. Then our Lord, who wanted his death to be avenged, did a great miracle, for when the men from the two hosts thought that the sun had set, they began to leave the field. And the sun, by the will of God, came back in the east and rose as if it were morning and the night had passed. And so it was plain day until the setting of the sun. And in this way, there was no night between the two days.

44. And when the emperor and Titus, his son, had seen the miracle, they were full of great joy and thought that God did not wish them to leave the field just yet. And so they returned and began to strike Pilate and his troops and Pilate struck them. And the battle continued until noon. And there died on the side of Pilate twelve hundred and fifty and on the side of the emperor one thousand and fifty.

### d. Pilate seeks mercy

*Pilate and Archelan retreat to Jerusalem, along with Joseph of Arimathea, and Vespasian's army besieges the city, digging trenches around the walls so that no one can escape. The inhabitants consume all their food and are then forced to eat grass. Trapped in the city are the wife of the king of Africa and her daughter along with a companion and her son. All are Christian. When the two children die of hunger, the queen and her companion cook and eat the bodies, fulfilling a prophesy. Pilate realizes that he can no longer avoid surrender.*

56. And then Pilate declared that what he had decreed before should be undertaken, and he and the king Archelan armed themselves with five thousand knights and went off to the trenches where the emperor was. And they demanded to speak to him in confidence. And immediately the emperor, with his son, Titus, and Jacob and Jaffet and ten thousand knights, came to where Pilate was. And once he had come, Pilate began to speak to him and said: "Sire, emperor, have pity on me and on all your people, please. And so take the city and treasure, whatever there is, and let us go into exile in foreign lands throughout the world." Then the emperor responded and said: "If you want to surrender the city to me and if you and all those within will do my bidding, I will willingly take you. But otherwise no, for I will have mercy for no one as you had none for Jesus Christ." And then the king Archelan said to the emperor: "Sire, I am the son of King Herod, your friend, who was king of Galilee, and then after his death I was king. So I beg that it be pleasing to you to have mercy on me, for neither my father nor I ever did anything

against your father or against you, nor did we consent to the death of Jesus Christ. And so I say to you that my father was of your father's court." Then the emperor responded to Archelan and said to him: "Are you then the son of Herod who caused the persecution of children in his desire to kill Jesus Christ, the prophet, in his childhood? He who shows no mercy should find no mercy. Your father wanted to kill Jesus Christ, the prophet, when he was born, and thus had all the children he could find who were up to two years of age killed so that he could kill Jesus Christ without showing any mercy. And the number [of children] he had killed was 144,000. And for this I will not show any mercy toward you because you will pay for the iniquities of your ancestors." And when King Archelan heard this, he was so angry that he almost went mad. And he got off his horse and took off his armor. And when he was unarmed, he unsheathed his sword and said to the emperor: "Never does God the Great want you or any pagan to be able to avenge my death." And then he put the point of the sword to his chest and pushed so hard that he made the sword go through the body, a quarter of the way. And he immediately dropped dead into the trenches. And when Pilate and his men saw the king Archelan thus dead, they were most angry and went back into the city and recounted to the people the response of the emperor and the death of Archelan. And then Archelan's people and all the populace were in great mourning and tore their robes and pulled out their hair and made such a great keening that never since has such great mourning been carried on in any place.

57. And when the next morning came, Pilate had Joseph of Arimathea and his seneschal and all his people come and he said to them: "Lord, you see well that we can't hold out any longer and that God has forgotten us, for never was any city in such great tribulation as this one here, for you see that we have no provisions and so we will die of hunger. So I pray you to advise us on what to do." Then Joseph said: "We wouldn't know how to advise you since the emperor does not want to show you mercy. Whoever advised you to be his enemy gave you bad advice for you could have known that you wouldn't be able to resist him and that we can no longer hold out for long."

58. Then Pilate said: "I know not what we could do except to the extent that in this city there is great treasure of gold and silver and precious stones. And the emperor and his people want to have it all. I know how [to arrange it so that] they will not get any of it and won't make any profit from us. We will have it all ground up in a copper mortar so that we can eat it and thus continue to stay alive. And when the emperor takes this city, he won't find any treasure because we will get as much mercy from him without the treasure as with the treasure." When he had given this advice, they all said that it was well said. And each went away to his home, and whoever had gold or silver or precious stones did as Pilate had said. And those who had too much

gave to those who had little and on this treasure they lived for twenty-one days. When the treasure was eaten, all the populace came to Pilate and said to him: "Sire, we have done as you had said regarding the treasure, and now it is all used up. What can we do now?" Then Pilate was in great discomfort and began to cry in front of all and said to them: "Lords, you made me your lord and your governor in this city, but from now on I can no longer govern you. So I beg your pardon, by God, that if I ever did you any misdeed, that you might forgive me [for it]." And when the Jews heard him, they were most discomfited and there was not one who did not cry, and due to the great sorrow they felt, they could not answer him. But all were lamenting most loudly because they thought all of them would be destroyed.

59. Then Pilate said to them: "Lords, be of good heart and let us put everything in the will of God the Great and surrender to the emperor and to his mercy, for it is better than if we die thus of hunger. For every day that goes by well over four hundred of us die in this city. And by chance he may take us in his mercy or in pity and we won't be wasting away. Thus we won't die of hunger. After this, Pilate went out of the city with all his men and came to the trench that the emperor had had made. And Titus, the new emperor, went along, exercising with his knights in the area. And Pilate recognized him by his armor, signified by an eagle. And then he made him a sign with his glove that he wanted to speak to him. And when Titus saw him, he came over with his knights. And Pilate said to him: "Sire, Titus, Emperor, we beg you that it please you to pray to your father that he have mercy on us. And may it please you to take some pity on this people who entreat you tearfully. And may it please you not to consider our iniquities but instead your goodness and nobility." And when Titus heard this, he sent to his father by way of two knights. When he had heard the knights, he [Vespasian] sent for all his people and commanded that they arm themselves. And when they were all ready, he came to the trenches where his son was. Then Titus said to his father: "Sire, behold Pilate, who has agreed to surrender the city to you if you but have mercy on them." And the emperor said that the time for mercy has passed and he means to take the city by force. Then Vespasian said to Pilate: "If you want to surrender the city and all those who are with you to my will, I am all ready to do so. But I truly tell you that I will have as little mercy for you and the others as you and they had for Jesus Christ when you sentenced him to death and hung him on the cross. And I want you to know that his death will be avenged on you. And because he found no mercy from you, you won't have any from me." When Pilate heard the Emperor's response, he and all his people were most angry and they did not know what to do or say, but said to the emperor: "Sire, take the city and what you find there and us also, and do according to your will as the lord that you are."

## e. Revenge against the Jews

60. Then Vespasian had them fill the trenches that he had had made. And when they were full, he sent Titus, his son, and Jacob and Jaffet and ten thousand knights into the city and told them that they should close the gates of the city, so that no Jews could get out or burrow out. And then Titus entered the city with his people and took Pilate and handed him under guard to ten knights and ordered that he be well guarded. And then he had all the Jews that he found, men and women, taken and tied up. And by number they found in all 70,600 of them. And when all that was done, he commanded that the gates be opened. Then the emperor and all those who were guarding the gates and walls of the city so that no Jew could flee entered into the city and went straight to the temple of Solomon. And there they rendered thanks to Jesus Christ for the victory he had given them. And they stayed there and conducted themselves happily. And all manner of people could come there except for Jews. And they brought enough provisions from all over.

61. And when the emperor saw that he was holding so many Jews prisoner, he said to his people, "Lords, since Jesus Christ so honored us that he gave us victory over our enemy, I want to avenge his death and so I want all these Jews to be sold. And it is my wish that just as they purchased Jesus Christ for thirty silver coins (*deniers*), that one give thirty Jews for one silver coin." Then he proclaimed that every man who would like to purchase Jews come to those whom he had ordained for selling them, for one could have thirty for one silver coin. There were thirty-five men [in charge of] selling them. And because they were selling them, he gave one silver coin to each. And he gave them the choice to take the ones who pleased them most.

62. When the proclamation was made, a knight came to the emperor and said to him: "Sire, I want one silver coin's worth." The emperor had thirty [Jews] handed to him. And when the knight had his thirty Jews, and had paid his silver coin, he held his lance in his hand and came before the Jews he had purchased, and struck one of them through the body with the blade so far that it went right through. The Jew fell to the ground dead. In pulling the blade out of the wound of the Jew, out came a rivulet of gold and silver. The knight was most amazed. Then he took another Jew and said to him: "I want you to tell me, if you know why this Jew seems to bleed gold and silver." The Jew said to him: "Sire, if you will keep me from death, I will tell you what that means without lying." The knight assured him and the Jew told him the story of how Pilate had made them eat gold and silver, precious gems and all the treasure so that the emperor and his people would not find it and they wouldn't get rich from it, and also so that they could live on it, "for we lived twenty-one days when we didn't have anything else to eat." Presently this

news came to be known to the emperor's people. Immediately, each wanted to buy some of the Jews, and the emperor received a silver coin handed over by each one. And when Jacob and Jaffet saw that all the Jews were being sold and that those buying them were killing them for the treasure they had eaten, they came to the emperor and said to him: "Sire, among these Jews there must be some who were good friends of God. For Joseph of Arimathea should be there, the one who took the body of Jesus Christ down from the cross and put it in his sepulcher with Nicodemus. And there should also be a woman who was queen of Africa, and a daughter of hers, and a woman who was the queen's companion, and a son of the companion, all of whom believed strongly in Jesus Christ. So we beg you, Sire, that it please you to show them mercy, for know that they never consented to the death of Jesus Christ."

63. Then the emperor said to them: "See if you can find them. And if you find them, have them come before me." Then Jaffet and Jacob looked all over the area where the Jews were, but they found only Joseph of Arimathea. And then they went off to the house of the queen for they had often been inside [the house] sharing consolation with them [the women]. They found [the queen] dead and the companion also, and so they returned to the emperor with Joseph of Arimathea. The emperor asked them if he was the one who took the body of Jesus Christ from the cross, and they told him yes. And then the emperor pardoned him as he had done for Jaffet and Jacob.

64. When the emperor saw that the Jews were either dead or sold, he asked of those who had sold them how many silver coins [worth of Jews] were left. They said that there were still at least six silver coins left [that is, one hundred and eighty Jews]. And then the emperor told them not to sell any more for he was keeping his six silver coins [worth of Jews]. So there was done in Jerusalem such a great killing of Jews that one could not walk without stepping on the dead, there were so many. It was done because of the recommendation that Pilate gave when he advised them to eat their treasure. For if they [the Jews] had not eaten it, those who bought them would have pardoned a great many more and they would have escaped. But for the love of treasure they killed a total of 72,350 to get at the treasure within their bodies.

65. When the killing of the Jews was complete, the emperor had their bodies carried outside the walls. Then he had the entire city wall knocked down so that there was not one stone left atop another, nor were any stones left standing elsewhere in the city except for the temple of Solomon and the tower of Zion that was David's, for God did not want it so. And then was fulfilled that which God spoke from his own mouth the day of Palm Sunday when he cried over the city. But before the city was knocked down, Titus, the son of the emperor, went by all the houses and had all the arms and all the equipment

taken and many other things that the emperor won there. But he didn't find any treasure because the Jews had eaten it. Yet it was bad for them because they all died for it, except for the six coins worth of Jews that the emperor retained and Joseph of Arimathea and the one who revealed that the Jews had eaten the treasure, for those two were pardoned.

66. When the emperor and Titus, his son, had completed the task and were well rested and their people also, they told Jacob and Jaffet and Joseph of Arimathea to lead them to where Jesus Christ was put on the cross, and to the mount, and to the river Jordan, and to the place where he resuscitated the leper, and to all the places where Jesus Christ had done great miracles. And they led them there, and at each place, everyone cried while adoring Jesus Christ in great honor and very great reverence.

67. After this, the emperor and his son and his people were thinking of returning to their homeland of Romania [Rome], so they brought along Pilate and the six silver coins worth of Jews and came to Acre. There, Vespasian made ready three boats, and in each boat he put two coins worth of Jews without any provisions and without anyone to steer them. Using other boats he had them put out to sea and had the sails raised. There he let them go, by chance, to wherever the will of God would have it. And because God didn't want all the Jews to die and perish, but wanted some to remain on earth, to remember, God willed that one of the boats arrive in Narbonne and another in Bordeaux and the other in England. And the Jews who were in the boats thought that God had made it happen by a miracle and by having mercy on them. But God did it so that in all the latter days there would be remembrance of his suffering and death. Then, after the emperor and Titus, his son, had boats outfitted and had a great quantity of provisions put in them, they also embarked and their men with them, and also taking Jacob and Jaffet and Joseph of Arimathea. And God gave them such a good wind that within nine days they arrived at the port of Barletta. And so they came to Rome healthy and happy.

### f. Pilate's punishment

*Clement baptizes the emperor and his court.*

69. Then after one day in the morning, when the emperor and Titus, his son, had heard mass [said] by the bishop [Clement], they returned to the palace. There, Vespasian sent for the senators of Rome. And when they had come, he commanded them to judge Pilate according to his crimes. The senators wanted to know what the crimes were. And when he told them what they

were, they withdrew into council. When they had held their council, they came before the emperor and said to him: "Sire, we well understand that according to the crimes of Pilate he must die. But, Sire, your father, Julius Caesar, ordained that each man living outside of Rome at the time he committed a crime against the emperor should meet his death and be adjudged in Vienne [a town in France] by the executioner of Vienne. We judge that he be brought to Vienne and that he die in this way: first, that the executioner prepare a stake in the middle of the plaza of Vienne, three *toises* high [about six meters]. And on top of the stake there should be a large bar fastened across the stake which should be about two meters in length and strong enough to attach Pilate to. Pilate should be put on the stake and attached firmly to the bar, straight up and naked, and he should be anointed with honey and oil. And inscribed on the highest part of the bar should be: "This is Pilate who failed to acknowledge Jesus Christ and renounced the emperor, his lord." And his face should be in the sun. When he has stayed there from nine A.M. until sundown, he should be taken down and one of his ears cut off, and then put in prison. He should be given enough to eat so that he doesn't fail in prison, so that he can live twenty-one days in torment as he lived twenty-one days on the treasure that the Jews had eaten because of famine. The ear should be put where Pilate can see it when he is on the stake. Then the next day, he should be given plenty of dinner and then returned to the stake well oiled. Let him stay there until sundown. Then he is to be taken down and have the other ear cut off and put with the first and be given enough to eat. The third day likewise, and his virile member [penis] shall be cut off; the fourth day likewise, and one hand cut off; the fifth day likewise, and his other hand cut off; the sixth day likewise, and a flap of skin should taken from his side, as deep as the kidney; the seventh day likewise, and another flap taken from the back; the eighth day likewise, and the sole of one foot taken off; the ninth day likewise, and the other sole taken off; the tenth day, a cut made from the belly button to the bottom; the eleventh day, another cut made across the same place so that he wears the cross as he made Christ carry it; the twelfth day, one of his arms should be cut off at the elbow; the thirteenth day the other, the fourteenth day, one of his shoulders; the fifteenth day, the other shoulder; the sixteenth day, have his beard burnt; the seventeenth day, one of his feet cut off; the eighteenth day, the other; the nineteenth day, have his thighs broken as he had done to the two thieves that he hung with Jesus Christ; the twentieth day, the body [of Pilate] with all the parts [that were cut off] should be dragged and hung, and his tongue cut out and held outside his mouth; and on the twenty-first day, have his head cut off and make him bleed so that he suffers longer. And he is to be put on the stake in the plaza so that there is remembrance of this and he is to be burnt and his ashes thrown into the Rhone. See here how we judge him to die in a bad and horrible way because he was a traitor to God and to you, and because he made all his people die."

*They take Pilate to Vienne but Pilate is carried away by devils lest he undergo contrition and convert to Christianity during his execution.*

## 115. A MIRACLE OF THE BLESSED VIRGIN MARY

*Collections of miracles performed by the Virgin Mary circulated throughout the Middle Ages and were used primarily by preachers. This collection was written sometime between 1435 and 1440 by the Dominican friar John Herolt, also known as Discipulus. The miracle related below is one that operates on the "eye-for-an-eye" principle of vengeance. Based on the idea that killing a murderer's child can avenge a child's murder, the woman in the story threatens to take away Mary's child if she loses her own child.*

Source: trans. C. C. Swinton Bland, Johannes Herolt, *Miracles of the Blessed Virgin Mary* (London: George Routledge and Sons, 1928), pp. 32–33. Modernized by Kelly Gibson.

15. A certain worthy and devout woman paid great honor to the image of the Blessed Virgin, worshipping her with salutations, prayers, and bending of the knee. Now one day when she had sent her little girl into the nearest village and the child was playing out in the open country, a wolf carried her off to a wood as she played. Some men followed him with shouts, but returned without saving the girl. One of them ran to the castle and brought word to the mother as she sat at the table about how her daughter had been carried off, saying: "Lady, a wolf has devoured your daughter." She, being exceedingly agitated, said to him: "Surely a wolf cannot have devoured my daughter."

Soon, however, she rose from the table, and, in much bitterness of heart, entered the chapel and plucked the image of the Savior from the bosom of his Mother. Before her with many tears, the mother broke out into these words: "Never, Lady, shall you have your Son back again, unless you restore my daughter to me."

O wonderful kindness and condescension in the queen of heaven to seem to fear she would lose her Son, unless the woman got back her daughter! She gave the order and released the girl. After following the wolf's track, they found the girl walking around among some bushes, and saw the marks of the wolf's teeth in her throat. The marks were only on the surface of the skin, where they remain to this day as a testimony to that great miracle.

Then, when they had taken the child to her mother, she immediately rejoiced when she saw her [daughter] and ran to the image. Replacing the Child in her bosom, she said: "Because you restored my daughter to me, I restore your Son to you."

## 116. A VISION OF PEACEMAKING IN THE *MIRACLES OF SAINT ROSE OF VITERBO*

*The holy virgin Saint Rose was born around 1233, in Viterbo, Italy, to a family – possibly farmers – of modest status. She reputedly worked miracles and lived as a hermit as a young child. Stories of those miracles were collected after her death in 1252. The miracle below was recorded in the* Acts *for her canonization process in 1457.*

Source: *Miracula ex Processu Canonizationis, Acta Sanctorum Septembris,* vol. 2 (Paris and Rome: Victor Palmé, 1868), col. 466. Trans. Kelly Gibson.

A certain Marietto [son] of Silvestro Boccafusa was vulnerable to a certain Raffaele Santori of Viterbo because of long enmity. Marietto's mother was greatly concerned that he would kill her son Marietto under some artificial pretense. That night, his [Marietto's] mother, lady Nicola, dedicated herself to the blessed virgin Rose, whereupon, for a brief while, the aforementioned virgin Rose appeared to the mother while she was falling asleep, announcing to her as follows: "Be of good mind because tomorrow morning peace will be made." After this, when the daylight was beginning to shine, Marietto and Raffaele made peace, exactly as the mother had seen at night in the vision about the peace that had been given up as completely hopeless. Marietto and his aforementioned mother, lady Nicola, attest to this.

# CHAPTER FIFTEEN: COURT CASES AND NOTARIAL PEACE ACTS

*Court records, notarized contracts, and other documents relevant to vengeance, emotion, and peacemaking from the later Middle Ages provide a clear picture of how individuals dealt with these issues on a practical, day-to-day level. Notices arising from secular peacemaking procedures (Doc. 117) and notarial peace acts (Doc. 120) during this time are extremely common, and indicate that peacemaking was practiced systematically in the later Middle Ages. They also provide a nice complement to the talk of peace found in sermons and narrative sources.*

*Frequently, malefactors had to escape temporarily from the wrath of their enemies, either by flight (Doc. 119) or by seeking sanctuary in churches (Docs. 119, 124, and 125), in order to give peacemakers time to work. Peacemaking itself was a community affair: it involved friends, neighbors, kinfolk, members of religious orders, notaries or other officials, and legally appointed procurators or legal representatives (Doc. 118). The process did not necessarily compete with the system of criminal law for jurisdiction over homicide. Instead, historians have argued that the two systems worked side by side. Inevitably, the process for handling homicide and other grave injuries by means of peacemaking procedures broke down from time to time, leading to lawsuits (e.g., Docs. 121–123).*

*The selections below offer examples from the Low Countries, Italy, France, and England.*

## 117. THE PEACE REGISTERS OF THE CITY OF TOURNAI

*The city of Tournai, in modern Belgium, kept "peace registers" recording the efforts made to promote peace in the city; the extracts below are from 1273–80. One section, entitled* Des fourjuremens, *or "the foreswearers," lists the names of people who came before the city leaders and swore not to give aid to a relative or friend of theirs who had committed a homicide, and not to retaliate for any reprisal killings (see Doc. 117b). The people listed in these oaths were probably coerced to some degree into foreswearing their kinsman or friend (notice the public nature of the events in Docs. 117b, e, f, and g). It is also possible that they wished to gain immunity themselves from any retaliation by the victim's kin or friends. Some of the entries in the registers include long lists of names of foreswearers, and these provide a useful sense of the size and nature of the groups of kin and friends who could be associated with vengeance. We have included one in full in this chapter (Doc. 117b).*

*The longer entries in this section (Docs. 117b, e, f, and g) probably involved more serious killings than in the others. Consequently, we have included several shorter entries that arose from less prominent killings (Docs. 117a, c, and d), so as to give readers a sense of the range of entries in these registers.*

Source: ed. Walter Benary, "Zwei altfranzösische Friedensregister der Stadt Tournai (1273–1280)," *Romanische Forschungen* 25 (1908), pp. 101–4, 106, 108. Trans. Daniel Lord Smail.

## a. Jakemins li Caudreliers foreswears Jehennet d'Eskelmes
### [No. 618, from 1273]

Jakemins li Caudreliers foreswore Jehennet d'Eskelmes by sworn faith that never would he give him aid, whatever might befall him, for the killing of the son of Estievenon dou Triesscon, whom he killed during one of the nights of Christmas in a bakeshop, where he was baking his bread, without calling out to him or speaking to him; and never did he who was killed see this Jehennet d'Eskelmes, so black was the night.

## b. The foreswearing of Watiers de la Plagne and company
### [No. 620, from 1273–74]

Milord Watiers de la Plagne, his valet, Alardins, Pieres de Guiegnies and Bourscardins de le Lokerie were foresworn by all the people whose names are listed below, and they should not help them in any way either through others or with their own goods: milord Alars de Haudion; Jehan his son; mister Pieres de Guiegnies; Willaume de le Porte; Liepus; Gillos his brother; Watiers de le Porte; Alars d'Esplechin; Bauduins d'Esplechin; Gosseaus de Calone; Watiers de St. Amant; Fasteres d'Orke; mister Jehans de Bauduimont; Jehans de Tressin; Fasteres de Tressin; Jehans de le Lokerie; Bouschars de Bauduimont; and he took Ghilebiert his brother on his oath; Estievenes Chokette; Charles d'Escaupont; Gilles de Popioele; Hues his brother; Watiers Froischars; Gilles Froischars; Watiers de le Haie; Hakous de Haudion; Mahius his brother; Gilles de Maude; Colars de Haudion; Sohiers his brother; Estievenes Lourdeaus; milord Amourris Blauwes; Adans his son; Jehans dou Gardin; Mikiols d'Jerembaudenghien; Pieres his brother; Sohiers des Campeaus; Watiers a le Take, the clerk of Wastines; Jehans de Holai, and he took his children on his oath; Gilles de Holai; Watiers de Holai; Sohiers de Borgies; Jehans his brother; Gillos des Campeaus; milord Reniers de St. Amant; mister Gossuins his brother.

[The men listed at the top of this act were killed in retribution the following year, as this entry reveals.] In the year of the incarnation 1274, the fifth day of March, there came into the open hall, before the jurors, Pieres de le

Plaigne, who was the brother of milord Watier; mister Gilles dou Lokeron and his two sons, Jakemes and Gilles; and Grars del Omit and Jehan his brother. They promised and swore on the relics of the saints that, whatever should happen in the future on behalf of milord Watier de le Plaigne, or anything that might come from those who were in his kin group, never would they involve themselves nor aid them, neither in counsel nor in any other way, nor wishing any evil to those of Tournai or their kin for the killing of milord Watier and his suite.

### c. The Polekins brothers foreswear Gillion Ghievart
### [No. 623, from 1273]

Gilles Polekins and Ghievins, his brother, foreswore Gillion Ghievart for the death of the son of Jehan Malvaisgarchon whom Gillion Ghievart killed.

### d. The de Poukes brothers foreswear Colart de Poukes
### [No. 624, from 1273]

Willaume de Poukes and Pieres, his brother, foreswore Colart de Poukes.

### e. Jehans Liepus foreswears his nephew
### [No. 628, from 1277]

In the year of the incarnation 1277, the fourteenth of October, Jehans Liepus a le Take, in the hands of Gossuin de Maubrai, the provost elected to this task, and in the open hall in the presence of the jurors, foreswore Watier Maughier, who was the son of his brother, in such manner that Jehans Liepus promised and swore on the relics of the saints that he would neither give comfort nor aid to Watier Maughier, his cousin, either from his own or from his family's goods, neither for his death nor for any threats nor for his wounding, or anything that might happen in the future, in whatever manner, for the killing of Gillon Kieville whom this Watiers killed.

### f. Willaume Castagne foreswears his nephew
### [No. 632, date unclear]

In the year of the incarnation, Willaume Castagne foreswore Willemet Roveniel, the son of his sister, for the death of Jakemon Rainbaut whom he helped to kill, and Willaume Castagne promised and swore in the hands of Jakemon Mouton, provost of the commune, before the jurors in the open hall, that he will neither be helpful nor comforting toward the aforesaid Willement, either from his own or his family's goods, in any manner, for the killing of Jakemon Raimbaut, whatever might happen to this Willemet.

### g. Henris Pourres foreswears Bauduin de Rengies
### [No. 641, from 1278]

In the year of the incarnation 1278, the last day of January, Henris Pourres the father, in the hands of Gillion Cardevake, the provost of the commune, in the open hall before many jurors, foreswore Bauduin de Rengies in this manner: he promised and swore that he would never give comfort nor aid to Bauduin de Rengies, either from his own or his family's goods, neither with weapons, horses, nor any other thing in any way, neither for threats nor the death nor anything that might happen in whatever manner, for the wounding he [Bauduin] gave to Ernaut de Dotegnies, the carpenter. In the same way foreswore all those who are named in the following [26 names follow].

## 118. TURA RANERII, OF FLORENCE, CREATES A PROCURATOR

*Peace acts and other contracts related to peacemaking procedures were very common in Florence and other Italian cities in the later Middle Ages, and involved all ranks of society. This document, from 1290, is a legal instrument whereby a Florentine named Tura Ranerii empowered a representative (called a "procurator") to act on his behalf in order to arrange a peace back in Florence with Ranerii's enemy, Giovannino Benvenuti, who had injured him. The act does not explain why Tura was in Siena, but it is possible that Tura was there on business, or, perhaps, was in self-imposed exile for some unrelated injury against another party.*

Source: ed. Gino Masi, *Collectio chartarum pacis privatae Medii Aevi ad regionem Tusciae pertinentium* (Milan: Vita e pensiero, 1943), p. 229. Trans. Daniel Lord Smail.

In the name of the Lord amen. In the year of the Lord 1290, the fourth indiction, in the month of November. Let it be evident to all who will consult this public document that, in the presence of the notary and witnesses identified below, Tura Ranerii of San Frediano in Florence, currently living in Siena, in the quarter of San Salvatore, creates and constitutes as his legitimate procurator, factor, and special agent Arriguccio, the son of Giovanni of Florence. He is to receive himself and on Tura's behalf a voluntary peace, conclusion, and remission from Giovannino Benvenuti of San Paolino for each and every injury and offense inflicted on Tura by the said Giovannino, however these may be done or defined. The special circumstance is that Giovannino was denounced by Ciccio the chaplain of San Fridiana and his associates during the government of Lord Antonio de Fuxeragho de Laude, the podesta of the commune of Florence. Last October, having suffered a double penalty, Giovannino went to Tura's house and, entering the house, attacked Tura with a knife. His mind clouded by wrath and evil intent, he threatened to slit Tura's veins. For this reason he was banished from the commune of Florence, following the order of the lord Antonio the podesta, under penalty of 500 small florins, and then fined 200 small florins, which were included in the penalty of banishment. All this is written out fully in a charter of banishment and condemnation. In Tura's name, the procurator is to receive and confirm a similar peace, with the appropriate guarantees, penalties, obligations, and renunciations, following the form of the act of peace and concord, as he should judge appropriate. He should do everything else in both their names, as a true and legitimate procurator wishes to do for the sake of the task of procuration, or whatever Tura himself would do if he could go himself. Tura grants to Arriguccius the procurator a full, free, and general mandate, and promises for all time to hold firm and steady to everything that is done or achieved by the procurator in the matters above. He obligates all his goods to this end.... Enacted in Siena, in San Salvatore, in front of Guidone Mallivali, shoemaker; Albertino Benedicti, and Casino Gratie, witnesses. I, Compagno the notary, son of Bornaccio of Siena, took part in the procuration made for Tura, and, by Tura's order and request, wrote and published what is read above.

## 119. CASES OF HOMICIDE IN THE CALENDAR OF CORONER'S ROLLS, LONDON

*The coroner was an English official in charge of undertaking inquests into homicides committed in the region assigned to him, and the coroner's rolls consist of a series of short entries summarizing his findings in each case. Extracts from the coroner's rolls for London between 1324 and 1340, given here, show how common it was for killers to take sanctuary in nearby churches so as to avoid prosecution or vengeance by relatives of the victim. Some finally just slipped away into the countryside and were not caught (Docs. 119b and d). Others "abjured the realm"; that is to say, they acknowledged their guilt, abandoned to the Treasury all their worldly goods (typically few in number, if any), and were banished from England (Docs. 119a, c, and e). Provisions were made to allow the abjurers the necessary number of days to travel to the coast and find a ship to cross the Channel. We cannot know how many actually left, and it is possible or even likely that any men who did leave eventually slipped back into the country and resumed their former lives. In some cases (Docs. 119b, c, and e), a lapse of several years exists between the killing and the confession.*

Source: trans. Reginald R. Sharpe, *Calendar of Coroners Rolls of the City of London, A.D. 1300–1378* (London: R. Clay, 1913), pp. 84–85, 111, 124, 198, 259–60.

## a. The death of John le Belringere
### [Roll C, no. 16]

On Friday the morrow of the Ascension [24 May] the year aforesaid [1324], it happened that a certain John le Belringere lay dead in the high street of Douegate before the gate of the house held by Roger de Haveryng of Benedicta Box in the parish of All Hallows at the Hay in the Ward of Douegate. On hearing this, the aforesaid coroner and sheriffs proceeded thither and having summoned good men of that Ward and of the three nearest Wards, namely, Vintry, Bridge and Walebroke, they diligently enquired how it happened. The jurors say that when on the preceding Thursday a certain John de Wheteley of Chester and the said John le Belringere sat playing and drinking in the said house, strife arose between them, so that the said John de Wheteley drew his knife called a "Twytel" [a small knife that, in other cases, made wounds 1 inch long and 6–7 inches 'deep] and fatally struck the said John le Belringere therewith on the throat inflicting a mortal wound an inch and a half long and two inches deep, and when the said John le Belringere at length left the house he fell down outside the door of the house and forthwith died. Being asked who were present when this happened, the jurors say no one except those two, nor do they suspect anyone except the said John de Wheteley. Being asked what became of the said John, they say that he immediately fled to the church of All Hallows at the Hay, where the said coroner and sheriffs immediately came to him; that the said John confessed himself guilty of the felony and refused to surrender himself to the king's peace but asked to abjure the realm and did abjure it on Sunday the Feast of Pentecost following. He chose the port of Bristol to cross the sea in five days, namely, the first day to Wicombe, the second to Oxford, the third to Hegheworth, the fourth to Malmesburi, and the fifth to Bristol, thence to cross the sea at the first tide under penalty prescribed. The said John has no chattels.

## b. The death of Roger Herne
### [Roll D, no. 19]

On Tuesday after the Feast of Saint Matthias [24 Feb.], anno 18 Edward II [1324–25], a certain Robert Flemyng of the county of Surrey, fled into the church of

St. Mary de Aldermanneburi, and on the following Thursday confessed before the said coroner and sheriffs that he was a king's felon, inasmuch as about the Feast of the Nativity of Saint the John the Baptist [24 June] anno 14 Edward II [1321], he had feloniously killed Roger Herne de Bokham, county Surrey, in the High Street between Bokham and Guildeford. He refused to surrender to the king's peace, and precept was issued to the men of the Ward of Bassieshawe to safeguard him until, etc. Afterwards, namely, on the following Tuesday, he escaped. His chattels consist of a red hakeney [horse] worth 40 pence, for which Benedict de Folsham [the sheriff] will answer.

### c. The abjuration of William, son of William le Toliere, and Roger le Leche
### [Roll D, no. 35]

Abjuration of William, son of William le Toliere de Manneby, and Roger le Leche.

   On Thursday after the Feast of the Nativity of Saint John the Baptist [24 June] anno 18 Edward II [1325], a certain William, son of William le Tollere de Manneby of county York and Roger le Leche son of Roger le Walshe of Welyngtone "under Wrekene" in Wales fled into the church of St. Michael in the War of Bassieshaw, and then and there acknowledged themselves before the coroner and sheriffs to be felons of the lord the King inasmuch as about Christmas time anno 16 Edward III [1322] they had feloniously killed a certain William of York. They refused to surrender to the king's peace, and asked to abjure the realm, and they did abjure it the next day. To the said William was assigned the port of Dover whence to cross the sea at the first tide; to the said Roger was assigned the port of Harwich to cross the sea in three days, namely, the first to Brendwode, the second to [blank], the third to Harwich. Their chattels consisted of a tunic and hood worth 16 pence, a sword and two knives worth 4 pence. Total 20 pence, for which Benedict de Fulsham, the sheriff, will answer.

### d. The deaths of William Gilemyn and Robert de Staunton
### [Roll F, nos. 31–32]

31. Friday, after the Feast of Exaltation of the Holy Cross [14 Sept.] the same year [1337], William de Kyngesclere of county Southampton took refuge in St. Paul's church and confessed before Richard de la Pole, the king's butler and coroner of London, and William de Brykelesworth one of the sheriffs, that on Thursday in the week of Pentecost anno 11 Edward III [1337] he feloniously killed with a knife William Gilemyn of Kyngesclere in the vill of

Kyngesclere county Southampton, but refused to surrender. Chattels none. Afterwards, he escaped by night.

32. The same Friday, William de Westone of Burton county Staffordshire took refuge in St. Paul's and confessed before the aforesaid coroner and sheriff that on the aforesaid Thursday he had feloniously killed Robert de Stanton of Burton in the above vill of Burton, but refused to surrender. Chattels none. Afterwards, he escaped by night.

### e. The abjuration of John, son of Richard Taillard, for two murders
### [Roll H, nos. 31–32]

31. On Friday the Feast of Translation of Saint Thomas [7 July] anno 14 Edward III [1340], John, son of Richard Taillard de "Hameldone" [Hambleton] of county Rutland, confessed before John de Shirbourne, the coroner of the city, in St. Paul's church, that on the Sunday before the Feast of Pentecost [7 June] anno 6 Edward III [1332] he feloniously killed Geoffrey Pope, servant of Sir Oliver de Ingham, in the vill of "Borewelle" [Burwell] county Cambridgeshire with a knife, and according to custom, he abjured the realm, the port of Southampton being assigned to him, whence to cross the sea on the fourth day. Chattels none.

32. On the death of William Casse. Friday after the Feast of Translation of Saint Thomas [7 July] the same year, information given to the aforesaid coroner and sheriffs that William Casse, an apprentice of the Bench, lay dead of a death other than his rightful death in the rent of Mary Box in the parish of St. Mary de Stanynglane in the Ward of Aldresgate. Thereupon they proceeded thither, and, having summoned good men of that Ward and of the two nearest Wards, namely, Farndone Within and Crepelgate, they diligently enquired how it happened. The jurors say that on Monday after the Feast of SS. Peter and Paul [29 June] anno 14 Edward III [1340] a certain John, son of Richard "Taillard" of Hameldone county Rutland, called John Hytone, met the above William Casse about the third hour of the day, in Chepe opposite St. Vedast lane in the Ward of Farndone Within, and, at the instigation of Robert de Wyleby, Knight of county Northampton, struck him with a short knife, inflicting two wounds, namely, one on the left arm and the other under the left breast, of which he died on the Friday after the Feast of the Translation of Saint Thomas aforesaid. The said John "Tayllard" immediately took refuge in St. Paul's church, where he remained until the Friday on which death took place and then he abjured the realm before the coroner for the death of Geoffrey Pope, servant of Sir Oliver de Ingham, as above recorded. Four neighbors attached.

# 120. NOTARIZED PEACE ACTS AND RELATED ACTS FROM MARSEILLE

*The following acts, from the Archives Départementales des Bouches-du-Rhône, France (ADBR) and the Archives Municipales de la Ville de Marseille (AM), and dated between the years 1337 and 1361, provide a sampling of the kinds of notarized peace acts that were common in Mediterranean Europe in the later Middle Ages. The crimes detailed range from woundings to killings and involve both men and women. One act (Doc. 120h below) is a dowry contract that follows immediately on a peace act. The final act (Doc. 120j) is a highly unusual declaration of vengeance.*

Sources: as listed below. Trans. Daniel Lord Smail.

## a. Peace for the killing of Uguo Clalpin
### [ADBR 381E 38, folios 19v-21r, 25 April 1337]

In the name of the Lord amen. In the year of his Incarnation 1337, the fifth indiction, the 25th day of April, let it be known to all that among all the many gifts of God is judged to be the peace pleasing to God that suppresses hatreds and fosters friendships; the customary consolation among Christians; not un-like the cordon of divine scriptures as having been established in the reverence of Christ, who wished that his own blood be shed and nothing less than to be slain for the redemption of humankind, who by his voice and soul brought together peace and mercy, and gave, through preaching the most holy text, the greatest goodness for the salvation of souls, in saying "My peace I give to you, my peace I leave to you, and peace on earth to men of good will." So it is that since an enduring matter of dissension, through diabolical instigation, has for some time existed between Johan Bernis, blood cousin of the late Uguo Clalpin, son of [blank], murdered by the sword of Guilhem Garrigas, son of Andrieu Garrigas, a citizen of Marseille; and Peire Bernis, son of Johan; and Johan Bonaut, blood cousin of the late Uguo; and Ugua Romea, an aunt of Uguo; and Rixendis Berengiera, an aunt of the same Uguo of the said city, who are the closest kin of Uguo, since according to them there are no other kin most closely related, on the one hand – and on the other hand, Andrieu, maternal uncle of the late Uguo and father of Guilhem, as well as Guilhem himself – over a wound inflicted by Guilhem in the stomach of Uguo and over the death that followed from this; from the memory of this death, anger and hatred reverberated greatly between these parties and their kinsmen, up to this very moment, from which it was feared that evils might pile up upon worse evils. Behold in the year and day and hour as [written] above, at the beginning of this present public instrument, through the persuasion of those holy words of foremost distinction, and through the intervention of the noble esquire Berengier Uguolen, citizen of Marseille, following the celestial edict as a benevolent and noteworthy friend of the said parties, the above-named Johan Bernis, in his own name and that of his absent son Peire; Johane Bonaut; Hugua Romea; and Rixendis Berengiera, in their own names and in the names of all others present, absent, and future whoever they might be, led into a good frame of mind, because it would be unseemly (no less by virtue of the Holy Book) and contrary to fairness that Guilhem be harassed in whatever way for the sinful fault of the late Uguo himself, since on that occasion, as it is said, he had first assaulted Guilhem, throwing many stones at him and, as they say, through wounding him in the head, and whatever Guilhem did against Uguo he did, or so they say, in defending himself.... The aforesaid parties...in good faith and without any deception or force or fear, neither compelled nor entrapped nor subverted by any payment..., in the presence of the nobleman and the witnesses below, concerning the said death, foreswore from this point onward all hatreds and hateful deeds arising from this death.... Embracing each other bodily, they exchanged the kiss of peace, and the parties made promises to the other in turn, demanding and receiving for themselves and their families and their kinsfolk and friends to have, hold, and observe as valid, now and in perpetuity, both this true and holy peace and each and every thing contained in this instrument, and not to contravene them either by themselves or through other men or any other person related more closely than they under pain of a fine of 100 Marseille pounds assessed in the royal court of Marseille on each contravening party, if it should come about – but let it not be.... Concerning all and everything above Guilhem Garrigas asked that a public instrument be made for him by me, the notary below. Redacted in Marseille in the refectory of the church of the Carmelites in the presence and testimony of Brother Bertran Crota of the said order, Brother Peire Missonier of the same order of the convent of Marseille, of the said Berengier Uguolen, Johan Laurent, Martin Franquesa, Jacme Desdier, and Uguo Cadel, especially gathered and invited by the parties above. And I Bertomieu de Salins, public notary of Marseille, who was hired by the parties, wrote this public document. It was extracted for Guilhem.

### b. Peace between Jacme Gavot and Folco de Nercio
### [ADBR 381E 393, folio 121v, 1 March 1344]

2. In the year above, on March first, a peace was made between Jacme Gavot of Caudalonga, the shepherd of Antoni Frances, on the one hand, and Folco de Nercio of Marseille, over a public fight that took place between them and the wounds inflicted, as is said, by Folco on the body of Jacme Gavot; they

promised from now on not to assault one another; they each forgave the other in turn any injury and hatred,... Jacme confessing that he is the cause of his own wounding and was wounded through his own fault. Redacted in the house of myself, the notary below. Witnesses Audebert de Signa, Antoni Frances, Johan Durant.

### c. Peace for the killing of Guilhem Turel
### [AM II 42, folios 60r-61v, 10 April 1349]

3. The tenor of an instrument of peace for Guilhem Bascul. In the name of Lord God eternal and of our savior Jesus Christ amen. In the year of his incarnation 1349, the tenth of the month of April, which is Holy Friday, the first hour of the day. From the tenor of the present public writing let it be known to all present and future that, since a mortal fight or battle at one time took place between Guilhem Bascul of Marseille on the one hand, and Guilhem Turel of the same city on the other, who both live on the Carpenters' Street of Marseille – in this battle, so it is said, Guilhem Turel was wounded and fully murdered by Guilhem Bascul. And Guilhem Bascul was then arrested for the homicide and, because of it, banished and condemned by the court of Marseille for contumacy. So it is that, with the aid of the venerable and religious man Brother Guilhem of Marseille, prior of the convent of Dominicans of Marseille, and of certain other common friends of the parties involved, Isnart Bayle, as a cousin and as one closer in grade of kinship to his cousin the late Guilhem Turel than all other kin and affines [relatives by marriage] now living – as Isnart himself claims, on oath, in his own name and of his children, and in the name and place of Laurens Gartin of Marseille, also a cousin of the late Guilhem Turel, and of the remaining friends, relatives, and affines of the late man and of Isnart Bayle himself and his successors – Isnart Bayle of Marseille, considering and pondering how our Lord Jesus Christ, son of God, king of kings and lord of lords, to whom everyone owes obedience, coming to his death, he prayed for those persecuting him, saying "Father, forgive them this sin since they know not what they are doing," and to his disciples he gave the sign of peace, saying "My peace I give to you." All these things having been pondered by Isnart Bayle, for the sake of God and his passion on this holy day, mercifully inclined by the contemplation of the piety of Guilhem Bascul, there in the courtyard of the church of the Dominicans of Marseille, before all the people gathered therein to hear the holy words, on bended knees, humbly and tearfully requesting pardon and peace, through the kiss of peace he made an intervening and perpetual peace, end, and remission and concord for the wounds and death and all the injuries, harms, offenses, and insults in word or deed brought by Guilhem Bascul

against the late Guilhem Turel; Isnart Bayle, in the names of those above and for himself and his heirs and successors and friends whoever they may be, through solemn intervening covenants, promising that he would not proceed further with the indictments made on these occasions by himself or by others, nor would he draw up others anew, nor consent that any be drawn up, nor even will any of those on his side make an effort that [a suit] be brought against Guilhem Bascul by any court, judge, or chief, by the inquisition or in any other way; instead he will in perpetuity hold and take and observe this peace, end, and remission as well as concord and all and everything written above as secure and settled, by himself and his family, and neither will he himself nor others break [the peace] for any reason or cause, in law or in deed, for which he pledges in security and bond all the goods he owns now and will own, under pain of restoration for all legal damages and expenses and further deeds and under an entire renunciation of all rights that may be and under a legal agreement; and Isnart Bayle also promised to fashion and procure with all his ability that his sons, when they will be of legal age, and Laurens Garsin when he will return to Marseille, and others on his side to whom he will write, will hold, ratify, and confirm this peace, settled and secured in perpetuity by legal bonds, covenants, and legal agreements; and so, Isnart Bayle, in the names of the others, promised to heed and observe without violation all and everything as contained in this public instrument and not to do or to come against it in any way, and with the holy Gospels of God touched bodily by him with his right hand, he freely swore an oath and expressly renounced any canonical and civil and municipal right contained in the book of statutes and customs of Marseille and other places, by virtue of which he or anyone above might be able to act or come against the said peace on his own behalf or on behalf of others, for any reason or cause, whether in law or in deed. And concerning all and everything above he asked and conceded to the plaintiff Guilhem Bascul a public instrument and public instruments that could be transcribed, made, reestablished, corrected, and emended; that instrument or instruments having been produced in court or otherwise as often as there will be a need for the counsel and writing skill of a single wise man and of several wise men, the substance of the deed not changed in any way. Redacted in Marseille, in the courtyard of the Church of the Dominicans of Marseille. Witnesses called and brought to these agreements included Brother Guilhem of Marseille, prior of the Dominicans of Marseille; Brother Guilhem Betonin, of the said order; Uguo Esteve; Jacme Gili; Antoni Bonfilh; Peire Bonfilh, son of Jacme Bonfilh; Bernat de Soluiers [the last five witnesses named were carpenters] and many others of Marseille; and I, Augier Aycart, notary public of Marseille, who wrote this etc. An instrument was made.

## d. Peace for the killing of Adalays Rogeria
### [ADBR 381E 79, folios 67v–68r, 9 June 1353]

In the year above, on the ninth day of June, around nones [fifth hour of the day, or ninth hour after sunrise]. Let it be known to all etc. that, with diabolical instigation, Adalays Rogeria, the wife of the baker Jacme Rogier, a citizen of Marseille, proffered many insulting and harsh and contumacious words to Antoni Bort, a citizen of Marseille, who was there and listening, because of which Antoni, moved by wrath, drew his sword and wounded Adalays through a single wound to the head, from which Adalays, for reasons owing as much to the poor care taken of her as to the raging heat of this present summertime, after fifteen days, entered upon the path of all flesh. Behold now that Jacme, the husband and dearest friend of Adalays, heeding and considering that Antoni had come to the delivery of the wound not so much as it were through fault; and instead moved by sadness and by Adalays's own fault – therefore, out of fear for the divine preference and heeding and considering that God does not wish the death of a sinner but rather that he live and be turned around, heeding also, according to the holy word, that merciful saints follow a merciful path – therefore, Jacme, along with Peire Durant and Raymon Durant and Guilhem Durant and Raymon Uguo, blood cousins of Jacme, heeding the holy word "Wish not to give an evil for an evil," for they themselves and all and every kinsmen and successors of theirs, in admiration of piety and mercy, promised and offered the kiss of peace to Antoni, present and receiving for himself and all his kinsmen; they forgave any injury and offense brought against Adalays by Antoni, and promising and swearing on the holy Gospels of God, with the sacred scriptures corporally touched by their hands, for themselves and their families, under pain of forfeiture of all their present and future goods, that they would never contravene the said peace and the peaceable forgiveness of injuries. Renouncing etc. Swearing etc. Antoni asked for an instrument concerning these matters. Redacted in Marseille, on the doorstep of the house of the Dominicans. Witnesses: lord Uguo de Geminis, jurist; Brother Guilhem Beton, Dominican; Esteve Broquier; Jacme Arvieu; Simon de Rabes. It has been transferred to the great cartulary.

Immediately afterward let it be known to all etc. that, since Antoni Bort is caught up with many diverse matters to the extent that he cannot conveniently remain in the city of Marseille, therefore Antoni made, constituted, and formally ordained as his certain, true and authoritative special procurator, namely Carle de Rabes, his cousin, present and receiving, to receive, negotiate, and fulfill in his name and for him a peace and concord with Bertranda, the wife of Guilhem Brize, the sister and nearest relative of the late Adalays Rogiera. Promising etc. Redacted as above. Witnesses as above.

### e. Peace between Guilhem Johan and the brothers Peire and Guilhem Tallarone
### [ADBR 381E 79, folio 125r-v, 8 December 1353]

The year as above, the eighth day of December, hour around terce [the third hour of the day]. Let it be known to all etc. that since a matter of conflict has arisen between Guilhem Johan, alias Chilpa, a laborer and citizen of Marseille, and his kinsmen on the one hand, and Peire Tallarone and Guilhem Tallarone, brothers, and their kinsmen on the other, arising from a certain public battle that took place between them, in which battle Peire Tallarone was wounded by Guilhem Johan with a single wound on the left arm. Behold now that Guilhem Johan, for himself and his kinsmen, and Peire Tallarone, in his own name and of his brother and their kinsmen, over these hatreds and hostilities that took place among themselves, unanimously and freely made and agreed between themselves a peace and concord, and as a true sign of the agreement the one kissed the other. And they promised for themselves and their men to have and hold this peace as valid and firm, and if ever one should harm the other, or arrange to have the other harmed, either in his person or goods, by word or by deed, etc. And if they should move against etc. Obliging etc. Renouncing etc. Swearing etc. And since Guilhem Johan was condemned by the royal court to pay twenty-five pounds for this wounding and to make good the costs of damages and other sufferings endured by Peire because of the wound, Peire and Guilhem, at the intervention of common friends, for the cost of damages and other things agreed freely among themselves that Guilhem would be held to give, pay, and transmit to Peire for these damages and other things sixteen royal pounds, to be paid between now and the upcoming festival of Pentecost. Guilhem immediately promised, for himself and his family, to pay and transmit the money to Peire or his family before the deadline above. In peace etc. Obliging etc. Renouncing etc. Swearing etc. The noblemen Montoliu de Montoliu and Aragon de Rabastenc, along with Johan Bertran and Uguo Botelhier, constituted themselves as guarantors and peacemakers and liquidators for this debt on behalf of Guilhem and his party and for all the things above that are to be paid over, as was firmly undertaken and promised by him. Renouncing etc. and especially etc. Redacted in Marseille in the house of Peire de Rabastenc. Witnesses: Peire de Rabastenc, of Marseille; Guilhem Martha, notary of Marseille; Jaufres de Rellania, of Limoysa. An instrument was made for the amount of the debt owed to Peire Tallarone.

### f. Peace between Uguo Blanc and Peire Gontard
### [ADBR 381E 86, folios 35r-37v, 29 May 1354]

In the name of our lord Jesus Christ amen. In the year of his incarnation 1354, the seventh indiction, the 29th day of the month of May, the hour of day around crepuscule [the hour just after sunset]. Let it be known etc. that a celestial goodness is constructed and fostered through the oneness of a loving peace, with the disturbances of hatreds and enmities having been cast down; the intercourse of peace, and the trust of good will between those present and equally the successors to follow; and so chiefly through this intermediary activity, [so] pleasing and mirthful to God and the angels and his entire celestial court, the occupations of the ancient enemy who is wont to beget storms of discords among Christians [are] undermined, and especially through the elimination of wicked attacks, the glories of the peaceful are brought back to the augmentation of consolation; [and] although the lesions caused by the injuries were conceived and executed through the work of the wicked devil, through the guidance of a true knowledge for the reverence of that man who wished that his own blood be spilled for the redemption of humankind and nothing less than to be killed, who wished to pray for peace and mercy and that one ought not give offences for offences, since the merciful, in his ineffable sight, deserve auspiciously to follow mercy from desire, just as is believed; by preaching the holy word [when] visiting his divine apostles, he gave his peace to them, and left among them [his peace] to be served tenaciously and in many lands, to be sown among the company of the faithful in the hope of attaining the inestimable reward. And since a matter of dissent was sown by the creative sower of discords between, namely, Uguo Blanc, skin-preparer [*conreator*: someone who scraped and treated skins before tanning], citizen of the city of Marseille, on the one hand; and Peire Gontard, laborer, citizen and resident of the city on the other, over the wound to the body of Peire Gontard that was inflicted, as is said, by Uguo, in consideration of which wrath, anger, and hatred had arisen and echoed between the parties from which it was feared that evil matters might often in all possibility be heaped up on other evils and in the future might even fall back on worse evils. So it is that in the year, day, indiction, and hour as above, under the motivation of the divine mystery and heeding the aforementioned holy words, Peire Ferrier, a citizen of Marseille, coming and establishing himself in the presence of myself, the notary below, and of the witnesses below, and also of Peire Gontard, resident of the city, lying as one infirm and wounded, as he says, by Uguo Blanc, currently detained in the royal jail, in the house of Peire [Gontard]; Peire Ferrier, as I was saying, asked Peire Gontard, with insistence, again and again, out of reverence of God and with the entreaties of the same Peire Ferrier and of others standing around there, he ought to forgive, as I said, Uguo Blanc for any injury that he committed, by words or deeds, against the identity of Peire Gontard, by wounding or otherwise, and for whatever other reason; Peire Gontard, without any impetuosity, freely, and from his own free will, having listened to and understood these words spoken and proposed by Peire Ferrier without commands, out of reverence for God and for the love of him shown by Peire Ferrier and the others standing there, forgave, forswore, and yielded to Uguo Blanc, absent but as one present, and also to those entreating and receiving in the name and on behalf of Uguo Blanc – me, the notary below, and Guilhem de Anjou, godfather and affine of Uguo Blanc – any injury, wrath, and hatred which he has and could have by reason of the wound and for any other reason or cause, offering a peace and concord to Uguo Blanc with all right and manner by which it can and ought to become better and more useful.

And these things Peire Gontard said and forgave once, twice, three times, and often in the presence above, through forbearance, and by offering peace to Uguo Blanc, and on his behalf to the said notary and to Guilhem de Anjou, intervening and receiving on the name and on behalf of Uguo Blanc.

Guilhem de Anjou, godfather and affine of Uguo Blanc and in his name, requested that a public instrument containing all and everything above be made for himself and for Uguo Blanc by me, the notary below.

Redacted in Marseille, in the house of Peire Gontard. Witness lord Peire Galbert, curator-chaplain of the church of St. Cannat. Witness Peire Ferrier. Witness Guilhem Naulon. Jacme Novel, apothecary. Raynaut Esteve; Peire Durant; Antoni Gayroart, laborers and citizens of Marseille. I Johan Silvester, public notary of Marseille, wrote this. A public instrument of these things was made by me for Uguo Blanc.

## g. Peace for the killing of Adalays Borgone
### [ADBR 355E 290, folios 20r-21r, 4 April 1355]

An instrument of peace for Pons Gasin. In the name of our Lord God eternal and our savior Jesus Christ amen. In the year of his Incarnation 1355, the fourth day of the month of April, the hour of day around terce, let it be known to all present and future that when Pons Gasin, laborer of the city of Marseille, was arrested by the royal court of the city for wounds inflicted on the body of the late Adalays Borgone of the same city, and for this was banned and condemned for contumacy by the court; and since, for the above, a hatred and capital enmity has sprung up, namely between Uguo Sycart, brother of the late Adalays Borgone, and the brothers Bertran and Johan Borgon, sons of the late Adalays, on the one hand; and Pons Gasin on the other; so it is that with the involvement of the gentlemen Johan Girman, Salvaire Chapus, and Johan Martin, laborers and citizens of the said city, and of many other common friends of the parties, desiring to bring the parties in this way to unanimity through the mediation of divine regeneration; the parties considering and heeding moreover how our Lord Jesus Christ, son of God, King of kings, and Lord of lords, to whom all things owe obedience, coming to his death, prayed for his persecutors, saying "Father, forgive them this sin, for they know not what they do," and to his disciples he gave the way of peace, saying "Peace I give to you, my peace I leave to you"; and all these things above having been considered by the parties above, and by each of the two parties, moved to the honor of God and the mercy of his passion, they made, through the exchange of the kiss of peace, a perpetual peace, end, and forgiveness and concord for the wounds and death and all other injuries, ill-wills, attacks, and insults by word or deed inflicted on the identity of the late Adalays Borgone by Pons Gasin, and for all things related to and emerging from those things. And the parties desired that the peace be observed by themselves and their families and whatever successors and others; the parties forgiving for themselves and their families, as was said earlier – namely the one party the other and the other the one, alternately and in turn – all injuries and enmities whatsoever that on account of this or alternately of another thing they have or could have, for these causes or for any others whatsoever. And the parties promised for themselves and their heirs and successors whomsoever in equal fashion and their kinsmen, with binding oaths – namely the one party to the other and the other to the one, alternately and in turn – that each would have, hold, and observe inviolately the peace, end, and forgiveness and concord and all and everything contained in this present public instrument as valid and firm in perpetuity, and never to move against or contravene it, either by themselves or through another man or men in their names and in the names of either of these parties, for any excuse, reason, or cause, whether by law or by deed, and not to bring about any damage, alternately and in turn, to the other's goods or identities in any way; and the parties also promised in good faith for themselves and their families as above to pay the penalties, expenses, and interest suffered through either of the parties within the law or outside, through litigation or from any other circumstance, of the peace and concord. Concerning which damages, expenses, disturbances, burdens, and other things, the parties promised to believe and hold, for themselves and their families as above – namely the one party to the other and the other to the one, alternately and in turn – and by their own, only by simple word alone without any kind of proof required from it. And for all the above contained in this public instrument, in its entirety and in its parts, being heeded, fulfilled, and inviolately observed and not being contravened in anyway by themselves, another, or others in their names of each of the same parties for any excuse, reason, or cause, by law or by deed, the parties obligated for themselves and their families as above – namely the one party to the other and the other to the one, alternately and in turn – all their goods, in their entirety and individually, movables and immovables, and moving (in and out of their possession) both in the present and the future.... Moreover, with this agreement made between the parties that the peace shall remain always unbreached and firm as above by virtue of the oath offered above by them, and under pain of a hundred royal or Marseille pounds as applied by the curator of the port of Marseille and demanded from them and each of them, so often, how often, and whensoever against the things above or any part of the above shall have been committed or even agreed upon by the parties or their families or one of them. Which penalty committed and exacted once or often, nevertheless the parties for themselves and their families as above wished to observe the peace and all and everything contained in this present public instrument now and always inviolately. Each party asked that a public instrument be made of all and everything above by me, the notary below, and that it might be written down, made, remade, corrected, and emended once and many times according to the advice of a single wise man or of many wise men, produced in court or not produced, as often as there will be need, nevertheless the substance of the deed unchanged in any way. Redacted in Marseille in the church of the Augustinians in the chapel of Jacme de Galbert. In the presence and testimony of the noble damoiseau Johan Martin; Primar Mirapeis, jurist; Peire Durant; Jacme Raynaut; Jacme Giraut; and Johanet Girman, citizens of the city of Marseille, witnesses called and assembled for this. And of me, Peire Aycart, notary etc.

An instrument was made for Pons Gasin.

## h. A dowry act for Bertomieua Bohiera
### [ADBR 355E 290, folios 61r–62r, 4 April 1355]

8. The assignation of the dowry of the wife of Johan Borgon, laborer of Marseille

In the name of the Lord...on the occasion of the ill-will that sprang up between Uguo Sicart and the brothers Bertran and Johan Borgon of Marseille on the one hand, and Pons Gasin, laborer of the city of Marseille on the other, for making a peace and avoiding future danger, it was arranged by common friends of the parties for a marriage to be contracted by words of the present between, namely, Johan Borgon and Bertomieua Bohiera, daughter of Pons Bohier, laborer of the city and blood cousin of Pons Gasin, who was born from the ordinary and legitimate marriage that existed between Pons

Bohier and his wife Adalays; Pons Bohier, in observance of the peace, for himself and his family, all traps and frauds being remote, in good faith gave, constituted, and assigned and promised to give and pay to the same Johan Borgon, his future son-in-law, present and receiving, together with his own daughter, married in the face of the Holy Mother Church as is customary, in dowry and for dowry and in the name of and by reason of the dowry of Bertomieua his daughter and future wife of Johan Borgon and for supporting all the burdens of the marriage and so that the peace arranged between them might always remain unbroken and firm, namely fifty royal pounds to be paid to him in this fashion.... And Pons Gasin likewise in good faith and without any trickery or fraud, freely and from his own knowledge, for himself and his family, thanks to the peace made between them and in order that the peace made between them might always retain the strength of oak, he gave or donated to Johan Borgon, the future husband of Berthomieua Bohiera, present and receiving, in augmentation of Berthomieua's dowry, namely a certain vineyard of his together with all its rights and appurtenances situated in the territory of Marseille....

### i. Peace for the killing of Ugueta Roquiera
### [ADBR 355E 35, folio 62v, 6 August 1357]

In the year of the Lord 1357, the sixth day of the month of August, hour around the middle of terce. Let it be known etc. that since Jacme Roquier, laborer of Marseille, was arrested for beatings inflicted on the person of Ugueta, his late wife, and for those things a hatred, wrath, and ill-will sprang up between Uguo Borchart, maternal uncle, and Peire de Barioles and Pons Bochart, cousins of the late Ugua on the one hand, and Jacme Roquier on the other. So it is that the said parties wishing, out of reverence for God, to make a peace out of those things, in good faith the parties for themselves and their families, kinsmen of the parties, and friends, mutually made of all injuries, ill-wills, and enmities a perpetual peace, formal and irrevocable, an understanding, a forgiveness, etc.; a kiss of peace etc; promising etc.; in turn etc.; obliging etc.; renouncing etc.; swearing etc.

And this under pain of a hundred royal pounds determined by the royal court and any other court of the port of Marseille. Concerning this etc.

Redacted in Marseille on the doorstep of the Franciscans. Witnesses Laurent Vital; Guilhem de Bras, barber; and Esteve Johan, of Marseille, etc. An instrument was made for Jacme Roquier by me, Peire Aycart, notary.

## j. Guilhem de Bessa declares vengeance
### [ADBR 381E 83, folios 16v-17r, 27 April 1361]

In the name of our lord Jesus Christ amen. In the year of his incarnation 1361, the fourteenth indiction, the 27th day of the month of April, hour around vespers [evening, or the sixth hour of the day]. Let it be known to all present and future that with Guilhem de Bessa, of Auriole, the son of the late Uguo de Bessa of Auriole, in Marseille in the presence of myself, a notary, and of the witnesses below, this said Guilhem de Bessa, of Auriole, stated and asserted before me, the notary, and the witnesses below, that last Wednesday, which was this past 21st of the month of April, Raymon de Ornhon, from the same town, was accidentally and by happenstance struck on the head by a blow with a certain *piola* [an unknown type of weapon] while inside a certain open pen of Raymon's situated in the territory of the town of Nantes, in a place called *Fonte Grassa,* from which blow or wound inflicted on him he immediately brought his last days to a close. And since various people free of guilt and hardly at all culpable in these matters could perhaps be accused of the wounding and subsequent death of the late Raymon by reason of suspicion, and therefore the same Guilhem de Bessa, wishing to unburden his conscience and shed light on the circumstance of the death of the late Raymon, therefore the said Guilhem de Bessa, in good faith and without any deception or fraud, out of free knowledge and willingly and from a certain knowledge, not co-opted nor deceived, nor in any way oppressed by anyone or any people or deceptively led, but instead moved by his own spontaneous will, and since the truth of the matter holds itself thus from what is written below, according to the judgment of truth, he freely confessed and publicly recognized as truth, before me, the notary, and the witnesses below, that he cast and struck the said blow and wound inflicted on the person of the late Raymon on the head, from which he died, and that the said death of the late Raymon was fathered by the same Guilhem de Bessa and after his own inclination without any assistance, advice, involvement, or support of any person; all this was because in recent years the late Raymon, along with three associates, harshly beat Guilhem on the occasion of a certain beating; this beating he nurtured and nurtures in his own breast, wishing to have vengeance, and so fathered the said death; Guilhem even intends from his own ability to avenge himself on the other associates of the late Raymon who were involved in the beating of Guilhem, who even beat him; and Guilhem asserts that this confession is true and firm and from it he will never dissent but continually persist in it. And thus Guilhem swore to heed and fulfill on the holy Gospels of God, bodily touched with his hand, to excuse anyone with knowledge of the wound and death of the late Raymon who might be accused of aid, exertion, involvement, advice, assistance, or support; of this confession made by me as true and just, I [that is, Guilhem] allow that a public instrument or public instruments be made for any person or persons wishing to have the substance of these matters. Redacted in Marseille in my house, the notary's, in the presence and witnessing of Master Isnart Durant, stonemason; Masel Gines, notary; and Rostahn Alexi, laborer, citizens of Marseille, witnesses especially called and summoned. And of me, Peire Giraut, public notary of Marseille and of the counties of Provence and Forcalquier, constituted by royal authority, who was present at these matters and, required and demanded by Guilhem, wrote this public instrument concerning these matters and sealed it with my own seal. An instrument was made.

## 121. A LAWSUIT BY NICOLAU GUILHEM, A CUTLER OF MARSEILLE

*The need to make peace was worked firmly into the practice of criminal law, a situation that allowed the relatives of some victims to game the system, as we see in this lawsuit from 1353.*

Source: Archives Départementales des Bouches-du-Rhône, France, 3B 50, folios 196r–203r, case opened 12 February 1353. Trans. Daniel Lord Smail.

The case of Nicolau Guilhem, alias Garnier, cutler [knife-maker] of Marseille.

The year as above [1353], the 12th of February. Before the noble and worthy lord Guilhem de Montoliu, a licenciate in decretals, substitute for the lord palace judge sitting as a tribunal, there appeared Bertran de Vellans, a goldsmith of Marseille, procurator for and relative of Nicolau Garnier, his son-in-law. He offered to the lord judge the titles written below and requested that he be allowed to prove them this same day.

In a letter obtained from the serene princes, Lord Louis and Lady Jeanne, king and queen of Jerusalem and Sicily, a grace was accorded to Nicolau Guilhem, alias Garnier, both for the sentence of contumacy as well as for the wounding and the death that is said to have followed from it on the person of Antoni Jardin, late goldsmith. This grace ought to be executed by the lord officials of the royal court of the city of Marseille. What is more, as is permitted from suppliants, Bertran de Vellans, as procurator and relative of Nicolau Garnier, offers the titles written below.

1) First, he intends to prove that Nicolau Garnier, through the intervention of Bertran de Vellans, his procurator and relative, made a peace and

concord and a remission of rancor and hatred with Guilhem Cauderie and with the brothers Bernart and Jacme Bonaut for wounds inflicted, as is said, on the person of the late Antoni Jardin, and for the death that is said to have followed from it. 2) Next, that the said Guilhem Cauderie and Bernart and Jacme Bonaut were cousins or blood relatives of the late Antoni Jardin.

[Titles 3–5 are missing but we can extrapolate them from the context: 3) Next, these three were Antoni's closest relations, both inside and outside the city; 4) Next, when Antoni died, these three were judged to be his closest relatives in Marseille; 5) Next, all the aforegoing is the public voice and fame in Marseille.]

Against Bertran appeared Johaneta Jardina, claiming an interest in this suit, and requested that a copy of the said titles be given to her and an appropriate day be assigned to her for its deliberation.

And the said lord judge, having conceded the copy to Johaneta, assigned a period of deliberation from today until next Friday so that she might put together interrogatory questions should she wish to do so. And in addition, he ordered that Bertran's witnesses be cited, and he ordered the citation to be made by Giraut de Pahentis, a crier of the court, who was present. The witnesses ought to appear today, in vesper, and he entrusted to me, Johan Joli, notary of the palace court, the task of hearing the witnesses.

The year as above, the 13th of February, Bertran appeared before the lord judge and produced as witnesses Robert de Rocca, Peire Sanchols, and Ugueta Bertrana of Marseille, along with Antoni Raynaut and Rostahn Flordeleon, and requested that their oaths be taken in the absence of the adversary party, which was legitimately cited but chose not to appear. These witnesses took the oath to speak the truth about the titles in the hands of me, Johan Joli.

And immediately, Johaneta Jardina appeared before me, Johan Joli, notary of the present suit, and said that from now on she does not wish to carry on with the present suit nor take any part in it.

The year as above, the 13th of February, Peire Sancho, a witness for Bertran de Vellans, the procurator, testified on the titles of proof, which were read to him and diligently explained in the vernacular. And first, on the first of those titles, interrogated on his oath he said that he knows practically nothing about the things contained in the first title except that he heard it said by many people who live on the street of the Goldsmithery and elsewhere that Nicolau Garnier made a peace and every sort of concord with Guilhem Cauderie and Bernart and Jacme Bonaut, brothers, citizens and residents of the aforesaid city. Asked by whom he heard this said, he answered by Johaneta Jardina, wife of the late Antoni, and from certain other people, quite a few of them, whose names he does not remember. Asked many other things on the title he said he doesn't know.

On the second of the titles, interrogated on his oath, he said he knows a great deal about the things contained in the title, because at the time when the said Antoni Jardine was alive, he used to identify Guilhem Cauderie and Bernart and Jacme Bonaut, brothers, as his cousins, affines, and relatives, and in turn Guilhem, Bernart, and Jacme continually used to call the late Antoni Jardin cousin, and they were held as such by those acquainted with them in the city of Marseille. Asked how he knows this, he answered on his oath that he personally heard the late Antoni, Guilhem, Bernart, and Jacme call each other cousins, relatives, and affines in turn and on many occasions. Although many more questions were asked of him, he said he knows nothing further.

'On the third of the titles, interrogated on his oath, he said that he knows nothing further about what is contained in the title except that the witness believes and used to believe that Antoni Jardin, during the time that he was living, had no other male or female relatives, affines, cousins, or friends more closely related to him than the said Guilhem Cauderie and Bernart and Jacme Bonaut, brothers. Even so, the witness said that he doesn't know whether the late Antoni Jardin might have had other cousins or relatives more closely related outside the city of Marseille. He said he knows nothing more on the title.

On the fourth of the titles, interrogated on his oath, he said that what is contained in the title is true, namely, that at the time of Antoni's death, Guilhem, Bernart, and Jacme were said and publicly adjudged to be Antoni's most closely related cousins and relatives, and till now are presently adjudged by those knowing them.

On the fifth of the titles, interrogated on his oath, he said it is true that everything contained in fuller detail in his deposition is the public voice and *fama* [rumor, reputation] in the city of Marseille. Asked among whom the *fama* can be found, he answered on his oath among those acquainted with the late Antoni, Guilhem, Bernart, and Jacme Bonaut, brothers. Asked what is *fama*, he answered that it is the common and vernacular speech of the people.

And generally interrogated whether he was taught, instructed etc. or whether he is related to the plaintiff, he answered no to each one....

*Depositions were then given by Robert de Roca, a silver merchant, Antoni Ray-naut, and Johan de Belloloco, barber. All are nearly identical to that of the previous witness. Then follows a deposition by Rostahn Flordeleon, goldsmith, in which the witness denied knowing much of anything about the facts in the case. It is possible that Rostahn, who shared the profession of goldsmith with the murder victim, was not sympathetic to Nicolau Garnier.*

On the same day, Ugueta Bertranda, witness produced and sworn on behalf of Bertran de Vellans, interrogated on her oath on the titles read and
diligently explained to her in the vernacular, said that she heard the things
which are contained in the title being said by Johaneta Jardina and by many
others whose names she does not recall. She doesn't know anything more
on it.

On the second title, interrogated on her oath, she said that Antoni Jardin,
Guilhem Cauderie, and Bernat and Jacme Bonaut often got together, calling
one another in turn blood relatives and affines and first cousins; more she
doesn't know.

On the third title, interrogated on her oath, she said that Antoni Jardin
did not have any more closely related blood relatives than Guilhem Cauderie
and Bernat and Jacme Bonaut.

On the fourth title, interrogated on her oath, she said that she is ignorant
of whether Guilhem Cauderie and Bernat and Jacme Bonaut had other blood
relatives more closely related than Antoni Jardin or not.

On the fifth title, interrogated on her oath, she said that she believes the
*fama* to be what she herself attested. Asked what is *fama*, she said she does not
know.

She was not taught etc. nor is she related etc.

The year above, the fifteenth of February, Bertran de Vellans appeared
before the lord substitute judge and asked that Johaneta Jardina be cited for
the purpose of seeing the publication of the witness depositions produced for
Bertran. Johaneta has frequently made accusations against Nicolau Garnier
and has opposed the grace conferred upon him by the most serene princes,
the lords king and queen of Jerusalem and Sicily. She has been giving objec-
tions and exceptions for the purpose stalling the proceedings, and she has on
many occasions harassed and has intended to harass Nicolau, exhausting him
through toils and expenses, and causing him to be put in jail. For this reason,
he is asking the lord judge to assign to Johaneta a specific time period within
which she should propose any exceptions, should she have any, as to why the
said grace is not sufficient for extinguishing his debt, with the proviso, if it
please his lordship, that after the expiration of the assigned time period, he
should not listen to her any further.

And the said lord substitute ordered that Johaneta be cited to come tomorrow evening, in terce, for the purpose of hearing the publication of the
depositions and for proposing exceptions, if she has any, against Nicolau and
the grace made to him by the royal excellence arising from the killing of the
late Antoni Jardin. By way of a second delay, he assigned next Wednesday,
with the proviso that should she not appear that day, he would decline to

listen to her any further. He ordered that this citation be made by Giraut de Paherius, crier of the court.

The crier left and then, returning, told me, Johan Joli, notary of the palace court of Marseille, that he personally cited the aforesaid Johaneta in the manner above, just as the lord judge ordered. Johaneta, however, responded to the crier that she is no longer interested in proceeding with the present lawsuit nor does she wish to involve herself in any way.

The following day, in terce, which was assigned by the lord substitute judge, Bertran de Vallens, the procurator, appeared before the substitute judge. Johaneta, the adversary party, was absent, even though she was legitimately cited, and he accused her of contumacy. He asked and requested that the witness depositions be opened, read, and publicized, and an instrument concerning their publication be made for him.

And the lord substitute, given Johaneta's contumacy, ordered that the depositions be publicized, read, and opened. And immediately the words of those witnesses, that is to say one for all of them, were publicized by me, the notary. Bertran asked that an instrument concerning this be made for him if necessary. It was enacted in Marseille in the Palace Court. Witnesses Peire Lort, notary, and Pons Maurel, notary.

## 122. A LAWSUIT AGAINST LOIS ORLET OF MARSEILLE

*As becomes clear in this case from 1353, the victim, Johan, had the right to claim both medical expenses and future interest from the man who injured him, Lois Orlet, meaning that since Johan had become incapacitated, he was owed a sort of pension. The dispute in the document below turns on the appropriate amount of this pension.*

Source: Archives Départementales des Bouches-du-Rhône, France, 3B 52, folios 12r–20r, case opened 20 September 1353. Trans. Daniel Lord Smail.

For the court against Lois Orlet.

In the year of the Lord 1353, the 20th of September, the distinguished gentleman Uguo Borgondion, the royal treasurer of the court of Marseille, appeared in the presence of the noble and distinguished lords Simon de Giron, palace court judge, and Guilhem de Montoliu and Uguo de Gemenas, the other two judges of the courts of Marseille, sitting in judgment in the palace court, and presented to them a certain sheet of paper whose contents are below, saying "I request that you to carry out the things in it."

The tenor of the paper.

Uguo Borgondio, the royal treasurer of this city, acting on behalf of the courts as his duty requires, appeared in the presence of the noble and distinguished lords Simon de Girona, palace court judge, and Guilhem de Montolieu and Uguo de Gemeñas, the judges of the other two courts of Marseille and said that Lois Orlet, alias de Tos, was condemned in the amount of 40 pounds by the mighty lord Raymon de Monte Albano, knight and former vicar of the city, during his last parlement, since, with his sword, he cut off the left hand of Johan Robert. Following this, Robert de Duracio is said to have remitted Lois this condemnation if he should follow the conditions outlined in the remission. And since Lois has failed to fulfill these conditions, the treasurer is now asking the lord judges that they ought to acknowledge that Lois owes 40 pounds to the court and can no longer benefit from the remission for the reasons given above. If it be done otherwise, which the treasurer does not believe will happen, he will pursue an appeal to the superior court or otherwise follow through on it. Concerning all this the treasurer requested that a public instrument be made for him. The witnesses were Johan Maurel and Bertomieu Bonvin.

And the lord judges desired to notify the said Lois of the aforegoing and to see the remission of condemnation to find out if it is indeed conditional, as was proposed in the statement. They also want to hear if Lois has any legitimate reason for adhering to the payment of the condemnation.... They ordered that the notice be sent to Lois by Jacme de Fonte, a crier of the court, such that he or someone acting in his name appear before them today, in the hour of vespers, for speaking about his rights. They gave the same deadline to the treasurer for demonstrating his own claims.

The crier, going and then returning, reported to me, the notary, that he found Lois in person and gave him the notification just as the lord judges required in their order. I, Peire Amiel, the notary of the palace court, wrote this.

On the day and hour designated above, the treasurer appeared before the lord judges pursuing his petition, and produced a certain act written by the hand of the notary Peire Amiel containing the indulgence granted by lord Robert de Duracio and including the conditions which have not been fulfilled by Lois. For this reason he repeated his request, and noted the lapse of time.

On the other side there appeared the said Lois, saying that, because he was incarcerated – that is to say, because he had been imprisoned in the royal jail, and only just now released – he has been unable to consult with his lawyer or make a personal appearance in court. In no way can he defend himself from the treasurer's petition, and therefore he asked that a transcript of the treasurer's petitions be given to him and a period of time be granted for deliberating on and responding to it. As the proceedings allow, he named, as his procurators, actors, and defenders in this case, Lord Guilhem Johan and Johan Penchirat, who are present, and Guilhem Baxiani, who is absent though available, and each one of them singly. Enacted in the palace court. Witnesses Antoni Lort, notary, and Johan Maurel, notary.

And the lord judges, wishing to hear the truth on these matters, asked Lois, who was present and listening, if a remission of condemnation had been given him as has been proposed and if he has made peace with the injured party and if he reimbursed him for his expenses and future interest. He answered that a remission had been given him and that it is not the case that he has made peace with the injured party, although in fact he had asked the injured party, who is currently present, that he make peace with him. He asked that the party be compelled by the lord judges to make peace with him, saying that he would make satisfaction for the expenses and future interest that he requests, and pleads and requests as stated above.

Johan Robert, the injured party who is present here, said that Lois never asked him about the peace but he was asked by others in his name, nor has he made satisfaction for the expenses and future interest. He is prepared to make peace with him as long as his expenses and future interest are satisfied. A transcript of the aforegoing acts was granted to Lois so that he can deliberate on this and learn about his rights, and next Monday, at the hour of terce, was assigned to him and to the treasurer.

On the day and time assigned above, which is the 23rd of September, the treasurer appeared before the lord judges, asking and requesting that the judges issue a ruling in the case. On the other side, Master Guilhem Johan, as named above, appeared before the lord judges, saying that since he has only just been able to acquire the transcript which was granted to him, he has not been able to consult with his lawyer nor can he inform the lord judges on these matters, therefore he asked for another delay.

And the lord judges asked the notary of the case if it was by his doing that Lois did not receive the transcript until now, or whether it was something to do with Lois. The notary answered that it was not his fault but that of Lois.

Therefore, since things ought to go ahead, the lord judges declared and ruled that unless Lois can prove that it was not his fault that peace was not made and expenses and interest left unpaid to Johan, then the treasurer would be allowed to demand the payment of the fine, regardless of whether the remission had been made conditionally, as has been said. If, however, he can prove that the conditions were successfully met or that it was not his fault that they were not fulfilled, they would not require that the condemnation be paid. For the purpose of proving this, they gave him a deadline of five days hence, and in the meantime will proceed to an examination of witnesses by the notaries of the court if they shall be presented.

The year above, the 25th of September, in the hour of vespers, Master Guilhem Johan appeared before the lord palace judge, in the presence of the royal treasurer, and said that he wished to offer interrogatory questions to be made to the adversary party's witnesses and, concerning the remission, offered the following witnesses, namely, Marques de Jerusalem, Bertran Johan, and Guilhem Blanc. He asked that they be examined and heard concerning the conditions described above which he was asked about, namely, that Lois had asked Johan Robert many times, or had had him asked, to make peace with him and to arrange for payment of the expenses and interest. Also, that it was not his fault that the conditions were not fulfilled. The lord judge wished to take the sworn oaths of the witnesses. In the presence of the treasurer, they swore to tell the truth.

In the year of the Lord and the day as above, Lois, standing in the presence of the lord vicar, promised to pay the 40 pounds to the treasurer in case the lord judges of the court should rule thus. Lois's wife, Marques de Jerusalem, Bertran Johan, and each one of them singly promised before the lord vicar and me, the notary, to stand as guarantors for Lois's promise to pay the 40 pounds. The treasurer asked for an instrument concerning these matters. It was enacted in the court; the witnesses were Primarcus Mirapeis and Johan Maurel, notary.

In the year above, the 27th of September, the hour of vespers, Master Guilhem Johan appeared before the lord judge, in the presence of the treasurer, and said that he should be allowed to produce the three witnesses who swore yesterday in the presence of the treasurer and have not been interrogated yet. This was not his fault but was owing to the negligence of the treasurer, who delayed giving his interrogatory questions until the hour of vespers yesterday, and then gave them orally to Peire Amiel, the notary, and not in writing. This was not Master Guilhem's fault but the negligence of the treasurer and because the notaries are so busy with the general council meeting that is taking place today that they cannot hear and examine his witnesses. And to avoid losing his case owing to a violation of the deadline, he asked that another period of time be assigned to him for the purpose of proving his case. To avoid denying the possibility of proof to the defendant, the judge extended the deadline in the present case until next Monday.

The examination of the witnesses. On the same day, Marques de Jerusalem, a witness offered on behalf of Lois Orlet, was requested and interrogated on the oath that he swore above if he knows whether Lois had fulfilled the conditions outlined by the illustrious lord Robert de Duracio concerning the indulgence made by him to Lois over the wounding of Johan Robert, which were read to the witness in the vernacular by me, the notary. He said that he knows nothing more about this except that he brought two florins to Johan, who at the time was lying wounded in bed, to help with his expenses; the money had been given to him by the wife of Lois. The injured man refused to accept the money. Asked where this took place, he said in his house. Asked about those present, he said Antoni Guigo, but he doesn't remember the day or the hour, except that Johan was wounded this year.

On the same day, Bertran Johan, a witness offered on behalf of Lois Orlet, was requested and interrogated on the oath that he swore above if he knows whether Lois had fulfilled the conditions outlined by the illustrious lord Robert de Duracio concerning the indulgence made by the lord Robert to Lois over the wounding of Johan Robert, which were read to the witness in the vernacular by me, the notary, or if he knows whether it was not his fault that the conditions were not fulfilled. He said that it is true and that he knows a great deal about it. The witness had been asked and requested by Lois to arrange a peace on Lois's behalf with the wounded party, Johan Robert, for the amputation of Johan's hand by Lois. He went to Johan's house this year, while the ailing man was lying in bed, and begged and pleaded and even admonished him, on Lois's behalf, that, moved by a reverence for God, he make peace with Lois over the wounding. Johan answered that he couldn't do it just now, since his wound was recent. As far as the expenses go, he said that he had heard from the wife of Lois Orlet that, by way of expenses, she had sent Johan two gold florins on one occasion and five gold florins on another; the latter she had sent via Guilhem de Martel and Aragon de Rabastenc, just as Guilhem and Aragon later told the witness. Concerning the expenses, the witness went on to say that he himself, upon Lois's request, promised from his own apothecary shop whatever sugar, unguents, and plasters the wounded man could want for his wound. Lois reimbursed him with his own money. He doesn't know anything more than this. Asked when this took place, he said this year not too long ago, around eight days after the wounding. Asked about the day, he said he doesn't remember. Asked what time of day, he said around terce. Asked about the place, he said within the injured man's house, while he was in bed. Asked about those present, he said Brother Paul and Brother Bernard Rodel, Franciscans, who were there to help make peace. The witness said that he offered on Lois's behalf to give Johan for his expenses and future interest a certain vine and land belonging to Lois and located in the territory of Marseille called Ibeline. It is three acres in size or thereabouts and is worth 100 pounds. He offered to give him this property on Lois's behalf for the expenses and future interest, in perpetuity, in the presence of the Franciscans named above. Asked if he knew whether Johan Robert or someone else in his name took the two florins and the five florins, as he had described, he said yes, according to the attestations of Guilhem de Martel and Aragon de Rabastenc, as far as the five are concerned, and according to the attestions of Johan Robert's wife and Bertran de Castilhon as far as the two florins are concerned as well as the five. He was not taught etc., nor is he related to the defendant.

In the year above, the 28th of September, Guilhem Blanc swore to tell the truth. Asked if he knew whether Lois had fulfilled the conditions imposed by Robert de Duracio..., he answered that it is true and that he knows a great deal about it all. This year, the illustrious Robert granted remissions and indulgents to the people of Marseille for offenses, crimes, and excesses that would prevail once a peace was obtained and expenses reimbursed. The witness, together with Johan de Sant Jacme of Marseille, was elected by the lord vicar in the general council to make peace settlements between the injured parties and the assailants, following Robert's orders. Once he was elected, on a certain day which he does not remember, the pleas were made to him on behalf of the wife and friends of Lois Orlet, who were asking that a peace be made on Lois's behalf. Lois was hiding in the church of St. Victor of Marseille, or so they say. They asked that a peace be made with Johan Robert for the wounding and amputation of his hand. Responding to these pleas, the witness, together with Johan de Sant Jacme, his partner, asked Johan to come to the court, and they admonished him to do business with Lois Orlet for the wounding and amputation of his hand. After many words, he finally answered that he needed to think about it. These things having been arranged, a few days later – he doesn't remember just how many – since Lois's wife kept bothering them daily with her requests, the witness and his partner went to Johan's house to hear his response concerning the peace. They found him lying in bed, and, asking him about the peace, he finally, after many words, answered them that he might be inclined to make peace with Lois Orlet to do honor to God, the city council, and the two peacemakers, once his expenses and medications had been reimbursed and future provisions made for the duration of his life, his wife's, and his children's. Once this was related to the wife of Lois Orlet, following other exchanges, the wife, on behalf of her husband and for the purpose of establishing a peace, offered to give Johan in perpetuity 100 royal pounds in addition to the expenses which had been made by him, the doctors, and his family. These offers having been made, the peacemakers presented the offers to Johan, who finally, after many words, answered that he couldn't do it for 100 pounds, but he could do it for 100 gold florins. And there things lay. Asked about those present, he said a certain Franciscan named Brother Paul and a certain partner of his. Asked about the time, he said during the last reign, which was when Robert granted the remissions and indulgences. He was not taught nor is he related to the litigant etc.

The year and day above, the hour of terce, the procurator appeared above the judge and asked that the oaths of other witnesses whom he intends to offer be received and that their statements on the subject be received and heard. And, by an order of the judge, the treasurer was called to appear before him to see the taking of the witnesses' oaths, although he declined to attend. The judge entrusted to me, Peire Amiel, notary, the task of receiving the oaths and undertaking the examination of the defendant's witnesses in this case. And immediately the procurator called as witnesses Guilhem de Martel and Aragon de Rabastenc.

Guilhem de Martel, witness, swore to give truthful testimony. He was asked on his oath whether Lois had fulfilled the conditions imposed by the illustrious lord Robert de Duracio…. He said that it is true and that he knows a great deal about it, namely, that not too long ago, this year, the distinguished men Guilehm Blanc and Johan de Sant Jacme were elected in the general council to make peace for injuries and other things for which the illustrious lord Robert de Duracio had granted remissions. The witness, upon the request of Lois Orlet, who at that time was hiding in the church of St. Victor, repeatedly asked the two peacemakers to arrange a peace on Lois's behalf with Johan Robert for the wounding and amputation of his hand. In the end, Guilhem Blanc, one of the two peacemakers, said to the witness that, although on Lois's behalf they had offered to give Johan for his expenses and his future life earnings either 100 pounds or a certain piece of land belonging to Lois worth 110 pounds, Johan refused to agree on the expenses. He did, however, say that, together with Aragon de Rabastenc, he had on one occasion taken to Johan's house five gold florins and passed it over to him on behalf of Lois's wife for reimbursing his expenses. At the time, he refused to take the five florins, but said to the emissaries that they should take them to his *compère* [spiritual kinsman] Johan de Sant Jacme and, if Johan should advise that he should accept them for the wound, then they should give the five florins to Johan de Sant Jacme on behalf of the wounded man. So the witness and Aragon went to Johan de Sant Jacme and, running across him on the New Street, told him what the injured Johan had said, and offered the five florins for the expenses occasioned by the wound. On the spot, Johan de Sant Jacme had the five florins taken by Peire de Sant Jacme, his nephew, who was also there, so as to carry them to the wounded man. He also said that he had heard from Master Salves, a Jew, who was the surgeon assigned to Johan Robert, that he had been fully paid by Lois for his salary and efforts. He knows nothing further. He was not taught nor is he related to the defendant etc.

The year above, the last day of September, Aragon de Rabastenc, a witness for the plaintiff, swore to offer truthful testimony…

[Aragon's deposition, as recorded, is identical to the preceding one.]

The year above, the last day of September, in the hour of vespers. With the parties in the presence of the lord judge, the judge declared that owing to the lateness of the hour the case would be continued the following day in terce.

At this time and day, the 1st of October, in the hour of terce, the treasurer appeared before the judge in Lois's presence and requested that the witness depositions produced on Lois's behalf be published and read so that he can make his statements against them. For the other side there appeared Lois, temporarily revoking his procurators, and since he hasn't had a chance to consult his lawyer he asked that another delay be assigned before the hearing of the witness depositions. And for purpose of hearing the publication of the witness depositions or for explaining why they ought not to be heard, the judge assigned to Lois the same day, in the hour of vespers, to which they would proceed even if he is absent.

At the hour of vespers, Master Guilhem Johan, the procurator, appeared before the judge in the presence of the treasurer and asked that the depositions be opened and published, and once they have been published he requested that the judge issue a sentence in this case. And the treasurer asked for the same thing, preserving the right to protest the words or status of the witnesses. And the judge ordered that the depositions be opened, read, and published. I, Peire Amiel, the notary, proceeded to the publication as ordered by the judge. With this done, the treasurer, so as to show the rights of the court, presented the fourth condemnation of the royal court of Marseille, showing that part where the sentence of the court against Lois was entered and the format of Lois's absolution, through the sequence of which he requested that the judge issue a ruling in this case.

And Master Guilhem Johan said that for the entire period of time after the wounding he offered to make peace and was continuously prepared to make reasonable satisfaction to Johan following the format of the grace made to him by lord Robert and it wasn't his fault that the conditions were not met either before the grace or afterward. Then, following the sentence of the splendid and powerful lord Raymon de Monte Albino, former vicar of Marseille, he was absolved for the reasons given by the vicar, and the inquest and sentence were canceled, just as appears in the fourth condemnation produced above by the treasurer. He is prepared to prove the absolution if the judge wants to see it.

And, for the purpose of hearing his ruling, the judge assigned this day, in vespers.

The year above, the 16th of October, in terce, Master Guilhem Johan appeared before the judge, in the presence of the treasurer, and asked that the judge issue a ruling on the aforegoing. And the treasurer said that it seems to him that he should be able to demand the payment of the fine. And the lord judge said that, concerning the aforegoing, he took note of the remission made by Lord Robert de Duracio on the conditions described in it. He also saw the attestations of the witnesses produced on Lois's behalf, from which it seems to have been proven that he had very often asked Johan Robert to make peace with him, and that he would pay for his expenses, on account of which it may seem that Lois should no longer be pursued to pay this fine. However, since this has not actually been achieved, since Lois has not received a letter officially executing the remission of condemnation from the seneschal of Provence, he does not intend to prevent the treasurer from executing the condemnation nor similarly does he intend to do anything against the pardon and remission.

The treasurer asked that an instrument be made for him if necessary. It was enacted in the palace court in the presence of Antoni Lort and Guilhem Feniculi, notaries, and me, Peire Amiel, notary of the court.

In the year of the Lord as above, the 17th of October, in vespers, Johan Robert, the wounded man, came into the presence of the lord judges. Since he has been rendered helpless by Lois de Tos, owing to the wounding and the amputation of his hand, he requested that the value of the work which he cannot do and will not be able to do in the future be adjudged to him by the lord judges, in execution of the ruling issued on this matter by virtue of which Lois was condemned.

And the lord judges ordered that Lois de Tos be cited by Giraut de Paernis, crier, to appear in court this Saturday in vespers so as to hear the amount to be adjudged to him, and if he should not come they would proceed anyway.

## 123. A LAWSUIT BY ANHELLON FABER, A BUTCHER OF MARSEILLE

*This case from 1362 is a demonstration of how difficult it could be to get your enemies to make peace with you and also shows how, by withholding peace, enemies could make ongoing trouble.*

Source: Archives Départementales des Bouches-du-Rhône, France, 3B 62, folios 73r-75v, case opened 27 November 1362. Trans. Daniel Lord Smail.

On behalf of Anhellon Faber, butcher of Marseille.

The year of the Lord 1362, the 27th of November. Appearing in the presence of the eminent lord Pons de Montels, knight, vicar of the city of Marseille, and the nobleman lord Antoni de Sarciano, judge of the palace court of the aforesaid city, Anhellon offered and presented a written statement requesting the following:

In the presence of the distinguished and puissant men, Lord Pons de Montels, knight and vicar of the city of Marseille, and also Lord Antoni de Sarciano, jurist and judge of the palace court of this city, Anhellon Faber, a resident of this city, states that upon the instigation of a number of people, this same Anhellon, following an order of the lord vicar, was arrested and placed in the royal jail. The situation was that Anhellon had been accused in the court of the death of his wife, Dousiana, and then publicly absolved of this death by the lord vicar. Although Anhellon had made peace with all of the late Dousiana's relatives on the male and female side before the absolution, as he was bound to do, some of Dousiana's relatives from the city of Marseille requested a further inquest against Anhellon, saying that, since he hadn't made any peace with them, no such peace existed. Yet the ones making the complaint don't actually live in the city of Marseille. Following this, the general council of the city made a ruling that trouble-makers and those refusing to make peace with the friends and relatives of the victim for any injury whatsover ought to be exiled following an order of the said lord vicar, as the minutes of the council state. And Anhellon is prepared to make peace with all of Dousiana's relatives on the female and male side if there are any with whom he hasn't already done so, wherefore he requests that the lord vicar and the lord judge, as duty and their oath require, observe everything contained in the council minutes. At the same time they should revoke the order made to Anhellon that he be exiled from the city, and if they do otherwise, he shall appeal the decision. He requested that a public instrument of this be made, along with the response of the said lords vicar and judge.

And the said lords vicar and judge, persisting in their order that Anhellon must be exiled from the city for the whole of the present day, under penalty of amputation of a foot, responded that they are ready to listen to give Anhellon a favorable hearing, once the things that are presented in his statement be proven. Up till now, neither Anhellon nor his procurator, if he has chosen one, have shown them much of anything related to these matters.

Anhellon immediately said that, as long as a sufficient amount of time is given to him, he is prepared to prove the things contained in the statement to the satisfaction of the lords vicar and judge. He requested that a deadline be offered to him. They assigned to him a period of five days for proving the things contained in the statement through his procurator. For the purpose of proving the aforegoing, Anhellon elected his own brother, currently absent although available, as his procurator. *An act was made.*

In the year of our Lord as above, the 28th of November, in terce, Antoni Fabri, the brother and procurator of Anhellon Fabri, appeared before the lords vicar and judge, and his act of procuration was fully noted in the present acts. In addition to the things he is pleading, he asked that the said lords vicar and judge condescend, out of the duty of their offices, to compel certain relatives of Dousiana on the male or female side, to make peace with Anhellon according to the manner contained in the decision of the general council dedicated to the topic of making peace. To observe this decision, the vicar and judge should give orders to have Raymon Audebert, notary of the court, collect the information from the cartulary where the said decision was written and write it in the present acts so as to have the proper information about the claims made in the statement offered by Anhellon. The procurator is ready to give proof of the peace made by certain friends and relatives of the late Dousiana and also to prove that those who refuse to make peace were often asked to do so on Anhellon's behalf. Their names are Rixendis, the wife of Antoni Salusse, and Antoni Valentie, the nephew of the late Dousiana. He protested that it is not Anhellon's fault that a peace hasn't been arranged as required by the council.

And before anything else, the vicar and judge ordered me, Raymon Audebert, notary of the palace court, to extract the decision of the council from the council's cartulary and place it, word for word, in the present acts, according to the request made by the procurator. They ordered that the siblings Rixendis and Antoni be cited by Peire Augier, crier, to appear before them in the aforementioned court at the hour of vespers under penalty of 100 royal pounds, so as to give the required responses to the complaints about them made by the procurator.

Peire Augier, crier of the court, left and then, returning, reported to me, the notary, that he had personally cited the aforementioned siblings just as was required of him above by the vicar and judge.

Following the order of the vicar and judge, I, the notary Raymon, drew up and transcribed the act as below. This was the tenor of this decision:

So that the city of Marseille and its citizens might nourish a perpetual love, and so that every matter of hatred and anger might accordingly be eliminated and, from the hardships and dangers which have been provoked for so long, be calmed into peace and friendship, it pleases the entire council to require the lord vicar to bring however many trouble-makers there may be in the city of Marseille, for whatsoever reason, into a state of peace and concord and, out of honor and reverence for the crown and for the safety, salvation, and restoration of this city, to punish the obdurate and the disobedient with the penalty of perpetual exile from Marseille and its district....

In the year of the Lord as above, the 29th of November, Antoni appeared before the said lords vicar and judge, and repeated his request that Rixendis, the wife of Antoni Salusse, and Antoni Valentie, her brother, niece and nephew of the late Dousiana, wife of Anhellon, be compelled to make peace with the said Anhellon. As shown above, Anhellon is ready to make such a peace, and Antoni his brother, acting as procurator, is also ready to do so. If they refuse, they should, following the decision of the council, be perpetually exiled from the city and its district as disobedient people. The procurator also asked the vicar and judge to annul their order to Anhellon to leave the city and its district for the whole day on Saturday, which has already passed, and to grant him full authority and license, as an obedient son, to return to the city. He is ready, again and again, now and always, to make peace with the late Dousiana's niece and nephew, following the spirit of the council's decision.

And the vicar and judge, having heard the request made by Antoni Fabri, the brother and procurator of the said Anhellon, who is currently absent, and having seen and read the transcript of the decision, which makes it clear that the said niece and nephew and other citizens, associates, or injured parties should be forced to make peace or suffer exile, they ordered Rixendis, who was present, and under penalty of 200 pounds and the amputation of a foot, that she make peace with the said Anhellon or his procurator within the next two days or else leave the city and its territory as an exile. They ordered a crier of the court of Marseille who was present and listening to the order to go to Antoni Valentie, the brother of Rixendis, currently absent, and order him, under the aforegoing penalty, both monetary and corporal, to make peace with the said Anhellon or his brother within the said two days or else depart the city of Marseille and its district as one who is disobedient. In addition, he should not presume to come back at any time once those two days have passed unless he has already fulfilled what he was ordered to do by the vicar and judge. And for the purpose of listening to their response to the above petitions and requests made by the procurator, they assigned Thursday, in terce, as a deadline to the procurator. Concerning all of this, Antoni requested an instrument.

In the year as above, the 2nd of December, in terce. Antoni Fabri, the brother and procurator of Anhellon Fabri, appeared before the said lords vicar and judge sitting in law and asked that his petitions be vigorously executed. He is ready to hear the response of the vicar and judge. Since Rixendis, the niece of the late Dousiana, has not fulfilled the order given her by the said lords vicar and judge, rejecting it wholly in contempt of the court, the procurator, acting in the aforesaid name, requested that the court proceed against the said Rixendis as justice demands, and at the same time proceed against the said Antoni Valentie, Rixendis's brother, who, although he was sought out, has remained absent lest he be compelled to make peace through the fitting remedies of the law.

And the vicar and judge delayed the present case until the hour of vespers.

## 124. AN INQUEST INTO THE MURDER OF BERNART BERENGIER IN MARSEILLE

*Bernart Berengier was a minor cleric, as was one of his killers, Nicolau Jausap, which is why this case from 1400 ended up in ecclesiastical court and not in a secular court. Like Nicolau, many members of the minor clergy could and did marry; in this particular case, the term* clericus *meant that the men so called had learned to read and write and had undertaken a minimal set of vows. Most married clergy of this type lived lives indistinguishable from those of the laity.*

Source: Archives Départementales des Bouches-du-Rhône, France, 3B 5G 772, folios 24r-30v. Trans. Daniel Lord Smail.

Against Nicolau Jausap, otherwise called Binayga, a married cleric of Marseille, and against all those, all together and individually, who may in any way be found guilty of the things written below through influence, effort, aid, advice, dealings, and preferment.

In the year of the Lord 1400, Thursday, the 16th of December. If the guardians of justice should not suppress the growing number of evil-doers and extirpate them by means of the due precision of justice, doing honor to God and the prince, they would be committing grave, damnable, and rash things to their subjects who would then have no fear about pursuing their own misdeeds. Therefore an inquest, initiated both by the present episcopal court of Marseille and also by an order of the venerable and distinguished lord Gilibert de Ferratorio, jurist of the church of Toloney, prior of the vicar general and the official of the Marseille court..., is being made against Nicolau Jausap, otherwise named Binayga, a married cleric, and all those, all together and individually, who may in any way be found guilty of the things written below. It concerns this, namely, that it has just come to the attention of the said official and the present court, conveyed, that is, by a serious public *fama* [rumor, here a report] that is not to be endured and cannot be brushed aside, that the accused man ... wounded and killed Bernart Berengier, son of the late Raymon Berengier of the city of Marseille, a married cleric. He was joined by several of Bernart's capital enemies, namely Johaneta Rostahne, the wife of Uguo Rostahne, laborer of the city of Marseille, and Johanet Rostahne, the couple's son. Today, around the hour of the Ave Maria, armed with long knives known as "*bregomasses*," with blades longer than the legal limit [arms restrictions were common in the period], and with bucklers,... javelins or darts,... and various other arms of diverse types, wishing to carry their despicable dealings and damnable plot through to a conclusion and desiring to direct their illicit acts toward evil-doing, moved by diabolic inspiration, with their weapons drawn, they attacked Bernart Berengier with the aforesaid weapons at the corner of the street known since ancient times in the vernacular as the Corner of Cavalhon, as he was passing quietly through the street of Johan Ricau, as it has been known since the ancient times, in which the arrested parties live, going along peacefully and quietly toward his own home, located near there. The said Johanet struck Bernart first in the left arm with a dart and wounded him severely. Then Johaneta Rostahne struck him two blows with a great staff, one of them on the head, and the other on the shins, and from these blows he immediately fell prostrate on the ground before the house of Folco Arnaut of Marseille, Bernart's neighbor. As he was lying prostrate, Johanet Rostahne struck Bernart with two piercing blows on his left hip and wounded him lethally, causing a great deal of blood to flow. Finally, Nicolau Jausap struck and lethally wounded him on the head with two blows of the blade of his long knife or *bregomass*, as Bernart lay there prostrate on the ground, causing a great effusion of blood. From these blows and wounds as described, which the arrested parties inhumanly inflicted on the person of Bernart, the same Bernart is now lying heavily in bed, afflicted by the fear of death more than he hopes for life. Thus, he [Nicolau] is liable for the penalties prescribed by the sacred law against all those committing such rash ventures.

It has also come to the attention of the said lord official and the present court that Nicolau Jausap, as one both accused and guilty of the aforegoing, was fearful of the court and therefore, so as not to be caught and detained and otherwise punished for the aforegoing, went to the church of La Major of Marseille along with Johanet Rostahne and took refuge and sanctuary in the church, so that he might enjoy ecclesiastical immunity and liberty and an exemption from pontifical orders conceded to the Church in times past. From this we can infer that he is aware of and guilty of the aforegoing.

A zeal for justice and the duty of the office together with the enormity of the deed rightly compels the lord official of the present court to inquire into and gather the truth of the aforementioned, since it is an evil model and worthy of correction and punishment.... Therefore the episcopal court proceeds to an inquest against the accused in the manner written out below.

The tenor of the clerical privilege of Bernart Berengier. We, Guilhem, by divine sufferance the bishop of Marseille, make known to all that we confer a first clerical tonsure on our beloved in Christ, Bernart Berengier of Marseille, son of Raymon, suitable in letters and age, and born of a legitimate marriage, having first been proven by means of an examination, and it is our wish that he enjoy clerical privilege for this reason. In attestation of this, we had this, our letter, drawn up and sealed with our pontifical seal. Made and given the corridor of our episcopal house in Marseille in the year of the birth of the Lord 1373, the 4th of January.

The deposition of the accused. Since this astonishing crime has come to the attention of the aforesaid officials, these same officials...ordered and required me, Guilhem Barban, notary of the present court, present and listening, to go to the church of La Major so as to find out the truth of the matters contained in the inquest titles and whether Nicolau carries the habit and tonsure, and also if he wishes to benefit from clerical privilege as far as the contents in the inquest are concerned. I, the notary, wishing to obey the court and accept the orders of the lord officials, went immediately to the church, where I climbed the campanile of the church along with Lord Folco Amat, a priest and beneficed cleric belonging to the church. In the campanile I found Nicolau along with Johanet Rostahne. And I drew Nicolau to a spot located above the church's pavement in the presence of the witnesses whose names are written below. He was wearing a great multi-colored robe without any fringe made of a different cloth, a hood, and sandals made of bluish cloth. I asked him whether he was a cleric, and he answered "Yes, a married cleric." I also asked him if he was accustomed to wearing the clerical tonsure; he answered yes and immediately lifted the hood from his head and, having inspected it, I found that he was wearing the clerical tonsure. Asked further by me, the notary, if he wished to plead benefit of the clergy concerning those matters outlined against him in the inquest titles,... he answered yes. Asked if he had wounded Bertran Berengier, he said no. Although many other questions were posed to him, he admitted to nothing further.

Acted in Marseille above the floor of the said church in the presence of lord Folco Amat; Jacme de Paris, deacon of Toulon; and the aforesaid Johanet Rostahne, witnesses specially asked and called for this purpose. And I, Guilhem Barban, notary of the said court etc.

The information from the wounded man. Next, in the year above, the 17th day of the month of December, near the hour of prime, I, Guilhem Barban, notary of the present court, was ordered and commanded by the lord officials, together with Jacme Lucian, another of the servants of the court, to go to the house of Bernart Berengier, the wounded man, where he lives in the quarter of Cavalhon. The purpose was to gather from him complete information concerning who had wounded him. Immediately after arriving at his house, I, the notary, found Bernart lying wounded in bed in one of the rooms of the house, suffering from his injuries. After he took an oath on the holy Gospels, I interrogated him about the contents of the inquest in the presence of the witnesses specially called for this purpose, whose names are below. I first read out loud the contents of the inquest in the vernacular. Interrogated diligently on his oath, he said and attested that it is true, and that he knows a great deal about what is contained in the inquest that he can tell the present court. Yesterday evening, around the time of sunset, he invited

Nicolau Novel of Marseille to eat dinner with him in his house and in the church or house of St. Antoine. Following the invitation, he and Nicolau, at the hour of the Ave Maria, were coming along together toward the aforesaid house or church of St. Antoine, and walking along the broad street where his *compère* lives, namely Nicolau Jausap; once they got to the corner of the street where Johaneta Rostahne lives, he met up with Johanet Rostahn, son of Johaneta and of Uguo Rostahn of Marseille, armed with a long knife or *bregomass* with an illegally long blade, a buckler, and a javelin or dart. Johanet immediately asked him these words or ones similar: "O Bernart Berengier, now is the time that you'll speak to me or offer threats" and on the spot, his mind clouded by anger, he unsheathed the dart or javelin which he threw at the witness, and he, the witness, was struck a piercing blow in the left arm and horribly wounded, causing blood to flow. Next he drew his knife with which he struck the witness a blow to the head with the blade and horribly wounded him, causing blood to flow. Following this, Johaneta Rostahne, so as to assist her son Johanet, joined the fight bearing a great staff, and she struck the witness two blows, namely, one to the head and the other on the shins. Owing to these blows he fell prostrate on the ground before the house of Folco Arnaut, the witness's neighbor. Jorgi Marin then joined the fight and, holding a ball and chain, he struck the witness a blow on the left side from which he immediately fell prostrate on the ground. Following this Nicolau Jausap alias Binayga joined the fight bearing his sword or *bregomass* with an illegally long blade, and he immediately rushed out at him where he lay prostrate on the ground and struck the witness three blows, namely, one in the head with the blade and two piercing blows to the left hip, causing a great flow of blood. Asked if he wounded the wife of Johanet Rostahn on her face with a ball and chain, he said no. Asked if he was walking along armed with a long knife, a buckler, a ball and chain, or other defensive arms, he answered no. Asked about those present, he answered that he does not remember since, at the time of day at which the fight took place, so great a multitude of people came to the fight and especially so many women whose surnames and forenames he does not currently remember. Asked if he wishes to plead benefit of the clergy he responded yes. Asked if at the time of the fight or battle the witness was walking along wearing habit and tonsure, he answered yes. Although many other questions were posed to Bernart, he said that he doesn't know anything more about the things contained in the inquest.

These were enacted in the city of Marseille in a room of Bernart's house. The witnesses present, who were specially called for this purpose, were Jacme Bertran, Peire Garin, Bertomieu Andran, and Jacme Lucian, all citizens and residents of Marseille. And me, Guilhem Barban, notary of the court, etc.

Next, the lord official, so as to maintain the law of the present court and for ascertaining clear information about everything contained in the titles of inquest..., wished and desired that each and every person who is aware of and has knowledge about the things contained in the accusation be cited by one of the servants of the present court. Having been cited by me, the said notary, and following an oath taken on the holy Gospels by each and every one of them, they were heard and diligently examined one by one and apart. Their words and depositions were written into the present transcript, word for word, by me, the notary. And their examinations and the taking of their oaths was undertaken by me, the notary.

The report of the servant. In the year and day above, the 17th of December, Jacme Lucian, one of the servants of the court, reported to me, the notary, that he had personally cited the people whose names are written below to give true testimony concerning the contents of the accusation, namely, Rostahn de Sort, weaver; Guilhem Galian; Monet Berengier, son of Jacme Berengier; Raymon Santolh; Laurona Franca, wife of Raymon Franc; Garsens, the wife of Guilhem Galian; Antoneta Surllota, wife of Peire Surlloti of Marseille; Johan Alohier and Alazays his wife; Uguet Arnaut; Raymon Santolh; their wives and sons; and Batrona Milhona, just as he was ordered to do by the official. I, Guilhem Barban, notary, wrote this.

The examinations of the witnesses.

In the year of the Lord above, the 18th of December, Monet Berengier, son of Jacme Berengier, laborer of Marseille, twenty-eight years of age or thereabouts, a witness produced on behalf of the said court, having been cited and sworn, promised and swore, with his hand touching the holy Gospels, to say and attest the pure truth concerning the matters contained in the accusation, it having first been read to him in the vernacular. Diligently interrogated on his oath by me, the said notary, concerning the things written above and below, he said and attested that it is true, and that he knows a great deal about the things contained in it, namely, that last Thursday, which was the 16th of December, around the hour of the Ave Maria, the witness, as he was standing before his own house located in the broad street of Cavalhon, unloading two of his animals who were laden with grape juice, he saw a fight in the street between the people named in the accusation, namely, Bernart Berengier, Johanet Rostahn, and Nicolau Jausap, alias Binagya. And he saw Johanet throwing a javelin or dart at Bernart Berengier though he couldn't tell if he struck and wounded Bernart with the dart. It is true that the witness heard it said by other people who had come to the fight, whose names and forenames he doesn't presently recall, that Johanet Rostahn struck and wounded Bernart on the left arm, causing blood to flow. Next, he saw Bernart Berengier lying prostrate on the ground before the house of Folco Arnaut, his own neighbor. He also heard it said by the aforementioned people that Johaneta Rostahne, Johanet's mother, had knocked Bernart to the ground with a single blow from a staff. At any rate, with Bernart lying prostrate, he reported that Guilhalmona, Bernart's wife, threw herself on top of his body and shouted these words or similar ones out loud to the said Nicolau Jausap, namely, "O false friend, you are killing my husband." Despite these words, he saw Nicolau strike Bernart a blow to the head with the blade of the long knife or *bregomass* that was drawn in his hand, and he wounded him, causing blood to flow. Next he saw Johanet strike Bernart, lying there prostrate on the ground, behind the left hip, using his long knife or *bregomass*, and he wounded him, causing blood to flow. Asked if Jorgi Marin joined the fight against Bernart Berengier, he answered no. Asked if Uguo Rostahn, the father of Johanet Rostahn, and Guillelmet Rostahn his son joined the fight against Bernart, he answered that he didn't know. Asked about those present, he answered that he doesn't remember at present, since it was night and dark, and he didn't recognize the people and doesn't even know them. Although many other questions were asked of him, he answered to each one that he knows nothing other than what he attested above.

The same day, Laurona Franca, wife of Raymon Franc, laborer of Marseille, forty years of age or thereabouts, a witness produced on behalf of the said court, having been cited and sworn, promised and swore, with her hand touching the holy Gospels, to say and attest the pure truth concerning the matters contained in the accusation, it having first been read to her in the vernacular. Diligently interrogated on her oath by me, the said notary, concerning the things written above and below, she said and attested that it is true and that she knows a great deal about the things contained in the accusation. Standing before the house of Monet Berengier, the witness saw a big fight in the street between Johanet Rostahn and Nicolau Jausap alias Binayga on the one side and Bernart Berengier of Marseille on the other, and all this taking place last Thursday, around the hour of the Ave Maria. As Bernart was drawing back toward his house, Johanet Rostahn threw a javelin or dart toward him, and with the dart struck Bernart a blow on the left arm and wounded him, causing blood to flow. Next, she said Johaneta Rostahne, Johanet's mother, coming into the fight bearing a huge staff, with which she struck Bernart a blow to the head on the back side, and from this blow Bernart immediately fell prostrate to the ground before the house of Folco Arnaut, his neighbor. While he was lying there prostrate Guillelmona, Bernart's wife, came to the fight and, lying on top of Bernart's body, she cried out loud to Nicolau Jausap, who was holding a long knife drawn in his hands, using these or similar words, namely, "O, false friend, you are killing my husband." Despite these words, she saw Nicolau strike Bernart Berengier a blow to the head with his drawn knife and wound him horribly, causing a great effusion of blood. Subsequently she saw Johanet Rostahn strike Bernart with a blow to his left hip, using his long knife, which was drawn, and wound him horribly, causing blood to flow. Asked whether she knows or heard it said that Jorgi Marin joined the fight against Bernart, the witness answered no. Asked about those present, she said that she doesn't remember at present, since it was practically night and she did not recognize the people who came to the fight and doesn't know about them. Although many other questions were asked of her, she answered to each one that she knows nothing other than what she said and attested above.

The same day, Garsens, the wife of Guilhem Galian, citizen of Marseille, twenty-five years of age or thereabouts, a witness produced on behalf of the said court, having been cited and sworn, promised and swore, with her hand touching the holy Gospels, to say and attest the pure truth concerning the matters contained in the accusation, it having first been read to her in the vernacular. Diligently interrogated on her oath by me, the said notary, concerning the things written above and below, she said and attested that it is true and that she knows nothing beyond what is contained in it. Last Thursday, around the hour of the Ave Maria, as the witness was standing inside her house, located on the street of Cavalhon near the house of Bernart Berengier who was identified in the accusation, she heard a commotion in the street and immediately ran to the hallway of her house and saw a great fight. She immediately came down from her house and when she was in the street she saw Johaneta Rostahne, Johanet Rostahn's mother, striking Bernart Berengier twice with a great staff which she was holding in her hands, one of them, namely, behind the shoulder blades and the other on Bernart's shins. From these blows Bernart immediately fell prostrate on the ground before the house of Folco Arnaut. As he was lying prostrate, she saw Guillelmona, Bernart's wife, place herself on his body, crying out loud to Nicolau Jausap, who was holding a long knife or *bregomass* drawn in his hand, these or similar words, namely, "O false friend, you are killing my husband underneath me." Despite these words, she saw Nicolau strike Bernart, lying there prostrate on the ground, two blows to the head with his long knife, which was drawn, causing a great flow of blood. Then she saw Johanet strike Bernart, still lying prostrate on the ground, a piercing blow to the left hip with his long knife, which was drawn, and wounding him, causing blood to flow. Next, she saw Uguo Rostahn, Johaneta's husband, joining the fight carrying in his hand a dart or javelin, but even so she didn't see Uguo striking Bernart anywhere on his body. Asked who was present at the fight, she answered that she does not remember, since there was a great multitude of people who had come to the fight and especially the neighbors from the neighborhood, and she didn't recognize them because it was night. Although many other questions were asked of her, she answered to each one that she knows nothing other than what she said and attested above.

The same day Antoneta, the wife of Peire Surllot of Marseille, thirty years of age or thereabouts, a witness produced on behalf of the said court, having been cited and sworn, promised and swore, with her hand touching the holy Gospels, to say and attest the pure truth concerning the matters contained in the accusation, it having first been read to her in the vernacular. Diligently interrogated on her oath by me, the said notary, concerning the things written above and below, she said and attested that it is true and that she knows a great deal about the things contained in it. Last Thursday, a little before the hour of the Ave Maria, as the witness was standing inside her house, located in the street of Cavalhon touching the house of Uguo Rostahn, she heard a great noise in the street and immediately came down from her house. When she was in the street she saw Johanet Rostahn, the son of Uguo Rostahn, carrying in his right hand a long knife or *bregomass*, and in the other hand he was carrying a javelin or dart, and also Nicolau Jausap, alias Binayga, with his long knife or *bregomass* drawn. They were following Bernart Berengier who was drawing back toward his own home, and when he was before the house of Folco Arnaut, his neighbor, Johanet Rostahn threw the dart at Bernart and struck him a piercing blow on his left arm, causing blood to flow. Then she saw Johaneta Rostahne, the wife of Uguo Rostahn, joining the fight carrying a great staff, and she struck him a blow behind the shoulder blades, from which he fell prostrate to the ground before Folco's house. As he was lying prostrate, she saw Guillelmona, Bernart's wife, immediately lying on top of him, crying out loud to Nicolau these or similar words, namely, "Don't do this, friend, don't kill my husband from under me." The witness herself was holding Nicolau from behind by his cloak and was pulling or drawing him back by the robe so that he would not wound Bernart, saying to Nicolau these words or similar, namely, "O Nicolau, do not do this; don't you see that this is forbidden." Despite these words, she saw Nicolau strike Bernart as he was lying there on the ground two blows to the head with his long knife, wounding him with the blade and causing a flow of blood. And she also saw Johanet Rostahn strike Bernart a piercing blow on the left hip with this long knife, which was drawn, wounding him and causing a flow of blood. In addition to this, the witness said and attested that she saw Uguo Rostahn carrying a mid-sized sword into the fight, although she didn't see him hit Bernart with the sword. She also saw Guillelmet Rostahn, Uguo's son, carrying in his hands some stones, although he didn't throw them. Asked if Jorgi Marin was involved in the fight, she answered no. Although many other questions were asked of her, she answered that she knows nothing other than what she said and attested. Asked about those present, she answered that she doesn't remember at present, since it was night and she could hardly recognize the people.

The same day, Huguet Arnaut, son of Folco Arnaut of Marseille, twenty-five years of age or thereabouts, a witness produced on behalf of the said court, having been cited and sworn, promised and swore, with his right hand touching the holy Gospels, to say and attest the pure truth concerning the matters contained in the accusation, it having first been read to him in the vernacular. Diligently interrogated on his oath by me, the said notary, concerning the things written above and below, he said and attested that it is true and that he knows nothing other than what is contained in it except as follows. Last Thursday, the 16th of December, as the witness was sitting in his father's house eating dinner with him and his mother, he heard a great uproar and a shouting of people in the street. Hearing this, he swiftly went out to the hall, and saw Johaneta Rostahne, wife of Uguo Rostahn of Marseille, carrying a great staff, with which she struck their neighbor Bernart Berengier a blow to the head where the pulse is located. From this blow he immediately fell to the ground prostrate before the witness's house. Then he saw Johanet Rostahn, Uguo's son, strike Bernart a piercing blow to the left hip with his long knife, which was drawn, and he wounded him, causing blood to flow. Subsequently he said and attested that he saw a man whom he didn't recognize very well, owing to the obscurity of the night, who was wearing a coarse multi-colored robe and holding a drawn long-knife. He struck Bernart a blow to the head with it, using the blade, and wounded him, causing blood to flow. However, it is true that later that day or evening, the witness heard it said by many people whose names he currently does not remember that Nicola Jausap, alias Binayga, had struck and wounded Bernart that day or evening with his drawn knife. Although many other questions were asked of him, he answered that he knows nothing more about the contents of the accusation other than what he said and attested above.

The same day, Johan Alohier, laborer of Marseille, fifty years and more of age, a witness produced on behalf of the said court, having been cited and sworn, promised and swore, with his right hand touching the holy Gospels, to say and attest the pure truth concerning the matters contained in the accusation, it having first been read to him in the vernacular. Diligently interrogated on his oath by me, the said notary, concerning the things written above and below, he said and attested that he knows nothing about what is contained in the accusation.

The same day, Alaeta, the wife of Johan Alohier, fifty years of age or thereabouts, a witness produced on behalf of the said court, having been cited and sworn, promised and swore, with her right hand touching the holy Gospels, to say and attest the pure truth concerning the matters contained in the accusation, it having first been read to her in the vernacular. Diligently interrogated on her oath by me, the said notary, concerning the things written above and below, she said and attested that she knows nothing about what is contained in it.

I, Guilhem Barban, notary of the episcopal court, wrote this etc.

Accusation of homicide against Nicolau Jausap, alias Binayga. In the year of the Lord as above, the 21st of December, an inquest was made and this present accusation drawn up against Nicolau Jausap, alias Binayga, of Marseille, a married cleric. The court is proceeding both on its own authority and through the order of the worthy and honorable lord Gilibert de Ferraterio, jurist, prior of the church of Toulon, the vicar-general and official of Marseille. The issue is that Bernart Berengier, owing to the wounds to his body, specifically to his head, that were inflicted by Nicolau, as in the accusation above, ended his days today and suffered bodily death and has been cut off from his association with the living. On account of this, Nicolau has become liable to the penalty of the Cornelian law on assassins [a Roman law governing homicide; see Doc. 11e] along with other penalties prescribed by the holy laws.

Wherefore etc.

In the year of our Lord above, the 23rd of December, in vespers, appearing before the lord vicar-general and official of Marseille in the episcopal court, sitting as usual as a tribunal, there appeared the worthy gentleman Ricart Veteris, the sacristan of the church of La Major of Marseille, the treasurer and fiscal procurator of the episcopal court. He requested that Nicolau Jausap, alias Binayga, be cited by one of the servants of the present court or by letter, whichever seems best to the official, so as to respond to the inquest made above against Nicolau, under threat of severe penalty, on the day and hour to be assigned by the lord official.

Having heard and obligingly granted this request, as is fitting to both law and reason, the lord official ordered that Nicolau Jausap, alias Binayga, be cited by letter to respond to the inquest made above against him, under penalty of 400 marks of silver to be applied by the present court.

The tenor of the letter of citation.

Gilibert de Ferratorio, jurist of the church of Toulon, prior, vicar-general, and official of Marseille, to the chaplains who oversee the parochial churches of this city or to whomever this letter might reach, such as their substitutes. Greetings in the Lord. If a judicial penalty were not inflicted on criminals and instead gave way impotently, and the perversity of the evil were allowed to triumph over the sufferings of the good, therefore, so that a penalty should strike the agents of evil and evil deeds remain not unpunished, we desire, order, and require you and each of you, by virtue of the present letter and following the request of the treasurer and fiscal procurator of the episcopal court of Marseille, that on our behalf you cite

Nicolau Jausap of Marseille, alias Binayga, a married cleric, if you happen to be able to find him, or otherwise at his accustomed residence, and in addition publicly in your churches, during the mass, while the greater part of the people are present and participating in the divine services, so that this citation cannot remain unknown in any way, whom we cite by virtue of the present letter, that [he appear before us] by the fifteenth day after the citation, not including holidays. Of these fifteen days, after five he will be subject to a penalty of 100 marks of fine silver; after the next five, a penalty of 200 marks of fine silver; and after the remaining five and at the end of the period assigned, a penalty of 400 marks of fine silver to be paid to the treasury of the episcopal court and arising from an inquest just now made against him in the episcopal court concerning the wounding and the death that followed from it on the person of the late Bernart Berengier, a married cleric of this city, just as law and justice teach. Otherwise, we shall proceed, through justice, to issue a sentence of condemnation against Nicolau based on the contumacy alone.... Given in Marseille on the 23rd of December in the year of the Lord 1400. Bearing the seal of Gilibert. Signed by Guilhem Barbani on behalf of the court....

## 125. THE MARSEILLE CITY COUNCIL MAKES A RULING ABOUT BROKEN SANCTUARY

*The preceding cases, coupled with the Coroner's Rolls (Doc. 119) and other documents, show how common it was for individuals to seek sanctuary in churches following an assault or killing. This extract from the records of the city council of Marseille in 1403 shows what could happen if policing agents broke sanctuary and seized fugitives in churches.*

Source: Archives Municipales de la Ville de Marseille BB 32, folio 122r. Trans. Daniel Lord Smail.

The presentation of a contentious issue by the lord vicar was heard in the city council, for, as the duty of his office requires, and following the advice given to him to the effect that the church ought not to provide sanctuary, he intends and wishes to do justice over several willful murderers who at the time were in the church of St. Antoine. Bearing in mind that these men committed homicide willfully and deliberately, he went there and ordered them to be taken from the church, which was done, and he brought them to the jail so that justice could be administered. The lord bishop of Marseille, however, has suggested that one of them is a cleric, taken together with the others from the ecclesiastical immunity of the church of St. Antoine, and on account of this he has imposed a general interdiction on the city of Marseille, much to the city's harm and to the danger of souls…. It pleased the council, having reached a decision, to require the lord vicar, together with the lord syndics and the Six of War [the city's syndics], to go to the bishop for the purpose of having the interdiction removed inasmuch as it affects the city which, in this matter, is not at fault.

## 126. IGNORING DUE PROCESS DURING A FEUD IN THE PASTON LETTERS

*The Paston letters are a collection of approximately 780 letters written by and to members of the Paston family between 1422 and 1509. Along with wills, indentures, and petitions, the collection records the affairs of three generations of the family, who lived in a village, also named Paston, near the northeast coast of Norfolk, in England. This letter, written by William Tailboys to Viscount John Beaumont in 1449, describes an incident in the Tailboys and Cromwell feud, which was an extension of the parliamentary feud that was being fought between Lord Cromwell and the Duke of Suffolk. Cromwell had led a call to impeach Suffolk, then a minister of the king, blaming him for putting his own interests above those of the country and for making decisions that resulted in the loss of Normandy, Maine, and Anjou during the Hundred Years' War. Tailboys, a Suffolk supporter, had sent armed men to kill Cromwell as he was leaving Star Chamber, the seat of the king's council in Westminster, but failed. Tailboys was then imprisoned in 1450.*

Source: Arranged and ed. Alice Drayton Greenwood, *Selections from the Paston Letters as transcribed by Sir John Fenn* (London: G. Bell and Sons, 1920), pp. 43–44.

### [Letter 32]

To my right honourable and right worshipful lord, Viscount Beaumont.

Right honourable and my right worshipful lord, I recommend me unto your good lordship with all my service, ever more desiring to hear of your prosperity and welfare, the which I pray God encrease and continue to his pleasure, and after your own heart's desire; and thanking you of the good lordship that ye have shewed me at all times, beseeching you alway of good continuance.

Please it your good lordship to be remembered how afore this time Hugh Wytham hath said he would be in rest and peace with me, and not to malign against me, otherwise than law and right would. That notwithstanding, upon

Monday last past, he and three men with him came into a servant's house of mine in Boston, called William Sheriff, and there as he sat at his work struck him upon the head, and in the body with a dagger, and wounded him sore, and pulled him out of his house, and set him in prison without any cause reasonable, or without writ, or any other process shewed unto him; and that me seems longs [belongs] not for him to do, but as he says he is indicted, and as your good lordship knows well, I and all my servants are in like wise, but an any man should have done it, it longs either to the sheriff or to your bailiff, as I conceive, and other cause he had none to him as far as I can know, but only for the maliciousness of that he hath unto me, nor I can think none other but it is so. And now, yester night my lord Welles came to Boston with four score horses, and in the morning following, took him out of prison, saying afore all people, "False thief thou shalt be hanged, and as many of thy master's men as may be gotten," as your servant John Abbot can report unto your good lordship, and hath taken him away with him to Tattershall, what to do with him I cannot say, but as I suppose to have him to Lincoln Castle; wherefore I beseech your lordship in this matter to be my good lord, and that it please your good lordship to write a letter to the keeper of the castle of Lincoln, that it liked him to deliver him out of prison under a sufficient surety had for him, for and [if] they may keep him still by this mean they may take all the servants that I have, and so I may do again in like wise.

And also, as I am informed, without he be had out of prison in haste, it will be right grievous to him to heal of his hurt, he is so sore stricken; and if there be any service that your good lordship will command me to do in any country, please it you to send me word, and it shall be done to my power with the grace of God which have you my right honorable and worshipful lord alway in his blessed keeping. Written at Kyme, upon Wednesday next after our Lady's day, the Assumption [15 August].

Also, please it your good lordship to weet [that is, to know] after this letter was made there came a man from Tattershall, unto my fen, which ought me good will, and because he would not be holden suspect, he spake with women which were milking kyne, and bade them go to a priest of mine to Dokdyke, and bid him fast go give me warning, how that my lord Willoughby, my lord Cromwell, and my lord Welles proposed then to set a Sessions, and hang the said William Sheriff, and they might bring the intent about; and so, as I and your servant John Abbot stood together, the priest came and gave me warning thereof, which I trust for my worship your good lordship would not should happen, for it were to me the greatest shame that might fall, but and [unless] it please your good lordship to write to all your servants in this country, that they will be ready upon a day's warning to come when I send them word; I trust to God they shall not hang him against the law, but

I, with help of your good lordship, shall be able to let [prevent] it.
By your Servant,
William Tailboys.

# INDEX OF TOPICS

*Topics are listed by document number and, in some cases, by part number as well. Thus, "26a" is a reference to Document 26, "Einhard on the fear of family vengeance," and Part A of that document, "Vengeance gets in the way of military service." The goal of the index, in other words, is to guide readers with specific questions in mind to documents that have some bearing on those questions. In some of the categories referring to emotions or emotional states, we have included the full range of a given emotional spectrum in a single category. For example, "joy" is included in "grief/sadness" and "freedom from fear" is included in "fear." Only the documents themselves are indexed; editorial introductions are not included.*

# SOURCES

**Akehurst, F.R.P.** (translator)

"Guarantees of Peace in the Customs of Touraine and Anjou," from *The Etablissements de Saint Louis: Thirteenth-Century Law Texts from Tours, Orléans, and Paris* (Philadelphia: University of Pennsylvania Press, 1996). Copyright © 1996 by University of Pennsylvania Press; "Procedures for Private War in the Customs of Beauvaisis," from *The Coutumes de Beauvaisis of Philippe de Beaumanoir* (Philadelphia: University of Pennsylvania Press, 1992). Copyright © 1992 by University of Pennsylvania Press. Reprinted by permission of University of Pennsylvania Press.

**Barney, Stephen A., W.J. Lewis, J.A. Beach, and Oliver Berghof** (translators)

"Isidore of Seville on the Law of the Talion," from *Etymologies* (New York: Cambridge University Press, 2006). Reprinted by permission of Cambridge University Press.

**Barnish, S.J.B.** (translator)

"Law and the 'Accursed Custom' of Vengeance in Theoderic's Italy," from *Selected Variae* (Liverpool: Liverpool University Press, 1992). Reprinted by permission of Liverpool University Press.

**Benton, John F.** (translator)

"Feud between Bishop Gaudry and Baron Gérard in the *Autobiography* of Guibert of Nogent," from *Self and Society in Medieval France: The Memoirs of Guibert of Nogent* (New York: Harper and Row, 1970). Copyright © 1970 by John F. Benton. Reprinted by permission of HarperCollins Publishers.

**Blum, Owen J.** (translator)

"A Letter by Peter Damian on the Vengeance of Spiritual Leaders," from *Peter Damian, Letters 61–90* (Washington, DC: The Catholic University of America Press 1992). Reprinted by permission of The Catholic University of America Press, Washington, DC.

**Bornstein, Daniel E.** (translator)

"Dino Compagni on the Florentine Factions," from *Dino Compagni's Chronicle of Florence* (Philadelphia: University of Pennsylvania Press, 1974). Copyright © 1974 by University of Pennsylvania Press. Reprinted by permission of University of Pennsylvania Press.

**Bradley, S.J.A.** (translator)

"Vengeance for the 'Hard Man'," from *Anglo-Saxon Poetry* (London: Dent, 1982). Copyright © 1982 JM Dent. Reprinted by permission of JM Dent, an imprint of The Orion Publishing Group, London.

**Butcher, Carmen Acevedo** (translator)

"Aelfric's Sermon on Anger and Peace," from *God of Mercy: Aelfric's Sermons and Theology* (Macon, GA: Mercer University Press, 2006). Reprinted by permission of Mercer University Press.

**Caenegem, R.C. van** (translator)

"William of Malmesbury on the Consequences of Resisting Peace," from *English Lawsuits from William I to Richard I, vol. 1* (London: The Selden Society, 1990). Reprinted by permission of The Selden Society.

**Cusimano, Richard and John Moorhead** (translators)

"*The Deeds of Louis the Fat* by Suger of St. Denis," from *The Deeds of Louis the Fat* (Washington, DC: The Catholic University of America Press, 1992). Reprinted by permission of The Catholic University of America Press, Washington, DC.

**Dam, Raymond Van** (translator)

"Gregory of Tours on God's Vengeance," from *Glory of the Martyrs* (Liverpool: Liverpool University Press, 1988). Reprinted by permission of Liverpool University Press.

**Dobozy, Maria** (translator)

"From the *Sachsenspiegel*," from *The Saxon Mirror: A "Sachsenspiegel" of the Fourteenth Century* (Philadelphia: University of Pennsylvania Press, 1999). Copyright © 1999 by University of Pennsylvania Press. Reprinted by permission of University of Pennsylvania Press.

**Downer, L.J.** (translator)

"The Laws of Henry I of England," from *Leges Henrici Primi* (Oxford: Clarendon Press, 1972). Reprinted by permission of Oxford University Press.

**Drew, Katherine Fischer** (translator)

"The Laws of the Salian Franks," from *The Laws of the Salian Franks* (Philadelphia: University of Pennsylvania Press, 1991). Copyright © 1991 by University of Pennsylvania Press; "The Lombard Laws," from *The Lombard Laws* (Philadelphia: University of Pennsylvania Press, 1973). Copyright © 1973 by University of Pennsylvania Press. Reprinted by permission of University of Pennsylvania Press.

**Dutton, Paul Edward** (translator)

"Einhard on the Fear of Family Vengeance" and "Einhard on the Peace Inspired by the Relics of Saints Marcellinus and Peter," from *Charlemagne's Courtier: The Complete Einhard* (Peterborough, ON: Broadview Press, 1998). Copyright © 1998 by Paul Dutton. Reprinted by permission of University of Toronto Press.

**Ewald, Sister Marie Liguori** (translator)

"Jerome on Kindness and Cruelty," from *The Homilies of Saint Jerome, vol. 2* (Washington, DC: The Catholic University of America Press, 1964). Reprinted by permission of The Catholic University of America Press, Washington, DC.

**Habig, Marion A.** (editor), **Paul Oligny** (translator)

"A Sermon by Saint Francis on Hatred and Peace," from *Writings and Early Biographies: English Omnibus of the Sources for the Life of Saint Francis* (Chicago: Franciscan Herald Press, 1973). Reprinted by permission of Franciscan Press.

**Kagay, Donald J.** (translator)

"A Comital Peace Assembly of Barcelona," "Grant to the Norman Bishops of Fines Due from Breaches of the Truce of God" and "The Usatges of Barcelona," from *The Usatges of Barcelona* (Philadelphia: University of Pennsylvania Press, 1994). Copyright © 1994 by Donald J. Kagay. Reprinted by permission of Donald J. Kagay.

**Landes, Richard** (translator)

"Peace Oath Proposed by Bishop Warin of Beauvais to King Robert the Pious" and "Rodulphus Glaber on the Truce of God," from *The Peace of God: Social Violence and Religious Response in France around the Year 1000*, ed. Thomas Head and Richard Landes (Ithaca: Cornell University Press, 1992). Copyright © 1992 Cornell University Press. Reprinted by permission of Cornell University Press.

**Liuzza, R.M.** (translator)

"Heroic Vengeance," from *Beowulf: A New Verse Translation* (Peterborough, ON: Broadview Press, 2000). Copyright © 2000 R.M. Liuzza. Reprinted by permission of Broadview Press.

**McNamara, Jo Ann and John E. Halborg** (translators)

"Vengeance As the Devil's Work in the *Life of Saint Sadalberga*," from *Sainted Women of the Dark Ages* (Durham: Duke University Press, 1992). Copyright © 1992 Duke University Press. All rights reserved. Reprinted by permission of Duke University Press.

**McNeill, John T. and Helena M. Gamer** (translators)

"Emotion and Sin," from *Medieval Handbooks of Penance: A Translation of the Principal Libri poenitentiales and Selections from Related Documents* (New York: Columbia University Press, 1938). Reprinted by permission of Columbia University Press.

**Mommsen, Theodor E. and Karl F. Morrison** (translators)

"How the Emperor Conrad Pacified His Realm, According to Wipo," from *Imperial Lives and Letters of the Eleventh Century* (New York: Columbia University Press, 1962). Reprinted by permission of Columbia University Press.

**Muckle, J.T.** (translator)

Peter Abelard's "Story of My Adversities," from *The Story of Abelard's Adversities: A Translation with Notes of the Historia Calamitatum* (Toronto: Pontifical Institute of Mediaeval Studies, 1964). Reprinted by permission of the Pontifical Institute of Mediaeval Studies.

**Murray, Alexander C.** (translator)

"Gregory of Tours on Feuding and Vengeance," *From Roman to Merovingian Gaul* (Peterborough, ON: Broadview Press, 2000). Copyright © 2000 Alexander C. Murray. Reprinted by permission of University of Toronto Press.

**Pharr, Clyde** (translator)

"Criminal Justice and Vengeance in the Theodosian Code and Sirmondian," from *The Theodosian Code and Novels and the Sirmondian Constitutions* (Princeton: Princeton University Press, 1952). Copyright © 1952 in the name of the author, 1980 renewed in the name of Roy Pharr, executor. Reprinted by permission of Princeton University Press.

**Ross, James Bruce** (translator)

"*The Murder of Charles the Good* by Galbert of Bruges," from *The Murder of Charles the Good Count of Flanders by Galbert of Bruges, rev. ed.* (New York: Harper and Row, 1967). Copyright © 1967 by James Bruce Ross. Reprinted by permission of HarperCollins Publishers.

**Ryan, Frances Rita** (translator)

"An Account of the Speech of Pope Urban II by Fulcher of Chartres," from *A History of the Expedition to Jerusalem 1095–1127* (Knoxville: University of Tennessee Press, 1969). Reprinted by permission of University of Tennessee Press.

# READINGS IN MEDIEVAL CIVILIZATIONS AND CULTURES
Series Editor: Paul Edward Dutton

"Readings in Medieval Civilizations and Cultures is in my opinion
the most useful series being published today."
– William C. Jordan, Princeton University

**I – Carolingian Civilization: A Reader, second edition**
Edited by Paul Edward Dutton

**II – Medieval Popular Religion, 1000–1500: A Reader, second edition**
Edited by John Shinners

**III – Charlemagne's Courtier: The Complete Einhard**
Translated & Edited by Paul Edward Dutton

**IV – Medieval Saints: A Reader**
Edited by Mary-Ann Stouck

**V – From Roman to Merovingian Gaul: A Reader**
Translated & Edited by Alexander Callander Murray

**VI – Medieval England, 1000–1500: A Reader**
Edited by Emilie Amt

**VII – Love, Marriage, and Family in the Middle Ages: A Reader**
Edited by Jacqueline Murray

**VIII – The Crusades: A Reader**
Edited by S.J. Allen & Emilie Amt

**IX – The Annals of Flodoard of Reims, 919–966**
Translated & Edited by Bernard S. Bachrach & Steven Fanning

**X – Gregory of Tours: The Merovingians**
Translated & Edited by Alexander Callander Murray

**XI – Medieval Towns: A Reader**
Edited by Maryanne Kowaleski

**XII – A Short Reader of Medieval Saints**
Edited by Mary-Ann Stouck

**XIII – Vengeance in Medieval Europe: A Reader**
Edited by Daniel Lord Smail & Kelly Gibson